MW01195828

Praise for
Scorched Earth

"If doubts remain that World War II was the most devastating conflict in human history, *Scorched Earth* dispels them. Even more, Paul Thomas Chamberlin challenges the basic notion of a struggle between good and evil. There is little good here except that this war of annihilation finally ended after taking its tremendous toll. And while historians have long identified World War II as a seminal influence on our contemporary era, none have effectively argued that colonialism in its varied versions was its ultimate legacy—until now. In previous work, Chamberlin contested Cold War realism; likewise, here he upends common assumptions about the Good War. He demythologizes in a way that eloquently covers this epic conflict in all its details—experts and war buffs will find a lot of battle descriptions that are fresh here—while provoking us to rethink our understanding of history itself. Truly a tour de force!"
—Thomas W. Zeiler, author of *Annihilation*

"In a sweeping and vivid narrative, *Scorched Earth* challenges us to abandon the simplistic hero myths that have blinded us to World War II's devastating and continuing impact on our own time."
—Drew Gilpin Faust, author of *This Republic of Suffering*

"A well written, balanced, and provocative account of the twentieth century's greatest and most destructive war. Chamberlin covers all the major theaters of the war, smoothly integrating political and military developments. The author's unorthodox interpretation of the Second World War will challenge historians to reexamine long-standing assumptions and beliefs about the origins and nature of this critical conflict."
—Ronald H. Spector, author of *Eagle Against the Sun*

"The most up-to-date and enlightening global history of World War II. Chamberlin's briskly written *Scorched Earth* is an unflinching account of the role played by racism and colonial aspirations in the conflict's origins, brutal unfolding, and less-than-heroic outcomes."

—Brooke L. Blower, author of *Americans in a World at War*

"What more is there left to say about World War II? A lot, it turns out, as Chamberlin shows in his brilliant, panoramic new history of the most colossal, catastrophic war in human history. New insights leap from every page, introducing even seasoned readers to fresh perspectives on the war. By reimagining the war as a global struggle for supremacy between different types of empires, and by focusing our attention away from Europe and more towards the rest of the world, Chamberlin provides a breathtakingly new interpretation of World War II. A truly remarkable book."

—Andrew Preston, author of *Total Defense*

SCORCHED EARTH

Also by Paul Thomas Chamberlin

The Cold War's Killing Fields:
Rethinking the Long Peace

The Global Offensive: The United States,
the Palestine Liberation Organization,
and the Making of the Post–Cold War Order

SCORCHED EARTH

A GLOBAL HISTORY OF
WORLD WAR II

PAUL THOMAS CHAMBERLIN

BASIC BOOKS

New York

Basic Books
Hachette Book Group
1290 Avenue of the Americas, New York, NY 10104
www.basicbooks.com

Printed in the United States of America

First Edition: May 2025

Published by Basic Books, an imprint of Hachette Book Group, Inc. The Basic
Books name and logo is a registered trademark of the Hachette Book Group.

The Hachette Speakers Bureau provides a wide range of authors for speaking
events. To find out more, go to hachettespeakersbureau.com or email
HachetteSpeakers@hbgusa.com.

Basic books may be purchased in bulk for business, educational, or promotional
use. For more information, please contact your local bookseller or the Hachette
Book Group Special Markets Department at special.markets@hbgusa.com.

The publisher is not responsible for websites (or their content) that are not
owned by the publisher.

Print book interior design by Bart Dawson.

Library of Congress Cataloging-in-Publication Data
Names: Chamberlin, Paul Thomas, author.
Title: Scorched earth: a global history of World War II / Paul Thomas Chamberlin.
Description: First edition. | New York: Basic Books, 2025. | Includes
   bibliographical references and index.
Identifiers: LCCN 2024035650 (print) | LCCN 2024035651 (ebook) | ISBN
   9781541619265 (hardcover) | ISBN 9781541619289 (ebook)
Subjects: LCSH: World War, 1939–1945. | Imperialism—History—20th century.
Classification: LCC D743 .C426 2025 (print) | LCC D743 (ebook) | DDC
   940.53—dc23/eng/20250123
LC record available at https://lccn.loc.gov/2024035650
LC ebook record available at https://lccn.loc.gov/2024035651

ISBNs: 9781541619265 (hardcover), 9781541619289 (ebook)

LSC-C

Printing 1, 2025

To Leila and Mia

CONTENTS

CONTENTS

A NOTE ON NAMES

World War II presents an array of challenges regarding both proper and place names. Throughout the following pages I have tried to identify individuals according to their most common contemporary English usage (for example, "Adolf" instead of "Adolph," "Fumimaro Konoe" instead of "Konoe Fumimaro"). I have also sought to identify places as they were referred to by my sources (for example, "Manchuria" instead of "Northeast China," "Kiev" instead of "Kyiv," "Danzig" instead of "Gdańsk") except in extreme examples (for example, "Beijing" instead of "Peiping"). This usage should be understood as a reflection of my sources rather than as a political statement.

SOVIET UNION

SOVIET STRATEGIC OFFENSIVE
IN MANCHURIA 1945

SAKHALIN
ISLAND

MONGOLIA

Nomonhan
1939

MANCHUKUO

KURIL ISLANDS

MUKDEN
INCIDENT
1931

KOREA

JAPAN

MARCO POLO BRIDGE
INCIDENT 1937

CHINA

ICHIGO
OFFENSIVE
1944

Xuzhou 1937

Tokyo 1945

Hiroshima 1945

Nagasaki 1945

NANJING MASSACRE 1937

Shanghai
1937

Pacific Ocean

Chongqing
1937

Wuhan
1938

BH

Changsha
1937

IN

Okinawa 1945

Iwo Jima 1945

Imphal
1944

Kohima
1944

BURMA

Hanoi

Hong
Kong
1941

PHILIPPINES
(American)

Philippine
Sea
1944

Saipan 1944

Guam 1941

TH

Rangoon
1942

Bataan
1942

Manila 1945

FI

Leyte Gulf
1944

Peleliu 1944

Truk 1944

MA

Singapore
1942

BR

NB

SA

General Douglas MacArthur
Supreme Commander of Allied
Forces in the Southwest Pacific Area

Rabaul
1943

SOLOMON
ISLANDS

DUTCH EAST INDIES

NE

Batavia

Port
Moresby

Indian
Ocean

Guadalcanal
1942–43

Coral Sea
1942

AUSTRALIA

BLACKMER MAPS

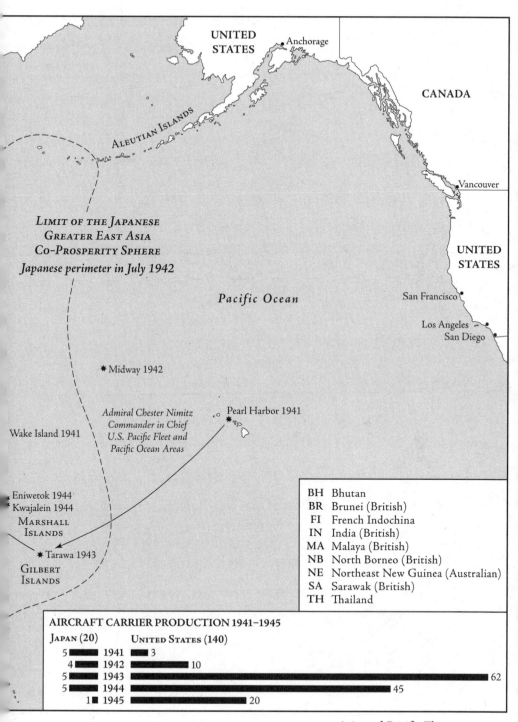

UNITED
STATES

• Anchorage

CANADA

ALEUTIAN ISLANDS

Vancouver

LIMIT OF THE JAPANESE
GREATER EAST ASIA
CO-PROSPERITY SPHERE

Japanese perimeter in July 1942

UNITED
STATES

Pacific Ocean

San Francisco

Los Angeles
San Diego

✳ Midway 1942

Admiral Chester Nimitz
Commander in Chief
U.S. Pacific Fleet and
Pacific Ocean Areas

Pearl Harbor 1941

Wake Island 1941

Eniwetok 1944
Kwajalein 1944
MARSHALL
ISLANDS

BH	Bhutan
BR	Brunei (British)
FI	French Indochina
IN	India (British)
MA	Malaya (British)
NB	North Borneo (British)
NE	Northeast New Guinea (Australian)
SA	Sarawak (British)
TH	Thailand

✳ Tarawa 1943
GILBERT
ISLANDS

AIRCRAFT CARRIER PRODUCTION 1941–1945

JAPAN (20)		UNITED STATES (140)	
5	1941	3	
4	1942	10	
5	1943		62
5	1944	45	
1	1945	20	

Asia and Pacific Theater

AN	Andorra
BEL	Belgium
DAN	Free City of Danzig
DEN	Denmark
EP	East Prussia (German)
FIN	Finland
LX	Luxembourg
NET	Netherlands
SLO	Slovakia (German)
SWIT	Switzerland

NORWAY

SWEDEN

GREAT
BRITAIN

DEN

DAN
Danzig
1939

North Sea

IRELAND

Rotterdam
1940

Hamburg 1943

Berlin 1945

Dunkirk
1940

NET

Market
Garden
1944

Nordhausen

Seelow Height
1945

London
1940

Aachen
1944

Torgau

Dresden
1945

Antwerp

Hürtgen Forest 1944

BEL

Remagen 1945

Elbe

**OVERLORD
1944**

LX

SEIGFRIED LINE

GERMANY

Paris
1940

St. Lô
1944

Caen
1944

Ardennes
1940

Battle of
the Bulge
1944–45

Rhine

SLO

Vienna •

Falaise
1944

SWIT

AUSTRIA

Atlantic Ocean

• Vichy

FRANCE

ITALY

YUGOSLAVIA

Ste. Maxime
1944

Rome
1944

AN

**DRAGOON
1944**

Anzio
1944

• Madrid

Monte
Cassino
1944

Salerno
1943

PORTUGAL

SPAIN

Mediterranean Sea

HUSKY
1943

Tunis
1943

Sicily
1943

TORCH
1942

TA

SM

Algiers
1942

Kasserine
Pass
1943

Malta
1940–42

Oran
1942

TUNISIA (French)

Mers
el-Kebir
1940

ALGERIA
(French)

Casablanca
1942

MOROCCO
(French)

IF	Ifni (Spanish)
SM	Spanish Morocco
TA	Tangier (International)

LIBYA (Italian)

IF

BLACKMER MAPS

FIN

Baltic Sea

ESTONIA

Leningrad
1941–44

Rzhev
1942–43

LATVIA

LITHUANIA

Smolensk
1941

Moscow
1941

Vyazma
1941

EP

Vilnius
1941

• Minsk

Katyn Forest
1939

*Bryansk
1941

**BAGRATION
1944**

*Treblinka
*Warsaw 1939/1942

Kursk *
1943

• Majdanek

*Kiev 1941/1943

POLAND

Dnieper

*Auschwitz

Vistula

HUNGARY

Odessa
1941

ROMANIA

Belgrade

Bucharest •

BULGARIA

• Sofia

Sevastopol
1942

*Kharkov
1942

Don

Volga

*Stalingrad 1942–43

SOVIET UNION

← *Furthest advance of Axis forces
into the Soviet Union*

Istanbul

L

GR

Black Sea

TURKEY

Mediterranean Sea

CY

Beirut •

S&L
(French)

• Damascus

IRAQ

Mersa
Matruh
1940

El
Alamein
1942

Suez Canal

Tobruk
1941–42

Alexandria

EGYPT *Nile*

AL	Albania
CY	Cyprus (British)
GR	Greece
S&L	Syria and Lebanon (French Mandate)

MAJOR ALLIED OPERATIONS

Operation Torch (North Africa)
November 8–16, 1942

Operation Husky (Battle of Sicily)
July 9–August 17, 1943

Operation Overlord (Battle of Normandy)
June 6–August 30, 1944

Operation Bagration (Soviet Union)
June 22–August 19, 1944

Operation Dragoon (Southern France)
August 15–September 14, 1944

**MILITARY AND CIVILIAN
DEATHS BY NATIONALITY***

Soviet Union	24,000,000
China	20,000,000
Germany	7,700,000
Poland	5,600,000
Dutch East Indies	3,500,000
Japan	3,100,000
French Indochina	1,500,000
India	1,500,000
Yugoslavia	1,000,000
Romania	833,000
Philippines	750,000
Hungary	580,000
France	567,600
Greece	550,000
Italy	457,000
United Kingdom	450,700
Korea	425,500
United States	418,500
Austria	384,700
Lithuania	353,000
Czechoslovakia	345,000
Netherlands	301,000
Latvia	227,000
Ethiopia	100,000
Malaya	100,000

* Data from the National World War II
Museum in New Orleans

Europe and Mediterranean Theater

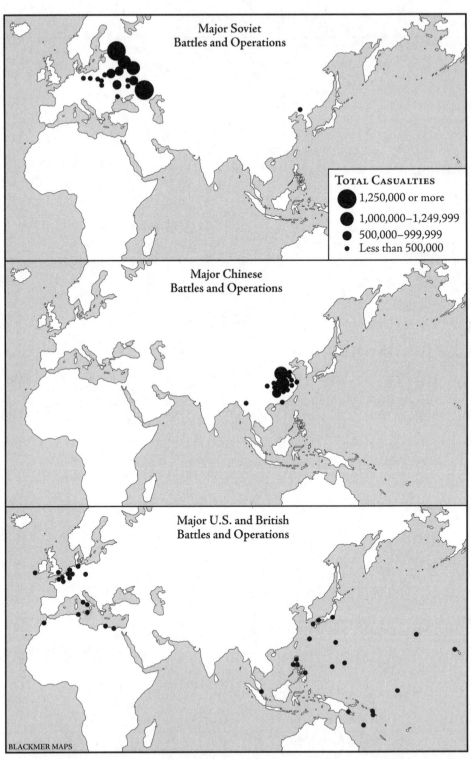

Geographic distribution of major battles and operations and relative size of casualties (Allied and Axis)

Introduction

UNTHINKABLE

MAY 22, 1945. THE THIRD REICH LIES IN RUINS. OVER TWO MIL-lion Soviet soldiers occupy the shattered capital of Berlin, site of the last great battle of World War II in Europe. Sixty miles to the west, American and British armies are camped along the Elbe River. Halfway around the world, Japanese leaders remain defiant even as American B-29 bombers burn Japan's cities to the ground. But it is only a matter of time until Tokyo, too, falls. The largest war in human history is entering its final months. Although they stand on the brink of victory, a growing sense of anxiety hangs over Allied leaders. Winston Churchill, prime minister of the British Empire, has just received a top secret paper prepared by his military staff. Code-named Operation Unthinkable, the study outlines a plan for a war against the Soviet Union to begin in just under six weeks. "The overall or political object is to impose upon Russia the will of the United States and the British Empire," the authors explain. But defeating the Soviets will be no simple task. British commanders estimate that the Red Army enjoys a numerical advantage of well over two-to-one, with 261 Soviet divisions against 103 US, British, and Polish counterparts. "If we are to embark on a war with Russia, we must be prepared to be committed to a total war, which will be both long and costly," they warn. "Our numerical inferiority on land renders it extremely doubtful whether we could achieve a limited and quick success." Furthermore, what slim hopes Western forces have depend on taking a drastic step. The remnants of Adolf Hitler's Nazi legions will have to be reconstituted, rearmed, and unleashed to fight alongside American and British soldiers against the Red Army.[1]

Churchill's blueprint for World War III may sound like alternative history, but it was very real. And the prime minister was not the only one thinking in these terms. Two years earlier, in the summer of 1943, Geroid Robinson, head of the Russian division of the research and analysis branch of the US Office of Strategic Services (OSS)—precursor to the CIA—had floated a similar plan "to turn against Russia the full power of an undefeated Germany, still ruled by the Nazis or the generals."[2] We now know that American and British leaders elected not to pursue these proposals. But the fact that they were even considered stands at odds with our prevailing picture of the Second World War. Why were Allied leaders contemplating a war against one another months, even years before defeating the Axis powers? Why were figures like Churchill considering joining forces with Nazi commanders to attack their Soviet allies?

THE SECOND WORLD WAR MAY BE THE SINGLE MOST STUDIED CONflict in human history—a subject search of Columbia University's library returned nearly 160,000 hits on the topic. However, despite this exhaustive attention, the vast majority of English-language accounts offer a surprisingly one-dimensional interpretation of the conflict, portraying it as a good war, a crusade against fascism, a battle of the free democratic world against a heinous totalitarianism. This interpretation, what we might call the orthodox explanation of World War II, emerged in the 1950s during the darkest years of the Cold War. Scholars across the West found themselves living in a world transformed by the conflict: the old empires of Europe had been brought to their knees; the record of Nazi war crimes had discredited eugenics and scientific racism; an ostensibly ideological struggle between the United States and the Soviet Union had come to dominate international affairs. The first generation of World War II scholars produced histories that reflected this zeitgeist. They framed the war as a democratic struggle against fascism while downplaying racial and colonial dynamics that no longer seemed relevant. They chose to celebrate the contributions of the Western Allies while marginalizing the more problematic roles of Soviet and Chinese forces. They crafted a story that transformed empires into nation-states and conquerors into liberators. Theirs was a history of the war presented as a parable about the evils of totalitarianism and the triumph of an American-led democratic order.[3]

For the last seventy-five years, this orthodox explanation of the war has maintained a stranglehold on our collective memory. While every other major conflict of the twentieth century has undergone multiple rounds of scholarly revisionism—including World War I, the Cold War, the Korean War, and the Vietnam War, to name a few— traditional explanations have remained entrenched in the case of World War II. Why have newer interpretations remained so elusive?[4] Part of the answer lies in the war's overarching moral clarity. Nazi Germany stands as perhaps the most abominable regime in human history. The Axis powers committed many of the vilest atrocities the world has ever seen. And no serious scholar laments the defeat of Nazi Germany, fascist Italy, and imperial Japan.

But the orthodox interpretation of the Second World War falls short in explaining phenomena such as Operation Unthinkable. Indeed, if we look more closely, we see that the reality of the Second World War was far messier than the prevailing good-versus-evil narratives have led us to believe. Most historians now agree that Hitler's legions were defeated not by freedom-loving American and British soldiers on the western front but by the slaughter of millions of Soviet soldiers driven by brutal communist leaders across the killing fields of Eastern

Europe. The Western Allies contributed to this victory less through pluck and democratic idealism than through savage firebombing raids and atomic attacks on Axis cities that incinerated hundreds of thousands of civilians.

This book argues that history's largest conflict was not the good war between democracy and fascism that history books often describe.[5] Rather, it was a massive, colonial race war marked by vicious atrocities and fought by rival empires across huge stretches of Asia and Europe. Although the war destroyed European and Japanese colonialism, it forged the new American and Soviet empires and created a system of highly militarized states armed with nuclear weapons and focused on waging perpetual war against entire populations.[6]

The fires of war that raged across much of the industrialized world burned away a five-hundred-year-old colonial order and opened the way for humanity to build the world anew. The old colonial powers fought to the point of exhaustion only to be consumed by the colossal energies of the Soviet Union and the United States. These continent-spanning superstates, commanding seemingly unlimited resources and manpower, each worked to build new hegemonic orders on the ruins of a world devastated by war. *Scorched Earth* is a history of this transformation. It is a story of both continuity and change that seeks to understand how a war launched by horse-drawn armies in pursuit of colonial aims destroyed the old imperial order and created a new world dominated by nuclear-armed superpowers capable of projecting cataclysmic violence across the entire planet.

This new world did not witness an age of peace, nor did it eliminate the scourge of colonialism. As declassified documents such as "Operation Unthinkable" reveal, well before the end of the war, American and British intelligence officers were considering plans to enlist the still-unvanquished German military in a new war against the Soviet Union. Special teams of Allied soldiers were combing through the former Third Reich in search of Nazi scientists and engineers who would be conscripted to build the arsenals of the future Cold War adversaries. Soviet leaders were busy installing puppet regimes across Eastern Europe to serve as a strategic glacis against a future assault from the Western powers and dispatching spies to penetrate their allies' weapons programs. While the superpowers prepared for the coming Cold War, governments in Britain, France, and the Netherlands laid plans to rebuild their colonial administrations in the Far East with the help of many of the same figures who had collaborated with Japanese forces during the wartime occupations. In this way, the upheavals of the Second World War set the stage for a half century of genocidal violence across Africa, Asia, Latin America, and the Middle East while Europe and North America perched on the brink of full-blown nuclear war.[7]

But it is not enough to simply acknowledge the often-ambiguous nature of the war's violence and the fraught nature of its legacies. A sustained reassessment of the Second World War requires a fundamental reexamination of our basic assumptions about the conflict—its place in world history and the underlying aims of its belligerents, as well as the stakes involved in its outcome. The first step in this process consists of approaching the war not as a historical singularity or an event unto itself but as a conflict that was caught up in the deeper currents of modern world history. The following chapters argue that World War II represented a critical episode in a much longer story of the rise and fall of great powers, colonial warfare, and racial violence.[8]

Orthodox scholarship, by framing World War II as a battle between nation-states and political ideologies, has downplayed the explicitly imperial dynamics that suffused the war and shaped its aftermath. The architects of the Second World War came of age in a world dominated by great European empires—it was in this imperial context that they devised the plans and strategies that gave birth to World War II. All of the war's major belligerents fought as empires in pursuit of imperial aims. Combat in Asia and Europe began as the result of Axis imperial conquests rather than ideological disagreements with the future Allied powers. Put simply, London and Paris declared war on Germany because the Wehrmacht invaded Poland, not because British and French leaders objected to the political tenets of Nazism or fascism more broadly. Likewise, Japan fought a war of colonial conquest across Asia, not an ideological crusade.

Approaching the Second World War as an imperial struggle helps to explain the genocidal brutality of the conflict. Through the nineteenth century, Western writers had become accustomed to the notion of "civilized" war: a type of conflict between established nation-states in which all sides respected a basic set of rules. Soldiers should wear uniforms, violence should be limited to identifiable fronts, civilians should be spared, prisoners of war should be treated humanely, and so forth. However, no such restrictions applied to colonial wars against nonstate peoples. Colonial warfare often took the form of wholesale destruction of non-Western societies that erased the distinction between civilians and combatants and promoted racialized violence. By the early twentieth century, most observers believed that such conflicts had been banished to the colonial hinterlands, far from the centers of Western civilization in Europe and North America and the cosmopolitan port cities of the Far East.

But they were mistaken. Colonial warfare provided a blueprint for much of the violence of the Second World War. The precursors of Auschwitz and Hiroshima can be found in the colonial world. The first concentration camps appeared not in Nazi Germany but in the British colony of South Africa during the Boer War. German soldiers launched their first war of extermination not in Eastern Europe but in the German South West Africa colony in 1901. The world's first concerted aerial bombing campaigns targeted not London or Rotterdam but cities in the colonies of Africa, Asia, and the Middle East. When American and British leaders sat down to plan the amphibious invasion of Normandy, they drew on a wealth of knowledge gained over generations of war in the colonial world. The Second World War fused the colonial war mentality that made little distinction between civilian and combatant with a total war strategy that marshaled the entirety of the state's resources for the purposes of mass, industrialized killing.

Berlin and Tokyo set in motion this fusion of colonial warfare and total war with genocidal campaigns aimed at transforming the heart of Europe and the bustling metropolises of Asia into new colonial spaces. Having launched the largest colonial campaigns in world history, German and Japanese leaders rejected the limitations of "civilized" war and unleashed the full terror of "savage" warfare on the peoples of Eastern Europe and East Asia. Soon, the Allied powers did the same, staging napalm attacks on population centers, sending marauding armies into conquered territories, and directing atomic strikes against Japanese cities. By the end of the war, civilian massacres had become integral to all sides' combat tactics. As theorists such as Hannah Arendt and Aimé Césaire would later argue, the war's worst atrocities are best understood as colonial violence returned home to the metropole.[9]

Positioning the Second World War within the broad landscape of world history also brings the conflict's impact on the postwar era into sharper focus. World War II constituted a pivotal moment in the evolution of the modern international order from the age of formal colonialism to the geopolitics of the Cold War. Orthodox accounts that downplay the war's colonial dimensions tend to overlook this transition, imposing an imaginary separation between the history of nineteenth-century imperialism and the dynamics of the Cold War. The effect has been to gloss over the imperial roots of superpower geopolitics and conceal the colonial foundations of our contemporary international order. The orthodox interpretation of the war thus becomes an instrument of absolution, purging the sins of empire and cleansing the postwar world of its residue.

This book seeks to peel back the layers of mythology surrounding World War II by offering a series of challenges to prevailing interpretations of conflict. It departs from a narrow focus on great leaders and military operations to examine the ways that history's largest conflict remade the relationships between empire, race, violence, war, and the state. Geographically, the book moves past the beaches of Normandy to give greater emphasis to the war's bloodiest theaters in Eastern Europe and East Asia. It breaks with the standard explanations of the war by arguing that race and empire formed the core dimensions of the conflict. It approaches World War II as a conflict thoroughly embedded in the longer sweep of world history. And in doing so, it works to excavate the war's colonial foundations and chart out its imperial afterlives.

IN BROAD BRUSHSTROKES, THIS BOOK ARGUES THAT WORLD WAR II was colonial in its origins, genocidal in its prosecution, and imperial in its outcome. The roots of German, Japanese, and Italian aggression can be traced back to nineteenth-century imperial politics. Although usually portrayed as rogue states, the Axis powers are better understood as heirs to the grand strategy of empire-building through colonial conquest. Expanding on a playbook written by the Western empires, the Axis powers fused concepts of racial hierarchy and colonialism with modern military technology to launch a series of spectacular offensives across Europe, Africa, and East Asia. This assault overwhelmed the bastions of the international order, toppling the French Third Republic and forcing the British Empire to adopt a defensive posture against the threat of German invasion. Having thrown world politics into chaos, German and Japanese leaders turned to their next targets, the Soviet Union and the United States.

The Nazi invasion of the Soviet Union and Japan's Pacific offensive dragged Moscow and Washington into the war. Berlin had opened the bloodiest theater of war in human history; Tokyo had opened the largest. As their adversaries rampaged across Eastern Europe and colonial Asia, American, British, Chinese, and Soviet leaders marshaled the vast resources of their domains in a desperate bid to stop the Axis onslaught. While Moscow built the Red Army into an enormous continental behemoth capable of overrunning the plains of Central Europe, Washington engineered a high-tech military leviathan designed to dominate the seas, stage amphibious assaults on any coast, and direct a rain of fire down on Axis cities. These rapid military buildups transformed both the Soviet Union and the United States into superpowers that eclipsed the British Empire and the older European great powers as the preeminent forces in international affairs.

The superpowers turned the tide of the war at the battles of Stalingrad and Guadalcanal in November 1942. These twin victories eviscerated Axis imperial ambitions and announced the ascendency of the new superpowers. The process of rolling back the Axis conquests hardened the United States and Soviet Union into neo-imperial superstates contending for dominant positions in the postwar international order. But competing postwar visions combined with the unequal burdens of fighting the Axis to place the superpowers on a path toward confrontation. While Soviet generals unleashed the crushing power of the Red Army in bloody land battles against the Third Reich, American forces staged amphibious operations to seize strategically vital territories across the Pacific, the Mediterranean basin, and Western Europe and deployed their massive new fleet to lay a maritime siege against Japan. As each power advanced, their armies established control over what would become postwar spheres of influence. In the closing days of the war, as the Red Army blasted its way through China, US forces launched atomic attacks on Hiroshima and Nagasaki that forced Tokyo into submission and blocked a Soviet occupation of the Japanese home islands. The end of the war found the Red Army camped across most of Eurasia and US forces commanding the seas from a network of bases stretching across the globe.[10]

Having slain the Axis beast, the Soviet behemoth and the American leviathan turned on one another, triggering a new forever war. This new struggle would be waged amid the ruins of World War II and a dying colonial order, and it would breathe new life into old imperial structures in the form of Cold War geopolitics. Armistice lines hardened into militarized frontiers as Soviet leaders installed puppet governments in shattered capitals across Hitler's former empire, from Warsaw to Sofia, and US forces garrisoned the fallen outposts of

Japan's Greater East Asia Co-Prosperity Sphere, from Guam to Okinawa. Armies that had been forged in the battle against the Axis now took stations along the front lines of the Cold War. Meanwhile, across Africa, Asia, and the Middle East, dozens of new states appeared inside borders drawn by the collapsing imperial powers. Over the next half century, old colonial fault lines and World War II battlefields reemerged as Cold War flash points. As leaders in Moscow and Washington engaged in an ideological struggle between communism and democratic capitalism, simmering ethnic and racial tensions metastasized into virulent new forms of nationalism that would gain power and influence in the twenty-first century.

Ultimately, *Scorched Earth* argues that the war's legacy was not the destruction of fascism, racism, and imperialism but rather the creation of a postwar order in which highly militarized, neo-imperial states were forced to prepare for perpetual warfare and the prospect of nuclear annihilation. Our collective amnesia regarding the war's colonial origins and its imperial fallout has stripped the conflict of its meaning, transforming it into a twentieth-century fairy tale. This book seeks to restore our understanding of the Second World War to its proper place in the wider landscape of modern world history. Viewed against this backdrop, the Second World War appears as the climax of centuries of colonial expansion and the catalyst for the reinscription of imperialism under the aegis of Cold War geopolitics.

Chapter 1

A WORLD OF EMPIRES

THE FIRST DELEGATES ARRIVED AT VERSAILLES JUST AFTER 2:00 P.M., driving up the tree-lined Avenue du Château before passing through the gates and clattering over the cobblestones leading to the palace. Outside, an estimated twenty thousand soldiers stood guard, holding back cheering throngs. Rays of sunlight pierced the clouds and glinted off bayonets as flags fluttered in the breeze and a dozen airplanes circled overhead. Within an hour, the last officials had arrived to take their places in the great hall. French prime minister Georges Clemenceau called the session to order and invited the German delegates to begin signing the document laid out before them. Less than forty minutes later, the ceremony was finished. The Treaty of Versailles brought the formal state of war between Germany and the Entente powers to an end. Clemenceau, British prime minister David Lloyd George, and American president Woodrow Wilson stepped out onto the terrace overlooking the palace gardens to be greeted by cries of "Vive Clemenceau!" "Vive Wilson!" and "Vive Lloyd George!" On June 28, 1919, after nearly five bloody years of war, joyous citizens across the Western world celebrated peace.[1]

While peace had come to the western front, war raged in the East. Even as the crowds cheered at Versailles, the town of Aydin in western Anatolia was burning. The chief of the Greek Red Cross reported that advancing Turkish troops had plundered the town, torching the Greek quarter and slaughtering their inhabitants. The corpses of massacred civilians littered ravines outside the town. "[Aydin] is a vast sepulchre," wrote one correspondent. "Here hundreds of Greek and Armenian women, children and priests lie in nameless graves. . . . The broken columns of a thousand shattered homes are the mute witnesses of the martyrdom of the population."[2] While Greek and Turkish forces fought for control of Anatolia, a series of anti-Jewish pogroms swept through Poland and Ukraine. Marauding Ukrainian soldiers had murdered over a thousand Jewish civilians in the town of Proskuriv in February 1919. By 1921, pogroms across the region had killed over one hundred thousand Jews and displaced millions more.[3]

The residents of Aydin and Proskuriv had been caught up in the great upheaval unleashed by the First World War as the defeated land empires of Europe and the Near East were torn apart. The Austro-Hungarian and Ottoman Empires were dismembered, their lands divided to form a series of new independent states and League of Nations mandates. Germany survived as a nation but was stripped of its overseas colonies and large sections of its eastern and western borderlands. The Russian Empire had been consumed by the fury of the Bolshevik Revolution, whose leaders had ceded a quarter of their prewar European territory, along with 40 percent of Russia's European population, in order to secure peace on the eastern front. From the wreckage of these empires there arose ten new states—Finland, Estonia, Latvia, Lithuania, Poland, Czechoslovakia, German-Austria, Hungary, Yugoslavia, and Turkey—and five League of Nations mandates—Palestine, Transjordan, Syria, Lebanon, and Iraq. These transformations were not bloodless. Even before the signing of the peace at Versailles, vicious interethnic power struggles had broken out across a vast arc of territory running north from Vienna, through Warsaw and Riga, and south across the Balkans, Anatolia,

Syria, Palestine, and Iraq. In the five years following the end of the First World War, over four million people were killed in civil wars or ethnic conflicts inside this territory. Millions more became refugees after fleeing before advancing armies or being forcibly displaced, victims of a savage round of ethnic cleansing sparked by the collapse of empires.[4]

Although the violence raging across Eastern Europe and the Middle East has received less attention from historians than the negotiations taking place at Versailles, it proved every bit as central to the world that emerged from the Great War. The architects of the Versailles Treaty hoped to create a new international order that would ensure peace and stability for generations to come. They understood their historic role as successors to the 1815 Congress of Vienna, which had given Europe nearly a century without a general war. Rather than stability, however, the next years witnessed profound strife born of sweeping political change, economic dislocation, imperial competition, virulent racism, revolution, war, and genocide. In less than a generation, the Second World War would weave these threads of empire, race, and violence together, with disastrous consequences for peoples around the globe. But the roots of this tragedy stretch far beyond the decisions of specific leaders. The origins of the coming war lay in the very structure of the Versailles order itself: an unstable imperial system constructed around racial hierarchies and maintained through colonial violence. All of the key elements that would fuel the future Axis reign of terror were present in the interwar period. It should come as no surprise, then, that an international order built on empire, race, and violence would help to give birth to a new set of far-right regimes steeped in racist rhetoric and intent on staging violent bids to seize the mantle of empire for themselves.

"VERY RARELY HAS PARIS GIVEN ITSELF UP TO JOY AS COMPLETELY AS it did to-night," wrote a correspondent for the London *Times* in the early hours of June 29, 1919. A booming cannon announced the signing of the peace treaty as hordes of joyous Parisians crowded the streets. So dense was the multitude that city officials were forced to reroute the torchlight military parade planned for that evening.[5]

The Treaty of Versailles aimed to do many things: to ensure collective security through the creation of the League of Nations; to set up mandates for colonial territories across large parts of Asia, Africa, and the Middle East; to establish German guilt for starting the war; and to prevent the resurgence of German military power that might one day plunge Europe back into a state of general war. But no task loomed larger than that of establishing a new international order in the wake of the largest conflict the world had ever seen. "We were journeying to Paris, not merely to liquidate the war but to found a new order in Europe," one British diplomat explained. "We were preparing not Peace only, but Eternal Peace."[6] Indeed, the most optimistic leaders at Versailles hoped to restore a balance of power to the continent and lay the foundations for long-term peace. Britain and France would serve as the central players in safeguarding this new order. On paper, such an arrangement seemed viable. Britain controlled the world's largest empire, numbering over 530 million people and spread across thirty-five million square miles of territory. London also commanded the largest fleet of warships on the high seas. France held colonies in Africa, the Middle East, and Indochina with a combined population of nearly 113 million. While its navy was considerably smaller than Britain's, France's army was the largest in Europe. Together, the two Western powers had orchestrated the defeat of the Central Powers and now appeared destined to control the postwar world. As long as the French army maintained its primacy on the continent and the British navy continued to dominate the oceans, this new order might succeed.[7]

Imperial power formed the geopolitical cornerstone of the post-1919 international order. Such an arrangement would have been self-evident to the leaders at Versailles. For centuries, the ability to project power across vast distances and over foreign peoples had represented a key component of national power. Empires dominated the international order and remained the central players on the world stage. One needed only to look at a map of the world circa 1919, with its continents divided into empires and colonies, or to peruse the headlines of one of the many newspapers for sale on the streets of London, New York, or Paris to see that imperial projects and the violence they entailed were hardly out of the ordinary. Students of international relations remained fixated on imperial politics. As the world's leading theorist of naval strategy, American captain Alfred Thayer Mahan had explained in his seminal work, *The Influence of Sea Power upon History*, strong navies allowed nations to expand trade, control overseas markets, and generate economic prosperity at home, which in turn increased power abroad. But a first-class navy required overseas possessions. "Colonies attached to the mother-country afford, therefore, the surest means of supporting abroad the sea power of a country," he wrote. Thus, production, shipping, and colonies contained the "key to much of the history, as well as the policy, of nations bordering upon the sea."[8]

And the seas were not the only arena of great power competition. In 1901, German geographer Friedrich Ratzel had popularized the concept of lebensraum, or "living space." Giving theoretical weight to long-standing notions of race and colonialism, Ratzel argued that an energetic, growing population needed room to expand. Three years later, British geographer Halford Mackinder published his seminal essay, "The Geographical Pivot of History," which identified the Eurasian heartland as the key to world power. "Who rules East Europe commands the Heartland," he wrote. "Who rules the Heartland commands the World Island; Who rules the World Island commands the World."[9] In the early 1920s, German geographer Karl Haushofer synthesized Mahan, Ratzel, and Mackinder's theories in his own version of Geopolitik, which played a formative role in shaping German ideas of world power.

The message for interwar leaders and would-be strategists seemed clear: great powers possessed empires. Colonial holdings showcased national prestige at the same time that they strengthened states' ability to project force around the globe by providing bases for military operations and fueling stations for ships. In times of peace, colonies provided resources such as fossil fuels and rare metals, both of which had grown increasingly vital in the industrial age. Agricultural products from the tropics such as rubber, timber, coffee, tea, and sugar were valuable commodities. Colonies also provided the promise of new territories for white settlers in search of new opportunities. Underdeveloped imperial domains served as safety valves for European nations suffering from the pressure of rapid population growth. Imperial rule provided an opportunity for colonizing nations to build new societies and demonstrate the power of their ideas. In this way, colonies served as what one historian has called "laboratories of modernity"— they were places where new medical and scientific practices could be tested, where new military equipment and tactics could be perfected, and where forms of social and political organization could be created.[10] Colonies also functioned as proving grounds for a nation's martial strength. Generations of American, British, and French soldiers who had been hardened by fighting wars against native populations along colonial frontiers would one day return home to test their skills on the battlefields of Europe. Far from ending the age of empires, then, the peace that followed the end of the First World War was built on imperial foundations and maintained through imperial power.

CONCEPTIONS OF RACIAL HIERARCHY ALSO SAT AT THE CENTER OF international relations through the interwar period. Although many leaders had abandoned the explicit racist language of the nineteenth century—at least in official discourse and polite conversation—their worldviews remained anchored in deep-seated notions of scientific racism and white supremacy. These ideas were echoed in the prevailing discourse on "Western civilization." While largely innocuous on its face, the concept of a unified West sitting atop a hierarchy of world civilizations evoked fixed racial and cultural differences between societies and served to justify the ongoing subjugation of colonized peoples under the auspices of the civilizing mission.[11] In the same way, eugenics and social Darwinism lent an air of academic credibility to imperialism and white supremacy. However, the devastation of the Great War appeared to deal a heavy blow to the superiority of the West. The European great powers had fallen into a fratricidal conflict that had destroyed vast stretches of the continent, ravaged economies, killed millions, and threatened colonial power structures. The years following the end of the Great War saw a stream of dire predictions about the decline of Western civilization. "It was not Germany that lost the World War," warned German historian Oswald Spengler. "The West lost it when it lost the respect of the coloured races."[12] Nascent anticolonial movements and rising immigration rates exacerbated fears of this decline.[13] As these perceived threats to Western civilization conjured racial, ideological, and imperial anxieties across much of Europe and North America, a range of commentators warned of a looming race war.[14]

Throughout the interwar period, mainstream thinkers continued to conceptualize race as a key factor shaping foreign affairs. Indeed, the Council on Foreign Relations' esteemed journal, *Foreign Affairs*, began life under the title the *Journal of Race Development*. The most widely used international relations textbook of the 1920s, Raymond Leslie Buell's *International Relations*, had an entire chapter titled "The Conflict of Color," which expounded on the threat of a coming race war. What religion and nationalism had been to earlier eras, Buell warned, race might be to the twentieth century. Alongside tensions between European non-Western peoples, Buell warned of racial disputes between white nationalities. A "nation intoxicated with racial theories is tempted to impose its racial 'superiority' upon the remainder of the world." Buell identified three leading figures working to promote these racial theories. The first, Houston Stewart Chamberlain, had been raised in Britain and later moved to Germany. A virulent antisemite, Chamberlain argued that the Aryan race and its Teutonic descendants were responsible for nearly all of humanity's achievements. In this view, race formed the foundation of all human history. His 1899 opus, *The Foundations of the Nineteenth Century*, had sold 250,000 copies across twenty-four editions by 1938. In it, he argued that "physically and mentally the Aryans are pre-eminent among all peoples; for that reason they are by right . . . lords of the world." Chamberlain's work became an international sensation, earning accolades from such figures as former US president Theodore Roosevelt and German kaiser Wilhelm II as well as publications such as the *New York Times* and the London *Spectator*.[15]

The second of the three figures came from the United States. In 1916, American eugenicist Madison Grant published his seminal *The Passing of the Great Race*. Like Chamberlain, Grant saw race as the key to explaining the broad currents of world history. In particular, he identified the "Nordic race" as the progenitor of all the world's great civilizations and praised racial prejudice as a natural means of preserving racial "purity." He was perhaps best known, however, for sounding the alarm about the dangers to Western civilization posed by immigration of non-European peoples. Like Chamberlain, Grant won praise from such mainstream publications as *Science*, the *Annals of the American Academy of Political and Social Science*, and the *Journal of Race Development*.[16]

Such ethnonationalist jeremiads thrived into the postwar era. Grant's most prominent disciple, Lothrop Stoddard—the third leading eugenicist—followed in his mentor's footsteps with his 1920 book, *The Rising Tide of Color Against White World-Supremacy*. Stoddard had earned a doctorate from Harvard while under the supervision of Archibald Cary Coolidge, who, in turn, was a founding member of the Council on Foreign Relations and served as the first editor of *Foreign Affairs*. Stoddard's book warned of a coming clash of civilizations between the West and the nonwhite world. Stoddard recast World War I as the "white civil war" that had weakened the "white world [and] opened up revolutionary, even cataclysmic, possibilities" as the "brown and yellow peoples of Asia" mobilized for independence. Although he warned that "colored armies" might one day conquer "white lands," the real threat, Stoddard wrote, came from "conquests like migrations which would swamp whole populations and turn countries now white into colored man's lands irretrievably lost to the white world." Above all, Stoddard insisted, the white world must develop a "true *race*-consciousness." Again, these racist diatribes earned praise from the *New York Times*—which claimed that the book provided a "new basis for history"—and even secured an endorsement from the sitting US president, Warren G. Harding.[17]

Well into the interwar period, then, American and British prophets of race war occupied a central place in mainstream political discourse. Their books sold thousands of copies across multiple editions, received positive reviews in leading newspapers and academic journals, and earned praise from sitting and former presidents. Grant's and Stoddard's writings shaped state and federal legislation and forced their way into public debate. As the *Chicago Defender* wrote in 1923, "Probably no two books in recent years have had as great an influence on American government policies." While Chamberlain's, Grant's, and Stoddard's influence diminished in the 1930s, their arguments had been instrumental in shaping a set of widely held worldviews that looked to race and racism as key tenets of international relations. In 1939, First Lady Eleanor Roosevelt hosted a luncheon attended by Stoddard along with Under Secretary of State Sumner Welles and other guests; as late as 1940, the *Washington Post* published glowing reports of Dr. and Mrs. Stoddard's spring parties in Georgetown.[18]

WHILE THE AMERICAN POLITICAL ELITE RUBBED ELBOWS WITH RAC-ist luminaries such as Grant and Stoddard, leaders in London and Paris were working to consolidate their hold over newly won colonial domains. Under the auspices of the League of Nations mandates, British and French diplomats carved up the Arab territories of the former Ottoman Empire. France assumed control of Syria and Lebanon; Britain took Palestine and Iraq. The mandates amounted to imperialism in all but name. As British and French forces marched into

Jerusalem, Baghdad, Damascus, and Beirut, they moved to crush all forms of nationalist resistance among the local population. The Western empires could kill rebels and imprison anticolonial politicians, but they could not destroy the seeds of nationalism that had taken root in the Arab world. In May 1920, Iraqi leaders began mobilizing against British authorities in Baghdad. This opposition quickly grew to include religious and tribal elements in the capital and beyond, each of which had its own grudge against the new mandate authorities. As the summer heat fell over the Euphrates valley, this political unrest erupted into armed revolt. British forces clamped down on demonstrations in the cities as rebel forces seized parts of the countryside. Although disunity and a swift British military response put down the revolt by late October, the cost had been high: some five hundred British and Indian troops had been killed, along with as many as six thousand Iraqis. For future generations of Iraqi leaders, the 1920 Iraqi revolt would be known as the bloody birth of a long history of nationalist resistance.[19]

Across the border in Syria and Lebanon, French officials also faced a rebellion. In the summer of 1925, anticolonial groups drawn from rural communities and led by veterans of the Great War launched a campaign of resistance against French authorities in Syria. By October 18, the rebels had reached the capital city of Damascus, where they were greeted by enthusiastic supporters. French authorities responded with a brutal bombardment of the city's old quarter. Over the next two days, French artillery shelled the ancient Souq al-Hamidiyeh while aircraft strafed busy streets, dropping bombs and leveling large sections of the center city. The attack killed an estimated 1,500 people and marked the first full-scale "aerial bombardment" of a major city in world history. Meanwhile, French counterinsurgency forces swept into the surrounding farmlands in search of insurgents. In the capital, barbed-wire barriers and checkpoints cordoned off neighborhoods with rebel activity while French legionnaires patrolled the streets in armored cars. Alongside these military operations, French authorities declared martial law. In 1926 alone, Damascus's military tribunal executed 355 Syrians—nearly one per day. Many of the condemned were hanged in the city's public square, their bodies left on display to send a macabre message to other would-be rebels. After skirmishes broke out between Syrian rebels and mandate forces in early May in the Midan neighborhood just south of Damascus's old city gates, French troops unleashed an even fiercer bombardment. For twenty-two hours, artillery rained shells down on Midan, destroying hundreds of buildings, killing one thousand people, and igniting fires that could not be extinguished because colonial authorities had cut off water to the neighborhood. As the fighting continued, the brutal French counterinsurgency took its toll. By the summer of 1927, French officials declared victory and congratulated themselves for pacifying the mandate. As the carnage on the streets of Baghdad and Damascus revealed, the colonial era was far from over.[20]

WHILE BRITISH AND FRENCH AUTHORITIES FOUGHT TO EXTEND control over their new mandates, the disintegration of the Austro-Hungarian, German, and Russian empires provoked a burst of violent state-building across much of Central and Eastern Europe. A complex mix of diplomacy, mass political mobilization, revolution, and war helped to create a total of nine new states across the region at the end of the Great War: Austria, Czechoslovakia, Estonia, Finland, Hungary, Latvia, Lithuania, Poland, and Yugoslavia. In the first months of 1918, communist and anticommunist forces fought a brutal civil war in Finland that killed thirty-six thousand people, amounting to 1 percent of the nation's population. To the south, across the new Baltic states, German mercenaries—many of them veterans of the Great War—rampaged through towns and villages, slaughtering civilians, raping women, and plundering the countryside. Through 1919 and into 1920, militias in Budapest massacred some five thousand suspected leftists in their efforts to destroy the communist regime. No small amount of this violence across Eastern Europe took the form of pogroms against Jewish communities. All told, the upheaval that accompanied this reordering witnessed twenty-seven violent transfers of power by 1920 and an estimated four million killed—a staggering total greater than the combined deaths suffered by Britain, France, and the United States in the Great War.[21]

But no conflict generated more bloodshed than the Russian civil war. The Russian Revolution, which toppled the czar's regime in 1917, plunged Europe's largest nation into a series of upheavals that would continue until 1923 and claim the lives of some three million people. Although the provisional government that first came to power sought to maintain Russian participation in the war against the Central Powers, the burden of fighting combined with internal challenges to strengthen the more radical Bolshevik party under the leadership of Vladimir Ilyich Lenin. In October 1917, the Bolsheviks staged an armed insurrection in Petrograd and proclaimed the creation of a new Soviet government. In order to buy time to consolidate their hold on power and eliminate counterrevolutionary challenges, Lenin and the Bolsheviks agreed to the Treaty of Brest-Litovsk, which ended hostilities with the Central Powers and surrendered massive stretches of Russian territory in the west. Confident that socialist revolutions would soon bring these lost territories back into the fold, Lenin and his top commander, Leon Trotsky, turned to the task of defeating the anti-Bolshevik "White" armies in a series of campaigns across large parts of Russia. Trotsky proved an able leader who managed to build the new Red Army into a formidable military force that turned the tide against the White forces. Meanwhile, Bolshevik leaders launched a reign of terror designed to root out domestic political opponents and bolster the party's hold on power. The turmoil of revolution, war, and bungled agricultural policies plunged Russia into a catastrophic famine in 1921–1922 that killed another two million people.[22]

Furthermore, the shock waves from the Bolshevik Revolution reached far beyond the borders of Russia. Bolshevik leaders insisted that theirs was only the first in a string of revolutions that would topple the existing political order across Europe and beyond. For their part, anticommunist leaders across the region feared that the revolutionary contagion might spread. In May 1920, Polish forces launched an invasion of Ukraine in a bid to restore the eastern borders of their historic kingdom. The attack provoked a Soviet counteroffensive that took the Red Army to the banks of the Vistula, threatening Warsaw itself. Although Polish forces rallied and saved the capital, the war inflamed fears that the Bolshevik Revolution would spread across Europe. In January 1919, the *Times* of London warned that the "danger of Bolshevist imperialism" represented the most "urgent" problem facing the peace conference at Versailles. Not since 1789 had a European revolution so threatened the regional status quo. Bolshevik rhetoric lauding Russia as "the citadel of world revolution" only fed these fears. Likewise, the creation of the Communist International as an organization charged with spreading the revolution abroad convinced European leaders that Lenin and his comrades represented an existential danger to the existing world order.[23]

MEANWHILE, ACROSS THE ATLANTIC, ANOTHER EMERGING POWER also threatened to unbalance the world order, albeit through thoroughly capitalist means. By the beginning of the twentieth century, the United States had emerged as an economic and industrial juggernaut—a sleeping giant that threatened to dominate the globe. The American population of 130 million outnumbered the combined populations of metropolitan Britain and France. Added to this was America's colonial population of nearly eighteen million—most of whom lived in the Philippines. However, America's real power came not from its formal colonial holdings but from its economic weight. By 1938, the US gross domestic product stood at $800 billion; the British Empire came in second at $688 billion; Germany's GDP stood at $375 billion, Japan's was $232 billion, and Italy's $143 billion. The Americans wielded their economic influence through a concerted strategy of Open Door diplomacy. For generations, US leaders had worked to break down economic barriers to American trade and secure overseas markets for US goods. When the nation had been a relatively weak power on the global stage, American efforts to gain footholds in overseas markets had been a matter of simple economic survival. However, as the United States expanded across North America, opened ports on the Atlantic and Pacific Oceans, and built its industrial economy into the largest and most efficient in the world, the Open Door strategy took on an altogether different tone of free-trade imperialism. The Great War accelerated this process, transforming the United States into the world's largest creditor. By 1919, the United States controlled a massive, though largely invisible, commercial and financial empire stretching around the globe.[24]

Through the interwar years, Washington played a central role in the international system despite the reluctance of American leaders to exercise direct political leadership. President Woodrow Wilson's efforts to draw the United States into a long-term commitment to maintaining collective security through the League of Nations failed in the face of congressional opposition, and many American leaders hoped to pull back from world affairs in the wake of the Great War. But no amount of diplomatic disengagement could counteract the gravitational pull of US commercial, financial, and industrial might.[25]

Furthermore, instead of genuine isolation, American leaders pursued greater engagement in world affairs where and when it suited their purposes. The United States took a leading role in working to secure long-term Anglo-American military supremacy on the high seas, guaranteeing that the existing balance of naval power remained unchanged. While the Treaty of Versailles had sought to cripple German military power and guarantee that the Great War's victors would maintain supremacy in Europe, the 1922 Washington Naval Treaty endeavored to prevent a new naval arms race and ensure US and British dominance over the seas. The treaty fixed the disbursement of British, US, and Japanese battleships at a ratio of five to five to three. Italy and France each received lower allocations of 1.75. The terms of the agreement also limited the number of aircraft carriers allowed to the major naval powers, again giving a decisive advantage to Britain and the United States over powers such as Japan, France, and Italy. While US and British leaders heralded the treaty as a triumph in efforts to block a new and dangerous arms race, other nations resented a post-1919 world order that seemed designed to relegate them to the status of second-class powers.

RATHER THAN STABILITY, THEN, THE INTERWAR YEARS WERE marked by a sense of revolutionary change and growing unrest. As the specter of Bolshevism took shape to the east, the colossal forces of American industrial capitalism threatened to subsume Europe from the west. All the while, the guardians of the Versailles order, Britain and France, busied themselves with their imperial ventures across Africa, Asia, and the Middle East. The Great War had ended, but geopolitical tensions remained high. A young Italian newspaper editor named Benito Mussolini, writing in 1918, captured the sentiment: "The whole earth trembles. All continents are riven by the same crisis. There is not a single part of the planet . . . which is not shaken by the cyclone. In old Europe, men disappear, systems break, institutions collapse." In the following years, the young editor watched as Britain and France expanded their empires while Italy was forced to settle for meager territorial gains. He railed against these perceived injustices and called on his countrymen to reclaim their imperial destiny. "Italy's hour has not yet rung," he thundered in May 1919, "but fate decrees that it surely will. . . . [Italy] feels the irresistible attraction of the Mediterranean which will itself open the way to Africa. A two thousand year old tradition calls Italy to the shores of the black continent whose venerated relics are reminders of the Roman Empire." In the coming years, these ideas would harden as Mussolini and his comrades in the National Fascist Party gained influence. The fascist leader had every intention, should he gain control of Italy, of rectifying the crimes of Versailles. As he announced in December 1921, "Either there will be a new war, or we will have a treaty revision!"[26]

MUSSOLINI WAS NOT ALONE. THROUGH THE 1920S, A GROWING NUM-
ber of political and military leaders across Europe and Asia began
working to reestablish order amid this chaos and to restore a sense
of national glory that they felt had been lost in the aftermath of the
Great War. Drawn to the politics of the far right, many of these aspiring leaders found inspiration in the legacies of empire, notions of
racial identity, the glorification of violence, and strident anticommu-
nism. In a world raked by revolutionary upheavals and social unrest,
these right-wing forces promised a return to traditional values and
national pride.

On the night of October 27, 1922, Mussolini, now head of the Italian National Fascist Party, staged his infamous "March on Rome" at
the head of thirty thousand black-shirted thugs. Divided and weak,
the Italian government collapsed before the fascist show of force.
By the end of the month, Mussolini had become Italy's new prime
minister. He quickly set about creating an authoritarian state, eliminating rivals, and crushing all opposition to his leadership. Having
conquered Italy, Mussolini now turned his gaze to the Mediterranean
and beyond. He exhorted his followers to seek out an Italian *spazio
vitale* (vital space). In order to become a great nation, he claimed, Italy
had to expand and seize new territories. Like many European leaders of his era, Mussolini believed in the concept of social Darwinism.
Races rose and fell in a mortal struggle; the strong survived, and the
weak perished. Italy, he warned shortly before coming to power, could
not "live eternally in its confines without the threat of suffocation and
death." The fate of Italy and the whole European race was at stake,
he explained later, evoking the "Black peril" and "Yellow peril": "The
entire white race, the Western race, can be submerged by the other
races of colour that multiply with a rhythm unknown to ours. Are the
Blacks and Yellows at the door? Yes, they are at the door." The solution, ultimately, lay in an effort to increase Italy's population. "The
military power of the state and the future of the security of the nation
are linked to the demographic problem," he wrote in 1934, "a vexing
problem for all the countries of the white race including our own."

Mussolini's goal, then, was to reclaim the lost glories of the Roman Empire, the pursuit of which would entail waves of cleansing violence that would at once purify the nation and give it the *spazio vitale* it would need to survive. There was no other choice.[27]

Weimar Germany also emerged as a hotbed of nationalist resentment. The Versailles Treaty had cleaved off 13 percent of Germany's pre-1914 territory, containing 10 percent of its population. One in ten Germans now lived outside the borders of the fatherland. Likewise, Germany had lost its overseas colonies in Africa and its concessions in China. But not all Germans were prepared to abandon the dream of empire. In the years following the armistice, the German Colonial Society established some 250 branches consisting of thirty thousand members who called for a return of Germany's overseas domains. Even more influential were those elements of German society that called for the restoration of Germany's lost continental empire. While academics such as Karl Haushofer lectured to packed halls on the geopolitical necessity of lebensraum, popular writers such as Paul Rohrbach and Hans Grimm celebrated Germany's imperial past and extolled their countrymen to rise to the challenge of reestablishing Germany as a great power. Grimm's 1926 novel, *Volk ohne Raum* (People without space), sold over three hundred thousand copies in its first decade in print.[28]

The most strident voices argued that Versailles had reduced Germany from an empire to a colony. Many Germans considered their nation heir to an imperial legacy stretching back to the coronation of Charlemagne in the year 800. For the better part of a thousand years, the Holy Roman Empire had sat at the center of European geopolitics. Prussian forces had been instrumental in the defeat of Napoleon at Waterloo in 1815, and a united Germany had nearly conquered the continent in the Great War. But defeat had brought this once-great empire to its knees. German nationalists resented what many felt was a punitive peace designed to cripple the nation and deprive it of its rightful place as the most powerful state in continental Europe. Foreign troops occupied sections of the Rhineland. That many of these troops were drawn from French colonies in North and West Africa triggered racialized fears throughout the country over the "subhuman beasts" who had been loosed among the population. German newspapers wrote of the "black horror on the Rhine" as a threat to German women, the German family, and German society itself.

Meanwhile, conspiracy theories circulated through the country about the Jewish, Marxist, and/or liberal "stab in the back" that supposedly constituted the real cause of Germany's defeat in the war. Building on these fantasies, journalists, writers, and a growing number of political leaders warned that the victorious Anglo-American "cartel" was engaged in the aggressive economic colonization of Germany. Together with local Jewish, Marxist, and liberal collaborators, these rapacious foreign powers, they claimed, were transforming Germany into a colony of Western capitalism. Widespread conspiracy theories placed Germany's Jewish minority at the vanguard of this colonial assault. As General Erich Ludendorff, German hero of the Great War, insisted, the Jews had "acquired a dominant influence in the 'war corporations' . . . which gave them the occasion to enrich themselves at the expense of the German people and to take possession of the German economy, in order to achieve one of the power goals of the Jewish people." Millions of Germans imagined that they, the indigenous peoples of Central Europe, were now targets of a hostile invasion led by Jewish colonizers, the British, French, and American governments, and capitalism itself.[29]

Among the thousands of Germans entranced by these fantasies was a young radical named Adolf Hitler. A failed artist from Austria, Hitler had served in the German army during the Great War. While convalescing after being wounded in a mustard gas attack, he became one of the millions of Germans who were shocked to learn of Germany's surrender in November 1918. After the armistice, he joined the German Workers' Party (precursor to the National Socialist German Workers' Party, or Nazi Party) while working in army intelligence and quickly moved into the party's inner circle. The young Hitler now threw himself into a quest to restore Germany's lost glory. He was particularly taken with tales of Germany's mythical past, a deep distrust of capitalism and the Versailles Treaty, and a raging antisemitism. In speeches delivered to growing crowds in Munich beer halls, Hitler electrified audiences, tapping into currents of anger and resentment that he then channeled into ever-broader support for the Nazi Party. In November 1923, Hitler and some six hundred Nazis burst into a political meeting being held in a Munich beer hall in an attempt to launch a coup that would topple the German government. Local police responded quickly, scattering the Nazis, rounding up their leaders, and putting an end to the so-called Beer Hall Putsch. For his involvement in the attempted coup, Hitler received a five-year sentence (of which he would serve less than a year) in Bavaria's Landsberg Prison. He spent his relatively comfortable incarceration poring over the works of philosopher Friedrich Nietzsche, historian Leopold von Ranke, and British imperialist and antisemite Houston Stewart Chamberlain. It was also in Landsberg that Hitler dictated his rambling manifesto, *Mein Kampf,* to his assistant, Rudolph Hess, a former student of Karl Haushofer.

Published in 1925, Hitler's book revealed a mind unhinged by racism and intoxicated by fantasies of imperial power. *Mein Kampf* blended Friedrich Ratzel's and Haushofer's arguments about Germany's need for lebensraum with tales of ancient German conquests in eastern lands, reframing them in the post-1919 realities of Weimar Germany. Dismissed by critics as a semicoherent collection of rants inspired by adolescent fantasies, the book found an audience with disgruntled right-wing Germans. Hitler based his argument on a reading of history as a great struggle between competing races. In this struggle, the Aryan master race was assailed by the degenerate race of Jews. At present, according to Hitler, the "blood Jew," working under the guise of Bolshevism, had "killed or let starve to death around 30 million people [in Russia] in truly satanic savagery in order to secure rule over a great people of a bunch of Jewish *literati* and stock-market bandits." It was the Nazi Party's "mission" to awaken the German peoples to their destiny, which simultaneously called for crusades to destroy "Jewish Bolshevism" and to seize lebensraum in the East.

> Germany will either be a world power or there will be no Germany.... We take up where we broke off six hundred years ago. We stop the endless German movement to the south and west, and turn our gaze towards the land in the east.... If we speak of soil in Europe today, we can primarily have in mind only Russia and her vassal border states.

For all its nonsensical rambling, *Mein Kampf* succeeded in linking antisemitism, Aryan nationalism, and anti-Bolshevism to the quest for German imperial expansion in Eastern Europe.[30]

DISILLUSIONMENT WITH THE STATUS QUO WAS ALSO MOUNTING halfway around the globe in Japan. Like their Italian and German counterparts, Japanese leaders had concluded that the Versailles order was a fundamentally unjust system engineered to relegate their nation to second-class status. Tokyo sought to build an empire as a means of challenging the world order and seizing what it saw as its rightful status as a leading power in global affairs. However, Japan's relationship with colonialism was complex. Although key forces in Japan had come to see imperial conquest as critical to the nation's survival as a great power, Japanese leaders also chose to cast their nation as a champion of anticolonialism—a crusader against generations of Western imperialism in Asia. As the most powerful state in Asia, Japan had forces that would, in theory, serve as a bulwark against Western imperialism. Paradoxically, Japanese leaders presented their empire as an anticolonial force aimed at toppling the old order built on white supremacy and replacing it with a new order dominated by Tokyo—thereby creating an Asia for Asians.[31]

Japan had suffered colonial incursions since the nineteenth century as Western powers sought to break into the fabled markets of

China and the Far East. Although Japan had initially sought to remain closed off from Western influence, Commodore Matthew Perry's 1853 expedition at the head of a small fleet of American warships forced the nation to open to Western trade. Whereas Chinese leaders continued to oppose nearly all forms of Western influence, Japanese leaders came to recognize the futility of outright resistance and instead chose to co-opt Western ideas and technology in an effort to transform their nation into a modern world power. Like their Western counterparts, Japanese leaders recognized that national power was linked to imperial power. Tokyo's first target was Korea, which Japan occupied in 1905. However, the real prize was China. For the Western powers, China was a massive untapped market across the eastern horizon; for Tokyo, China was the empire's commercial and strategic backyard. To compete against the Western empires, Japanese leaders studied Western strategy, particularly in regard to its naval applications. The American prophet of naval power Alfred Thayer Mahan gained a large following in the Japanese government, which launched a crash program to build a modern fleet of warships over the 1890s.[32]

Japanese leaders remained keenly aware that the rising power of the United States was a long-term threat to their plans to dominate the Far East. In the 1870s and 1880s, the Americans had begun creeping across the Pacific Ocean in a form of lily-pad imperialism, seizing territories in the Hawaiian Islands, Midway, Howland and Baker Islands, and Kingman Reef. Though minuscule in terms of territory, these dots of land served as coaling stations, supply depots, telegraph nodes, and guano fields, allowing the United States to project significant military and commercial power across the vast distances of the Pacific Ocean. Most dramatically, America's victory in the 1898 Spanish-American War brought the Philippines under American colonial occupation, transforming the massive archipelago into a launchpad for future US commercial, diplomatic, and military operations in East Asia.[33] Tokyo's fears were confirmed the following year when the McKinley administration issued the first Open Door note.

The Open Door policy represented a direct challenge to Tokyo's plans to create a formal colony in China and establish a sphere of economic influence. Rather than carving China up into colonies, Washington called on the great powers to create a level commercial playing field in Asia's largest market. While on its face this Open Door policy appeared anti-imperialist, it masked a deeper truth: as a rising industrial giant, the United States had the capacity to outcompete all of its rivals in an open market. An open door to the China market all but guaranteed that the United States would enjoy a decisive advantage in the Far East for decades to come. Japanese officials recognized that the United States was more of a commercial menace than a military threat. Although the United States claimed to eschew official colonialism—its colony in the Philippines notwithstanding—America's Open Door policy seemed engineered to secure a dominant position for the United States and the Western powers in the China market. While the Americans controlled much of North America and the Europeans maintained vast colonies around the globe, Japan's frontier lay in continental Asia. Washington's Open Door threatened to render Tokyo subject to the whims of Western fiscal policies and commercial domination. Ultimately, Japanese leaders recognized that in a world dominated by empires, their nation could either, in the words of one historian, "join the West as a 'guest at the table' or be served up with China and Korea as part of the feast."[34]

America's emergence as a Pacific power coincided with Japan's efforts to flex its own imperial muscle. In a stunningly short period of time, Japanese leaders working under Emperor Meiji had transformed their nation into an industrial power. To ward off further Western incursions, Japan had built a modern army and a powerful fleet of warships that could challenge any of its Western rivals. Tokyo's military forces were not just for show. Like their counterparts in London, Paris, Berlin, and Washington, leaders in Tokyo understood that empire formed the foundation of national power at the turn of the twentieth century. Japan had built an army and navy designed for waging colonial war. The coming years would witness the realization of Tokyo's imperial dreams. Japan defeated China in the First Sino-Japanese War (1894–1895) and joined the international expedition that crushed the Boxer Rebellion in China in 1901. More dramatically, Japanese forces won a war against Russia (1904–1905), marking the first victory of an Asian nation against a European great power in the modern era and electrifying anticolonial nationalists across Asia and the wider non-Western world. As Tokyo's power grew, Japanese forces laid claim to Taiwan and the Kuril, Ryukyu, and Nanpo Islands; gained control of Port Arthur; established a colonial presence in Korea; and exerted influence in Manchuria (northeast China). Japan also gained treaty privileges alongside Western powers in the Chinese treaty ports of Hankou, Fuzhou, and Guangzhou.[35]

During the Great War, Japan joined the Entente powers, emerging victorious in 1918. Although Tokyo had fought on the side of the victors, Japanese leaders—much like their Italian counterparts—felt slighted by the peace agreement struck at Versailles. While Britain and France gained effective imperial control of vast sections of the Middle East and Africa and the United States emerged as the world's preeminent financial power, Japan gained the measly German concession in China's Shandong Province. However, even this proved to be too much: China demanded the return of Shandong, the United States and its allies reaffirmed the principle of the Open Door, and Japan was forced to relinquish formal control of the territory in 1922. Making matters worse, the Western powers had rejected a Japanese proposal made in February 1919 to include a racial equality clause in the Treaty of Versailles. Under the terms of the new treaty, Tokyo suggested that "all alien nationals of state members of the League [should be accorded] equal and just treatment in every respect making no distinction, either in law or in fact, on account of their race or nationality." Though relatively modest on its face, the implications of the Japanese proposal—that race should no longer be used to grant privileged status to certain groups—were revolutionary. If successful, the racial equality proposal would have marked a significant stride toward the long-held Japanese goal of securing equal status with the

Western powers.[36] But the hope of a new world order based on equality between the races was not to be. The British, who were eager to expand their imperial dominions, and the Americans, who presided over a system of legal racial segregation at home and maintained colonies abroad, worked to defeat Tokyo's proposal. The victors of the Great War were prepared to imagine a future without military conflicts, but they refused to abandon an international order predicated on white supremacy.

Tokyo would not soon forget these betrayals. The experience of the Great War also drove home the central importance of strategic resources during wartime: access to oil, rubber, and iron could very well be decisive in future conflicts. The Japanese home islands remained desperately poor in terms of strategic resources, a fact that rendered Japan dependent on imports for vital war materials. This reality would have left Japan deeply vulnerable in the event of another world war. Meanwhile, Japan also faced the challenge of feeding a rapidly growing population. As military propagandist Sadao Araki demanded, "Why should Japan remain content with 142,270 square miles, much of it barren, to feed 60 million mouths, while countries like Australia and Canada had more than 3 million square miles to feed 6.5 million people each? . . . [The] United States possessed not only 3 million square miles of home territory but 700,000 square miles of colonies. If expansion westward to the Pacific Ocean was the manifest destiny of the nineteenth-century United States, then China was twentieth-century Japan's manifest destiny."[37] In an international system torn by fierce competition between the great powers over resources, military strength, and territory, Japan could not afford to remain passive.

While some Japanese leaders looked to the Versailles system of collective security as a potential check against unrestrained great power competition, radical factions within the Japanese government and military worried that the post-1919 international order left Tokyo at a decisive disadvantage. In particular, the Washington Naval

Conference consigned Japan to the status of a second-tier naval power, granting Tokyo only 60 percent of the warship tonnage allocated to the United States and Great Britain. As a resource-poor island nation off the shores of an Asia that remained heavily colonized by Western empires, Japan saw the Washington Naval Treaty's restrictions as a clear danger to its commercial ambitions and long-term hopes for security and prosperity. Indeed, Japan had only managed to avoid China's semicolonial fate through herculean efforts to transform itself into a modern industrial power with substantial military forces. If the post-1919 international order crippled Japan's continued growth, Tokyo might find itself outclassed and overwhelmed in a world that was still very much controlled by empires. Japan seemed to face a clear choice: either expand to become a world empire or stagnate and become a colony.

IF LATECOMERS SUCH AS GERMANY, ITALY, AND JAPAN HOPED TO establish themselves as great imperial powers, they would need to find some way to topple the post-1919 international order. The Versailles and Washington Treaties stood as bulwarks against revisionist states. But the treaties themselves were only paper—they were only as strong as the willingness of status quo powers such as Britain, France, and the United States to defend them. In this regard, American, British, and French leaders differed in their long-term goals. Prevailing sentiment in the United States favored a withdrawal from formal diplomatic and military commitments to the post-1919 order. British leaders remained focused on defending the home islands, maintaining its naval supremacy, and fostering a balance of power in Europe that would allow London to ensure that no continental challenger could threaten its interests. With Germany prostrate and Russia in the throes of a violent communist revolution, many British leaders considered the possibility of reintegrating Germany into the new regional order. In contrast, French leaders recognized that their nation sat on the front lines of any future clash with Germany—for leaders in Paris, then, the prospect of a resurgent Germany constituted an existential threat.[38]

More broadly, the international order created at Versailles faced an inherent structural problem: the interwar balance of power was only viable because it had locked out two of Europe's most important players, Germany and Russia. The devastation of the Great War had weakened the two great continental powers and cleared the way for Britain and France to assert their will. But this situation was only temporary. As Germany and the new Soviet Union recovered over the 1920s, they came to command ever-greater influence, destabilizing the Versailles order and placing a heavier burden on its protectors. London and Paris could not hope to contain German and Soviet power indefinitely—at least not on their own.[39]

Moreover, through much of the interwar period, Bolshevism and the threat of communist revolution appeared to be the greatest menace to the status quo. With this in mind, many leaders in London, Paris, and Washington viewed far-right groups such as Mussolini's fascists and Hitler's Nazis as potential allies in the struggle against the Bolsheviks. Whereas Lenin and his comrades had vowed to topple international capitalism and pledged support for foreign revolutions, right-wing nationalists of Mussolini's ilk were working within the established parameters of European diplomatic relations. Likewise, the fascists and their fellow travelers had declared themselves to be staunch adversaries of the revolutionary left. At the very least, the far right might be co-opted by the capitalist powers, whereas the Bolsheviks and their allies sought nothing less than total revolution.[40]

ANXIETIES ABOUT THE SURVIVAL OF WORLD CAPITALISM RECEIVED a massive jolt in October 1929 when the New York stock market crashed, sparking the greatest economic crisis of the twentieth century. Wall Street's collapse sent shock waves across an increasingly interconnected world economy, triggering sharp losses in European markets and marking the beginning of a period of economic turmoil that would last well into the 1930s. The global economic crisis shook the foundations of the existing international order at the same time that it fundamentally transformed the domestic political playing field in nations around the world and exacerbated imperialist anxieties. Many observers feared that the Great Depression heralded a general crisis for world capitalism. Market instability, collapsing currencies, global financial shocks, bread lines, and rampant unemployment seemed to confirm the worst allegations leveled by capitalism's critics. While internationally oriented capitalist economies were buffeted by the Depression, the Soviet Union remained only loosely connected to global markets and managed to weather the economic storm.

In states around the world, moderate leaders suffered while isolationists, ultranationalists, and militarists gained influence. The Depression weakened moderates and emboldened extremists. One strain of thought looked to isolationism and protectionism as a solution to the international financial crisis. Perhaps the world had become too interconnected, protectionists suggested, and a return to stability and prosperity required a retreat from the global economy. To this end, a growing number of commentators argued, empire might provide the key to economic self-sufficiency: colonies provided readily controlled commercial zones, cheap labor, and raw materials. Rather than subjecting one's own economy to the vagaries of a volatile global economy, imperial powers could create and maintain their own captive markets.[41]

As much of the industrialized world sank into the morass of the worldwide economic depression, far-right forces across Europe and Asia stepped forward to challenge the restrictions of the Versailles order. The 1930s would witness a series of bids by regimes in Berlin, Rome, and Tokyo to carve out their own empires in Europe, Africa, and Asia. These upstart powers would fuse the politics of revolution, war, race, and empire into a potent new force in world affairs that would upend the interwar status quo and plunge the globe into another catastrophic war. As tensions mounted and the spirit of hope that had accompanied the Treaty of Versailles receded, the assessment of French marshal Ferdinand Foch, supreme Allied commander in the Great War, would come to seem prescient. "This is not a peace," he had scoffed upon reading the treaty. "It is an armistice for twenty years."[42]

Chapter 2

DESTROYING THE VERSAILLES ORDER

THE CITY OF MUKDEN—MODERN-DAY SHENYANG—SITS IN THE LIAO River basin at the edge of the Changbai Mountains almost four hundred miles northeast of Beijing. Surrounded by vast stretches of monotonous farmland interrupted by the occasional temple or crumbling graveyard, Mukden showcased a China in the midst of dramatic transformation. Fortified walls circled the old city, guarding traditional temples and an aging imperial palace. Muddy sidewalks lined poorly lit streets bustling with pedestrians, bicycles, and taxis. In stark contrast to the chaos of the Chinese quarters, the Japanese concession appeared to be a bastion of modern organization. Dull architecture prioritizing efficiency over aesthetic appeal struck one Western journalist as "almost offensively new."[1] The Japanese presence in the city had grown steadily since Tokyo's victory in the 1905 Russo-Japanese War. Mukden had long been a power center in Manchuria, contested by local Chinese leaders and the Russian and Japanese empires. By the early decades of the twentieth century, the city had emerged as a critical hub for the South Manchuria Railway—the lifeline of modernity and industrialization linking the continental interior to the port of Dalian and the waters of the Yellow Sea.

Just past 10:20 p.m. on September 18, 1931, Lieutenant Suemori Komoto of the Japanese Kwantung Army placed a set of yellow packages filled with blasting powder along the tracks of the South Manchuria Railway line near Mukden. After priming the explosives, Komoto retreated and lay flat on the ground with his hands pressed firmly over his ears. The damage caused by the ensuing blast proved insufficient to derail a train that passed by a few minutes later, but Komoto's actions succeeded in plunging Japan and China into fourteen years of conflict that would kill millions. His task complete, Komoto led his unit to a nearby camp to relay a message to his commanders: "Engaged in action with Peitaying Chinese forces which set off explosion along railroad." With the successful execution of this false flag operation, which would become known as the Mukden incident, the Kwantung Army's plans for the conquest of Manchuria lurched into motion.[2]

The South Manchuria Railway bombing was the initial flash point in what would become the Second World War. The turmoil unleashed by the Great Depression ended the complacency of the 1920s and drove a number of governments around the world to adopt more aggressive policies aimed at building power in an increasingly tumultuous international system. In particular, governments in Germany, Italy, and Japan made preparations over the 1930s to seize their own colonies in an already-crowded geopolitical field. United by a shared desire to topple the Versailles order, these revisionist powers drew from the playbook of Western imperialism, claiming a need for more living space and advancing arguments about their unique racial and historical destiny. Put together, the bids of Berlin, Rome, and Tokyo to seize new colonial empires would bring about the collapse of the old order. Though none knew it at the time, the Japanese bombing of the South Manchuria Railway had provided the first spark for the approaching global conflagration.

JAPANESE ARMY OFFICERS HAD LONG SEEN MANCHURIA AS A NEW frontier for development that could save Japan from the depredations of the European great powers. The region comprised over four hundred thousand square miles of territory rich with reserves of iron and coal and abundant agriculture. If Japan could transform Manchuria into an industrial center and a colonial breadbasket, the empire might finally stand toe to toe with the likes of London and Washington. Tokyo would deploy its technological prowess to modernize Manchuria, the plan went, and, in doing so, relieve many of the demographic pressures and resource shortages facing the home islands. Railroads would form the critical infrastructure of this effort, providing transportation networks for commercial and industrial development as well as facilitating the rapid deployment of military forces in the event of a crisis. To this end, Tokyo created the South Manchuria Railway Company in 1906. Beyond developing Manchuria's transportation infrastructure, the company served as a vehicle for the consolidation of Japan's political and military sphere of influence in northeast China. Just as London had used the East India Company to build an empire in South Asia in the eighteenth century, Tokyo would deploy the South Manchuria Railway Company to colonize Manchuria in the twentieth century.[3]

By the 1920s, Japan's efforts had acquired no small amount of urgency. Manchuria remained a heavily contested imperial frontier at the crossroads of Japanese-controlled Korea, the eastern marches of the Soviet Union, and a China gripped by revolution. Japanese leaders remained wary of Soviet designs on Manchuria—which echoed older Russian claims on the region—as well as the influence of Bolshevik ideology. Like many of their contemporaries around the world, leaders in Tokyo feared the contagion of revolutionary socialism. Making matters worse, the Guomindang regime in Nanjing was working to consolidate all of historic China under a central government.

At the helm of the Guomindang's crusade for national unification sat Chiang Kai-shek. Born to a family of salt merchants outside of Ningbo in 1887, the young Chiang proved to be a headstrong and mercurial youth with an avid interest in military affairs and revolutionary politics. These interests led him to a military school in Tokyo, from which he graduated an undistinguished fifty-fourth out of a class of sixty-two. Nor was he an especially popular student—his comrades described him as standoffish. But what he lacked in charisma and brilliance he seemed to make up for in determination. He would need every ounce of this resolve in what would become a decades-long quest to unify China as a sovereign state and expel the last vestiges of imperial influence from the country. Although he would prevail, his triumph would prove as fleeting as it was costly.[4]

China in the late nineteenth and early twentieth centuries presented a sort of mirror image to Japan. Where Japan had unified and staged a remarkable modernization campaign, China had fractured and fallen behind the curve of industrial and technological modernity. Where Japan had built itself into a rising great power that could challenge the Western empires, China had found itself a colonial target largely at the mercy of imperial predations. The massive Taiping Rebellion (1850–1864)—a civil war that dwarfed the contemporaneous American Civil War—left perhaps as many as thirty million dead and devastated large parts of the country. The Boxer Rebellion (1899–1901) emerged as a challenge to foreign imperialism that provoked a nine-power military intervention, fundamentally weakened the ruling Qing dynasty, and left colonial forces more deeply entrenched inside China. Generations of upheaval destroyed centralized rule in China, fueled the rise of regional warlords, sidetracked development schemes, and left the nation open to outside imperialism. America's Open Door policy was formulated as a response to the chaos in China—an effort to block a potentially dangerous imperial free-for-all in East Asia and to devise a new sort of informal economic imperialism that would rely on commercial influence, manufacturing power, and economic power rather than gunboats and expeditionary forces.

Although less overt than traditional Western colonialism, Washington's Open Door imperialism still trampled on Chinese sovereignty. The nation could never truly be independent while outside imperial powers controlled the nation's critical ports, maintained special courts for their citizens, and exercised commanding influence over the economy. If China was to reclaim its sovereignty, its leaders had to reestablish central control and throw off the yoke of foreign imperialism. In 1911, a loose coalition of nationalist leaders and local demonstrators launched the Xinhai Revolution, which toppled the ailing remnants of the Qing dynasty. Sun Yat-sen emerged as the intellectual leader of the revolution. Sun served as the provisional president of the new Republic of China in early 1912 before stepping aside as part of a negotiation that placed a military regime in power. In August 1912, he became leader of the new Guomindang (GMD) party. While successful in national elections, the nationalists failed to dislodge the ruling military regime, and Sun was forced to flee to Japan in 1913. Sun continued to push for a genuine republican revolution from exile until 1917, when he returned to lead the GMD in its struggle for China. The power struggle between feuding factions and warlords kept China divided into the 1920s. In 1923, Sun, aging and in failing health, reached out to the Chinese Communist Party to form a coalition of progressive forces. Sun's health continued to decline, and in March 1925, he passed away while undergoing treatment for cancer.[5]

Chiang Kai-shek's chance had arrived. He had worked his way up through the ranks of the GMD to become Sun's most prominent military deputy, but Chiang still faced a formidable rival for leadership in the person of Wang Jingwei. Initially, Wang—a handsome, brilliant, and charismatic politician—seemed to be the favorite to succeed Sun. In the wake of Sun's death, Chiang emerged as the leader of the right-wing faction of the GMD while Wang ascended to leadership of the party's left wing. While Wang set up a government in Wuhan, Chiang—frequently referred to as "Generalissimo"—launched the Northern Expedition, a sweeping military campaign to scatter the Communist Party and bring regional warlords to heel. In April 1927, Chiang's forces seized the critical port city of Shanghai. Soon after taking the city, Chiang's troops, working hand in hand with the local mafia, launched a vicious massacre of suspected communists. GMD forces slaughtered thousands on the streets of Shanghai, a great many of whom were certainly innocents. The victories of the Northern Expedition and the carnage in Shanghai established Chiang as the preeminent figure in the GMD, with a firm grip on military power. Wang chafed at having been eclipsed, but his attempts to push Chiang aside proved fruitless. Chiang moved the national capital to Nanjing and launched a decade of rule that would see the nationalist government further consolidate control over China.[6]

While many in China celebrated the promise of a new, modern nation, leaders in Tokyo recognized Chiang and the resurgence of Chinese nationalism as a dire threat. Chiang and his comrades remained steadfast in their determination to push foreign influence out of China. If the GMD succeeded in unifying a population of 470 million Chinese against Japan's population of 64 million, Tokyo's great power ambitions could be crushed. While still years away, the prospect of a unified, modern China could doom Tokyo's imperial designs on Manchuria. In response to Chiang's rise, Japanese officials decried China's "extreme anti-Japanese policy, which resulted in the boycott of Japanese goods and in many cases of public insult of the Japanese people." The economic dislocations of the Great Depression only deepened these imperial anxieties and increased the urgency among expansionist elements in Japan to find foreign markets for Japanese goods.[7]

MEANWHILE IN TOKYO, A GROWING MINORITY OF RIGHT-WING nationalists and militarists had begun calling for a more aggressive foreign policy. Increasing economic strife exacerbated by the outbreak of the Great Depression in 1929–1930 bolstered these militant factions and broadened their base of public support. As the 1930s began, rampant unemployment and poverty, declining exports, and social unrest had empowered the more radical elements in Tokyo. A critical turning point arrived in April 1930 when Prime Minister Hamaguchi Osachi signed a revision of the Washington Naval Treaty expanding Japan's warship tonnage from a previous ratio of 10 to 6 to a new ratio of 10 to 6.975. Although the new agreement benefited the Japanese navy, it angered the militarists in Tokyo, who denounced the revised terms as insufficient and an affront to Emperor Hirohito's authority. When an assassin shot Hamaguchi in November, right-wing groups throughout the country celebrated. This strain of radicalism gained traction in the military among officers who hoped to reorient Japan away from internationalism and toward a more nativist course. One group of young officers calling themselves the Cherry Blossom Society planned to launch a coup in March 1931 that was thwarted only by the refusal of senior army brass to support the conspirators.[8] The coup had failed, but other forces along the empire's frontier were preparing to transform Japanese society.

If the geopolitical situation in Manchuria had created a powder keg, Tokyo's rising militarism lit the fuse. To secure its position in Manchuria, Japanese leaders had created the Kwantung Army—a force of imperial soldiers charged with defending Japan's interests in China, particularly the South Manchuria Railway. As a major presence in the region, the Kwantung Army's duties expanded to include not just the maintenance of a military presence but also police operations, economic and industrial development, financial investment, and the deployment of political influence. Over the 1920s, its officers became embroiled in the political intrigues unfolding among Chinese warlords in Manchuria and among political leaders in Tokyo. By 1928, Japanese officers had become so deeply involved in Manchurian politics that they hatched a successful plot to assassinate the warlord Zhang Zuolin. Their efforts backfired, however, when Zhang's son and successor chose to align his forces with the Guomindang. The Chinese government's efforts to claim sovereignty over Manchuria in 1931 increased the sense of urgency among many Kwantung Army leaders. So, too, did the sporadic clashes between Japanese forces, Korean colonists, local farmers, and Chinese soldiers over the summer of 1931.[9]

The lack of civilian control in Tokyo exacerbated matters. Although officially the supreme leader of Japan, Emperor Hirohito occupied a largely ceremonial position. Real power was split between Japan's civilian political leaders and military officials. Although Japan allowed for universal male suffrage and maintained an elected parliament in the form of the National Diet, the military functioned largely outside of civilian control. Unlike the era's other great powers, Japan lacked a single charismatic leader such as Stalin, Hitler, or Franklin Roosevelt. Instead, a rotating coterie of prime ministers, generals, admirals, and ministers directed Japan's foreign affairs through the 1930s and into the 1940s. It was not until 1941 that General Hideki Tojo assumed the position of prime minister, a position that he held until 1944. While a general political consensus had ensured a measure of harmony between the Japanese military and civilian leadership in previous generations, over the course of the 1920s young officers in both the army and navy had increasingly embraced a more radical vision of Japan's place in the world that spurned internationalism and cooperation with the other great powers. With official representation of both army and navy leaders in the ruling Japanese cabinet, the military could exercise veto power over government decisions by forcing the collapse of any ruling coalition. The government's failure to rein in the military after the assassination of Zhang Zuolin in 1928 revealed that Tokyo lacked both the will and the means to bring the Kwantung Army under control.[10]

Added to this volatile mix were apocalyptic, ultranationalist ideologies concerning a coming clash of civilizations that had gained increasing purchase in the ranks of the Imperial Japanese Army. One of the most vocal prophets of these visions, Kanji Ishiwara, arrived in

46

Manchuria in 1928 to assume the position of lieutenant colonel in the Kwantung Army. The previous year, Ishiwara had forecast a coming world war that was to be the "final war of mankind." Modern aircraft would wage a "war of destruction from the air" that would culminate with the "unification of mankind." In preparation for this coming Armageddon, he believed, Japan had to establish itself as the leader of a pan-Asian civilization, while the United States would assume leadership over a unified Western coalition. Manchuria, as Japan's imperial frontier, represented the first stage on the road toward global war with the United States. To establish control over Manchuria, he warned in May 1931, it might be necessary for the military to "create the occasion with a plot and force the nation to go along." In this way, the Japanese Empire could "hope for the achievement of great things by having the Kwantung Army take the lead." Together with Colonel Seishiro Itagaki, Ishiwara would mastermind the bombing of the South Manchuria Railway line.[11]

Meanwhile, the Manchurian Youth League—a nationalist organization founded in 1928 to promote Japanese interests in China—printed pamphlets designed to fire up Japanese support for the conquest of northeast China. "Manchuria and Mongolia," the league told its followers, "are our first line of defense. Not only are they invaluable to our military because of their stores of raw materials, but they play a central role in our national existence because of their industrial materials and food surpluses." The league warned its members that the "era of colonization that began in the 18th century" was ongoing as the great powers conquered the continents and seized islands across the world's oceans. Indeed, it now seemed as if "every reef in the boundless oceans [was] occupied." The people of Japan must act, the pamphlet argued, to defend the empire's rights from being "snatched away." In August, Itagaki reminded an assembled audience in Dalian of Manchuria's importance as the industrial base of Japan's power. "Even if there should be a protracted war between Japan and the United States," he explained, "we will not need to worry because we will be able to lead China."[12]

As the summer heat set in across Manchuria in 1931, the more radical officers in the Kwantung Army were growing increasingly restless under the restraint of more cautious civilian authorities in Japan. The killing of a Japanese scout by Chinese forces in July might have served as the necessary provocation for war had cooler heads not prevailed in Tokyo. Nevertheless, tensions remained high. On September 10, 1931, Chinese officials notified the US consulate in Nanjing that the Kwantung Army had launched a series of deliberate "provocations in Manchuria in order to provide excuses for the use of force, as well as an intensive propaganda campaign to blind the eyes of the world to the facts of the situation." According to US officials, Chinese authorities seemed convinced that Japan was "preparing the ground for military intervention in Manchuria." Eight days later, the Mukden bombing plunged Japan and China into war.[13]

In the hours after the railroad bombing, Japanese soldiers attacked Mukden, firing rifles and artillery into the city. Chinese authorities ordered their forces to remain in their barracks and refrain from retaliation, fearing that the Japanese troops had "apparently run amuck." However, as the clashes continued into the early hours of September 19 and Japanese soldiers took positions outside the city gates, it became clear that the fighting was no accident. The Kwantung Army moved swiftly. The residents of Mukden spent a sleepless night as Chinese and Japanese forces clashed and Japanese artillery pummeled the suburb of Peitaying. Kwantung troops began by seizing the commercial district of Mukden before moving to secure the Japanese residential district, and then the city's arsenal and aerodrome. The *North China Herald* reported that the Japanese, having taken Mukden by 6:30 that morning, now intended to disarm all Chinese forces in Manchuria. Meanwhile, Japanese units attacked Changchun, Port Arthur, and Liaoyang.[14]

As the fighting continued, a picture began to emerge of the Kwantung Army having taken its own initiative to launch a war of conquest. The US consul in Mukden, Andrew Lynch, noted that the Japanese diplomats with whom he spoke seemed genuinely surprised by the outbreak of hostilities: "I very much doubt their having prior knowledge of the actual moving of troops." Rumors of atrocities added an ominous tone to the reports of violence in Manchuria. Lynch reported multiple instances of Japanese forces killing Chinese troops who had surrendered, shooting policemen, and beating civilians. In one instance, Japanese soldiers supposedly threw grenades into laborers' quarters, killing twenty. However, considering the amount of territory and the size of the population that had switched hands "literally overnight," Lynch was surprised at the relatively low level of bloodshed.[15]

Officially, Japanese leaders continued to blame Chinese authorities for provoking the conflict. The Foreign Ministry insisted that "deep-rooted anti-Japanese feeling in China," driven by the Chinese government and the nationalist regime, had forced the Kwantung Army to "resort to measures of self-defence." Meanwhile, military leaders argued that the prevalence of Chinese guerrilla operations necessitated the conquest of the whole of Manchuria, which in turn required the creation of what would become the puppet state of Manchukuo. Tokyo insisted that it was the revolutionary regime in Nanjing, rather than Japanese expansionism, that had been responsible for violence. Nanjing, it claimed, had "ceased to recognize [Japanese] rights and interests and gradually intensified its policy of shutting Japan out of Manchuria. To cope with this policy, Japan finally resorted to the use of military power, taking the opportunity presented by the local clash to destroy oppression and thus restore her rights."[16]

However, the Kwantung Army's pretense carried little weight with outside observers. Only days after the Mukden incident, the American chargé d'affaires in Tokyo noted that the Japanese seizure of so much of Manchuria seemed "out of proportion to the alleged cause. . . . It seems probable that the [railroad bombing] was seized upon by the Army authorities and the whole area occupied as a military measure to force a general liquidation of outstanding issues." These suspicions were confirmed in the coming weeks as Japanese operations escalated. US officials were particularly appalled by the October 8 bombing of the city of Jinzhou by Japanese aircraft. The attacks, which killed a Russian professor, fourteen civilians, and one soldier, drew strong protests from the US secretary of state, Henry Stimson. "Bombing of an unfortified and unwarned town is one of the most extreme of military actions, deprecated even in time of war," Stimson fumed. Jinzhou lay fifty miles from the Japanese railway zone, firmly within Chinese-administered territory. The real motivation, Stimson suggested, seemed to be preventing Chinese authorities from re-establishing administrative control over Manchuria.[17]

Japanese leaders offered classic colonial arguments to justify their seizure of ever-larger chunks of Manchuria. In late December 1931, Tokyo insisted that local Chinese authorities had "fled or resigned," leaving the population to the mercy of bandits—many of whom were, paradoxically, under the direction of the Chinese military authorities in Jinzhou. The current turmoil had, "in spite of her wishes, created a new responsibility and a wider sphere of action for Japan . . . [forcing Tokyo] to assume the duty of maintaining order and private rights throughout a wide area." Far from seeking conquest, Tokyo had a moral responsibility to assume control of Chinese territory: "It would have been a breach of that duty to have left the population a prey to anarchy—deprived of all the apparatus of civilized life."[18] Tokyo's justifications echoed those of generations of Western empires that had colonized vast stretches of Africa, Asia, and the Middle East in the name of securing order, peace, and civilization.

Indeed, Japanese expansionists insisted that they were merely following a blueprint laid out by the Western great powers. In particular, voices in Tokyo and beyond argued that Japanese actions in Manchuria amounted to an Asian Monroe Doctrine—a reference to the 1823 policy whereby the United States claimed a position of great power primacy over North and South America and warned outside powers not to interfere in the Western Hemisphere. Surprisingly, the idea for a Japanese Monroe Doctrine was first floated by President Theodore Roosevelt in 1905: "The future policy of Japan towards Asiatic countries should be similar to that of the United States toward their neighbors on the American continent. . . . A 'Japanese Monroe Doctrine' in Asia." But US support proved short-lived. The adoption of an anti-imperialist foreign policy under Woodrow Wilson and the 1919 Treaty of Versailles recast Japanese great power ambitions as a threat to the international order. For Japanese leaders, this about-face proved doubly insulting. Not only were the Western powers seeking to block Tokyo from joining their ranks, but the United States, of course, still invoked the Monroe Doctrine as a claim to supremacy in North and South America. "Many Japanese," wrote historian John Murnane, "began to ask how it was that the United States could claim an 'open door' in China, while maintaining a 'closed door' in the Western Hemisphere." The string of US military interventions in Latin America in the 1910s and 1920s added further evidence of an international double standard working against Tokyo. As Stanford professor and adviser to the Japanese government Katsuji Inahara wrote in 1928, "When [Japan] proved herself so successful in her economic enterprises in South Manchuria, Europe and America became hostile to her. Japan was severely criticized by her Western colleagues for doing what they were doing." Three years later, in response to the Manchurian crisis, Inahara argued, "As long as the United States maintains the Monroe Doctrine—that is, a 'closed door policy'—and still insists on enforcing the Open Door policy [in China], it is only natural and should not be objectionable at all that Japan, acting on the principle of equality, should establish its own Monroe Doctrine—that is, 'a closed door policy'—and further demand that the Open Door policy be applied to Central and South America."[19]

In late January 1932, Tokyo expanded its war beyond Manchuria by launching an attack on the international city of Shanghai. While Japanese soldiers battled Chinese defenders across the cobblestone streets, aircraft bombed Shanghai, igniting raging fires amid the wooden houses of the city. As night fell, Japanese forces began shooting out streetlights in a bid to deter Chinese snipers from harrying their advance. Stimson worried that the ongoing situation in China ultimately presented a threat to the existing balance of power in Asia and the wider world. Nanjing, he wrote, now faced the potential choice of having to either "arm herself and become a military nation or . . . be thrown into total subservience to a more military nation like Japan. Either of these results would be extremely injurious to the peace of the world and to the freedom of commerce which Britain and [the United States] had been striving for in the Far East. They would tend directly to destroy thus the work which [the United States] had been trying to do in the last thirty years in protecting the integrity of China and the Open Door." To challenge this threat, Stimson told British officials at the beginning of the Manchurian crisis that "the White races in the Orient had got to stand more or less together." Far Eastern powers, he feared, could not be expected to conduct themselves like their Western counterparts. The provisions of the post-1919 international order, he wrote in his diary, "no more fit the three great races of Russia, Japan, and China, who are meeting in Manchuria, [than] a stovepipe hat would fit an African savage."[20]

While Stimson worried about threats to Western interests in Asia, Japanese officials continued tightening their hold on large parts of Manchuria. On February 18, 1932, Tokyo announced the creation of the new state of Manchukuo. Nanjing condemned Tokyo's actions as a violation of the Covenant of the League of Nations and denounced the new entity as a puppet state. This stance was shared by the Western powers, which refused to recognize Manchukuo. British officials in particular worried that Tokyo's actions—especially its assault on Shanghai—were a grave threat to the League of Nations and the system of international order it represented. "Anything which tends to throw doubt on the sanctity of the Covenant or to bring the League of Nations into disrepute," the British secretary of war told Parliament, "must necessarily be a matter of the gravest importance to this Government and to the people of this country."[21]

By early February, Japanese forces had seized nearly half a million square miles of territory and routed large-scale Chinese resistance. These victories proved wildly popular in Japan. Leaders in Tokyo who had initially opposed the Kwantung Army's reckless aggression now found themselves unable to resist the combination of military pressure and popular enthusiasm. As the army consolidated its hold on northeast China, "war fever" swept across Japan. Mainstream newspapers were caught up in a wave of "imperial jingoism" that silenced critics of the war. Popular songs, magazines, and dailies invoked memories of the Russo-Japanese War and called on the Japanese people to "defend the Manchurian lifeline!" Meanwhile, right-wing military societies launched a campaign of assassinations against moderate civilian leaders, killing the governor of the Bank of Japan and the director-general of the Mitsui Group. The greatest shock came on May 15, 1932, when officers from the Imperial Japanese Navy assassinated Prime Minister Inukai Tsuyoshi, who had attempted to rein in military power. Though the killers did not appear to be working on behalf of the senior military brass, their murderous actions helped to widen the rift between the military and civilian leadership in Tokyo. In seizing Manchuria, the militarists in the Imperial Army had conquered not only northeast China but also the hearts and minds of the Japanese people. In doing so, the militarists transformed themselves into a near-irresistible force in the Japanese government.[22]

By early 1932, the British and the Americans had come to recognize that Japan's actions in China posed a serious threat to two of the cornerstones of the post-1919 international order: the Open Door principle and the authority of the League of Nations. By creating facts on the ground, the Kwantung Army could establish a puppet state in Manchuria, destroy the principle of the Open Door, and make a mockery of the league. Japan's decision to withdraw from the league the following year underscored the weakness of the organization in the face of the Manchurian crisis. Though still implicit, Japanese imperialism offered an even more profound challenge to the international status quo. By brushing aside American and British objections, Tokyo had initiated a campaign that would overturn the established racial order in the Far East. Secretary Stimson wondered if tensions between Japan and the Western powers might be leading to an inevitable clash of civilizations.[23] The rising power of the Japanese Empire would soon challenge Western colonial influence in the Pacific. And for the time being, there seemed to be little that either Washington or London could do about it.

FIVE THOUSAND MILES TO THE WEST, BENITO MUSSOLINI'S REGIME was also preparing to seize new colonies. The fascist leader had long eyed the Mediterranean as Italy's zone for expansion. If Rome was to transform the sea into an Italian lake, it would have to strengthen its presence in Africa. Mussolini's gaze had initially fallen on North Africa, but its arid landscape would not support the heavy agrarian colonization that he envisioned. The arable land the dictator sought lay farther to the south, across the sands of the Sahara. Italy already had a foothold in the Horn of Africa in Eritrea and Italian Somalia. However, larger tracts of land lay inland in the independent empire of Ethiopia. Furthermore, time might have been running out for Italy to expand. Ethiopian emperor Haile Selassie had emerged as a powerful figure in the region who appealed to anticolonial elements inside Italian-controlled territories. Ethiopia had repelled an Italian imperial invasion in the 1890s, a national disgrace that Mussolini was only too eager to avenge. Likewise, the competition among European states for colonies remained a constant concern. In February 1932, Italy's director general of political and commercial affairs for Europe, the Levant, and Africa wrote that Ethiopia was the only place where Italy could create "a true colonial Empire. . . . The places in the sun and especially the places in the African sun (those that interest us most) are all taken." The Italian governor of Eritrea added a social Darwinist argument in favor of colonial war. "Superior races," he explained, "have the right and the duty to impose themselves and to superimpose themselves and to substitute themselves for their inferiors." The regime set to work preparing its forces for an aggressive colonial war in East Africa.[24]

By the beginning of 1935, Rome's plans for the war had come into focus. Italian forces would launch an invasion of Ethiopia from Eritrea and Somalia. Swift-moving ground troops would be supported by aircraft equipped with chemical weapons that would overwhelm native resistance. Once subdued, Ethiopia would be incorporated into Italy's growing African empire. Sporadic skirmishes along the border—most notably the November 1934 clash at the fort of Wal Wal that killed one hundred Ethiopians and thirty Italians—would form the pretext for the invasion.[25]

Italian forces crossed into Ethiopia on October 3, 1935, and drove deeper into the country as quickly as the terrain would allow. Mussolini's forces embarked on a vicious colonial war waged by a modern, mechanized army against indigenous forces armed with a significant arsenal of modern weapons. However, the Italians enjoyed the advantage of an air force, with which they planned to terrorize the population. "Everything must be destroyed with incendiary exploding bombs," explained the commander of the Italian army, Marshal Pietro Badoglio. "Terror must be disseminated throughout the Empire." Italian aircraft strafed enemy soldiers, bombed Ethiopian cities, and staged mustard gas attacks.[26] Ethiopian troops put up a determined defense, but they were outgunned by Italian forces, which took the capital, Addis Ababa, in May 1936. The initial conquest only marked the beginning of the violence.

The Italians now confronted a concerted resistance movement. Ethiopian fighters were no mere victims in the brutal warfare. Rebels gained the reputation for using dumdum bullets—explosive ammunition that left horrific wounds. In perhaps the best-publicized Ethiopian atrocity of the war, Ethiopian forces murdered and mutilated sixty-eight Italian employees of the Gondrand transport company. The photographs of the victims enraged Mussolini, who ordered Badoglio to retaliate with "inexorable energy." As they had done in their initial invasion, Italian commanders launched poison gas attacks against rebel forces in the outlying hinterlands, using aircraft and chemical weapons as a substitute for larger deployments of ground troops.[27]

With his forces in retreat, Ethiopian emperor Haile Selassie turned to the international community to address Italy's blatant violation of Ethiopian sovereignty. On June 30, 1936, Selassie addressed the League of Nations in Geneva. Ethiopia was the victim of a savage colonial attack made in a gross violation of international law, he argued. Moreover, Italian forces made no distinctions between civilians and combatants; they had "attacked populations far removed from hostilities, in order to terrorize and exterminate them." The Italians had used poison gas in a brutal campaign of annihilation: "The deadly rain that fell from the aircraft made all those whom it touched fly shrieking with pain. All those who drank the poisoned water or ate the infected food also succumbed in dreadful suffering." At stake, he insisted, was the Versailles system of collective security upon which the entire international order rested. "I decided to come myself to bear witness against the crime perpetrated against my people and give Europe a warning of the doom that awaits it, if it should bow before the accomplished fact." At the end of his address, as applause from supporters—and jeers from the Italians and their allies—swept through the chamber, the emperor reportedly added prophetically, "It is us today. It will be you tomorrow." The league's vote to lift sanctions on Italy and issue de facto recognition of Italian suzerainty over Ethiopia represented a crushing blow to Selassie, the Ethiopian people, and the League of Nations. Mussolini's land grab in Ethiopia put the league's pretensions of collective security on a deathwatch.[28]

Italian forces now rushed to consolidate their hold over their new colony of Italian East Africa. As counterinsurgency operations and poison gas attacks continued in the countryside, imperial authorities settled into their offices in the cities. However, tensions in Addis Ababa remained high. The situation in the capital exploded on February 19, 1937, when insurgents staged a grenade attack on Italian officials during a public ceremony, gravely wounding the Italian viceroy. In response, Italian troops turned machine guns on the assembled crowd, to devastating effect. "The dead fall upon the dead," one witness wrote. "Human blood streams like floodwater from the rain." In the following days, Italian forces unleashed a reign of terror on the city. "Comrades," Federal Secretary Guido Cortese told an assembled group of fascists, "today is the day we should show our devotion to our Viceroy by reacting and destroying the Ethiopians for three days. For three days I give you *carta bianca* to destroy and kill and do what you want to the Ethiopians." Witnesses described "torrents" of blood flowing through the streets amid the "screams of women and children mingled with the diabolical concert of modern arms." Victims were shot, clubbed, run down in the streets, and tied to vehicles and dragged to their deaths. Meanwhile, groups of men with torches and flamethrowers set fire to thousands of houses in the poorer sections of the city, many with their inhabitants still inside. British intelligence officials reported that many who tried to escape were shot or thrown back into the flames. Over the course of three days, more than nineteen thousand people, comprising perhaps 20 percent of the city's population, were massacred in Addis Ababa.[29]

Italy's brutal invasion and occupation of Ethiopia made a mockery of the League of Nations' ostensible role as an arbiter of the post-1919 world order. In the same stroke, Mussolini's colonization of Ethiopia revealed British and French reluctance to use force in defense of post-Versailles visions of collective security. Even so, the Italians were hardly alone in marshaling savage violence on colonial battlefields of the 1930s. Indeed, while Mussolini's forces rampaged through Ethiopia, British authorities launched a sweeping counterinsurgency against an anticolonial revolt in Palestine in 1936. British troops razed hundreds of Palestinian houses, destroyed crops, and executed scores of suspected rebels. In the course of the crackdown, British colonial authorities reduced to rubble a substantial section of Jaffa's Old City. During the three-year revolt, British forces killed an estimated five thousand Arabs.[30] From the standpoint of international law, the key difference between Mussolini's war in Ethiopia and Britain's war in Palestine lay not in the levels of brutality but in Italy's challenge to the established order. Because the Versailles Treaty had granted Britain mandate authority in Palestine—against the wishes of the majority of that region's inhabitants—British violence was marked as a legitimate police action of a mandate power. In contrast, Italy's war in Ethiopia enjoyed no such sanction. Nevertheless, even this breach proved insufficient to earn the league's lasting sanction.

As Japan and Italy launched their bids for empire, German leaders waged a different battle to circumvent Versailles's restrictions and rearm. Defeated in the Great War, demilitarized, deprived of its colonies, stripped of parts of its eastern and western provinces, and saddled with burdensome war reparations, Germany's Weimar Republic was in no shape to withstand the onslaught of the Great Depression. As unemployment and inflation skyrocketed, increasing numbers of Germans concluded that the time had come for radical change. While socialists, communists, and anarchists assailed the Weimar government from the left, Adolf Hitler's Nazi Party emerged as a powerful force on the political right, winning 18 percent of the vote in the 1930 Reichstag elections. Two years later, the Nazis won 37 percent of the vote, making them the largest party in the Reichstag and paving the way for Hitler's rise. In the coming months, Hitler and the Nazis ruthlessly consolidated control over the German state, dismantled the republic, and created the Third Reich.[31] Hitler had come to power promising not only to restore Germany's rightful place among the great powers but to make Germany the leading power in Europe and the world. However, during his first few years in office, Hitler made the strategic decision to downplay his expansionist goals while he centralized control over German society and rebuilt the economy. Nazi policies focused on eliminating German socialists, fanning the flames of antisemitism, instituting policies of racial hygiene, and establishing concentration camps for political prisoners and others deemed undesirable. Alongside political repression, Hitler instituted an ambitious rearmament program that aimed to transform the Germany military into one of the most powerful fighting forces in the world.

However, before he could conquer Europe, Hitler faced two key challenges closer to home. First, he needed to tighten his hold over the German state and the Nazi Party. As a revolutionary organization fighting for power during the 1920s and early 1930s, the Nazis had relied on their paramilitary wing, the Sturmabteilung (SA, a.k.a. Brownshirts), which routinely engaged in street violence, attacked opponents, and intimidated voters. Once in power, however, Hitler found that the SA had become something of a nuisance. Not for the first time, onetime allies in revolution became rivals following their victory. The approximately three million men in the SA ranks far outnumbered the one hundred thousand men in the German military—a fact that rankled German military leaders. Likewise, the leader of the SA, Ernst Röhm, had built up a devoted following that challenged Hitler's total control of the party. Röhm's calls for an ongoing revolution further threatened the Nazi leadership, which was now focused on institutionalizing their control of the German state. By the early summer of 1934, the situation had become intolerable. On the morning of June 30, 1934, the Schutzstaffel (SS)—a rival paramilitary organization under the command of Hitler's deputy Heinrich Himmler—launched a purge of the SA. Röhm and the other leaders of the SA were rounded up while Hitler announced that the organization had been plotting a coup. That evening, Hitler's lieutenant Joseph Goebbels gave the order to begin executing the prisoners. The following afternoon, Röhm was shot and killed in his prison cell in Munich in what came to be known as the Night of the Long Knives. President Paul von Hindenburg's death from lung cancer the following month allowed Hitler to merge the offices of president and chancellor, granting the Führer total control over the state.

Having consolidated control over the state, Hitler and the Nazis faced a second challenge in the form of rearming the military. The Treaty of Versailles had capped the German army at one hundred thousand men, imposed strict limitations on the size of the German navy, and prohibited Berlin from maintaining an air force. While these restrictions had held through the 1920s, Hitler was intent on throwing off the shackles of Versailles. Heavy spending on the military supported conquest, conquest granted lebensraum, lebensraum ensured ethnic survival. Soon after coming into office in 1933, Hitler had informed his advisers of his plans to begin rearmament. Eight months later, he told the world that Germany would no longer allow itself to be relegated to the status of a second-tier power and promptly withdrew from the League of Nations. On March 16, 1935, Hitler announced that he would terminate Versailles's restrictions on the German military, increase the army to 480,000 men, and reinstitute mass conscription. Hitler explained that Germany's European neighbors had forced the Reich to "take the necessary measures to put an end to her defenselessness." The Soviet army alone numbered nearly a million men, he explained. "This is the German nation's great day," the Nazi newspaper *Korrespondenz* wrote in celebration of the announcement. "We believe that this day will herald a new era of peaceful cooperation among European peoples."[32]

Some voices outside Germany also wondered whether the time had come to ease the treaty's limitations on German power. The *Washington Post* argued that Hitler's pledge to rebuild his military represented "the most honest fulfillment of a definite pledge to the German people." To many in the world community, the paper explained, "the German case for rearmament is very strong." In any case, the paper continued, "soon or late, by concession of the victors or by assertion of the vanquished, the intolerable stigmas of the treaty of Versailles were due for obliteration."[33]

By 1936, THE WORLD STOOD ON THE BRINK OF THE ABYSS. THE POST-1919 international order had started to collapse beneath the threefold assault from Berlin, Rome, and Tokyo. Hitler, Mussolini, and a clique of Japanese militarists had concluded that imperial conquest was the key to securing their nations' rightful status as great powers. The road to empire required the use of unrestrained violence and the destruction of the existing international order, which had trapped Germany, Italy, and Japan in subservient positions. This same order had banished colonial violence to the far corners of Africa, Asia, and the Middle East. As Haile Selassie had predicted, the conquest of Ethiopia served as a harbinger of the brutalities to come. In the coming years, the citizens of London, Berlin, Leningrad, and dozens of other cities would experience the horrors of indiscriminate colonial violence already familiar to the residents of Addis Ababa, Jaffa, and Mukden.

Chapter 3

A NEW ORDER
IN EAST ASIA

O N THE MORNING OF DECEMBER 13, 1937, THE RESIDENTS OF CHI-
na's capital city, Nanjing, awoke to a nightmare. As Japanese troops
swarmed through the city's gates, the defending garrison disintegrated. Terrified soldiers tore off their uniforms, discarded their
weapons, and fled before the invaders. Black smoke lifted into the sky
as whole districts burned. Many of the fires had been set by retreating
Chinese forces determined to destroy any infrastructure or supplies
that might be of use to the attackers, leaving the Japanese nothing
but scorched earth. Hastily erected barricades did little to slow the
attackers, who began ransacking homes and shops in search of food,
liquor, and spoils. The persistent crackle of gunfire filled the air, adding to the mass hysteria. Soon the attackers turned their fury on the
population. Women of all ages were dragged off to be gang-raped or
violated in their homes. Chinese men suspected of being soldiers were

shot on sight or rounded up and herded into groups to be used for bayonet practice. Citizens who resisted the Japanese or tried to defend their families were butchered. In the days and weeks that followed, survivors described streets strewn with the burned corpses of men, women, and children. *New York Times* reporter F. Tillman Durdin, witness to the slaughter, described a ghastly scene: "The unrestrained cruelties of the Japanese are to be compared only with the vandalism in the Dark Ages in Europe or the brutalities of medieval Asiatic conquerors."[1]

The outbreak of the Second Sino-Japanese War in 1937 heralded eight years of ferocious violence that would consume huge sections of the world. Driven by both their desire to consolidate control over Manchuria and their fears of a closing window of opportunity, Japanese leaders launched a vicious campaign designed to destroy Chiang Kai-shek's regime and render the whole of China prostrate before the power of the Japanese Empire. If successful, they would overturn the existing regional order, seize a commanding position over East Asia, and drive the Western empires out of the region. If they failed, Japan would be crushed between the rising power of a unified China, a revolutionary Soviet Union, and the irresistible force of American capitalism. Like the Western empires they emulated, Japanese leaders combined their drive for imperial conquest with a vision of racial hierarchy. A victorious Japanese Empire would not only drive the white colonial powers from Asia but also place the Yamato race in a position of supremacy over the other peoples of the Far East. If all went according to Tokyo's plan, Japan would be to East Asia what the United States had become to Latin America.

IN THE YEARS LEADING UP TO 1937, JAPAN'S PUPPET STATE OF MANchukuo buzzed with activity. Workers laid railroads across the landscape, new factories belched clouds of smoke into the skies, and Manchuria emerged as the most advanced industrial region in all of China. In Manchukuo, Tokyo found not only the living space it sought but also a stage for the demonstration of Japan's civilizing mission. Like British officials in India and French officials in Indochina, Japanese leaders could trumpet their efforts to bring modernity to the colonized peoples of Asia. But like all colonial projects, Japan's empire had a dark side. Tokyo's venture in Manchukuo relied on harsh violence against the local population. After the September 1932 massacre of some 2,700 civilians outside of Fushun who had been accused of harboring "bandits," Japanese officials issued a report titled *Outline for Guiding Manchukuo*, which explained, "Racial struggle between Japanese and Chinese is to be expected. Therefore, we must never hesitate to wield military power in case of necessity." Moreover, Japanese dominion in Manchuria came with the price of increased vulnerability. Investments in Manchukuo transformed Japan from an island nation surrounded by the Sea of Japan and the Pacific Ocean into a continental power forced to defend frontiers abutting not one but two massive nations: China and the Soviet Union.[2]

Many Japanese leaders remained convinced that their traditional rivals in Moscow constituted the most significant threat to the empire. The Bolshevik Revolution had momentarily weakened Russia but raised the long-term menace of communist revolution along the borders of the Soviet Union. Meanwhile, revolutionary transformations continued to sweep through China. The rise of the Guomindang regime in Nanjing and Chiang's crusade to unify China under his central administration remained an existential threat to the Japanese Empire. Ultimately, Manchukuo could only survive as long as the rest of China remained divided. Although sporadic clashes between Japanese and Chinese troops continued after 1932, Tokyo focused its energy on development in Manchukuo, and Chiang turned his attention to rooting out the remnants of the Chinese Communist Party. In 1934, Chiang's Fifth Encirclement Campaign drove the CCP out of Jiangxi, forcing the communists to embark on what would come to be called the Long March. After twelve months and thousands of miles, the survivors set up their headquarters in the remote city of Yan'an, where, under the leadership of Mao Zedong, they would rebuild themselves into a massive revolutionary army.

Meanwhile, Japan continued to push Chiang to recognize the puppet regime in Manchuria. Tokyo sent diplomatic feelers to Nanjing and upgraded its consulate to a full embassy—all to no avail. Chiang and the GMD remained adamant in their refusal to cede the territory to the Japanese Empire. Nanjing's refusal reinforced the conviction in the Japanese military that Manchukuo remained dangerously exposed. While one faction in the military saw Moscow as the greatest threat, a second group called for total mobilization of Japan's resources against all potential enemies. This power struggle erupted in February 1936 when the first faction staged a coup, which culminated in the assassination of a number of ministers and the seizure of the War Ministry and general staff. In response, the total mobilization faction staged a counterattack, soon regained control of the government, and rounded up the coup's architects.[3]

With the supporters of total mobilization in control, Tokyo embarked on an even more ambitious policy of imperial expansion. In the grandest sense, Japanese leaders sought a new balance of power in East Asia. The most ambitious among them believed that the days of Western preeminence were over and that their nation stood poised to lead the peoples of the Far East in a new order. As Foreign Ministry official Amo Eijiro explained in the spring of 1934, Japan would no longer accept Western interference in East Asian affairs. Going forward, the great Western powers must accept Tokyo as the dominant player in the Far East. Amo's proclamation reaffirmed Tokyo's vision of a Japanese Monroe Doctrine and represented a direct challenge to the existing balance of power. Although Tokyo backed down in the face of US and British objections, its long-term goals remained unchanged. Indeed, by 1936, Japan had effectively withdrawn from the Washington treaty system. Tokyo's decision in November to join the Anti-Comintern Pact, aligning with Germany and Italy against Moscow, confirmed that Japanese leaders had chosen to cast their lot with the revisionist powers of Europe.[4]

Over the spring and summer of 1936, Japanese leaders developed a series of plans aimed at securing strategic supremacy in East Asia. As an April 1936 navy document explained, the nation's goal must be to "establish peace in East Asia, advance the welfare of the people, and completely achieve a position as a stabilizing power in East Asia." The focus of Tokyo's efforts would first fall on Manchukuo, which would be developed into an economic and military power closely tied to Japan. China would follow in the spirit of "co-existence and co-prosperity," albeit under Japanese tutelage. The long-term prize, however, was the Western colonies of Southeast Asia: French Indochina, British Malaya, Dutch Indonesia, and the American-controlled Philippines. "The Southern countries are the areas we should regard as most important for strengthening our national defence and solving the population problem and economic development," the document explained. Without this southern advance, the Japanese vision for Manchuria and China would be imperiled. Therefore, the document insisted, "it is our country's inevitable mission to expand our power, based on the Imperial spirit, in the Southern area, and to improve the peoples' welfare and realize co-existence and co-prosperity." However, a move into Southeast Asia risked provoking conflict with the Western imperial powers. "We will watch and be on strict guard against British maneuvers to bring pressure on Japan, using world power, especially America, Russia and China," the document explained. Ultimately, Tokyo's forces must prepare to "resist traditional American policy in the Far East."[5]

In its bid to overturn the international balance of power, Japan mounted an explicit challenge to the existing racial order. In June 1936, the army general staff drew up its own policy document titled *General Principles of National Defence Policy*. The document explained that the "first order of business" was to "establish our status as protector and leader of East Asia. To do this we must have the power to expunge the pressure of the white races in East Asia." Russia represented the first target. Once Moscow was neutralized, the document predicted, Japan would "expel the power of Britain from

East Asia." But none of this could happen without China. "Friendship between Japan and China is the key to administering East Asia, and the restructuring of China is our mission. However, it will be difficult to realize without sufficient power against the pressure of the white races." After forging an alliance with China and defeating Russia and Britain, Japan would turn to the last and ultimate foe: "We will plan a resurgent development of strength and prepare for a great decisive war against the United States."[6]

Five weeks later, a joint conference of Tokyo's top leadership drew up a sweeping statement on grand strategy titled *Fundamentals of National Policy*. Japan's ultimate goal was to "expand [its] national destiny. Japan should be the stabilizing power in East Asia." To accomplish this goal, Japanese forces must "secure the position of Japan on the East Asiatic continent," which would serve as the core area of Japanese power. Japanese forces would then turn to "advance and develop in the Southern area." Japan's southern advance was likely to spark resistance, which made it all the more critical for Tokyo to forge a close alliance between "Japan, Manchukuo and China for preparations against Britain and the United States." In the meantime, the army should prepare for a conflict with Russia while the navy must take steps to "ensure naval supremacy in the Western Pacific against the United States Navy."[7]

Collectively, the leadership of the Japanese army, navy, and government articulated a wildly ambitious vision for regional supremacy that tied Japanese security to imperial conquest in Manchuria, Southeast Asia, and the Pacific. Each region was dependent on the others, and the preservation of Japan's great power status required active campaigns to carve out a sphere of influence. These campaigns, in turn, all but guaranteed a conflict with the Western colonial powers.

Moreover, Japan's ambitions went beyond the realm of geopolitics. Japanese leaders hoped to topple the existing imperial order built on the basis of white supremacy in the Pacific. For nearly five hundred years, the European great powers had treated Asia as a theater of colonization and imperial competition. Naturally, Tokyo leaders placed the Japanese people atop this new racial hierarchy. Like their German counterparts, Japanese leaders remained fixated on "blood and soil" rhetoric. As a 1943 report put out by the Ministry of Health and Welfare would explain, "We, the Yamato race, are presently spilling our 'blood' to realize our mission in world history of establishing a Greater East Asia Co-Prosperity Sphere. In order to liberate the billion people of Asia and also to maintain our position of leadership over the Greater East Asia Co-Prosperity Sphere forever, we must plant the 'blood' of the Yamato race in this 'soil.'"

Though rooted in cultural notions of the Japanese family, these ideas bore more than a passing resemblance to the racial hierarchies that had structured Western imperialism for centuries. Japanese imperialism married elements of European colonialism, scientific racism, Japanese culture, and Pan-Asianism.[8] But first, Japan would be drawn into a massive conflict in China.

ON THE EVENING OF JULY 7, 1937, A BATTALION OF JAPANESE TROOPS reported a missing soldier while conducting maneuvers near the Marco Polo Bridge—a twelfth-century stone bridge spanning the Yongding River and leading to the Wanping fortress some fifteen miles outside of Beijing. Alarmed by the disappearance and by reports of shots being fired in the area, Japanese commanders launched an aggressive search. Although the missing soldier reappeared twenty minutes after the search began, his commanding officer failed to report his return for another four hours. By that time, the situation had escalated. Chinese soldiers outside of Wanping began firing at Japanese troops but were forced to retreat. Initially, the incident appeared as little more than a dustup—hardly the sort of clash over which world wars were started. Indeed, skirmishes of the sort had become fairly routine since 1931. But the political landscape in China had changed.[9]

Following the 1933 truce that halted the fighting in Manchuria, Chiang Kai-shek had focused his energy on the communists. He remained convinced that the failure to destroy the CCP in the near term would guarantee a communist victory in the long term. However, strong voices inside China disagreed. In particular, Generals Zhang Xueliang and Yang Hucheng—warlords from Manchuria and Shaanxi, respectively, who had joined forces with the Nationalists—remained convinced that Chiang's obsession with fighting the communists played into the hands of Japanese forces seeking to keep China divided. In December 1936, Chiang, unaware that he was walking into a trap, traveled to Xi'an in a bid to bring Zhang and Yang back into the fold. After negotiations failed, Zhang tried to capture the Generalissimo and force him to come to terms. Chiang initially eluded capture but was found the following day in a damp cave, shivering in his pajamas. Zhang and Yang insisted that the Generalissimo, under threat of execution, form a united front with the communists against the Japanese. After two weeks of negotiation, Chiang relented. The communists would forge a united front with the GMD and come under nominal command of the government in Nanjing. By ensuring the CCP's survival and reorienting Nanjing toward confrontation with Tokyo, the Xi'an Incident transformed the course of history in China, East Asia, and ultimately the world.[10]

By the summer of 1937, Chiang and the GMD were prepared to resist further Japanese provocations. Rather than allowing local commanders to broker a ceasefire, Chiang instead chose to make a stand. In the half decade since 1931, Chinese forces had grown in strength, the civil war with the communists had been paused, and a growing number of great powers had granted recognition and support to the Nanjing government. However, if the Generalissimo accepted a ceasefire with the Japanese, he risked denunciation from his ostensible allies in the CCP, who would accuse him of backing down in the face of Japanese aggression. Moreover, the fighting at Marco Polo Bridge threatened not Manchuria but Beijing—the historic political capital of China, a place of tremendous cultural importance, and a key junction in China's rail network. For Chiang to have simply backed down might have meant risking his leadership. Chiang recognized an opportunity to force a showdown with Tokyo, present Nanjing's case to the international community, confirm his own commitment to resisting foreign imperialism, and compel the Japanese to back down.[11]

But Tokyo remained obstinate. In June 1937, Prince Fumimaro Konoe had become prime minister in Tokyo. Chosen for his aristocratic lineage and universal likability and in the hope that he would serve as a bridge between the military and civilian leadership, Konoe proved inadequate. Lacking charisma and eager to compromise, he quickly fell under the sway of hawks in the military. A more aggressive stance toward Nanjing was not entirely out of line with Konoe's own thoughts. Though he had flirted with socialist ideas in his youth, Konoe had grown into a proponent of Japanese expansion. Konoe dismissed Woodrow Wilson's calls for a new, liberal world order as a cynical bid to distract from the Western powers' true goal of maintaining imperial power. He believed that the world was divided into haves and have-nots: the former maintained extensive colonial possessions; the latter remained locked out of this system of imperial spoils. One day, he argued, these injustices would "compel Japan to attempt to overthrow the status quo as Germany did before the [Great War]." In 1933, he had published an essay arguing that Japan's population growth required an "adjustment of the world system. . . . We have chosen to advance into Manchuria and Mongolia as our only means of survival." In a speech two years later, he called for an end to US and British "monopolization" of the world's resources. Far from restoring civilian control in Tokyo, the Konoe era (1937–1940) would be remembered as the moment when the militarists led Japan over the brink.[12]

Ironically, a full-scale war in China was precisely the sort of strategic morass that the Konoe government should have sought to avoid. Renewed hostilities with Nanjing ran counter to nearly all of Japan's long-term goals of establishing a cooperative relationship with China, gaining control of Southeast Asia's vital natural resources, and supplanting the Western powers in the Far East. A war with China threatened to drive Nanjing into the arms of Japan's greatest rivals—the Soviet Union, Great Britain, and the United States—and further alienate Japan in the eyes of the international community. Furthermore, such a conflict would fan the flames of Chinese nationalism. A war with China would tie down a large contingent of the Japanese army, strain the nation's resources, and divert Tokyo's attention away from its efforts to expand its influence in Southeast Asia. Finally, a campaign that weakened the GMD would empower Mao Zedong and the CCP—a nightmare scenario for Japan's anticommunist leaders. Indeed, with the benefit of hindsight, Tokyo's decision to go to war with China in 1937 appears to be a colossal blunder.[13] Nevertheless, Japan's colonial ambitions combined with militarist sentiment to lead the nation into a bloodbath.

As is often the case with military quagmires, Japan's war began with impressive victories. Beijing fell quickly after Chinese forces withdrew in late July. Japanese troops surrounded the city while artillery pounded Chinese barracks to the northeast. Meanwhile, a column of Japanese soldiers pursued retreating Chinese as they moved south while another contingent of Japanese troops took Tianjin. In a mark of the brutality to come, retreating Chinese soldiers under the command of the East Hopei Autonomous Government butchered nearly three hundred Japanese and Korean civilians in nearby Tongzhou. Reports of men, women, and children being rounded up and shot by firing squads filtered out over the following days.[14] As the retreat continued, it became clear that Chiang's troops were badly outmatched. But these initial victories gave little indication of the long years of ferocious warfare that lay ahead.

Recognizing that he had little hope of defending the north, Chiang chose to regroup and mount a stalwart defense of Shanghai. He appears to have believed that his troops would fare better in an urban battle, where Japanese advantages in mechanized warfare would be less pronounced. Moreover, Shanghai constituted a major strategic prize:

a key port city with a large concentration of commercial and industrial activity that sat astride supply lines to the Soviet Union. The city also hosted large communities of foreigners in the International Settlement along the western banks of the Huangpu River. The celebrated Bund was lined with neoclassical and Romanesque buildings overlooking the waterfront that housed foreign banks, newspapers, stock-trading houses, and consulates. Thousands of foreigners from the world's great powers lived and worked in Shanghai. A bloody struggle for the city would arouse international interest in China's plight far more than clashes in faraway Manchuria.[15]

The situation came to a head on August 9 when Chinese guards gunned down a Japanese naval officer and his chauffeur outside the Hongqiao Aerodrome. Japanese authorities cited gruesome reports of the bodies, riddled with bullets, as evidence of the viciousness of Chinese forces. Meanwhile, Chinese authorities threw up barricades, planted minefields, and prepared defenses around Shanghai, and a large flow of refugees flooded over the bridges into the International Settlement. At 2:00 p.m. on August 12, the ranking officer at the US consulate in Shanghai reported the sighting of a large flotilla of Japanese warships in the harbor. Rumors of a Japanese aircraft carrier floating off the coast and Japanese troop transports steaming toward the mouth of the Yangtze River added to concerns, as did news of Japanese efforts to convert a nearby golf course into a makeshift airfield.[16]

The battle for Shanghai began the following day as Chinese soldiers fought off Japanese marines trying to land in the city. On August 15, Japanese aircraft attacked Chinese airfields outside of Nanjing, Nanchang, and Shanghai. Chiang sent an estimated 190,000 Chinese troops, including many of his best units, into the city. While Japanese soldiers were better trained and better equipped, Shanghai's dense streets lined by brick buildings provided a citadel of fortifications for the Chinese defenders, forcing Japanese units to fight street by street with small arms. Outside the city, Japanese divisions battled Chinese troops across a complex patchwork of canals, creeks, rice paddies, and town walls. The fighting raged through August and September as Japanese units pushed their way deeper into Shanghai. By October 1, the Japanese had reached Suzhou Creek, where the defenders had established a heavy line of fortifications. A maze of barbed wire, trenches, pillboxes, and bunkers greeted Japanese attackers on the far side of the creek as Chinese soldiers laid down a hail of gunfire. As Japanese forces continued their creeping advance into November, Shanghai's defense became increasingly untenable. After Japanese troops landed at Hangzhou Bay in November, Chinese commanders started pulling out of the city to avoid encirclement.[17]

The fighting proved particularly deadly for civilians. A botched Chinese air raid against the Japanese cruiser *Izumo* on August 14 sent one bomb crashing into the side of the Palace Hotel and Nanking Road. "Flames from a blazing car played over distorted bodies," the *North China Herald* reported. "In shapeless heaps where they had been huddling in shelter bodies in coolie cloth turning scarlet lay piled up in the entrances to the main doorways and arcades of the Palace and Cathay Hotels. Heads, legs, arms lay far from smashed masses of flesh." Survivors "cried piteously for aid." Witnesses placed the death toll at six hundred, with another one thousand wounded. Another pair of bombs struck the congested intersection of Avenue Edward VII and Yu Ya Ching Road, killing 445 and wounding 828. "The bodies were most horribly mangled, some of them being without heads and limbs or otherwise mutilated," the paper explained. "The pavement was running in blood" and the "smell of burned flesh" clung to volunteers working to rescue the survivors. Another bombing on August 24 along Nanking Road killed 170 and wounded nearly 500 more. Reporters described "heaps of mangled bodies" lying amid shattered glass and debris. Victims died in a "hail of shell fragments . . . in the streets, on balconies and in the shops where assistants and customers were tangled in death." Outside, a burst water main sent a torrent of water into the air, showering the dead and running "red in the gutters." Allegations of war crimes added to the grim toll. Tillman Durdin witnessed the summary execution of two hundred men on the Bund while Japanese sailors in the ships anchored nearby watched and cheered. "The men were lined up against a wall and shot. Then a number of Japanese armed with pistols trod nonchalantly around the crumpled bodies, pumping bullets into any that were still kicking." All told, the fighting killed some three hundred thousand people.[18]

The fury of the Battle of Shanghai played a critical role in forging Chinese national unity. The conflict between China and Japan was no longer confined to the northeast but rather an expanding war that would engulf the whole of China. But this unity had come at a staggering price. Tens of thousands of Chiang's best troops had been killed, wounded, or captured in Shanghai, and the Chinese would now have to scramble to field effective units in what promised to be a long, bloody war. Although they were victorious in Shanghai, the Japanese had also suffered heavy losses, with eleven thousand killed and thirty-one thousand wounded. Having invested so many lives in Shanghai, Japanese leaders now chose to unleash a full-scale assault against the GMD. As Tokyo's troops turned west toward Chiang's capital in Nanjing, many thirsted for vengeance.[19]

As Japanese columns bore down on Nanjing, Chiang faced a terrible choice: whether to sacrifice even more of his troops in a doomed defense or to abandon the capital and move his government west into China's vast interior. Many of Chiang's advisers insisted that the defense of Nanjing was not only impossible but strategically pointless—it would squander large numbers of troops on a cause that was already lost. But Chiang's war was not purely military. He faced a battle for the hearts and minds of the Chinese people. To abandon Nanjing without a fight, he concluded, would risk appearing weak in the face of the Japanese assault. He therefore resolved to sacrifice the capital along with thousands of his troops in a hopeless defense of the city. Nanjing would become a tragic symbol of Chinese resistance against the Japanese attack. But not even Chiang could have known how terrible and how effective this gambit would be. Having taken Shanghai, Japanese units now beat a bloody trail west toward Nanjing, raping and killing villagers along the way and pillaging towns in their path. In one widely reported account, two Japanese lieutenants staged a competition to determine who could be the first to kill one hundred Chinese soldiers using their swords. Meanwhile, Chinese forces launched a "scorched earth" policy, in reporter F. Tillman Durdin's words, designed to leave "the districts to be occupied by the Japanese only blackened wastes of no use to the conquerors."[20]

The impending massacre would be born of a tragic combination of factors. In a general sense, Japanese racial hostility toward the Chinese forged a degree of brutality that might not have otherwise been possible. Making matters worse, by framing their campaign as a police action in response to uncivilized Chinese provocations rather than as a war, Japanese leaders justified a disregard for international law. Indeed, much like colonial powers before them, the Japanese ignored the laws of war in pursuit of imperial conquest. Furthermore, the largely unplanned and haphazard advance of the Japanese army led to a lack of supplies, forcing Japanese units to sack the surrounding countryside in search of provisions. In addition, the lack of a large number of military police allowed individual units to run amok. Finally, the race to Nanjing encouraged a frenzied atmosphere among battle-wearied troops already eager to punish the Chinese after the ordeal of Shanghai. Durdin, who had made his way to Nanjing, described a scene of medieval brutality: "The Chinese defense within a city wall, the wholesale Chinese burning of villages, mansions and populous business districts for miles around the metropolis and the slaughter, rape and looting by the Japanese after their occupation of the city all seem to belong to a more barbaric, vanished period. . . . [Japan's] victory was marred . . . by barbaric cruelties, by the wholesale execution of prisoners, the looting of the city, rape, killing of civilians and by general vandalism, which will remain a blot on the reputation of the Japanese Army and nation." While Chinese soldiers initially put up a solid defense at the city walls, Japanese artillery and aircraft quickly wore them down. After Japanese troops managed to scale the wall at the west gate of the city, Chinese forces panicked. Soldiers fled en masse, throwing off their uniforms and scrambling to disappear into the civilian population. "I witnessed the wholesale undressing of an army that was almost comic," the reporter wrote. "Some soldiers disrobed completely and then robbed civilians of their garments." Japanese forces massacred any suspected Chinese soldiers that fell into their hands. "In one slaughter a tank gun was turned on a group of more than 100 soldiers at a bomb shelter," the reporter explained. "Nanking's streets were littered with dead." In some places "heavy military traffic had been passing through, grinding over the remains of men, dogs and horses."[21]

Japanese forces had been ordered to show no mercy to those captured. "Kill all POWs," read one battle report. "As a method, we suggest tying them up in groups of less than twenty and shooting them one by one." Some units were ordered to use bayonets. "We see prisoners everywhere, so many that there is no way we can deal with them," wrote one Japanese commander. "The general policy is: 'Accept no prisoners!' So we ended up having to take care of them lot, stock, and barrel [sic]. But they came in hordes, in units of thousands or five-thousands; so we couldn't even disarm them."[22]

Alongside news of these massacres came horrifying reports of widespread rape. As one soldier reported: "We took four people captive—parents and daughters. We played with the daughters as if they were whores and killed the parents because they kept on telling us to release the daughters. We had our kicks until the unit was ordered to leave; then we killed the daughters." German business-man John Rabe, who remained in the capital to help run the Nanjing Safety Zone, recorded the chilling details in his diary: "Last night up to 1,000 women and girls are said to have been raped. . . . You hear nothing but rape. If husbands or brothers intervene, they're shot." The International Military Tribunal for the Far East—convened in 1946 by the Allied powers to investigate war crimes by the Japanese—offered the following conclusion:

Individual soldiers and small groups of two of three roamed over the city murdering, raping, looting, and burning, there was no discipline whatever. Many soldiers were drunk. Soldiers went through the streets indiscriminately killing Chinese men, women and children without apparent provocation or excuse until in places the streets and alleys were littered with the bodies of their victims. According to another witness, Chinese were hunted like rabbits, everyone seen to move was shot. At least 12,000 non-combatant Chinese men, women and children met their deaths in these indiscriminate killings during the first two or three days of the Japanese occupation of the city. . . . There were many cases of rape. Death was a frequent penalty for the slightest resistance on the part of a civtion [sic] or the members of her family who sought to protect her. Even girls of tender years and old women were raped in large numbers throughout the city, and many cases of abnormal and sadistic behaviour in connection with these rapings occurred. Many women were killed after the act and their bodies mutilated. Approximately 20,000 cases of rape occurred within the city during the first month of the occupation.

The highest estimates of the dead reached a staggering two hundred thousand to three hundred thousand killed over six weeks in Nanjing. As the tribunal later explained, "This war was envisaged by Japan's military leaders as a punitive war, which was being fought to punish the people of China for their refusal to acknowledge the superiority and leadership of the Japanese race and to cooperate with Japan. These military leaders intended to make the war so brutal and savage in all its consequences as to break the will of the Chinese people to resist."[23]

The horrors in Nanjing gave Chiang his rallying cry. "The war will not be decided in Nanking or any other city," he announced after the capital fell. "It will be decided in the countryside of our vast country and by the inflexible will of our people. We shall fight on every step of the way and every inch of the 40,000,000 square *li* of our territory."[24]

AFTER THE FALL OF NANJING—AND THE HORRIFIC MASSACRE THAT followed—Chiang Kai-shek's forces staged a fighting retreat into the interior of the continent, contesting the Japanese army as they moved west from the coast. Chiang attempted "to slow everything down . . . fighting a long war of attrition" and transforming "defense into offense." Although it lacked Japan's modern mechanized military forces, China's landmass was thirty-five times the size of Japan and its citizenry was larger by a factor of seven. Chiang's strategy aimed to set China's demographic and geographic mass against Japan's technological and organizational supremacy. Chinese bodies would be thrown against Japanese firepower across the vast expanses of mainland China in a brutal struggle for supremacy in Asia. Chiang ordered his generals to employ a troop advantage of six or nine to one in large confrontations with Japanese forces, often in the form of human wave attacks.[25]

By the late spring of 1938, Japanese commanders had conquered most of coastal China north of Shanghai. This zone was the most easily accessible, relatively developed section of central China. Japanese ships, aircraft, and troops had little trouble moving through this area. In particular, Japanese forces relied on China's rail networks to transport troops and supplies through the country. Japan occupied key industrial centers of Manchuria, Beijing, Shanghai, and Guangzhou, but much of the countryside beyond the railhead remained outside of Tokyo's control. It was into these vast inland expanses that the Chinese armies were forced to withdraw. If Japanese forces hoped to deliver a knockout blow to the Chinese armies and destroy Chiang's government, they would have to follow. In the wake of his retreat from Nanjing, Chiang set up his new wartime capital in the city of Chongqing. Deep in southwest China, some 1,300 miles from Shanghai, Chongqing lay beyond the reaches of the Imperial Japanese Army. In the course of this retreat, Chiang's regime abandoned 87 percent of China's industry. Tokyo had destroyed China's economy and occupied many of its key cities, but it now assumed the heavy burden of occupying massive stretches of territory and fighting a war of attrition against a stubborn regime fortified deep in China's inaccessible interior.[26]

Wuhan now emerged as the new center of Chinese resistance. Located 430 miles inland from Shanghai, the city commanded a key point along the Yangtze River and a vital junction along China's railroad. If Japanese forces captured Wuhan, they would deal a heavy blow to Chiang's continued resistance and gain control of a critical transportation hub deep in China's interior. At the same time, Wuhan gave the Guomindang an opportunity to prove that its troops could withstand the onslaught of the Japanese army. Chiang's armies would stage their defenses around the city of Xuzhou, some three hundred miles to the north. If Xuzhou fell, Japanese forces would control the Tianjin-Pukou railway and a direct route to Wuhan.

In March 1938, Japanese forces launched their campaign to take Wuhan by attacking Chinese defenders around Xuzhou. The battle soon came to focus on the garrison town of Taierzhuang, which separated the northern and southern arms of the Japanese advance and blocked the encirclement of the Chinese defenders. Fierce fighting raged for two weeks as Chinese and Japanese troops struggled for control of streets, ruined houses, and courtyards. Close-quarter skirmishes negated Japanese advantages in firepower. On April 7, Japanese forces abandoned the attack, giving Chiang his first victory in the war. Foreign observers noted the stiffening of Chinese resistance and, for the first time, wondered about Tokyo's ability to win the war. The US ambassador to China explained that the victory had "changed [the atmosphere] from . . . pessimism to one of dogged optimism . . . based more upon the hope of wearing out the Japanese than any expectation of being able by force to drive [them] out." At the end of the month, British foreign secretary Lord Halifax noted that "[Chiang] has now become the symbol of Chinese unity." The China Weekly Review was even more optimistic: Taierzhuang had crushed "Japan's high hopes for a quick, decisive and overwhelming victory in China . . . smashed their morale, exposed the myth of their invincibility."[27]

While the victory at Taierzhuang boosted Chinese morale, it was not enough to save Xuzhou. Japanese commanders hurled troops against the Chinese defenses, tightening the circle around the doomed city. On May 15, with the situation becoming hopeless, Chiang ordered his forces to abandon Xuzhou. Three days later, Chinese columns escaped under the cover of a sandstorm, leaving the city and its remaining residents to the fury of marauding Japanese troops. A Reuters correspondent flying in a Japanese aircraft over the battlefield described pillars of smoke rising along the horizon from dozens of towns and villages caught in the fighting. "Wherever one could see inside [Xuzhou], and in the neighborhoods around it, the bayonets of Japanese guards gleamed in the sunshine around great shell-holes and ruins of what once were buildings." As the "dull thud of exploding bombs" rumbled in the distance, retreating Chinese troops and pursuing Japanese tanks and cavalry threw up great clouds of dust. "Peering down from the aeroplane," the correspondent wrote, "one could see men fighting, swarming and dying like so many ants, along the dusty roads and the green fields." The Battles of Taierzhuang and Xuzhou had transformed Japan's imperial adventure in China into a grinding war of attrition. As Mao Zedong, leader of the ragtag Chinese Communist Party, observed, China would win the war, but "it [could not] win quickly, and the War of Resistance [would] be a protracted war."[28]

But the war of attrition was already taking a terrible toll on the Chinese people. The rampaging Japanese armies provisioned themselves from the territory they overran. While Chinese leaders realized that they could not stop the Japanese onslaught, they could deprive the invaders of the spoils of victory. But denying resources to the enemy also meant destroying the means of sustenance for the local population. As Chinese general Xue Yue explained, "Scorched earth policy . . . has been our major strategy. We have destroyed China—removed every stone, burnt down every farm, torn up every railway track upon which we could lay our hands." One of the deadliest single acts of the war came in June 1938 when Chiang's forces decided to breach the dikes holding back the waters of the Yellow River near Huayuankou in order to slow the Japanese advance toward Wuhan. Chinese commanders "use[d] water as a substitute for soldiers" by flooding vast sections of the North China Plain. This gambit created a new geographic obstacle for the Japanese armies, but it also drowned hundreds of thousands of civilians. Though only a few feet deep in many areas, the floodwaters were often inescapable. Those who survived the initial surge faced the longer-term threats of starvation and disease in the drowned, desolate plains. Official estimates of the death toll numbered eight hundred thousand; millions more had become refugees.[29]

The deaths of hundreds of thousands of Chinese civilians bought Chiang and the defenders in Wuhan a mere five months. Slowed by the floodwaters, Japanese forces paused until summer rains raised the water level enough to allow gunboats to push forward. Japanese troops marched through the blistering summer heat along both sides of the Yangtze, fighting Chinese soldiers as well as bouts of malaria, dysentery, and cholera. By October, enough Japanese troops had reached Wuhan's approaches to render the city undefendable. On October 25, Wuhan's defenders heard the thunder of Japanese naval artillery some seventeen miles away as warships bombarded Chinese defenses at Kotien, one of the last bastions guarding the city. As the morning sun crept above the horizon, the shelling drew nearer and fires broke out throughout the city. Refugees, wounded soldiers, and retreating troops clogged the routes out of the city as Japanese planes streaked overhead. A riverboat carrying some two thousand refugees was struck, killing most of those aboard and leaving dozens of bodies floating in the waters of the Yangtze. A flotilla of junks loaded with refugees managed to escape. Faced with a hopeless situation, Chiang chose to abandon the city. The war had become a stalemate. Chiang had failed to stop the Japanese advance and had been driven deep into China's interior, but his regime had not collapsed. Tokyo had won every major campaign, but its forces were now stretched thin.[30]

Nonetheless, the stalemate perpetuated the mass slaughter of thousands of Chinese civilians and soldiers. As Japanese forces continued their pursuit of Chiang's armies, they approached the provincial capital of Changsha. On November 9, Chiang ordered that the city be burned, just as Russia had decided to destroy Moscow before Napoleon's advance in 1812. Chiang's forces stashed tanks of gasoline in major public buildings and prepared to torch the city if the Japanese continued their advance. Over the night of November 12–13, faulty reports of an imminent attack convinced Chinese commanders to torch Changsha. Twenty-thousand people died and two hundred thousand lost their homes in an inferno that reduced many of the city's ancient landmarks, mansions, and public buildings to ashes. "When I arrived five weeks later the city was still dead," one British observer wrote. "The main streets were not only destroyed, they were obliterated without trace in the indistinguishable acres of rubble and ash."[31]

While Chinese commanders unleashed scorched-earth strategies on their own population, Japanese forces continued their brutal campaign. Leaders in Tokyo insisted that they were fighting a colonial war in China, arguing that Chiang's regime was not a "modern" state and therefore the rules of war did not apply. Under this logic, Japanese commanders staged chemical weapons attacks against Chinese forces over the course of 1937 and 1938. Japanese units used poison gas 375 times during the Wuhan campaign alone. Meanwhile, beginning in May 1938, Tokyo directed a terror bombing campaign against Chongqing with the goal of pummeling the regime into submission. Japanese bombers operating from airfields in occupied China staged hundreds of raids against Chiang's mostly defenseless capital. The first major raid, on May 3, killed 673 people. The aircraft appeared at 12:45 p.m., sending the city's residents scrambling for shelter. One man told the story—related by his father—of hearing an explosion and watching as a group of workers "turned into bloody, fast-flying bits of flesh." A raid the following afternoon killed over three thousand people. "Outside, bomb shrapnel was flying, window glass was shattering, and falling to the floor," one citizen recalled, "and there were the sounds of the enemy planes buzzing and machine-guns firing."[32]

At the end of 1938, Tokyo expanded its pacification operations to include an "annihilation" campaign against guerrilla groups fighting in Hebei Province. Japanese commanders authorized their troops to eliminate "enemies pretending to be local people" and "all males between the ages of fifteen and sixty whom we suspect to be enemies." In recognition of Japan's continuing military progress in China, on December 22, 1938, Prime Minister Konoe proclaimed Tokyo's intention to create a "new order in East Asia" and to bring about the "complete extermination of the anti-Japanese Kuomintang Government." Konoe's new order in East Asia offered a clear challenge to the existing balance of power in the Far East. With its poison gas attacks, terror bombing of civilians, and annihilation campaigns, Japan was following in the footsteps of the Western colonial powers that it sought to replace.[33]

RIVAL POWERS WERE BY NO MEANS EAGER TO WELCOME JAPAN INTO their ranks. Soviet leaders in particular worried about the presence of hostile Japanese forces on their eastern borders. Tokyo's seizure of Manchuria placed an aggressive, highly militarized empire along the three-thousand-mile-long border of Outer Mongolia. In response, Moscow stationed soldiers along the border to defend Soviet claims in the East. By 1938, Soviet and Japanese forces were skirmishing in sporadic clashes along the disputed frontier. More significant fighting broke out again in May 1939 as part of what came to be known as the Nomonhan Incident. In all, 1,000 Soviet tanks joined some 57,000 troops against 30,000 Japanese soldiers. As the fighting raged through the summer, Japanese commanders formed a "suicide corps" to drive Soviet troops back across the Kalka River. Both sides launched cavalry charges across the prairie while aircraft bombed enemy positions overhead. The clashes propelled Soviet commander General Georgy Zhukov to prominence as the Red Army gained the upper hand. By the time a ceasefire was brokered in mid-September, the Japanese had lost some 17,000 troops while Soviet losses stood at 9,284. In the meantime, the Nomonhan Incident forced Japanese commanders to halt their offensives in China to concentrate on the battle with the Soviets.[34]

Japanese operations in China had also attracted the attention of leaders in London and Washington. Fighting in key Chinese cities such as Shanghai and Nanjing raised concerns about damage to Western property and the danger to British and US citizens. In retaliation for London's efforts to stabilize Chinese currency, Japanese troops ringed the British concession in Tientsin with an electrified fence and began conducting strip searches of British citizens entering and leaving. Japan's military operations in China also drew protests from US officials, who feared that Tokyo was working to purge US influence from the country. Japanese diplomats insisted that the interferences were the "temporary" results of wartime necessity and that their government had no intention of driving the Americans out of China. As Foreign Minister Hachiro Arita told US ambassador Joseph Grew in May, "The Japanese Government in establishing the new order has no intention of excluding trade and other legitimate economic activities in China of the countries of Europe and America." But Grew found Arita's statements "ambiguous and vague." By midsummer, American patience had worn thin. On July 26, Secretary of State Cordell Hull informed the Japanese ambassador to Washington of his intention to terminate the treaty of commerce and navigation between the two countries. Japanese officials recognized that the deterioration of economic relations between Tokyo and Washington now threatened Japan's supply of oil and scrap metal. "Even if we can purchase [oil and scrap] for the next six months," Emperor Hirohito wrote in early August, "we will immediately have difficulties thereafter. Unless we reduce the size of our army and navy by one-third, we won't make it."[35]

By the summer of 1939, Japanese leaders found themselves caught in a vicious circle. Japanese military operations in China required a steady supply of resources such as oil and scrap metal, but the war had inflamed tensions with the Western powers that supplied those resources. Meanwhile, Chiang's stubborn resistance guaranteed that victory in China remained out of reach. Tokyo could abandon its military adventure in China and repair relations with the West, but doing so would entail abandoning Japan's ambitions to become the leading power in Asia. On the other hand, Tokyo could continue its imperial war in China, but it faced the risk of having its vital military resources choked off. Japan's last hope, it now seemed, lay in an even bolder gamble. The Japanese navy determined in April 1939 that Tokyo should accelerate its plans to expand its influence in the "Southern Area," a.k.a. Southeast Asia. Naval leaders called on Tokyo to secure the region's vital raw materials and establish control over regional trade networks before Japan faced shortages of critical war materials. At the same time, they explained, Japan should begin "preparatory projects aimed at driving out British and French political and economic power in the future from the Southern Area" and rendering the Dutch dependent on Tokyo for the administration of the Dutch East Indies. Likewise, Japan must work to build ties with "native peoples" through diplomacy, cultural and academic outreach, and education initiatives. Academic, agricultural, banking, commercial, and industrial interests should work with the Japanese government to overhaul Tokyo's influence throughout the region in the interest of fostering "neighbourliness and co-prosperity."[36]

The Imperial Navy's calls for a southern advance resonated with those in Tokyo who had long advocated for the creation of a Japanese Monroe Doctrine. In August 1939, Professor Kamikawa Hikomatsu of Tokyo Imperial University called for Western recognition of a Japanese Monroe Doctrine. Kamikawa drew parallels between Japanese operations in China and nineteenth-century American continental expansion and argued that Japan should be afforded a sphere of influence in East Asia that was analogous to the US sphere of influence in the Western Hemisphere, which dated back to the nineteenth century. The Japanese and American doctrines were "essentially similar, the only difference being that the Japanese 'Monroe Doctrine' has East Asia for its field of operation and the original Monroe Doctrine the American continents." Japan must insist on the Western great powers following a policy of "non-colonization, non-territorial acquisition and non-intervention" in East Asia. Tokyo was simply following in Washington's footsteps by proclaiming a hands-off policy in its sphere of influence. Pushing a line with which many in Tokyo agreed, he insisted that US refusal to recognize Japan's great power prerogatives in the Far East while simultaneously claiming regional supremacy in the Western Hemisphere amounted to rank hypocrisy.[37]

Although they won few adherents in the wider international community, such arguments laid out a coherent justification for Japan's actions in the Far East: Tokyo sought nothing more than the same imperial privileges that the Western great powers had claimed for centuries. Japanese leaders understood their actions in China to be firmly in keeping with long-standing patterns of Western colonialism. Why, Tokyo demanded, must Japan stand aside while the Western powers carved up Asia into colonies? At stake was Japan's bid to upend the colonial status quo and replace the Western imperial powers in East Asia. Rapidly changing events on the other side of the world in Europe would soon give Japan its chance.

THE VICIOUS FIGHTING IN CHINA WAS A HARBINGER OF THE approaching global cataclysm. As German diplomat Paul Scharffenberg wrote upon witnessing the aftermath of the Nanjing massacre, "We Germans in Nanjing . . . all think that the war in Asia is fundamentally different from the ones with which we are familiar. . . . It seems as if we are back in the Thirty Years' War." Indeed, to many Western observers, the savage violence raging in China hearkened back to an era of warfare that made no distinction between soldiers and civilians, men and women, children and the elderly.[38] The

Japanese invasion of China revealed key patterns that would repeat around the world in the coming years. Convinced of their own racial superiority and the geopolitical necessity of empire, leaders in Tokyo had launched a brutal war of annihilation to secure control of their colony in Manchukuo and destroy the rising power of a unified China. Japan's campaign devastated entire cities and vast stretches of the countryside, slaughtering millions of Chinese in the process. And this was only the beginning: in the space of twenty months, Scharffenberg's own government would launch a racialized war of annihilation in a bid to carve out a new empire in the heart of Europe.

Chapter 4

BLOOD, SOIL, AND EMPIRE

A S THE FIRST LIGHT OF DAWN CREPT OVER THE PORT OF DANZIG ON September 1, 1939, the old German battleship *Schleswig-Holstein* glided into position overlooking the Polish Military Transit Depot on the Westerplatte peninsula. In an instant, the morning stillness broke as the big ship's 28cm guns thundered to life. In the next seven minutes, the battleship hammered the Polish position with five metric tons of shells. "They dropped a lot of iron on Westerplatte," one survivor explained. A second, larger bombardment followed, raining another forty-six tons of munitions on Polish defenses. "The soldiers cling to the walls of the trench," wrote a Polish lieutenant. "A hail of shrapnel, splinters of tree branches and entire treetops rain down from the sky. Fountains of sand, a whirling cloud of smoke, the stench of sulphur and hot iron." To the southwest, thousands of German infantry poured across the frontier. After long years of planning, Adolf Hitler's bid to create a thousand-year Reich was in motion.[1]

Over the next five and a half years, the Third Reich would wage a vicious war to remake the structure of world power. The Nazi regime would deploy modern military technology in pursuit of nineteenth-century dreams of race and empire. In doing so, Hitler and his minions would unleash a reign of medieval brutality on the peoples of Europe. Hitler's new order would witness the restoration of slavery in Europe, the prosecution of genocide on a massive scale, and the introduction of a savage new machinery of colonial violence. All this was necessary, Hitler argued, in order to defend European civilization against the mortal threats of revolutionary Bolshevism and American capitalism and to restore the Aryan race to supremacy in world affairs. The struggle for Europe had begun.

SINCE THE 1920S, HITLER HAD ARTICULATED A CONSISTENT VIEW OF foreign policy centered around the two core concepts of "blood and soil." Blood, for Hitler and his followers, denoted a worldview that reduced human history to a struggle between different races. The course of world events, the rise and fall of empires, international affairs, contemporary politics, and the destinies of entire civilizations could all be explained as a struggle between competing races. A master race descended from Nordic and Aryan bloodlines was responsible for all of humanity's great accomplishments. The Aryan, Hitler argued, was "the Prometheus of mankind." He traced the fall of the Roman Empire to a decline in racial purity of the Romans. "All great cultures of the past perished only because the originally created race died out from blood poisoning," he explained in *Mein Kampf.* "Blood mixture and the resultant drop in the racial level is the sole cause of the dying out of old cultures." Germany's current woes, he wrote, stemmed from the dispersion of the German people across much of Central and Eastern Europe and the so-called colonization of the German *volk* by outsiders—most notably the Jews. Hitler ranted that Jewish people were "a parasite in the body of other nations," living off the labor of others and weakening the host.[2]

Soil formed the second fundamental theme in Hitler's world-view. To flourish, races needed living space, lebensraum. Soil and agriculture ensured purity and vitality of the blood. Without living space, the German race would be suffocated and forced to live at the mercy of the other, lesser races of Europe. The Nazi quest for blood and soil demanded conquest. *"Only an adequately large space on this earth assures a nation of freedom of existence,"* Hitler wrote. *"Land and soil are the goal of our foreign policy"* (italics in the original). If Germany's enemies refused to surrender, they had to be destroyed through the instrument of racial warfare. War, for Hitler, was not only necessary but desirable: armed conflict would unify the German people, harden their resolve, and remake the Third Reich into the world's most powerful empire. War, then, would become Hitler's instrument to purify the blood and conquer the soil for the Nazis' new empire.[3]

Furthermore, he felt that a rebuilt German empire might very well be necessary to counter a growing communist influence in Europe. The economic turmoil of the Great Depression, the Bolshevik Revolution, and the rising power of the Soviet Union led some world leaders to look on the prospect of a resurgent Germany as a counterweight against the greater threat of communist revolution—a drum that Hitler was eager to beat. At a meeting with Hitler on March 25, 1935, British leaders tried to reason with the Führer regarding the scale of German rearmament, but Hitler insisted that Germany sought only to defend itself against rival powers, notably the Soviet Union. "Hitler added that there could be no question of German hegemony over Europe," the official report stated. "What was in question, was the hegemony of Russia or the hegemony of a combination of smaller States with France." Hitler warned that Moscow was driven by "Bolshevist doctrines" that propelled the Soviet Union toward war. He also added—in an observation that he would apparently forget six years later—that "the risks for Russia in a possible war were smaller than those for other Powers. Russia could with impunity allow the occupation of great tracts of her territory as large as Germany; she could permit bombardment of great regions; she could therefore wage war without risking destruction."[4]

Indeed, the looming presence of the Soviet Union assumed a prominent place in Hitler's mind. Under the brutal leadership of Joseph Stalin, the Soviet Union had transformed itself from a backward agrarian empire into a rising industrial powerhouse. All the while, Moscow had directed the Comintern (the Communist International) in a bid to spread the revolution to the wider world. The Great Depression further exacerbated fears that the world order was ripe for a left-wing revolution. But in Germany, the Nazis had established themselves as a right-wing bulwark against this creeping socialism. Hitler's hostility toward Moscow remained firmly rooted in the matrix of Nazi race theory. As he explained in *Mein Kampf*, Soviet leaders "belong[ed] to a race which combine[d], in a rare mixture, bestial cruelty and an inconceivable gift for lying." They were "the scum of humanity." The Soviet government was dominated by "the international Jew" who had instrumentalized Bolshevism in a bid for "world domination" that had now set its sights on Germany. This "striving of the Jewish people for world domination . . . [was] just as natural as the urge of the Anglo-Saxon to seize domination of the earth."[5]

If Stalin's Soviet Union embodied the menace of left-wing revolution, the United States occupied a more complicated place in Hitler's worldview. On the one hand, Hitler admired the United States and its control of a vast continental empire that granted the nation "immense inner strength." Germany, he noted, would do well to emulate the American example by building a land empire in Europe. The United States, he said, contained a large stock of racially pure Germanic inhabitants who "rose to be master[s] of the continent." American leaders had fashioned this racial purity using a system of segregation and restrictive immigration policies that Hitler praised as a model for others to follow. On the other hand, the United States represented a rising presence in world affairs that "threaten[ed] to nullify all the previous state power relationships and hierarchies." Writing in 1925, German geographer Karl Haushofer had warned, "Germany will have to decide where she stands; does she want to be a satellite of the Anglo-Saxon powers and their super-capitalism, which are united with the other European nations against Russia, or will she be an ally of the Pan Asiatic union against Europe and America?"[6]

Haushofer's vision was no mere fantasy. In the decades after the First World War, an informal network of American and British elites envisioned an Anglophone world order rooted in notions of Anglo-Saxon racial identity and justified through the vocabulary of liberal democratic government. Coalescing around organizations such as the Council on Foreign Relations in New York and the Royal Institute of International Affairs in London, this movement pushed for closer ties between the Atlantic powers and sought to inculcate a shared sense of racial and cultural heritage across the English-speaking world. While some efforts focused on high-level diplomacy and military cooperation, academics developed courses on the history and literature of "Western civilization," which promoted a shared identity between nations such as Great Britain, France, Italy, and the United States that stretched back to ancient Rome and Greece. Anglophone nations would still sit at the heart of this Atlantic community—the embodiment of Western civilization and the guardians of democracy in the international arena. These interwar ideas and the groups that promoted them helped to lay the groundwork for a new liberal world order that would emerge in the postwar world.[7]

Hitler and his supporters were determined to build a German Reich strong enough to resist the Anglo-American ascendancy. Once again, they looked to earlier Western imperial examples to justify their ambitions. German political theorist and Nazi Party member Carl Schmitt argued that the means of resisting American hegemony lay in the creation of a German *Grossraum*—a greater Germany over which Berlin would maintain supremacy free from foreign intervention. The precedent for this *Grossraum*, Schmitt argued, lay in the Monroe Doctrine, which the United States had pursued since 1823. "Theodore Roosevelt, Woodrow Wilson and the current President Franklin D. Roosevelt, in transforming a specifically American spatial conception into a transnational and trans-ethnic world ideology, have attempted to use the Monroe Doctrine as an instrument for the domination of the world market by Anglo-Saxon capital," Schmitt wrote. The solution was for Germany to create its own Monroe Doctrine for Central and Eastern Europe. Hitler would echo Schmitt's reference to the Monroe Doctrine in an April 1939 speech in which he declared, "We Germans employ exactly the same doctrine for Europe, in any case for the interests and territories of the greater German Reich." Nazi foreign minister Joachim von Ribbentrop would make a similar reference the following year.[8]

On its own, Hitler argued, Germany could never hope to challenge American capitalist production and world influence, nor could other European powers who might hope to "prevent the world hegemony of the North American continent." The vast expanses of land under the control of millions of Americans "of the highest racial quality" rendered the United States a juggernaut in world affairs. "In the future," Hitler wrote, "the only state that will be able to stand up to North America will be the state that has understood how . . . to raise the racial value of its people. . . . It is, again, the duty of the National Socialist movement to strengthen and prepare our own fatherland to the greatest degree possible for this task." Only by rebuilding the German economy could the Nazis hope to survive the deluge of American economic influence. Making matters worse, Berlin faced this challenge under the burden of reparations payments and amid the wreckage of the Great Depression. In response, the Nazis faced a sprint to build the Third Reich into an economic power before it could be consumed by the rising force of American capitalism.[9]

Hitler also maintained a grudging respect for Great Britain. Although he viewed London as a rival, he hoped that the British, with their traditional focus on overseas empire and naval power, might choose to accommodate the rise of a German land empire in Europe and accept a division of the colonial spoils between two great world empires.[10] He praised London's ability to govern a vast empire and expressed a desire to see British rule in India continue. Beyond these complementary imperial interests, Hitler believed that racial affinity between Anglo-Saxons and Germans could allow Britain to maintain a secondary role in world affairs once the Third Reich had claimed its rightful and supreme position.

But Hitler held nothing but disdain for France. The French, he insisted, not only sought to keep Germany divided and weak but had also allowed their nation to become racially contaminated. "What France, spurred on by her own thirst for vengeance and systematically led by the Jew, is doing in Europe today is a sin against the existence of white humanity and some day will incite against this people all the avenging spirits of a race which has recognized racial pollution as the original sin of humanity." Though the Third Reich's lebensraum lay to the east, it was the hated French—"the mortal enemy of our nation"—and their quest for European hegemony that had robbed Germany of its destiny. If they hoped to claim their empire, Hitler wrote, the Nazis must first bring about the "annihilation" of French power before turning to the east. As early as 1925, then, Hitler had articulated a rough blueprint for the coming war in Europe.[11]

As part of the Nazi quest to transform Germany into a world power, the regime launched a vicious campaign to root out perceived racial enemies at home and purify the German population. Although the Nazis had attacked racial minorities for years, a critical turning point arrived in September 1935 with the institution of the Nuremberg Laws. Announced in the old capital of the Holy Roman Empire, the new laws were designed to defend the purity of German blood against the contamination of Jews living in the Reich. The laws forbade intermarriage between Germans and Jews and restricted German citizenship to those deemed racially pure. In the face of this institutionalized antisemitism, many Jews who could afford to do so chose to flee Germany. Beginning in 1933, Nazi officials also instituted a "racial hygiene" policy aimed at eliminating undesirable genetic characteristics from the population. Forced sterilization, incarceration, and euthanasia programs targeted individuals with congenital diseases, physical and mental disabilities, and populations deemed racially undesirable, such as the Roma.[12]

In the broadest terms, Hitler believed it was the Nazis' destiny to prepare Germany to lead a racially cleansed Europe that could challenge the rising power of the United States. The Third Reich faced a rapidly closing window of time to rebuild its economy, reconstitute its military, purify its population, and conquer an empire in Eastern Europe before it was subsumed beneath the forces of Western capitalism or Eastern Bolshevism. This nexus of cash, steel, blood, and soil formed the dark heart of Nazi strategy in the run-up to the Second World War.

THE THIRD REICH'S NEW MILITARY FORCES RECEIVED THEIR FIRST taste of battle not in the eastern domains of Hitler's future lebensraum but in the brutal civil war raging in Spain. The Spanish Civil War (1936–1939) pitted Republican defenders of the democratically elected left-wing regime against right-wing nationalist rebels fighting under Francisco Franco. In short order, the conflict escalated to a proxy war as German, Italian, and Soviet forces as well as international volunteers joined the fighting. The conflict foreshadowed greater violence to come as fascists battled communists over the fate of Spain.

Germany's involvement began in July 1936 in response to Franco's request for aid from Berlin. Hitler recognized an opportunity to fight communist influence in Western Europe, gain a potential ally in Spain, and distract the European powers from Germany's resurgence. In its diplomatic dimensions, the Nazi intervention in Spain forged a critical relationship between Germany and Italy by convincing Mussolini—who had initially been wary of Nazi Germany—of his shared interests with Hitler in resisting communism and fighting for a new order in Europe. The fact that Hitler seemed happy to concede Spain and the Mediterranean as lying within the Italian sphere of influence surely helped relieve Mussolini's reservations. This

Rome-Berlin axis, first declared in October 1936, laid the foundations for an alliance that would survive until 1943.[13]

The Spanish Civil War also served as a laboratory for new types of violence that would come to characterize the approaching war in Europe. Moscow, Rome, and Berlin each sent significant numbers of warplanes and pilots to fight in the war. The war in Spain also drove rapid developments in aircraft technology as Soviet and German engineers sought to field new and improved designs, and it introduced Europeans to the horrors of large-scale aerial bombing. While Nationalist air raids on Madrid in 1936 and 1937 killed several hundred, Republican forces retaliated by slaughtering thousands of Nationalist political prisoners. As part of their intervention in support of Franco's Nationalists, the Nazi government formed the Condor Legion—a special air unit composed of some ninety planes and aircrews along with artillery and two companies of light tanks. The legion's most notorious operation focused on the intensive bombing of the town of Guernica in April 1937, which killed at least 150 people. "I walked through streets thick with blood and saw bodies of the dead—many of them dismembered," wrote one witness. "There were bodies of old men, women and children." While such a toll now seems modest in comparison with the destruction that awaited British, German, and Soviet cities, the carnage at Guernica became a potent symbol of the terrible civilian suffering that aerial bombing could unleash. "No more horrible story has blackened history," wrote the *Manchester Guardian*.[14]

Meanwhile, Hitler continued his quest to establish an empire in the East. On November 10, 1937, the Führer held a meeting with the heads of the Luftwaffe (air force), Wehrmacht (army), Kriegsmarine (navy), and Foreign Ministry in the offices of the chancellery in Berlin. His goal was to discuss long-term plans for the Reich—plans that he insisted should be put into place even in the event of his death. The minutes of the meeting—which became the famous Hossbach Memorandum—represent a distillation of many of the ideas from

Hitler's earlier writings into the format of a policy brief. "The aim of German policy was to make secure and to preserve the racial community [*Volksmasse*] and to enlarge it," the Führer explained. "It was therefore a question of space." Without this space, the nation could not survive. Germany, he insisted, was "living in an age of economic empires in which the primitive urge to colonization was again manifesting itself." Only by seizing its own empire in the East could the Reich hope to prosper. However, Britain and France were the "two hate-inspired antagonists" that blocked Berlin's path. "Germany's problem could only be solved by means of force," Hitler explained. Adding a sense of urgency, as other states rearmed, Germany faced a short window of time in which to act. The Reich had to "take the offensive" before its enemies reached their full strength—sometime between 1943 and 1945. "One thing only was certain," Hitler insisted. "We could not wait longer."[15]

The immediate objects of Hitler's imperial ambitions lay to the southeast: Austria and Czechoslovakia. Together, the two countries contained an estimated ten million ethnic Germans whom Hitler hoped to bring into the Reich, along with vast stretches of territory for his growing empire. Though he had insisted that war would be necessary to achieve his goals, Hitler's early victories came through diplomacy. Hitler's home country of Austria contained many who were sympathetic to the Reich. Indeed, Austria had a violent Nazi Party that, while officially outlawed, continued to call for unification with Germany. In July 1934, Austrian Nazis had staged a failed coup that resulted in the assassination of Chancellor Engelbert Dollfuss. His successor, Kurt Schuschnigg, struggled to maintain Vienna's independence in the face of domestic turmoil and mounting pressure from the Third Reich. In February 1938, Schuschnigg sat down for a meeting with Hitler and German military brass in Berchtesgaden. The Führer had grown tired of the impasse with Austria. "I have achieved everything that I set out to do and have thus perhaps become the greatest German of all history," he announced. "The German Reich is a major power, and no one can or will try to interfere when it puts things in order at its borders." Hitler's tirade continued for two hours. Three days later, Schuschnigg relented: Vienna would follow Berlin's lead on foreign policy, lift the ban on the Austrian Nazi Party, and release all Nazi prisoners held in Austrian jails. Schuschnigg staged one last attempt to foil the Reich's plans through a plebiscite that would affirm Austrian independence, but Hitler managed to block it. Schuschnigg, defeated, announced his resignation. At 5:30 the next morning, thousands of German soldiers marched into Austria as cheering crowds showered them with flowers. Throngs of pro-German demonstrators brandishing torches and Nazi banners took to public squares throughout the country shouting "Heil Hitler!" and "One people, one Reich!" The next evening, March 13, Germany's annexation of Austria, the Anschluss, became official.[16]

The Führer's sights now fell on Czechoslovakia and the approximately three million Germans living in the Sudetenland. Pan-German sentiment had swelled in the wake of the Anschluss as ever-greater numbers of ethnic Germans in Czechoslovakia cried out for "home rule." Crowds at pro-German rallies roared Nazi slogans such as "Ein Reich, ein Volk, ein Führer!" (One empire, one people, one Führer!) Hitler was determined to use mounting tensions with Czechoslovakia to start his long-anticipated imperial war. Momentum lay with Germany, and her rivals were still weak and preoccupied with more pressing concerns. Hitler seems to have believed that the British army would need three to four years to prepare for war and that the Royal Air Force would need only one or two. As a result, the Führer insisted, London hoped to "postpone at all costs any European conflict which might lead to a weakening of the whole position of the democratic powers." Germany therefore, to Hitler's mind, should provoke a conflict sooner rather than later. Hitler planned to deliver an unacceptable set of demands to Czechoslovakia and then use Prague's resistance as a pretext to launch an invasion that would, in turn, spark a general war. However, Hitler's generals, who feared a larger war with Britain and France, remained hesitant. So, too, did his key ally, Mussolini, who urged the Führer to agree to negotiations with London and Paris.[17]

British prime minister Neville Chamberlain largely agreed with Hitler's analysis of the situation: the British were not yet ready for a full-scale war. As the Czechoslovakian foreign minister later explained, Britain and France "could not fight and Germany knew it." Rather than give Hitler the war he sought, the British leader was prepared to accept Germany's demands—which included the cession of the Sudetenland to the Reich—sacrificing Czechoslovakia for the greater goal of preventing a wider European war. The fact that French leaders seemed reluctant to confront Berlin also played a critical role. "If France did not go to war in order to protect Czechoslovakia," explained Lord Chancellor Frederic Maugham in a cabinet meeting on September 14, "it was clear that we could not be expected to do so." In a series of negotiations that culminated in a conference held in Munich at the end of September, Chamberlain struck a deal with Hitler that gave in to nearly all of the dictator's demands.[18]

In a speech broadcast on September 28, Chamberlain explained his reasoning: "How horrible, fantastic, incredible it is that we should be digging trenches and trying on gas masks here because of a quarrel in a far-away country between people of whom we know nothing." However, there were lines beyond which London refused to be pushed. Chamberlain would not stand by if a hostile power sought "to dominate the world by fear of its force." Munich, then, represented the limit of Western forbearance. The German ambassador to Washington noted an apparent stiffening of anti-German sentiment in the United States. Explaining the mood in late September, he warned that Hitler could expect resistance if he chose to move beyond the Sudetenland. Even US leaders seemed to be running out of patience for Berlin. If Hitler pushed any further, he could expect war.[19]

Hindsight would soon reveal the folly of appeasement. The Sudetenland represented merely the prelude to the Führer's imperial ambitions. As one US diplomat wrote, "I put forward that it is not realistic to assume that with the gaining of its now proclaimed objectives in Czechoslovakia, Germany will be satisfied so far as her territorial objectives are concerned." Rather than saving the peace, appeasement made a larger war all but "inevitable." But prevailing opinion among the great powers favored Chamberlain. Although the prime minister would later be skewered for this last effort to prevent a global war, Hitler would offer a different assessment. Looking back years later, the Führer seems to have been convinced that his greatest mistake lay in backing down from war in 1938, when Germany's military advantage over its rivals was at its peak. Ironically, in the dictator's mind, his dream of empire was foiled not by Churchill, Stalin, or Roosevelt but by Chamberlain. The next time, however, Hitler would get the war he wanted.[20]

In the early morning hours of September 1, 1939, 1.5 million German troops prepared to cross the frontier into Poland from the north, west, and south. Against them stood a Polish army of 1.3 million—the fourth largest in Europe. Planners in London and Paris hoped that the Poles could hold out for months and allow the full weight of French and British forces to enter the fray. But the raw numbers were deceiving. Polish officials faced an impossible situation. Their forces were sorely outmatched in terms of technology, coordination, and strategy. Whereas Germany, the aggressor, could choose the time and place of the attack, Polish defenses were strained. Full military mobilization would shut down the Polish economy and weaken the nation before a single shot was fired. Then, too, if Warsaw concentrated its forces in one area, it would leave much of the country open to attack, but if Polish troops tried to defend the entire frontier, the Wehrmacht could quickly overwhelm them at any given point.[21]

Moreover, German leaders were not simply seeking minor territorial gains. The Third Reich was fighting a full-scale war of imperial conquest. As Hitler had explained in a meeting in May 1939, "Danzig is not the subject of the dispute at all. It is a question of expanding our living space in the East." Germany must attack Poland "at the first suitable opportunity" with a full understanding that such an action would very likely start a war with France and Britain. In a meeting with Italian officials August 12–13, 1938, Hitler laid out his reasoning:

> As matters now stand, Germany and Italy would simply not exist further in the world through lack of space; not only was there no more space, but existing space was completely blockaded by its present possessors; they sat like misers with their heaps of gold and deluded themselves about their riches. The Western Democracies were dominated by the desire to rule the world and would not regard Germany and Italy as their class. This psychological element of contempt was perhaps the worst thing about the whole business. It could only be settled by a life and death struggle.

Italy would claim the Mediterranean, the dictator explained, while Berlin would reconstitute and expand the eastern borders of the Reich. By late August, Berlin believed that it was ready for the war. "Our enemies are little worms," he told his top generals. "I saw them in Munich."[22]

Watching the collapse of the Polish defenses from Warsaw, American correspondent Edward Beattie noted the Luftwaffe's punishing superiority. "The campaign was already lost because the waves of bombers were systematically destroying every means of gathering the forces to fight it." Eight-year-old Josef Musial wandered through the town center of Wielun following a German air raid. "It was badly destroyed," he later wrote. "Everywhere lay corpses and body parts torn off: arms, legs, a head." Some 1,600 townspeople had been killed. "I have seen shells falling in the center of the town, the mutilated corpses of women and children, houses in flames, the bombing of refugee trains from an altitude of 60 yards, the machine-gunning of men and women fleeing on the roads, and the shelling of hospitals flying the Red Cross," a Polish diplomat told reporters at the end of the month.[23]

Poland's situation was even more hopeless than the war's first days made it seem. The Nazi invasion of Poland marked the culmination of a delicate series of diplomatic negotiations between the great powers over the preceding weeks. Initial discussions between London, Paris, and Moscow aimed at creating an alliance to counterbalance the rising power of Berlin. However, these talks fizzled. Stalin worried that British and French leaders were maneuvering to force the Soviets to shoulder the burden of fighting a potential war with Germany—a fear that would be borne out in the coming years—while British and French officials proved unable to secure agreements from Poland and Romania to permit Soviet forces to travel through their territory in the event of war.[24]

In the midst of this failed diplomacy, Moscow received an overture from Berlin. The resulting Molotov-Ribbentrop Pact of August 1939 combined a pledge of nonaggression between Berlin and Moscow with an agreement to divide Poland between the German and Soviet empires. Moscow would gain control over Latvia, Estonia, and Finland while Berlin would claim Lithuania and Danzig. The pact represented a major coup for Hitler, who secured his eastern flank, allowing him to concentrate on fighting a war with France and Britain. Stalin, on the other hand, gained control over large stretches of Polish territory, which he hoped might serve as a buffer against a possible future clash with Germany. The pact also gave Stalin time to build up his military forces. More broadly, the agreement with Hitler squared with Stalin's deeper ideological belief that it was in the Kremlin's best interest to allow the capitalist powers of Europe to destroy themselves rather than launch a combined attack against the Soviet Union: better for the British, French, and Germans to exhaust themselves fighting one another than attack the Soviet empire in the East.

No doubt the Munich agreement of the previous year had reinforced Stalin's convictions on this point. Chamberlain's willingness to deal with Hitler suggested that there might exist some potential for long-term cooperation between London, Paris, and Berlin.

From Moscow's perspective, Munich could be read as an indication that the Western imperialist powers were laying the groundwork for an anti-Bolshevik entente. Indeed, following the failure
of the London-Paris-Moscow talks, the Kremlin worried that an
Anglo-German alliance was a very real possibility. If Hitler seized
Poland, and London chose to continue its policy of appeasement,
Stalin would face a hostile Germany allied with Britain and camped
along the borders of the Soviet Union. Better to strike a deal with Hitler and allow Germany to turn its wrath toward France and Britain
while Moscow rebuilt its military forces. "A war is on between the
two groups of capitalist countries . . . for the redivision of the world,
for the domination of the world!" Stalin announced on September 7,
1939. "We see nothing wrong in their having a good hard fight and
weakening each other."[25]

In accordance with the nonaggression pact, Stalin launched
his own invasion aimed at expanding the western marches of the
Soviet empire and reclaiming territories that had been surrendered
under the terms of the 1918 Treaty of Brest-Litovsk. Sixteen days
after the German invasion, the Red Army marched into Poland from
the east. Behind the front lines, Soviet state security forces, the People's Commissariat of Internal Affairs (NKVD), conducted a campaign to eliminate Polish leaders, intellectuals, and civil servants. In
this task, they often proved brutally efficient. Soviet officials forced
nearly 140,000 veterans, policemen, government workers, and their
families onto trains headed for prison camps in Siberia—part of the
gulag that Moscow had used to crush the kulaks (small landowners)
a decade before. By the end of the year, Soviet forces had herded tens
of thousands of Poles into internment camps. The Soviets focused
on detaining military officers, police, and intelligentsia. As NKVD
chief Lavrenty Beria explained, these groups were "just waiting to
be released in order to enter actively into the battle against Soviet
power." The solution, Beria said, was "to apply to them the supreme

punishment: shooting." The following month, Soviet guards began busing the first groups of prisoners from the camps to the edge of the Katyn Forest. Upon arrival, the prisoners were stripped of their valuables, led into a building, and murdered. One executioner at the Kalinin prison shot some 250 prisoners per night. The bodies were then thrown into mass graves. Over the course of April and May 1940, Soviet forces massacred nearly twenty-two thousand prisoners in this manner.[26]

While the NKVD staged its massacres in Poland, Stalin took advantage of the agreement with Germany to expand the Soviet empire in the Baltic. In late September 1940, Moscow presented Estonia with an ultimatum demanding that leaders in Tallinn allow Soviet military forces to establish bases in their country. Soviet officials presented similar demands to Latvia and Lithuania in October. "I tell you frankly a division into spheres of influence has taken place," Stalin explained on October 2. This expansion, the dictator claimed, was defensive: "The Germans might attack. For six years German fascists and the communists cursed each other. Now in spite of history there has been an unexpected turn, but one cannot rely upon it." Meanwhile, Stalin also tried to force Finland into a mutual assistance pact. When Finnish leaders refused to concede to Soviet demands, the two countries prepared for war. On November 30, 1940, the Red Army attacked, starting the Winter War. Moscow's expectations of a short war were quickly dispelled as Finnish troops mounted a fearsome defense. Soviet forces suffered high casualties—and international embarrassment—but by March 1941, Moscow had gained the upper hand. For a time, however, it appeared as if the Winter War might spark a larger conflict with the Western powers. News that British and French leaders were considering an intervention in support of Finland fed Stalin's fears that the Western powers were hoping to either draw the Soviet Union into the war against Germany or forge an anti-Soviet coalition of capitalist states. The Red Army's victory in March foreclosed such possibilities, but Stalin's suspicions of capitalist machinations continued.[27]

BRITAIN AND FRANCE CONFRONTED THE GRIM REALITY OF NOT ONE but two totalitarian states rampaging through Poland. Having failed to draw Moscow into an anti-German coalition, London and Paris were left to bear the brunt of the struggle against Hitler's war machine. While British military planners urged a swift mobilization and attack, French generals favored a slower, more deliberate approach. Nevertheless, both London and Paris declared war on Berlin on September 3, 1939. French troops supported by British aircraft could pressure the Germans along the Siegfried Line, but they were unlikely to force a German withdrawal anytime soon. In the meantime, Poland fought on in hopes of eventual liberation after a German defeat. British strategists envisioned the war lasting some five years and entailing "extreme" effort. Western leaders initially planned for a war that would not be entirely unlike the First World War, with large French and British forces tying down the German army near the Franco-German border while the British navy enforced a blockade aimed at starving the Reich of resources. The deployment of larger air forces, Italy's alliance with Germany, and Moscow's neutrality complicated matters, but British and French leaders believed that they had the situation in hand.[28]

Polish resistance to the Reich's larger program of expansion bolstered Hitler's convictions that the nation must be destroyed. The Wehrmacht, he determined, would unleash a campaign of colonial violence in their newly conquered territory designed to destroy Polish culture, scatter the population, and clear out living space for German colonists. In late August, the dictator ordered the military to show no mercy:

> Our strength lies in our speed and our brutality. Genghis Khan hunted millions of women and children to their deaths, consciously and with a joyous heart. History sees in him only the great founder of a state. . . . The aim of the war lies not in reaching particular lines but in the physical annihilation of the enemy. . . . I have put my Death's Head formations at the

ready with the command to send every man, woman and child of Polish descent and language to their deaths, pitilessly and remorselessly. . . . Poland will be depopulated and settled with Germans.

Nazi victory would be followed by colonization. Like earlier European imperialists who had moved into Africa, the Americas, Asia, and the Middle East in bids to subdue "uncivilized" populations, Nazi leaders resolved to colonize Poland. As Hitler explained to Goebbels, the Poles were "more animals than men." By driving out the Slavic populations, the Reich would clear the way for an expanded German empire. The Nazis' repertoire of colonial violence would be fashioned on the Polish killing fields. "Poland," two Holocaust historians wrote, "was thus destined to become a 'laboratory' for the Nazi experience in racial imperialism" designed to transform Hitler's theories of imperialism, nationalism, and ethnic conflict into reality.[29]

DRIVEN BY THE FÜHRER'S CALLS FOR ETHNIC STRUGGLE AND WAR OF annihilation (*Vernichtungskrieg*), German troops unleashed a punishing assault on the Poles. Even sporadic resistance from civilians was often met with brutal collective reprisals. German forces summarily executed suspected attackers and then razed their houses and sometimes entire villages. After Polish forces killed an estimated one thousand ethnic Germans in retaliation for guerrilla attacks in the city of Bydgoszcz, advancing Wehrmacht troops retaliated by massacring some five thousand Poles in the city and the surrounding area. However, this initial violence was only the beginning.[30]

Behind the frontline soldiers followed the Einsatzgruppen— special units created by Himmler and his deputy Reinhard Heydrich. These units were given the grisly task of slaughtering the groups deemed most dangerous by the Nazi leadership, as part of an operation code-named Tannenberg. As Heydrich explained, Hitler had authorized the Einsatzgruppen to carry out the "extraordinarily radical

. . . order for the liquidation of various circles of the Polish leadership, [killings] that ran into the thousands." The Polish intelligentsia sat at the top of the list. The elimination of doctors, lawyers, leaders, and intellectuals was a key part of Hitler's larger vision of eradicating the Polish nation to make room for his new empire: "Only a nation whose upper levels are destroyed can be pushed into the ranks of slavery," he argued. Heydrich told military leaders that the Einsatzgruppen's task was "fundamental cleansing: Jews, intelligentsia, clergy, nobles." Likewise, the army chief of staff, Franz Halder, told officers that "it was the intention of the Führer and Göring to destroy and exterminate the Polish people." Locating these individuals proved hard work, however. The second category of people targeted by the Nazi death squads—Poland's Jewish population—proved far easier to track down. Einsatzgruppen commanders unleashed troops with flamethrowers to torch synagogues, conducted searches of suspected Jews on the streets, and terrorized the population in an effort to drive them out of German-controlled areas. At one point, Hitler mused that surviving Jews might be forced into a sort of "nature preserve" to the east.[31]

Hitler's invasion of Poland constituted nothing less than a racialized war of colonial conquest. In late September, Hitler mused that Poland might be split up: the Jews would be driven to the east, a Polish section would serve as a buffer in the middle, and the west would become "a German granary, a strong peasantry, to resettle good Germans from all over the world." The Führer envisioned a wholesale erasure of the Polish state. "In thirty years' time," one of Hitler's aides noted, "people will drive across the country and [see] nothing to remind them that once upon a time these regions had been the subject of disputes between Germans and Poles." The Poles would be reduced to a nation of slaves. "The Führer has no intention of assimilating the Poles," Goebbels explained. "They are to be forced into their truncated state and left entirely to their own devices."[32]

The Wehrmacht's brutal advance through Poland brought German forces face-to-face with the devastated population now at their mercy. "These people are not one level of civilisation, but many levels of civilisation, behind the Germans," one Wehrmacht soldier wrote. "Two thousand years ago our ancestors lived better—and above all more cleanly." Another soldier wrote of the conditions in Poland as being "as primitive as one imagines them to be in darkest Africa— but these people here are Europeans." Toward such peoples, many Germans felt scant pity. Describing a typical reprisal raid against a village suspected of harboring resistance fighters, one officer wrote, "When the action is over, the entire village is set on fire. No-one is left alive, even all the dogs are shot." Following the fall of Warsaw on September 27, Jadwiga Sosnkowska, a Polish nurse, remembered walking through the hospital where she worked: "Long rows of more than a hundred yards of mutilated bodies of soldiers, women and children. . . . I saw the most terrible sight—a river of blood literally flowing down the corridor, washing the bodies of the dead, dying and still living martyrs." Pianist Wladyslaw Szpilman emerged from hiding to find that "decaying bodies were piled up in the streets." He watched in horror as "people, starving from the siege, fell on the bodies of horses lying around. . . . You had to hold a handkerchief to your nose—the nauseating stink of eight rotting bodies seeped through the blocked up cellar windows." Surveying the devastation, he wrote, "The city no longer existed."[33]

Indifferent to the suffering of the Poles and basking in the glow of their own victory, German leaders laid plans for absorbing Poland into the Reich. The ethnic cleansing of the Polish population formed the first order of business. A secret research document from the Academy of German Law on resettlement expressed concern that this "mass of Poles is a great inconvenience, an obstacle to the Germanization of the country, and under certain circumstances a danger." The new territories acquired could barely accommodate the numbers of Jews, Polish intelligentsia, and Polish leaders that needed to be driven from the Reich. Forced labor could help, but it was not in itself a solution. Further conquest was necessary: "A resettlement of many millions can only be undertaken after victory . . . which could create space for surplus Poles, be it in Siberia . . . [or] eastwards of the White Russians. A resettlement of several million Jews, perhaps in Madagascar, could also create space."[34]

AS HE WATCHED HIS ARMIES TEAR THROUGH POLAND, HITLER savored the realization of his long-held dream of carving out a new Nazi empire in the heart of Europe. Years of feverish work to reconstitute the German military and condition the German people for conquest had paid off. Now, across the devastated Polish countryside, the Führer's vision of blood, soil, war, and genocide was taking shape. But he was not alone. Stalin's Red Army was also marching through the eastern half of Poland. Germany's eastward expansion brought the Bolshevik menace to the new borders of the Third Reich. However, before he could turn to his larger goal of striking at the communists in the East, Hitler had to look toward his western flank, where Britain and France were preparing to join the war. If the Führer hoped to achieve his ambition of building a thousand-year Reich, he would first have to defeat the guardians of the old Versailles order.

Chapter 5

EMPIRE BESIEGED

A S NIGHT FELL OVER THE LOW COUNTRIES ON MAY 9, 1940, ALLIED troops heard a "vast murmuring" from the German lines across the frontier. Thousands of men, horses, and motor vehicles were moving through the darkness on the other side of the border. An hour past midnight, Belgian observers concluded that an invasion was imminent—and three and a half hours later, German paratroopers began landing in the Netherlands. But it was not until 6:30 a.m. that the commander of French forces, General Maurice Gamelin, was awoken from his bed. In short order, Gamelin was up and striding through the halls of his fortress, "humming with a pleased and martial air." The general had good reason to be confident. Revered by his peers, Gamelin had distinguished himself as one of the architects of the First Battle of the Marne, which had stopped the German drive on Paris in 1914. France had spent the last twenty years preparing for this day. To the south, the Maginot Line—a vast, near-impenetrable system of fortifications—guarded the French border with Germany. In the north, French, British, Belgian, and Dutch divisions had mobilized to engage the spearhead of a German invasion through the Low Countries. Against 2,439 German tanks, the French army fielded 3,254 tanks, many of which were of superior quality. Combined with the Belgians, the British Expeditionary Force (BEF), and the Dutch, Allied strength comprised some 4,200 armored vehicles. If the First World War was any guide, the French could expect a long struggle, for which Gamelin was prepared. Using the formidable army at his command, Gamelin would once again halt the Wehrmacht's advance while Britain used its mastery of the seas to starve the Third Reich into submission. The fight was sure to be bloody and long, but as Gamelin had told the French government the preceding August, the army was ready.[1] The long months of waiting had come to an end and the battle to decide the fate of Europe had begun.

The catastrophe set to befall the Western allies would transform not only the balance of power in Europe but Europe's position in the world order. France served as one of the two pillars of the Versailles order. While the British navy patrolled the seas, the French army held the line on the continent. France's crushing defeat would bring the entire international system crashing down and send shock waves across the continent and around the world. The battles along the frontiers of Belgium, France, Germany, and the Netherlands in the spring of 1940 set in motion a series of events that would topple the old order, pose a direct threat to the survival of the British Empire, convince Japan and Italy to launch imperial offensives in North Africa and the Pacific, persuade the United States to mount a bid for world hegemony, and push Nazi Germany to attack the Soviet colossus in the East. Ultimately, the French collapse would serve as the catalyst for the transformation of the international system away from a world of formal empires and toward the neo-imperial order of the Cold War.[2] But none of this was knowable on that fateful morning in May 1940.

AS THE SPRING THAW ARRIVED ACROSS WESTERN EUROPE, OBSERVers around the world seemed to sense the enormous gravity of the approaching hostilities. In question was not just the leadership in Europe but the fate of Western civilization and the shape of an emerging global order. "This is the fateful hour," proclaimed the editors of the *New York Times*. Hitler's bid for mastery over Europe represented a dire threat not just to the regional balance of power but to the future of the democratic world. The newspaper admonished Americans not to be complacent. The people of the United States, "who live behind the defenses of the Western European nations which are the outposts of our own kind of civilization must watch with deep anxiety." In April, the leading international relations journal *Foreign Affairs* published an essay by American journalist Dorothy Thompson. She had watched Hitler's rise to power before being expelled from Nazi Germany in 1934. Thompson claimed that a revolution was underway in European civilization. The Nazis had turned away from the West and its bourgeois decadence. Instead, she explained, Germany, along with Russia, had descended into totalitarianism, a fascination with militarism, and an "oriental despotism." Now, the crazed leadership in Berlin had entered into a war with the Western powers. As a result, she warned, "the west confronts the greatest danger in her whole history."[3]

In the same issue, French economist André Siegfried warned that Europe faced a struggle between the Third Reich and the Western powers for leadership of "White civilization." For generations, the European colonial empires had maintained a "major defense line behind which white civilization has been able to live and prosper." But now that line was embattled, particularly in Asia, where millions of colonized people were rising up to challenge the old imperial order. The rise of anticolonial nationalism represented a challenge both to the existing geopolitical order and to the deeper notion of "white supremacy" that justified Western powers' exploitation of societies across Africa, Asia, and the Middle East. In the long run, Siegfried wrote, the "United States might itself become the leader of the white race and itself take over the responsibilities of empire, either jointly with England or in place of England."[4]

British planners also recognized the imperial dimensions of the conflict. Shortly after Hitler's invasion of Poland, officials in the War Office outlined a plan to send four divisions to France to fight against Germany. However, they warned that British leaders must not forget the wider empire in the midst of the European conflict. In particular, London should remember "that our strategy in the Middle East must be an Imperial strategy," the report explained. "The Suez Canal is in the centre of the British Empire." In early May 1940, the British chiefs of staff concluded that Germany sought a short war. Although the Wehrmacht could stage an invasion of France, officials believed that France could hold off a direct offensive. In light of the formidable French defenses, the War Cabinet feared that Berlin would instead bypass France and launch an attack on the British Isles. London should also prepare for attacks against British assets in the Mediterranean and Middle East, the chiefs advised. Although Britain's immediate fears of a cross-channel attack failed to materialize, what happened was perhaps even more catastrophic.[5]

Early reports from the front seemed encouraging. French and British forces had sent their best units forward into the Netherlands and Belgium to block the expected main thrust of the German advance. Meeting at the Belgian town of Hannut, French and German forces waged a climactic battle. "The scene was hell itself," wrote American reporter G. H. Archambault on May 13, "with tanks engaging at close range, charging one another, firing projectiles on all sides, with some catching fire and exploding." Although the French appeared to win this initial engagement, Archambault also noted reports of heavy fighting to the south, in the Ardennes forest.[6]

In fact, it was precisely in the Ardennes sector that the Wehrmacht was mounting its decisive assault. The dramatic tank battle in the north was merely a diversion. The main thrust of the German attack had slogged through the Ardennes as part of a massive line of armored vehicles snaking through the supposedly impenetrable forest. For three days and nights, drivers chewed amphetamines to stay awake and refueled whenever they were forced to stop as part of what one described "the greatest traffic jam known to that date in Europe." All of this came as the result of a freak series of events that had led Berlin to overhaul its original plan of attack aimed at the north. In January 1940, a plane carrying the German war plans had lost its way in the fog and been forced to make a crash landing across the border in Belgium. With their original plans in Allied hands, German leaders were compelled to revise. Instead of a frontal assault through northern Belgium and the Netherlands, German planners devised a bold gamble: the main Wehrmacht force would attack through the Ardennes, slipping between the Allied strongpoints in the north and the Maginot Line in the south to strike at the weak center of the French lines along the Meuse River. The German attackers were outnumbered nearly two to one in the north and south, but this imbalance allowed the Wehrmacht to send its forty-five finest divisions against eighteen mediocre Allied divisions in the center—no reserves were held back. The Luftwaffe also sent waves of aircraft to support the attack, betting everything on the offensive and holding few of its reserves back.[7]

This gamble paid off. German forces smashed through the few defenders they encountered on their way through the Ardennes and emerged at the French border near Sedan and Dinan. French troops tried to slow the German advance by demolishing roads, erecting barricades, and fighting wherever possible, but the Allied forces lacked effective antitank weapons. A concerted bombing attack might have slowed the Wehrmacht, General Heinz Guderian later noted, but Allied leaders failed to recognize the severity of the German thrust—German commanders considered it a miracle that the Allied air forces had not staged a more serious attack on the vulnerable panzers. A second miracle arrived with the failure of French commanders to bolster their defenses along the Meuse river. The French had had months to prepare their defenses and days since the invasion to reinforce their positions, but they had failed to do so. "Here and there a few French machine-guns were firing from small, ludicrous concrete emplacements on the west banks of the Meuse. That was all," remembered German general Günther Blumentritt. "We simply could not grasp this miracle—and feared that it was a French ruse." As German artillery directed heavy fire against the pillboxes across the river, soldiers rowed rubber dinghies to the opposite shore to clear a bridgehead. By midnight, German engineers had finished their first bridge across the Meuse, piercing the French defenses and clearing the way for their panzers to roll forward. Once in open country, the full fury of the German armored assault was unleashed. Disobeying direct orders to halt while the Wehrmacht consolidated its position near Sedan, Guderian swung north in a headlong dash toward the channel coast designed to cut off the frontline British and French armies in the Low Countries. The German panzers raced forward behind the Allied lines, leaving infantry and supply trucks scrambling to catch up.[8]

While the Wehrmacht consolidated its bridgehead across the Meuse, the Luftwaffe launched a brutal assault on the city of Rotterdam. German commanders had threatened to destroy the port city unless the Dutch surrendered. Following the government's refusal to lay down arms on May 14, German aircraft began pummeling Rotterdam's historic quarter. Lacking any defense against the bombers, Rotterdam's population could only scramble for shelter. A visiting American journalist wrote that the German attack left "only a scar of a city—its main business and financial district a pile of bricks and mortar serving as headstones for hundreds of dead." Days later, smoke still drifted over the harbor and hundreds of bodies lay entombed in the ruins.[9] By destroying the city, the Germans had sent a message to all who dared resist the Third Reich. Rotterdam had joined Chongqing as an early victim of the terrifying violence of strategic bombardment. A form of warfare once consigned to colonial battlefields would henceforth become a mainstay of the Second World War in metropolitan Europe and Asia.

WHILE FIRES STILL BURNED IN ROTTERDAM, THE BRITISH AMBASSADOR to the United States, Lord Lothian, spoke to an audience on the other side of the Atlantic Ocean at the Waldorf Astoria Hotel in Manhattan. Convened to commemorate the English-Speaking Union's two decades of charitable educational activities, the event soon turned to focus on the darkening clouds of war in Europe. Lothian stressed the common civilizational bonds shared by the English-speaking peoples of the United States, Britain, and the Commonwealth. The "decisive battle has begun in the West," he warned his audience.

> On the one side are those ideals of individual freedom, national self-government and democracy which have slowly evolved under Christian influence and for which the English-speaking world unflinchingly stands. On the other side is a system which respects none of those spiritual values and has subordinated everything else to preparing for aggressive war and which uses violence to the limit and utterly regardless of any moral restraint in order to establish its pagan dominion over mankind. . . . The next thirty days may determine whether there is to be any effective barrier left to the domination of all Europe, Asia and Africa by the dictatorships, leaving America isolated and alone to champion a free way of life. . . . We live in the greatest era of history. There stand before us two naked alternatives. On the one side Western civilization may, for a time, take a plunge back into a darker age than we have ever known before. On the other we may rise to levels of national unselfishness, and vision, and dedication which may give to mankind the greatest new birth of freedom it has ever known.

The ambassador's speech laid out London's argument for Washington's entry into the war: the Anglophone world represented a single civilization organized around democracy and the English language; Anglophone civilization was threatened by a barbaric totalitarianism; leaders in Washington had to now choose whether to join London in the struggle for democratic civilization or allow the world to sink into a new dark age.[10]

Lothian's words echoed long-running efforts to forge a common cause between the American and British empires. Through the interwar years, many US and British leaders had envisioned an Anglophone world order rooted in vague notions of Anglo-Saxon racial identity and justified through the vocabulary of liberal democratic government. Institutions such as London's Royal Institute of International Affairs and New York's Council on Foreign Relations pushed a worldview that bound notions of social and political progress to British and American national power and called for the formation of a new Atlantic community of nations. Building on earlier visions of an imperial civilizing mission, these ideas saw London and Washington as the torchbearers for a liberal world order.[11]

Lothian's speech also reflected the increasingly dire situation in France. On May 15, as German panzers drove toward the channel coast, France's prime minister, Paul Reynaud, warned the US ambassador to France, William Bullitt, that the "greatest battle in history was in progress." French forces desperately needed more aircraft from Britain and the United States to slow the German advance. German tanks had broken through at multiple points and were now driving toward Paris. "The situation could not be more grave," Bullitt warned. The following day, British prime minister Winston Churchill flew to Paris in hopes of bolstering French resolve. There he found a demoralized government and French armies in retreat. Barring some miracle on the battlefield, London was likely to find itself fighting alone against the Nazis. Churchill pledged to "fight until England is burnt to the ground," but the situation appeared grave.[12]

By May 18, the Wehrmacht's objective of reaching the channel coast and cutting off the French and British armies had become apparent. Reynaud emphasized France's increasingly dire situation to Ambassador Bullitt. The world had witnessed a new military revolution: the era of slow, plodding advances was over. Mechanized warfare had allowed the Germans to move at incredible speeds, flanking and surrounding defenders before the latter realized their danger. If France fell, Reynaud warned, Britain would be isolated and Hitler would move into Latin America with the long-term goal of install-ing a Nazi regime in the United States. Although it was now too late for the United States to send the massive amounts of aid needed to reverse the situation, the prime minister pleaded for US officials to issue a declaration that Washington considered the survival of France and Britain to be in its vital interests. While Bullitt agreed that Hitler would likely turn toward the United States at his first opportunity, he worried that the American public was not prepared to enter the war.[13]

Two days later, an advance battalion from Guderian's Second Panzer Division reached the waters of the English Channel. Forces from Rommel's Seventh Panzer Division were also driving toward the coast. The finest French and British armies were now trapped in an ever-shrinking pocket of territory around Dunkirk and Calais. While Hitler and his commanders celebrated the news of their stunning suc-cess, British and French leaders scrambled to organize an operation to break out of the encirclement. The German lines were still tenuous, but the Allies were slow, disorganized, and unable to mount a success-ful counterattack. Nevertheless, the rapid advance had thrown the German forces into disarray. The Führer ordered his armies to halt for repairs and in order to allow their supply chains to catch up with the armored units. Years later, Hitler's generals would blame the Führer for ordering the pause and allowing the British to escape. However, at the time much of the German leadership recognized that they needed to consolidate their gains after a series of risky operations. The Wehr-macht's lines were dangerously overextended, their tanks were in need of repair, and their crews needed rest. In addition, the marshy land in front of them would slow their tanks, and the danger of an Allied counterattack remained.[14]

In the meantime, the German pause allowed British and French forces to pull back to the coast as leaders in London dispatched ships to evacuate their defeated armies. British leaders had concluded that France was likely to collapse and that they must save what was left of the army around Dunkirk and Calais. "On the broader issue," Sec-retary of State for Foreign Affairs Lord Halifax argued, "we had to face the fact that it was not so much now a question of imposing a complete defeat upon Germany but of safeguarding the independence of our own Empire and if possible that of France." Halifax went on to argue that London ought to consider striking a peace deal with Hitler in order to spare the British people the ordeal of a German invasion.[15]

With their position on the continent in jeopardy, British leaders looked to the empire. The fall of France did not guarantee defeat in the larger war, planners argued. London must concentrate on waging a successful defense of the British Isles while preparing its larger empire to meet the threat of future attacks. Defeat in Europe would embolden Italian and Japanese leaders seeking to seize British colonial possessions in Africa, Asia, and the Middle East. "We must therefore fight our enemy everywhere we can," British planners wrote. In time, the colonies could be used as launchpads for counterattacks against the Axis powers.[16]

Across the Atlantic, US officials had also begun drawing up contingency plans in the event of a total Allied defeat. The day after German forces reached the English Channel, US Army chief of staff George Marshall received an unsigned memorandum calling for Washington to take control of British and French colonial possessions in the Atlantic in order to prevent Nazi incursions into the Western Hemisphere. On May 28, the US War Plans Division of the War Department submitted a proposal to do just that. Two weeks later, the US naval attaché in London warned that the collapse of the British Empire would open the door to Axis incursions into the Caribbean and South America, compromising US continental security and closing off the Panama Canal.[17]

While US military leaders prepared to defend the Western Hemisphere, groups of demoralized British soldiers at Dunkirk braced for the Nazi onslaught. As Captain Basil Bartlett entered Dunkirk on May 27, a wave of Luftwaffe bombers roared overhead, sending him running for cover. "There were huge columns of flame and smoke coming from the docks," he wrote later. Bartlett spent the night with his men on the beach, sharing water, biscuits, and pieces of chocolate.

German flares and the glow from burning buildings lit the surrounding dunes, but they escaped into the shadows. Some men dug graves for themselves in the sand. The next day, Bartlett ventured back into the city, which was now choked by black smoke. "Tangled wires and dead horses and blazing masonry made it impossible to move about except on foot," he wrote. As the midday heat settled over the beaches, soldiers took shelter from falling bombs and strafing Messerschmitts.[18]

On the German side of the front, American reporter Ralph Barnes made his way toward Dunkirk. Along the road, he passed battlefields littered with the hulks of destroyed tanks and artillery, ruined towns, collapsed bridges, and POW camps crowded with British and French soldiers. Belgian and French refugees streamed away from the front in great, ragged hordes. Barnes saw fresh graves, unburied corpses, and the rotting bodies of cattle and horses. The "rattle and roar of battle on land and in the air is about us and above us," he wrote. Seven miles to the west, a great column of smoke hung over the burning Allied bastion of Dunkirk. German warplanes roared overhead, their bombs making a low rumble in the distance. The fighting had left the town of Bergues in ruins. While flames consumed the Hôtel du Roi, the town hall stood ready to collapse. Shell holes pockmarked the town's medieval church. Survivors hid like "frightened animals. . . . They peer[ed] from doorways and cellarways of houses and shops," he wrote.[19]

But British forces managed to stave off total catastrophe. Dunkirk lay close enough to English airfields for the Royal Air Force to provide air cover for the beleaguered troops on the beaches. Meanwhile, the Royal Navy organized a massive flotilla of hundreds of ships and pleasure craft to evacuate nearly 340,000 Allied soldiers from the beaches. Among them was Captain Bartlett, who managed to board a destroyer. However, as his ship made the perilous journey across the channel, it was torpedoed by German boats and then raked with machine gun fire. Bursting onto the deck of the burning sinking ship, Bartlett stumbled across "a mass of twisted steel and mangled bodies."

Fortunately, another British ship arrived to rescue the survivors. "I suppose that, in history, this campaign will count as a first-class defeat," he wrote.[20]

THE BRITISH EVACUATION FROM THE BEACHES OF DUNKIRK HAD staved off disaster. Although they had abandoned most of their equipment, nearly two hundred thousand British soldiers made it back to England. Their return, Churchill explained, "has revolutionized the Home Defence position. . . . We have a mass of trained troops in the country which would require a raid to be executed on a prohibitively large scale." With this infusion of soldiers, British leaders could now focus on shifting troops around the empire, reconstituting another expeditionary force to be sent to France, and bolstering British defenses against a German invasion. Berlin must now realize, Churchill argued, "that the armed forces in Great Britain are now far stronger than they have ever been."[21]

Churchill's hopeful assessment masked the grim reality that now confronted London: Germany had cut the Allied armies to shreds, France perched on the brink of collapse, and the mighty British Empire found itself besieged. London now faced the choice of whether to cut its losses and abandon France or to send reinforcements into a collapsing fortress. The British chiefs of staff understood that total defeat of France would be catastrophic for Britain. The Nazis would install a pro-German government and transform France into a base from which to attack the United Kingdom. However, the chiefs feared that French leaders had already accepted defeat. The French army had proven incapable of defending its positions against the Germans and had suffered heavy losses. It therefore seemed doubtful that British reinforcements could turn the tide of battle. "Any forces despatched to France can virtually be written off," the chiefs warned. In his darker moments, even Churchill confronted the grim reality of the situation. "You and I will be dead in three months' time," he told his chief military assistant on June 12.[22]

The prime minister's visit to French headquarters in mid-June confirmed the mounting danger of a total collapse. French commanders warned that the army was disintegrating and Marshal Philippe Pétain, who would replace Reynaud as prime minister on June 16, appeared to favor a negotiated surrender to the Nazis. Nevertheless, Churchill observed that Reynaud remained defiant, as did a young general named Charles de Gaulle, "who believe[d] much can be done."[23]

Such optimism for the Allied cause was in far shorter supply on the continent. A correspondent for the *Chicago Tribune* described Dunkirk as "a pile of rubbish. . . . The wreckage of bomb shattered buildings chokes its streets." Smoke poured from a burning French tanker, while the bodies of French soldiers blackened in the June heat. Elsewhere, the charred corpses of soldiers that had been caught in the burning city still lay where they had been killed. The "stench was almost overpowering," the correspondent wrote. Bullets, spent shells, and grenades covered much of the ground. The wreckage of cars and trucks caught in the Luftwaffe's bombardment cluttered the roads. Hundreds of dead French cavalry horses floated in the canals. The Wehrmacht now controlled many of the key ports along the English Channel. American reporter Ralph Barnes reported that, despite wrecked buildings and bullet-scarred walls, the port of Boulogne remained largely intact. Abandoned Allied field guns still littered the area while crowds of demoralized civilians queued for bread rations. German soldiers manned antiaircraft guns protected by sandbags along the docks. Calais had suffered far more damage and remained mostly deserted aside from the wrecks of Allied vehicles. "There was a weird silence of death about this once bustling port," wrote Barnes. The one waterfront cafe that remained open sold drinks to suntanned SS soldiers who told Barnes, "We are here ready to go to England."[24]

To the south, the Wehrmacht drove on toward Paris. On June 13, German forces sighted the Eiffel Tower looming in the distance, well within range of their artillery. The following morning, American correspondent Demaree Bess watched from his hotel as authorities lowered four large French flags around the Rond-Point of the Champs-Élysées. German troops were set to enter Paris. The invaders had been notified that the city had surrendered and that the army had abandoned the capital. Bess joined onlookers watching the German troops as they marched into the city along the rue La Fayette. The soldiers "were young and alert and freshly shaved," the journalist wrote. "To the amazement of Parisians, who had read so much of Germany's mechanised army, those first units were all drawn by horses." Swastika banners flew from the capital's major landmarks: the Quai d'Orsay, the Arc de Triomphe, city hall. "Paris was a ghost city when I entered," wrote another reporter. Seventy percent of the population had fled. The stunned citizens who remained gazed in disbelief at the Nazi soldiers roaming through the streets. On June 16, Pétain declared his intention to seek an armistice with Germany. France had fallen.[25]

In response to France's catastrophic collapse and the disintegration of the international order, the acting chief of the US War Plans Division, Major General George Strong, recommended a series of emergency measures. First, Washington must adopt a defensive position in the Far East, hunkering down and maintaining as many of its possessions as possible while trying to avoid a direct clash with Tokyo. Second, the United States should halt any further arms deals or aid agreements with the Allied powers in "recognition of the early defeat of the Allies." Any equipment or cash Washington sent to Europe could very likely end up in the hands of the Wehrmacht. In the same vein, American leaders must now recognize the "probability that [Americans] are next on the list of victims of the Axis powers." To this end, Strong called on Washington to mobilize the army and National Guard for the defense of the Western Hemisphere, to ramp up production of war materials for a coming conflict, and to prepare "for 'protective seizure' of British and French colonies in the New World." Planners worked from the assumption that both London and Paris would surrender and that their fleets would fall into German hands. In this event, the United States and Canada would be tasked with defending the Western Hemisphere against the combined might of Germany, Japan, and, in the worst-case scenario, the Soviet Union. Hawaii and the Panama Canal appeared to be likely targets of a future assault that would drive US forces back across the Pacific to bases in Hawaii and Alaska while the bulk of the US fleet defended the Caribbean.[26]

Prominent voices in the United States now called on the nation to prepare to join the war against Hitler. Speaking at Columbia University's 186th commencement ceremony in early June, the university president, Nicholas Murray Butler, invoked Edward Gibbon's *The History of the Decline and Fall of the Roman Empire* to describe the drama unfolding across the Atlantic. "What will the Gibbon of 500 years hence have to say concerning those happenings which are now shaping the history of the modern world in this twentieth century?" he asked the assembled audience. Germany's victory constituted a dire threat to democracy around the world. As a consequence, he warned, "the progress of civilization is hanging in the balance." Butler exhorted his audience to take action in defense of liberal civilization. "The call is for every civilized human being who believes in justice, in liberty and in public morals," he declared. "The bell is ringing!"[27]

Striking a similar tone, *Washington Post* reporter Barnet Nover warned that the fall of France extinguished the last light of democracy in continental Europe. Now, he wrote, "the pall of darkness extends over the whole of that land mass from the Atlantic to Asia, from the Arctic to the Mediterranean." Hitler's victory meant the triumph of a monstrous and savage will to violence over democracy, morality, and law. If Britain also fell to the Nazi juggernaut, he wrote, "it will mean in a very real sense the end of European civilization." The United States must not be lulled by a sense of complacency, but Nover questioned whether the nation would rouse itself from isolation and prepare to defend the last bastion of democracy against the Nazis. He was not alone.[28]

Life magazine's Walter Lippmann, America's most widely read columnist, wrote in June, "The controlling power in western civilization has crossed the Atlantic. America, which was once a colony on the frontiers of Europe, is now, and will in the next generations become even more certainly, the geographic and the economic and the political center of the Occident." The United States was destined for global leadership. "What Rome was to the ancient world, what Great Britain has been to the modern world, America is to be to the world of tomorrow." Washington was to become nothing less than the "controlling power in western civilization." Lippmann's predictions echoed the sentiment of Ambassador Lord Lothian, who had implored a skeptical Franklin Roosevelt to join with the British Empire to meet the rising threat of Nazi Germany earlier in the year. "The British for a thousand years had been the guardians of Anglo-Saxon civilization," Roosevelt recalled Lothian saying. Lothian had also said, Roosevelt remembered, "that the scepter of the sword or something like that had dropped from their palsied fingers—that the U.S.A. must snatch it up—that F.D.R. alone could save the world." But not everyone was so cynical. Less than two weeks after Germany's invasion of Poland, Hamilton Fish Armstrong and Walter Mallory—leading members of the Council on Foreign Relations—had offered the council's services to the State Department for the purposes of postwar planning. The conflict might very well serve as a catalyst for the United States to assume a dominant position in world affairs, and Washington should not let such an opportunity slip away.[29]

The following month, Lippmann warned that the economic impact of a German victory would fundamentally undermine the American standard of living and push the nation toward revolution and disorder. Totalitarian powers now stood on the brink of seizing control of three of the world's great industrial centers: Western Europe, Russia, and Japan. Only the United States remained outside of their grasp. If Britain fell, Lippmann argued, the United States would be doomed to economic isolation. "The fact is that a free economy, such as Americans have known, cannot survive in a world that is elsewhere under a regime of military socialism. . . . The America we have known will be destroyed by a social convulsion from within because we are isolated and impoverished and demoralized," he wrote. To pretend otherwise, Lippmann insisted, was to indulge in a complacency that was as foolish as it was dangerous.[30]

Lippmann's assessment was widely shared by US officials, who concluded that Washington must take a lead role in shaping the postwar order. In particular, Under Secretary of State Sumner Welles determined that the United States must not repeat Woodrow Wilson's mistakes—this time, Washington would prepare in advance and build a consensus among the White House, State Department, and Congress. On June 18, former US secretary of war Henry Stimson delivered a radio address on the impending fall of France. He warned that the United States faced perhaps "the greatest crisis in its history." The fall of France threatened not only American security but democracy and self-government around the world. Fascist powers were on the march in Europe, Asia, and Africa. Nazi hegemony in Europe would divide the world into two camps, "half slave and half free." To meet this threat, Stimson called on the United States to give all possible assistance to the British navy and to prepare its own forces for battle against the fascist states. The following day, Stimson received a call from President Roosevelt asking him to once again become America's secretary of war.[31]

While American officials worried about the escalating conflict in Europe, voices in the international socialist movement predicted a sea change in world affairs. In May 1940, exiled Russian revolutionary Leon Trotsky convened an emergency meeting of the socialist Fourth International at a secret location somewhere in the Western Hemisphere. While the conference's fanciful calls for a worldwide proletarian revolution fizzled, Trotsky's assessment of the war's causes carried greater weight. "The immediate cause of the present war," he argued, "is the rivalry between the old wealthy colonial empires, Great Britain and France, and the belated imperialist plunderers, Germany and Italy." British naval hegemony had foundered, opening a path for new challengers in Germany, which was focused on dominating Europe, and the United States, which was intent on establishing control over the world. Germany had launched a naked grab at imperialist expansion in Europe, Trotsky insisted. Meanwhile, the United States was preparing to assert its hegemony over the international system. "History is bringing humanity face to face with the volcanic eruption of American imperialism," he explained. The Atlantic world would be consumed by the war against Germany, and the Pacific world would soon see the outbreak of a war between the United States and Japan. The end result, he insisted, would mean the eclipse of the British Empire: "American imperialism, which emerged as the world's creditor from the last war, expects to emerge from this one its undisputed master."[32]

For their part, British leaders remained keenly aware of the dangers they faced. On June 19, 1940, the British chiefs of staff warned that, following the collapse of French resistance, the Nazis would now attempt an invasion of Great Britain. Such an attack could deal a knockout blow to London long before the arrival of any American aid. In preparation for the "imminent threat of invasion," British leaders should plan for a concerted aerial campaign aimed at air defenses and population centers. The chiefs also called for the arrest and internment of Italian and German men in Britain to prevent a potential fifth column. All measures had to be taken to defend the nation against the looming threat of invasion. The next three months would be critical.[33]

ON JUNE 22, 1940, FRENCH LEADERS SURRENDERED. FRANCE'S FALL sent shock waves across the Atlantic. Perhaps the greatest immediate threat to Anglo-American security concerned the fate of the French fleet. While the Wehrmacht was a formidable force on land and in the air, Germany lagged far behind the British and the Americans at sea. However, France's collapse raised the terrifying prospect that Germany might seize control of the French fleet—intact and undamaged—and redirect it against the Western powers. But even as the Third Republic prepared to surrender, the French foreign minister assured US diplomats that the French fleet would never surrender to the Nazis. French ships would be sent overseas or scuttled, he insisted. Such assurances fell flat, however, when US officials received a draft of a French-German armistice agreement that demanded that the fleet be recalled to French ports—well within the reach of the Third Reich.[34]

In a heated exchange with the French ambassador on June 24, US under secretary of state Sumner Welles complained that, regardless of Berlin's promises, the terms of the armistice effectively gave Germany control of the French fleet. The French ambassador protested, but Welles responded by reminding him of Germany's assurances in the wake of the 1938 Munich agreement. Three days later, Secretary of State Cordell Hull gave the unfortunate French ambassador an even more severe tongue-lashing. By allowing the fleet to return to its home ports, he insisted, French leaders risked handing "Germany a cocked gun to shoot at us."[35]

Certainly, the mood in France gave US officials cause for alarm. On July 1, US ambassador William Bullitt spoke to a number of high-level officials in the newly created French collaborationist government, located in the city of Vichy. What he heard was terrifying. French leaders were utterly defeated, both morally and physically. The Vichy government aimed to turn its back on generations of French history and embrace its role as a "province of Nazi Germany." Having accepted this fate, Vichy leaders "hope[d] that England [would] be rapidly and completely defeated by Germany." Indeed, Marshal Pétain and Admiral François Darlan, head of the French navy, believed that Hitler would make short work of the British. Darlan—the man who would be in charge of sinking French ships in the event of an attempted German seizure of the fleet—gave London a mere five weeks before defeat and seemed to express "considerable pleasure" in speaking of British "asphyxiation" at the hands of a Nazi siege.[36]

To some observers, Vichy leaders appeared to prefer to keep their empire and be ruled by the Nazis rather than surrender their colonies and fight for independence. Pétain, for instance, believed that Algeria would remain in French hands despite the occupation. This desire to maintain control of the empire was also evident in Darlan's discussion of the French fleet—the force necessary to maintain France's control of its overseas colonies. The admiral argued that the Germans would never gain control of the fleet: it would be sent to French colonies in the New World. But Darlan would never send French ships to Britain. Once the British gained control of French ships, the admiral insisted, London would never return them to France. Bullitt observed that Darlan seemed to think that "if Great Britain should win the war [France's] treatment . . . would be no more generous than the treatment accorded by Germany." When Bullitt suggested that Vichy leaders would like to see Hitler conquer Britain so that France could then become Germany's "favorite province, [Darlan] smiled again and nodded." Darlan also predicted that Hitler would attack the United States soon after defeating Britain and that Washington, too, had little hope. Bullitt was profoundly disturbed by his conversations with the Vichy leadership. His conclusions suggested that Washington could have little faith in French leadership going forward: "The simple people of this country are as fine as they have ever been. The upper classes have failed completely."[37]

As Nazi officials settled into their occupation, US diplomats sent a warning to Berlin. Citing the Monroe Doctrine, Washington refused to tolerate the transfer of any French colonies in the New World to German control. In his reply on July 2, Nazi foreign minister Joachim von Ribbentrop feigned surprise at the American warning. Unlike Britain and France, he explained, Germany had never held colonies in the Western Hemisphere. Further, Ribbentrop added disingenuously, Berlin had no intention of acquiring them. He then concluded with a thinly veiled threat: "The Reich Government would like to point out . . . that the nonintervention in the affairs of the American continent by European nations which is demanded by the Monroe Doctrine can in principle be legally valid only on condition that the American nations for their part do not intervene (*einmischen*) in the affairs of the European continent."[38]

By the beginning of July, British leaders had concluded that they could no longer afford to stake their survival on Vichy's promises. On July 3, British forces seized French vessels in British ports while a British flotilla encircled a large contingent of the French fleet off the coast of Algeria at Mers el-Kebir. The British commander delivered an ultimatum, calling on the French admiral to accept one of four alternatives: to fight alongside the British navy against the Axis, to sail to a British port to await repatriation, to sail across the Atlantic to a French port in the West Indies, or to have their fleet sunk.[39]

The French commanders refused to accept any of the options. Just before 6:00 p.m., the British ships opened fire. The French fleet, crowded into the harbor, could offer only a token response. British shells ignited the old battleship *Bretagne*'s magazine, sending up a massive explosion that killed nearly one thousand sailors aboard. The French fleet's flagship, *Dunkerque*, was forced to ground herself to avoid being sunk. In all, 1,297 French sailors were killed in the attack. Vichy leaders were incensed, and the British found it hard to relish their victory. "We all felt thoroughly dirty and ashamed," the British commander wrote to his wife. Nevertheless, Churchill's government insisted that the neutralization of the fleet, though regrettable, had been a necessary precaution.[40]

Beyond removing the possibility that the French fleet might fall into German hands, the attack also convinced observers in the United States that London remained determined to continue the fight against the Third Reich. "The British have obviously become tough," wrote journalist Barnet Nover. "They ask for no quarter and they will give none. They regard themselves, and with reason, as the last bastion of civilization, left alone to hold back the forces of darkness." American officials agreed. As London dug in its heels, the Roosevelt administration concluded that concerted support for Britain was the best course for protecting long-term US interests in Europe.[41]

While Britain's stiff resistance impressed many Americans, leaders in the Soviet Union balked at the notion of supporting the

Western powers. Stalin recognized the danger posed by a victorious Germany, but he hoped to maintain the Nazi-Soviet Pact as the genesis of a new regional order in Europe. On July 1, 1940, Britain's newly arrived ambassador to Moscow, Stafford Cripps, delivered a message from Churchill to Stalin warning of the threat posed by the Third Reich and urging Moscow to join London in opposing Hitler. Stalin dismissed the proposal, explaining that he had no interest in restoring the "old equilibrium in Europe, which worked against the USSR. As earlier negotiations showed, the British and French did not want to meet [the Soviets] halfway on this question." Two weeks later, Soviet minister of foreign affairs Vyacheslav Molotov passed a summary of the Cripps meeting to the German ambassador as a demonstration of Moscow's determination to maintain its agreements with Berlin.[42] The Kremlin leadership remained convinced that their best bet lay in standing aside, biding their time, building their strength, and allowing the British and Germans to tear each other apart. It would take nearly a year for the folly of this approach to become apparent. By then it would be too late.

THE DESTRUCTION OF THE FRENCH FLEET RENDERED AN INVASION OF Britain nearly impossible in the near term—deprived of captured French vessels, Germany lacked the necessary ships to stage a full-scale amphibious assault. London's move also convinced American policymakers that Britain could serve as a strategic asset in the coming war against Germany. For all its cruelty, then, the sinking of the French fleet off the coast of Algeria represented a decisive moment in the war. But such realizations had yet to dawn on a German leadership still flush with victory. Hitler had initially hoped that the shock of French collapse would convince the British to accept a negotiated peace: London would acknowledge German hegemony in continental Europe, and in return, the Führer was prepared to allow Britain to keep its overseas empire. Indeed, Hitler believed that it might even be advantageous to have a robust Britain to ensure stability in the wider world while the Wehrmacht fought its campaign against the Soviet Union in a bid to carve out a new German empire in Eastern Europe. So confident was Hitler that the British would come to the table that, as late as mid-June 1940, Berlin had failed to create any substantial plan for a cross-channel invasion. In July, a frustrated Führer lamented that "the outcome of the war had already been decided," but the British "were still not aware of it."[43]

Churchill was holding out hope that the Americans and the Soviets might emerge as new sources of aid against the Reich. Churchill's refusal to strike a deal baffled the Führer and forced the German military staff to come up with a concrete plan to knock Britain out of the war. Chief of Operations Staff Alfred Jodl suggested a plan that included a naval blockade and strategic bombing designed to cripple British industry and terrorize the population into submission. Alternatively, Germany could launch attacks on key outposts of the British Empire such as Gibraltar and the Suez Canal. But Hitler doubted indirect attacks would be enough. To defeat Britain, Germany must invade England and crush the British army. However, before the Wehrmacht could attempt an amphibious invasion—code-named Sea Lion—the Luftwaffe must establish air superiority over southern England and the Kriegsmarine must clear the English Channel of British warships. Moreover, all of this would have to be accomplished before winter storms made such an amphibious assault too risky.[44]

Nevertheless, Luftwaffe chief Hermann Göring remained confident: his forces had made short work of French air defenses in May, and he saw no reason to believe that the British would present a greater challenge. On August 1, the German staff presented a strategy aimed at achieving four goals: the annihilation of the Royal Air Force (RAF); the protection of an invasion force crossing the channel from the British fleet; the destruction of British harbors; and terror attacks against British cities, to be used as reprisals. The Luftwaffe's campaign to knock out the RAF began in earnest in mid-August. In one of the largest raids of the war against Britain, on August 15, approximately one thousand German aircraft attacked targets from southern England to Scotland. Massed waves of Luftwaffe planes targeted harbors, airfields, and factories in a bid to bring Britain to its knees. One American reporter described waves of aircraft swooping like "flocks of hungry seagulls" above the cliffs overlooking the English Channel. A massive dogfight above Croydon Airport left the tangled wreckage of downed warplanes strewn over the ground. "One hundred machine guns rattled above the din of the engines, drowning London's wailing sirens and the shouts of mechanics," the reporter wrote. "Red flames, clouds of black smoke, dust and debris hurtled toward the sky." When the day ended, the British Air Ministry claimed to have shot down 144 German aircraft with a loss of nineteen British pilots and twenty-seven planes. Even more aircraft likely disappeared beneath the misty waters of the channel.[45]

The Luftwaffe's efforts to destroy the RAF in daylight raids were taking a heavy toll on German pilots and aircraft, and with each passing week, German plans to force a British surrender grew dimmer. In early September, a frustrated Hitler ordered the Luftwaffe to shift its attention from raids against British airfields to massive nighttime attacks on London and other cities. The imprecision of night attacks rendered cities one of the only viable targets in the darkness. But this reorientation brought civilians squarely into the Luftwaffe's bombsights. Night raids on September 7 bathed London in a fiery glow as the low rumble of bombs came from the south. Stunned men and women in formal evening dress moved through the streets. "The children! Oh, the children!" moaned one distraught woman. Londoners crammed into air-raid shelters filled with the smell of "smoke and dust and unwashed clothing and bodies." A wave of dive-bombers sent flocks of seagulls bursting from their roosts along the river as they streaked through the sky, occasionally illuminated by searchlights. Farther south, in the Elephant and Castle district, German bombs slammed into two houses, killing three women, a baby, an elderly man, and a pilot home on sick leave. Horrified residents looked on, some searching the ruins for survivors.[46]

The Nazis were not alone in attacking civilian population centers. Small-scale British raids against German cities had begun in August, but Hitler's announcement of Germany's strategic bombing campaign opened the floodgates. In short order, Churchill and his colleagues abandoned their reservations about bombing civilians and about strategic bombing as a cornerstone of their war against Germany. One RAF raid on September 11 sent thermite bombs smashing into the Reichstag, igniting a blaze that was quickly extinguished. Incendiary bombs also tore through St. Hedwig Hospital and residential sections of Berlin. Another barrage hit the Brandenburg Gate, narrowly missing the US embassy. Twelve-foot craters pockmarked the Avenue of Splendor. Like the citizens of Damascus in the 1920s and of Rotterdam in May 1940, the citizens of London and Berlin now came to know the horrors of strategic bombing.[47]

For all its horrors, the Luftwaffe's attacks on British cities signaled German failure: unable to destroy the RAF, the Luftwaffe had turned in frustration to strategically futile attacks on British civilians. Though Churchill and later historians would portray the Battle of Britain as a closely fought engagement, in fact, London enjoyed decisive advantages. Britain's extensive network of radar installations and observer posts gave the RAF advance knowledge of Luftwaffe attacks and allowed the British to pick and choose their engagements. RAF pilots operated from their home airfields, while Germans were forced to fly out of makeshift airstrips in occupied countries. British Spitfires and Hurricanes faced the sole task of destroying Luftwaffe aircraft, while German fighters also had to defend their accompanying slow-moving bombers. German pilots who were shot down over Britain or forced to make a crash landing were captured or killed and therefore lost to the Luftwaffe. In contrast, many downed British pilots were able to return to their units and rejoin the battle. Germany's only hope, then, lay in destroying British airfields or overwhelming the RAF through massive production of fighter aircraft. The Third Reich achieved neither goal. At the beginning of August 1940, RAF fighters outnumbered their Luftwaffe counterparts 1,377 to 869; by the end of the month, the RAF fielded 1,422 fighters against the Luftwaffe's 735; by early November, the RAF's advantage stood at 1,796 to 673.[48]

After weeks of heavy fighting and heavier losses, it became clear to German planners that they had failed to establish control over either the air or the sea. In mid-September Hitler postponed Operation Sea Lion indefinitely. On "the afternoon of Sunday, the fifteenth of September, Adolf Hitler met his first defeat in eight years," wrote American journalist Ralph Ingersoll. "The battle that was fought in the air over London between September 7 and 15 may go down in history as a battle as important as Waterloo or Gettysburg. Like Gettysburg, it may be recorded as a battle that the loser had won and didn't know it."[49]

THE FALL OF FRANCE HAD KNOCKED OUT ONE OF THE TWIN PILLARS of the Versailles order and destroyed the fragile balance of power that had existed since 1919. In its place, the Axis powers would race to establish new orders across Europe, Africa, and Asia while the British Empire scrambled to reinforce its strained defenses around the world. Still many months away from entering the war, the Soviet Union and the United States waited in the wings, rushing to mobilize their massive resources to meet the challenges looming on the horizon. The French collapse created the conditions for the series of ongoing regional conflicts across Europe and Asia to coalesce into a global war. A growing chorus of voices now warned that Germany's stunning victory heralded the beginning of a transformation of imperial power not seen in centuries.

Chapter 6

COLONIAL RAMPARTS

ON NOVEMBER 12, 1940, THE CHIEF OF US NAVAL OPERATIONS, Admiral Harold Stark, completed a strategic analysis of the current Axis threat to the United States. He likely had no inkling that he had outlined what would become Washington's core strategy for the Second World War. The admiral opened with a startling judgment, that the survival of the British Empire was essential to preserving American national security: "If Britain wins decisively against Germany we could win everywhere; but . . . if she loses the problem confronting us would be very great; and while we might not *lose everywhere*, we might, possibly, not *win anywhere*." Stark warned that Britain's defeat would force the United States to fall back to a defensive position in the Western Hemisphere, economically isolated and unable to sustain the military budgets necessary for long-term security. Moreover, even if Britain survived, London could not win the war alone. Germany's stranglehold on Western Europe showed no signs of slipping, and Japanese forces were threatening Western colonies in the Pacific.

Looking forward, Stark wrote, American leaders had four choices: (A) accept isolation and resort to a policy of hemispheric defense,

(B) launch an all-out war against Japan, (C) conduct a war against Japan and Germany simultaneously, or (D) join Britain in the war against Germany while fighting limited defensive operations in the Pacific. Stark argued that plan D offered the best chance of defending US national interests. Despite its restrained tone, Stark's memorandum was nothing short of monumental: more than a year before the Pearl Harbor attacks, the US government had embarked on a path to enter the war with the central strategic goal of defeating Germany first. The United States, a nation born out of a revolution against the British Empire, would accept that same empire's survival as necessary both for defending American security and for launching counterattacks against the Axis powers.[1]

Stark's assessment—soon to be known as the "Plan Dog" memo—reflected the rapidly evolving state of the world conflict. With German divisions halted along the French side of the English Channel, the European war had reached an impasse. Hitler stood in a commanding position over much of Europe, but Britain's stubborn resistance deprived Germany of a complete victory in the West. With both sides unable to break the deadlock, the strategic focus of the war was shifting to the colonial world. Having lost their French allies, British leaders redirected their attention from fighting a continental war in Europe to waging an imperial war of attrition. Allied forces conducted a series of offensives aimed at closing the ring around the contested borders of the Axis empires while using the colonial world as a launchpad for their military operations. This peripheral strategy sought to dominate lines of communication—vital transportation routes that allowed powers to move troops, supplies, and information between military bases and forces operating in the field—and secure a network of colonial bases from which to launch strikes against Axis positions. Meanwhile, Churchill orchestrated a diplomatic campaign aimed at pulling the United States into the Allied war effort. In the near term, US participation provided much-needed aid to the struggling British Empire. In the long term, however, US entry into the war laid the foundations for a new international order in which

Washington would replace London as the capital of a postwar global empire.

However, Axis leaders also recognized the colonial world as a key theater in the war. The fall of France and collapse of the Versailles order sent shock waves across the globe. With Europe in turmoil, Western colonies scattered across Asia, Africa, and the Middle East appeared ripe for the picking. Japanese and Italian leaders, eager to expand their empires, scrambled to seize new territory amid the resulting chaos. Meanwhile, anticolonial nationalists recognized an opportunity to assert their own claims to independence. Revolutionaries and anticolonial leaders joined the battle as allies, collaborators, and adversaries. The stage was now set for a series of interconnected battles across the colonial world that would determine the outer limits of Axis expansion and lay the foundations of postwar American global hegemony.

WATCHING FROM WASHINGTON AND EMBASSIES AROUND THE GLOBE, US officials remained keenly aware that the crisis in Europe had destabilized the colonial world. With France defeated and Britain besieged, Western colonies across Africa and Asia appeared open to attack. In late May, State Department adviser Stanley Hornbeck warned that Japan was now in a position to threaten British, Dutch, French, and US possessions in Southeast Asia. In the near term, Britain and China were serving as barriers between the United States and the German and Japanese threats, but if either power collapsed, Washington would be faced with a direct threat to American security. Secretary of State Cordell Hull also understood the global impact of the war in Europe. A victorious Germany would seal Europe off from the world economy while extending a system of imperial control across Asia and Africa. Even if Berlin was unable to directly attack the United States, American economic prosperity would be compromised. Japanese leaders also recognized these prospects, Hull warned, and were now in the process of deciding whether to join Germany in this bid to tilt the scales of world power. The response of Joseph Grew, US ambassador to Japan, was equally grim. The "tragedy" unfolding in Europe was having a major impact in Tokyo. US and British efforts to encourage Japan to abandon its China adventure had foundered. German victories in Europe had undermined moderates in Tokyo and strengthened factions that hoped to expand the war in the Far East.[2]

In response to these mounting threats, Roosevelt ordered the US Battle Fleet to remain in a forward position operating out of the base at Pearl Harbor—a signal to Tokyo that the United States was prepared to take military action in response to further Japanese expansionism. The redeployment served as a public show of force, but in private, some naval officers expressed reservations. The fleet's forward deployment left American ships vulnerable to a potential attack. By stationing the fleet in the waters around Hawaii, the White House had painted a huge target on the base at Pearl Harbor.[3]

From their vantage point in Tokyo, Japanese leaders recognized that the fall of France and the Netherlands had created an opening to transform the strategic balance in East Asia. The Japanese war minister insisted in late June that Tokyo "must not miss this golden opportunity to implement its policies." But this window would not remain open forever. Indeed, on July 2, the Roosevelt administration announced that it would cease exports of a long list of arms, ammunition, and war matériel. Washington was slowly choking off the flow of vital military resources to Japan and, in doing so, closing Japan's window of opportunity to seize an empire in the Pacific. In response, the Japanese naval general staff submitted a draft paper, "The Principles to Cope with the Changing World Situation," calling on the empire to break out of its economic dependence on the Western powers by seizing European colonies in the south and forming a military alliance with Germany and Italy.[4]

The expansionists in Tokyo received another boost on July 16–17 when the army forced the collapse of the moderate government and replaced it with a new regime led by Prince Konoe, a staunch imperialist. On July 23, Konoe delivered a radio address in which he called on the empire to seize the opportunity created by France's collapse to build a new order in the Far East. As Japan's ambassador to London later explained, "Many on the Japanese side were seized with panic about what would happen to British colonies in Asia, and feared what would become of the Japanese Empire once Dutch and French colonies were occupied by Germany." The Konoe government determined that Japan must hurry to lay claim to French Indochina and the Dutch East Indies before Germany could consolidate a new empire in Southeast Asia.[5]

However, such a move risked provoking a war in the Pacific. The Japanese navy warned that Tokyo would be forced to go to war in retaliation for a full embargo of vital strategic commodities such as petroleum. American or British efforts to strengthen their colonial garrisons in the Far East would also require a military response from Tokyo. The best course of action, planners explained, would be to pick the Western powers off one by one. But above all, Japan must avoid a drawn-out war of attrition with the United States. As the official Japanese operational history later explained, the navy might defeat the American fleet in an early decisive sea battle, but victory was unlikely in the event of a protracted war. "If Japan waited for the inevitable expansion of the United States' war preparations, she would be overwhelmed. It would be better to start war before the United States was fully prepared."[6]

On August 1, 1940, Foreign Minister Yosuke Matsuoka declared Tokyo's intention to build "the Greater East Asia Co-Prosperity Sphere"—an expansive economic bloc linking Japan to the Dutch East Indies, French Indochina, Manchuria, and China. The Co-Prosperity Sphere served as a blueprint for Japanese imperial ambitions, claiming a sphere of influence across much of Asia and the Pacific, justified under the auspices of Pan-Asianism. Matsuoka explained that Japan's new order was designed to destroy "the white race bloc" and "shatter the White man's mastery over the Orient," creating a new regional order in Asia purged of Western colonial rule. However, the Co-Prosperity Sphere encapsulated a deliberately vague set of conflicting ideas crafted to appeal to imperialists and militarists in Tokyo as well as anticolonial groups in the Dutch East Indies and Indochina—it was simultaneously a response to the rapidly changing situation in Europe, a challenge to US hegemony in the Pacific, a call for liberation from Western imperialism, and a mission statement for Japan's new imperial order in Asia.[7]

The stage was set for Tokyo to make its move. During the night of September 22, Japanese units crossed into French Indochina and attacked the French garrison at Lang Son, seizing the key railroad corridor leading into Hanoi. Japanese artillery and air strikes drove the defenders back from the border as air-raid sirens wailed through the capital. A trainload of one hundred French wounded that made its way back to Hanoi indicated the severity of the fighting. Meanwhile, a Japanese battle fleet steamed toward the port of Haiphong. Reports from the front told of piles of Japanese bodies, their hands cut off to allow for later identification of the dead upon their return to Japan. Posters went up throughout Hanoi warning those without essential business in the capital to leave in anticipation of heavy bombing raids. French commanders stood down on the twenty-sixth. "Two thousand Japanese troops landed in Indo-China yesterday under the powerful but silent French guns commanding the entrance to the Red River and marched across the hot countryside into Haiphong," reported the Associated Press.[8]

Tokyo combined this military offensive with a major diplomatic stroke. On September 23, the British passed information to the US embassy in Moscow that Tokyo had entered into an agreement with Berlin to "keep the United States fleet 'occupied' in the Pacific" in exchange for German supplies. Four days later, Japan signed the Tripartite Pact with Germany and Italy—which built on the Anti-Comintern Pact and the Pact of Steel—to forge the Axis alliance. The three governments explained that lasting peace required that "all nations of the world be given each its own proper place" and pledged cooperation "in regard to their efforts in Greater East Asia and the regions of Europe . . . to establish and maintain a new order."

Germany and Italy would take the lead in creating this new order in Europe while Japan assumed leadership over the new order in Asia. The Axis threat was now worldwide.[9]

BRITISH LEADERS NEEDED NO REMINDER OF THE GLOBAL NATURE OF war. The fall of France forced London to pivot away from its plans to fight a continental war in Europe and instead prepare for a protracted imperial war. British colonies around the world would provide strategic reserves of resources and manpower as well as naval bases for its fleet, and serve as launchpads for future campaigns against the Axis powers. As one strategy paper explained, London must enforce "as rigid an economic blockade as possible, to include the Middle East and Mediterranean areas." Germany's control of Europe had increased Hitler's resources, but the Wehrmacht still lacked access to large quantities of oil. At current rates, British planners predicted that Germany would run out of oil by June 1941. However, an attritional strategy of this sort would only work if London defended its colonies and maintained the ability to project naval and air power in sufficient strength to block Axis shipping. Planners argued that naval and air power together with an economic blockade would ultimately allow Britain to prevail in a war against Germany.[10]

British strategy would concentrate on Germany, defend the home islands, and hold the line in the Middle East, Malaya, West Africa, Iraq, and Palestine. The Middle East formed the linchpin of this imperial strategy, serving as a crossroads for all of the other theaters. As the chief of the Imperial General Staff wrote, the Middle East represented "a vital interest, second only to security at home." Italian operations in North Africa constituted the most immediate threat, but Germany posed the greater long-term danger. Britain had to continue building its forces with the aim of defeating Italy in 1941 and mounting "an offensive in all spheres with the greatest vigour in 1942." Meanwhile, the growing Japanese threat in the Far East was a vexing problem for Britain's already-strained forces. But there was reason for hope,

British planners explained. American and Soviet participation in the war would transform the strategic dimensions of the conflict. As strategists wrote in August, the "entry of America into the war on our side would have a profound effect."[11]

In key respects, the United States was already involved in the war. The Roosevelt administration had abandoned neutrality in 1939 when it instituted the "cash-and-carry" policy, whereby Washington would sell arms to Britain as long as London paid for weapons in cash and carried them back across the Atlantic on British ships. By May 1940, Churchill had begun pleading for old US destroyers to help ward off German submarine attacks until new British vessels, then under construction, could be launched. While sympathetic, Roosevelt feared that the Nazis might soon overwhelm British defenses, at which point the warships would end up in Hitler's hands. However, London's perseverance during the Battle of Britain, the sinking of the French fleet at Mers el-Kebir, and the heart-wrenching images of the Blitz wore away at Washington's reservations. By early August, Roosevelt had begun searching for a way to send the ships to Britain. But congressional opposition to European entanglements remained a significant obstacle. Cabinet officials floated the prospect of dispatching the destroyers to Britain in exchange for leases on British military bases in the Western Hemisphere. On August 15, Churchill agreed to grant a ninety-nine-year lease on British bases in the New World in exchange for fifty American ships and swore never to surrender the fleet to Germany. Rather, should the home islands be overrun, Churchill would continue the fight from the outposts of the British Empire.[12] This conviction, combined with his belief that the United States and Soviet Union would eventually be drawn into the war, bolstered the prime minister's determination to fight on.

The destroyers-for-bases deal was a pivotal moment in the transformation of American global power: the United States officially bound its national security to the fate of the British Empire. While London struggled for its survival, US military forces moved into British colonial territories in anticipation of confronting the Axis menace.

Moreover, the ninety-nine-year lease on British bases indicated that this was not merely a short-term deal. Rather, it hinted at a sweeping reorientation of US national security policy. In the coming years, this passing of the torch would repeat itself in parts of Asia and the Middle East as US forces established a global military presence. This principle—more than the value of the antiquated ships themselves—represented the true significance of Roosevelt's deal. However, Roosevelt was careful to explain that the United States sought bases rather than domains. "I'm not purchasing any headaches for the United States," Roosevelt told British ambassador Lord Lothian. "We don't want your colonies."[13] Nevertheless, as British troops moved out of colonial outposts in places such as Newfoundland and Bermuda, US military forces moved in. The decline of Pax Britannica had set the stage for the rise of Pax Americana.

While the destroyers-for-bases deal sealed the security partnership between London and Washington, British officials had also offered to share top secret technical information with the United States. In August, British scientist Henry Tizard arrived in the United States at the head of a mission bearing a cavity magnetron along with a trove of technical data. The magnetron would prove to be the key piece of technology necessary for the development of compact radar devices, which would later be installed on Allied aircraft and small ships. London had opened its book of technological secrets in anticipation of a durable military-technological partnership with Washington. And this was just the beginning.[14]

Meanwhile, London continued its efforts to fortify its Mediterranean empire. "We are endeavoring to assemble a very large army in the Middle East," Churchill wrote to Roosevelt in October, "and the movement of troops thither from all parts of the Empire, especially from the Mother country, has for some months past been unceasing." These efforts had placed considerable demands on shipping and industry that could only be sustained through US assistance. Beneath the linguistic embellishments, Churchill made it clear: Washington's support was instrumental for British imperial defense.[15]

On the other side of the Atlantic, a growing number of American leaders were coming to the conclusion that the survival of the British Empire was necessary for the preservation of US national security. Admiral Harold Stark's twenty-six-page Plan Dog memo of November 1940, which served as the basis for Washington's Europe-first strategy, offered the most impactful assessment. "I believe that the continued existence of the British Empire," Stark wrote, "combined with building up a strong protection in our home areas, will do most to ensure the status quo in the Western Hemisphere, and to promote our principal national interests."[16]

Later that month, the New York–based Council on Foreign Relations—which had stepped in to fill a planning role as the US government geared up for greater involvement in the war—released a report on the Western Hemisphere. The paper called for a sweeping reassessment of American strategy. The first task for Washington, it argued, must be to ensure the security of the Western Hemisphere. After this, however, the paper called on policymakers to seek a dominant position in world affairs: "The United States (more than any other nation on the globe) can exercise a considerable amount of free will in determining 'the shape of things to come'—the type of international world in which we shall have to live." Although the United States was still over a year away from direct military involvement in the war, a growing chorus of voices had already begun laying plans for postwar hegemony.[17]

Meanwhile, Churchill continued his dogged efforts to pull Washington into the war. In a December request for further US assistance, the prime minister again emphasized the bonds of Anglo-Saxon civilization between the United States and Britain and Washington's interest in supporting the defense of the British Empire. "[The] vast majority of American citizens have recorded their conviction that the safety of the United States as well as the future of our two democracies and the kind of civilisation for which they stand are bound up with the survival and independence of the British Commonwealth of Nations," he insisted. Although Hitler's Fortress Europe remained impregnable, he said, British forces would continue using sea and air power to block the spread of German influence into Africa and Southern Asia.[18] The empire would stand as the bulwark holding back the Nazi war machine.

By mid-December, this strategy of Anglo-American cooperation had come into sharper focus. In a conversation with reporters, Roosevelt explained that most Americans now understood that Britain was serving as a bulwark against further Axis expansion. Therefore, America's best defense lay in the effort to "do everything to help the British Empire help itself." Put differently, the president argued, "the best defense of Great Britain is the best defense of the United States." To this end, Roosevelt likened the current situation in Europe to a neighbor's house catching on fire. "If you have a hose and connect it with his hydrant, you may help him to save his house. You don't say to your neighbor that your hose cost $15 and that he must pay $15." On December 29, Roosevelt made this same case to the public. The vast distances of the Atlantic and Pacific Oceans were no longer sufficient to protect the nation. The rise of the Axis powers represented a dire threat to US security. The British Empire and its formidable navy remained the surest guardian of the oceans. "In a military sense," Roosevelt explained, "Great Britain and the British Empire are today the spearhead of resistance to world conquest." But if Britain should fall, he warned, the Axis powers would dominate Europe, Asia, Africa, and Australasia and be in a position to threaten the Western Hemisphere. "It is no exaggeration to say that all of us in the Americas would be living at the point of a gun." To guard against this threat, Roosevelt insisted, the United States must become "the great arsenal of democracy." The nation would turn its vast industrial potential toward war manufacturing aimed at arming the British Empire in defense of civilization and against the Axis scourge.[19]

The public response to Roosevelt's "Arsenal of Democracy" address was overwhelmingly positive. Telegrams to the White House read one hundred to one in favor of the policy; 61 percent of those polled agreed with the president. Eight days later, Roosevelt ascended the dais before the assembled houses of congress to deliver his 1941 State of the Union. The president announced a new national policy based on the promotion of "four freedoms": freedom of speech, freedom of religion, freedom from want, and freedom from fear. Roosevelt's vision represented nothing less than a mission statement for US power in the postwar world.[20] In March, Congress approved the Lend-Lease Act, which provided military aid for nations deemed vital to American security.

Roosevelt's effort to transform the United States into the arsenal of democracy was not purely altruistic, nor was it simply an emergency response to the world crisis. Rather, in keeping with their goal of projecting American power across the global arena, US leaders intended to use the lend-lease agreements to kick open the doors of the British imperial preference system and gain access to colonial markets. As a proposed draft of the agreement with Britain explained, Lend-Lease would bar London from allowing "discrimination" against either US or British trade, in hopes of bettering "world-wide economic relations." This provision would prevent London from maintaining preferential trade relationships with its colonies—a cornerstone of the imperial system—and remove restrictions on the importation of American goods. Washington's efforts drew protests from British leaders, who argued that their nation would require preferential trading arrangements once the war had ended. However, such objections were met with little sympathy in Washington. As Assistant Secretary of State Dean Acheson explained, "The British should realize that an effort of the magnitude of the lease-lend program on our part imposed upon them the obligation of continuing good will in working out plans for the future."[21]

Washington would pay and perhaps even fight to save London from the Nazis. But in exchange, the Americans sought the dissolution of Britain's imperial economy and the creation of postwar US economic hegemony. German leaders also picked up on this passing of the torch from British to American hegemony: "The Lend-Lease

Act is nothing more than a legalization of a practice that, for some time, has been a fait accompli," the German foreign office told Japanese officials. "Its true objective is the inheritance by the United States of British assets through the prolongation of the war."[22]

In fact, prevailing sentiment in the White House appeared to be moving toward an even grander strategic vision. As Roosevelt wrote in January, "I believe that the fundamental proposition is that we must recognize that the hostilities in Europe, in Africa, and in Asia are all parts of a single world conflict." As a result, he explained, "our strategy of self-defense must be a global strategy which takes account of every front and takes advantage of every opportunity to contribute to our total security."[23] In the seven months since the fall of France, the administration had embraced a globalized conception of American security backed by a determination to defend American interests around the world.

Perhaps the most enduring statement of this new, muscular American internationalism arrived in the form of a February essay titled "The American Century" written by *Life* magazine publisher Henry Luce. Although most Americans had not yet realized it, Luce wrote, they had already joined the war. "We are in a war to defend and even to promote, encourage and incite so-called democratic principles throughout the world," he explained. The generations of splendid isolation that the American people had enjoyed came to an end with the First World War. However, after that conflict, the nation had failed to accept its position of world leadership, and this failure had resulted in the present global upheaval. Now, however, the nation had an opportunity "to accept wholeheartedly our duty and our opportunity as the most powerful and vital nation in the world and in consequence to exert upon the world the full impact of our influence, for such purposes as we see fit and by such means as we see fit." The United States must embrace the responsibility of shaping the "world-environment in which she lives." His conclusion would shape decades of American foreign policy that followed. "The 20th Century is the American Century," he wrote.[24]

Luce's essay captured the evolving national mood as the United States moved into position to vie for global supremacy. Washington would first partner with and then eclipse the British Empire as the dominant power in global affairs—a remarkable transformation in itself. Indeed, as late as 1938, US war planners had maintained contingency plans for a war against Britain as part of a larger security strategy of hemispheric defense.[25] Now, three years later, Washington was preparing for a ninety-nine-year deployment of US military personnel to British bases in the Western Hemisphere, where they might remain until the year 2040. Washington and London had also embarked on a program in which the two powers would share major weapons engineering research. Meanwhile, the United States was remaking itself as an arsenal for British imperial forces battling Nazi Germany and preparing to use this aid to force open the closed markets of the British Empire to American trade. Roosevelt was engineering not only a policy of active involvement in the war against Germany but a new global national security strategy designed to survive well into the twenty-first century. America's new global hegemony—Luce's American Century—would be built on the foundations of the dying British Empire. The concept of US global leadership had grown from a loose set of ideas articulated by the likes of Walter Lippmann and Lord Lothian in the 1930s to an expanding military, ideological, economic, and strategic blueprint in late 1940.

NEVERTHELESS, THIS VISION OF A FUTURE AMERICAN HEGEMONY remained contingent on the survival of the British Empire in what was rapidly becoming a global war. British commanders fought with an army of colonial soldiers. Short on manpower, London drew from the massive populations of the colonies to continue the war against the Axis. "From next to nothing the army of the Nile had risen to half a million men," wrote journalist Alan Moorehead, "English, Australians, New Zealanders, South Africans, Indians, Poles, Czechs, French, Palestinians, Cypriots, Sudanese, Belgians, Ethiopians, East and West Africans." Comprising some thirty-five million square miles of territory and home to over half a billion people, Britain's empire was a prize of incalculable strategic value. The critical first step in its defense lay in the Mediterranean and Middle East—a region straddling vital transportation routes and containing massive oil fields. With this in mind, British leaders cobbled together a Mediterranean strategy drawn from a patchwork of wartime exigencies, imperial interests, and postwar planning.[26]

The fall of France had dashed London's hopes of stopping German expansion in northern Europe, leaving British leaders with few options for mounting a direct challenge to the Nazis. Instead, British forces pursued a peripheral strategy focused on maintaining control of the seas and protecting the empire. The Mediterranean offered London an ideal theater in which to implement this approach. Rather than fighting the vaunted Wehrmacht head-on, British forces operating out of colonial bases and supported by their formidable navy would face the weaker Italian army. The British chiefs were confident in their ability to counter the Italians, defend their empire, and eventually stage an attack on Italy itself. If British forces could knock Mussolini's regime out of the war, the Axis would suffer a serious blow. In addition, control of the Mediterranean might provide an avenue to attack German-occupied Europe from the south.

British chiefs of staff explained that London's goal must be to use its naval supremacy to choke off vital war supplies to the Axis powers, most importantly petroleum. It therefore remained essential that the British hold their naval base at Alexandria to prevent Axis control of Middle Eastern oil fields and shipping through the Mediterranean. Planners insisted that the empire held the advantage in a prolonged conflict, provided it could maintain control of Egypt and the eastern Mediterranean. "The security of our position in the Middle East is of the utmost importance to our strategy," they wrote, "not only as a base from which to exercise and intensify economic pressure, but as a barrier to prevent our enemies from breaking the blockade." For the time being, London would fight a war of attrition.[27]

The struggle began in one of the more remote outposts of the empire with an Italian attack on British Somaliland in early August 1940. Like his counterparts in Tokyo, Mussolini had recognized an opportunity to expand his empire in the wake of France's crushing defeat. The Italians quickly overwhelmed the meager British defenses, which numbered some 4,500 British and Commonwealth troops, 75 percent of whom were African soldiers or irregulars. Over the next eleven days, the invaders pushed British colonial forces back toward the port city of Berbera on the shores of the Gulf of Aden. By August 15, British commanders were scrambling to coordinate a hasty seaborne evacuation to the colony of Aden. As the last British ships pulled away from the harbor the morning of August 19, the HMS *Hobart* fired on key buildings in the city, rendering them useless to the Italians. Although the Berbera evacuation paled in comparison to Dunkirk—one magazine dismissed Somaliland as "'perhaps the least valuable' territory in the British Empire, with its 'burning heat and so parched and barren a ground' making it difficult for Europeans to survive"—the defeat represented yet another setback for London.[28]

Mussolini's invasion of Egypt constituted a more serious threat. Left unchecked, the Italian invasion would threaten British control of Alexandria and the Suez Canal and sever the strategically vital lines of communication connecting the Mediterranean Sea to the Indian Ocean. On September 9, Italian units crossed the Libyan border. In August, British forces had pulled back to defensive positions around Mersa Matruh to prepare for a counteroffensive. "The aim must be to destroy Italian forces in the desert," the War Cabinet explained, "but as a last resort the line of the [Nile] Delta must be held at all costs." In the event of a further retreat, British forces were ordered to poison all water supplies between Mersa Matruh and Alexandria. If Italian forces reached the delta, the British planned to flood the surrounding territory in a bid to drown the assault.[29] Although Mussolini envisioned a larger offensive, Italian commanders remained cautious, pushing their forces only as far as Sidi Barrani before halting.

The initiative now passed to British forces under the command of Lieutenant-General Archibald Wavell. Wavell had devoted his life to defending the empire. He had fought in the Second Boer War and along the North-West Frontier in India before serving in France during the First World War, losing his left eye in the Second Battle of Ypres. He then served in various staff positions after the war before returning to colonial duty in Palestine, which was in the throes of the bloody Arab Revolt. Despite this long military service, he remained a man of academic bearing. His critics accused him of being too hesitant and too conservative. His defenders argued that he was a faithful soldier continuously thrust into all-but-impossible situations who handled his commands with meticulous attention to detail. "My trouble," he himself confessed, "is that I am not really interested in war."[30]

Wavell's ground forces launched their attack in the early hours of December 9 and made rapid progress throughout the day. A dust storm slowed the advance, but British forces had closed in around Sidi Barrani by nightfall. The Italians were caught off guard. Advancing British forces captured thousands of demoralized prisoners. The general commanding Italian forces at the Nibeiwa camp was found dead in the door of his tent. Upon entering Sidi Barrani, Australian journalist Alan Moorehead—traveling with Wavell's troops—described a desolate collection of twenty houses, one bombed-out shop, and "two small brothels of unexampled dreariness." Shelling had reduced many of the buildings to rubble, and destroyed vehicles littered the streets. Oil spills and the resulting fires stained the sand "a grimy stinking black." The Italians had abandoned their breakfasts along with piles of clothes, fresh loaves of bread, wheels of Parmesan cheese, chocolates, coffee, jam, and cigarettes. The doctors in the Italian field hospital had been in the middle of an appendectomy when the attack began—their unfortunate patient's body still lay sliced open on the operating table. "We are trying to fight this war as though it is a colonial war in Africa," one abandoned Italian letter read. "But it is a European war in Africa fought with European weapons against a European enemy. . . . We are not fighting the Abyssinians now."[31]

Churchill now urged Wavell to give pursuit. "Nothing would shake Mussolini more than a disaster in Libya itself," he wrote. The prime minister suggested an assault on a Libyan port. Wavell's forces were driving the last Italians out of Egypt, but an extended offensive into Libya entailed significant logistical challenges. Tanks, trucks, and troops would have to be supplied along miles of narrow coastal highway that not only was an obvious attack route but was also vulnerable to counterattack. Nevertheless, on December 11, Wavell sent an armored division and an infantry brigade in pursuit of retreating Italian forces, capturing some fourteen thousand outside of Sollum. British forces then paused for sixteen days to bring up ammunition and supplies from Mersa Matruh and the harbor at Sollum. Before dawn on January 3, 1941, British forces attacked the seaport of Bardia, crossing the defensive tank ditch and cutting through the barbed wire surrounding the Italian positions. In the early evening of the following day, British tanks and infantry entered Bardia. By January 5, Wavell's forces had taken another forty-five thousand prisoners.[32]

While British forces finished mopping up in Bardia, Wavell continued his drive west toward the port of Tobruk. Once again, Wavell took his time moving ammunition and supplies into position. At 5:30 a.m. on January 21, British armor, artillery, and infantry launched an attack on Tobruk. The attackers made rapid progress and seized the harbor the next day. Moorehead "felt suddenly sickened at the destruction" he saw while walking through the fallen town. Soldiers and stray cats wandered amid the ruins of shops and houses against a backdrop of still-burning fires. The path to the Italian stronghold at Benghazi now appeared open, and the larger goal of seizing the capital city of Tripoli seemed to be within reach.[33]

But Churchill and Foreign Secretary Anthony Eden were about to derail the North Africa campaign. On January 29, 1941, the new Greek government requested assistance in repelling an attack by Italian forces. Churchill and Eden sensed an opportunity to open a new front in Europe against Germany. With British forces making good progress in North Africa, an impatient Churchill and his advisers concluded that the time had come to strike a blow against Axis forces in the Balkans. Wavell pushed back, explaining that the campaign in North Africa was not over. After fighting for eight months, his troops needed rest and resupply. Still, Churchill argued that Greece had to take first priority. Political considerations weighed heavily in London. Churchill insisted that the empire must live up to its commitments to Greece's defense. Moreover, a successful Allied intervention in the Balkans would deal a significant blow to the Axis and go some way in convincing the Americans to join the war. But British commanders had good reason to be skeptical of the prime minister's plan to intervene in Greece. Churchill had been one of the key architects of the disastrous 1915 Gallipoli campaign, leading his critics to accuse him of harboring a dangerous fixation on Greece. Moreover, to divert troops from Libya before they had neutralized the Italians would place the entire Mediterranean campaign in jeopardy.[34]

Ultimately, political considerations trumped military logic. After Churchill bulldozed the British chiefs into accepting his Greek gamble, Wavell relented. The first of some fifty-eight thousand British and Commonwealth forces began landing in Greece on March 7 and made their way north to defensive positions along the Aliakmon Line southwest of Thessaloniki. Although they expected to meet large concentrations of Greek troops, British planners hoped that the terrain might blunt the force of German armor. Even so, the commander of the British expedition had already made contingency plans for an evacuation. At dawn on April 6, German forces crossed into Greece to attack Greek and British defenders along the Metaxas and Aliakmon Lines. Greek resistance, though valiant in places, soon collapsed before the German onslaught. With the Wehrmacht advancing, British commanders were forced to stage a fighting retreat to avoid envelopment. The British managed to save a large number of troops, but they were forced to abandon much of their equipment. By April 30, the British had evacuated some forty-two thousand troops—in addition, two thousand had been killed and another fourteen thousand had been captured.[35]

The Greek debacle dealt a serious blow to London's position in the Mediterranean. The most immediate implication concerned the fate of Wavell's Western Desert campaign in North Africa. The diversion of troops to Greece stalled the British drive into Libya and bought critical time for Axis leaders to reinforce their position. On February 6, Wavell received a telegram announcing the dispatch of a German commander, Lieutenant-General Erwin Rommel, to Tunis. Though he was relatively unknown at the time, British forces would soon come to recognize the name. Hitler's decision to intervene was driven less by strategic interest in North Africa than by the fear that defeat in Libya would gut popular support for Mussolini's regime in Italy. Operation Sonnenblume was designed to stiffen Italian Libya against the British without drawing large amounts of resources away from German operations in Eastern Europe. However, Rommel had bigger things in mind. The ambitious young general was not content to play defense against Wavell's now-undermanned troops in North Africa. "We could have defeated and destroyed the British Field Army, and that would have opened the road to the Suez Canal," he later wrote. The Wehrmacht, with complete control of the "Mediterranean coastline," could then charge into the Middle East, sweep through Iraq and Persia, and attack the Soviet Union from the south. Along the way, the Germans would seize massive oil fields and sever a key transportation link between Russia and the West.[36]

Instead, German leaders forced Rommel to fight with only a meager supply of tanks and men. So short was Rommel on armor that his troops began mounting dummy tanks on Volkswagen chassis to trick British intelligence into thinking that they faced a larger force. Rommel would use deception, maneuvers, and tenacity in a race to seize as much of North Africa as possible before the British managed to shore up their defenses. "If Wavell had . . . continued his advance into Tripolitania [in early February]," Rommel wrote, "no resistance worthy of the name could have been mounted against him—so well had his superbly planned offensive succeeded." However, the disastrous British intervention in Greece gave Rommel his opportunity to step into the breach. On March 24, German forces launched a successful attack on the lightly defended British fort at El Agheila. The Afrika Korps drove British troops back across Libya. On April 2, Wavell ordered British troops to pull out of Benghazi. By April 10, German forces had reached the Egyptian border and laid siege to Tobruk. While British defenders would hold Tobruk for 241 days, the Western Desert campaign's momentum had shifted toward the Axis.[37]

Rommel's panzers were not the only threat to the British Empire. Although London had managed to keep a lid on anticolonial movements in Egypt, Iraq, and Palestine through the 1930s, mounting Axis power in the Mediterranean and Vichy control of Syria and Lebanon created a revolutionary situation that Germany might be able to exploit. On April 1, while Rommel's panzers blasted their way toward the Egyptian border, a group of generals led by Rashid Ali al-Gaylani staged a coup against Nuri al-Said's pro-British government in Iraq. Rashid Ali's group were nationalists who recognized that the British Empire, assailed by the Axis in Europe and the Mediterranean, might be weak enough to drive out of Iraq. British officials now came to fear coordination between the Iraqis and Germans. If the Iraqi crisis was a harbinger of a broader anticolonial uprising in the Arab world, Britain's empire was in trouble. Not only would the British lose their holdings in the Middle East, but Nazi Germany might gain a base from which to attack Egypt from the east, sever British communications with India, and link up with Japanese forces in the Indian Ocean. With this nightmare scenario in mind, British leaders resolved to crush the uprising in Iraq.[38]

The first British troops landed at Basra in mid-April to reinforce the garrison in Iraq. British officials began evacuating women and children from Baghdad while Iraqi troops prepared to move into position near the British air base at Habbaniya. On the morning of May 2, British commanders launched air attacks against the Iraqi encampments. The Iraqis responded with artillery fire. Meanwhile, the British chiefs warned of a possible German airborne assault on oil facilities in Syria or northern Iraq. It remained essential, they said, "to deny to [the] greatest extent possible Iraq oil to [the] enemy." The chiefs cautioned that Rashid Ali had been working "hand-in-glove with [the] Axis powers" and only swift action in Iraq had prevented more substantial coordination. After a four-day battle, Iraqi units withdrew from their positions around the air base. Churchill pushed a reluctant Wavell to crush the regime. "Rashid Ali and his partisans are in desperate straits," the prime minister insisted. "There can be no question of negotiation." British forces must move swiftly to install a friendly regime in Baghdad: "Every day counts, for the Germans may not be long."[39]

On May 18, British reinforcements moved toward Iraqi positions in Fallujah, sitting astride the approaches to Baghdad. The following day, British aircraft began bombing the city. After thirty minutes of fighting, British ground troops took the bridge spanning the Euphrates River and accepted the surrender of the Iraqi garrison soon after. British forces now prepared to advance on the capital. Sensing an opportunity to strike a blow against the British Empire, Hitler issued a directive calling for support of the uprising in hopes that it would spread to the wider region and tie down large numbers of British troops. The ultimate goal was to "wreck . . . the English position between the Mediterranean and the Persian Gulf, in conjunction with an offensive against the Suez Canal." But Hitler's orders came too late. As British forces entered the outlying districts of Baghdad on May 30, Rashid Ali fled for Iran. An armistice was signed the following day and the regent reinstated. London's quick action along the imperial periphery had blocked a potential Axis advance into Iraq at the cost of crushing a local nationalist movement. However, as Churchill later explained, the Iraqi rebellion was "but one small sector of the immense emergency in the Middle East."[40]

Indeed, London's position in the region remained precarious. As British forces moved into Baghdad in late May, German paratroops staged an assault on the island of Crete. The Germans suffered heavy losses at the hands of the British defenders, who had learned of the invasion through intercepted messages. "Sometimes a whole sector of the sky, crowded with parachutists, would fill the sights of a machine-gun, so that all were killed in the air and the parachutes would deposit only inert, clumsy bodies on the ground," wrote Alan Moorehead. Paratrooper losses were so serious that they convinced Hitler that airborne assaults were unfeasible going forward. Nevertheless, the attackers managed to seize the island, forcing Allied troops to stage yet another seaborne evacuation. Combined with Rommel's success in Libya, Axis victories in Greece and Crete raised the very real possibility of a German assault on Egypt from the east. Although British forces had crushed the Iraqi uprising, Syria and Lebanon remained in Vichy hands. The Axis use of Syrian airfields to refuel German and Italian aircraft only added to Vichy's record of caving to Axis pressure. On May 8, Churchill's chief military adviser, General Hastings Ismay, explained that a "supreme effort must be made to prevent the Germans getting a footing in Syria," from which they could attack Egypt's "eastern flanks." Again, Wavell resisted London's efforts to pull troops and resources away from the Western Desert campaign, but Churchill remained adamant that British forces must fan out throughout the Mediterranean. On May 28, he warned Wavell that the fall of Crete would give Germany control of the shipping lanes to Libya. In order to protect their position in Egypt, British forces must occupy Syria before the Germans regrouped.[41]

Early on the morning of June 8, Allied troops based in Iraq and Palestine invaded Syria and Lebanon in a bid to capture Damascus, Rayak Air Base, and Beirut. The attackers made good progress in the first five days, pushing Vichy forces back toward Damascus, but failed to overwhelm the defenders. Hardening resistance and a series of counterattacks slowed British operations over the next week. However, by June 21, Allied forces had begun to turn the tide, taking both Damascus and Sidon. At the gates of Sidon, Moorehead found the bodies of two Senegalese soldiers "jumbled in a horrible death"—colonial soldiers killed fighting in defense of Vichy's empire. On his first night in the fallen city of Damascus, the journalist marveled at the twinkling lights—it was the first time in a year he had slept in a city with no blackout. The next day he drove through the ancient city, through "endless bazaars and byways," while machine gun fire cracked in the distance. Over the next three weeks, Allied troops took Palmyra, Deir ez-Zor, and Damour and advanced to the gates of Beirut. On the evening of July 11, Vichy commanders requested a ceasefire, and they signed a draft armistice the following morning.[42] While the British victories in Iraq, Syria, and Lebanon had strengthened Egypt's eastern flanks against a feared German invasion, the diversion of forces from Wavell's Western Desert campaign weakened the units fighting to hold back Rommel's forces. Churchill had taken British troops from an area where the Germans were fighting in order to protect an area where they were not.

One day after the official armistice was signed in Syria, shorthanded British forces launched Operation Battleaxe in a bid to relieve the siege of Tobruk in Libya. Wavell had been doubtful about the offensive, warning that British armor was too slow to be effective against German tanks and insisting that reinforcements be made available. In the face of these reservations, British leaders launched Battleaxe on June 15. The operation quickly degenerated into a fiasco, with Rommel's troops threatening to envelop the British attackers. Following Battleaxe's failure, Churchill removed Wavell. "At home we had the feeling that Wavell was a tired man," the prime minister later explained. Foreign Secretary Anthony Eden remarked that Wavell seemed to have "aged ten years in the night." Churchill opted not to comment on how London had squandered the hope of a quick victory in Libya by dispatching Wavell's troops to futile battles in Greece and Crete.[43] As the Western Desert campaign drifted toward an uneasy stalemate between British and German forces, an even more momentous affair was set to commence in the cold waters of the North Atlantic.

ON AUGUST 7, 1941, THE USS *AUGUSTA* DROPPED ANCHOR IN PLA-centia Bay, Newfoundland. Emerging into the morning sun, the *Augusta*'s most important passenger, Franklin Roosevelt, made his way to the ship's forecastle to fish in the cool waters below. Fortune smiled on the president. He "caught a large and ugly fish which could not be identified by name and which he directed be preserved and delivered to the Smithsonian Institute." An afternoon expedition yielded only a few "wormy" cod and flounder. But Roosevelt had not sailed to Newfoundland in order to catch ugly fish, let alone wormy flounder. Two days later, the HMS *Prince of Wales* pulled alongside the *Augusta* to deliver Winston Churchill and an escort of top British leaders. Roosevelt and Churchill's meeting, orchestrated with the utmost secrecy, would have sweeping implications for the postwar world.[44] Over the coming days, the two leaders would discuss their plans for fighting the war and shaping the global order that would follow it.

The resulting Atlantic Charter represented a milestone in the war and in the longer history of American foreign relations. The issue of Washington's nonbelligerency took priority for Churchill, who hoped to secure a firm commitment from Roosevelt to enter the fray. Although the prime minister was disappointed in this regard, he succeeded in reaching a general set of principles to guide the Anglo-American war effort against the Axis powers. The charter renounced the idea of territorial aggrandizement through force, supported the "right of all peoples to choose the form of government under which they will live," called for free trade and free navigation of the seas, supported international economic collaboration and improved labor practices and social security, called for the "final destruction of the Nazi tyranny" and the creation of world peace, denounced international aggression, and called for the creation of a "permanent system of general security."[45]

Although no signed copy of the Atlantic Charter was ever produced, the document would come to embody Washington's rationale for fighting the war and its vision for a postwar global order. In broad brushstrokes, the charter made it clear that if and when the United States joined the war, it would be fighting not to restore the prewar status quo but to establish a new, American-led international order built on ideals of free-trade capitalism, political self-determination, and collective security. The United States would sit at the center of this new world order: New York and Washington would control the global economy; the US Navy would command the seas; the American political system would become the archetype for postwar governments around the world; and, as would ultimately be decided, the United Nations would build its headquarters in Manhattan. The charter traced a schematic for a new American empire without colonies that would be structured by the power of the US dollar. The war would give Washington the military forces to project American power across every ocean and into every continent, thereby claiming a sphere of influence that was planetary in scope. The Atlantic Charter's implications for world politics were clear: going forward, US supremacy would no longer be hemispheric but global.

IF THE FOURTEEN MONTHS FOLLOWING THE FALL OF FRANCE HAD witnessed some of the darkest days of the war, it also saw Britain lay the groundwork for future Allied victories against Germany, Italy, and Japan. London devised a workable, albeit plodding, strategy that focused on military operations along the edges of the Axis empires. German forces held a position of strength in continental Europe, but the Allies could pick away at strategic points along the imperial periphery from a ring of colonial outposts running west from Singapore, through Sri Lanka, Iraq, Palestine, Lebanon, Egypt, Malta, and Gibraltar, and south to Pretoria. Control of this outer ring gave Britain and its allies the ability to project military force from multiple points across the globe. As British military forces conducted these colonial campaigns along the periphery, Churchill secured Roosevelt's commitment to underwrite the Allied war effort—and this was only the beginning. The United States was now on a path to join Britain in the battle against Germany.

Still months away from the United States joining the war as an active belligerent, the Roosevelt administration signaled its intention to treat the global conflict as a catalyst for the construction of an American-led international order. Starting with the Plan Dog memo, carrying through the destroyers-for-bases deal and Lend-Lease, and culminating in the Atlantic Charter, American leaders laid out a program for the creation of a new American hegemony. If it was successful, Pax Americana would replace Pax Britannica, and Washington's Open Door would replace London's imperial preference system in the postwar world. America would step into Britain's shoes as the preeminent power in world affairs, exercising a dominant influence across the political, economic, and military spectrum. In this imperial succession, the British would serve as Greeks to America's Romans. As Harold Macmillan, the British minister resident in the Mediterranean and future prime minister, explained, "We . . . are Greeks in this American empire. You will find the Americans much as the Greeks found the Romans—great big, vulgar, bustling people, more vigorous than we are and also more idle, with more unspoiled virtues but also more corrupt. We must run [Allied military operations in the Mediterranean] as the Greek slaves ran the operations of the Emperor Claudius."[46]

But the American bid for global supremacy would not go unchallenged. Indeed, while Churchill and Roosevelt met in the waters off Newfoundland, German commanders were fighting the largest colonial campaign of all: the brutal conquest and depopulation of Eastern Europe.

Chapter 7

A WAR OF ANNIHILATION

A s December 1940 began, Berlin prepared for its second winter at war. Cold and darkness had descended across the capital, with blackout curtains shrouding windows through the night. Inside this dark metropolis, Adolf Hitler was growing restless. Despite Germany's stunning victory in France, the British Empire remained defiant. Italy's bumbling campaign in the Mediterranean was little more than a sideshow, and Japan's war in China seemed to be a world away. Meanwhile, across the Third Reich's eastern frontier, almost within reach, lay the great prize that had occupied the Führer's dreams since the 1920s: the Soviet Union. A massive transcontinental empire covering over 8.6 million square miles of territory and home to 195 million people, the Soviet colossus seemed formidable. But Hitler had reason to be optimistic. Germany had defeated Russia in the First World War only to lose in the West. In this war, however, German forces had trounced the combined armies of Britain and France. And the extent of Moscow's authority remained uncertain. Soviet leaders ruled over an empire containing more than one hundred different ethnic groups, many of whom had been forcibly incorporated into the Bolshevik state. Indeed, the Bolsheviks had only recently consolidated control over many of their western territories. Millions of Belorussians and Ukrainians had lived under Moscow's control for less than a generation. For the residents of the Baltic states, Soviet rule was only months old. Whether these people would fight to defend Joseph Stalin's brutal regime in Moscow remained an open question. Making matters worse, Stalin had conducted a series of purges through the 1930s that had devastated the Red Army, the very forces that would now be called on to defend the nation against a Nazi invasion.

Behind the Red Army lay that which Hitler coveted most: living space. The invasion of the Soviet Union would mark the culmination of Germany's imperial ambitions. The attack on Poland, the fall of France, and the Battle of Britain had been merely the prelude to Hitler's goal of building a new Nazi empire in the East. The conquest of the Soviet Union, Hitler believed, would transform the Third Reich into the thousand-year empire he had envisioned. With the capture of the vast eastern plains, Berlin would seize a sprawling colonial domain, gaining control of the rich black soil of Ukraine and mastery over the oil fields of the Caucasus.[1]

The lands set to become the battleground between Berlin and Moscow constituted an ancient imperial frontier linking Europe to the vast Eurasian steppe. For hundreds of years, armies of Goths, Huns, Slavs, and Mongols had marched across these plains. Napoleon had met defeat on this same route, and in more recent decades, German, Polish, and Russian forces had fought over these territories. Now, Hitler planned to win mastery over Eastern Europe once and for all. German forces would smash their way through the Red Army and topple the Bolshevik regime. Russians and their Slavic cousins were to be enslaved or driven from their homes across the Urals, clearing vast stretches of Eastern Europe for German colonization. In the process, the Jewish peoples of the East were to be exterminated. At its core, Nazi leaders envisioned Barbarossa as a *Vernichtungskrieg*, a war of annihilation engineered to slaughter hundreds of millions of men, women, and children and pave the way for German imperial hegemony in Europe.[2]

But the Führer's window of opportunity would not remain open forever. British leaders were mobilizing their forces throughout their scattered global empire and staging sporadic strikes along the periphery. Across the Atlantic, the United States had begun to stir, edging ever closer to joining the war against the Axis. And across the eastern frontier, Stalin and his comrades were hard at work rebuilding the Red Army. If Hitler was to create his thousand-year Reich, he had to act before the rising powers in Moscow and Washington grew stronger. As Christmas 1940 approached, the Führer gathered his generals and ordered them to begin preparations for the largest invasion in world history, code-named Barbarossa.

THE THIRD REICH'S WAR IN THE EAST MARKED THE CULMINATION of Hitler's colonial ambitions and the apogee of the centuries-old Western imperial project. In this respect, the Führer drew on long-standing imperial impulses dating back to the nineteenth century and earlier. The British Empire served as perhaps the closest inspiration. As Hitler liked to explain, London had managed to control four hundred million South Asians with 250,000 colonial officers: "What India was for England, Russia will be for us." But where other Western powers such as Britain and France had sailed across the oceans in search of colonies, Germany would fight a war of annihilation to transform Europe itself into a colony. Here, the United States stood as a prime example. Through violence and ethnic cleansing, Europeans had driven Native American peoples from huge stretches of the continent, opening up new lands for settlement. "Here in the east a similar process will repeat itself for the second time as in the conquest of America," Hitler insisted. "Our Mississippi must be the Volga, not the Niger."[3]

Moreover, in the eyes of Nazi leaders, the American model of continental imperialism had proven so successful that Germany had no choice but to try to replicate it. Washington's global ascendence as an economic and industrial power increasingly threatened to overwhelm the nations of Europe. The only way to avoid becoming vassals living under US hegemony, Hitler and his colleagues concluded, was to consolidate their hold over all of Europe, building the Old World into a new unified power that could outcompete the United States. As Hitler explained, the Third Reich must "exploit the advantages of continental hegemony. . . . When we are masters of Europe, we have a dominant position in the world. . . . We'll be four hundred millions, compared with the hundred and thirty million Americans." But time was of the essence. The Americans were on track to enter the war in force in 1942. The Third Reich had to complete its conquest of Eastern Europe in 1941 and prepare to meet the American challenge. "The struggle for hegemony of the world will be decided in favor of Europe by the possession of the Russian space," Hitler insisted. "Thus Europe will be an impregnable fortress, safe from all threat of blockade." In this way, Germany would seize its rightful place as the leading imperial overlord in Europe.[4]

German leaders also saw themselves as locked in a clash of civilizations with the peoples of Asia. The consolidation of a Nazi empire across Europe would serve as a bulwark against an imagined racial peril in the East. "We'll take away [Russia's] character of an Asiatic steppe, we'll Europeanize it," Hitler explained in October 1941. Germans would then repopulate the "Russian desert." In yet another allusion to the US example, the Führer called on German settlers "to look upon the natives [of Russia] as Redskins."[5] In this task, Germany would serve as Europe's guardian standing on the front lines of a civilizational war. "The safety of Europe will not be assured until we have driven Asia back behind the Urals. No organized Russian State must be allowed to exist west of that line. . . . They are brutes in a state of nature. The danger would be still greater if this space were to be Mongolized. Suddenly a wave comes foaming down from Asia and surprises a Europe benumbed by civilization and deceived by the illusion of collective security!"[6] Hitler also consistently conflated racial fears of Jews, Slavs, and Asians with political opposition to Marxism as part of a crusade against "Jewish-Bolshevism" and the "Asiatic hordes" that lay beyond the Urals. Germany's bid for lebensraum—in Hitler's mind—represented a defensive effort to push back these threats at the frontiers of European civilization.

As part of this effort to prosecute a racial war aimed at destroying the foundations of Russian society, Hitler granted special responsibilities to Heinrich Himmler, Reichsführer-SS and leader of the Einsatzgruppen. Himmler's death squads would be responsible for tracking and eliminating designated racial and ideological enemies in rear areas as the Wehrmacht advanced. As General Alfred Jodl, chief of the Wehrmacht high command, explained in early March, "The Jewish-Bolshevist intelligentsia, hitherto the 'oppressor' of the people, must be eliminated." As plans for Barbarossa took shape, the Einsatzgruppen began training three thousand men to be deployed in four detachments along with Army Groups North, Center, and South and with Romanian forces participating in the invasion. Another group would be stationed in Poland in July. Many of those recruited had police backgrounds, while a high percentage of the leadership had earned law degrees or doctorates.[7]

While the Einsatzgruppen were specifically charged with liquidating the Third Reich's racial and ideological enemies, the Wehrmacht also followed a policy of systematic atrocities. "The intelligentsia put in by Stalin must be exterminated," Hitler told his military leaders in March 1941. Likewise, Field Marshal Walther von Brauchitsch, commander in chief of the German army, insisted that German forces had to "realize that this struggle is being waged by one race against another, and proceed with the necessary harshness." In May, General Erich Hoepner, commander of the Fourth Army, told his troops that the "war against the Soviet Union is an important part of the struggle for the existence of the German people. It is the old battle of Germans against the Slavs, the defense of European culture against

Moscovite-Asiatic inundation, the repulse of Jewish-Bolshevism." All energy must be focused "toward the merciless and complete annihilation of the enemy."[8]

Alongside Eastern European Jews, the Nazis' most-hated opponents were Soviet commissars: political officers tasked with enforcing the ideological doctrine of Red Army units. In an infamous order issued on June 6, 1941, the German high command directed Wehrmacht officers to employ the harshest measures against captured commissars, disregarding the principles of international law. Commissars in particular represented "a menace to [German] safety and to the rapid pacification of the conquered territories." Ultimately, the document explained, "the originators of the asiatic-barbaric methods of fighting are the political commissars. They must be dealt with promptly and with the utmost severity. Therefore, if taken while fighting or offering resistance they must, on principle, be shot immediately."[9]

German commanders decreed that this same ruthlessness should apply to partisans operating behind the front lines as well as to Jews. In the fall of 1941, Field Marshal Walter von Reichenau, commander of the German Sixth Army, issued a series of instructions on conduct of German troops in the eastern theater of the war. "The most essential aim of war against the Jewish-bolshevistic system," he wrote, "is a complete destruction of their means of power and the elimination of asiatic influence from the European culture." German soldiers should not consider themselves subject to the rules of war. Instead, they "must have full understanding for the necessity of a severe but just revenge on subhuman Jewry" and must remain focused on the "annihilation of revolts in hinterland which, as experience proves, have always been caused by Jews." German troops should not feed or aid Soviet troops or citizens unless they were working in support of the Wehrmacht. Partisans should be shot along with any citizens found in possession of "arms of any kind or explosives." Captured partisans should be interrogated and then hanged or shot in the vicinity where they had been caught. "This is the only way to fulfill our historic task to liberate the German people once forever from the Asiatic-Jewish danger."[10]

REDUCED TO ITS MOST BASIC FORM, BARBAROSSA WOULD BE A MAD dash to destroy the Red Army, seize farmland and natural resources, exterminate the Nazis' ideological and racial opponents in Eastern Europe, and prepare for a war against the United States and Great Britain. Indeed, a Wehrmacht report to Hitler in early December 1940 identified the "main war industrial centers" of Ukraine, Moscow, and Leningrad as key military objectives. To this Hitler added that the most critical goal must be to "achieve the annihilation of the Russian army and to prevent its regeneration." However, General Georg Thomas, chief of the Defense Economy and Armaments Office, emphasized that the *"main mission of the organization* will consist of *seizing raw materials and taking over all important concerns"* (italics in the original).[11]

Although Barbarossa appeared to solve a number of Germany's most pressing problems, this reality made the operation all the more risky. Berlin's sense of urgency forced Germany to launch an invasion—not unlike the invasion of France the year before—that gambled everything on the promise of a quick victory. German commanders would lead a force only slightly larger than the one that had conquered France in 1940 into a territory that was nearly ten times as vast. The Wehrmacht had traveled 250 miles in its drive to the channel coast to defeat France in 1940. In contrast, Barbarossa's ultimate objective of Moscow lay 650 miles from the starting lines. The oil fields of the Caucasus were even more distant. Meanwhile, the Soviet population of 171 million was more than twice the size of Germany's population of 80 million. Despite these daunting challenges, Nazi leaders banked on rapid victory. After all, France had been a far tougher opponent than Russia in the First World War—many in Berlin assumed that this same calculus would hold true for the present conflict. As a result, Hitler predicted victory in a mere four months.[12]

Logistical shortages further undercut Barbarossa's chances of success. German forces, already saddled with a sprawling occupation across large sections of Western and Central Europe, lacked the resources to stage a successful invasion of the vast Russian steppe. Ironically, however, Nazi leaders saw Barbarossa as the means to solve the supply problems that the invasion would exacerbate. Part of the rationale for seizing Ukraine and driving toward the Caucasus was to feed and fuel the German forces charged with taking these territories. This supposed necessity led to a brutal conclusion. With the "Hunger Plan," Nazi leaders determined that something on the order of twenty to thirty million Soviet citizens had to die in order to feed the Wehrmacht and the people of Germany. One high-level planning memorandum from early May 1941 read, "The war can only be continued if all armed forces are fed by Russia. . . . There is no doubt that as a result many millions of people will be starved to death if we take out of the country the things necessary for us." The following month, Alfred Rosenberg, head of the Reich Ministry for Occupied Eastern Territories, explained, "We see absolutely no reason for any obligation on our part to feed also the Russian people with the products of that surplus territory." In the minds of Nazi planners, mass starvation across Eastern Europe would not be the unfortunate by-product of Barbarossa: it would be the campaign's goal.[13]

ONE FACTOR WORKING IN GERMANY'S FAVOR WAS THE NIGHTMARISH state of affairs in the Soviet Union in the years leading up to Barbarossa. The Soviet Union must be understood as an empire in its own right—both as a successor to the Russian Empire of the czars and as an expansionist power seeking to capitalize on the existing upheaval in Europe. Many general histories of World War II gloss over the fact that the western reaches of Soviet territory were often recent and not always willing additions to the USSR. Bolshevik leaders had worked to reconstitute the territories of the old Russian Empire during the 1920s. Ukraine had been part of the Soviet Union for eighteen years and in that time had been the victim of a horrific man-made famine. The Ukrainian Holodomor, which killed an estimated 3.3 million people, was largely the result of forced Soviet collectivization. In some parts of Soviet Ukraine, historian Timothy Snyder writes, hunger became so acute that "a black market arose in human flesh." Stalin's regime had also been an eager participant in the dissolution of Poland and the conquest of the Baltic states. As a result, eastern Poland had been in Soviet hands for less than two years following the 1939 invasion, and Latvia had been forcibly incorporated in August 1940.[14]

Ukrainian peasants were not the only victims of Soviet state terror. Starting in 1936, Stalin led a series of purges that targeted an array of ostensible enemies of the regime including kulaks, ethnic minorities, political opponents, and, notably, officers in the Red Army. Beyond removing a significant number of experienced officers, the purges bludgeoned army morale and cowed many leaders who remained. Furthermore, the Soviet decision to move their forces into occupied eastern Poland meant that a large number of Red Army units would be deployed in poorly prepared forward positions in unfamiliar, hostile territory. Indeed, in order to occupy these new areas, the Red Army was in the process of pulling up its established defensive lines in the east and moving them forward when Germany attacked. Stalin had also chosen the summer of 1941 to launch a sweeping reorganization of the Red Army—a fact that would help to sow confusion in the opening phase of the war.[15]

Making matters worse, Stalin dismissed numerous warnings of an impending German attack. For years, the Soviet leader had watched as the Nazi threat grew in the West. Above all, he feared that Hitler would forge an alliance with France and Britain and launch an attack on the Soviet Union. Marxism-Leninism and its prophecy of an inevitable clash between capitalism and communism seemed to predict just such a struggle. In addition, Neville Chamberlain's decision to appease Hitler at Munich in 1938 suggested that London and Paris would continue to stand aside as Nazi forces marched east. The Molotov-Ribbentrop Pact, then, came as a relief to Stalin, although it would later be revealed as a huge strategic misstep. The outbreak of war between Germany and the Western powers bought the Soviet dictator time to build his forces and consolidate his defenses in Eastern Europe. Stalin hoped that Britain and Germany would wear each other down while the USSR grew stronger. The Kremlin was therefore wary of British attempts to cajole Moscow into joining the fight against Hitler. For the time being, Germany remained dependent on Soviet aid and focused on the war with Britain. Stalin found it inconceivable that Berlin would risk creating a second front before defeating Britain. "Germany is involved up to its ears in the war in the West," Stalin explained in mid-1941, "and I believe that Hitler will not risk creating a second front for himself by attacking the Soviet Union. Hitler is not such a fool as to think that the Soviet Union" could be defeated as easily as Poland, France, and Britain. Even so, Stalin believed that it was only a matter of time before Germany turned east. Indeed, *Mein Kampf* was a readily available declaration of Hitler's desire to destroy the Soviet Union. However, the Soviet leader considered it far more likely in the near term that London would attempt to trick Moscow into entering the war against Germany.[16]

These strategic calculations that Hitler would not yet dare attack and that Churchill would try to deceive Moscow into war colored intelligence warnings of a German buildup along the Soviet frontier. Also, Berlin went to great lengths to conceal its intentions. An Oberkommando der Wehrmacht directive from September 1940 called on the military to veil its buildup. Wehrmacht commanders dictated that "the actual preparations for deployment in the East should be represented as a diversionary maneuver to divert from plans which are being pursued for an attack against England."[17]

AS THE WARM SUMMER NIGHT DESCENDED ON MOSCOW ON JUNE 21, 1941, General Ivan Tyulenev left the capital's military headquarters. "Moscow was so beautiful on that last peaceful June evening," he later remembered. But the general was troubled as he made his way to his home outside of the city. Intelligence from the western borders indicated that German forces were preparing to attack. Moscow's air defenses maintained a state of high readiness, but many officials still doubted the likelihood of hostilities. At 3:00 a.m. the telephone rang, summoning Tyulenev to the Kremlin. "War!" he thought as he made his way back to headquarters. At the general staff offices he learned that the Germans were bombing Kaunas, Rivne, Sevastopol, and Odessa.[18]

Nearly seven hundred miles to the west, panzer commander Hans Schäufler watched as German artillery opened up against Red Army positions across the Bug River in Poland. "Shell after shell rocketed" overhead as the "silver bodies" of Luftwaffe formations drifted across the skies above. "Clouds of smoke and fountains of earth shot skyward on the far bank." By noon, Schäufler's troops were crossing pontoon bridges and trudging through the "knee-deep sand of the Bug lowlands." Operation Barbarossa, the largest invasion in history, moved some three million men, 3,600 tanks, and six hundred thousand horses into Soviet-controlled territory in a bid to annihilate the Red Army. The Germans were entering an almost unimaginably vast realm that stretched across the marshes and forests of the East European Plain, rambled over the Urals, and then opened up to the even more expansive steppe of Siberia before plunging to the shores of the North Pacific. Bounded by the frozen tundra and Arctic ice in the north and the arid Central Asian plateaus in the south, this new battlefield spanned the breadth of Asia and much of Eastern Europe. The Wehrmacht faced a long charge of some 300 miles to their first objective of the Dnieper River; Moscow lay some 350 miles beyond that; and the waters of the Volga River flowed some 450 miles farther to the east.[19]

The Luftwaffe began bombing Soviet positions near the border at 3:30 in the morning, hitting sixty-six airfields on the opening day of the offensive and destroying over one thousand aircraft. The Soviets' advance deployment had left large concentrations of planes crowded around airfields that were still under construction. Making matters worse, many of the Red Army's airfields were located within artillery range of the German frontier and lacked adequate communication with Soviet headquarters. These initial strikes gave the Luftwaffe control of the skies going forward. Barbarossa also overwhelmed the Red Army's ramshackle communication network. In some places, Soviet units were forced to use civilian telephones to report the attacks. It would take four hours for Moscow to begin to formulate a coordinated response, by which time many Wehrmacht units had already penetrated the Soviet lines.[20]

As his forces streamed across the frontier, Hitler told the German people that he intended to smash the "Soviet Russian–Anglo-Saxon plot" to encircle the Third Reich. Germany was fighting to save Western civilization, he thundered. "The task of this front, therefore, no longer is the protection of single countries, but the safeguarding of Europe and thereby the salvation of all." Hitler would thus join American and British leaders as a claimant to the cause of defending Western civilization against an ostensible threat from what he deemed to be the uncivilized non-Western world. Soviet leaders reached for historical parallels, referencing Napoleon's invasion from 129 years before. While Red Army units struggled to hold back the rampaging Wehrmacht, Soviet foreign minister Vyacheslav Molotov denounced the German invasion: "This is not the first time that our people have had to deal with an attack of an arrogant foe," he told the Soviet people. "At the time of Napoleon's invasion of Russia our people's reply was to war for the fatherland, and Napoleon suffered defeat and met his doom." Hitler would suffer the same fate, Molotov insisted.[21]

WATCHING FROM LONDON AND WASHINGTON, BRITISH AND AMERIcan leaders recognized that Operation Barbarossa had transformed the war. If the Soviets survived the German assault, the resulting bloodbath in Eastern Europe would tie down the Wehrmacht and allow Western armies to fight a primarily littoral war relying on air and sea power, attacking German forces at times and places of their choosing. In addition, the Western powers could channel aid to the Red Army, ensuring that Soviet soldiers bore the brunt of fighting the Wehrmacht.

As Churchill explained, the German invasion of the Soviet Union would take pressure off Britain and place both London and Washington in a position to begin providing military aid to Moscow. "The Soviet Union will then need our aid in reconstruction far more than we shall need theirs," he said. Soviet officials worried that the British would seize the opportunity to shift the burden of fighting the war onto the Red Army. As Moscow's ambassador to London, Ivan Maisky, explained, "For many this feeling is mixed with the secret thought that now it would be possible to dump the main weight of the struggle with the German military machine onto the shoulders of others." Stalin agreed that London would likely stand aside as the Germans and Soviets tore each other to shreds. "It seems they want us to be weakened," he wrote. Even worse, Stalin feared that Nazi leaders might seek a deal with London that would pit Britain and Germany against the Soviet Union. Stalin warned that Berlin was working "to set up a general coalition against the USSR, draw Great Britain and the United States into this coalition, intimidating the ruling circles of these countries beforehand with the spectre of revolution, thereby completely isolating our country from the other Powers."[22]

A young senator from Missouri named Harry Truman expressed a similar idea in even blunter terms. As he told the *New York Times* shortly after Germany's invasion, the United States should let the two dictatorships wear each other down. "If we see that Germany is winning," he suggested, "we ought to help Russia and if Russia is winning we ought to help Germany and that way let them kill as many as possible." No one would have guessed that this same man would be meeting with Stalin four years later to negotiate the fate of the postwar world.[23]

President Roosevelt offered a more diplomatic assessment. "Now comes this Russian diversion," he wrote on June 26. "If it is more than just that it will mean the liberation of Europe from Nazi domination."

Henry Morgenthau Jr., secretary of the Treasury, provided the most direct appraisal, telling the president that "this was the time to get Hitler." But some officials urged caution. One young American diplomat working in the Berlin embassy named George Kennan warned that London and Washington should not rush to identify their moral struggle with Moscow. "Russia has tried unsuccessfully to purchase security by compromising with Germany and by encouraging the direction of the German war effort toward the west," he wrote. And in the long run, Soviet leaders had no desire to see London and Washington emerge in a stronger position after the war was over. While this stance should not prevent the Western powers from giving material support to the Red Army, Kennan explained, Western leaders should be under no illusion that Moscow shared their larger aims.[24]

On July 23, Acting Secretary of State Sumner Welles delivered a statement denouncing the German invasion. He explained that Barbarossa confirmed Hitler's aim of "world domination." As a result, the United States now faced the question of "whether the [plan] for universal conquest, for the cruel and brutal enslavement of all peoples and for the ultimate destruction of the remaining free democracies which Hitler is now desperately trying to carry out, is to be successfully halted and defeated." Speaking on behalf of the president, Welles made it clear that the United States was moving toward war: "Hitler's armies are today the chief dangers of the Americas."[25]

Hitler's attack forged what was to become the largest military alliance in world history, between the United States, Great Britain, the Soviet Union, and China. On the afternoon of June 29, Foreign Minister Molotov summoned the US ambassador, Laurence Steinhardt, to the Kremlin. Steinhardt made it clear that Washington was sincere in its desire to provide military aid to Moscow. Although the United States had offered basic goods such as gasoline and tires, Molotov explained that the Red Army's greatest need was for military equipment such as artillery, antiaircraft cannons, fighter planes and bombers, factory equipment, and chemicals.[26] Such shipments, the foreign minister added, could be delivered through the Persian Gulf and

Iran. Less than a week into the war, the foundations of Lend-Lease aid to the Soviet Union were already being laid. Roosevelt's arsenal of democracy would also arm Moscow.

BUT IN THE NEAR TERM, PROMISES OF AMERICAN AID COULD DO LIT-tle to replace the Red Army's catastrophic losses. The Wehrmacht's withering assault took a horrific toll on frontline Soviet troops. "The enemy was bombing Minsk savagely," Marshal Georgy Zhukov later wrote. "The whole city was in flames. Thousands of peaceful inhab-itants hurled their dying curses at the Nazi brutes." General Dmitry Pavlov's Western Army Group suffered some of the heaviest mauling at the hands of Germany's Army Group Center. German infantry and panzers commanded by Field Marshal Fedor von Bock, Her-mann Hoth, and Heinz Guderian staged a series of encirclements that trapped most of Pavlov's forces in a massive "cauldron" between Bia-lystok and Minsk. Red Army soldiers faced marauding panzers, artil-lery barrages, and blazing forest fires. Estimated Soviet losses ran to 340,000 troops, nearly five thousand tanks, and over nine thousand pieces of artillery. Pavlov was relieved of command, arrested, and charged with cowardice and incompetence. Moscow needed a scape-goat, and Pavlov, who was executed in July, played the role. Stalin also created his martyrs. While German forces surged around them, the defenders inside the nineteenth-century Brest Fortress staged a hope-less defense. For a week, Soviet forces, cut off from their comrades, fought from the old fort's bastions and casements against German artillery and air strikes. Reports later surfaced that small groups of soldiers hidden in the depths of the fortress and its cellars held out into late July.[27]

Nevertheless, Barbarossa's opening phase appeared to many to be a stunning victory for the Germans. On July 3, the German army chief of staff Franz Halder concluded that the Red Army was all but defeated. "It is thus probably no overstatement to say that the Rus-sian Campaign has been won in the space of two weeks," he wrote.

Zhukov likewise admitted the defeats of late June and early July were catastrophic. The Wehrmacht's tank and air forces had overwhelmed the Soviet defenders. But even in defeat, the Red Army had bloodied the German assault. Zhukov explained that the Soviet's strategic defense had four major objectives: slowing the Nazi advance to buy Moscow time to call up more troops in the East; inflicting "maximum losses on the enemy, to harry and exhaust him and thereby to restore . . . the balance of strength"; to evacuate the population and industry "deep into the country's interior zone"; and to build Soviet forces for a counteroffensive. Even at this early stage, the Soviets had begun to fight the war of attrition that would eventually destroy the Wehrmacht.[28]

Behind the lines, the Nazi regime had launched its extermination campaign. As the Wehrmacht advanced, Einsatzgruppen—Nazi death squads—scoured the occupied territories, searching for Soviet officials, commissars, and Jews. With the help of local collaborators, Nazi officials managed to kill perhaps a million Jews in the space of six months. Most were simply shot and thrown in mass graves—a grimly efficient system. The 139 Einsatzgruppen members stationed in the Lithuanian city of Kaunas coordinated the slaughter of a reported 133,346 people. Outside Vilnius, Einsatzgruppe A orchestrated the murder of over seventy thousand Jews. The killers marched small groups into death pits in the neighboring forest, ripped out the victims' gold teeth, and massacred them. Alongside the Einsatzgruppen, Reichsführer-SS Heinrich Himmler dispatched the Waffen-SS and twelve battalions of the Order Police to "pacify" rear areas. One SS commander told his troops that "not one male Jew is to be left alive, not one remnant family in the villages."[29]

These systematic atrocities functioned as an integral part of Barbarossa. On July 19, the German field commandant in charge of Minsk ordered the creation of a Jewish ghetto. The city's Jews were given two weeks to relocate or risk being shot. Authorities set up barbed-wire barriers around the ghetto and residents were only allowed out as part of forced labor details. Laborers received one hundred grams of bread per day, along with porridge. Those who could not work received nothing. Widespread hunger, overcrowding, and lack of sanitation led to typhus outbreaks. Police staged nightly raids into the ghetto, and bands of soldiers frequently entered to kill, rape, steal, and pillage. After capturing a dozen suspected insurgents in late October 1941, Nazi officials publicly hanged the prisoners and ordered their bodies to be left on display. German authorities in the ghetto also staged periodic *Aktions*—systematic sweeps aimed at liquidating the Jewish population using Latvian, Lithuanian, and Ukrainian police. Households were ordered out into the streets and those without work cards were selected, loaded into trucks, and driven to pits outside of the city. There, they were told to disrobe and then led to the edge of the pits and shot. Later *Aktions* were early experiments in the use of specialized gas vans, which released their exhaust into a compartment filled with sixty to one hundred victims, who perished en route to mass graves or the extermination camp in Maly Trostenets near Minsk.[30]

An account of a 1942 assault on the Jewish ghetto in Rivne, Ukraine, by Nazi *Schutzstaffel* (SS) troopers provided a chilling description. At 10:00 p.m., an SS detachment surrounded the neighborhood and threw on electric floodlights. Squads fanned out through the streets, pounding on doors, shattering windows, and forcing their way into the houses. "In the street women cried out for their children and children for their parents." The SS troopers drove the crowd through the streets and onto a waiting freight train. "Car after car was filled," the engineer who wrote the account explained. "Over [the train] hung the screaming of women and children, the cracking of whips and rifle shots." The violence continued through the night as "wounded people dragged themselves across the lighted streets. Women carried their dead children in their arms, children hugged and dragged by their arms and feet their dead parents down the road toward the train."[31]

The Nazis established similar ghettos in cities throughout occupied Polish and Soviet territory: Bialystok, Bobruisk, Brest, Gomel, Kaunas, Klimavichy, Lakhva, Mogilev, Pinsk, Polatsk, Vitebsk, and Slutsk each had its own ghetto where thousands of victims suffered systematic violence at the hands of the Nazis and their allies. The leader of Einsatzgruppe D testified that his forces "liquidated approximately 90,000 men, women and children." Most were Jews but many were "Communist functionaries." Death squads entered towns or villages and called on all the Jews to assemble for "resettlement." The victims were then stripped of valuables and clothing and marched to a killing grounds, "which usually was located beside a deepened anti-tank ditch. They were shot, kneeling or standing, and the corpses were thrown into the ditch." Groups of men performed the actual shooting "in order to avoid direct personal responsibility." Squad leaders then inspected the corpses and shot any survivors.[32]

Although Einsatzgruppen and SS death squads received the lion's share of the blame for these atrocities, the Wehrmacht played a central role in the killings. German soldiers coordinated with the death squads, rendering assistance and support, and often participated in the actual killing. Soviet POWs, in particular, suffered horribly at the hands of the Wehrmacht. Many were simply shot when they tried to surrender. German troops had explicit orders to execute Soviet commissars immediately, and some soldiers also received instructions to kill women captured in uniform. Suspected partisans were also subject to summary execution. Soviet soldiers who survived their initial capture faced a prolonged ordeal. Many Germans looked on the captured Soviet soldiers as members of strange Eastern races. "We saw Asia in what we believed to be the heart of Europe," one German soldier remembered of his first sight of Soviet POWs. The Wehrmacht took over 360,000 POWs in the first three weeks of the war. This number more than doubled by early August. Such massive numbers strained the already-insufficient German supply networks. Army Group Center allotted a mere seven hundred calories per prisoner per day. In response, some German commanders complained that the prisoners were too weak for forced labor. But the Nazi war machine, focused on race war and the depopulation of the eastern steppe, saw little reason to feed the thousands of Soviet prisoners under its control. As a result, somewhere around 60 percent of the nearly six million Soviet POWs in German custody perished.[33]

WHILE THE NIGHTMARE OF GENOCIDE AND NAZI RACIAL IMPERIAL- ism took shape in newly occupied rear areas, the battle continued at the front lines. Despite Hitler's victory declaration, much fighting still lay ahead. On July 3, Stalin delivered his first address to the Soviet people since the beginning of Barbarossa. Although the nation confronted a grave danger, he said, no army was invincible. Napoleon and Kaiser Wilhelm had both been defeated. The same fate awaited Hitler. The nation must prepare for a war of scorched earth. In the event of retreat, Soviet citizens must destroy anything that might be of use to the Germans. Machinery, vehicles, and fuel must be destroyed. Livestock should be scattered and crops destroyed or turned over to state authorities. "To the enemy must not be left a single engine, a single railway car, not a single pound of grain or gallon of fuel," the dictator insisted. Bridges, roads, telegraph lines, forests, and stores must all be destroyed. "This war with Fascist Germany cannot be considered an ordinary war," Stalin said. "It is not only a war between two armies, it is also a great war of the entire Soviet people against the German fascist forces." But there was hope, he continued. Moscow now had stalwart allies in London and Washington. Moreover, "our forces are numberless. The overweening enemy will soon learn this to his cost."[34]

On its face, however, the situation appeared hopeless. Hitler's armies continued their bloody march deep into Soviet territory, annihilating the Red Army units that stood in their path. Nevertheless, signs of fatigue had begun to appear. Months of fighting since the invasion had strained German troops and supply lines. Evidence of stiffening resistance also gave German leaders cause for concern. The sheer size of the Soviet Union, too, unnerved many German troops.

"The spaces seemed endless, the horizons nebulous," remembered one general. "We were depressed by the monotony of the landscape, and the immensity of the stretches of forest, marsh and plain. Good roads were so few, and bad tracks so numerous, while rain quickly turned the sand or loam into a morass." Another German soldier marching to the front in mid-July remembered "dust, mud, burning heat, thunderstorms and endless open space." His column passed countless Soviet and German graves. "Skeletal remains of horses left a lingering stench along our path," he wrote, "the smell that would remind us forever of the Soviet paradise into which we found ourselves marching deeper."[35]

Compounding the problem, German leaders systematically over-estimated the damage they were dealing to Soviet forces. Among the most celebrated Soviet accomplishments in the early days of the war was the herculean effort to dismantle western factories and move their components east to locations in the Urals, Siberia, and Kazakhstan. Between 1,500 and 2,500 factories were stripped of their vital machinery, hauled vast distances, and rebuilt in locations out of the Wehrmacht's range. These evacuations, in conjunction with a massive effort to ramp up production in existing eastern factories, allowed the Soviets to increase overall war production even in the midst of the German assault. Soviet factories produced 1,800 tanks in the first half of 1941 and 4,700 in the second half of the year; aircraft, artillery, and rifle production all doubled over the six months following the invasion. The effect, in Zhukov's words, was to transform "the country into a single military camp." Meanwhile, bands of Soviet partisans stalked through the forests and marshes behind German lines. The sheer speed of the Wehrmacht's advance had left thousands of soldiers stranded—many would join local guerrillas in attacks against German forces. In the coming months, the Nazis' brutal occupation policies would only serve to drive more fighters to the partisans' ranks.[36]

And unbeknownst to German leaders, Barbarossa's tipping point was approaching. In early July, German forces reached the walled city of Smolensk, some three hundred miles east of their starting points in Poland. Straddling the banks of the upper Dnieper River, the city held a key railway junction that blocked Army Group Center's approach to Moscow. Soviet leaders recognized the city as a crucial bastion standing in the way of the Nazi advance—their best shot at stopping or at least slowing Barbarossa's crushing momentum. Meanwhile, German leaders hoped to stage a repeat of their massive encirclement of the Red Army west of Minsk. With the shock of the German surprise attack having worn off and Soviet forces having mobilized their reserves, Smolensk would serve as the first true test of the two armies.

The clash at Smolensk would reveal that the Wehrmacht remained a fearsome force capable of pummeling the Red Army in one battle after another. However, the Germans were losing the strategic initiative as the steady drain of men, machines, and supplies blunted their ability to fight the war of maneuver on which Barbarossa's success depended. While the Wehrmacht could win individual engagements, it lacked the resources and units to win a grinding war of attrition. Smolensk would prove to be the tipping point in Barbarossa's transformation. The Wehrmacht had strained its supply chain and depleted its reserves in the drive east. Now, as the summer offensive dragged on, the Germans would find themselves bogged down in the vast spaces of Russia.[37]

Over the course of July 10–11, Guderian's panzer forces crossed the Dnieper west of Smolensk and prepared to attack Soviet positions. Guderian remembered "the beautiful sunshine" as he surveyed the landscape where Napoleon had set up his headquarters nearly 129 years earlier. German vehicles threw up thick clouds of dust that clogged engines as they attacked two Red Army divisions encamped in the nearby woods. Guderian knew nothing of the Soviet reserve armies that were preparing to shore up the defenses near Smolensk. To the Germans' surprise, the supposedly defeated Red Army launched a series of heavy counterattacks on July 13. Three days later, German observers sighted Soviet reinforcements to the east. Soviet attacks continued from positions near Yelnya. In one engagement, the Tenth Panzer Division destroyed fifty Soviet tanks at the cost of a third of its vehicles. But the going was tough. Guderian complained that the area's roads were "swampy and impassable," making all movement "exhausting and time-consuming." By the end of the month, German leaders concluded that they would not be able to reach the Volga by the planned date of October 1. Their new objectives were to advance to the line running from Leningrad to Moscow and to conquer Ukraine. Meanwhile, Guderian's forces continued suffering heavy casualties and their supply of ammunition dwindled. Halder, too, noted his concern over growing German casualties; some units had lost half of their officers. Still, the Wehrmacht continued to rack up battlefield victories against the Red Army, bolstering German convictions that victory remained within reach.[38]

The newly arrived commander of the Soviet forces, General Semyon Timoshenko, deployed the Thirteenth, Nineteenth, Twentieth, Twenty-First, and Twenty-Second Armies in a line to defend the city sector and held back the Fourth and Sixteenth Armies in reserve. Although this concentration of forces proved insufficient to hold Smolensk, which fell on the sixteenth, Soviet commanders managed to slow the German advance and inflict heavy casualties on the attackers. Nevertheless, the Luftwaffe had moved closer to Moscow, allowing German bombers to stage nightly raids on the Soviet capital and forcing the general staff to work out of a basement bomb shelter. In short order, the staff moved its night command post to the Belorussky Subway Station, separated from women and children taking shelter on the platform by only a thin plywood partition. Zhukov would later cite the battle as a key moment in the shift from a war of movement to a war of attrition. "Smolensk played a crucial role in the initial period of the Great Patriotic War," he explained. Though the Germans won the battle, "the enemy striking groups had been exhausted." The general estimated German losses at 250,000 officers and men.[39]

At Smolensk, then, the Wehrmacht had come face-to-face with the enormity of their Soviet adversary. As they marched deeper into Soviet territory, German lines of supply grew longer and more tenuous. "The Russian rearguard elements continued to withdraw before us, attempting to burn many of the few mud and straw huts in our path and always leaving an ever-present cadre of snipers, who slowly extracted a deadly price from our ranks at the cost of their own lives," wrote one soldier. As a German tank officer later explained, "Now it was clear to every one of us that this Russia would be a very hard nut to crack." An army commander writing home from the front lamented, "All past campaigns seem like child's play in comparison with the present war. Our losses are heavy." German commanders shared many of these frustrations. One general complained that "one has the impression that even if Moscow was taken, the war would go on from the depths of this unending country."[40]

These misgivings reached all the way to the top of the Wehrmacht. On August 11, Halder wrote that it was "increasingly plain that we have underestimated the Russian Colossus, who consistently prepared for war with that utterly ruthless determination so characteristic of totalitarian states. . . . At the outset of war we reckoned with about 200 enemy divisions. Now we have already counted 360. Those divisions indeed are not armed and equipped according to our standards, and their tactical leadership is often poor. But there they are, and if we smash a dozen of them, the Russians simply put up another dozen." These accounts reveal that the attrition of Army Group Center had compromised Barbarossa's goal of a swift victory in the East. Perhaps the most pithy assessment came from a German tank commander who observed that the Wehrmacht needed to stop this bloodletting at the hands of the Soviets "if we do not intend to win ourselves to death."[41]

The Wehrmacht's frustrations squared with Moscow's assessments of the battle: Soviet commanders would come to see Smolensk as a victory, albeit a painful one. As Timoshenko told Stalin, "We have completely upset the enemy offensive. The seven or eight tank and motorised divisions and two or three infantry divisions put into action against us have been deprived of offensive capabilities." Zhukov noted that two months into the war, Berlin had achieved none of its strategic objectives of destroying the Red Army, capturing Moscow, and reaching the Volga. Instead, the Germans were taking heavy casualties and quickly losing hold of the strategic initiative. The Wehrmacht remained deadly, but the Red Army could now mass its forces to counter the brunt of the expected German offensive against Moscow.[42]

The Battle of Smolensk, then, marked the point at which the Nazi-Soviet war passed from Hitler's war of maneuver to Stalin's war of attrition. Germany's spectacular victories, which destroyed no fewer than twenty Soviet field armies in 1941, were offset by Moscow's ability to create a staggering fifty-seven new armies by the end of the year. Despite the Wehrmacht's significant and all-too-ephemeral advantages in the opening months of Barbarossa, German forces were only destroying Red Army units at a third of the rate necessary to exhaust Soviet manpower. Indeed, in spite of Germany's growing list of battlefield victories, Barbarossa was grinding down the Wehrmacht, not the Red Army.[43]

Nevertheless, each German victory brought new populations into Hitler's genocidal empire. At the end of July, Nazi authorities forced the approximately 1,200 Jewish residents of Smolensk into a ghetto surrounded by barbed wire in the northeastern Sadki district of the city. Jews were ordered to wear a yellow Star of David on their clothing and prohibited from having contact with any Russian citizens. The following month, Einsatzgruppen raided the neighborhood searching for "officials, agents, criminals, members of the Jewish intelligentsia, and others." Police shot seventy-four people in this initial round and thirty-eight more "intellectuals" soon after. Only workers received a bread ration; other residents were forced to barter with local Russians. These harsh conditions led to widespread malnutrition and typhus and dysentery outbreaks that grew worse over the winter, killing some two hundred residents.[44]

THE BLOODBATH AROUND SMOLENSK FORCED A RECKONING AMONG both the German and Soviet leadership. On July 30, Hitler ordered Army Group Center to hold and mop up the remaining Soviet forces around the city while Army Groups North and South continued pushing forward. The more astute German leadership had begun to recognize that war could no longer be won quickly. Having failed to force the complete collapse of the Soviet central front, German commanders turned to seizing the resources necessary to support a prolonged campaign on the eastern front. At the top of their list were Leningrad's war industries, the Ukrainian breadbasket, and the oil fields of the Caucasus. The pivot to the northern and southern sectors also helped to alleviate growing concerns about the danger of exposing Army Group Center's flanks following the heavy losses at Smolensk.[45]

The closing days of July also revealed a grim truth to leaders in Moscow: the Soviet Union might very well survive, but only by sacrificing millions of lives and abandoning key Soviet cities to the enemy. On July 29, Zhukov reluctantly told Stalin that Kiev should be surrendered to the Wehrmacht. Soviet forces could not defend the city against the coming German assault, and any attempt to do so would sacrifice men and weaken the southwestern front. Instead, the Red Army should withdraw to stronger defensive positions on the eastern banks of the Dnieper River. Stalin, infuriated, immediately rejected the idea. After further consideration, Stalin removed Zhukov as chief of the general staff and sent him to take command of Soviet forces preparing for the Yelnya Offensive southeast of Smolensk.[46] Events would prove Zhukov correct, but not before another catastrophic Soviet defeat.

In the face of Zhukov's warnings, Stalin remained determined to fight the approaching German forces around Kiev. The third-largest city in the Soviet Union and the capital of Ukraine, Kiev held deep cultural and political significance for the nation. Stalin balked at the thought of simply abandoning the ancient city to the Nazis. By early September, Red Army leaders were pleading with the dictator to authorize a withdrawal to the east banks of the Dnieper, warning of catastrophic losses of men and matériel. However, "the mere mention of the urgent need to abandon Kiev," remembered one deputy, "threw Stalin into a rage and he momentarily lost his self-control." Instead, the dictator insisted that the city be defended even in the face of a possible encirclement—a fate that Soviet armies had already suffered in multiple battles in the previous weeks. "Stop looking for lines of retreat and start looking for lines of resistance and only resistance," Stalin thundered. Under Stalin's express orders, the Soviet armies braced themselves for the Nazi onslaught bearing down on Kiev.[47]

Although Soviet commanders ordered a withdrawal on September 17, it came too late for the doomed forces around Kiev. The city fell on September 19 as Wehrmacht forces drove hard to complete the encirclement of four Soviet armies in the vicinity. Nevertheless, the Soviet forces trapped in the Kiev cauldron put up a savage defense. "They are driven back with such losses that one wonders how they can find the courage and the men to keep coming on," one German soldier marveled. "The [Soviet] dead stretched for miles. . . . Their dead, particularly where there had been a fierce battle, formed a carpet." The encircled Soviet forces did not take prisoners—captured Germans were slaughtered; many were mutilated. One group of German prisoners were hung by their hands from trees and burned alive. Wehrmacht units retaliated by executing some four thousand Soviet prisoners and dumping their bodies in antitank ditches. Such actions convinced soldiers on both sides that surrender was futile. Meanwhile, Soviet troops retreating from Kiev left a series of timed bombs set to detonate after the Germans took the city. Arsenals, ammo dumps, and Kiev's Grand Hotel exploded in the following days, killing hundreds of Germans and civilians and igniting fires throughout the city.[48]

Enraged German authorities took their anger out on Kiev's Jewish population. On September 28, Nazi officials ordered the city's Jews to assemble at the intersection of Melnikov and Dokterivska Streets the next morning. In a scene that resembled many others across the

East, the assembled crowds were marched to a ravine called Babi Yar on the outskirts of the city. Witness accounts described how Nazi death squads separated the victims into groups of fifty men, women, and children and forced them to lie face down in the pit. Men with submachine guns then opened fire, and police and prisoners covered the bodies with a mixture of chloride and lime before forcing another group of fifty to lie on top of the corpses. One boy, covered in blood and sand, who protested that he was not a Jew was promptly shot in the face. The executioners fortified themselves with wine throughout the two-day massacre. In this way, the Germans slaughtered over thirty-three thousand people.[49]

The Battle of Kiev was an epic tragedy for the people of Ukraine, for the Red Army, and for Stalin's regime. The Wehrmacht killed or captured well over six hundred thousand Soviet troops, largely because Stalin refused to allow his forces to retreat to stronger defensive positions. But once again, attrition's grim calculus applied even to a victory as triumphant as the one at Kiev. As had been the case at Smolensk, German armies captured the city. But the battle cost the Wehrmacht that which it could least afford to lose: troops and time. Conversely, it took from the Red Army that which it could most afford to sacrifice: space and manpower.

While Army Groups Center and South continued their bloody offensives toward Moscow and through Ukraine, Army Group North swept through the Baltic republics. The local populations—only recently incorporated into the Soviet Union—often welcomed German forces as liberators from the Stalinist regime. However, their hopes for independence were sorely disappointed as German authorities incorporated the Baltic region into the Nazi empire. As elsewhere, the Wehrmacht's invasion spelled doom for the local Jewish populations. In Kaunas, Lithuanian nationalists unleashed a wave of attacks on the city's Jews that Nazi occupation forces organized into a coordinated purge. German authorities created a ghetto in the northern Slobodka section of the city. Jewish leaders organized a functioning resistance organization inside the ghetto charged with helping hundreds of residents escape to join partisan bands operating in the forests outside Kaunas. Nazis and their local collaborators murdered an estimated fifty thousand Jews from Kaunas and the surrounding areas at a killing ground located in the city's old Ninth Fort. Of the city's prewar population of forty thousand Jews, only two thousand would survive the war.[50]

Similar scenes unfolded on the streets of Vilnius, where, on September 6–7, approximately forty thousand Jews were forced into a ghetto in the old quarter. The ghetto was ringed by barbed wire, the windows looking out were covered, and foot traffic was restricted to a single gate on Rudnicka Street. Starting in September, German authorities conducted a series of attacks on the ghetto, murdering approximately one thousand residents on a near-weekly basis. On October 1, 1941, authorities launched an *Aktion*, rounding up several thousand Jews, driving them to a nearby killing grounds at Ponary forest, and shooting them. Two weeks later, the Nazis emptied the smaller of Vilnius's two ghettos, herding the residents to Ponary and shooting between six and eight thousand of them. Another five to seven thousand were killed at the end of the month. Altogether, the Nazis and their local collaborators killed something on the order of 95 percent of Lithuania's over two hundred thousand Jews between 1941 and 1944—the most extensive Holocaust of the war.[51]

While German authorities murdered Baltic Jews, the Wehrmacht marched toward Leningrad. Nestled on a narrow passage of land running between the Neva River and Lake Ladoga to the west and the cold waters of the Gulf of Finland in the east, the city carried enormous significance. Founded by Peter the Great, the former capital of the Russian Empire had witnessed the birth of the Bolshevik Revolution and served as home to the Soviet Baltic Fleet. To Hitler, Leningrad represented a Bolshevik salient thrusting into northern Europe. While the city prepared its defenses, the directors of the Hermitage carefully packed the museum's artistic treasures away on trains heading east to the Urals. Klodt's horses were also taken down from the Anichkov Bridge and buried, safe from artillery fire, in the nearby palace gardens. Meanwhile, parents scrambled to load their children onto buses and cars leaving for the countryside before the Nazis completed their encirclement. The authorities also rushed to tear down steel plants and machine factories before moving them east, beyond the Wehrmacht's reach. Red Army officials rushed to complete trenches and train volunteer defense battalions. "The enemy is at the gates," Stalin's propagandist Andrei Zhdanov warned. "Either the working class of Leningrad will be enslaved and its finest flower destroyed, or we must gather all the strength we have, hit back twice as hard and dig Fascism a grave in front of Leningrad."[52]

In Leningrad, the Nazi empire's logic of war and genocide merged. Rather than losing thousands of troops into a bloody urban battlefield, the Wehrmacht planned to blockade the city, starve its inhabitants, and free up army units for the planned assault on Moscow. On September 4, Axis forces began shelling the Soviet Union's second-largest city. Four days later, the Luftwaffe launched its first bombing raid, igniting fires in a large supply of stored food. But German forces and their Finnish allies stopped short of a full-scale assault on Leningrad, opting instead to encircle the city and place it under siege. Hitler envisioned an even crueler fate for the city than conquest. As Halder wrote in July, "It is the Führer's firm decision to level Moscow and Leningrad and make them uninhabitable, so as to relieve us of the necessity of feeding the population during the war." Hitler announced his plan for Leningrad on September 22: "The Führer has decided to erase the city of Petersburg from the face of the earth. I have no interest in the further existence of this large population center after the defeat of Soviet Russia." Hitler and his generals intended to starve the city not into submission but into oblivion.[53]

As the siege tightened around Leningrad, thirty-four-year-old Elena Kochina, her husband, and their infant daughter, Lena, found themselves trapped. At night German bombers unleashed "a fiery rain of gas and incendiary bombs" upon the city. As Elena and her daughter huddled in the "grave-like cold of the bomb shelter," she wrote in her diary, "Rats crawled along the pipes like tightrope walkers." Meanwhile, her husband stayed on the building's roof in order to smother any flames started by the bombs and watched as fires raged throughout different parts of the surrounding city. As autumn set in, the city doled out ever-more-meager bread rations and hunger began to set in. In October, Elena's milk ran dry and she was no longer able to nurse her daughter. As the weeks wore on, famine seized hold of Leningrad. By December 10, the entire city's malnourished residents limped through the streets. "Some have swollen up and shine as if they're covered with lacquer," Elena wrote. "Others have dried up." By the end of the month, residents of the city were dying in waves. Elena watched the men carting bodies through the streets. "There are a lot of corpses. Death is not a casual visitor now," she wrote. "People die easily, simply, without tears. The dead are wrapped in sheets, tied up with a rope, and carried off to the cemetery where they are stacked in piles . . . [and] buried in common graves."[54]

WHILE LENINGRAD STARVED, WEHRMACHT PLANNERS BEGAN PREPArations for a late-fall offensive against Moscow. Delayed by the heavy fighting around Smolensk, Bock's armies now faced a new enemy: the dreaded autumn rains. Torrential downpours turned the Russian dirt roads to a thick morass of mud that threatened to swallow vehicles, horses, and men and slowed any advance to a crawl. Army Group Center's pause had also allowed Soviet leaders to prepare three major defense lines along what Zhukov described as "the distant approaches to Moscow: the Western Front, the Reserve Front and the Bryansk Front." Put together, these three rings of defense numbered some 800,000 soldiers, 770 tanks, and 9,150 pieces of artillery. Red Army leaders also assembled reserve units in the rear. Meanwhile, workers in Moscow and its surrounding districts labored around the clock, digging trenches and erecting barricades. Key government buildings were camouflaged and a blackout was enforced at night. "The city and its environs were transformed into a fortified camp," Zhukov boasted.[55]

While Moscow's residents transformed the city into an urban fortress, the Wehrmacht resumed its advance toward the capital. On September 6, Hitler called for "a decisive operation" against the Timoshenko Army Group: "This [army group] must be beaten to destruction in the limited time available before the onset of winter weather." The Führer remained focused on the goal of annihilating the Soviet forces now assembled along the approaches to Moscow. Red Army forces commanded by General Ivan Konev deployed to defend the rail hubs at Vyazma and Bryansk from Bock's Army Group Center. Guderian's panzers led the assault at the southern end of the battlefront on September 30. Two days later, German forces some three hundred miles to the north launched Operation Typhoon while a third force prepared to attack the center of the Soviet lines in hopes of staging a double encirclement. The German offensive proved to be a stunning success, tearing through the defenders' ranks and trapping six Soviet armies. One Soviet journalist described a scene of utter chaos:

> Exodus! Biblical exodus! Vehicles are moving in eight lanes, there's the violent roaring of dozens of trucks trying to tear their wheels out of the mud. Huge herds of sheep and cows are driven through the fields . . . thousands of wagons . . . crowds of pedestrians. . . . This isn't a flood, this isn't a river, it's the slow movement of a flowing ocean. . . . We have been transported back in time to the era of biblical catastrophes.

Even so, thousands of troops were enveloped in the Wehrmacht's crushing offensive. The Germans captured a staggering 760,000 prisoners.[56]

The Vyazma-Bryansk encirclements ranked among the Red Army's most catastrophic battles of the war. Unlike in the early battles of Barbarossa, Stalin's forces had not been surprised, nor had they lacked time to prepare. Indeed, Germans noticed Soviet troops preparing extensive fortifications and massing armies across the front. A growing number of Germans recognized that these were not the actions of a defeated enemy. "The real hardships were about to start," wrote one soldier. "The experience so far was only a prelude." Another soldier noted the presence of "Asians, lots of Asians, who . . . fight with utmost determination and devilish cunning." These attacks took a steady toll on the Germans, forcing some to fall back. "A little later those dogs attack again," the soldier wrote. "Only by giving it all our all are we able to keep the fanatical howling horde at bay. . . . It looks like we'll be burying corpses!" German troops continued suffering losses even in victory. Combined with the deteriorating weather, these losses degraded German morale. "Suddenly our task in Russia seemed insurmountable." Roads turned into rivers of mud; tanks, trucks, horses, and men all sank into the morass. "The whole of Russia, so it seemed to us, was one great basin of sticky mud and we were in the middle of it," the soldier complained.[57]

Once again, Nazi leaders declared victory. But soldiers fighting on the ground told a different story. Guderian noted a sense of exhaustion in the field that contrasted sharply with the mood at headquarters, where the "superiors were drunk with the scent of victory." The endless fighting was draining Guderian's strength. Although replacements had arrived, they were not of the same quality as the Wehrmacht's battle-hardened veterans. Progress slowed as vehicles sank into the mud, engines froze or ran out of fuel, and men without winter gear shivered and suffered frostbite in the cold. Checking on his forces, Guderian despaired:

> Only he who saw the endless expanse of Russian snow during this winter of our misery and felt the icy wind that blew across it . . . who drove for hour after hour through that no-man's land only at last to find too thin shelter with insufficiently clothed, half starved men; and who also saw by contrast the well-fed, warmly

clad, and fresh Siberians, fully equipped for winter fighting—only a man who knew all that can truly judge the events which now occurred.

Making matters worse, Guderian's forces were now encountering large numbers of Soviet T-34 tanks, which proved superior to German panzers. "The prospect of rapid, decisive victories was fading," Guderian wrote. "Hitler was living in a world of fantasy." The Wehrmacht's opportunity to "strike a single great blow is fading more and more, and I do not know if it will ever recur," he worried.[58]

As the Germans drew closer, terrified Muscovites did their best to prepare for a lean winter. Residents made coffee from acorns, kept chickens in their yards, and grew onions in their window boxes. Meanwhile, peasants from the countryside drove half-starved cattle, goats, and pigs through the streets to be slaughtered to fill the city's meat lockers. Officials converted Moscow's factories from civilian production to arms manufacturing: the typewriter factory turned out machine guns; a bicycle workshop made flamethrowers. Meanwhile, Soviet leaders drew up a list of everything that was to be destroyed if the city fell to the Germans and assigned demolition teams for the task. All food stores, factories, bakeries, butcher shops, power stations, bridges, telephone exchanges, and transport hubs would be razed if the Nazis took the city. Stalin was determined to leave nothing of value for the invaders. Volunteers organized resistance parties that would stay behind to wage an urban guerrilla campaign against the occupation.[59]

On October 10, Stalin appointed Zhukov commander of the western front. While the Wehrmacht mopped up the remnants of the Soviet forces trapped in the Vyazma pocket, Soviet leaders scrambled to bolster the defensive lines guarding the capital. Engineers worked to set up tank traps and fortifications along likely attack routes while infantry and artillery pulled back to create a more organized front blocking the approaches to the capital. Zhukov credited the forces at Vyazma for buying time to prepare the defenses around Moscow. On October 20, Soviet leaders declared "a state of siege in Moscow and its environs." While air raids on Moscow escalated, continued fighting near Bryansk and Tula blunted the German march on the capital.[60]

On the heels of their victories at Vyazma and Bryansk, Germany's Army Group Center struggled to resume its drive toward Moscow. The brutal autumn weather lashed the Germans with rain, wind, cold, and snow. "The rain again sheeted down, the temperature dropped, the rain gave way to hail, then snow. Then it rained again," remembered Wehrmacht doctor Heinrich Haape. "Marching troops and men on horseback squelched forward through the clinging mud, but vehicles sank three feet deep into the quagmire." Trucks were abandoned, hopelessly mired in the muck. The retreating Red Army also did everything in its power to slow the Germans. As Haape's unit advanced, three soldiers stumbled into a freshly laid minefield. "Two had been killed instantly; the right leg of the third man had been torn out of the hip socket and portions of his entrails were hanging from his horribly gashed belly. He was screaming in agony." The doctor rushed to the wounded soldier, but there was little he could do. As the soldier stared at his mangled body, Haape administered a lethal dose of morphine and waited as he slipped away. His column then wheeled to avoid the minefield and resumed its grim march toward Moscow.[61]

To the south, in Odessa, the rains turned the countryside into an ocean of mud through which the Wehrmacht was now forced to march. "Every few hundred yards there is a broken-down vehicle; or a dead horse with a swollen belly; or a corpse," wrote military surgeon Peter Bamm. "Crows rise with a heavy flapping of wings. Tattered grey clouds chase without pause high above the living and the dead; high above beasts and men." In November, falling temperatures froze the mud, making roads once again passable, but now the Germans found that their equipment was freezing. As one panzer commander, Hans von Luck, wrote, "We were soon forced to thaw the water in the morning with blow lamps . . . [or] leave the engines running throughout the night. . . . No western or southern European or American can imagine what it means to fight in temperatures of 40 C below zero and in icy gales." Exhausted, short on supplies, lacking reserves, their equipment frozen solid, and stranded hundreds of miles into the heart of European Russia, the Wehrmacht marched onward.[62]

While German forces trudged ever deeper into Russia through mud, slush, and snow, the Red Army continued gathering strength. Stalin had ordered the creation of ten new reserve armies to be brought from the east to defend Moscow. Bock's forces exhausted themselves driving forward in one final push toward the capital while Zhukov massed fresh armies for a counterattack. By early December, Soviet workers had excavated nearly a hundred miles of antitank ditches, established seventy-five miles of barbed-wire obstacles, and amassed seventy-five new divisions, forty-four of which were still held in reserve.[63]

Meanwhile, an autumn of hard fighting had ground the German forces down. In late November, the German minister for armaments and ammunition, Fritz Todt, warned Hitler that the war could "no longer be won militarily." Germany lacked the capacity to field a military force capable of defeating the Soviet Union in a war of attrition. The prospect of American entry into the war only made matters worse. The only possible outcome, he explained, was a political settlement. Guderian offered a similarly gloomy assessment. "Our attack on Moscow had broken down," he wrote. "All the sacrifices of our brave troops had been in vain. We had suffered a grievous defeat."[64]

Soviet leaders sensed that the invaders were reaching the point of exhaustion. Wehrmacht forces were spread thin and running short on reserves. Although German and later Western accounts of Barbarossa would point to the Russian winter as Soviet Union's savior, Zhukov insisted, "It was neither rain nor snow that stopped the fascist troops near Moscow." Rather, it was the steadfast defense of the Red Army and the people of the Soviet Union that defeated Hitler's army at the capital's gates. The Germans, he explained, had underestimated the strength of the Red Army. Stubborn resistance by the Soviet forces at Vyazma combined with the actions of the defenders guarding Moscow had overwhelmed the Nazis' already strained resources. In contrast, Zhukov was able to send fresh reserves from the east to attack the Wehrmacht's flanks. On November 29, the general gave Stalin the encouraging news: "The enemy has been bled white," he told the dictator. It was now the Red Army's turn to attack.[65]

On December 5, 1941, the Red Army launched its counteroffensive. Soviet troops marched through a meter of snow in temperatures of 5 degrees Fahrenheit. Soon, six Soviet armies were attacking German positions, forcing the Wehrmacht to shift its units to protect weak areas and pull back to more defensible positions. Three days later, Guderian outlined the situation: "We are faced with the sad fact that the Supreme Command has overreached itself by refusing to believe our reports of the increasing weakness of the troops and by making ever new demands on them, by having made no preparations for the cruel winter weather and by being surprised when the Russian cold reached −32 degrees. The troops were no longer strong enough to capture Moscow. . . . I hope that I shall be able to hold with what is left of my forces. The Russians are pursuing us closely and we must expect misfortunes to occur."[66]

OPERATION BARBAROSSA GAVE HITLER AND HIS COTERIE THAT which they coveted most: a continental empire forged by war and genocide, coupled with a chance to destroy the Bolshevik citadel in the East. The awful power of the Nazi war machine was on full display as German panzers roared across the plains of Eastern Europe, slaughtering millions of Soviet soldiers and citizens in their path. But for all of its success on the battlefield, the fearsome Wehrmacht proved unable to deliver a knockout blow against the Red Army. As they drove deeper into the Russian interior, Hitler's legions were swallowed by the vast expanses of the Russian steppe. Meanwhile, these same expanses gave Stalin and his generals ample room to retreat, regroup, and raise new armies to be hurled against the Nazi invaders.

Millions of Soviet soldiers perished in the suicidal efforts to defend their homeland, but millions more stepped forward to take their place. The bloodbath of the eastern front took shape as an epic clash between continental empires, comprising the single deadliest battle-front in world history. The world's two greatest land powers were now locked in a grinding war of industrial attrition that would drag on for another three and a half years, generate some forty million deaths, and decide the fate of European civilization.

Meanwhile, half a world away, another battle was beginning, this one between maritime empires vying for supremacy in the Pacific. While Soviet troops pounded the Wehrmacht along the icy approaches to Moscow, Japanese warplanes struck the American fleet anchored in the shallow waters of Pearl Harbor: the centerpiece of a stunning transhemispheric offensive against the Western-controlled territories of Guam, Hawaii, Hong Kong, Malaya, the Philippines, Singapore, and Wake Island.[67]

Chapter 8

JAPAN'S GRAND OFFENSIVE

A T 5:30 IN THE PREDAWN HOURS OF DECEMBER 7, 1941, A PAIR OF floatplanes rocketed off the Japanese cruisers *Chikuma* and *Tone* to scout the approaches to Hawaii. Violent waves sent plumes of water crashing across the decks as the ships rocked back and forth in the rough swells of the central Pacific some 230 miles north of Oahu. Across the task force's six aircraft carriers, pilots received their orders. "The rise or fall of the empire depends upon this battle," fleet commander Isoroku Yamamoto had remarked. "Everyone will do his duty with utmost efforts." Crews made their final preparations as the aircraft warmed their engines in the darkness. At 6:00, the initial aircraft launched into the air. Less than two hours later, Second Lieutenant Margaret Olsen of the US Army Nurse Corps was bathing infants in the station hospital in Schofield Barracks, Pearl Harbor, when an explosion shook the building. The sound of fighter planes roared in the skies overhead. "Stay away from the windows and doors!" a corps-man yelled. "The Japs are bombing Pearl Harbor." Olsen ran to the pharmacy to get more drugs for the wounded. Outside, she looked up and saw planes streaking low across the sky. "You could see the rising sun [symbol on the planes]," she remembered, "and you could see the pilot." Soon, litters with injured personnel filled the floor of the station hospital. Most were suffering from shrapnel wounds in the abdomen. "They were having breakfast, and they just mowed 'em down," she explained. "I was just mad 'cause they upset Christmas. It upset everything for us."[1]

Five thousand miles to the west, eleven-year-old Oscar Villadolid woke up to go golfing with his father in Manila—the capital of America's colony in the Philippines. "The sun had just filtered through the early morning mist when Dad and his companions took turns teeing off," he remembered. As they finished the sixteenth hole, Villadolid "heard the thunderous drone of planes high up in the sky somewhere over Manila." Looking up, the boy noticed "red balls" on the wings of the planes. "Hapon! Hapon!" his father shouted in Tagalog as the golfers scrambled for cover. "Guerra na! Guerra na!"[2]

Fifteen hundred miles southwest of Manila, in the British colony of Singapore, Yeoh Siang Aun was awoken at 4:00 a.m. by wailing air-raid sirens. Looking up, he saw the predawn skies illuminated by searchlights that every so often reflected off planes flying overhead. "And then we suddenly heard the swish . . . as if bombs dropping," the young student recalled. "Nobody had put off the lights. From the hill behind the Medical College, we could see the lights of the harbour."[3]

Sixteen hundred miles north of Singapore, Punjabi soldiers were already fighting against Japanese forces in the British colony of Hong Kong. Just before 5:00 a.m., British commanders ordered the Royal Engineers to detonate the frontier belt of demolitions east and north of Fanling. Three hours later, Japanese planes began attacks on the Kai Tak Airport. "Cruising leisurely over the field," British reports read, "the Japanese airmen bombed these targets with no more difficulty than if they had been on bombing practice on a range in peace time."[4]

The Pacific empires were now at war. Japan had staged an audacious attack across nearly eight thousand miles of the ocean, opening the broadest battlefront in world history. While many American accounts of the attacks focus exclusively on the Pearl Harbor operation, the opening blows of the Pacific War constituted something far more ambitious: a coordinated, multipronged assault on the bastions of Western imperialism across nearly a third of the globe. Japan's grand offensive struck Washington and London's most strategically significant Pacific outposts in an all-out effort to topple the Anglo-American supremacy in the region.[5] If successful, Japanese forces would achieve the unprecedented feat of destroying four centuries of Western colonial rule in Asia and replace it with a new racial and geopolitical order controlled by the imperial overlords in Tokyo. The battle for the Greater East Asia Co-Prosperity Sphere had begun.

As 1940 drew to an end, President Franklin Roosevelt confronted a world filled with problems. On December 14, Ambassador Joseph Grew sent the White House a blunt cable from Japan: Washington and Tokyo were headed toward a showdown. Years of patient diplomacy had been scrapped by militant factions in Tokyo. Grew warned that no moderate Japanese leaders could oppose expansionism and hope to stay in power. As a result, "Japan has become openly and unashamedly one of the predatory nations and part of a system which aims to wreck about everything that the United States stands for." The war in Europe added a layer of complexity to the coming US-Japanese confrontation, and Washington must soon decide how to manage the crises in both the Atlantic and the Pacific. Ultimately, unless Washington was prepared "to withdraw bag and baggage from the entire sphere of 'Greater East Asia including the South Seas' (which God forbid), we are bound eventually to come to a head-on clash with Japan."[6]

After more than a month of consideration, Roosevelt responded to Grew. "I believe that the fundamental proposition is that we must recognize that the hostilities in Europe, in Africa, and in Asia are all parts of a single world conflict," he wrote. American interests were threatened in both Europe and Asia, and the nation was already preparing to defend itself. "Our strategy of self-defense must be a global strategy which takes account of every front and takes advantage of every opportunity to contribute to our total security." Washington's priority must be to ensure the survival of the British Empire, which in turn depended on both the defense of the home islands and control of imperial resources and supply lines. "Our strategy of giving them assistance toward ensuring our own security must envisage both sending of supplies to England and helping to prevent a closing of channels of communication to and from various parts of the world." The president remained confident that London would eventually prevail, but he warned that "she may not have left the strength" to restore the prewar order in the Far East.[7] In the near term, then, the United States would work to save London's global empire. However, after the Axis defeat, Roosevelt's cable implied, Washington might find itself in a position to define the postwar order in the Far East.

Nevertheless, for the time being, Japan remained a serious threat to the American position in the region. No problem seemed more vexing than that of the US colony in the Philippines. The distant islands had long troubled US strategic planners. On the one hand, the Philippines functioned as a launchpad to Asia. The islands and the 1898 Spanish-American War that had brought them under US control had transformed the United States into an empire. During its four decades of control, US colonial authorities had built a network of fortifications across the islands, including harbor defenses at Manila and Subic Bays, forts on Corregidor and Grande Islands, and a number of airfields, bases, and training camps. From these bases, the United States could project commercial influence and military power into the Far East. Along with bases in Guam and Hawaii, the Philippines formed the infrastructure of US imperial power in the Pacific. On the other hand, the US installations in the Philippines were a vulnerable salient thousands of miles across the Pacific, surrounded by threats. In the event of a war, US planners warned, the archipelago's seven thousand islands and twenty-two thousand miles of coastline would be nearly impossible to defend against an invading force—particularly one such as the Japanese navy, which was operating from nearby bases in the Western Pacific.[8]

Further complicating matters, strong voices in the US military insisted that the Philippines must be defended in the event of a war. Among the loudest advocates of defending the islands was General Douglas MacArthur. A leading contender for the title of most ego-tistical officer in the US military, MacArthur had spent part of his childhood in the Philippines while his father, Lieutenant General Arthur MacArthur, had served as governor general of the islands from 1900 to 1901. After a decorated career in the US Army, during which he had served as superintendent of West Point and army chief of staff, Douglas MacArthur had retired to accept a post as the top military adviser to Manuel Quezon, president of the Philippines. In this role, he launched an impassioned campaign to convince US lead-ers to commit to defending the entire archipelago. In the face of the general's bullying and preoccupied with events in Europe, American strategists relented.

The Philippines were not the only problematic US possession in the Pacific. For half a century, Hawaii had occupied a key position in the US-Japanese imperial rivalry. President William McKinley had annexed Hawaii during the Spanish-American War. McKinley's decision had been driven in no small part by Japanese efforts to exert control over the islands. Compounding US fears, people of Japanese ancestry comprised the largest ethnic group in Hawaii. By 1920, they made up 40 percent of the population. Although Japan had relin-quished its claims to the islands, Hawaii remained as a sort of colonial crossroads between Japan and the United States.[9] As such, Roosevelt's decision to move the Pacific Battle Fleet to Hawaii as a show of force aimed at Tokyo carried added symbolic weight, as did Japan's even-tual decision to attack the American fleet at Pearl Harbor.

Moreover, although Americans would come to see Hawaii as integral to the United States in the years following the war, this was not the case prior to 1941. Hawaii existed in a sort of limbo between outright colony and statehood. Instead of referring to the islands as a colony, US officials were encouraged to employ the euphemistic "territory." Nevertheless, many Americans continued to refer to the Kingdom of Hawaii as a colony. For example, the *Daily Boston Globe* wrote in 1937 that Congress was considering granting statehood to the "colony" of Hawaii. However, given its large nonwhite population, many Americans remained staunchly opposed to accepting Hawaii as the forty-ninth state. As a result, residents of the islands had no voting rights in Congress and were subject to control from Washington. This marginal status prompted the American Civil Liberties Union to include Hawaii in a pamphlet lamenting the "deplorable state" of democratic rights in "America's colonies" in February 1939. Hawaii, the pamphlet explained, was best understood as a "colon[y] with territorial status." Indeed, the annexation of the islands "was the first of [the United States'] major imperialist ventures." As atlas publisher Rand McNally explained in 1942, "Although Hawaii belongs to the United States, it is not an integral part of this country. It is foreign to our continental shores, and therefore cannot logically be shown in the United States proper." Even after the Pearl Harbor attacks, then, US mapmakers remained reluctant to include the islands as part of the nation.[10]

Like the Philippines, Hawaii constituted an important link in the chain of US military bases in the East. Roosevelt's decision to deploy the US Battle Fleet to Pearl Harbor in 1940 had sent a message to Tokyo that the United States was prepared to defend its Pacific possessions. However, the US military presence in Hawaii—not unlike the stationing of US forces in the Philippines—created a dilemma for planners. Although envisioned as a deterrent to Japanese aggression in the Western Pacific, the Pearl Harbor deployment left US ships exposed to a potential Japanese attack. In 1932, the navy had conducted a live war game simulating a possible clash in the Pacific in which an attacking force of aircraft carriers staged a successful strike on Pearl Harbor. However, rather than taking note of the base's vulnerability, navy officials dismissed the results.[11]

A second warning arrived in September 1940 when the commander in chief of the US fleet, Admiral James O. Richardson, questioned Roosevelt's decision to keep the Pacific Battle Fleet around Hawaii. He explained that the base facilities in the area were simply inadequate for fleet operations: they were congested, exposed, and unable to accommodate large ships. Moreover, he argued, in the event of hostilities, the fleet would be forced to return to the West Coast in order to be fully armed and mobilized. A month later, Richardson told Roosevelt himself that while the fleet's presence might intimidate a civilian government, the military leadership in Tokyo would not be impressed. If Washington hoped to send a message to the Japanese, Richardson advised, the best course of action would be to recall the fleet to the West Coast, where it could be readied for war. Roosevelt disagreed, insisting that Japan had been restrained by the presence of the fleet in Hawaii. Four months later, Richardson was removed from command.[12]

Yet another warning arrived in January 1941 when the secretary of the navy, William Franklin Knox, notified Washington of the threat of a carrier-based attack against Pearl Harbor. "If war eventuates with Japan," Knox wrote to Secretary of War Henry Stimson, "it is believed easily possible that hostilities would be initiated by a surprise attack upon the Fleet or the Naval Base at Pearl Harbor." The greatest danger would come from aerial attacks launched from aircraft carriers. That same month, Ambassador Grew informed Washington of a report "that the Japanese military forces planned, in the event of trouble with the United States, to attempt a surprise attack on Pearl Harbor using all of their military facilities."[13]

But top US officials downplayed the possibility of a surprise attack on Hawaii. In May 1941, Army Chief of Staff George Marshall described Oahu as "the strongest fortress in the world." Moreover, withdrawal from the Pacific bases in the Philippines and Hawaii would send a message to the American people that Washington was retreating from its standoff with Tokyo. By early 1941, Roosevelt, fresh on the heels of an unprecedented third victory in a presidential election, sought engagement with the mounting world crisis, not withdrawal. Washington had long recognized the problem of Japanese expansionism, but the president favored a passive policy of "strangulation" designed to choke off the flow of economic resources to Japan and rein in Tokyo's ambitions. This approach, supported by the symbolic power of the fleet's forward deployment to Pearl Harbor, took advantage of US economic supremacy over Japan and allowed Washington to focus on the Europe-first strategy outlined in Admiral Harold Stark's Plan Dog memo.[14]

Washington now worked to forge a close military partnership with London aimed at defending the US sphere of influence across the Western Hemisphere and maintaining the integrity of the British Empire. In January 1941, US and British military planners met in Washington under the auspices of the secret ABC-1 Talks to hammer out a long-term strategy for defeating the Axis powers. The group agreed on a plan for close coordination at every level, from top-level planning to field command. They identified their three top strategic priorities as security of the Western Hemisphere, the defense of the United Kingdom and the British Commonwealth, and security of sea communications. Once again, well before officially entering the war, US military leaders had committed to using their power to preserve America's hemispheric superiority and defend the British Empire. The talks also reaffirmed Washington's support for a Europe-first strategy. Allied forces would play for time in the Pacific while working to hold the line against further Japanese expansion. "If Japan does enter the war, the Military strategy in the Far East will be defensive," the planners decided. In this regard, British and American colonies in Singapore, Malaya, the Philippines, and Hawaii would serve as the first line of defense against the Japanese Empire.[15]

With the bulk of the fleet deployed to defend and supply the British Isles, London's strategy in the Pacific relied on the heavily fortified base at Singapore. In the event of a war with Japan, British forces would use Singapore to anchor their defenses while the fleet made the long journey from Europe to Southeast Asia. But the fall of France and the resulting crisis in Europe had forced London to concentrate its resources in the Atlantic, leaving its forces in the Far East depleted. "In present circumstances," the chiefs of staff admitted in June 1941, "we cannot send a Fleet to the Far East." Making matters worse, recent Japanese advances into French Indochina represented a clear danger to British colonies across the region and to the Singapore base. Nevertheless, London's lines of communication to Australia, New Zealand, and India all depended on holding the island as a base of British naval strength. British leaders were left with no other choice but to strengthen Singapore's defenses and hope for the best while trying to delay a Japanese attack. Ultimately, by focusing their efforts on Europe, American and British leaders accepted that their operations in the Pacific would depend on a shoestring budget.[16]

JAPANESE LEADERS RECOGNIZED THAT THE KEY TO BUILDING THEIR Co-Prosperity Sphere lay in knocking out American and British bases in Southeast Asia and the Pacific and destroying the military infrastructure of Western colonial rule. Only then could the empire secure the strategic resources it needed to continue fighting the war in China. Access to the rich oil fields in the Dutch East Indies sat at the top of Tokyo's list. But Dutch officials in Batavia rebuffed Japanese demands, leading to a breakdown of negotiations on June 18, 1941. Following the failure of this diplomacy, Japanese forces entered Indochina in preparation for a broader thrust into Southeast Asia.[17]

Four days after the failure of Japanese negotiations with the Dutch, Germany launched Operation Barbarossa. Like the fall of France the previous year, the Wehrmacht's invasion of the Soviet Union presented another opening for Japanese action in the Far East. While voices in the army pushed for an attack on the Soviet Union, the navy continued pushing operations aimed at Southeast Asia. Much would depend on the outcome of the struggle in Eastern Europe. Army Minister Hideki Tojo predicted that the Soviets would continue retreating until Stalin's government collapsed. It was possible, however, that the Red Army would engage the Wehrmacht in a "decisive battle," which would play into German hands. Alternatively, Soviet forces might stage a fighting retreat while wearing down the Nazi invaders—a strategy that favored the Red Army. In light of this uncertainty, Tokyo adopted a wait-and-see policy toward the German-Soviet war. In the interim, Japan would accelerate its southern advance by establishing bases in Indochina and Thailand aimed at securing control of the Co-Prosperity Sphere.[18]

On July 28, 1941, Japanese troops began disembarking from ships at Nha Trang, Indochina. Meanwhile, workers cleared out docks and warehouses in Saigon's port in preparation for more Japanese landings in the southern capital. Although Vichy officials were cooperative, it remained clear to all that this was a military occupation. "The Japanese Government is giving clear indication that it is determined to pursue an objective of expansion by force or threat of force," the US State Department announced. Privately, Admiral Stark warned Japanese ambassador Kichisaburo Nomura that the United States would devastate Japan in the event of a war between the two nations. "While you may have your initial successes due to timing and surprise, the time will come when you too will have your losses, but there will be this great difference. You will not only be unable to make up your losses but will grow weaker as time goes on; while on the other hand we will not only make up our losses but will grow stronger as time goes on. It is inevitable that we shall crush you before we are through with you."[19]

On August 1, the White House responded to Tokyo's occupation of Indochina by leveling an oil embargo on all petroleum products to Japan. The clock was now ticking. Japanese leaders calculated that their current petroleum reserves would be exhausted in less than two years. Washington's embargo represented a direct threat to one of Japan's most vital strategic commodities. One Japanese official explained that his nation was "like a fish in a pond from which the water was gradually being drained away." Making matters worse, the German offensive in the Soviet Union had slowed, and it now began to appear that Stalin's regime would survive. Japanese officials watched US tankers brimming with oil steaming into Soviet ports on the Pacific and US naval vessels bringing reinforcements to the Philippines. Admiral Nobutake Kondo, commander of the Japanese Second Fleet, outlined these fears. "If we don't start war now," he warned, "we shall be 'gradually pauperized,' until finally we don't have the slightest chances of success. . . . If [the Americans] further reinforce their buildup, we won't be able to cope with it." Tokyo recognized that the Western powers were building a fortified ring around Japan and preparing to strangle the Co-Prosperity Sphere in its cradle. Any offensive against the Soviet Union would need to wait. The southern advance must take top priority.[20]

As Admiral Kondo explained in mid-September, "We stand a chance of success in a quick and decisive war." But in a drawn-out conflict, the United States "would rapidly outbuild Japan and the disparity between naval ratios will progressively widen so that Japan will not be able to cope with it." Captain Shingo Ishikawa, chief of the navy's planning section, echoed this sentiment. "Our empire is under siege by enemies," he wrote in his diary, "and by resorting to war we will be taking a desperate action to break through and seek our survival. And this step must be taken just as soon as possible because of accelerated Anglo-American military and economic oppression of Japan."[21]

As a joint army and navy document from early September explained, the empire must launch its bid as soon as possible in order to preserve its freedom of action. A subsequent conference held in October concluded that Japan would need to occupy the oil fields of the Dutch East Indies no later than March or April 1942 if it hoped to bring production online and ensure a sufficient supply of oil to continue fighting. Any delay beyond this time could prove fatal. This left Tokyo with mere months to either convince Washington to lift the embargo or seize oil fields in the Dutch East Indies. Tokyo would not place its faith in diplomacy. Japanese commanders would begin preparations for war.[22]

However, a direct assault on Batavia's oil fields was unfeasible. Even if Japanese troops succeeded in seizing the Dutch East Indies, Tokyo's lines of communication would be fatally exposed to attacks from US forces in the Philippines and British forces in Malaya. The only way to guarantee access to the archipelago's vital resources was to first neutralize the threat from the Anglo-American colonies. Japanese planners concluded that their best chance was to launch a sweeping campaign to conquer Thailand, the Gilbert Islands, Guam, and Wake Island before turning to seize Malaya, Singapore, the Philippines, the Dutch East Indies, and Burma. Tokyo would then present the British and the Americans with a fait accompli. Tokyo hoped that Washington and London would then agree to a negotiated settlement rather than risking a bloody and protracted war to reclaim their distant Pacific colonies.[23]

Nevertheless, if the United States chose to fight, the Japanese fleet would activate a war plan in development since 1907. During the opening phase of the conflict, Japanese submarines would lie in wait for the US fleet as it set off across the Pacific, launching a relentless stream of torpedo attacks designed to wear US forces down. As US ships approached Japanese waters, the Imperial Navy's main fleet would sail out to engage them in a decisive battle. The American fleet would be swarmed by Japanese aircraft launched from bases and carriers while cruisers and destroyers mounted night attacks on the hapless US vessels. Japanese forces would choose the time and place of the battle and fight with the advantages of short supply lines and air superiority. In this way, Japan would deliver a crushing blow to the American fleet and secure supremacy across the Western Pacific. Though devastating on paper, this ambush plan was by no means guaranteed to work. US forces might choose not to launch a direct attack across the broad expanses of the Pacific Ocean and instead stage an island-hopping campaign, inching ever closer to Japan while avoiding Tokyo's trap.[24]

As the long-anticipated war with the United States drew closer, some officials in the Japanese navy came to doubt their chances for success. The interception scheme was a plan to win a battle, not a war. Even if Japan managed to intercept and destroy the US fleet, America remained a massive economic power capable of rebuilding its forces and waging a drawn-out war of attrition in the Pacific. Japanese leaders estimated that the United States possessed triple the ship-building capacity of Japan. While Tokyo could secure initial operational victories, Japan had little hope of winning a protracted conflict against the US Navy. But public admission of these doubts would undercut the navy in its interservice rivalry with the army. As one Japanese official later explained, "After so many years of clamoring about its 'invincible fleet,' [the navy] was hardly in a position to say it could not take on the United States."[25]

Ironically, the one officer who did voice his objections to fighting a war with the United States was the same man who would mastermind Tokyo's opening attack: Admiral Isoroku Yamamoto. The admiral was convinced that chances of victory were vanishingly slim. "If we are ordered to do it, then I can raise havoc with them [the American navy] for the first six months or a year," he had told Prince Konoe in September 1940, "but I have absolutely no confidence as to what would happen if it went on for two or three years." After receiving his orders, he warned, "To fight the United States is like fighting the whole world. But it has been decided. So I will fight the best I can. Doubtless I shall die on board *Nagato* [his flagship]. Meanwhile Tokyo will be burnt to the ground three times."[26] Having failed to convince Japan's leaders of the folly of war, Yamamoto set about devising a plan that offered the best hope of success. After watching Japan lose one war game after another against the US Navy, he became convinced that the interception strategy would not work. Instead, he insisted that Japan's best chance for success lay in launching a crippling initial strike against the American fleet that would prove so demoralizing that the United States would lose the will to fight a longer war. In early 1941, he argued that Japan must "fiercely attack and destroy the U.S.

main fleet at the outset of the war, so that the morale of the U.S. Navy and her people" would be utterly devastated: "We should do our very best at the outset of the war with the United States . . . to decide the fate of the war on the very first day."[27]

The targets for this surprise attack would be Western colonial bases across the Pacific: British Malaya, Hong Kong, Guam, Pearl Harbor, the Philippines, Wake Island, and Singapore. Indeed, every territory that the Japanese military would strike on December 7–8 was a Western colonial possession. This choice of targets conformed with Japan's larger goal of replacing the Western empires in Western Pacific. Japanese leaders hoped that, following this opening strike on military installations in the Pacific, Allied leaders would choose to cut their losses. The United States lay thousands of miles away from Asia and the Americans had little need of the region's resources. Leaders in Tokyo determined, therefore, that the seizure of a Japanese sphere of influence posed little threat to US vital interests. With its fleet decimated and the Third Reich occupying most of Europe and patrolling the Atlantic, the Americans, they hoped, would not have the heart to fight a bloody war in the Far East to help the British, French, and Dutch regain control of their colonies.[28]

However, leaders in Tokyo failed to account for the sea change that had taken place in Washington's conception of American vital interests. The Roosevelt administration had come to see its overseas concerns as comprising far more than a sphere of influence in the Western Hemisphere and a handful of islands across the Pacific Ocean. Rather, as documents such as the Atlantic Charter suggested, US leaders had increasingly come to perceive their vital security interests as encompassing the very structure of the global order itself.

THROUGH THE FALL OF 1941, US INTELLIGENCE PICKED UP NUMEROUS signals pointing to the approaching attack. In late October, the US consulate in Saigon reported Japanese troop concentrations in Indochina, particularly near the southern borders. Alongside these troops,

Tokyo had sent new military equipment, including aircraft, tanks, and artillery. The Japanese had also accelerated construction of airfields, radio stations, barracks, and a pier at Vung Tau. "The stage is clearly being set for the accommodation of a large army with which to attack Thailand." Meanwhile, cryptographers in the Magic code-breaking program reported that Tokyo considered the present negotiations with Washington to represent their "last possible bargain." Puzzled US officials predicted that Japan might be preparing an attack on Yunnan Province, Malaya, Thailand, or the Philippines. But critical pieces of information were still missing.[29]

In mid-November, Washington's commercial attaché in Japan warned that Japanese leaders were approaching their breaking point. It had been three months since Japan had received any supplies of petroleum, copper, iron, steel, or aluminum. Tokyo could only sustain present levels of production for ten to twelve months, and Japan would run out of fuel within two years. "No nation can erect a wall around its national defense structure," he explained. Japan now faced three options: surrender its dreams of becoming a great power, "make an all-out effort to establish her Greater East Asia Co-Prosperity Sphere and finish the China Affair," or reach a diplomatic settlement with the United States.

[By] pooling her entire resources and taking a desperate gamble on victory in a short "blitzkrieg" she could, from an economic standpoint, wage what might be termed a fairly efficient war for a few months, at the end of which time she would be economically bankrupt. The remaining alternative is to forego [sic] her aggressive action in the Far East and "make the best out of a bad bargain." . . . This leaves only two moves, i.e., war or an agreement with the United States. A decision must be made in the very near future. On this decision rests the nation's destiny.

By the end of the month, the White House concluded that war was imminent. Reports of Japanese troop movements streamed into

Washington, indicating a likely offensive somewhere in Southeast Asia. Dutch sources warned of the arrival of a Japanese expeditionary force near Palao; British officials reported that Japan had evacuated all but four hundred of the seven thousand Japanese citizens in the Dutch East Indies; the US consulate in Hanoi relayed a rumor that Tokyo was preparing to attack Thailand in early December; and the US consulate in Saigon reported the arrival of tens of thousands of Japanese troops and the seizure of all pier space in the harbor. On November 25, Roosevelt held a meeting with Secretary of State Cordell Hull, Secretary of the Navy William Franklin Knox, Army Chief of Staff George Marshall, Admiral Harold Stark, and Secretary of War Henry Stimson. The president explained that the United States was "likely to be attacked perhaps (as soon as) next Monday." The attack would come as a surprise, most likely somewhere in Southeast Asia. "The question," Marshall later recalled, "was how we should maneuver [the Japanese] into the position of firing the first shot without allowing too much danger to ourselves."[30]

The next morning, Roosevelt and Hull agreed that the Nomura negotiations had failed and that war was "possible at any moment." That same day, Hull delivered what amounted to an ultimatum to Ambassador Nomura. Washington's proposal required Tokyo to withdraw its troops from China and Indochina, pledge to not interfere in the internal affairs of neighboring countries, and enter into a nonaggression pact with the Western powers in exchange for a resumption of trade with the United States. Upon receiving Hull's note, leaders in Tokyo concluded that there was now no other choice besides war. The United States had not negotiated in good faith and had instead coordinated with the other Western empires to encircle Japan and force Tokyo into a subservient position in the Far East. "If the Japanese Empire accepts the United States' terms, Japan cannot hope to maintain self-existence and self-defense or the security of Greater East Asia," officials concluded. "Moreover, all the efforts which have been exerted during the past four years to obtain a settlement of the China Incident will come to naught. This is unbearable for Japan, and her prestige and very existence are at stake." On December 7, at the urging of Tokyo's military leadership, the emperor agreed to go to war with the United States. The following day, one hour after Japanese forces began their attack, Tokyo declared war.[31]

Sunday, December 7, was warm and pleasant in Tokyo. American journalist Otto Tolischus noted that it was a quiet news day aside from the announcement that Japanese troops were marching in the south. "All Japan seemed to be waiting for something," he later remembered. Tolischus spent the day writing a story about Ambassador Joseph Grew. His piece opened with the mood in the Japanese capital, as he saw it. "[The] descendants of the Samurai are reviving the old cry against the 'foreign barbarians' and propose to return to a new kind of isolation not only of Japan, but of the entire Orient, in the name of the 'Greater East Asia Coprosperity Sphere' put under Japanese control and dedicated to the exclusion of all Occidental influence. . . . As a result, the long-predicted war between the white and yellow races in general, and war between Japan and the United States in particular, has become an imminent possibility." Early the next morning, loud pounding at his door woke Tolischus. He opened his bedroom door to find four men standing outside. "We are from the Metropolitan Police," they announced. "Put on your coat. The procurator wants to see you." The men were in high spirits. "There has been a battle," they told the confused journalist. "Manila, Singapore, and Hong Kong have been bombed."[32]

Over a seven-hour period, Japanese forces struck targets in Thailand, Malaya, Hawaii, the Philippines, Guam, Hong Kong, and Wake Island. The offensive began with attacks on Thailand and Malaya before dawn. Around 2:00 a.m., Japanese troops attacked the Thai frontier and staged landings along the coast. Thai soldiers attempted a defense but were quickly overwhelmed by the Imperial Japanese Army. By 7:30, the Thai government had ordered its troops to stand down. Thailand, the only Southeast Asian nation never to have been colonized by a Western power, was forced to submit. Meanwhile, Japanese forces to the south staged landings along the Malay Peninsula at Singora and Kota Bharu. Local resistance and rough tides delayed the Japanese landings in some areas, but the peninsula's long beaches proved impossible to defend. As infantry stormed the beaches, Japanese aircraft attacked Singapore and Tengah Air Base. British newspaper editor Jimmie Glover was awoken by a thundering crash. "Good heavens, that's bombs," his wife Julienne exclaimed. "The Japs are here." Glover watched searchlights sweeping across the night sky as the explosions continued.[33]

Halfway across the Pacific, Commander Mitsuo Fuchida's plane broke through a bank of clouds to look out over Kahuku Point at the northern tip of Oahu. Peering through his binoculars, Fuchida sighted eight American battleships anchored in Pearl Harbor and gave the order for his pilots to attack. The commander's plane circled to the east as he kept an eye on the unfolding battle. Soon, columns of black smoke began to rise over the army air base at Wheeler Field as waterspouts shot up among the battleships. Aboard the battleship *Arizona*, American sailor George Phraner was scrambling to carry ammunition to the ship's forward five-inch gun when the first bombs hit. Below deck, he found himself shrouded in darkness and choking on smoke. Struggling for air, he climbed a scorching-hot ladder to escape, his hands sizzling against the handrails. Gasping as he reached the deck, he looked over "to see nothing but a giant wall of flame and smoke." He later recalled, "Behind me a marine lay dead on the deck, his body split in two. I began to realize there were dead men all around me." Over the next seventy-five minutes, two waves of Japanese warplanes pummeled the base, damaging all eight battleships—four of which were sunk—as well as three cruisers and three destroyers, destroying 169 aircraft, and killing 2,403 people. Fortunately for the Americans, the fleet's three aircraft carriers were at sea. As a result, they remained unscathed, and their absence helped convince the commander of the Japanese force, Admiral Chuichi Nagumo, to call off a third wave of attacks for fear that the American ships might be lurking nearby, preparing for a counterattack. George Charland, a marine serving at the base, was given the grisly task of searching the harbor for bodies, and body parts, of those who had been killed. "Our orders were: 'If you find survivors, pick them up. If you find dead body parts, pick those up, too.'"[34]

While the Pearl Harbor operation seized Washington's attention, Tokyo's attack against the Western empires in the Pacific was only just beginning. As Fuchida's bombers flew away from the carnage on Oahu, Japanese aircraft from Saipan prepared to strike US installations on Guam and Wake Island. Japanese forces bombed Guam for two days before staging a dawn landing on the island's northwestern and eastern beaches that quickly overwhelmed the small force of US Marines. American defenders fought off a similar assault on the beaches of Wake Island that same day and managed to hold out until Japanese reinforcements arrived on December 23. By seizing the islands, Tokyo severed communications with the American colony of the Philippines. Japanese commanders planned to attack the Philippines at daylight on the eighth—three hours after the Pearl Harbor attack, owing to the differing time of sunrise between the Central and Western Pacific—but a dense fog shrouded their airfields, forcing further delay.[35]

However, Japanese commanders need not have worried. MacArthur's headquarters in the Philippines was in a state of chaos as reports of attacks across the Pacific streamed in. The general and his closest staff would wait five hours before authorizing air strikes against Japanese air bases in Formosa, by which time it would be too late. US aircraft—including the much-vaunted B-17s—were still being fueled and loaded with bombs when the first wave of Japanese bombers appeared in the skies over Luzon. "I have never been able to get the real story of what happened in the Philippines," Commanding General of the US Air Forces Henry "Hap" Arnold later wrote.[36]

Tokyo was also perplexed by the Americans' lack of resistance. Japanese pilots, running some six hours behind schedule, were astonished to find that the US defenses around the Philippines had not yet been activated. "We met no opposition," returning pilots remarked. "What is the matter with the enemy?" The Japanese attackers had found the American planes "lined up on the target fields as if in peacetime." The raid destroyed seventeen of the army's B-17 bombers, fifty-three P-40 and three P-35 fighters, and twenty-five to thirty other aircraft. Many of the remaining planes were badly damaged and US airfields were wrecked. Eighty servicemen were killed. Thanks to MacArthur's dithering, the strongest American air force unit outside the United States had been decimated while it sat on the ground.[37]

Japan's attacks shook leaders in Washington, who suddenly found their nation at war. President Roosevelt was clearly rattled by the news. Labor Secretary Frances Perkins remembered watching the president struggle to articulate the reality that the navy had been caught off guard. Nevertheless, Perkins also sensed "a wave of relief." For months, the administration had agonized over the question of how to respond to an expected Japanese attack that was limited to European bases in the Pacific. Roosevelt doubted that the American people would be willing to go to war to defend British forces in Singapore. However, by attacking the Philippines and Pearl Harbor, Tokyo had solved the president's dilemma. As Harry Hopkins, adviser to Roosevelt, explained, the decision between war and peace was now "entirely out of [Roosevelt's] hands, because the Japanese had made the decision for him." Across the Atlantic, Winston Churchill struggled to contain his enthusiasm. "Now at this very moment I know the United States was in the war," he wrote, "up to the neck and in to the death. So we had won after all!"[38]

The following afternoon, Roosevelt stood at the podium before a joint session of Congress. "Yesterday, December 7, 1941—a date which will live in infamy—the United States of America was suddenly and deliberately attacked by naval and air forces of the Empire of Japan," he intoned. Japanese forces had bombed "the American island of Oahu," he told the assembled representatives, causing "severe damage to American naval and military forces." The president chose to focus his address on the Pearl Harbor attacks, using a pencil to cross out the reference to the Philippines that had appeared in an earlier draft. In doing so, Roosevelt relegated the attack on America's largest colony to a later point in his speech as part of a list that began with Malaya, Hong Kong, and Guam and ended with the Philippine Islands, Wake Island, and Midway Atoll. The president's primary intention in highlighting Hawaii and downplaying the Philippines was almost certainly to simplify his message for the broadest possible audience, but in doing so, he also reframed Japan's offensive against the centers of Western colonialism in Asia as an attack on the United States proper. In this new formulation, the US forces would be fighting a war not to restore Western control of colonial territories in the Pacific but rather to avenge the "unprovoked and dastardly attack" on "the United States of America."[39]

All but one member of Congress voted in favor of declaring war on Japan. Three days later, Germany declared war on the United States. The years of waiting had come to an end, and the nation was at war. The three days between December 5 and December 8 witnessed two of the most decisive turning points in the war: the Soviet halting of the Wehrmacht before the gates of Moscow and the American entry into the war. The clock was now ticking on the German, Italian, and Japanese forces to make good on their offensives in Eastern Europe, North Africa, and the Pacific before the full weight of Soviet and US counterattacks could be brought to bear on the Axis powers.

AS THE UNITED STATES BEGAN MOBILIZING FOR WAR, BRITISH LEADERS moved to strike back against Japan. With tensions rising in the Pacific, the admiralty had deployed the battleship *Prince of Wales*, the battle cruiser *Repulse*, and four destroyers to the base in Singapore. Following the Japanese air raid on the city, British leaders sent the squadron—Force Z—out of Singapore harbor to intercept Japanese forces attacking Malaya. "We are off to look for trouble,"

Repulse's captain told the crew. "I expect we shall find it." Although the British ships lacked air cover, the admiralty had reason to be confident: no battleship at sea had ever been sunk by aerial attacks, although the previous day's raid on Pearl Harbor should have given London pause. At dusk on December 9, Japanese planes sighted the British squadron heading north. Shortly after 2:00 a.m. a Japanese submarine located the ships, but all five of its torpedoes missed. As dawn approached on December 10, twelve reconnaissance planes and eighty-five attack aircraft took off from Saigon. Spotter planes found Force Z and radioed its location to the bombers. At 11:13 a.m., the first Japanese planes staged a bombing run on the *Repulse* to little effect. A wave of torpedo bombers followed thirty minutes later, scoring two hits on the *Prince of Wales* that immobilized the battleship's port propeller. Enemy aircraft now swarmed around the two ships, sending salvoes of torpedoes into their armored hulls. The doomed vessels began taking on water and listing heavily. The *Repulse* capsized at 12:33 p.m. as desperate sailors tried to escape. At 1:20 p.m., the *Prince of Wales* also capsized. British aircraft arrived as the last "flight of Japanese bombers jettisoned their bombs and disappeared over the horizon," the official British history explained, and found the sea below strewn "with men and wreckage." In all, some 837 sailors perished.[40]

The sinking of the capital ships shocked British leaders. As Churchill told Foreign Secretary Anthony Eden, "The loss of the *Prince of Wales* and *Repulse* together with United States losses at Pearl Harbour gives [the] Japanese full battle-fleet command of [the] Pacific. They can attack with any force overseas at any point." Churchill now expected Tokyo to attack the Philippines, Burma, and Singapore.[41] More broadly, Japan's grand offensive sounded the death knell of the battleship era. The success of Japan's carrier force at Pearl Harbor and the destruction of the *Prince of Wales* and *Repulse* revealed the new power of military aviation and the vulnerability of the old battleships. Ironically, the Allies would learn the lessons of their defeat while the Japanese would fail to learn the lessons of their victory.

Going forward, the United States would reorient its Pacific War strategy around a growing fleet of aircraft carriers to fight the war in the Pacific even as Japan continued to look to battleships to deliver a decisive victory in the war at sea.

Having crippled the British and American battle fleets in the Far East, Tokyo unleashed its armies on the colonial defense forces of Burma, the Dutch East Indies, Hong Kong, the Philippines, and Singapore. Tempered by years of bitter fighting in China, Japanese troops made short work of the untested and increasingly isolated colonial garrisons standing in their way. The British colony of Hong Kong lay in an especially vulnerable position. A British possession since 1842, Hong Kong comprised a mere twenty-nine square miles of territory at the mouth of the Pearl River Delta. By 1937, British leaders recognized the futility of trying to defend the colony against a concerted attack and chose to station only a small number of troops in the territory. Japan's occupation of Guangzhou and parts of Guangdong Province in 1938 placed the Imperial Army on Hong Kong's doorstep. The loss of the *Prince of Wales* and the *Repulse* then rendered the colony's situation hopeless. "Hong Kong is isolated and must fight to the end," a grim Churchill explained on December 12.[42] Over the next two weeks British, Canadian, Chinese, and Indian troops waged a desperate defense of the territory as Japanese forces fought their way into the territory before the British surrender on December 25.

Victorious Japanese units committed systematic atrocities against captured troops. One Indian radio overseer witnessed the cold-blooded murder of 180 Chinese prisoners on the football field in King's Park. "Japanese officers tried out their swords on the victims," one witness explained, killing as many as four hundred per day. At the marina, prisoners had their hands tied and were then tossed into the sea. Another witness reported seeing a European in civilian clothes strapped to a rattan chair on the side of the road, his face and head horribly burned. Not far away, a man and woman lay in a pool of blood. As the slaughter continued, Japanese troops shot an elderly European couple outside of a shop after forcing them to embrace.

"Their corpses were left at the same spot for about 2 or 3 days," the witness noted. Following the fall of Hong Kong, Japanese troops decapitated fourteen Indian officers along with a company of Punjabi soldiers captured near Lei Yu Mun. Another Indian soldier reported an incident in which two British officers "were taken by a Japanese soldier into a tea shop and given tea to drink. The Japanese then shot the [officers] and displayed there [sic] bodies to Indians to show what could be done to Europeans."[43]

On the basis of such reports, the British foreign secretary, Anthony Eden, drew parallels between the violence in Hong Kong and the Nanking Massacre of 1937. Fifty officers had been bound "hand and foot then bayoneted to death." Japanese authorities refused to give survivors permission to bury the dead. Women "both Asiatic and European were raped and murdered. . . . One entire Chinese district was declared a brothel regardless of the status of the inhabitants." Those soldiers who survived the initial bloodbath were then forced into a prison camp of ramshackle huts with no sanitation and no access to medical supplies. Disease, dysentery, and death soon swept through the camp.[44]

The racial dimensions of the fall of Hong Kong were not lost on Western observers. As one journalist explained, "It was plain that humiliation was part of the Jap [sic] scheme to convince the natives that the white man had been conquered." Gwen Dew, an American reporter, was among the Westerners captured in Hong Kong. "They paraded us, the hungry, bedraggled two hundred of us, through the crowded Chinese section," she wrote. "We were the perfect picture of the Fall of the White Man in the Far East. A white man lying disemboweled in the dirt, a white woman snatched naked and gang-raped, a parade of whites carrying their own pitiful burdens—these pictures delighted the Jap [sic] heart. . . . They are determined upon the rape, the ruin, and the subjugation of the world—particularly the white world." Clifford Matthews, a student at Hong Kong University, had volunteered to fight the Japanese before being captured. In defeat, he later explained, the Chinese "could see that we were nothing special, we were just human beings. [What] was clear to me [was] that there will be another world after the war."[45]

Likewise, the Japanese conquest of Rabaul in the Australian-controlled Territory of New Guinea inflamed Western racial anxieties. Japanese forces under the command of General Tomitaro Horii attacked the settlement's small garrison of some 1,500 soldiers on January 23, 1942. Like their counterparts in Hong Kong, the defenders at Rabaul had no hope of fighting off the Japanese onslaught. Australian troops tried to defend the beaches against the Japanese landings, but they were soon overwhelmed. Hundreds of Australians took to the jungles to continue guerrilla operations, but they lacked the training and equipment to mount effective partisan attacks. Bouts of malaria, scarce food, and exhaustion sapped their will to fight. After Horii's forces located their hideouts with the help of local villagers in early February, most of the Australians surrendered.[46]

The fall of Rabaul put Japan in a position to threaten Australia and New Zealand. If the Allies failed to halt Tokyo's advance, Japanese soldiers might soon be marching through the streets of Sydney or Auckland. While Western observers had expressed horror at Tokyo's conquest of neighboring countries in Asia, the prospect of Japanese forces occupying white-majority nations sparked a firestorm of racial anxieties. As Admiral Ernest King warned to President Roosevelt in early March, "Australia—and New Zealand—are 'white men's countries' which it is essential that we shall not allow to be overrun by Japan—because of the repercussion among the non-white races of the world."[47]

MEANWHILE, JAPANESE FORCES CONTINUED THEIR ATTACKS ON Allied positions in Singapore and the Philippines. Again, the prospect of Japanese armies seizing European cities, soldiers, and civilians struck terror in the hearts of European authorities. On December 17, British leaders in Singapore suggested that all "white women and children" should be evacuated "in view of the bestiality and brutality of the Japanese." However, Governor Shenton Thomas pointed out that "if Asiatics see Europeans leave, then looting and panic will break out." Rather, the European population faced the obligation of staying and helping the "Asiatics to remain." On the other hand, the Japanese capture of "women and children would lead to atrocities, humiliation and indignities. . . . To abandon Asiatics to Asiatics is quite different to leaving behind Europeans, especially when the enemy is the Japanese, with the memory of Nanking behind us."[48]

As General Yamashita Tomoyuki continued his march south through Malaya, British and Commonwealth forces retreated to Singapore. As they approached the city, exhausted soldiers saw immense columns of smoke rising from burning oil tanks in the Seletar Naval Station. On January 31, British commander Arthur Percival ordered his forces to cross the Johor Causeway connecting the island to the mainland. After the last troops had crossed, British and Indian sappers detonated explosives on the causeway, severing Singapore from the mainland. "Singapore itself was in a state of almost complete chaos," journalist George Seabridge, witness to the events, wrote. Many of the British and Australian troops deserted, and some engaged in looting. Malayan workers fled and a general mood of panic set in. As the fighting raged, propaganda pamphlets and radio broadcasts called on the Indian troops to defect to the Japanese side: "They flogged the point that they were fighting only the white man," wrote Seabridge, "that the British were putting Asiatic troops in the front line as cannon fodder, while the white soldiers remained skulking in the background. They promised that any Asiatic soldier who gave himself up would be unharmed." Captured Indian soldiers were set free—"unless you want to come with us and fight the white man."[49]

Patients and staff at Singapore's British Military Hospital were not so lucky. The first Japanese troops entered the hospital on the afternoon of February 13 and began bayoneting doctors and wounded. One witness described a scene in which a doctor and the patient he had just anesthetized both lay dead—the first shot through the heart, the second stabbed to death. Another two hundred people were forced out of the hospital, tied up, and imprisoned overnight, and then bayoneted in groups of three the next morning. When a larger group of the prisoners tried to escape, they were shot with machine guns. Only four survived. For the next three days, Japanese soldiers looted the hospital while the wounds of survivors went untreated and the bodies of those murdered—many wearing Red Cross armbands—blackened in the tropical heat. A high-ranking Japanese medical officer who arrived at the hospital offered no apology when he surveyed the scene.[50]

Lance Corporal Stephen Taylor, serving with the Malay States Volunteer Forces recalled the confusion and demoralization of the troops as Japanese shells pounded their defenses. "It was all very unpleasant and disconcerting as the enemy could never be seen," he wrote. As he made his way through the city's streets he passed neighborhoods of ruined houses. The docks were strewn with burning warehouses and ammunition fires. Taylor managed to escape by sea and eventually reach Australia. "Our last view of Singapore was terrible," he wrote in his after-action report, "and seen from the sea it seemed to be enveloped in enormous fires." One lance bombardier fighting in the city judged that "Singapore was fast becoming a death trap." As his unit withdrew toward the harbor, they "saw death and destruction everywhere as [they] drove to the beach and dead still littered some of the streets." Taylor and most of his comrades made it off the island, gaining a haunting vista of the destruction left behind: "Big fires were burning and lit up the town—it looked like Dunkirk all over to me."[51]

The fall of Singapore on February 15 dealt a crushing blow not only to Western imperialism in East Asia but also to the notion of white racial superiority. Churchill bemoaned the loss of Britain's Far Eastern citadel as the "worst disaster" in British military history. "How came 100,000 men (half of them of our own race) to hold up their hands to inferior numbers of Japanese?" the distraught prime minister asked his physician. The US State Department's Far East Division had warned that the battle for Singapore was "more than a focal point in military strategy—it [was] a symbol—a symbol of power, the determination, and the ability of the United Nations to win this war." The fall of Singapore would devastate "the prestige of the white race and particularly of the British Empire and the United States."[52]

Non-Western players also recognized the implications of Japan's victory. One Japanese commander announced that the fall of Singapore represented a key step in the struggle to secure "Asia for the Asians." Mohan Singh, the first leader of the Indian National Army, wrote that the "Asians in general, and the Japanese in particular, began to assume the air of being more civilised and more intelligent than the British and began to treat them as if they were an inferior race." Similarly, S. C. Goho, the president of the Indian Association in Singapore, observed that the cowardly retreat of the British Empire "brought great disgrace on the white race generally."[53]

Allied troops would receive another drubbing in Burma in the coming weeks. London now understood that the security of its Eastern colonies was in jeopardy. The British chiefs of staff warned that the fall of Malaya would give Japanese forces a clear run to the Indian Ocean. Tokyo could launch attacks on Ceylon and India, foment rebellion in the Raj, disrupt Indian Ocean communications, and cut Burma off from any hope of resupply. Worse still, they wrote, the "loss of Ceylon would imperil the whole British war effort in the Middle and Far East." And Burma's defenses were already collapsing. Japanese forces under the command of General Shojiro Iida had attacked the British colony from Thailand in mid-January. By February 21, British and Commonwealth forces had been driven back to the banks of the Sittang River, marking the last major geographic obstacle along the eastern approaches to the capital, Rangoon. The city served as the terminus of the Burma Road, which connected China to the Bay of Bengal. If Japanese troops could seize Rangoon, they would sever one of Chiang Kai-shek's vital lifelines to Western aid and fatally undermine the British position in Burma. British commanders had ordered the defense of the main rail bridge spanning the Sittang River to the east, but Iida's troops had inflicted heavy casualties on the defenders. Fearful that they were on the brink of collapse, panicked British commanders ordered the destruction of the bridge at 4:15 a.m. on February 23, stranding the entire Seventeenth Indian Division on the opposite bank. Eight thousand men attempted a desperate swim across the kilometer-wide river. Fewer than half succeeded.[54]

The mood in Rangoon was nothing short of apocalyptic. The city's residents—already traumatized by Japanese bombing raids—fell into despair. Wealthy families sent women and children away from the capital. As Indian night-soil collectors fled the city, stinking piles of filth and garbage littered the streets. The nights belonged to looters and arsonists; the local prison and lunatic asylum threw open their doors. One rumor claimed that the zoo had loosed its panthers to prowl the streets. Remaining officials razed any resources and installations that might be of value to the Japanese. Telephone and telegraph stations, troop barracks, oil storage, and port facilities all went up in flames as the British torched the mechanical vestiges of imperial modernity. Meanwhile, in London, Chief of the Imperial General Staff Alan Brooke pondered what appeared to be the coming collapse of the empire: "I have during the last ten years had an unpleasant feeling that the British Empire was decaying and that we were on a slippery slope to decline! I wonder if I was right. I certainly never expected that we should fall to pieces as fast as we are and let Hong Kong and Singapore go in less than three months."[55] On March 7, British forces abandoned the ruins of Rangoon after destroying everything they thought might be of value to the Japanese.

Burma was now gripped by an epic refugee crisis as the British along with hundreds of thousands of Indian workers fled west toward India. As many as five hundred thousand people attempted the exodus. Europeans made up about 4 percent, Indians the rest. The fortunate ones made it out by boat, but most were forced to take to the roads, trekking through what one writer called a "green hell" of torrential rains, forbidding mountains, and malarial jungles. "In endless streams they came," wrote one observer, "women tired out and hobbling along by the aid of sticks; men carrying babies in panniers from their shoulders, others carrying small children on their backs." Along the way, refugees faced attacks from strafing Japanese planes, marauding Burmese villagers, and clouds of biting insects. More deadly, however, were the rampant malnutrition, dysentery, and cholera-infested drinking water. The monsoon rains that arrived in May only made things worse, spreading disease and washing out roads. A government estimate placed the number of the dead at eighty thousand. Starving people resorted to eating rancid food and collapsed from dysentery. The dead were often left by the roadside to rot in the tropical heat or simply sink into the mud.[56]

Having neutralized US and British colonial forces in Malaya, the Philippines, and Hawaii, Japan was free to launch an invasion of its ultimate target: the resource-rich Dutch East Indies. The archipelago of some seventeen thousand islands presented myriad challenges for attacker and defender alike. On December 16, Japanese forces under the command of Lieutenant General Hitoshi Imamura landed on the beaches of northern Borneo to seize the oil facilities at Miri. On January 11, Japanese forces attacked Sulawesi and Tarakan. Some of the Dutch defenders worked to demolish the oil fields, depriving Tokyo of an immediate petroleum supply and sending up billowing clouds of smoke that evoked a scene, one observer commented, out of some "misplaced corner of hell." American sailors could smell the burning fields some twenty miles out at sea. Another contingent of Japanese troops attacked Sumatra, home to 40 percent of the colony's oil. Two weeks later, Japanese forces landed on Java. Although guerrilla operations continued, the last major Dutch resistance ended in March. Japan's occupation of the islands would have sweeping implications for Indonesian history. Many Indonesians cheered the arrival of the Japanese as liberators, but their experiences as subjects of Tokyo's Co-Prosperity Sphere would help generate an anticolonial resistance against both Japanese and Dutch authorities.[57]

As European colonies fell one after another before the Japanese onslaught, US forces in the Philippines clung to an ever-shrinking foothold in the archipelago. Unable to halt the advance of Japanese ground forces commanded by General Homma Masaharu, General MacArthur ordered his forces to prepare five defensive lines designed to slow the Japanese advance while US and Filipino troops pulled back to the Bataan Peninsula and the fortress island of Corregidor. These tactics proved effective in preventing a complete collapse, but, deprived of reinforcements, the Philippines garrison remained doomed. Washington's war plans called for US troops in the Philippines to hold out until the navy could relieve them. However, the destruction of the Pacific Battle Fleet at Pearl Harbor left the navy without an effective means of supporting the US colony. Filipino president Manuel Quezon and MacArthur issued an ever more urgent string of pleas to the White House for aid. Roosevelt had little to offer the leader of America's largest colony besides words. "Those Americans who are fighting now will continue to fight until the bitter end," he wrote on February 9. "So long as the flag of the United States flies on Filipino soil as a pledge of our duty to your people, it will be defended by our own men to the death."[58]

General MacArthur also pushed leaders in Washington to redirect their efforts from the Atlantic to the Pacific theater. In the wake of its grand offensive, Tokyo had stretched its forces across "two thousand miles of sea with the whole line subject to American sea thrust." The general begged Army Chief of Staff George Marshall to attack these lines rather than take the defensive: "Theories of safety first will not win against such an aggressive and audacious adversary as Japan. . . . The only way to beat him is to fight him incessantly." Marshall thanked the general for his suggestions but explained that they were not feasible. Tokyo's capture of Guam, Wake, and the Marshall and Gilbert Islands had given Japan air superiority over the entire region. Then, too, in the wake of Pearl Harbor, the US Navy lacked the offensive capabilities to stage an attack that could relieve the Philippines.[59] Just as important as Marshall's stated reasons, however, was the reality that the White House had long ago made the decision to pursue a Europe-first strategy. A full-scale assault on Japanese forces in the Philippines would shift scarce resources away from Roosevelt's primary concern: the Atlantic theater.

MacArthur's troops were left to wage a hopeless struggle—albeit one that their commander had pushed for by insisting that the United States defend the Philippines in the event of a war with Japan. Moreover, the general made a number of questionable decisions in the face of impending defeat. In the first two months of 1942, MacArthur accepted a confidential payment of $500,000 from President Quezon. Major General Richard Sutherland, MacArthur's chief of staff, received $75,000. MacArthur would carry the secret of this payment, equivalent to nearly $8 million in contemporary dollars, to his grave. He also chose to make only one visit to the front during the four-month battle for the Philippines, leading many of his troops to nickname him "Dugout Dug." Together with his delay in launching air raids against Formosa on the opening day of the war, the general's record in the Philippines was far from distinguished. Nevertheless, MacArthur retained both his massive ego and his gift for self-promotion. "Of 142 communiques released by his headquarters between December and March," writes historian Ronald Spector, "109 mention only one individual: MacArthur." The general's messages gave scant credit to field commanders and units, instead referring to "MacArthur's right flanks" or "MacArthur's men." Nevertheless, the general appeared determined to remain in the Philippines. On February 22, Marshall issued a direct order demanding that MacArthur evacuate to Australia. Washington could not allow Homma's army to capture a four-star general in the field. Meanwhile, officials in Washington downplayed MacArthur's more controversial actions in the Philippines: the United States needed a hero.[60]

The lionization of MacArthur came as a slap in the face to the American and Filipino soldiers stranded in Bataan. "A foul trick of deception has been played on a large group of Americans by a commander in chief and small staff who are now eating steak and eggs in Australia," wrote one US general on the island. "God damn them!" With all hope lost, seventy-eight thousand half-starved US and

Filipino troops in Bataan surrendered on April 9. Homma's staff had planned for half that number. Moreover, Japanese leaders had not accounted for the scale of malnutrition among the POWs. Making matters worse, Homma was in a hurry to clear the enemy prisoners from the field so that he could begin his final attack on the fortress island of Corregidor. The following day, Americans and Filipino POWs began a forced march to a prison camp some sixty miles away. The exhausted prisoners stumbled through blistering heat with little water and less food. Japanese guards administered random beatings and bayoneted stragglers. Men survived by drinking from pools of water contaminated by dead bodies and manure. Some of those who collapsed were run over by trucks and tanks. One survivor recalled seeing a guard throw a sick man in front of a column of tanks. "There must have been ten tanks in that column, and every one of them came up there right across the body," he remembered. "When the last tank left there was no way you could tell there'd ever been a man there. But his uniform was embedded in the cobblestone." By the time the prisoners reached the camps, at least five thousand Filipinos and five hundred Americans had died or been murdered. The American troops on Corregidor held out for nearly another month, but with no chance of reinforcements or resupply, it was only a matter of time before their defenses broke.[61]

With Corregidor's surrender on May 6, the last fortress of Western imperialism in the Far East fell to Japan. In the space of five months, Japan had conquered vast swaths of colonial Asia, ending over four centuries of Western colonial rule. In its place, Tokyo sought to build a new empire in the guise of the Co-Prosperity Sphere and a new racial order dominated by the Japanese. Japan's conquests destroyed not only the infrastructure of Western imperialism but also its symbolic power. Watching as Japanese troops stormed across the Pacific, Australian journalist Ian Morrison recognized the transformation of the racial order in Asia: "The privileged status of the white man in the Far East is a thing of the past."[62]

Chapter 9

THE BATTLE FOR THE PERIPHERY

OKYO'S EMPIRE REACHED ITS APEX ON THE MORNING OF MAY 4, 1942, as a detachment of Japanese marines splashed onto the beaches of Tulagi. Just over three miles long and half a mile wide, the island is ringed by coral reefs and shaded by palm trees and lush mangroves. From 1897 to 1942, Tulagi served as the capital of the British Solomon Islands Protectorate. Axis leaders surveying a map of the recent gains would have been pleased. Over the five months before the invasion, Japan's grand offensive had devastated the outposts of Western colonialism across the Far East. As Tokyo's forces swept across the Pacific, London and Washington scrambled to defend their lines of imperial communication running through the Indian Ocean, the South and Central Pacific, and the Mediterranean. The German and Japanese victories of 1941 and early 1942 placed Axis militaries in control over one-third of the world's population and mineral resources. The Wehrmacht still camped outside the gates of Moscow, and the approaching spring thaw promised a renewed offensive. While the largest concentration of Axis ground troops remained engaged along battlefronts in China and the Soviet Union, German, Italian, and Japanese armies now threatened the Central Pacific, India, the Middle East, and the Mediterranean. The prospect of a coordinated German-Japanese offensive against India and the Middle East threatened to give the Axis a commanding hold over the world's peoples and strategic commodities.

But what should have been a day of celebration for the Japanese took a dark turn with the appearance of US warplanes in the skies above Tulagi at 8:45 a.m. The Americans sank a handful of ships and forced the remaining invaders to turn back. Although the clash at Tulagi was comparatively small, it marked the beginning of a far larger struggle between the US and Japanese fleets: the Battle of the Coral Sea.[1]

Historians often remember the Battle of the Coral Sea as the first major clash fought between aircraft carriers, an event that heralded the dawn of a new era in naval warfare. But it was much more than that. Although the preceding five months had witnessed a string of stunning Axis victories, the next six saw the turning of the tide in the world war. More broadly, the second half of 1942 witnessed a sweeping transformation of the international order from a system governed by colonial empires to a new world dominated by the emergent superpowers. By November, Allied forces had begun retaking territory in Africa, Eastern Europe, and the Pacific, inflicting heavy losses in an escalating war of attrition that eventually ground down the Axis armies. These battlefield victories were fueled by the vast resources of the Soviet Union and the United States—twin superstates spanning entire continents and commanding seemingly unlimited industrial resources and manpower. The mobilization of their energies over the course of the war propelled the Allies to victory and transformed both nations into superpowers capable of eclipsing the older colonial powers and dominating the postwar world. Ultimately, the battles of the second half of 1942—Coral Sea, Midway, Stalingrad, and Guadalcanal—would raise both the Soviet Union and the United States to the status of planetary powers: colossal empire-states capable of exercising hegemonic power across the economic, military, ideological, and political spectrum. Whereas regional clashes between the British, French, German, and Japanese empires had shaped the first stage of the war, this next stage would witness the deployment of Soviet and US power on a scale never before seen in history.

JAPAN'S TRANSPACIFIC OFFENSIVE HAD ACHIEVED VIRTUALLY ALL ITS operational goals by early 1942. Japanese forces occupied Batavia, Hong Kong, Manila, Rabaul, Rangoon, and Singapore; seven Allied capital ships had been sunk, mauling the British and US fleets. Nevertheless, strategic success remained elusive. Far from being demoralized by the Pearl Harbor attack, the United States now appeared determined to wage an all-out war against Tokyo. Faced with this dilemma, Japanese leaders considered five possible options. The first called for a pause to allow Japanese forces to consolidate control over their newly conquered territories, fortify defenses, and replace heavy losses of aircraft and pilots. However, this conservative course earned limited support. Japanese leaders understood that they would likely lose a long war of attrition and were therefore reluctant to surrender the initiative to the Allies. A second option envisioned a southern offensive against Australia to preempt Allied efforts to transform the continent into a launchpad for a counterattack. In this case, however, the army balked at the idea of invading Australia while the battle for China still raged. The third plan called for an offensive against New Guinea that would neutralize a potential staging area for an Allied counterattack and give Japan a base from which to stage raids on Australia. A fourth plan entailed an attack on the US possessions of Midway and Hawaii in the Central Pacific, which would draw the US Navy into a final, decisive battle and give Japan control of two military outposts in the Central Pacific.[2]

The fifth option proposed a naval offensive aimed at destroying the British Eastern Fleet, capturing Ceylon, and linking up with German forces in the Middle East. The Indian Ocean offensive carried high risks but promised great rewards. Any attempt to establish supremacy in the Indian Ocean would require a massive extension of Japan's already-sweeping naval commitments. Moreover, if the fleet became bogged down fighting the British, US forces might take the offensive in the Pacific. Nevertheless, the key British base in Ceylon seemed unlikely to offer much resistance to a Japanese attack, and the port of Diego Suarez in Madagascar lay in the hands of Vichy officials who seemed more likely to surrender than offer a stout defense. Further, if Japanese forces defeated the British fleet in a decisive engagement, they would crush the world's most celebrated navy, sever Britain's lines of communication with India, and deal a fatal blow to the British position on the subcontinent. More promising still was the possibility of linking up with German forces in the Middle East.[3]

Internal rivalries further complicated Tokyo's decision. While the navy pushed to expand overseas operations, army leaders chafed at the notion that they ought to play a supporting role to the admirals' conquests and insisted that their soldiers had their hands full fighting on the empire's most important front, China. Beyond these interservice rivalries, different bodies within the Imperial Navy itself pushed different plans. The naval general staff favored the thrust toward Australia, while Yamamoto's Combined Fleet staff pushed for an attack on the US fleet in the Central Pacific. An observer might be excused for thinking that Japanese military factions were more focused on fighting one another than the Allies.[4]

THE PEARL HARBOR ATTACK HAD IGNITED A VIRULENT WAVE OF anti-Asian racism in the United States. As one American newspaper correspondent wrote of the Japanese, "The kind of human being that he himself has become is wrong and has no place any more on earth." A 1942 parade through the streets of New York City featured a float, according to one newspaper, depicting an "American eagle leading a flight of bombiners down on a herd of yellow rats which were trying to escape in all directions."[5] Perhaps most troubling of all, the Roosevelt administration issued Executive Order 9066, which authorized the forced removal of civilians of Japanese ancestry from areas of military importance. Government authorities used the order to force some 112,000 people into internment camps scattered across the United States—a blatant violation of civil liberties and a stain on the nation's history.

Meanwhile, Allied leaders searched for a means to respond to Pearl Harbor. The stunning success of Japan's grand offensive forced a series of strategic reassessments among Britain and the United States. Although Allied leaders had agreed on the principle of a Europe-first strategy, both London and Washington recognized the urgent need to block a Japanese thrust into the Indian Ocean that would link the Axis empires. The Allies, in Roosevelt's estimation, must defend their "vital flanks": China, Burma, and India in the East and Australia and New Zealand in the West. At stake were control of three of the world's most strategically vital bodies of water and the survival of the British Empire in the Middle East and India. In effect, US and British forces would mount a series of interventions across the colonial world to secure forward bases for a larger offensive aimed at rolling back Axis gains in Africa, Asia, and the Middle East.

To coordinate their strategy going forward, Churchill and Roosevelt agreed to hold a conference of their general staffs in Washington in late December 1941. As he sailed across the Atlantic, Winston Churchill sketched out a lengthy strategic assessment. "Hitler's failure and the losses in Russia are the prime factor in the war," he wrote. Germany's days of "cheaply won successes" were now over, replaced by the "shock of a Winter of slaughter" and the steady attrition of fuel and supplies. He argued that London and Washington had to do everything in their power to ensure that Soviet resistance continued while at the same time bolstering the defenses around their lines of communication in the Atlantic, Mediterranean, and Pacific.

Churchill was convinced that Anglo-American forces must establish full control over the coast of North Africa as part of a larger campaign to secure the Suez Canal and establish supremacy over the Mediterranean.[6]

Japan presented a more complicated if less immediately dangerous problem. The sinking of the *Prince of Wales* and the *Repulse* had crippled the British war effort against Japan. For the time being, the United States remained the only power that could challenge the Japanese in the Pacific. London's resources would be best spent reinforcing the British position in the Indian Ocean with three aircraft carriers to protect lines of communication with India. Churchill argued that Allied forces must keep Japan engaged along a broad front in order to create a steady drain on Tokyo's aircraft and ships, grinding Japanese forces down to the point where Allied forces could reach the Japanese home islands. At that point, the Allies would unleash a rain of fire on the population: "The burning of Japanese cities by incendiary bombs will bring home in a most effective way to the people of Japan the dangers of the course to which they have committed themselves, and nothing is more likely to cramp the reinforcing of their overseas adventures."

Looking ahead, the prime minister identified 1943 as the year in which the Allies would turn the tide. London and Washington would regain naval superiority in the Pacific in 1943 and sever Tokyo's supply lines to its overseas possessions. The Allies would establish control of the northern coast of Africa and command the Mediterranean. Most dramatically, forty British and US armored divisions, supported by one million infantry, would stage landings in German-occupied Europe. All of these plans depended on "the command of the sea, without which nothing is possible."[7]

Churchill's strategic vision—shared by many in London—echoed themes that had been articulated in the 1930s by British military theorist B. H. Liddell Hart, who had called for an "indirect approach" to warfare. The key, he argued, was "not so much to seek battle as to seek a strategic situation so advantageous that if it does not of itself produce the decision, its continuation by a battle is sure to achieve this." Britain, as a maritime power, came to this approach naturally. Invoking Francis Bacon, Liddell Hart outlined what he termed the "British way in warfare": "He that commands the sea is at great liberty, and may take as much or as little of war as he will. Whereas those that be strongest by land are many times nevertheless in great straits." Historically, Liddell Hart explained, Britain had been most successful when it commanded the seas and used its financial power to support continental allies. This approach granted London the flexibility to launch naval attacks whenever it pleased against "the enemy's vulnerable extremities," maintain its overseas colonies and trade, and avoid the worst of the bloodbaths on the continent. Furthermore, this indirect approach placed London in a position to make the most of the peace. As Liddell Hart argued, war must always be waged with the goal of fashioning a more advantageous situation after victory: "The object in war is to attain a better peace—even if only from your own point of view. Hence it is essential to conduct war with constant regard to the peace you desire." Britain and its allies must fight not simply to defeat the enemy but to secure the best possible geostrategic positions in the postwar world.[8]

Applied to the current war, Liddell Hart's dicta bore striking resemblance to Churchill's strategic vision. London and Washington must establish control of the seas while sending sufficient aid to ensure that Soviet and Chinese armies wore down Axis forces in Eastern Europe and Asia. British and American forces should seize strategically vital areas not only for the purpose of choking off the Axis powers but also with the goal of preserving the British Empire and establishing supremacy after hostilities ceased. US plans for preliminary operations aligned with much of the British strategy. Since Stark's 1940 Plan Dog memorandum, leaders in Washington had agreed that Germany represented the greatest threat. The chiefs of staff working under the auspices of the Joint Board—predecessor to the Joint Chiefs of Staff—also agreed with British planners that lines of communications across the Atlantic, Indian, and Pacific

Oceans must be maintained. American leaders also recognized that Soviet forces had tied down the bulk of the Wehrmacht in Eastern Europe, diverting German forces from other fronts.[9]

Despite agreement on broad war aims and overall command structure, the First Washington Conference revealed divisions between the two allies. As Churchill explained in his opening meeting with Roosevelt, London hoped to launch a joint campaign to conquer North Africa in the coming year. But US officials were wary of Britain's proposed Mediterranean operations. To many, it appeared that London sought to draw the US military into defending the British Empire in the Near East. Army Chief of Staff George Marshall's senior strategic adviser, General Stanley Embick, insisted that British plans in North Africa were "motivated more largely [sic] by political than by sound strategic purposes." Embick warned that control of North Africa would not be sufficient to restore lines of communication in the Mediterranean and rejected the notion that the area could serve as an effective springboard for an invasion of Europe. A US invasion of North Africa, he warned, "would prove to be a mistake of the first magnitude."[10]

However, the British chiefs presented the Mediterranean option as a part of a broader strategy aimed at "closing and tightening the ring round Germany" stretching from Archangel in Northwest Russia, through the Black Sea and Anatolia, along the northern seaboard of the Mediterranean, and around the western seaboard of Europe. While they ramped up war production, the Allies had to work to maintain lines of communication around the world while gradually wearing down German resistance with aerial bombing, a continental blockade, subversive operations, and propaganda. To do this, the chiefs explained, London and Washington must tighten control of sea routes across the Atlantic, Indian, and Pacific Oceans and through the North Sea to the Soviet Union.[11] Left unsaid was the understanding that Anglo-American control of all of the world's most important shipping routes would leave the two powers in a commanding position over the postwar order.

ALTHOUGH US AND BRITISH OFFICIALS DIFFERED ON THE QUESTION of North Africa, they shared the broader goal of establishing Allied control of the seas. While German and Italian forces had been attacking British shipping in the Atlantic and Mediterranean since the beginning of the war, Japan's grand offensive introduced new challenges in the Indian and Pacific Oceans. This danger increased after the fall of Singapore on February 15. Having breached the Malay Barrier and mauled the British fleet, Japanese forces turned to attack Allied forces in the Indian Ocean. The British colony of Ceylon was Tokyo's prime target. First colonized by the Portuguese in the sixteenth century, Ceylon had been a British crown colony since 1815. The island, which commanded the sea lanes to India, the Bay of Bengal, and the passage to the Arabian Sea, was home to two good harbors at Colombo and Trincomalee. If Japanese forces captured the colony, they would be in a position to cut off British communications with India and project power across much of the Indian Ocean and into the Middle East.

In late March, Admiral Nagumo Chuichi led a large force of five carriers, three battleships, and supporting ships into the Indian Ocean to stage raids on Colombo and Trincomalee while a second fleet of cruisers and destroyers attacked British shipping vessels. Their goal was to force the British fleet out of eastern waters and fortify their flanks along Malaya, Sumatra, and Java. The British defenses consisted of five aging battleships, two carriers, and an assortment of cruisers and destroyers that were no match for Nagumo's forces. Shortly before 8:00 a.m. on Easter Sunday, April 5, Nagumo's carrier planes struck Colombo. For the next half hour, British and Japanese fighters battled over the city while Japanese planes bombed and strafed the harbor, rail yard, and airfield below. That afternoon, Japanese planes attacked and sank two British cruisers. British carriers failed to locate the Japanese as Nagumo's force swung toward Trincomalee. Two days later, Churchill wrote to Roosevelt warning of the danger. "It is not yet certain whether the enemy is making a mere demonstration in the Indian Ocean or whether these movements are the prelude to an invasion in force of Ceylon," he explained. "In existing circumstances our naval forces are not strong enough to oppose this." At 7:25 on the morning of April 9, Nagumo's aircraft bombed the naval installations, airfield, and docks at Trincomalee. Later that morning, Japanese aircraft sank the British light carrier *Hermes* along with four smaller ships. Recognizing their inability to withstand the Japanese assault, the British admiralty ordered its four Revenge-class battleships to withdraw to Kenya. Meanwhile, Japanese cruisers and destroyers sank twenty-three freighters in the area between April 4 and 9. For the cost of a handful of planes, Nagumo had smashed British defenses and forced the fleet to retreat.[12]

On April 15, Churchill warned Roosevelt that the Japanese were threatening to take Ceylon and invade eastern India, "with incalculable internal consequences to our whole war plan. . . . But this is only the beginning. Until we are able to fight a fleet action there is no reason why the Japanese should not become the dominating factor in the Western Indian Ocean. This would result in the collapse of our whole position in the Middle East." The loss of the Indian Ocean communications, moreover, would disrupt oil shipments from Iran and cut off the Persian Gulf supply route to the Soviet Union. Years later, Churchill would remember Japan's attack on Ceylon as the "most dangerous moment of the War, and the one which caused me the greatest alarm. . . . The capture of Ceylon, the consequent control of the Indian Ocean, and the possibility at the same time of a German conquest of Egypt would have closed the ring and the future would have been black."[13]

Fortunately for the British, Nagumo's fleet pulled back. Japanese carriers had been at sea since November; after striking Pearl Harbor, Rabaul, Colombo, and Trincomalee, Nagumo's ships needed to be refitted and rearmed, and his crews needed rest. The Japanese withdrawal saved the British position in the Indian Ocean. London now rushed to reinforce its lines of communications and bolster its defenses in South Asia. With the eastern fortress of Singapore fallen and the northern fortress of Ceylon in jeopardy, British sights now focused on the third key Indian Ocean base, on Madagascar. Colonized by the French at the close of the nineteenth century, the island was home to one of the best harbors in the western Indian Ocean, Diego Suarez. British officials recognized that the Japanese capture of the colony would give the Axis powers a triangular hold over the entire ocean. Japanese ships could cut Britain's last secure link with India and the Middle East, leaving the Atlantic—still infested with German U-boats—as Britain's last lifeline. South African prime minister Jan Smuts argued that Madagascar represented "the key to the safety of the Indian Ocean. . . . All our communications with our various war fronts and the Empire in the East may be involved." British fears had been exacerbated by the interception of a message from Tokyo's ambassador to Germany suggesting that Berlin had encouraged Japan to occupy the colony. Making matters worse, the Vichy administration on Madagascar showed no sign of standing up to the growing German pressure to give Japan access to Diego Suarez. If Vichy's earlier capitulation to Tokyo in Indochina was any guide, Japanese forces would have little trouble seizing the harbor.[14]

After weeks of preparation, British forces landed on the beaches of Courrier Bay on the northwest coast of Madagascar at dawn on May 5, 1942. Vichy defenders offered negligible resistance as the attackers seized the Windsor Castle battery and issued a surrender ultimatum. By 4:00 p.m., commandos had taken control of the northern section of Diego Suarez. The following day, British soldiers and Royal Marines occupied the nearby city of Antsiranana and captured the local Vichy authorities inside. By the morning of May 7, British forces had taken complete control of the harbor.[15] Having captured Diego Suarez, the British took their time conquering the rest of the island. Vichy governor Armand Annet led a low-level resistance against the British until his surrender in November 1942. Although it went largely unheralded at the time, the British seizure of Madagascar was a critical step in blocking a potential Japanese move into the Indian Ocean. Together with the reinforcement of Ceylon, the Madagascar operation marked the western boundaries of Japanese naval operations and secured British imperial communications with India and the Middle East.

WHILE BRITISH FORCES ESTABLISHED A NEW DEFENSIVE PERIMETER in the Indian Ocean, the United States worked to frustrate Japanese moves in the Pacific. A mere eight weeks after the Pearl Harbor attacks, the US Navy launched its first offensive operation against Japan's Co-Prosperity Sphere. Intelligence reports indicated that Japanese forces were building bases in the Marshall and Gilbert Islands that, if completed, would threaten Allied links to Australia. Just after 5:00 on the morning of February 1, 1942, a carrier task force organized around the USS *Enterprise* and commanded by Admiral William Halsey launched an attack on Kwajalein, Roi, Taroa, and Wotje in the Marshall Islands. US aircraft struck their targets around 7:00 a.m. as the sun crept over the horizon. Meanwhile, a second task force organized around the USS *Yorktown* attacked Japanese positions on Jaluit, Makin, and Mili in the Gilbert Islands. Attacks on Rabaul, Wake and Marcus Islands, Lae, and Salamaua followed in the coming weeks. Although these raids failed to inflict serious damage, they demonstrated that the American carriers remained a threat to Japanese forces in the Pacific.[16]

The most dramatic blow came on April 18, when a force of American B-25 bombers led by Lieutenant Colonel James Doolittle staged a raid on Tokyo and several other Japanese cities. Doolittle's planes took off from the carrier USS *Hornet* on a one-way mission that flew over Japan on their way to airfields in China. The raid did little significant damage beyond killing a number of civilians. Moreover, all of Doolittle's planes were lost. Nevertheless, news of the attack boosted morale in the United States. American citizens savored their first taste of revenge after the Pearl Harbor attacks. However, while the Americans celebrated, Japanese forces unleashed brutal reprisals against Chinese civilians suspected of helping the American pilots. Chiang Kai-shek informed Marshall that the Japanese were "slaughtering every man woman and child" in the areas where Doolittle's planes had crashed. The highest counts cited 250,000 Chinese killed in retaliation for the raids.[17]

Ultimately, the raid's principal strategic impact was symbolic: Doolittle's bombers had exposed Japan's vulnerability to attack. Just as Japan's carriers could strike at Pearl Harbor, American carriers could attack Tokyo. For the first time since the thirteenth century, foreign invaders had threatened Japan. The shock of this new vulnerability helped to convince Japanese leaders of the urgency of eliminating the US carriers in the Pacific. At the same time, this shift toward the Pacific drew Japanese attention away from operations in the Indian Ocean that might have led to a linkup with Germany in the Middle East.[18] The Doolittle raid underscored Tokyo's continuing dilemma: despite achieving overwhelming operational success in its offensives, Japan had made no significant progress toward winning the war. What was needed, Japanese leaders concluded, was a decisive battle against the Americans that would destroy the enemy's carrier forces once and for all.

BY THE END OF APRIL, TOKYO'S OPTIONS HAD NARROWED TO A thrust into the South Pacific or an operation designed to draw the US carrier fleet into a decisive battle in the Central Pacific. In typical fashion, Japanese leaders chose to pursue both. The South Pacific operation involved a continued drive south in an effort to isolate and neutralize Australia as a potential Allied base. While the Japanese army remained steadfast in its refusal to plan a full-scale invasion of the continent, Japanese leaders hoped to seize positions in the surrounding islands as a defensive barrier to major Allied operations. The construction of naval and air bases on Tulagi and at Port Moresby, New Guinea, would give Japan the ability to strike at any Allied forces moving to or from the northeastern shores of Australia. US carrier raids in February and March increased the urgency of these operations. The Port Moresby attack, to be led by Vice Admiral Shigeyoshi

Inoue, had originally been planned for late May. However, in early April, Yamamoto—still intent on luring the United States into a fleet battle—made a push to stage an attack on Midway. The naval general staff moved the Port Moresby operation up to early May, less than a month away. Moreover, the operation would be supported by the relatively inexperienced Fifth Carrier Division, composed of the carriers *Shokaku* and *Zuikaku*, rather than battle-tested First and Second Divisions, which were now being prepared for the Midway operation. Any remaining uncertainty about the primacy of the Midway operation disappeared following the shock of the Doolittle raid. Inoue and the Moresby operation would be consigned to secondary status to facilitate Yamamoto's fleet action at Midway.[19]

Meanwhile, US cryptographers working in Hawaii and Washington had managed to partially decipher Japanese naval codes. Using a series of Japanese messages transmitted between April 19 and 22, US code breakers retrieved a list of designators for Japanese targets: MO and RZ for Port Moresby, RXB for Tulagi, RY for another island in the Gilberts. Furthermore, the code breakers also determined a rough calculation of the size of the Japanese force, which would include the Fifth Carrier Division along with cruisers and the light carrier *Ryukaku*. By the end of April, US leaders had a fairly clear picture of Japanese plans. The staff of Admiral Chester Nimitz, commander in chief of the US Pacific Fleet, drew up an estimate of the situation on April 22. They concluded that on May 3 Japan would likely launch an offensive in the Coral Sea that could sever communications with Australia. For the Pacific Fleet, checking the Japanese advance remained a priority second only to the defense of Midway and Hawaii. "The Japanese are flushed with victory," the report explained. However, US forces now had the advantage of fairly accurate knowledge of Japanese plans. The best opportunity to attack the Japanese force, the estimate concluded, would be after its troop transports passed "south of the island barrier off the Papuan Peninsula."[20]

Nimitz decided to act and sent two task forces grouped around the carriers *Lexington* and *Yorktown* to attack the Port Moresby operation.

At 7:00 p.m. on May 3, Admiral Frank Jack Fletcher, commander of the *Yorktown* group, learned that Japanese forces had begun their advance on Tulagi. "This was just the kind of report we had been waiting 2 months to receive," he remembered later. The next morning, the *Yorktown* began launching a combat air patrol followed by torpedo planes and bombers charged with attacking the Japanese. At 8:45, the strike groups reached Tulagi and commenced their attack. US planes managed to sink a destroyer, a transport, and two patrol boats before returning to the *Yorktown*. The invasion forces called off the Tulagi operation and returned to their base at Rabaul. The stage was now set for a historic battle between the US and Japanese carriers. As the sun rose over the Coral Sea on May 7, search planes for both sides combed the skies. Japanese aircraft located an American oil tanker and destroyer, crippling the former and sinking the latter. Meanwhile, US planes located the small Japanese carrier *Shoho* and began launching attacks. A series of direct hits mauled the Japanese carrier, which burst into flames and began listing to starboard. Within minutes, the carrier sank with much of her crew. The sinking of the *Shoho* marked the first major Japanese loss of the Pacific War.[21]

As dawn broke the following morning, US and Japanese planes resumed their search for the opposing carriers. Bombers from the *Yorktown* sighted the Japanese carriers *Shokaku* and *Zuikaku* around 10:30 a.m. As the American planes began their bombing runs, the *Zuikaku* pulled into a rain squall, masking the ship from the US aircraft. Fogged bombsights and windshields hampered the planes bombing the *Shokaku*, which suffered serious damage but remained afloat. Meanwhile, over the southern horizon, Japanese aircraft had located the *Lexington* and *Yorktown*. The US aircraft defending the carriers were poorly deployed to intercept the Japanese attackers, which were flying seven thousand feet above the American planes. The *Yorktown* suffered one direct hit that tore through her flight and hangar decks before exploding and killing thirty-seven sailors. At 11:20 the *Lexington* received the first of two torpedo hits in rapid succession, followed soon after by a series of bombs. Crews reported that the fires raging belowdecks had been brought under control by 12:40. Seven minutes later, however, a massive explosion from fuel leaks rocked the *Lexington*. "From this time on," her captain later explained, "the ship was doomed." Despite desperate efforts to extinguish the flames, the fires raged out of control. At 5:07 p.m., Admiral Fitch gave the order to abandon ship. Later that evening, a US destroyer torpedoed the burning ship, sending it to the bottom of the sea. The *Lexington* constituted a quarter of US carrier strength in the Pacific, and her loss would be sorely felt. In terms of ships lost, the Battle of Coral Sea represented a tactical victory for Japan. Nevertheless, for the first time, the US Navy had fought the Japanese to a draw. Inoue was forced to cancel the Port Moresby invasion. Moreover, the loss of the *Shoho* and damage to the *Shokaku* would leave Japan shorthanded in its next battle in the Pacific. "This was a red letter day for our forces operation in the Coral Sea area," concluded Nimitz.[22] Although Allied forces were still outmatched in a straight fight with the Japanese navy, the odds were starting to turn in their favor.

FOLLOWING THE BATTLE OF THE CORAL SEA, JAPANESE LEADERS remained confident. The Americans, they concluded, had gotten lucky, attacked the fleet when it was vulnerable, and inflicted significant but not irreparable damage. Furthermore, Tokyo's initial estimates assumed that the United States had lost both of its carriers in the battle. As a result, Yamamoto saw no reason to postpone the Midway operation. Indeed, the fighting in the South Pacific underscored the need to eliminate the remaining US carriers in order to safeguard the Co-Prosperity Sphere. As one Japanese assessment explained, "The enemy is growing desperate to check his decline as his outer shell crumbles under our successive blows, and as India, Australia and Hawaii become directly threatened." With the US Navy focused on defending Australia, the report argued, "the time [was] ripe to strike at Midway and the Aleutians."[23]

Like Hawaii, Midway was a remnant of nineteenth-century US imperialism in the Pacific. First claimed by the United States in 1859, the atoll was thought to be a potential source of bird guano, prized for its use as fertilizer. By the end of the century, US leaders recognized Midway's value as a coaling station and a prime site for telegraph facilities. With the development of air travel, the island became a waypoint for transpacific flights. But the Americans were not the only ones interested in Midway. In 1904, President Theodore Roosevelt stationed a small force of marines on the island to defend against Japanese poachers. In the years before World War II, Midway assumed the role of a Pacific outpost guarding the approaches to Hawaii. For the Americans, Midway provided a stopover for flights to the South Pacific and a fueling station for ships. For the Japanese, Midway represented a launchpad for an invasion of Hawaii. As such, it remained an obvious target for a Japanese attack.

In late May, the Japanese fleet set out for Midway under Yamamoto's command. The plan called for a diversionary attack on the Aleutians followed by the invasion of Midway at dawn on June 6. Following the seizure of the island, Japanese forces would deploy to intercept the expected American counterattack. Submarines waiting along the potential attack routes would alert Yamamoto's forces to the American approach; the Japanese would then launch air and submarine attacks on the US fleet before sending in their battleships to deliver the coup de grâce. Critically, Yamamoto's plan depended on engaging the Americans after taking Midway, not before. In fact, the possibility of an American attack on the invasion fleet prior to the fall of Midway had appeared during Japanese war games conducted on the flagship *Yamato* in early May. When the officers commanding the American "Red" force positioned their ships to intercept the Japanese "Blue" fleet before it reached Midway, the game's judge, Admiral Matome Ugaki, dismissed the move as impossible and forced Red to pull back. When the Red fleet attacked the invaders, sinking two Blue aircraft carriers, Ugaki declared the results invalid. The entire exercise seemed designed to confirm Japanese assumptions that their fleet was invincible—not unlike the Americans' 1932 war games that exposed the dangers of a Japanese carrier raid on Pearl Harbor.[24]

However, US code breakers had once again given American forces a critical advantage in identifying the location, timing, and size of Japan's next attack. In the weeks following the Battle of the Coral Sea, US leaders had puzzled over Tokyo's intentions. Some officials feared that Japan intended a follow-up operation against Port Moresby, while others pointed to possible attacks on the Aleutians, Hawaii, Midway, or even the US West Coast. Tokyo's penchant for multipronged offensives and feints also raised the possibility that an attack on one area might be a diversion in preparation for a larger offensive elsewhere. American code breaker Joseph Rochefort, working in Hawaii, provided the critical missing piece of information. By mid-May, multiple Japanese communications had referenced "AF" in connection to a coming offensive. Allied code breakers in Hawaii and Melbourne agreed that AF was the Japanese code for Midway, but the head of the US cryptography operations in Washington disagreed and insisted that the South Pacific remained the most likely target of Tokyo's next attack. On May 18 or 19, Rochefort sent an unencrypted message falsely claiming that the US base on Midway was running short on water. Several days later, US intelligence intercepted a Japanese message noting that AF was experiencing a water shortage. Rochefort's subterfuge confirmed AF as Midway and resolved the question of Japan's next target.[25]

Rochefort's evidence persuaded Nimitz. "Unless the enemy is using radio deception on a grand scale," he wrote on May 16, "we have a fairly good idea of his intentions." Tokyo was likely to attack Midway and possibly Oahu in early June. The following day, he added that the United States must not risk falling into Japan's trap. The US fleet should make a concerted defense of the Hawaiian area by employing "strong attrition tactics and not repeat not allow our forces to accept such decisive action as would be likely to incur heavy losses on our carriers and Cruisers." Over the coming days, the plans for the Midway operation took shape. To meet the Japanese, Nimitz planned to deploy the *Enterprise, Yorktown,* and *Wasp* along with supporting ships. The three carriers, joined by aircraft from Midway, would match the four Japanese carriers expected to participate in the attack. Repair crews would have to work around the clock to patch the *Yorktown's* damage from the Battle of the Coral Sea, but Nimitz expected the carrier to be ready by the end of the month. He also realized that battleships, being highly vulnerable to air attack, had become a liability in carrier battles. All US battleships in the area would be moved to the West Coast, out of harm's way. Nimitz remained keenly aware that he was working with limited resources: "Common sense dictates that we cannot now afford to slug it out with the probably superior approaching Japanese forces. We must endeavor to reduce his forces by attrition." The US carriers would lie in wait for the Japanese fleet at a point north of Midway, where they hoped to remain undetected. Meanwhile, nineteen submarines patrolled the waters around the island.[26]

The largest fleet in Japanese history, consisting of over two hundred ships and over seven hundred aircraft set out from Honshu, Hashirajima, Saipan, and Guam in late May. The armada included eight aircraft carriers, eleven battleships, twenty-two cruisers, sixty-five destroyers, and twenty-one submarines. Yamamoto commanded the main force, Nagumo headed the carrier striking force, and Vice Admiral Boshiro Hosogaya led the northern force tasked with attacking the Aleutians. As rough seas buffeted the armada, heavy American radio chatter indicated that US forces might have detected the fleet. The need to maintain radio silence, however, kept much of this information from Yamamoto. Undaunted, the admiral forged ahead.[27] As planned, Japanese ships struck targets in Unalaska on June 3. Three days later, Japanese troops began landing in the Aleutian Islands, occupying both Attu and Kiska. Meanwhile, the main thrust of the operation continued toward Midway.

At 4:00 a.m. on June 4, pilots aboard Nagumo's carriers rushed to battle stations. The fog enshrouding the Japanese force had lifted, and

Japanese deck crews now hurried to prepare the aircraft for launch. Nagumo sent 108 of his nearly 225 warplanes to attack US installations on Midway, holding the rest back for a second strike and for fleet protection. Crews armed the remaining Japanese bombers with torpedoes. At the same time, almost two hundred miles to the east, aircrews on Midway began launching combat air patrols and reconnaissance planes to search for the expected Japanese fleet. B-17 bombers also took off to search for Japanese ships sighted the day before. At 5:45 a.m., an American patrol sighted Japanese planes 150 miles out of Midway. Seven minutes later, another plane reported the location of two Japanese carriers. In response, Midway's bombers set off to attack the Japanese carriers while the fighters defending the island prepared to engage with the approaching Japanese planes. The attackers shot down fifteen of the twenty-seven aircraft defending Midway and severely damaged seven more, but they reported forty-three Japanese aircraft destroyed. Japanese bombs did significant damage to the installations on the island but failed to knock out the base. As the surviving attackers turned away from the island, their commander called for a follow-up strike. Nagumo's carriers now braced for the attack from Midway's bombers.[28]

Multiple waves of US bombers attacked Nagumo's ships, inflicting little damage while suffering heavy casualties from Japanese fighters and antiaircraft guns. These failed strikes convinced Nagumo that the Americans represented only a negligible threat. At 7:15, the admiral gave the order for his crews to rearm their torpedo planes with bombs for a second attack on Midway. The order would leave the carriers vulnerable while the crews changed out the explosives, but Nagumo was willing to take the risk. Soon after, a Japanese patrol plane reported American ships approaching. Japanese commanders asked for clarification while they continued rearming their planes. One hundred miles to the northwest, Admiral Raymond Spruance, commander of Task Force 16 ordered an attack on Nagumo's carriers with his sixty-eight dive-bombers, thirty torpedo planes, and twenty fighters. At 8:30, Admiral Fletcher ordered the Yorktown to launch half of its bombers against the Japanese carriers. Aircraft from the *Hornet* failed to locate the Japanese ships, and the planes from the *Enterprise* found the reported location of the carriers empty and were forced to begin searching for Nagumo's ships. As a result, the planes from the *Yorktown* and *Enterprise* reached Nagumo's carriers at approximately the same time. The first to arrive was a low-flying squadron of torpedo bombers from the *Enterprise* that was almost totally destroyed by the Japanese Zeroes. However, the torpedo planes' low-altitude approach cleared the higher altitudes for a run by American dive-bombers.[29]

At 10:22, an observer on the Japanese carrier *Kaga* sighted enemy dive-bombers streaking toward the deck. Three initial strikes missed their target, but a fourth sent a five-hundred-pound bomb crashing through the flight deck. Bombs struck the *Kata*'s forward elevator and the ship's command center. As the attacks continued, flames set off explosions of the ordnance on the flight deck and hangar. At the same moment, three American bombers attacked the *Akagi* with one-thousand-pound bombs, each of which ripped into the carrier's flight deck. The strikes ignited munitions and fuel tanks, setting off a catastrophic series of secondary explosions. Aboard the *Akagi*, Mitsuo Fuchida heard the "terrifying scream of the dive-bombers" followed by the "blinding flash" and a "weird blast of warm air." The shocked airman looked at the flight deck, now strewn with wreckage and twisted metal. "Planes stood tail up, belching livid flame and jet-black smoke." As US bombs pummeled the *Kaga* and *Akagi*, another wave of American planes attacked the *Soryu*. Three bombs tore into the carrier, setting off explosions in her bomb and torpedo storage rooms that quickly spread to the ship's fuel tanks. "Fires enveloped the entire ship in no time," Nagumo's report noted. Twenty minutes after the first bombs struck, the *Soryu*'s commanders gave the order to abandon ship. In the space of five minutes, Japan had lost three of its carriers.[30]

Nagumo's last remaining carrier, the *Hiryu*, now launched an attack on the American carrier *Yorktown*. Just before noon, Japanese dive-bombers scored three hits on the carrier, knocking out six of the

Yorktown's boilers along with its communications and starting several fires. The carrier's crew managed to restore power to the engines and bring the flames under control, but a second wave of attacks from the *Hiryu* hit the *Yorktown* with two torpedoes, causing catastrophic damage. At 3:00 p.m., the crew was ordered to abandon ship. While the crews aboard the *Hiryu* prepared for a third attack, planes from the *Enterprise* sent four bombs crashing into the flight deck, igniting fires that soon reached the bombs and torpedoes stored in the hangar. At 2:30 the next morning, after fires disabled the carrier's engines, the *Hiryu*'s commander ordered the crew to abandon ship before committing ritual suicide. The *Yorktown* remained afloat through the night, but a Japanese submarine attack the following day finally sank the battered carrier.[31]

With evening approaching on June 4, US commanders decided to withdraw. The Americans had scored a resounding victory, sinking or disabling all four of Nagumo's carriers and killing most of Japan's elite naval pilots. Nevertheless, Yamamoto's battleships remained a serious threat to the US carriers, especially in a night engagement. The two fleets launched probing actions the following day, but the battle had already been decided. As Yamamoto's fleet turned back toward Japanese waters, the scope of the defeat sank in. "It was a defeat almost unprecedented in the history of naval warfare, in scale and intensity," Staff Officer Masataka Chihaya later explained. The "American air forces appeared like the proverbial bolt out of the blue from a corner of the heavens, one formation close after another." In the wake of Midway, "the battle between the two navies was completely broken. They became the offensive, we the defensive. Our doom was sealed."[32]

The US Strategic Bombing Survey reached a similar conclusion that "the carrier action at Midway was perhaps the decisive battle of the war."

The Japanese expansion to the east was stopped and Midway Island was saved as an important American outpost. To the Japanese this battle was disastrous. The loss of 4 of their finest aircraft carriers, together with 250 aircraft and some 100 of their first-line pilots deprived them of the powerful striking force with which they had achieved their conquests and with which they had planned to cut down United States efforts to counterattack. . . . All efforts to regain what had been lost were insufficient, and from this date the balance of power in the Pacific shifted steadily to the United States side.

Only six months after Japan's grand offensive, the Co-Prosperity Sphere had been fenced in behind Madagascar and Ceylon in the west, Port Moresby and Australia in the south, and Midway and Hawaii in the east.[33]

As devastating as the loss of four carriers at Midway had been, Tokyo faced an even grimmer calculus in the long term. During the first six months of the war, Japan sank three US aircraft carriers; they would sink three more before the war came to an end. Painful as these losses were, American shipyards would more than make up for them. By the end of the war, the US Navy would launch twenty-six new Essex- and Independence-class carriers. Japanese shipyards only managed to complete seven large carriers during the war. Alongside these larger carriers, the United States built a staggering eight battleships, thirteen heavy cruisers, 110 escort carriers, 202 submarines, and 349 destroyers. Japanese production simply could not keep pace with this flood of new American warships. Although Japan would win naval victories in the coming years, Midway marked a decisive turning point not only in the war at sea but in the battle of the shipyards. Japanese naval forces had indeed become a "wasting factor," as Churchill had predicted. The stage was now set for the war of attrition that Yamamoto had feared.[34]

The Battles of Midway and the Coral Sea signaled the dawn of a new age of American hegemony on the high seas. The US Navy that emerged after 1942 drew on the extensive resources that could only be mobilized by a rising superpower such as the United States. This new post–Pearl Harbor fleet combined the nation's vast natural resources with state-of-the-art technology, mass industrial production, and the most sophisticated logistical supply chain in history to project overwhelming force across the reaches of the world's oceans. The stunning American victory at Midway heralded the start of an era of US maritime supremacy that would survive well into the twenty-first century.[35] While the Americans prepared to exert dominion over the waves, the Soviet Union gathered an army capable of overrunning huge stretches of Eurasia.

Chapter 10

RISE OF THE SUPERPOWERS

N LATE JANUARY 1942, HITLER'S SOON-TO-BE MINISTER OF ARMA-
ments, Albert Speer, gazed out the window of a Heinkel bomber
flying to Dnepropetrovsk, Ukraine. The Nazi architect was eager
to join his staff working to repair the devastated Soviet railroad network. "Beneath us the dreary, snow-covered plains of southern Russia
flowed by," he wrote later. "On large farms we saw the burned sheds
and barns." It was a scene of desolation, with few vehicles moving
along the roads below. "The great stretches of land we passed over
were frightening in their deathly silence, which could be felt even
inside the plane. Only gusts of snow broke the monotony of the landscape." Watching the windswept expanses drift by, Speer realized just
how overextended the Wehrmacht's forces were.[1]

While Japanese forces rampaged across colonial Asia, German
and Soviet armies remained deadlocked in a brutal contest on the

plains of Eastern Europe. Through 1941 and 1942, Axis and Allied forces fought along a great crescent stretching from Tunisia in the west, through the Mediterranean, Middle East, and Caucasus, and arcing north deep into Russia. In line with Churchill's strategy of closing the ring around the Axis powers, British and Commonwealth forces fought a bitter desert battle to defend Egypt and the Levant from Rommel's Afrika Korps. Twelve hundred miles to the north, Stalin's armies fought across the Pontic-Caspian steppe to block a renewed German offensive aimed at the Caucasus. At stake were the vast oil fields of the Middle East and Baku, control of the Mediterranean and the Suez Canal, and the possibility of a link between Germany and Japan in Southwest Asia.

As this raging maelstrom of violence devastated huge sections of Eastern Europe, it transformed the Soviet Union into a military-industrial colossus. To counter the Axis threat and drive the Nazi invaders from their territory, Soviet leaders built the Red Army into the largest military force in human history, numbering nearly ten million soldiers at the end of 1942. At the same time, Moscow orchestrated a miraculous industrial mobilization that replaced much of the older military equipment lost in the opening stages of the war with new weapons systems, many of which outclassed their Axis counterparts.[2] Months of brutal combat also hardened the Red Army into a lethal fighting force. This combination of manpower, industrial might, and improved command and doctrine would turn the tables on the eastern front and propel the Soviet Union to superpower status. Just as the Battles of Midway and the Coral Sea presaged the coming era of American naval hegemony, the Battle of Stalingrad would signal the emergence of Soviet supremacy over the Eurasian heartland.

As the bitter Russian winter fell over the eastern front, leaders in both Moscow and Berlin confronted a new reality. "We are at the turning point now," Stalin told British foreign secretary Anthony Eden on December 16, 1941. There was good reason to hope that the spring might bring victory. Stalin proposed two agreements between London and Moscow. The first concerned military aid, while the second proposed the creation of new spheres of British and Soviet influence in Europe. Stalin called for London to recognize the Soviet Union's June 1941 borders consisting of eastern Poland, western Belorussia and Ukraine, Bessarabia, parts of Finland, and the Baltic states. Britain would be given bases on the continent, and Germany would be dismembered and demilitarized. "It is very important for us to know whether we shall have to fight with Britain over our western frontiers at a peace conference," said Stalin. British leaders hedged before finally making a noncommittal reply in April. London's reply "lacks the question of the security of frontiers," Stalin noted, "but this is not bad, perhaps, because it gives us a free hand." As a result, he explained, the issue of postwar frontiers "will be decided by force."[3]

Across the front lines, the Third Reich faced a three-part crisis. Barbarossa had failed and the Wehrmacht was now fighting to stave off a defeat of Napoleonic proportions. At the same time, Japan's attack on Pearl Harbor—and Hitler's declaration of war on the United States—raised the prospect of a two-front war. Compounding Berlin's dilemma, two years of fighting had depleted German labor and resources: Hitler's empire faced shortages in manpower, industrial production, and food. If the Nazis hoped to prevail, they would need to withstand the Soviet onslaught and survive the Russian winter in the near term; however, in the longer term, Germany would need to prepare for a protracted global war. Hitler's dreams of a lightning victory over the Soviet Union had collapsed before the gates of Moscow. Henceforth, Berlin's only hope lay in seizing resources—notably the Ukrainian breadbasket and the oil fields of the Caucasus—to provision a European fortress. The eastern frontier with the Soviet Union would be fortified along the Ural Mountains while the Nazis prepared to defend Western Europe against the Western Allies. Germany found itself encircled and locked into the war of attrition that Hitler had hoped to avoid.[4]

In the face of this crisis, German leaders outlined three inter-connected campaigns designed to achieve lasting victory in this new global war: one industrial, one racial, and one military. The war in the East had plunged the Third Reich into a crisis of industrial production. Not only was Germany deprived of the bounties of the eastern territories such as grain and oil, but now the Wehrmacht found itself mired in a war of attrition with the massive Red Army. In response, Nazi industrial planners launched a campaign aimed at consolidating the resources of these newly conquered eastern territories. Even before the Battle of Moscow, officials had warned of the need to replenish the Reich's dwindling resources. Nazi quartermaster general Eduard Wagner worried that German oil supplies might run out by January 1942 if the Wehrmacht failed to capture eastern oil fields. In November 1941, Hermann Göring ordered that the "eastern territories . . . be exploited economically as colonies and using colonial methods." The German empire had only a short window of time to construct a new industrial infrastructure capable of sustaining a drawn-out global war. Even so, some feared that the war was already lost. Fritz Todt, Hitler's armaments minister, warned that the wisest course of action would be to seek an armistice with Stalin. However, Todt's death in a mysterious plane crash in February 1942 removed one of the most prominent voices of dissent. In his place, Hitler appointed his own close confidant, Albert Speer. In contrast to Todt's gloomy predictions, Speer promised an industrial miracle that would save the German war effort.[5]

Even so, a sense of urgency hung over Hitler's capital as Nazi officials descended on a waterside villa in the suburb of Wannsee to plot their second campaign, the next stage of Hitler's war against the Jewish people. Originally scheduled for December 9, 1941, the meeting had been postponed following the Wehrmacht's defeat at Moscow. Now, on January 20, 1942, the Wannsee Conference's attendees confronted a changed war. Barbarossa had failed, and Germany now faced a long fight against both the Soviet Union and the United States. A rapid victory in the East would have given Germany its massive empire in Europe and bought time for the regime to coordinate the ethnic cleansing of the region. But the defeat outside Moscow scuttled these plans. The Reich's trains were needed to send soldiers and supplies to fight the Red Army, not to ship Jews to Siberia.

The day after declaring war on the United States, Hitler told a group of Nazi officials that the time had come to destroy the Jews. He could no longer afford to wait until after the defeat of the Soviet Union to activate his plans to exterminate the Jewish peoples of Europe. What was needed, Nazi officials decided, was a final solution to Europe's racial problems. Until now, most of the Holocaust's killings had taken place on an ad hoc basis as SS death squads and German soldiers slaughtered Jews and other victims as opportunities presented themselves. But as the tide of the war began to turn against Germany, Nazi leaders concluded that the Holocaust must accelerate. The Third Reich would now move toward the systematic extermination of the Jewish peoples of Europe using an increasingly centralized machinery of genocide. Going forward, the regime would begin transferring Jews and other groups deemed undesirable to a network of death camps located in Poland, where they would be executed en masse or worked to death. As Germany's chances of winning the war diminished, the Nazi genocide intensified.[6]

Ultimately, Hitler's vision of building a racially pure Fortress Europe hinged on the success of Germany's third major campaign, the military struggle against the Soviet Union. The Führer was convinced that the Wehrmacht must reach a decision on the East in the coming year if the Reich had any hope of winning the war. German commanders had taken their best shot against Moscow and been stopped. In contrast, the warmer climate to the south would allow for a longer campaign season and, hopefully, give the German commanders enough time to defeat the Soviets before the next winter. The Wehrmacht's great offensive of 1942, Operation Blue, took the form of a renewed campaign against southern Russia with the eventual goal of capturing the oil-rich Caucasus, which would give the Reich the petroleum it needed to fight a global war. On April 5, Hitler issued Directive 41, which laid out the plans for the next stage of the war. Soviet forces had spent their strength on the winter counterattacks, he argued, and were now vulnerable. The Wehrmacht must "wipe out the entire defense potential remaining to the Soviets" and "cut them off . . . from their most important centers of war industry." German troops in the northern and central regions would shift to the defensive to allow for a full-scale offensive in the south aimed at "destroying the enemy before the Don River" and securing "the Caucasian oil fields and the passes through the Caucasus mountains." German forces must seek to annihilate the Red Army as it crossed through the Don River basin, neutralize the industrial city of Stalingrad, and clear the path to the Caucasus.[7]

First, however, the Wehrmacht would need to eliminate Soviet forces along its southwestern flank in the Crimea. Axis forces had been fighting for control of the peninsula since the autumn of 1941, but stubborn Soviet resistance remained in the Kerch Peninsula in the east and in the western city of Sevastopol. So long as the Red Army maintained positions in Crimea, Stalin could threaten German forces by pushing west in the Caucasus. Moreover, the peninsula represented an important coastal zone of what was to be Hitler's eastern empire—Sevastopol would become a "German Gibraltar," the wider region would be settled by "pure Germans," and the Third Reich would extend its hold over the Black Sea. On May 8, 1942, German forces commanded by General Erich von Manstein mounted a full-scale assault on Soviet defenders in the Kerch Peninsula. Fierce German attacks forced the Soviets to stage a hasty evacuation across the Kerch Strait. Manstein then turned to attack the fortress of Sevastopol. Under siege since the previous October, the city now witnessed some of the heaviest fighting of the war. The Wehrmacht amassed its largest concentration of artillery of the war and brought up the largest gun ever fired in combat, the Schwerer Gustav railway gun. Still, Soviet defenders held out for another month before their ammunition ran out. In all, Soviet troops at Sevastopol managed to tie German forces down for 247 days—the Battle of France had lasted a mere 46 days. Nevertheless, the struggle for Crimea cost the Soviet Union dearly: nearly four hundred thousand Soviet troops had been either captured or killed.[8]

While fighting raged in the Crimea, German and Soviet forces clashed at Kharkov. German and Soviet commanders had both identified the Ukrainian city as a key location for an offensive in the south. Both sides maintained salients across the jagged battle lines drawn during the previous winter's fighting, and both sides hoped to deliver a knockout blow to their opponent. On May 12, Soviet forces under the command of Marshal Semyon Timoshenko struck first. The initial attack overwhelmed the unprepared German offenders and made rapid progress. However, this success led Timoshenko's forces to outrun their reserves, leaving them dangerously exposed. Punishing German air strikes and concentrated fire from 88mm antiaircraft guns slowed the Soviet advance on May 15. Two days later, the Germans launched a counteroffensive that sliced through the Soviet lines, and on May 22, German forces completed an encirclement of the Soviet Sixth Army. By May 26, the tattered remains of the Sixth Army had been forced into a shrinking pocket a mere two miles wide. Marshal Fedor von Bock watched from a nearby hill as German bombers streaked overhead and artillery shells rained down on the masses of troops and vehicles caught in the destruction. Above the explosions, Bock might have heard the screams of men and horses as yet another Soviet army was wiped out. It was an "overwhelming picture," he wrote in his diary. Field Marshal Paul Ludwig von Kleist wrote that in "places of the heaviest fighting the ground is so thickly covered with the bodies of man and horses, as far as the eye can see, that it is only with difficulty that you can find a path for your tank."[9]

The German victories at Kerch, Sevastopol, and Kharkov added to a still-expanding list of battlefield triumphs. Indeed, for a moment in the summer of 1942, it appeared as if the Wehrmacht might regain its standing as a near-unstoppable force. However, like the Wehrmacht's victories of 1941, the battles of 1942 did little to transform the under-lying strategic reality of the war in the East. Germany could win bat-tle after battle, annihilating entire Soviet armies in the process, but it could not stop the Soviet colossus. With each victory, the Wehrmacht sacrificed irreplaceable manpower, drained its strategic resources, and drove deeper into the Russian quagmire. This brutal calculus would soon reach its peak in the ruined city of Stalingrad.

On June 28, 1942, the Wehrmacht launched Operation Blue. Hitler and the German high command had made the fateful deci-sion to mount not one but two major prongs of attack, dividing Army Group South into two subgroups, A and B. Army Group A would strike south into the Caucasus in an effort to seize the region's rich oil fields; Group B would attack east toward the Volga. The oil fields of Maykop, Grozny, and Baku represented key objectives. However, the Führer explained, a "concentration of enemy forces is taking place in the Stalingrad area, which the enemy will probably defend tenaciously." German forces could not ignore this Red Army buildup and expose the eastern flanks of its offensive in the Caucasus. By splitting Army Group South into two groups, Hitler and his com-manders dispersed their strength and multiplied the Wehrmacht's already-formidable logistical challenges.[10]

In spite of these challenges, the twin German offensives made rapid initial progress. On August 9, forces from Group A seized the city of Maykop and its surrounding oil fields after heavy fighting. Hit-ler's long-held goal of gaining control of Russia's petroleum reserves seemed within reach. However, German engineers quickly discovered that the retreating Soviet troops had sabotaged the facilities, setting fires, pouring concrete into the wells, and ensuring that it would be at least six months before the Nazis were able to restore production. As in the previous summer, German forces had taken vast chunks of ter-ritory. But this time, the Soviet armies refused to be trapped. In July, Stalin had rescinded his "stand fast" orders and authorized Red Army commanders to stage strategic withdrawals. Operation Blue's goals of encircling and destroying the Red Army in the south depended on the Soviets' standing and fighting. "The Army High Command," Field Marshal Bock complained in August, "would like to encircle an enemy who is no longer there."[11]

More broadly, the campaign presented the Wehrmacht with a dilemma. "It had overrun a great deal of territory and eaten up a large chunk of its limited supplies of fuel and transport," writes historian Robert Citino. "It could not stay where it was, in the great flat plain between the Donets and the Don; it certainly had no intention of retreating to a more defensible position. Before it lay a yawning void, apparently empty of Soviet troops as far as the Don itself. The only realistic choice was to go forward." On August 1, Hitler and the German commanders made another pivotal decision, this one to shift their focus from the Caucasus to Stalingrad. Group A was still making good progress in the south, but Group B's advance had slowed. At the same time, continuing indications of a Red Army buildup to the east helped push the Germans toward Stalingrad. In the long run, they reasoned, the annihilation of the Soviet forces in the east would help secure the offensive in the south. Nevertheless, this push to take Stalingrad stripped Group A of vital petroleum, ammunition, and reinforcements. In contrast to its rapid initial progress, the German thrust into the Caucasus now began losing momentum. Soviet resistance, rougher terrain, and dwindling petroleum slowed Group A as it pushed farther south. By early November German forces had nearly reached the city of Ordzhonikidze, which controlled the strategically vital road to Baku. However, less than two kilometers outside the city, under withering fire from Soviet defenders, out of fuel, and facing the oncoming winter, German tanks ground to a halt.[12]

Germany's remaining hopes for a decisive victory in 1942 now hinged on the battle for Stalingrad. Although Nazi leaders had not initially identified Stalingrad as a significant strategic goal, its location as a potential staging point for a Soviet counterattack, along with the symbolic significance of seizing a city bearing Stalin's name, soon elevated its importance. By the end of June, General Alfred Jodl, chief of operations for the German high command, argued that "the fate of the Caucasus will be decided at Stalingrad." The campaign, spearheaded by General Friedrich Paulus's Sixth Army, got off to a slow start because of insufficient fuel supplies. Only after Hitler and the German high command shifted emphasis from the Caucasus to the Stalingrad offensive did Paulus's troops begin to make substantial progress. This delay gave the Soviets additional time to reinforce their defenses. Even so, the Germans managed to encircle and destroy a large number of Soviet troops outside of Kalach. The Wehrmacht continued its march eastward, but it was running out of time. "East of the Don, only more steppe awaits us," wrote German soldier Joachim Stempel. "The ground is flat and devoid of trees; it possesses a depressing boredom—heat, dust, and wide spaces without shadow." Nevertheless, Stempel could not help but worry about the coming winter: "Snow, winter storms, icy frost. Don't think about it! Not now, while we're sitting on our motorcycles, sweating."[13]

As German forces continued their drive toward Stalingrad, Soviet commanders prepared to meet them. Through July, Soviet officials anticipated a renewed German attack on Moscow and chose to concentrate their forces along the central front. By September, however, it had become clear that the thrust of the Wehrmacht's operations was taking place in the south. In response, the Soviet general staff redeployed forces for a defense of Stalingrad. News that the Wehrmacht had crossed the Don River and was marching toward the city prompted Stalin to issue a new order aimed at galvanizing Soviet resistance. "Our Motherland is experiencing days of grave adversity," he proclaimed. "It is time to stop retreating. Not one step back!" Alongside this bluster, Stalin ordered the creation of penal battalions, which would be assigned the most dangerous tasks, and the deployment of blocking detachments with orders to shoot those who retreated. The Sixty-Second Army, commanded by General Vasily Chuikov, would bear a large share of the burden of defending the city.[14]

While Stalin's order may have stiffened Soviet resolve, it did not stop the Nazi advance. On August 23, Luftwaffe commanders launched a massive air raid on the city. "It was beautiful and sunny," wrote Ezri Ioffe, director of the Stalingrad Medical Institute. Air-raid sirens wailed as waves of bombers streaked overhead. "It actually looked like the sky was covered with airplanes," remembered one local woman. "They bombed us mercilessly, and there was fire all around." The survivors emerged to a darkened landscape of ruined buildings, shattered glass, and raging fires. Columns of dark smoke towered over the river where German bombs had ignited the oil tanks. Soviet officials claimed as many as forty thousand people had been killed in the raid. That same day, panzers from the Sixth Army broke through Soviet defenses in the northern suburbs of Stalingrad and drove to the banks of the Volga. Soldiers gazing across the waters saw, for the first time, Barbarossa's original geographic objective.[15]

Arriving at the suburbs of Stalingrad in late August, German soldier Joachim Stempel noted the multiple echelons of fortifications facing the Wehrmacht. "Dug-in tanks are scarcely visible, with their guns aimed just over the cover. Flamethrowers turn the entire killing ground that we have to cross into a sheet of flame." In the distance, he watched massive columns of black smoke rising over "a bright gleam of fires [that] cover the entire city." After several days of fighting, Stempel grew concerned about high casualties. Three-quarters of his regiment's officers had been killed or wounded; Stempel's own driver had had one of his arms torn off. "How are we to carry on like this in the days and weeks to come?" he wrote. A panzer officer wrote of the brutal fighting in the "ruins, cellars, and factory sewers." After fighting to take the Barrikady gun factory, Wilhelm Hoffmann wrote, "Every time you move you have to jump over bodies." Hoffmann's fellow soldiers had begun calling Stalingrad "the mass grave of the Wehrmacht." Soviet soldiers "are not men, but some kind of cast-iron creatures; they never get tired and are not afraid of fire. . . . Every soldier sees himself as a condemned man."[16]

But men were not the only ones fighting for Stalingrad. Soviet women dug ditches, manned antiaircraft batteries, and fought alongside men. However, no role was more celebrated than that of female snipers. Women proved particularly adept at lying concealed for long hours waiting for a shot. Soviet forces had employed female snipers since the beginning of the war, but the fighting in the ruins of Stalingrad revealed their full potential. The most famous, Tania Chernova, claimed to have killed eighty Germans in three months of fighting.[17]

Amid the burned-out rubble of Stalingrad, the Red Army unleashed the horrors of urban warfare. Street by street, building by building, Chuikov and Paulus fed their troops into the Stalingrad meat grinder. Soviet troops were ordered to "hug" the Germans—to fight in such close quarters as to neutralize the Wehrmacht's superiority in aircraft and artillery. Soviet forces were able to use the eastern banks of the Volga as a sprawling rear area from which they ferried replacement troops to the front. In this way, Chuikov managed to hold on to pockets of the city, forcing Paulus and the Sixth Army into a brutal battle of attrition. The city's position, spread out along the river, prevented the Wehrmacht's preferred tactic of encircling the enemy and allowed Soviet forces to stage deadly ambushes in the ruins. Frustrated, filthy, and suffering mounting casualties, German soldiers began referring to the battle as the "rat's war."[18]

Still, the Germans pushed forward toward the river. "The fighting is meter by meter. It really is a bestial battle for every bit of ground," wrote Stempel. "Directly in front of us are the big, wide, and confusing factories and workshops." German forces watched through binoculars as newly built tanks drove out of the factories and disappeared "into the maze of ruins." He marveled at the Soviet willingness to sacrifice men and materials. "Smoke and dust rise against the skies and darken the piercing sun. And yet we see again and again that newly completed T-34 tanks leave the factories," some rolling "straight into battle." As the days turned to weeks, the bloodbath wore on. "The fight rages for each house, each factory hall, for railroad cuts and walls, for each cellar," Stempel wrote. "What we all fear seems likely to come true—that we'll be fighting here in winter."[19]

While German forces blasted their way deeper into the ruins, the Soviet leadership developed plans for a strategic counteroffensive: Operation Uranus. The origins of the plan remain disputed, but the general outline called for Chuikov's forces to continue their stubborn defense of Stalingrad, pinning down Paulus's Sixth Army, while the Red Army moved up its reserves. Once their troops were ready, Soviet commanders would launch pincer attacks to the north and south, driving forward to surround and destroy the Sixth Army inside Stalingrad. The ruined city would become a massive trap for Paulus's army. The overextended Sixth Army had deployed most of its forces to spearhead the attack on the city and left allied Romanian troops to guard its flanks. If Soviet forces could encircle the Germans fighting in Stalingrad, these second-rate Axis satellite troops would crumble, trapping Paulus's army inside the city.[20]

On the night of November 18, a white fog, "thick as milk," fell over Stalingrad and a heavy snow blanketed the ground. At 7:30 the next morning, thousands of Soviet guns and rockets opened up on the German lines. Soviet commanders had moved 160,000 men, ten thousand horses, 430 tanks, and six thousand guns across the Volga in the preceding weeks. By 9:00 a.m., Soviet infantry were advancing. The attack slammed into the Romanian Third Army, which was guarding the northwestern approaches to the city. Soviet heavy tanks routed the Romanians and drove hard to the southeast. The following day, November 20, the Stalingrad Front—"fronts" being the Soviet designation for army groups—attacked from the south, heading toward Kalach. This second pincer tore into the Romanian Fourth Army, which disintegrated before the Soviet onslaught. The two Soviet armies met on November 23 southeast of Kalach, closing the pincers on some three hundred thousand German troops still fighting in Stalingrad.[21]

Paulus was now cut off and facing disaster. Some officers began calling for the Sixth Army to stage a breakout. However, any attempt to withdraw faced steep obstacles: most of Paulus's forces were tied down fighting in the rubble of Stalingrad, his fuel supplies were dangerously low, and he had sent most of his horses away. Making matters worse, the winter weather slowed all movement. Hitler ordered Paulus to hunker down in the city rather than attempt to break out of the encirclement. Indeed, a similar tactic had worked at the Battle of Moscow the previous winter. In the meantime, German leaders would stage an operation to save Paulus's troops. Herman Göring, chief of the Luftwaffe, insisted that his forces could supply the Sixth Army by airlift. Field Marshal Erich von Manstein would mount an offensive to reestablish a land connection to Paulus. Hitler's refusal to admit defeat hung over all of these decisions: "To think that I will come back here again next time is madness," Hitler told Kurt Zeitzler, chief of the army general staff. "We won't come back here, so we cannot leave. Also too much blood has been shed to do that." Germany could not fail because failure would signal the unraveling of Hitler's empire.[22]

The Germans now braced for the dual onslaught of the Red Army and the Russian winter. "Soldiers of the Sixth Army," Paulus told his men the morning of November 27, "the Army is surrounded. That is not your fault. . . . [The enemy] will not achieve his aim, which is to annihilate us. There is much more that I must ask of you: to go through exertion and privation in the cold and snow; to stand fast and to hit back against greatly superior forces. The Führer has promised us help. . . . Have no doubt, the Führer will get us out." As days turned to weeks, however, hope waned. Manstein's efforts to blast his way to the Sixth Army failed, and Göring's promised air bridge proved entirely insufficient. On Christmas Day, a lull in the fighting allowed groups of doomed soldiers to huddle together, shivering in the cold while softly singing "Stille Nacht." By late December, starving Germans were grateful for "dainty morsels" of decomposing horse flesh. "If you were really lucky you might find a single pea or a bit of noodle floating in your soup," wrote one German tanker. "We looked like skeletons or walking corpses, some of us on a ration of just a handful of oats and a little water." Ernst Panse was among the thousands of

German soldiers trapped in Stalingrad, battling icy winds and frigid cold and surviving on rations of "only 100 grams of bread, 60 grams of meat or fat, six cigarettes, half a liter of tea or coffee, and, if it was available, half a liter of horse meat soup." Thousands of men, he wrote, were "killed, frozen to death, starved, or devoured by lice."[23]

By late January 1943, all hope had been lost. "Troops are without ammunition and food," Paulus wrote. Thousands of wounded lay untreated for want of bandages or medicine, and the front was disintegrating. "Collapse is inevitable. The army requests permission to surrender." The Führer refused and instead promoted Paulus to field marshal. No German officer of that rank had ever been captured. In effect, Hitler was ordering Paulus to commit suicide. However, the new field marshal had other ideas. On the morning of January 31, as a cold sleet fell from the winter sky and gunfire crackled in the distance, a delegation of Soviet officers approached the German headquarters at the Univermag department store. Five SS officers brandishing submachine guns guarded the entrance to the basement. After presenting their credentials, the Soviets were led into a dark basement lit only by dim lamps and flickering candles. Nazi banners covered the walls, but the floor was strewn with dirt and debris. Paulus waited alone in his room, wearing an unbuttoned greatcoat. He explained that he had recently been promoted but had not yet received his new uniform. After searching Paulus for weapons, Soviet officers took the field marshal into their custody.[24]

Paulus's surrender sent a shock wave through the Third Reich. For the first time, a full German army had been lost in battle. However, Stalingrad's greatest significance lay not in the obliteration of the Sixth Army but in the strategic transformation of the eastern front and the broader war. The Red Army had pulled even with Wehrmacht and was now on track to surpass the German war machine. Much like the American victory at Midway in the Pacific, the Soviet triumph at Stalingrad created a rough parity between the opposing forces that the Allies, with their superior human and industrial resources, could now move to exploit through a war of attrition.[25]

As Hitler watched the collapse of the Wehrmacht at Stalingrad, his mind reeled with the apocalyptic implications of the defeat. Russia, he warned the German people, sought "to conquer Europe, to destroy its culture, to exterminate its people, and to gain slave labour for the Siberian tundra." The choice was simple: "Either there is a victory of Germany, of the German Wehrmacht, of our allies, and of Europe, or the Asiatic-Bolshevik wave will break into our continent whose culture is the world's most ancient." The war that the Nazis had unleashed now assumed the specter of a titanic struggle for the defense of European civilization against an imagined horde of Eastern barbarians.[26]

WHILE THE RED ARMY PUMMELED THE WEHRMACHT ON THE EASTern front, Rommel's forces continued their struggle for control of North Africa. In November 1941, British forces mounted Operation Crusader, which relieved the besieged fortress of Tobruk and pushed Rommel's Afrika Korps back to El Agheila, Libya. For the moment, London had managed to fend off a German assault into Egypt. However, Britain's position in the Middle East remained precarious. In particular, colonial officials worried about the potential for Axis-backed insurrection in the region. The empire had stamped out uprisings in the Iraq and Palestine mandates, but other trouble spots remained.

Like many leaders in the colonial world, Iran's monarch, Reza Shah, harbored sympathies for Germany and remained eager to assert national independence from British influence. British concerns grew deeper in June 1941 when Rashid Ali, leader of the Iraqi Revolt, and some of his supporters fled across the border into Iran. The German invasion of the Soviet Union sounded yet another alarm in London: as the Wehrmacht tore through southern Russia, it drew ever closer to the vital oil fields of Iran. On the other hand, if Moscow held out, the Persian Gulf and the port of Abadan would serve as a vital shipping route for Allied aid to the Soviet Union. In July, London and Moscow delivered a joint ultimatum to Reza Shah calling for the expulsion of all Germans from the country. Although the shah tried to negotiate, London and Moscow had already resolved to take action. On August 25, 1941, British troops marched into southern Iran while the Red Army moved across the northern border. In one of their first official acts, the Allies placed large parts of Iran under occupation and deposed the shah.[27]

Wartime hardships and colonial politics were also straining Allied positions in the Mediterranean. By early 1942, Egyptians faced shortages of basic commodities such as sugar, flour, and cloth. Bread riots in Cairo coincided with news that German forces were once again advancing toward the border. In the midst of this crisis, Egyptian prime minister Hussein Sirri Pasha severed diplomatic relations with Vichy France, igniting a firestorm that ultimately led to his resignation on February 2. Fearing greater unrest, British authorities ordered King Farouk to invite the opposition Wafd Party to form a new government. When the king balked, British tanks and soldiers surrounded the royal palace, forcing Farouk's hand. Although the British move forestalled the immediate political crisis, it sowed the seeds for later unrest.[28] In Iran, Iraq, Palestine, and Egypt, the British had chosen to tighten imperial control as a bulwark against Axis incursions. For London, victory against the Axis required a heavier—rather than lighter—hand in the colonial world.

British leaders weren't the only ones struggling with the dilemmas of the Mediterranean war. Although they made for good press, Rommel's exploits in North Africa had achieved little in the way of concrete strategic success. German panzers had roared across vast stretches of sand, kicking up great clouds of dust and burnishing Rommel's fame, but they had not managed to dislodge the British from Egypt. Nor had they managed to break the defense of Tobruk. Moreover, long advances strained the logistical capabilities of both sides. By the time Rommel's tanks neared the Egyptian border, they were running desperately short of fuel. Indeed, neither army could fight effectively when it reached the outer limits of its supply line. The fortress of Tobruk remained key to the campaign. So long as British forces held, they could threaten any German thrust toward Egypt. To reinforce Tobruk, British commanders had erected a stout line of defense near Gazala bristling with barbed wire and machine gun nests and crisscrossed by deep trenches. Their aim was to force Rommel's Afrika Korps into a static war of position that would neutralize the Germans' tactical advantages. Rommel had no intention of falling into the British trap. On May 26, Axis forces launched Operation Theseus in a bid to crush the Gazala Line and blast open a path to Tobruk. The operation began with a diversionary Italian attack at the northern end of the line. While their allies pounded at the British fortifications, Rommel's forces swung south in a broad arc to attack the defenders from the rear. As the sun rose on the morning of May 27, British forces watched a wall of dust drifting toward their positions. As the cloud drew closer, the defenders realized they were looking at "the whole of Rommel's command in full cry straight for [them]." General Claude Auchinleck, commander of British forces in the Middle East, reported that the main attack now appeared to be coming from the south, but he did not rule out the possibility of a northern thrust as part of a dual pincer movement.[29]

By May 28, British troops were struggling to hold off a fearsome onslaught by the bulk of Rommel's forces near the junction of Knightsbridge. Both sides suffered significant casualties in the tank battles, but the defenders managed to blunt Rommel's initial assault. Nevertheless, the Afrika Korps had established a position on the southern flank of the Gazala Line. Making matters worse, casualties suffered in the repulse of the initial assault had seriously weakened British defenses. Rommel now began attacking British positions piecemeal. On June 8, Free French troops fighting with the Allies under Charles de Gaulle were forced to withdraw following a stand at Bir Hakeim; by June 19, the last defenders at Acroma had pulled back, clearing the path for Rommel to begin attacks on Tobruk. Two days later, British commanders lost radio contact with the garrison at Tobruk. Small groups of the defenders managed to escape by sea and eventually made their way to Alexandria. However, the bulk of the thirty-three thousand soldiers in Tobruk surrendered to the Germans. After months of fighting, Rommel had taken the port. The Germans were now within striking distance of the Egyptian frontier and threatening Alexandria and the broader Middle East.[30]

While the fall of Tobruk set off a panic in Cairo and a round of recriminations in London, Berlin celebrated. Hitler hailed the victory as "destiny's gift to the German nation" and told Mussolini that the loss of the city might lead to the "collapse of the entire oriental structure of the British Empire." Although some voices called for a pause to allow the depleted Axis forces to refit and resupply, Hitler and Rommel remained eager to press on toward the Egyptian frontier. On June 23—two days after capturing Tobruk—Rommel struck out toward Sollum and Sidi Barrani. British forces now scrambled to pull back to a defensive position. The defenders mounted a half-hearted defense of Mersa Matruh that collapsed on June 29. German forces advanced, but they were now running short on fuel and water and operating at the end of a long supply line. Nonetheless, Rommel charged forward once again, toward the British defenses at El Alamein. Triumphant Axis propaganda declared that German forces were fighting in Egypt "with the aim of driving the English out of Egyptian territory and continuing operations against England so as to free the Near East from English domination."[31]

In fact, the Western Desert campaign was about to turn decisively against the Axis. The fall of Tobruk and Rommel's invasion of Egypt were thunderous operational victories, but they did little to shift the deeper strategic realities of the war. The Afrika Korps had reached the outer limits of its supply line and would now confront well-provisioned British forces in much stronger defensive positions. The Allies were growing stronger while the Wehrmacht—even in victory—bled soldiers, tanks, and resources. The situation had become so dire that the Germans had come to depend on raiding Allied provisions to maintain their own supplies. Auchinleck had made the difficult decision to trade space for time. Rather than sacrifice British forces in a panicked effort to defend scattered desert outposts, journalist Alan Moorehead wrote, the general "allowed the Germans to come on, hoping that they would wear themselves out." By conserving his forces, even if it meant falling back to the Suez Canal, Auchinleck ensured his troops "would live to fight another day when they were stronger and the enemy weaker." Moorehead characterized Auchinleck's thinking thus: "If I lose the Delta I have always the hope of winning it back again. If I lose the Eighth Army then I lose everything." This strategy of playing for time made even more sense when viewed in the context of the global war. While Rommel's forces had been blasting their way toward Tobruk, the US Navy had won its pivotal victory against the Japanese carrier fleet at the Battle of Midway. As the strategic balance in the Pacific shifted, the United States prepared to enter the war in the Mediterranean. Indeed, the fall of Tobruk proved to be the final straw in pushing US leaders to agree to a joint plan to invade North Africa. First, however, Rommel's forces would crash full force into the British defenses at El Alamein.[32]

ON JUNE 30, GERMAN FORCES APPROACHED EL ALAMEIN, A LONELY railway stop less than two miles from the coast. Moorehead was struck by the battlefield's natural beauty. "First there was the green-blue sparkling sea itself," he wrote, "then the snow-white beach and the sand dunes, then inside the dunes the grey salt flats that were pitted with shell holes and bomb craters and looked as the surface of the moon might be." Beyond the flats, "ultramarine salt lakes" baked in the July sun, the dunes of the yellow desert fading into the distance. For all its natural beauty, El Alamein constituted a formidable defensive position. The town perched atop a narrow strip of solid land some thirty to forty-five miles wide, bounded in the north by saltwater marshes and the Mediterranean Sea and in the south by the steep cliffs of the Qattara Depression, which sloped down into another set of wetlands. Rommel would have no choice but to hurl his depleted panzer forces against Auchinleck's fortifications head-on. Not only would the attackers be forced into this narrow strip of land, but they would also have to surmount three fortified ridges, Miteiriya, Ruweisat, and Alam el-Halfa, the last of which rose some 430 feet above sea level. "We are 130 kilometers from Alexandria," the German Ninetieth Light Division reported. "West and south-west of El Alamein the enemy has established his last, albeit heavily fortified, position before the Nile crossing, which he will presumably defend to the last with all the forces at his disposal."[33]

Rommel planned to stage a frontal assault on the center of Auchinleck's line just to the south of the town of El Alamein. After spearheading the attack, the Ninetieth Division would encircle the town while a second force circled right to envelop British forces in the south. Rommel expected the defenders to flee in the face of this overwhelming attack. The operation began at 3:15 a.m. on July 1 and quickly came under heavy fire from British artillery. Far from running away, the British managed to stop the Germans in their tracks. The main thrust of the assault captured a British strongpoint at Deir el Shein, but at the heavy cost of eighteen tanks. Rommel tried to break through Auchinleck's defenses again on July 2 and 3, but each time, the Germans ran into punishing British fire and were forced to halt. Fighting raged for three more weeks, but Wehrmacht forces were unable to force a British collapse. Rommel found himself in a battle of attrition he could not win. "The front had now solidified," he later complained. "In operational terms, the British were in their element. . . . In this *Stellungskrieg* [war of position], the decision went to the side that fired off more ammunition." The First Battle of El Alamein amounted to a strategic victory for the British.[34]

Although Auchinleck's meticulous preparations had stopped Rommel, Churchill concluded that it was time for a change. In August, the prime minister arrived in Cairo to assess the situation. He wrote of his concern that Auchinleck may have "lost the confidence of the Desert Army." In truth, Churchill was annoyed that his Middle East commander had not launched a counteroffensive after halting Rommel's attack. Never mind the fact that British forces needed time to restore their strength and rearm; never mind the fact that the logistical situation now heavily favored the British. Churchill transferred Auchinleck to India and designated General William Gott as his replacement. However, Gott was killed soon after when German fighters shot down his plane. In his place, Churchill appointed General Bernard Montgomery.[35] Montgomery had the good fortune to assume command of a theater that had already turned in the Allies' favor. Auchinleck had broken Rommel's momentum at the First Battle of El Alamein and an influx of new supplies—including some from the United States—were bolstering the British advantage in manpower, firepower, and provisions. Though none of this was directly Montgomery's doing, he would receive the credit.

First, however, Rommel staged one last bid to break through the British defenses and reach the Suez Canal. Afrika Korps found itself in a "race against time," Rommel later wrote. As London and Washington rushed reinforcements to North Africa, Rommel found himself with a shrinking window of time before the resupplied Allied forces would overwhelm his Axis troops. "So we intended to strike first." Rommel planned to send a motorized force around El Alamein's supposedly impassable southern flank in a repeat of the Gazala offensive. Late on the night of August 30, Axis forces attacked the southern end of Montgomery's line at El Alamein. Slowed by minefields and artillery barrages, the Germans pushed forward. Flares lit the skies while the RAF carried out targeted air strikes against the attackers. This delay fatally undermined the German plan—having lost the element of surprise, Rommel turned to a last-ditch effort to seize the Alam el Halfa ridge, the anchor of the El Alamein position. At 1:00 p.m., blanketed by a heavy sandstorm, German troops charged toward the ridge. Again, however, waves of British aircraft rained bombs on the Germans, inflicting heavy casualties. Meanwhile, Axis forces were running out of fuel. The air strikes continued through the night while the defenders kept the German positions illuminated by parachute flares. On September 3, Rommel began pulling back, leaving scores of burning vehicles behind. "With the failure of this offensive our last chance of gaining the Suez Canal had gone," Rommel wrote. Allied production would now begin flowing into North Africa and "finally turn the tide against us."[36]

Key to the Allied position in North Africa was the survival of the British garrison on Malta. Together with Gibraltar and the Suez Canal, Malta represented one of the three keys to control of the Mediterranean. While the British base at Gibraltar controlled the western passage to the Atlantic and the Suez Canal formed the eastern link to the Red Sea and Indian Ocean, Malta sat at the midpoint and functioned as a vital supply depot for shipping and, in Churchill's words, an "unsinkable aircraft carrier" for the RAF. Control of Malta gave British planes and ships the ability to menace Axis shipping to Rommel's forces in North Africa and to protect their own supply lines to Egypt. Berlin, London, and Rome all recognized the island's importance and, from June 1940 to November 1942, fought a bitter struggle for its control. Italy's Regia Aeronautica and the Luftwaffe pummeled Malta with some fifteen thousand tons of bombs, making it possibly the most heavily bombed location of the war. Nevertheless, the island survived nearly two and a half years of siege. As the battle for the Mediterranean reached its climax in the autumn of 1942, British air and naval forces operating out of Malta had reduced the flow of Axis supplies to North Africa to a trickle.[37]

While Rommel's troops rationed fuel in their positions facing El Alamein, the strategic initiative in North Africa passed to the Allies. Montgomery set October 23 as the date for his attack: British forces needed time to train, and his sappers needed the light of a full moon to clear a path through Axis minefields to the west. This delay prompted grumbling in London—an impatient Churchill was anxious to score a win against Rommel before the Americans joined the war in the Mediterranean—but Eighth Army's commander remained firm. Montgomery also hoped to break with previous offensives that had concentrated on the south and then turned north toward the sea. Instead, he planned to focus his attack in the north. Montgomery reversed the traditional method of aiming one's attack on the enemy's armor and instead planned to concentrate on Axis infantry while blocking Rommel's tanks. British forces staged an elaborate deception operation consisting of camouflaged supply dumps, mock-up vehicles, and a dummy pipeline. Montgomery hoped to convince Rommel that the British offensive was likely to start in November and target the southern end of the Axis lines. British plans also depended on close support from the RAF, which now controlled the skies above Egypt. "If we are successful it will mean the end of the war in North Africa," he told his men. "It will be the turning point of the whole war."[38]

At 9:40 p.m. on October 23, bathed in moonlight, Montgomery's forces launched their assault. British artillery delivered a thunderous barrage against the Axis lines while engineers cleared two paths through the enemy's minefield. By 5:30 the next morning, the corridors had been cleared and British armor, bolstered by newly delivered American Sherman tanks, was surging forward to secure a bridgehead on the other side. Rommel, who missed the opening of the battle while receiving medical treatment in Austria, described the barrage as a "tornado of fire" that "grew to World War I proportions." Frontline Italian troops fled in terror as Allied forces overran their positions. German units fought back, but the attackers' material superiority threatened to overwhelm the defenders. "Rivers of blood were poured out over miserable strips of land," Rommel wrote. "Load after load of bombs cascaded down among my troops." Making matters worse, fuel shortages limited Rommel's ability to bring up reinforcements. Allied troops withstood the German counterattacks and gradually pushed deeper into Axis positions. At 1:00 on the morning of November 2, Montgomery's troops opened the next phase of the battle in the form of Operation Supercharge: a combined force of infantry and tanks punched through the German lines to establish a bridgehead for three armored divisions that then fanned out to sever Germany lines of communication and force an Axis collapse. "The battle is going very heavily against us," Rommel wrote the following day. "We're simply being crushed by the enemy weight."[39]

Rommel was now forced to retreat. His troops were running out of fuel, British tanks were massing inside his lines, and the RAF continued its heavy bombardment. However, Hitler demanded that Afrika Korps hold its position: "There can be no other thought but to stand fast and throw every gun and every man into the battle. . . . As to your troops, you can show them no other road than that to victory or death." Rommel, shocked by the Führer's intervention, scrambled to shore up his lines, but the situation was hopeless. British commanders estimated that their force of six hundred tanks faced a mere eighty surviving panzers. Hitler's "Victory or Death" command forced Rommel to hesitate one more day before ordering a retreat on November 4. Had he not waited, Rommel wrote, "the army would in all probability have been saved, with all its infantry, in at least a semi-battleworthy condition." Even so, the Germans executed a fighting withdrawal, retreating west across North Africa before finally arriving in the Axis stronghold of Tunisia. Montgomery's cautious pursuit aided Rommel's escape. Nevertheless, the Second Battle of El Alamein marked a critical moment in the struggle for the Mediterranean.[40]

CHURCHILL, EVER EAGER TO TRUMPET THE ACCOMPLISHMENTS OF the British Empire, praised the victory at El Alamein as nothing less than the turning point of the war: "Before Alamein we never had a victory. After Alamein we never had a defeat." The prime minister's statement contained a healthy dose of hyperbole. Somewhere between thirty-five thousand and forty thousand of Rommel's troops were killed, wounded, or captured at El Alamein. Axis casualties at Stalingrad were twenty times higher, numbering something on the order of eight hundred thousand. Nevertheless, November 1942 witnessed a sea change in the Second World War. Put together, the Allied victories at Stalingrad and El Alamein marked the farthest advance of Hitler's and Mussolini's empires. Although the scale of the fighting on the eastern front dwarfed the conflict in North Africa, Rommel's and Paulus's defeats were rooted in the same underlying dynamic:

for all their supposed tactical skill on the battlefield, German armies could not overcome the Allies' material advantages. Like the Battle of Midway, the struggles for Stalingrad and North Africa turned on the massive economic, technological, and military resources of the rising superpowers. Making matters worse, commanders such as Zhukov and Montgomery were starting to close the gap in operational prowess. The Axis powers had always been in a race against time, but by November 1942, it was becoming increasingly apparent that they were falling behind.[41]

Chapter II

THE PATH TO GLOBAL HEGEMONY

As the sun dropped below the horizon on August 6, 1942, eighty-two US ships approached the Solomon Islands. Haze hung in the humid air as darkness closed over the fleet. Aboard the transports, marines tried to sleep, wrote letters, or listened to juke-boxes in the mess halls. At 2:40 a.m. the next morning, the advance ships closed toward Cape Esperance at the northwestern tip of Guadalcanal. Twenty minutes later, as the dank smell of the jungle swept over the ships' decks, the first wave of marines were roused from their bunks. Just before sunrise, the American warships opened fire on the beaches of Guadalcanal and neighboring Tulagi. As landing ships loaded with marines pitched back and forth in the waves, aircraft streaked overhead to strafe Japanese positions. By 9:15 a.m., the marines were scrambling across the empty beaches of Guadalcanal. "The heat was terrific," remembered one marine. "Sweat was pouring like rivers off the brows. They reached the other side of the field going on to encounter the thickest jungle in the tropics." The lightly armed Japanese construction crews had retreated into the jungle. The next day, the marines would find the nearly completed airfield abandoned along with stocks of rice, beer, and sake.[1]

If the Allied victories at Midway, El Alamein, and Stalingrad halted the Axis onslaught, a string of American amphibious invasions in the late summer and autumn of 1942 placed the Axis empires on the defensive. By November, the United States would be fighting two large infantry campaigns against great power opponents in theaters separated by over ten thousand miles. The only other power to have attempted anything comparable was the British Empire, which had lost the battle for Malaya and only just held on to Egypt the previous year. Now, Allied troops were poised to seize Axis territory in both North Africa and the South Pacific. In August, US Marines landed on Guadalcanal, initiating a grueling six-month campaign that would stretch Japanese forces to their limit. Three months later, US troops landed in Morocco and Algeria in the first stage of a series of campaigns against Axis forces in North Africa, Sicily, and Italy. In doing so, the United States took the first steps on a path to securing control of the Pacific and the Mediterranean and placing its armies in control of much of Western Europe and East Asia after 1945. The Mediterranean and the South Pacific would serve as cornerstones for the Allied war effort and postwar American hegemony.

America's rise to global hegemony emerged from contentious debates between the Allied powers. While most US military leaders favored an early direct assault on Germany in the form of a cross-channel invasion of France, London advocated a peripheral approach aimed at safeguarding lines of imperial communication and securing strategic dominance in the postwar order. Concerted pressure from British officials ultimately convinced Roosevelt to back this peripheral strategy and assume the mantle of global empire. This new Pax Americana would rest on the foundation of a massive navy and a sprawling network of bases—both of which US leaders created to defeat the Axis empires.

But this peripheral strategy carried long-term costs. London and Washington conducted these campaigns as a series of massive colonial interventions, dominating the seas and intervening when and where they chose while relying on the Soviets and Chinese to grind down the Axis armies in the continental slaughterhouses of Eurasia. By pursuing an indirect approach, Washington and London shifted the bloodiest fighting onto their allies' shoulders, ensuring that Stalin's forces would occupy the Eurasian heartland at war's end and sowing lasting resentments in the Soviet Union and China. Stalin and Chiang repeatedly expressed their frustration with this peripheral approach, but American and British leaders made the calculated decision to pursue this strategy in an effort to minimize their own casualties and secure their postwar interests. Thus, although the battles in the South Pacific and North Africa were dwarfed by the contemporaneous struggle at Stalingrad, they would play an outsize role in shaping the structure of power in the postwar order.

ON JUNE 20, 1942, A TRAVEL-WORN WINSTON CHURCHILL MET WITH Franklin Roosevelt in a small room at Roosevelt's Hyde Park estate. The prime minister had endured a twenty-seven-hour flight to Washington, a rough landing in New York, and a dizzying motor tour of the overlooks along the Hudson River. Now, stepping into the shaded meeting room, he complained about the stifling heat, which did not seem to bother the Americans. The two leaders had much to discuss: the Battle of the Atlantic was still raging, top secret research on what would become the atomic bomb had begun, and, perhaps stickiest of all, there was the question of when and where the Americans would enter the European war. Their conversation focused on the atomic bomb project, but Churchill also pushed Roosevelt to come to a decision regarding a second front in the war against Hitler. Late that night, the two men boarded a train for Washington, DC. If the prime minister had felt late June in the Hudson Valley was uncomfortably warm, he found the capital sweltering. Though he was grateful for the

White House's air-conditioning, Churchill would soon be embroiled in some of the most contentious arguments of the war.[2]

While Roosevelt and Churchill had been motoring along the banks of the Hudson River, the American and British chiefs in Washington had been arguing over strategy. The Americans had agreed on a Europe-first strategy in 1940, but the exact details of how a war would be fought remained undecided. Military leaders such as Army Chief of Staff George Marshall favored a direct attack on Nazi forces in northern Europe. A landing in northern France represented the shortest route from Britain to Hitler's Fortress Europe. Marshall and the majority of the American brass argued that any other approach threatened to scatter Allied resources across peripheral theaters that would contribute little to the broader struggle to defeat the Third Reich. Only an invasion of northern Europe offered the prospect of a decisive victory that would prevent the United States from becoming mired in a drawn-out war in Europe. In contrast, Churchill and the British chiefs advocated just such a peripheral strategy. The so-called British way of war aimed at using the formidable Royal Navy, sustained by the colonies, to fight offshore while supporting continental allies who would provide the manpower for Europe's bloody land battles. Further, British commanders doubted the feasibility of staging a successful invasion of France anytime soon. London feared that any premature assault on northern Europe would result in a second Dunkirk at best.[3]

In contrast, US military leaders worried that the invasion of North Africa would ensnare the US forces in Britain's imperial ventures in the Middle East and force an indefinite postponement of any cross-channel invasion of northern France. Moreover, if Washington and London delayed opening a second front in Europe, Stalin might opt to cut a deal with Hitler. Since the late summer of 1941, Roosevelt had been convinced that the Soviet Union was the linchpin of the Allied effort to defeat Germany. As he had explained to Churchill in April, the Soviets "were killing more Germans and destroying more equipment than you and I put together." In addition, the army's War

Plans Division had explained in the fall of 1941 that a Soviet defeat would render the Third Reich "practically invulnerable." If it seemed that London and Washington were stalling, Moscow might seek a negotiated settlement with Berlin. The opening of a second front in Europe might very well be instrumental in keeping Stalin engaged in the battle against Hitler.[4]

In February 1942, US military intelligence echoed this assessment. Current levels of Lend-Lease aid to Moscow amounted to "a mere trickle." Making matters worse, Soviet leaders suspected that the Western powers were hoping to grind Russian manpower down in a prolonged war against Germany. "Accordingly, it is logical for a Russian official to assume that the capitalistic nations, finding themselves colleagues by chance of the USSR in the battle against Germany, will only give sufficient supplies to keep Russia in the combat against the Reich as long as possible." Regardless, the report warned, US leaders should harbor no illusions about their allies in the Kremlin: "Independent action, imperialist expansion, and communistic infiltration must always be expected from the U.S.S.R."[5]

The ideal solution appeared to be an early cross-channel invasion of Europe that would place large numbers of Western troops on the continent, relieve pressure on Moscow, and demonstrate Anglo-American resolve. However, few military leaders in the United States or Britain believed that such an invasion could succeed in 1942. British leaders insisted that any attempt would result in a disaster that would crush hopes for a future landing. Even US leaders who supported a landing in northern France worried about its chances of success: General Dwight Eisenhower—future supreme commander of Allied forces in Western Europe—believed that the odds stood five to one against a successful operation. Nevertheless, he believed that even a failed operation would be justified if it helped keep "8,000,000 Russians in the war." Roosevelt also worried about waning public support for the Europe-first strategy. Following the Pearl Harbor attack, many Americans saw Japan as the primary threat. The longer Roosevelt waited to enter the European theater, the greater political pressure he would face to focus primary attention on defeating Tokyo. Compounding matters, George Marshall, Henry Stimson, and the Joint Chiefs had begun to argue that US forces should place priority on defeating Japan if their British allies refused to back a cross-channel attack. Roosevelt's time for a decision was rapidly running out.[6]

But fate soon intervened. The same morning that Churchill and Roosevelt's train pulled into Washington, news arrived that Tobruk had fallen. The entire Allied position in North Africa now appeared to be in jeopardy. At Churchill's request, Roosevelt agreed to send some three hundred new Sherman tanks to British forces in Egypt. More broadly, the fall of Tobruk gave a new urgency to British calls for a US invasion of North Africa. But the president had larger things in mind. As Stimson wrote, after a long day of meetings, Roosevelt "suddenly suggested that we might throw a large American force into the Middle East and cover the whole front between Alexandria and Tehran." The president's tilt toward the British position infuriated George Marshall, who warned that any large operations in the Middle East would squander Allied resources and divert Western armies from the "decisive theater," Western Europe.[7]

Roosevelt was now caught between his military advisers and Churchill. Three weeks later, on July 12, Churchill delivered an ultimatum. The North African invasion "affords the sole means by which United States forces can strike at Hitler in 1942," he told the senior British officer in Washington, Field Marshal John Dill. "However, if the President decides against [the invasion] the matter is settled. . . . Both countries will remain motionless in 1942, and all will be concentrated on [a cross-channel attack] in 1943."[8] Because British forces would have constituted a majority of the troops employed in a 1942 cross-channel attack, London held a de facto veto over the operation. The president had been backed into a corner. Unable to attack France in 1942 and unwilling to wait until 1943 to enter the European theater, Roosevelt had only one remaining option: an invasion of North Africa. Against the wishes of US military leaders, the United States would join Britain in the battle for the Mediterranean, a move that would ultimately postpone a cross-channel attack until 1944.

The news that his allies had chosen to attack North Africa rather than France enraged Joseph Stalin. While hundreds of thousands of Soviet soldiers were being cut down in an effort to block the Wehrmacht's drive into the Caucasus, British and American forces were preparing to seize weakly defended Vichy colonies in Morocco and Algeria, reinforce the British Empire's control of the Suez Canal, and establish Anglo-American control over the Mediterranean. Stalin concluded that his capitalist allies were conspiring to prolong the attrition of the Red Army while gobbling up strategic territory in the West—an appraisal that aligned with then-senator Harry Truman's 1941 call to aid both the Nazis and Soviets in hopes that the two powers would kill each other off. Since the 1930s, the Soviet dictator had suspected that British leaders hoped to draw Moscow into a war with Germany in order to weaken both powers and allow London to exploit the resulting carnage.[9]

As Soviet war correspondent Ilya Ehrenburg predicted in May 1942, "The British would only establish a second front if it became clear that the Russians were either being defeated or were about to be victorious." According to the Soviet ambassador to London, Ivan Maisky, Stalin's suspicions were well founded. In early August, Maisky wrote that Churchill did indeed "wish to weaken both the Soviet Union and Germany." But the ambassador explained that this was a "variable factor. Bourgeois Britain is without a doubt interested in seeing both the Soviet Union and Germany weaken simultaneously, but it is certainly not interested in a Nazi victory." Above all, British leaders hoped to see Germany defeated. London would continue its efforts to strengthen the Red Army as long as the Wehrmacht remained a threat in Europe. However, this same fear of the German military had led Churchill to focus on an air war and peripheral attacks rather than a cross-channel invasion. In any event, the ambassador wrote, London had already made its decision—Maisky urged

Stalin to focus on requests for military aid rather than an invasion of France.[10]

After a dinner at the British embassy in Cairo on the evening of August 10, Churchill and his entourage set off on a flight to Moscow by way of Tehran. The prime minister would deliver the news to Stalin in person. As his plane passed over the sparkling waters of the Caspian Sea and the curving channel of the Volga, the prime minister reflected on his historic visit: "I pondered on my mission to this sullen, sinister Bolshevik State I had once tried so hard to strangle at its birth, and which, until Hitler appeared, I had regarded as the mortal foe of civilised freedom. . . . We had always hated their wicked regime, and, till the German flail beat upon them, they would have watched us being swept out of existence with indifference and gleefully divided with Hitler our Empire in the East." But now, Britain's former imperial rival was an ally against the Third Reich. However, Churchill knew that he must deliver the unwelcome news that there would be no second front in 1942. "It was like carrying a large lump of ice to the North Pole," he wrote. Churchill opened the meeting with a frank discussion of the reasons why London and Washington would not be launching a cross-channel invasion in 1942. Stalin tried his best to look surprised. The dictator chided Churchill for being so afraid of the Germans and downplayed the dangers of a cross-channel attack on France.[11]

The conversation then turned to the plan to invade French North Africa, rechristened Operation Torch. Churchill explained that although a cross-channel invasion would not be possible, British and American forces could mount an offensive in North Africa. To illustrate his point, the prime minister sketched a picture of a crocodile. Torch, he explained, would circumvent the snout to attack the soft underbelly. Stalin appeared to approve. The North Africa attack, the dictator observed, would strike at Rommel's rear, keep Spain out of the war, drive a wedge between Vichy and Berlin, and threaten Mussolini's Italy. While Stalin continued to push for a cross-channel invasion, he knew that the British had made up their minds. On August 16,

Churchill left Moscow knowing that he had disappointed Stalin but feeling that the visit had gone as well as he could have hoped.[12]

Three days later, a primarily Canadian force of six thousand troops attacked the French channel port of Dieppe. The attackers met heavy German resistance and were forced to withdraw after nearly two-thirds of their number were killed, wounded, or captured. "What I don't understand is why Dieppe?" wrote one British general after the operation. "A raid is either 'to obtain information' and destroy some worthwhile objective or it is to train one's own troops. In the latter case one would not select a strongly defended sector. In the former, what was the objective?" Churchill later wrote that the operation was necessary as a means to gauge the prospects for a later cross-channel attack: "Military opinion seemed unanimous that until an operation on that scale was undertaken, no responsible general would take the responsibility of planning for the main invasion." Further, the prime minister claimed that the raid provided a "mine of [tactical] experience" and forced the Germans to keep a larger number of troops stationed in France, thereby relieving pressure on the Soviet Union.[13]

The Dieppe operation also served the political purpose of relieving Soviet and American pressure for a cross-channel invasion. Days after the raid, the US ambassador in Moscow reported "unusually wide" coverage of Dieppe in the Soviet newspapers along with claims that the "French masses were ready for invasion." Roosevelt's envoy Averell Harriman noted that "since Dieppe there has been far less public clamor [in London] and more sober thinking regaining a second front." The raid gave the impression that the Western Allies were preparing to open a second front in Europe while at the same time demonstrating that the time was not yet ripe for an invasion.[14]

Churchill's visit to Moscow, together with the news of the Dieppe raid, may have softened the blow, but Stalin's resentment over the lack of a second front continued into the fall. In an October exchange with Ambassador Maisky, Stalin charged Churchill with working toward Moscow's defeat in hopes of striking a negotiated settlement with Germany. Maisky replied that Churchill still sought the destruction of the Third Reich, but the British government had chosen to fight an "easy war." Stalin's anger cooled, but he still expressed doubts about Torch's ability to relieve pressure on the Red Army. The following month, the dictator told an audience that had the Allies attacked France, "the German-fascist army would already have been on the verge of disaster."[15] Clearly, Stalin did not believe that the coming Anglo-American operations in North Africa would constitute a genuine second front against the Third Reich.

ALTHOUGH US FORCES WOULD NOT EXECUTE A CROSS-CHANNEL invasion of France until 1944, by the end of 1942 they had already launched what was to become arguably the pivotal campaign of the Pacific War. Scattered across over one thousand miles of the South Pacific, the Solomon Archipelago consisted of over nine hundred islands. The six main islands rose into lush green peaks above the blue sea. The waters of the New Georgia Sound ran through the center of the archipelago, forming a corridor running to the southeast. Most of the land was covered in dense jungle fed by frequent rain and tropical humidity and teeming with mosquitoes, crocodiles, and giant bush rats. The Solomons formed an unlikely setting for one of the greatest battles of the war. The islands were so remote that they had been lost to Western explorers for two hundred years after the Spanish first visited in 1567. The British Empire had declared the archipelago a protectorate in 1893, but colonial presence remained relatively sparse. A half century later, the islands' eleven thousand square miles of land were home to perhaps one hundred thousand Indigenous Melanesians and a mere 650 Westerners. That was about to change.[16]

While most American leaders remained committed to the Europe-first strategy outlined in the 1940 Plan Dog memorandum, the US victory in the Battle of Midway shifted the balance of naval forces in the Pacific. No longer was Washington focused simply on limiting its losses in the East: US leaders could now consider launching a limited offensive against the Japanese Empire. General Douglas

MacArthur and Admiral Ernest King were eager to follow up on the Midway victory while the United States still held the initiative. Nevertheless, the Americans lacked a clear plan. With the fleet still recovering from the destruction at Pearl Harbor, American planners ruled out a direct attack across the Central Pacific. Meanwhile, Japanese activity in the Aleutians seemed too remote to demand concerted action in 1942. The best option for a campaign, US leaders decided, lay in the South Pacific. The Japanese base at Rabaul posed a significant threat to Allied lines of communication with Australia and was the anchor of Tokyo's position in the region.[17]

Indeed, in the wake of Midway, Japanese leaders hoped to bolster their ring of outer defenses around their new empire. To the west, the capture of Singapore had given Japan control of a key point linking the Indian Ocean to the Co-Prosperity Sphere. To the east, Tokyo's forward base at Truk Atoll gave the Japanese navy a formidable presence in the Central Pacific. Japan's greatest vulnerability lay in the south. The failure of the Port Moresby operation after the Battle of the Coral Sea left the empire's southern flank exposed to a potential attack from forces in Australia, but Tokyo had not yet given up. In late July, Japanese forces carried out an unopposed invasion of Buna on the northern coast of New Guinea and advanced south to the settlement of Kokoda. From there, Japanese soldiers followed an arduous trail through the Owen Stanley Mountain Range on their way to stage an overland attack on Port Moresby. For the next two months, Australian soldiers fought a bitter defense along the Kokoda Track as Japanese forces tried to push through to reach Port Moresby. Dense malarial jungle, dysentery, and rugged terrain took a grueling toll on both armies as they fought along the mountain trail.

Rabaul anchored this southern line, but the base lay within striking distance of the Solomon Islands in the southeast. Japanese leaders hoped to build a network of airfields on the islands that would strengthen Rabaul's outer defenses and shield the base from Allied attacks. In May 1942, Japanese scouts had identified the flat plain on the northern edge of Guadalcanal as a promising site for an airfield.

British coastwatchers had reported increased Japanese activity on Guadalcanal, alerting Allied planners of Tokyo's plans. If Allied forces could seize the airstrip before it was operational, they would not only neutralize a threat but also gain a critical base in the battle for the Solomons. Accordingly, US commanders moved Guadalcanal to the top of the list of targets for the attack.[18]

On August 7, 1942, the American invasion fleet attacked Guadalcanal. As the sun rose over the beaches, thousands of marines rushed forward, overwhelming the surprised defenders and seizing the critical airfield. Although the landing had caught Tokyo off guard, Japanese commanders at Rabaul were quick to launch a counterattack against what they assumed was merely a raid designed to distract them from larger operations in New Guinea. Twenty-seven bombers escorted by eighteen fighters took off from Rabaul to attack the US fleet, but they did little damage. Meanwhile, a Japanese flotilla of five heavy cruisers, two light cruisers, and a destroyer commanded by Vice Admiral Gunichi Mikawa set out to attack the invasion force. Mikawa's ships steamed southeast through the waters of New Georgia Sound with plans to attack the Americans at night in hopes of avoiding American carrier planes.[19]

In fact, the US carriers were already preparing to leave. Just past 6:00 p.m. on August 8, the commander of the American carrier force, Vice Admiral Frank Fletcher, announced that he would be pulling his ships back from the Solomon Islands. Since the initial plans for the invasion had been drawn up, Fletcher had insisted that his carriers could stay in the area for only three days. He had already lost the *Lexington* and *Yorktown* at Coral Sea and Midway and now placed priority on preserving the surviving carriers under his command. After staying at Guadalcanal for a mere thirty-six hours, Fletcher explained that the loss of fighter planes and low fuel forced him to withdraw. The commander of the marines onshore, General Alexander Vandegrift, was livid, but he could do nothing to stop Fletcher's withdrawal. Meanwhile, Mikawa's cruisers were racing through New Georgia Sound toward the Allied fleet anchored around Savo

Island, north of Guadalcanal. A US reconnaissance plane had sighted the Japanese force that afternoon, but its report was delayed by nine hours. The Allied fleet's first indication of the attack came at 1:45 a.m. when a destroyer caught sight of Mikawa's ships in the darkness. The Allied ships were poorly deployed and failed to communicate with one another once the attack began. In the confusion that followed, Mikawa's ships pummeled the Allied cruisers with heavy gunfire and torpedo attacks. The Japanese force sank three American cruisers and one Australian cruiser and damaged two more, one so badly that it was later scuttled. Having torn through the Allied fleet, Mikawa could have pressed on to attack the transports and supply ships at Guadalcanal. However, the Japanese commander worried that daylight might bring attacks from the American aircraft carriers. Unaware that Fletcher was already gone, Mikawa chose to retreat at 2:25 a.m.[20]

In less than an hour, the Battle of Savo Island had decimated the American flotilla and put the entire operation at risk. Rear Admiral Richmond Turner realized that his remaining ships were now exposed. He continued unloading supplies for the troops on Guadalcanal until noon on August 9 but then withdrew. A group of marines returning to the beaches at sundown found the bay all but empty. "Only a few blackened smoking hulls were visible to their left, toward Savo as they faced the water," Private Robert Leckie remembered. "Otherwise there was nothing. The marines were all alone." The marines lacked barbed wire and radio equipment; ammunition and food were in short supply. Fortunately, the airfield was nearly complete, and on August 20, the first flight of warplanes arrived. Japanese commanders still believed that the Guadalcanal invasion was merely a raid. Tokyo did not expect a US offensive before the summer of 1943, and Turner's withdrawal supported the view that the Americans did not intend to remain in the Solomons. The Japanese army calculated that they would only need six thousand troops to retake the island. In the early hours of August 21, an advance team of one thousand soldiers led by Colonel Kiyonao Ichiki staged a night attack on the American lines along the Ilu River—which the Americans had dubbed Alligator Creek. Lit by a green flare launched as the signal to begin the attack, Ichiki's forces threw themselves against the American defenses. "They came flowing across the sandspit, sprinting, hurling grenades, howling," wrote Leckie. "Then the Marines opened fire, the flare-light faded and the re-enveloping night seemed to reel with a thousand scarlet flashes. Machine guns chattered and shook. Rifles cracked. Grenades whizzed and boomed. Fat red tracers sped out in curving arcs and vanished." In the morning, a group of tanks mopped up the last remaining resistance. When it was all over, the marines found over seven hundred Japanese bodies piled along the banks of the river and on the beach. The Japanese dead lay so thick that General Vandegrift wrote that "the rear of the tanks looked like meat grinders."[21]

Having failed to secure an easy victory, both sides now prepared for a drawn-out fight. Two days after the slaughter at the Ilu River, Admiral Yamamoto sent a force commanded by Admiral Nagumo and composed of the heavy carriers *Shokaku* and *Zuikaku* along with the light carrier *Ryujo* and supporting vessels. The two US carriers under Fletcher's command, *Saratoga* and *Enterprise*, along with the battleship *North Carolina* and supporting vessels, deployed to the east of the Solomons, sailed to meet them. The two sides spent much of August 23 searching for one another as the Japanese force approached from the north. The next morning, Nagumo sent the *Ryujo* ahead to lure the enemy away from his fleet carriers. The Americans sighted the *Ryujo* first and sent a wave of bombers to pummel the small carrier. Soon after, scout planes located the larger *Shokaku* and *Zuikaku*, which were moving into position to launch strikes on the *Enterprise*. Japanese aircraft began their attack on the *Enterprise* at 4:41 p.m. A heavy screen of antiaircraft fire limited the damage, but the carrier still suffered three serious hits in the next ten minutes. The Battle of the Eastern Solomons ended as an American victory. The *Ryujo* sank later that evening, joining seventy-five aircraft. The loss of seasoned pilots hit Japan particularly hard. The Americans lost twenty aircraft, and the damage to the *Enterprise* forced the carrier to return to Pearl Harbor for repairs. More importantly, the battle had blocked Tokyo's attempt to achieve a decisive American defeat at Guadalcanal. "Our plan to capture Guadalcanal came unavoidably to a standstill," one Japanese officer wrote in his diary. The struggle for the Solomons had become a battle of attrition that favored the Americans.[22]

Even so, the troops fighting on the island faced horrendous conditions. Guadalcanal's climate consisted of suffocating heat and humidity interrupted by torrential rain squalls. Infantry on both sides were plagued by tropical diseases and fungal infections as they pushed through dense jungles inhabited by swarms of mosquitoes, lizards, and crocodiles. In the early months of the battle, supply shortages sometimes forced marines to subsist on four tablespoons of maggot-infested rice per day. Just as bad were the nightly bombardments from Japanese warships, which kept the marines in a state of sleep-deprived terror. Some men lost forty pounds while stationed on the island. Japanese soldiers, who relied on tenuous supply lines, faced even worse conditions.[23]

The Imperial Navy's failure to drive the US fleet from the Solomons now threatened the security of the Co-Prosperity Sphere. Air patrols operating out of newly finished Henderson Field gave US forces aerial supremacy around Guadalcanal through the daylight hours. Japanese aircraft flying from Rabaul were at a distinct disadvantage to American planes based on Guadalcanal. Moreover, downed Japanese pilots were usually lost, whereas the Americans were often recovered. Unable to wrest control of the seas and the skies from the Americans, Japanese commanders were forced to focus on ground attacks aimed at recapturing Henderson Field. But the soldiers needed reinforcements and supplies that could only be delivered through the perilous waters of New Georgia Sound. As a result, Japanese leaders were forced to resort to nighttime runs using fast destroyers to ferry troops and supplies to Guadalcanal. The destroyers could only transport 150 men and thirty to forty tons of supplies—a fraction of what slow transport vessels could deliver. Further, by employing destroyers as ferries, the Japanese navy pulled the warships away from other duties such as escorting convoys.[24]

Japanese commanders understood that the prospect of slowly feeding men and supplies via destroyers into the tropical slaughterhouse of Guadalcanal, while steadily losing aircraft, pilots, and ships, was not a winning formula. If Tokyo hoped to maintain its ring in the south, it would have to find some way to break the deadlock. On the night of September 12, General Kiyotake Kawaguchi and two thousand soldiers launched a frontal assault on the thousand-meter-long ridge overlooking the southern edge of the airfield. Waves of attackers charged American lines as green flares lit the moonless sky. The initial attack threw the defenders back but soon degenerated into chaos in the darkness. By sunrise, the marines had retreated to a second line of defense. Both sides spent the day regrouping until Kawaguchi launched a renewed attack at 6:30 in the evening. Intense fighting raged through another night, but the marines managed to hold the ridge. Perhaps half of Kawaguchi's force had been killed or wounded in the fighting. The weeklong retreat that followed would kill even more.[25]

Kawaguchi's defeat convinced Tokyo that the Americans had established a strong presence on Guadalcanal, which constituted a real threat to the security of the Co-Prosperity Sphere. If Japanese commanders hoped to regain the island, they would need to mount a concerted naval, air, and infantry campaign. Accordingly, Tokyo shifted its efforts from the attack on Port Moresby in New Guinea to the struggle for the Solomons. Encouraging news arrived on September 15 when the Japanese submarine *I-19* sank the USS *Wasp*. The American fleet carrier had been escorting a convoy of transports carrying a marine regiment to Guadalcanal when it was intercepted by the *I-19*. The Japanese submarine fired a devastating salvo of six torpedoes—three slammed into the *Wasp*, one hit the destroyer *O'Brien*, and another hit the battleship *North Carolina* six miles away. The explosions ignited the fuel reserves aboard the carrier and quickly spread. Thirty-five minutes later, commanders gave the order to abandon ship.[26]

Both sides now recognized the strategic significance of Guadalcanal and accelerated their efforts to build up their forces on the island. By October 23, Tokyo had deployed some twenty-two thousand soldiers against a near-equal force of twenty-three thousand Allied troops. As part of its efforts, the Japanese navy staged frequent attacks on Henderson Field in an attempt to deplete the Americans' ability to use land-based aircraft to attack transport convoys. Marine patrols along the Matanikau River through early October forced Japanese landings to the western side of the island and established a defensive buffer around Henderson Field. Meanwhile, the US Navy tried to stanch the flow of Japanese reinforcements and supplies. On the night of October 11, US warships set out to intercept a Japanese force of three heavy cruisers and two destroyers, commanded by Admiral Aritomo Goto, en route to Guadalcanal. The American ships, under the command of Admiral Norman Scott, laid a trap for Goto's force fourteen miles northeast of Cape Esperance, Guadalcanal. Scott's ships had the advantage of radar, giving them the element of surprise against the Japanese cruisers. Even so, the difficulty of fighting at night led to a confused battle. Over the course of several hours, fire from Scott's ships inflicted significant damage, sinking the heavy cruiser *Furutaka* and a destroyer, mortally wounding Goto, and forcing the surviving ships to withdraw. Nevertheless, the Japanese troop transport made it through to Guadalcanal.[27]

By mid-October, the commander of the Japanese Seventeenth Army on Guadalcanal, General Harukichi Hyakutake, was ready to launch another assault on Henderson Field. After cutting tracks through the jungle, Hyakutake planned to attack along three axes from the south and west while the Japanese navy bombarded the marine defenders and aircraft prepared to land at the airstrip. The western prong of the attack began on October 23 when a force of nine tanks attempted to cross the Matanikau River. Marine artillery blasted the Japanese armor to pieces, halting the western assault in its tracks. Hours later, as sheets of rain poured down, a second Japanese force attacked the Americans' southern flank. The assault came close to breaking through, but the defenders managed to hold. At daybreak, the marines looked out over a battlefield strewn with over one thousand Japanese corpses. A third attack on the night of October 24 also failed. In all, as many as 3,500 Japanese soldiers may have died in the battle.

Leaders in Tokyo now understood that what they had thought was a small raid was in fact a critical battle for the defense of their South Pacific empire. "We must be aware," Japanese general headquarters warned, "of the possibility that the struggle for Guadalcanal in the southeast area may develop into the decisive struggle between America and Japan."[28]

While Hyakutake's infantry hurled themselves at the American lines, a force of three fleet carriers, one light carrier, and four battleships commanded by Vice Admiral Nobutake Kondo waited 350 miles to the east near the Santa Cruz Islands. The opposing American force, commanded by Admiral Thomas Kinkaid, consisted of two fleet carriers—the *Enterprise* and the *Hornet*—one battleship, and supporting vessels. On October 26, aircraft from the two opposing forces launched multiple waves of attacks against each other. American planes succeeded in dealing significant damage to two of Kondo's carriers, but the *Hornet* was hit by multiple Japanese torpedoes and had to be abandoned before it eventually sank. The *Enterprise* also suffered serious damage. The Japanese won a hard-fought victory in the Battle of Santa Cruz Islands, but it came at a near-crippling cost. Two of Tokyo's carriers were damaged and needed repairs that would keep them out of commission into 1943. Worse still, Japanese aircrews had suffered heavy losses. The Japanese had lost ninety-seven planes to the loss of eighty-one US aircraft—more troubling was the loss of 148 Japanese aircrew to the loss of 20 American personnel. Tokyo had no good way of replacing these seasoned aviators. Indeed, though still operational, the *Zuikaku* was pulled out of the South Pacific for lack

Adolf Hitler and Benito Mussolini in Munich, Germany *(US National Archives)*

Japanese infantry ready to storm Kiangwan *(US National Archives)*

Japanese field battery, 1932 *(US National Archives)*

German bombing of Rotterdam, 1940 *(US National Archives)*

British prisoners at Dunkirk *(US National Archives)*

Adolf Hitler in Paris
(US National Archives)

Smoke over Tower Bridge,
London, 1940
(US National Archives)

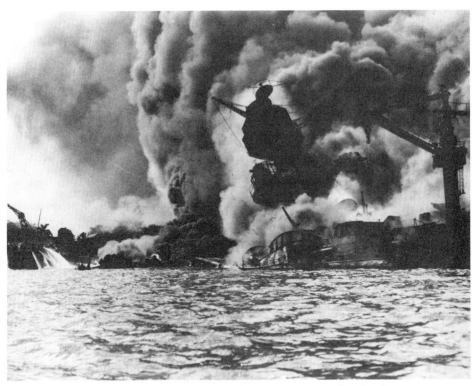

USS *Arizona* burning after Japanese attack on Pearl Harbor *(US National Archives)*

Japanese casualties after the Battle of the Tenaru, Guadalcanal *(Library of Congress)*

American casualties on Tarawa, 1943 *(US National Archives)*

Essex carriers: *Wasp, Yorktown, Hornet, Hancock, Ticonderoga,* and *Lexington,* 1944
(US National Archives)

Normandy invasion *(US National Archives)*

Normandy beach *(US National Archives)*

US soldiers fighting in Aachen, Germany, 1944 *(US National Archives)*

The Allied invasion devastated large sections of Normandy *(US National Archives)*

German SS troops on patrol in Warsaw *(US National Archives)*

Ruins of Cologne, 1945 *(US National Archives)*

Churchill, Roosevelt, and Stalin at Yalta *(US National Archives)*

Marines advance through ruined landscape of Enewetak Atoll *(US National Archives)*

Allied landing craft at Okinawa *(US National Archives)*

Patton's soldiers at Bastogne *(US National Archives)*

Ruins of Nuremberg *(US National Archives)*

Remagen bridge *(US National Archives)*

US soldiers inspect V-1 rockets at Nordhausen *(US National Archives)*

Rows of dead inmates at Nordhausen *(US National Archives)*

Soviet soldier raising a flag over the Reichstag *(TASS)*

American and Soviet soldiers embrace following link-up outside of Torgau, Germany, 1945 *(US National Archives)*

Montgomery, Eisenhower, and Zhukov in Frankfurt, 1945 *(US National Archives)*

B-29 Superfortress enroute to bomb targets in Japan *(US National Archives)*

Mushroom cloud
over Hiroshima
(US National Archives)

of pilots. "Considering the great superiority of our enemy's industrial capacity," one Japanese destroyer captain observed, "we must win every battle overwhelmingly. This last one, unfortunately, was not an overwhelming victory."[29]

Nevertheless, the Imperial Navy had finally achieved its goal of blunting the threat of US carriers in the Pacific, albeit temporarily. Yamamoto rushed to stage one last push to wrest control of Guadalcanal from the Americans. On November 12, a convoy of eleven transports carrying thirty thousand soldiers set out for the island. Their approach was covered by a force of battleships commanded by Vice Admiral Hiroaki Abe, which would stage a heavy bombardment of Henderson Field designed to ground if not destroy the US aircraft in the area. After learning of Yamamoto's plan from signals intelligence, the US Navy sent a force of cruisers commanded by Rear Admiral Daniel Callaghan to intercept Abe's battleships. Callaghan's cruisers would be heavily outgunned, but, the planners thought, a successful night attack aided by new radar equipment might be enough to drive off the Japanese force. At 1:30 a.m. on November 13, the two fleets approached each other through a driving rainstorm. US radar detected Abe's ships, but Callaghan's inexperience and reluctance to trust the new devices led the American admiral to hesitate. As the rain cleared, Japanese spotters sighted the black shapes of American warships through the darkness. The Japanese ships threw on their searchlights to reveal the American ships inside the Japanese formation. What followed, according to one American officer, amounted to "a barroom brawl with the lights out." Both sides scrambled to sort friend from foe as their guns raked each other at close range. Thirty-four minutes later, both Callaghan and Admiral Norman Scott were dead. However, all but two of the US warships remained operational. Callaghan's force had mauled the battleship *Hiei* and sunk several supporting ships, leading Abe to call off the attack. Later that morning, bombers from Henderson Field located the crippled *Hiei* and delivered the coup de grâce.[30]

That still left the transport ships and the supporting force commanded by Admiral Kondo, consisting of the battleship *Kirishima* and two heavy cruisers. To meet them, US commanders sent the battleships *Washington* and *South Dakota*, under the command of Rear Admiral Willis Lee. Unlike Callaghan, Lee was eager to test his radar equipment in a night battle with the Japanese. He was about to get his chance. Lee's and Kondo's forces spotted each other at 11:00 p.m. on November 14 and began firing. While Japanese ships concentrated their fire on the *South Dakota*—which had lost the use of its main guns after an electrical failure—Lee directed the *Washington*'s guns using radar targeting information. The *Washington* sent over twenty sixteen-inch shells into the *Kirishima*, devastating the flagship and forcing Kondo to withdraw. The *Kirishima* sank a few hours later. The Naval Battle of Guadalcanal proved to be the breaking point in the struggle for the island. The loss of two battleships in twenty-four hours combined with the repeated failures to take Henderson Field convinced leaders in Tokyo that Guadalcanal had become a quagmire—sucking in ships, soldiers, and resources out of proportion with its value. Although the Japanese navy would win the naval Battle of Tassafaronga two weeks later and its troops would remain on Guadalcanal until early February 1943, the outcome of the struggle was decided in November.[31]

The defeat on Guadalcanal served as a stark indication that Japan was losing the battle of attrition against the Americans. The Allies lost 7,100 servicemen during the battle; Japan lost over 30,000 killed, including a large number of its most experienced aircrews. The Battle of Midway had brought US and Japanese forces in the Pacific closer to parity and left the strategic initiative up for grabs. The marines had seized this initiative on Guadalcanal, placing Tokyo on the defensive. A decisive Japanese victory in the Solomons might have convinced US commanders to revert to a strategy of holding the line in the Pacific until Germany was defeated. But Japanese leaders had been slow to recognize the significance of the Solomons campaign and had failed to deliver a crushing blow to the Americans. Although naval clashes around Guadalcanal resulted in a tactical draw, Washington was winning the strategic battle. Tokyo's failure at Guadalcanal left a breach in the empire's defenses and guaranteed that the United States would be able to leverage its greater productive power to overwhelm Japan in a war of attrition. Washington could now pummel its way through Tokyo's outer defenses using an increasing superiority in ships, aircraft, and manpower. The US victory at Guadalcanal drew Tokyo into a war of attrition that it had no hope of winning.[32]

EVEN AS THE GUADALCANAL CAMPAIGN APPROACHED ITS NOVEMBER climax, Allied forces were preparing a second major amphibious operation halfway across the globe in North Africa. Since the fall of France in the spring of 1940, American officials had recognized that the British Empire offered the best launchpad for a war against the Axis powers. The destroyers-for-bases deal of September 1940 had given the United States control of British colonial positions in the Western Hemisphere, and the 1941 Atlantic Charter had articulated a joint Anglo-American vision for international order. And American marines on Guadalcanal were engaged in a fierce battle with Japanese forces for control of the British Solomon Islands Protectorate. With Operation Torch in the autumn of 1942, the US military launched an invasion of North Africa that restored British imperial influence in the Mediterranean and laid the foundations for American postwar hegemony throughout the region. The battle for North Africa served as a master class in which London instructed Washington on the finer points of naval imperialism—a complex strategy that relied on using maritime power to control sea lanes, launch and sustain large-scale amphibious invasions, and balance continental powers against one another to neutralize challenges to Anglo-American supremacy.

General Dwight Eisenhower commanded the Allied landings in Morocco and Algeria in the predawn hours of November 8, 1942. Three assault forces landed on the beaches outside Safi, Casablanca, Oran, and Algiers, adjusting the timing of their attacks to account for moonlight, tide, and wind conditions. Hollis Stabler, a Native American soldier in the US Army, was part of the force charged with seizing the harbor at Safi. At sunrise on November 8, Stabler and his fellow soldiers were assembled on the deck of their ship for their first look at Africa. "Everything looked gold except the buildings," he remembered. "They were snow white." Eisenhower had hoped that the Vichy authorities would offer little resistance to the Americans. He was disappointed. Associated Press correspondent Harold Boyle joined American troops storming the beaches of Casablanca. "We plunged from the sides of the settling craft up to our armpits in the surf and struggled to the reef," he wrote. "Waves washed over our heads, doubling the weight of our 60-pound packs with water." Boyle and the soldiers around him struggled through jagged coral toward the shore and then scrambled for whatever cover they could find. While 75mm shells whistled overhead, Boyle found shelter with a group of Moroccan Arabs watching the battle.[33]

American troops landing near Algiers splashed onto the same beach that the French had invaded at the start of their 1830 conquest and colonial subjugation of Algeria—a symbolism that could hardly have been lost on the local Arabs who turned up to watch the battle. US officials blanketed the airwaves with propaganda calling on French soldiers to join in the liberation from the Vichy regime and printed thirty million pamphlets reminding the defenders of the historic ties between the United States and France. Although the landings themselves were haphazard, the operation proved successful. The biggest threats to most of the invaders came in the form of sporadic sniper fire. Eisenhower's forces quickly seized the port facilities and pushed inland to take control of French administrative centers in Casablanca, Oran, and Algiers. American troops raced to capture oil facilities and power stations while British fighter planes began landing at the recently seized airfield at Maison Blanche. Meanwhile, the landing at Oran met determined resistance from French warships, but the defenses were no match for the Americans. Even so, the Allied invasion force suffered 1,887 casualties.[34]

Vichy authorities in Algiers surrendered to American forces at 8:00 p.m. on November 8, and hostilities ceased in Oran and Casablanca over the next two days. Allied plans to install Free French leader Henri Giraud as leader of French North Africa ran into trouble when Giraud refused to join the operation unless he commanded it. Giraud eventually relented and flew to Algiers on November 9, but once there, he proved unable to rally French support. Instead, Vichy prime minister François Darlan, who was visiting his hospitalized son in Algiers, emerged as Vichy's negotiator. The prime minister's presence placed Eisenhower in a difficult position: the best way to avoid potentially bloody clashes with French forces in North Africa was to strike a deal with Darlan that would keep the Vichy leader in power. However, doing so would undercut Allied claims to have liberated North Africa from Vichy. In the end, Eisenhower agreed to recognize Darlan as the new high commissioner of France in Africa. The general explained, "Our basic orders required us to go into Africa in the attempt to win an ally—not to kill Frenchmen." Nonetheless, Eisenhower understood that the deal would "create great revulsion" in Britain and the United States.[35] The embarrassment of having collaborated with the collaborators was partially absolved with Darlan's curiously fortuitous assassination on Christmas Eve at the hands of a twenty-year-old French monarchist. Nevertheless, the Darlan deal would unleash a lasting controversy over Allied operations in North Africa.

That still left the matter of the stronghold in Tunisia, where defending Axis forces enjoyed considerable geographic advantages. The country's borders were guarded by the Atlas Mountains in the northwest and lower hills in the south that would drive attacking forces from Algeria and Libya into narrow, easily defended passes. Making matters worse, Axis ships from Sicily could make the short trip to the ports of Tunis and Bizerte overnight, using the cover of darkness to avoid Allied air patrols. The Allies' best hope lay in attacking Tunisia before Axis leaders had a chance to reinforce their positions. However, American planners had elected to stage their easternmost landings at Algiers in order to reduce the chances of exposing the invasion force to Axis aircraft based in Sicily. As a result, Allied forces had to cross over five hundred miles of rough terrain to reach Tunis.[36]

And Hitler had no intention of surrendering his foothold in North Africa without a fight. On November 9, Field Marshal Albert Kesselring began transferring Luftwaffe units to Tunisian airfields. Two nights later, German paratroops occupied Tunis. In the following days, German troops moved into Bizerte and west along the coastal road to defend the passes through the mountains. As Axis forces took control of key strategic points along the approaches to Tunis, skirmishes broke out between advancing Allied units and German troops. Together with logistical delays, these attacks postponed a concerted Allied push toward Tunis until late November. Once underway, American tanks made some progress before running into stiff German counterattacks that erased many of these gains. Through the first half of December, Allied forces struggled to hold their positions against the Wehrmacht's assault. On December 24, Eisenhower called off the offensive—the drive on Tunis had ground to a halt. Axis forces in North Africa would hold out for nearly five more months.[37]

As a fierce sandstorm tore across the desert in the early hours of February 14, 1943, German engineers crept out to dismantle the Allied minefields guarding the approaches to the Faïd Pass. By 4:00 a.m., a force of one hundred creaking panzers was driving toward the front. The Americans had spread their forces thin across a 250-mile front stretching from the Mediterranean in the north to the edge of the Dorsal mountains in the south. The poorly supplied and inexperienced Americans were completely unprepared for the onslaught. At 6:30, the attackers fell upon the American camps. Panzers made short work of American Sherman tanks as their crews scrambled to meet the assault. One American captain compared the oncoming Germans to packs of wild dogs rushing toward their prey.

German dive-bombers screamed through the skies above, strafing bewildered Allied troops below. A hasty American counterattack was mauled by a line of German 88mm guns concealed along a ridge. In short order, the golden sands were littered with the blackened, smoking hulks of American tanks. Survivors streamed west to escape the advancing troops. One witness described the retreat as "a dryland Dunkirk." German forces continued their attacks over the coming days, but their lines were becoming overextended and their fuel supplies were running low. On February 23, Rommel chose to withdraw. Despite ravaging the Americans, German troops had suffered a steady loss of men and equipment, many from Allied air and artillery strikes. Rommel was also wary of the British Eighth Army approaching from the east. Although it would go down as a momentous tactical victory for the Germans, the Battle of Kasserine Pass did little to alter the basic strategic dimensions of the war in North Africa. Nevertheless, the Americans were humiliated by the thrashing. Eisenhower promptly sacked the American commander, General Lloyd Fredendall, who had spent the battle hiding in his subterranean bunker seventy miles from the front. In his place, Eisenhower promoted General George Patton.[38]

Meanwhile to the south, Montgomery was nearing the end of his drive across North Africa, a slow four-and-a-half-month-long affair that allowed Rommel's vastly outnumbered forces to escape and launch their counterattack against the Americans at Kasserine Pass. Now, as his Eighth Army entered Tunisia, he confronted the Mareth Line—a network of fortifications between the Mareth Hills and the Mediterranean Sea built by the French during the 1930s and now defended by German and Italian troops. Tangles of barbed wire snaked across the rocky terrain, beneath which lay some two hundred thousand land mines. Bunkers connected by a network of trenches concealed thousands of troops poised to contest the British drive north toward Tunis. Despite heavy numerical advantages, Montgomery's initial efforts on March 19 at staging a frontal assault against the dug-in Axis defenders foundered in the face of heavy resistance. Only after sending a flanking force around the Mareth Hills to attack the Axis defenses from the west were the Allies able to break through. They paid a heavy price of four thousand casualties but managed to force the defenders back while taking seven thousand prisoners.[39]

Hard fighting lay ahead, but there remained no serious doubt about an ultimate Allied victory in Tunisia. Perhaps the most decisive action against the Axis forces came not by land but by air and sea as Allied ships and aircraft, aided by Ultra intercepts, choked off the flow of supplies to Rommel's forces in Tunisia. With the blockade tightening and Allied armies threatening the frontiers, Rommel concluded that the battle for North Africa was lost. On March 9, he traveled first to Italy and then to Ukraine to try to convince Hitler to withdraw. The Führer refused, however, and removed Rommel from command, placing him on medical leave. The change in command could do nothing to reverse the tides of battle. Allied forces continued to drive forward, squeezing the defenders into an ever-shrinking foothold. In mid-May, having exhausted their stores of fuel and ammunition, some 275,000 German and Italian troops surrendered.[40]

ALLIED LEADERS HAD NOT WAITED FOR VICTORY IN NORTH AFRICA to begin planning for the next phase of the war. On January 11, 1943, with the Axis surrender in Tunisia still months away, a plane carrying Franklin Roosevelt took off from Miami on a five-thousand-mile trip across the Atlantic. After a stop in Gambia—where he became the first American head of state to visit Africa—he arrived in Casablanca, where he would meet with Churchill, Giraud, de Gaulle, and Sultan Muhammad V of Morocco at the Anfa Hotel. Stalin declined an invitation so that he could continue overseeing the Battle of Stalingrad. The orange groves and palm trees surrounding the hotel were ringed with barbed wire and patrolled by soldiers and Secret Service agents. Inside the building, Allied leaders deliberated on their next steps in the war. While London had prevailed in the debate over Torch, US military leaders still hoped to launch a cross-channel attack in 1943.

General George Marshall insisted that the Allies must not become mired in never-ending campaigns in the Mediterranean at the expense of operations in Europe and the Pacific. Once again, however, London outmaneuvered Washington. British planners had arrived in Casablanca far better prepared than their American counterparts. As the US Army's head planner, Albert Wedemeyer, later explained, "We lost our shirts. . . . One might say we came, we listened, and we were conquered."[41]

Convinced that victory in North Africa was now a foregone conclusion, British leaders pushed for an attack on Italy that would knock Mussolini out of the war. But such an operation would postpone a cross-channel invasion of France to 1944. Alan Brooke explained that the Allies' main assets consisted of the Red Army, the escalating American and British aerial bombing campaign against Germany, and the Western powers' ability to launch amphibious operations against the continent. However, he warned that the Wehrmacht would quickly respond and concentrate forces against any invasion; the Allies must therefore launch any amphibious assault "at the place where the enemy was least able to concentrate large forces." Admiral Ernest King, chief of US naval operations, grumbled that it was now clear that the British intended to use "the geographic and manpower position of Russia to the maximum." If the campaigns in the Mediterranean and on the eastern front compelled the Germans "to withdraw their forces from France, the British would be willing to seize this opportunity to invade the Continent." But London planned to wait for German defenses to weaken before it attempted a cross-channel attack.[42]

Top American military planners worried that British leaders were drawing the United States into a strategy designed to defend London's imperial interests. The Joint Strategic Survey Committee (JSSC) charged with long-term planning warned that Britain believed the Mediterranean to be "essential to the maintenance of their present Imperial power"—Churchill ultimately hoped to preserve and even expand the empire in the Mediterranean. British leaders, the

JSSC wrote, believed that a peripheral strategy was necessary not only to secure specific territories but to avoid the mass casualties of a cross-channel attack, which would lead to "a decline in Imperial strength." Rather than a frontal assault on the Third Reich, the committee wrote, London preferred to mount campaigns along the periphery while allowing "military attrition and civilian famine" to drain both German and Soviet strength in hopes of securing a favorable European balance of power at the end of the war. Britain was fighting in the Mediterranean, per B. H. Liddell Hart's dicta, as part of a larger strategy to secure a favorable postwar situation.[43]

Although leaders such as Marshall decried this strategy as both cynical and dangerous, other American officials were coming to the conclusion that the present world crisis had forced Washington to enter the Machiavellian realm of great power politics. In September 1941—three months before Pearl Harbor—Lieutenant Colonel Paul Robinett, assistant chief of staff for intelligence, had written in his diary that British power was on the decline and rival empires were poised to take its place. "Germany and Russia are fighting for world domination," he wrote. "Whichever wins will be a long way on the road to domination." The United States could no longer afford to sit on the sidelines: "If any one power dominates Asia, Europe and Africa, our country will ultimately become a second class power even if we gain South America and the whole of North America." Such thinking dovetailed with the writings of geostrategists such as Halford Mackinder and the forthcoming work of Nicholas Spykman. Beyond arguing that Washington must play an active role in global affairs, a growing number of officials argued that Soviet power constituted a long-term threat to US interests. Indeed, beginning in early 1942, army intelligence had warned that a Soviet victory in the war would allow Moscow to dominate its neighbors in Eastern Europe, the Middle East, and East Asia and spread communist influence into all three regions. In May 1942, General George Strong, chief of army intelligence, had warned a group of his colleagues that Washington might be forced to step into the role vacated by the declining British

Empire. The United States, he insisted, "must cultivate a mental attitude which will enable us to impose our own terms, amounting to perhaps a pax Americana." Likewise, Brain Trust member Adolf Berle wrote in his diary in late October 1942 that the "organizing principle" in postwar Europe "will either be on Stalinist lines or it will be along liberal and individualist lines."[44]

Voices in the State Department also urged greater consideration for Soviet power in the postwar world. In December, one official warned of the prospect of a communist-controlled Germany that would remove any pressure on Moscow to maintain good future relations with Washington and be "disastrous for any hope of a stable world after the war." US forces must stage a prompt entry into the war in Europe "so that peace would not find the Soviet armies alone on the continent." If Germany were to collapse before a large-scale Anglo-American invasion, Soviet prestige would become so great as to make it nearly impossible for Washington and London to challenge "any line of policy which the Kremlin may choose to adopt."[45]

By the beginning of the Casablanca Conference, these concerns about Moscow's postwar intentions had begun to shape US war plans. As Admiral King told the other chiefs on January 16, "Unless the U.S. and Britain make some definite move toward the defeat of Germany, Russia will dominate the peace table."[46] In this regard, it had become apparent that Washington and London faced a troubling dilemma. The reports from Stalingrad indicated that the Red Army, having long borne the brunt of the struggle against Nazi Germany, was now in the process of turning the tide in the war. Continued Soviet participation in the war remained critical because a separate German-Soviet peace would give Hitler a free hand to reinforce his western flank. However, an overwhelming Soviet victory in the war threatened to give Stalin a controlling hand over continental Europe—an outcome that both Washington and London considered catastrophic. Nevertheless, the Western Allies were still more than a year away from mounting a cross-channel invasion of France that would establish a meaningful Anglo-American military presence in Western Europe.

Ultimately, Western leaders hoped to find some means of keeping the Soviet Union in the war without creating the circumstances whereby the Red Army would overrun the continent.

To this end, Allied leaders understood the importance of Lend-Lease aid to the Soviets. As Marshall explained on January 17, aid to the Soviet Union was of "paramount importance in order to assist the Russian Army to absorb the strength of the German ground and air forces." Washington and London "must devise means to enable Russia to continue aggressively through 1943 by providing them with supplies." However, one area where London and Washington could directly contribute to the war in Western Europe was in the realm of a sustained strategic bombing campaign. While disagreement existed between British support for massed night attacks and American plans for daylight raids, both governments embraced the tactic of waging a brutal bombing campaign that would generate massive civilian casualties. As Britain's air chief marshal, Sir Charles Portal, had explained on January 16, the key to defeating Germany lay in attacking its oil facilities and staging relentless bombing raids aimed at crushing German industry and destroying German morale by "producing heavy casualties in her population and great misery by the destruction of their dwellings." Under such pressure, he argued, "it seemed fairly certain that a point would be reached at which Germany would suddenly crack."[47]

But Western forces could not simply stand aside in the event of a German collapse. As Marshall argued on January 18, in the event of a sudden collapse of Axis resistance, "we should make every effort to cross the Channel." President Roosevelt seconded this point, insisting that American and British forces must prepare for an emergency cross-channel invasion "in case Germany cracks." To this end, Washington would assemble a large number of lake and river craft and send them to Britain. A similar response would be necessary if German forces withdrew from France. The Western Allies must be in a position to take advantage of such contingency. Although concerns about providing general security certainly motivated some of these plans, equally if not more important was the unspoken desire to prevent Soviet forces from occupying Western Europe. As Roosevelt noted, the dispatch of these invasion vessels should be undertaken "quietly"—a consideration designed to keep Soviet officials in the dark. In the coming months, these contingency plans would grow into a full-fledged operational plan code-named Rankin.[48]

THE CASABLANCA CONFERENCE, THEN, SAW THE CREATION OF A WAR plan that bore a striking resemblance to Stalin's long-standing fears: London and Washington would continue seizing territory through operations around the periphery while bankrolling the attrition of German and Soviet forces on the continent. Once Germany appeared ready to collapse, British and American troops would mount a rapid invasion of France in order to claim a sphere of influence in Western Europe. Although Marshall had pushed for a cross-channel invasion of France in 1943, British leaders vetoed such an operation. In practice, then, the Americans and the British would bide their time and intervene against Hitler's Fortress Europe only when victory was certain and casualties would be comparatively low. In the meantime, the Red Army would be worn down in the slaughterhouse of the eastern front.

As the conference drew to a close, Allied leaders appeared at a joint press conference to announce the results of the meeting. Aware that their further delay in launching a cross-channel attack would infuriate Stalin, Roosevelt and Churchill offered one more sop to the Soviet dictator. "The elimination of German, Japanese, and Italian war power means the unconditional surrender of Germany, Italy, and Japan," Roosevelt announced. Although the president claimed that the declaration was an off-the-cuff remark and Churchill later maintained that the statement had caught him by surprise, both men were being disingenuous. After careful consideration, Roosevelt and Churchill issued the declaration in an effort to reassure Stalin that they had no intention of striking a separate deal with the Third Reich that would leave the Soviets alone in the war against Germany—Eisenhower's deal with Vichy leader François Darlan had been a one-off. In return, Washington and London hoped to receive a reciprocal promise from Moscow that the Soviet Union would not make its own peace with Berlin.[49] Stalin would continue receiving Lend-Lease aid from the West along with a measure of relief from the stepped-up strategic bombing campaign, but the Red Army must continue charging into the meat grinder of the eastern front while British and US forces secured hegemony over the Mediterranean and prepared their forces for a cross-channel invasion in 1944.

As Churchill and Roosevelt said their farewells and prepared to leave Casablanca, it was clear that the mood in the Allied camp had changed. Eventual Allied victory was no longer seriously in doubt, but the shape of the postwar peace remained very much an open question. The pivotal battles of late 1942—the Midway-Guadalcanal-Stalingrad-North Africa nexus—showcased a sweeping transformation in international power. France had fallen. Germany's invasion of the Soviet Union had failed. Japan's forces had faltered at Midway and been beaten back at Guadalcanal. Meanwhile, Britain had been unable to regain control of North Africa on its own. The traditional imperial systems, dominant for the last five hundred years, were no longer capable of commanding the course of history. Only the Soviet Union and the United States—continent-spanning, neo-imperial superstates—were able to turn the tide. Going forward, the key to world power would lie not in exploiting colonies and proclaiming racial supremacy but in wielding a vast machinery of economic, ideological, and military power to construct and dominate the international order itself. While the coming Pax Americana had been forged in the waters off Midway, Guadalcanal, and North Africa, the Soviet colossus had emerged from the burning ruins of Stalingrad. The dawn of the superpower age had arrived.

Chapter 12

COLONIAL INTERVENTIONS AND CONTINENTAL SLAUGHTERHOUSES

O N JUNE 26, 1943, YALE UNIVERSITY GEOGRAPHER NICHOLAS SPYK-
man died from heart complications at the age of forty-nine. In the
closing months of his life, Spykman delivered a lecture that would
be edited and published posthumously as *The Geography of the Peace*.
In the book, Spykman outlined a sweeping geostrategic vision for US
national security. The key to world power, he argued, lay in what he
called the Eurasian rimlands—a belt of territory running from Western Europe and through the Middle East and South Asia before curving north along the Pacific coast of Asia. The rimlands commanded
the main approaches to Europe, the Middle East, and Asia and strad-
dled vital shipping routes. Many of the largest battles of the Second
World War were already raging across these territories, and their outcome would likely determine the winner in the global conflict. Going

forward, Spykman argued, US national security must take an active role to ensure that no hostile power or combination of powers could dominate these rimlands. "Who controls the rimland rules Eurasia," he wrote, "who rules Eurasia controls the destinies of the world."[1]

Few writers have so powerfully captured the strategic spirit of their times. In the years ahead, Spykman's ideas would prove seminal to the formulation of America's Cold War policy of containment against the Soviet Union. In the present war, Spykman had articulated a core thread of the American and British strategy to defeat the Axis and shape the postwar peace. Indeed, even as Spykman lay dying in New Haven, American leaders called for the creation of a worldwide network of bases across the Eurasian littoral—Spykman's rimlands—that would allow the Western Allies to project military force around the globe. From this empire of bases, Washington could counter Axis and later Soviet power, promote American commercial interests, and defend a dramatically enlarged sphere of influence.[2]

Together with a concurrent set of technological breakthroughs, the creation of this network of bases placed the United States in a position to exert unprecedented strategic influence around the globe. Over the course of 1943, Allied forces combined historic feats of engineering, research, and mass production to roll out a series of advanced weapons systems. Armed with this array of world-beating technologies, the Allied powers—and the United States in particular—acquired the ability to deploy military forces in strength to nearly any ocean, airspace, or coastline in the world, allowing the United States and Britain to secure control of multiple theaters along the Eurasian periphery. These new force-projection capabilities would prove critical to defeating the Axis powers, but they would play an even greater role in structuring US global power in the postwar world.

As this revolution in national security affairs took hold, however, it became painfully clear that the Western Allies were fighting a very different war than their Soviet and Chinese counterparts. While American and British forces staged a series of naval campaigns and amphibious operations in the Atlantic, Mediterranean, and Pacific,

Soviet and Chinese troops remained locked in bloody land battles with Axis forces across Eastern Europe and mainland Asia, suffering massive casualties while grinding down the German and Japanese armies. These continental slaughterhouses stood in stark contrast to the heavily mechanized peripheral warfare practiced by the American and British imperial forces along the Eurasian rimlands—a dynamic that generated lasting resentments among the Allies.

Nevertheless, the war had shifted in the Allies' favor. If the battles of 1942—Midway, El Alamein, Torch, Stalingrad, and Guadalcanal—shifted the strategic initiative away from the Axis, the campaigns of 1943 tilted the scales firmly in favor of the Allies. Victories in the Battle of the Atlantic, Kursk, Italy, and Tunisia over the course of 1943 combined with the steady growth of the American and Soviet militaries to begin rolling back Axis gains. However, as the danger of Axis victory subsided, leaders in London, Moscow, and Washington began to devote ever more attention to the approaching struggle to determine the fate of the postwar world.

ONE OF THE FIRST ALLIED BREAKTHROUGHS OF 1943 CAME IN THE ongoing Battle of the Atlantic. Since the start of the war in Europe, British leaders had viewed the Atlantic as a critical theater of operations. Control of the ocean was vital not only for defending the home islands but also for securing lines of communication to the colonies and to the United States. Having staved off the threat of a German invasion, British leaders hoped to enforce a naval blockade against the Third Reich. However, Hitler's successful conquest of much of Europe left the Reich in control of considerable resources, rendering Germany all but blockade-proof. Further complicating matters, German leaders worked to set up a counterblockade against Britain. Although the Kriegsmarine could not hope to challenge the strength of the Royal Navy's surface fleet in open battle, the Reich entered the war with a formidable U-boat fleet commanded by Admiral Karl Dönitz and deployed across the Atlantic and the North Sea.

Dönitz called for a war of attrition against British shipping—if U-boats could sink British merchant ships faster than they could be replaced, London would be forced to sue for peace. Although this tonnage war lacked the glamour of a climactic battle between capital ships, it played to the Kriegsmarine's only strength. Dönitz innovated on the First World War–era strategy of deploying submarines in groups that would lie in wait along British shipping lanes. Dönitz's new wolf packs launched nighttime coordinated surface attacks designed to overwhelm Allied countermeasures. The fall of France expanded Dönitz's opportunities by opening naval bases on the western Atlantic coast. In short order, German U-boats were prowling the Atlantic in search of British shipping.

Few of the war's theaters provided as bleak an experience as the North Atlantic. The sailors serving aboard Allied convoys faced weeks of grueling voyages across tempestuous seas, battered by swirling winds and frigid waves, living perpetually in fear of attack by German submarines. One British officer serving aboard a corvette described the "long nightmare" of an Atlantic crossing: "Five hundred miles, and six days, of screaming wind and massed, tumbling water, of sleet and snow storms, of a sort of frozen malice in the weather which refused us all progress." Calm seas brought some relief from the elements but raised the danger of U-boat attacks. Frank Holding, a steward on the British steamship *Beatus*, remembered watching the reflection of the moonlight on the waves, "You're thinking 'Someone's out there.'" Soon after, a crew member sighted a torpedo streaking by the ship's bow. "The next thing I heard was this explosion and a sound like breaking glass from down near the engine room. The ship stood still. . . . We knew we were sinking." The crew rushed to a lifeboat and into the frigid water. As the *Beatus* sank beneath the waves, they listened to the shouts from a surfaced U-boat stalking the rest of their convoy across the dark ocean.[3]

Dönitz's strategy also complicated Allied efforts to send supplies and troops to Britain and rendered any potential amphibious operation in Europe or the Mediterranean significantly more dangerous.

To counter the U-boat threat, British naval commanders concentrated shipping into convoys escorted by destroyers or corvettes. British ships also employed early sonar technology designed to detect submerged U-boats. Unfortunately, these devices only worked if the U-boats were submerged and became useless for a period of time after the detonation of depth charges. By launching nighttime surface attacks, German U-boats could beat British sonar. With British shipping losses at over six hundred thousand tons per month in the spring of 1941, in July President Roosevelt took the first steps toward entering the European war by ordering US ships to provide security for British convoys in the western Atlantic. Weeks later, on September 4, the destroyer USS *Greer*, on its way to Iceland, received a report from a British search plane that a U-boat was nearby. While the RAF plane dropped depth charges, the *Greer* began a search for the German submarine. The U-boat commander, unaware that the *Greer* was an American ship, fired two torpedoes, prompting the destroyer to begin dropping its own depth charges. Neither ship was damaged, but the incident led Roosevelt to announce that US ships would henceforth fire on potential threats. German admiral Erich Raeder read this as a declaration of war, but Hitler ordered restraint—with its hands full fighting on the eastern front, Germany had no need of another enemy in the West. Even so, some three months before Pearl Harbor, the United States had joined the Battle of the Atlantic.[4]

The next eighteen months were difficult for the Allies. German wolf packs continued their rampage against Allied shipping, sinking millions of tons of ships and materials and killing tens of thousands of sailors. The official US entry into the war initiated a massacre of unescorted merchant ships in American coastal waters as US officials elected not to organize convoys or order blackouts along the Atlantic seaboard. American ships, silhouetted against the glow from cities along the East Coast and Gulf of Mexico, made easy targets for Dönitz's U-boats. Harsh winter weather brought some respite for the convoys crossing the rough waters of the Atlantic, but losses increased as summer approached. The Allies were helped by their ability to decipher German naval codes under the Ultra program, but British authorities were forced to use the intelligence sparingly for fear of alerting Berlin that its codes had been cracked. At the same time, German success at deciphering British codes countered some of the advantages gained from Ultra.

However, in the area of signals intelligence, the Allied powers enjoyed a decisive advantage over their adversaries. Ultra intelligence, combined with the successful Magic program aimed at breaking Japanese codes, provided the Allies with a wealth of information about Axis plans, from troop strength to submarine deployments, battle plans, and the movements of enemy commanders. Having already proved invaluable in the Pacific battles of the Coral Sea and Midway, cryptanalysis was employed to devastating effect in the Battle of the Atlantic. Although the exact impact of these Allied intelligence breakthroughs remains a subject of scholarly debate, there is little doubt that they saved thousands of lives and hastened the end of the war by a matter of months if not years.[5]

By the summer of 1942, the mid-Atlantic had become the most dangerous territory for the U-boat attacks. Shore-based Allied bombers such as the B-17 Flying Fortress and the B-24 Liberator lacked the range to cover the central stretches of the Atlantic. As a result, Dönitz had begun concentrating his wolf packs in these waters, where they faced little danger from the skies. The solution, for Allied engineers, was to replace one of the B-24's bomb bays with an extra fuel tank. The modified Liberator could now reach targets some 1,200 miles from its home airfield. Allied aircraft were also fitted with high-power searchlights capable of illuminating U-boats sailing on the surface at night. Meanwhile, Allied convoys began employing high-frequency direction-finding devices to detect radio transmissions from German submarines and triangulate their positions. The development of the cavity magnetron allowed for the construction of smaller, more accurate radar devices that could be placed on ships and aircraft.[6]

Many of the most effective antisubmarine weapons were low-tech, low-cost modifications of existing equipment. To answer the call for more escort vessels, British leaders began commissioning corvette warships, early versions of which were modified whaling vessels. In contrast to relatively expensive multipurpose ships such as destroyers, corvettes were tailored for escort duty. They pitched and rolled in rough seas and were slower than most other warships. However, they could be mass-produced at low cost and were effective at fighting submarines. Churchill lauded them as "cheap and nasties." Like the smaller corvettes, escort carriers also emerged as an improvised solution to the challenge of convoy protection. Allied engineers designed the new classes of small carriers to provide air cover for convoys. The earliest versions were converted cargo ships that plodded across the ocean and deployed only about fifteen aircraft. American sailors nicknamed them "baby flattops." Although they lacked the glamour and firepower of fleet carriers, escort carriers carried enough antisubmarine aircraft to make a U-boat captain think twice before attacking a convoy. In all, the US Navy built more than 120 escort carriers for service in the war. With a growing number of the small carriers roaming the seas and filling the skies with submarine-hunting warplanes to join the long-range B-24s, the mid-Atlantic air gap gradually closed.

The convergence of these new technologies proved decisive in the Battle of the Atlantic. The climax of the U-boat campaign arrived in the spring of 1943 as Dönitz sent Germany's largest-ever fleet of submarines into the Atlantic, and Allied commanders resolved to fight their way through the wolf packs. The convoys suffered heavy losses in March before an April lull while Dönitz's fleet rearmed. The battle resumed in May, but now the convoys—guarded by warships and long-range aircraft—were prepared. German wolf packs continued sinking Allied ships but at a cost of significant losses. Convoys HX 237 and SC 129 lost five ships but managed to sink four U-boats. On May 19, Dönitz learned that the U-boat on which his son was serving had been lost. The Kriegsmarine could not afford to trade submarines for cargo ships. At the end of the month that German sailors would dub "Black May," Dönitz ordered his U-boats to withdraw. Although neither side yet realized it, the Allies had effectively won the Battle of the Atlantic.[7]

While the story of Allied convoys fighting German wolf packs has gained a near-mythical status in Western histories of the war, assertions that the Battle of the Atlantic nearly starved the United Kingdom are overblown. During the deadliest month of the struggle, March 1943, British convoys lost a total of 67 out of 910 ships, meaning that nearly 93 percent of British ships traveling in convoys completed their voyage during the battle's darkest period. The previous month, February 1943, over 97 percent of the ships in British convoys survived. Furthermore, from 1942 on, US and British shipyards were more than making up for these losses. In March 1943 alone, the admiralty reported a net shipping increase of 401,000 tons. Gains in net tonnage were small consolation to the tens of thousands of Allied sailors, pilots, and merchant mariners killed on their ships or drowned in the icy waters of the Atlantic. However, Dönitz's crews faced an even bleaker fate. Of the forty thousand sailors who served on German U-boats, twenty-eight thousand died, a full 70 percent of the force. Such losses led U-boat crews to call their vessels "iron coffins."[8]

MEANWHILE, HALFWAY AROUND THE GLOBE, ALLIED FORCES FIGHTing in the Pacific benefited from a parallel set of advances. On July 31, 1942, the *Austin (TX) Statesman* ran a single-column article announcing the launch of the navy's newest aircraft carrier, the USS *Essex*, at Newport News, Virginia. "The first of a new carrier class bearing her name, the *Essex* will glide into the James river without benefit of formal speeches or fanfare," the newspaper reported. The *Essex* was the latest in a line of US Navy ships to bear the name, the first of which had fought in the Barbary Wars of the early nineteenth century. The new carrier would be commissioned at the end of December and see its first deployment in May 1943. With the public barred from attending the launch owing to wartime security measures, the event went largely unheralded.[9] However, the introduction of the Essex carriers—twenty-four of which would be built by the end of 1945— marked a pivotal moment in the war.

The Essex class was the most numerous class of capital ships during the war and the largest carrier fleet in history. The new carriers weighed a massive twenty-seven thousand tons—nearly 30 percent heavier than the Yorktown-class ships. The Essex ships had larger flight decks and greater fuel storage, and could operate a complement of one hundred aircraft. The carriers were covered in thicker armor and had new hulls that were subdivided into flood-resistant compartments, rendering the ships nearly unsinkable. In addition to these defenses, the ships bristled with antiaircraft guns and carried radar systems designed to give early warnings of possible attacks. Workers labored in around-the-clock shifts to build the new carriers at remarkable speed. The USS *Franklin* was finished in a mere fourteen months. The new carriers helped to give the United States unprecedented naval dominance. None of the Essex carriers would be sunk despite suffering direct hits from bombs, torpedoes, and kamikaze units. The ships gave the US Navy the ability to project forces across the Pacific Ocean and served as centerpieces of the island-hopping campaigns. In the years to come, the Essex carriers would become a cornerstone of US global hegemony, serving in the Korean and Vietnam Wars, acting as recovery ships for the Apollo space program, and remaining active into the 1970s.[10]

Adding to American superiority was a new generation of warplanes including the TBF Avenger torpedo bomber and the F6F Hellcat and the F4U Corsair fighters. The Hellcat improved on the earlier design of the F4F Wildcat in nearly every respect. In addition to having heavier armor, the new Hellcats outclassed Japanese Zeroes in climbing, diving, and turning capabilities. The first F6Fs appeared on the new USS *Essex* in February 1943 and were beginning to dominate the skies above the Pacific by November. By the end of the war, Hellcat pilots would claim to have shot down 5,163 enemy planes with the loss of only 270 of their own—an imposing nineteen-to-one record against enemy aircraft. In all, US factories would build over twelve thousand Hellcats.[11]

The introduction of these new warships and aircraft, combined with improved radar and better use of intelligence, allowed US forces to reverse Tokyo's early advantages. Since the beginning of the war, the US fleet had mainly concentrated on defensive operations designed to protect Allied bases and lines of communication. However, with the arrival of the Essex carriers in the summer of 1943, the balance of power in the Pacific shifted. It was now Japan's turn to play defense. By November, the American carrier fleet enjoyed an eleven-to-six advantage over its Japanese counterpart, and Admiral Nimitz determined that the time had come to rethink strategy. Using task forces composed of fast carriers and supporting ships, the Americans would launch an offensive across the Central Pacific aimed at destroying Tokyo's fleet and striking at the heart of the empire, the Japanese home islands. Dual lines of attack would focus on neutralizing Japan's strongholds at Rabaul and Truk while securing a string of bases across the ocean. Nimitz's carrier task forces would function as fast, long-ranged battle groups that relied on the independent initiative of their commanders at the operational level and of their pilots at the tactical level. Mobility would remain critical both in attacking enemy forces and in reducing the carrier's vulnerability to counterattacks.[12] As they established control of the skies over the Pacific, the new carrier groups would give US forces the ability to strike deep into the Co-Prosperity Sphere, sever Tokyo's lines of communication, and stage amphibious landings on Japanese-controlled islands. The days of trading lost aircraft carriers with Japan were over.

While American shipyards assembled this massive new fleet, an army of engineers was hard at work building a worldwide network of military bases linked by strategic and commercial air routes. In February 1943, a US Joint Strategic Survey Committee paper called for the creation of such a network in "the interests of national security and the maintenance of the Monroe Doctrine," to be used for "international military purposes and U.S. commercial interests." Several months later, Admiral King—speaking off the record with reporters—explained, "After this war, whether we are criticized for imperialism or not, we have got to take and run the Mandated Islands, and perhaps even the Solomons. We have got to dominate the Pacific. . . . We are in a world in which people play for keeps, and if we intend to survive as a great power we have got to take care of ourselves." Two months later, the Army Air Forces proposed the construction of some forty-five thousand aircraft designed to destroy the Japanese Empire in the near term and to counter the growing power of the Soviet Union over the long term. The report warned that "Russia may have sufficient provocation to alone occupy and assume control of not only all of Germany, but all of Central and Eastern Europe."[13]

Although Washington could not hope to match the Red Army on the ground, American aircraft operating out of a global network of bases could bolster US influence in Europe. With victory still years away, some US leaders were already planning to transform the infrastructure created for the war into what historian Daniel Yergin has called an "imperial system of overseas bases encircling the earth," from Newfoundland to Iceland, Bermuda to French Guiana, Ascension Island to Dakar, through Western Europe, and across the far islands of the Pacific Ocean.[14]

Ultimately, this effort to garrison the global littoral squared with the Anglo-American approach to both winning the war and securing postwar hegemony that had been coalescing since the fall of France. The campaigns in the Mediterranean and Pacific would leave the Western Allies in possession of a string of military installations stretching around the globe purpose-built to launch aerial, naval, and amphibious attacks deep into the Eurasian landmass. Control of this network would allow Western forces to make the most of their technological advantages and continue to pursue their strategy of peripheral operations. In the postwar world, these new bases, combined with existing colonial infrastructure, could be repurposed to deter or confront future adversaries such as the Soviet Union. And in times of peace, this global footprint would enhance the reach of

Anglo-American commercial, political, and cultural influence. All of which would contribute to the ongoing transition from British to American hegemony in the postwar world. As Edward Mead Earle, a Princeton professor working with the Office of Strategic Services, explained in September 1943, "Our interest demands that the United States, not Great Britain, become the stabilizing balance wheel of the world."[15]

THE DESTRUCTIVE POTENTIAL OF THIS NETWORK OF AIR AND NAVAL bases was demonstrated with the commencement of a colossal aerial offensive against the Third Reich in mid-1943. Both Churchill and Roosevelt understood that the absence of a true second front in Western Europe guaranteed that the Red Army would face the overwhelming majority of the Wehrmacht through 1943. In lieu of a cross-channel attack, British and American planners at January's Casablanca Conference had promised a massive strategic bombing campaign against the Third Reich. The offensive aimed at the "progressive destruction and dislocation of the German military, industrial and economic system, and the undermining of the morale of the German people to a point where their capacity for armed resistance is fatally weakened." The campaign would also force Germany to use the Luftwaffe to defend its own cities rather than to support troops fighting in Russia and the Mediterranean.[16]

The most enthusiastic supporters of airpower in London and Washington hoped that strategic bombing might deliver a knock-out blow to the German war effort. These ambitions drew on long-standing expectations about the power of strategic bombing to win wars. Writing in the years after the end of the First World War, early prophets of airpower had predicted that aerial warfare would prove so destructive as to render warfare obsolete. British strategist J. F. C. Fuller wrote that a war might be "won in forty-eight hours and the losses of the winning side may be actually nil!" Italian theorist Giulio Douhet argued that more effective aerial bombing would devastate "moral resistance" and force war to become more "civilized." Leading American strategist Billy Mitchell wrote in 1930 that airpower would lead to "the betterment of civilization, because wars will be decided quickly and not drag on for years." Theorists were not the only ones offering such predictions. "I think it is well also for the man in the street to realize that there is no power on earth that can protect him from being bombed," British prime minister Stanley Baldwin told the House of Commons in 1932. "The bomber will always get through. . . . The only defence is in offence, which means that you have got to kill more women and children more quickly than the enemy if you want to save yourselves. I mention that so that people may realize what is waiting for them when the next war comes." Of particular interest was the notion of using bombing campaigns to counterbalance the strategic threat from the revolutionary Soviet Union. With this in mind, Arthur "Bomber" Harris, deputy director of plans in the British Air Ministry, had called for the creation of a new fleet of bombers that could reach Soviet cities from bases in the Middle East. Likewise, many commentators envisioned military aviation as a means of projecting colonial power across vast distances. This notion of "air policing" found a receptive audience among imperial authorities who hoped to use bombing to crack down on colonial revolts.[17]

With the outbreak of World War II, prophecy gave way to practice. Having endured the Luftwaffe's assault during the Battle of Britain, British leaders looked to strategic bombing as perhaps the best way to strike back at Germany. Arthur Harris, who had risen to become chief of RAF Bomber Command, pushed for a merciless bombing campaign against Germany in retaliation for the Blitz. As he explained, "The Nazis entered this war under the rather childish delusion that they were going to bomb everyone else, and nobody was going to bomb them. At Rotterdam, London, Warsaw, and half a hundred other places, they put their rather naive theory into operation. They sowed the wind, and now they are going to reap the whirlwind."[18] Harris and the most vocal champions of airpower predicted that strategic bombing could win wars by devastating an enemy power's industrial base and demoralizing its population. However, others remained skeptical. Instead, they looked to airpower as a means of providing tactical support for ground and naval forces. The tension between the tactical and strategic use of aircraft would continue throughout the war.

Regardless of its war-winning potential, in the absence of a genuine second front in northern Europe, strategic bombing remained London and Washington's principal means of attacking the Reich. While it lacked the punch of a full-scale invasion of Western Europe, the Combined Bomber Offensive represented at least a minor concession to Stalin's demands. By day, US bombers would attack German factories; by night British aircraft would pummel German cities. These around-the-clock operations were designed to terrorize the German population, decimate German war industry, and degrade the strength of the Luftwaffe. In practice, strategic bombing proved difficult and expensive, and its effects were debatable. Heavy cloud cover over northern Europe frequently restricted operations, and the bombs themselves remained frustratingly inaccurate. One British study found that most aircrews were lucky if they placed their bombs within three miles of their targets. An American study found that only 13.6 percent of bombs landed within one thousand feet of their targets. To achieve these disappointing results, aircrews suffered heavy casualties from the Luftwaffe and antiaircraft fire. British raids against Germany in the summer and fall of 1943 frequently resulted in unsustainable losses of between 6 and 8 percent of the attacking planes. Combined with the massive resources consumed by aircraft production and operation, strategic bombing proved incredibly costly.[19]

One area where bombing did succeed was in killing large numbers of civilians. On the night of July 24, 1943, the RAF launched Operation Gomorrah—a series of devastating raids over eight days against the German city of Hamburg. Using radar and visual guidance, 728 planes attacked the city in less than an hour, killing an estimated 1,500 people along with 140 animals in the Hamburg zoo.

Three nights later, 787 bombers returned. The unseasonably hot and dry weather transformed the city into a tinderbox. The RAF struck Hamburg's working-class districts with concentrated bombing that ignited scores of fires. The rubble-strewn streets blocked fire trucks from reaching many of the blazes. Halfway through the raid, the individual fires began to combine into a single massive firestorm. The inferno sucked in oxygen, whipping up high winds that spread the conflagration even farther. The firestorm raged for the next three hours, incinerating sixteen thousand apartment buildings and killing an estimated forty thousand people—nearly all of whom were civilians. Following the raid, 1.2 million survivors fled the city. Such levels of destruction were no accident. As Harris explained in October, "The aim of the Combined Bomber Offensive . . . is the destruction of German cities, the killing of German workers and the disruption of civilized community life throughout Germany. . . . It should be emphasised that the destruction of houses, public utilities, transport and lives; the creation of a refugee problem on an unprecedented scale; and the breakdown of morale both at home and at the battle fronts by fear of extended and intensified bombing, are accepted and intended aims of bombing policy. They are not by-products of attempts to hit factories." But instead of admitting these realities, Harris's commanders at the Air Ministry chose to present the destruction as collateral damage—the unintended consequence of total war.[20]

In retrospect, it would seem that this type of terror bombing did little to undermine German willingness to continue the war. As historian Richard Overy wrote, "No European society collapsed under the impact of bombing." Just as the Luftwaffe had failed to break British morale during the Blitz, the RAF was now failing to crack German support for the Reich. Moreover, some officials argued the question of morale meant little in a dictatorship. A potential German dissident had more to fear from the Gestapo than from Allied bombers. Furthermore, the bombing campaign led many Germans to rally around Hitler and the Nazis. As a committee of scholars convened in 1943 to assess the impact of strategic bombing concluded, Soviet progress in the East remained the decisive factor in the war: "Bombing alone cannot bring about [German] defeat in the spring of 1944." In 1945, the US Strategic Bombing Survey would conclude that the German people's "morale, their belief in ultimate victory or satisfactory compromise, and their confidence in their leaders declined, but they continued to work efficiently as long as the physical means of production remained. The power of a police state over its people cannot be underestimated."[21]

Instead, attacks on German cities diverted airpower from other more effective uses, such as tactical support of ground troops and concentrated attacks on German industry. Historian Adam Tooze has shown that the Allied bombing campaigns were in fact hurting Germany's war production. Beginning in March 1943, the RAF dropped thirty-four thousand tons of bombs on factories and cities in the Ruhr valley. The Battle of the Ruhr killed thousands and resulted in a dramatic reduction of manufacturing. Falling steel output forced Berlin to cut its ammunition program, and aircraft production dropped off.[22] But by sending bombers to attack German cities, incinerating civilians rather than factories, RAF Bomber Command gave the Third Reich's war industry a reprieve.

Nevertheless, the Combined Bomber Offensive served the political goal of demonstrating the American and British contribution to fighting against the Third Reich. The argument that the air war represented a genuine second front against Germany made little headway in Moscow, but it at least provided Western officials a response to Soviet charges that London and Washington were not carrying their share of the burden. Left unsaid was the understanding—hearkening back to Harris's calls from the 1930s—that the same devastation visited on Hamburg might one day be unleashed on Soviet cities in the event of a future conflict between Moscow and the Western powers.

WHILE ALLIED WARPLANES FIREBOMBED GERMAN CITIES, WESTERN leaders deliberated over their next moves in the Mediterranean. The conquest of Tunisia put US and British troops in a position to stage an amphibious attack across the ninety-six miles of water separating Sicily from North Africa. If Allied forces could neutralize the Axis air bases on Sicily, they would finally secure shipping lanes through the Mediterranean, safeguarding a vital route for Lend-Lease supplies to the Soviet Union and clearing the approaches to the Suez Canal. An invasion of Sicily would also place tremendous pressure on Mussolini, Hitler's only major ally in Europe. While such an operation would again fall short of a true second front against the Third Reich, eliminating Italy proved appealing. Moreover, the Sicily invasion would provide another opportunity for the Allies to hone their amphibious operations in preparation for a larger cross-channel invasion of France. However, further operations in the Mediterranean would delay the Allied invasion of northern France until 1944. Many American planners continued to suspect that their British allies hoped to postpone a cross-channel attack indefinitely. Prior to Casablanca, George Marshall had accepted the idea that the Allies would follow the Tunisia campaign with an invasion of Sicily in order to secure their lines of communication through the Mediterranean. However, he worried that Sicily might instead become the prelude to an invasion of the Italian Peninsula. The inter-Allied debates at Casablanca had failed to resolve the issue, ensuring that the question remained open.[23]

The Third Washington Conference, held in May, showcased these divisions alongside the Allies' changing fortunes. Churchill announced that the Allies seemed to be gaining the upper hand against Hitler's U-boats in the Battle of the Atlantic and that the Soviets appeared ready to take the offensive in the East. Now, British and American forces were poised to take Italy, the "great prize" of the Mediterranean campaign. The invasion of Italy would divert German units from the eastern front, Churchill argued, while sending "a chill of loneliness over the German people, and might be the beginning of their doom." Roosevelt remained focused on a cross-channel invasion as the "most effective way of forcing Germany to fight" and relieving pressure on Moscow, but all parties now realized that no such invasion would be possible in 1943.[24]

Marshall expressed his concern that further operations against Italy would "establish a vacuum in the Mediterranean" that would prevent any cross-channel attack and prolong the war for the foreseeable future. Brooke countered that an invasion of Italy remained the best option. A cross-channel attack, he argued, could secure a bridgehead, at most: "No major operations would be possible until 1945 or 1946." To Marshall, this sounded very much like a plan to delay an invasion of northern France indefinitely. US secretary of war Henry Stimson worried that the British were playing a dangerous game by delaying a second front and forcing the Soviets to do most of the "real fighting." The opponents of the cross-channel operation, he told Roosevelt on May 17, "are trying to arrange this matter so that Britain and America hold the leg for Stalin to skin the deer and I think that will be dangerous business for us at the end of the war. Stalin won't have much of an opinion of people who have done that and we will not be able to share much of the postwar world with him."[25]

As the conference continued, the British chiefs argued that a cross-channel operation "could only form a very small part of the whole continental land war." Instead, Allied efforts should focus on aiding the Soviet Union. The conditions for a successful amphibious attack on northern France "could be created only by the Russian Army." Moreover, Brooke argued that the Allies must press the offensive in the Mediterranean in order to divert German forces for a future attack on France. If a cross-channel attack was to take place in 1944, he explained, the Allies should aim for June to coincide with the Red Army's summer offensive. After days of debate, the chiefs finally reached a compromise: Allied forces would stage an invasion of Italy but would also commit to the date of May 1, 1944, for a cross-channel assault.[26]

All of which meant that it would be at least another year before British and US forces arrived in France. Given the building momentum of the Red Army's operations in the East, a year was a long time.

Adding to Western concerns, the Allies had still not come to an agreement regarding the occupation of Germany. As Roosevelt's special assistant Harry Hopkins explained in March, "Unless we acted promptly and surely I believed one of two things would happen—either Germany will go Communist or [an] out and out anarchic state would set in. . . . Indeed the same kind of thing might happen in any of the countries in Europe and Italy as well." It was therefore crucial to draft a formal agreement between the Allied powers regarding the fate of a defeated Germany. "It will, obviously, be a much simpler matter if the British and American armies are heavily in France or Germany at the time of the collapse but we should work out a plan in case Germany collapses before we get to France." Two weeks later, Marshall expressed similar concerns to the president. The United States must have "a sizable American representation on the ground" when Germany collapsed. "I also gave him as my personal opinion the fear that if we were involved at the last in Western France and the Russian Army was approaching German soil, there would be a most unfortunate diplomatic situation . . . with the possibility of a chaotic condition quickly following."[27]

London and Washington's peripheral operations had made rapid progress by the summer of 1943, placing the Western powers in a position to exert strong influence in the Atlantic and Pacific Oceans, the Mediterranean Sea, and across North Africa. Nevertheless, with the Red Army preparing a new offensive, the prospect of Soviet domination over the Eurasian landmass loomed in the near future. Roosevelt's closest advisers, such as Hopkins and Marshall, recognized that the clock was ticking on Washington's bid to build a postwar order modeled on the terms of the Atlantic Charter. For the time being, however, Allied forces would focus on the impending invasion of Sicily.

IN THE EARLY HOURS OF APRIL 30, 1943, THE BRITISH SUBMARINE *Seraph* slipped silently through the waters off Huelva, Spain. As the submarine approached the darkened coast, sailors aboard hauled a six-foot canister marked "Optical Instruments" up to the ship's gun platform. At 4:15 a.m., the crew opened the canister and with some effort removed a large bundle wrapped in a blanket. The sailors unfastened the bindings to reveal a cadaver in the early stages of decomposition, clad in a British Royal Marines uniform complete with a Mae West life jacket. Attached to the corpse was a briefcase marked "Royal Cypher." After paying their respects, the crew lowered the body into the water, where it tossed in the waves, floating with the current toward shore. Later that morning, local fishermen discovered the corpse along with a set of fake British documents detailing a planned Allied invasion of Greece. Spanish authorities passed the plans to German intelligence agents, who relayed the information to Berlin, prompting a buildup of German forces in the Balkans. Operation Mincemeat—the British deception scheme to direct German attention away from the invasion of Sicily—was a complete success.[28] The Allies would not let it go to waste.

Ten weeks later, on the night of July 9, thousands of Allied paratroopers staged an airborne assault on Sicily. The attack got off to a rough start when many of the gliders were released too soon and forced to ditch in the sea while others came under heavy fire from German defenses. The troops that survived managed to cut telephone lines and attack a few German patrols. However, the bulk of the invasion arrived in the form of a 2,590-ship fleet carrying 180,000 troops. The developing American and British expertise at amphibious operations was on full display. Disorganized Italian forces mounted a haphazard defense of the coast as Allied troops stormed ashore, establishing strong beachheads and seizing the vital port of Syracuse. The invaders overwhelmed the Axis defenses, but Allied commanders proved overly cautious. Rather than pressing his advantage, General Bernard Montgomery adopted a conservative, methodical approach. Making matters worse, the Americans and British chose not to attack on the Strait of Messina, which separated Sicily from the mainland. The plodding advance coupled with the failure to block the strait allowed some fifty-five thousand German and seventy thousand Italian soldiers to escape into Italy, along with some ten thousand vehicles. What might have been a crushing Allied success instead became, in the words of one historian, a "hollow victory."[29]

Nevertheless, London and Washington had reason to celebrate. Repeated military setbacks in North Africa and the Mediterranean, heavy losses on the eastern front, and humiliations at the hands of Hitler had taken their toll on Mussolini's popularity in Italy. Now, the invasion of Sicily had brought the war to Italian soil. On July 24, as Allied forces continued their conquest of the island, the Grand Council of Fascism convened in Rome to consider the dictator's fate. The king along with senior leadership concluded Mussolini had entered into a subservient position to Germany, led the nation into a disastrous war, and lost the support of the Italian people. "You believed yourself a soldier," the president of Italy's parliament fumed. "Let me tell you, Italy was lost the very day you put the gold braid of a marshal on your cap." The meeting concluded with a successful vote of no confidence in the prime minister, removing Mussolini from power. "Dear Duce," the king stated, "things don't work any more. Italy has gone to pieces. The army is morally prostrated. The soldiers no longer want to fight. . . . In this moment you are the most hated man in Italy." At the close of the meeting, the disgraced dictator was arrested.[30]

With Mussolini imprisoned, Italian leaders found themselves caught between the seemingly unstoppable advance of Western forces in the south and their brutal German ally in the north. If Italy remained in the war, it risked being crushed by the Allies; if it surrendered, it would likely be occupied by the Germans. Prime Minister Pietro Badoglio's new government dithered for nearly six weeks, waiting until September 3—and the arrival of Allied ground forces in Calabria—to sign an armistice. Badoglio had hoped for a massive Allied invasion that would effectively rescue Italy from German vengeance. Rather than preparing a robust defense of the capital, he waited until the evening of September 8 to announce Italy's surrender and ordered his soldiers to refrain from taking "the initiative in hostilities against German troops." At 5:00 the next morning, the prime minister and his advisers fled the city, hoping to return with the arrival of Allied forces. In response, German forces under the command of Albert Kesselring launched Operation Achse—the rapid occupation of Italy. Bewildered Italian soldiers surrendered en masse to German troops, turned over their equipment, and in many cases were then taken as POWs to be shipped off as slave labor in the Third Reich. On September 12, German airborne troops raided the Alpine prison holding Mussolini, liberated the dictator, and rushed him away to be installed as the head of the new puppet Republic of Salò.[31] This debacle created the very situation Marshall had feared: Italy was set to become a bloody and indecisive battlefield between Allied and German forces, drawing troops and resources away from the cross-channel invasion of France.

WHILE ANGLO-AMERICAN FORCES MOVED TO SECURE THE MEDITER-ranean, the European war's focus remained on the eastern front. On the heels of their victory at Stalingrad, Soviet forces had mounted a series of winter offensives that achieved meaningful gains but failed to rout the invaders. Hitler's forces were battered but still far from beaten. In February, while a deep winter still gripped the front, Field Marshal Erich von Manstein launched a daring counteroffensive, retaking Kharkov and Belgorod and inflicting over eighty thousand Soviet casualties. The spring thaw found German and Soviet forces locked in a twisting, uneven battlefront stretching from Rostov to Leningrad. The center of the front was dominated by a massive bulge at Kursk that pushed west into the German lines between Belgorod and Orel. The salient formed an obvious point of attack for any future offensive—a fact that was very much on the minds of German and Soviet leaders as they planned their next moves.

Manstein made the initial push for the Kursk operation, arguing that the Wehrmacht should mount a spring offensive following the victory at Kharkov. German forces were in no condition to stage an attack on the scale of Barbarossa or Operation Blue. Instead, German commanders envisioned a more limited assault against the Kursk salient designed to shorten Axis lines, destroy a large number of Soviet troops, stymie the Red Army's summer offensive, and demonstrate to the world that the Wehrmacht was still a dangerous force. "The victory of Kursk must be a signal to the world," Hitler said. Initially planned for May, the operation was delayed to June to allow for a buildup of German troops and the deployment of new Panther and Tiger tanks. Manstein opposed the delay, but the Führer insisted that his new tanks be used at Kursk. General Heinz Guderian, for his part, opposed the entire operation. "Why do you want to attack in the East at all?" he asked Hitler. "Do you think anyone even knows where Kursk is? It is all the same to the world whether we hold Kursk or not."[32]

This delay coupled with the obvious nature of the objective gave the Red Army ample time to prepare an extensive network of defenses. Meanwhile, Soviet spies inside British decryption operations at Bletchley Park confirmed Moscow's suspicions of a German attack. Marshal Georgy Zhukov was convinced that the Germans would attempt a large-scale offensive against Kursk. Rather than attempting to strike the first blow, Soviet forces should prepare to absorb the initial German assault and then retaliate with an overwhelming counterattack. "It will be better," Zhukov wrote, "if we wear the enemy out in defensive action, destroy his tanks, and then, taking in fresh reserves, by going over to an all-out offensive we will finish off the enemy's main grouping." To this end, Soviet engineers built a fortress of antitank defenses, minefields, and strongpoints across the area. Red Army commanders deployed heavy artillery, antitank weapons, armor, and infantry to block potential German advances while commando units staged infiltration operations across German lines to conduct reconnaissance and sabotage roads and bridges. The Central and Voronezh Fronts would defend the salient reinforced by the Bryansk and Western Fronts to the north and the Southwestern and Southern Fronts in the south. Meanwhile, the Steppe Military

District would serve as a massive reserve force waiting in the east. In all, the Red Army fielded nearly 2.3 million troops in the region against 900,000 Germans, giving the Red Army a nearly three-to-one advantage in men and armor.[33]

The battle began early on the morning of July 5 when Soviet aircraft and artillery launched a largely ineffective barrage against assembling German forces. Soon after, General Walter Model's Ninth Army attacked the northern edge of the salient, charging directly into Soviet defenses. Hard fighting limited Model's advance to a mere five miles on the first day. German Tiger tanks mauled the defending T-34s, which were forced to dig into earthworks for protection. The northern spearhead penetrated another five miles before it was stopped at Ponyri. While Model's forces tried to break through, the Bryansk Front staged a counterattack against Orel that threatened to cut off the Germans fighting at Ponyri. Model had no choice but to pull back to cover his flank. Manstein's southern pincer made better progress, driving some fifteen miles into Soviet lines by the second day of the battle. On July 11, Manstein's tanks reached the town of Prokhorovka. The following day, Soviet commanders launched a concerted counterattack designed to encircle and trap the Wehrmacht forces inside the salient. Some of the heaviest fighting took place at Prokhorovka, where the reserve forces of the Steppe Front met Manstein's panzers in what would be billed as the largest tank battle in history. Soviet T-34s caught the Germans by surprise but suffered massive and disproportionate losses in the process. "It wasn't a battle, it was a slaughterhouse of tanks," remembered one Soviet tanker. "Everything was burning. An indescribable stench hung in the air over the battlefield. Everything was enveloped in smoke, dust and fire, so it looked as if it was twilight." Red Army forces took disproportionately high casualties, but the Bryansk Front's progress in the north now threatened to collapse the German pocket.[34]

As the Kursk offensive became bogged down, German leaders received another piece of bad news: the Allies had staged successful landings on Sicily and Mussolini's position was in doubt. On July 13,

Hitler ordered Manstein and Field Marshal Günther von Kluge to call off the Kursk operation and transfer the II SS Panzer Corps to Italy. Manstein protested, insisting that "victory was within reach. Breaking off action now would be throwing away victory." But the Führer had made up his mind. From the beginning, Hitler had planned to call off the offensive in the event of a major Allied operation in the West. Moreover, the fighting near Orel had helped convince Kluge that the operation had failed and that the Ninth Army must now be saved from encirclement.[35]

Kursk would stand as a sobering failure for Germany. The Werhmacht had inflicted far heavier casualties on Soviet forces: the Red Army suffered some seventy thousand killed and lost 1,600 tanks to fifteen thousand Germans killed with a loss of around 300 armored vehicles. But the Wehrmacht had thrown its best forces at the Red Army during a summer offensive and had been stopped. While formidable on the battlefield, the new Tiger and Panther tanks could not alter the fundamental calculus of the war. The failure at Kursk revealed that the balance of power on the eastern front had shifted decisively against Germany. The defeat at Stalingrad had been no fluke, and the Wehrmacht should expect things to get tougher going forward. "And so the last German offensive in the east ended in a fiasco," Manstein later wrote, "even though the enemy opposite the two attacking armies of Southern Army Group had suffered four times their losses in prisoners, dead and wounded. . . . The initiative in the Eastern theater of war finally passed to the Russians."[36]

ALTHOUGH STALIN COULD JUSTIFIABLY CONTEND THAT THE RED Army was carrying most of the burden in fighting the Wehrmacht, none of the principal Allied leaders had more reason for complaint than Chiang Kai-shek. China had spent nearly four and a half years fighting alone against Japan before Tokyo's Grand Offensive of December 1941 brought Britain and the United States into the war. And Allied leaders recognized that China was playing a critical role in the war against Japan by tying down the bulk of the Japanese army and serving as a base for operations against Tokyo. The US chiefs acknowledged that "keeping Russia and China actively in the war effort is essential to our successful conclusion of the war in any reasonable time." Likewise, Admiral King explained in May 1943, "The retention of China as a base for the defeat of Japan was as essential as the continuance of Russia in the war as a factor in the defeat of Germany."[37]

Despite this understanding of China's importance in the larger war, Chiang ranked a distant fourth behind Roosevelt, Stalin, and Churchill in the hierarchy of Allied leaders. Indeed, of the $48 billion the United States spent on Lend-Lease aid, $31 billion went to the British Empire, $11 billion reached the Soviet Union, $3 billion went to France, and a paltry $1.6 billion went to China. Making matters worse, Roosevelt's choice to command the US military mission to China, General Joseph Stilwell, clashed with Chiang. The fifty-nine-year-old Stilwell—nicknamed "Vinegar Joe" for his abrasive demeanor—initially seemed like an ideal candidate. He spoke and read Chinese and had spent a good part of the 1930s in the country. However, Stilwell evinced little respect for Chiang, giving him the derogatory nickname "Peanut" and deriding the Generalissimo as unreliable, ineffective, and incompetent. Chiang reciprocated this antipathy, especially after the disastrous 1942 campaign in which Stilwell insisted on sending an expeditionary force composed of China's best soldiers into Burma against the Imperial Japanese Army. Chiang had expressed strong reservations about the offensive, arguing that his armies were best used defensively. As he warned Stilwell, "Once the cream of Chinese troops . . . is defeated, it would be impossible to counterattack not only in Burma but also in the whole of China." A defeat in Burma would have a "grave effect upon the Chinese people." But Chiang ultimately relented in the interest of maintaining the alliance with Washington. It was a decision he would regret.[38]

Stilwell arrived in Burma on March 11, 1942, determined to launch a counteroffensive to retake Rangoon. It was already too late.

British defenses were disintegrating, and the introduction of Chinese divisions did little to slow the Japanese onslaught. Within a matter of days, Chiang's forces faced the threat of encirclement and were forced to retreat. Although Western newspapers portrayed Stilwell as a heroic general leading a valiant withdrawal, the Chinese assessment was harshly critical. Chiang placed the blame squarely on the American general: "The responsibility for the enormous sacrifice of our forces in Burma lies entirely with Stilwell's command failures. Rather than admitting his own mistakes, he just blames our senior commanders. When we began to lose, he was all in a fluster and only thought about fleeing to India, having no concern for our forces."[39]

While Stilwell squandered thousands of Chiang's best troops in Burma, Japanese armies rampaged across southeast China. Launched in response to the Doolittle raid of April 18, 1942, the Zhejiang-Jiangxi campaign had aimed to capture the American pilots responsible, punish any Chinese citizens who had aided them, and seize any Chinese airfields that might serve as bases for attacks on Japan. Japanese units cut a trail of destruction through the provinces of Zhejiang and Jiangxi, razing villages and massacring their inhabitants. "They shot any man, woman, child, cow, hog, or just about anything that moved," remembered one Catholic priest in the county of Yihuang. "They raped any woman from the ages of 10–65, and before burning the town they thoroughly looted it. . . . The men of the Roman Legions could not have been more barbaric." Marauding soldiers slaughtered entire herds of livestock, torched crops, poisoned wells, and destroyed irrigation systems in a bid to terrorize the local population. "They killed my three sons; they killed my wife, Angsing; they set fire to my school; they burned my books; they drowned my grandchildren in the well," remembered one schoolteacher. Another priest claimed that entire towns had been wiped off the map: "The whole countryside reeked of death in every form." In Nancheng, soldiers lined up a group of men suspected of helping the American pilots and staged contests to see how many could be killed with a single bullet.[40]

In late June, Japanese commanders directed their infamous biological weapons program, Unit 731, to launch a series of attacks on the local Chinese population. In a good month, the program's facilities were capable of producing 650 pounds of plague bacteria, 1,500 pounds of anthrax, and some 2,000 pounds each of typhoid and cholera. Scientists working with Unit 731 ran gruesome experiments on convicts and POWs that included transfusions of horse blood, vivisections, and inoculations with plague pathogens. As part of their campaign, Unit 731 dispatched agents to poison wells and rivers with plague, anthrax, typhoid, and cholera. Other groups left biscuits laced with typhoid near villages in hopes of infecting starving locals. The scale of devastation before the start of the campaign rendered accurate recordkeeping impossible, but reports of widespread epidemics spread across the countryside. "We avoided staying in towns overnight because cholera had broken out and was spreading rapidly," wrote an Australian journalist. "The magistrate assured us that every inhabited house in the city was stricken with some disease." But the Japanese soon began to fall victim to their own weapons. Under interrogation, Japanese soldiers reported over 10,000 deaths as a result of cholera epidemics during the campaign. The highest casualty estimates place the number of Chinese deaths from the entire campaign at 250,000.[41]

However, Japanese leaders were finding that wholesale atrocities against civilian populations paid meager strategic dividends. Indeed, over the long term, mass killings usually strengthened local resistance. Japanese commanders looked to break the stalemate by launching a large-scale offensive against Chiang's capital, Chongqing, deep in the western interior. Over the spring of 1942, Tokyo had amassed sixteen divisions for a planned five-month campaign, but the war in the Pacific had intervened. The escalating battle for Guadalcanal had forced Japanese commanders to cancel the Chongqing offensive in order to divert troops to the Solomon Islands. A smaller campaign launched in February 1943 along the Hebei-Shanxi border killed or captured an estimated thirty thousand Chinese fighters. Subsequent operations targeted Henan Province in May and western Hubei Province in June. Japanese commanders mounted their largest operation of 1943 against the city of Changde in November. A total of six divisions attacking from the north and east converged on the city. Despite persistent attacks from Allied aircraft, Japanese units managed to seize control of the Changde on December 3. Six days later, however, Chinese reinforcements recaptured the city, dealing an operational defeat to the Japanese. Despite inflicting heavy casualties on Chinese forces and civilians and winning a long series of battle-field victories, the Imperial Japanese Army proved unable to break the strategic stalemate. Ongoing Chinese resistance combined with the mounting Allied offensives in the Pacific to ensure that Japanese forces remained mired in an unwinnable war in China.[42]

Nevertheless, numerous warning signs indicated that Chiang's regime faced domestic trouble. In May, the American chargé d'af-faires in Chongqing, George Atcheson Jr., had written that, although Chinese leaders remained determined to fight the Japanese, the nation faced a rapidly deteriorating economic situation, a precari-ous military position, and a growing danger of food shortages, all of which combined in a "vicious circle." The cost of living in China had increased eightyfold since 1937 and continued to increase at a rate of 10 percent per month, and agrarian unrest was on the rise across much of the countryside. Making matters worse, ongoing Japanese operations threatened the nation's food supply, exacerbat-ing the regime's economic woes. "A number of intelligent Chinese of affairs with sober, conservative and balanced minds have variously estimated to me that under present conditions China 'can last' only from 6 months to a year," Atcheson warned. Chiang himself echoed these sentiments in December, warning Roosevelt that "the danger to the China theater lies not only in the inferiority of our military strength, but also, and more especially, in our critical economic con-dition which may seriously affect the morale of the army and people, and cause at any moment a sudden collapse of the entire front." More-over, even if Chiang's regime could continue its resistance until Japan's defeat, it would face the threat of a renewed battle with Mao Zedong's communist forces for control of postwar China. The longer the war continued, the grimmer Chiang's prospects appeared.[43]

IF 1942 WITNESSED THE HIGH TIDE OF THE AXIS ASSAULT, THE FIRST half of 1943 saw significant strides toward reversing those gains. By the early summer, Allied navies dominated the key shipping routes across the Atlantic, Pacific, and Indian Oceans and the Mediterranean; Allied aircraft were pushing ever deeper into German-controlled ter-ritory; Axis armies had been driven from North Africa and Sicily; the Soviets had repulsed the Wehrmacht's last large offensive on the east-ern front; and Chiang's regime still survived. However, the battles of 1943 highlighted the vastly disparate price in blood being paid by the big four Allied powers. While hundreds of thousands of Chinese and Soviet infantry were cut down in the continental slaughterhouses of China and Eastern Europe, American and British forces mobilized imperial assets to conduct heavily mechanized campaigns by air and sea along the periphery of the Axis empires, which were designed to minimize casualties while securing hegemony over vast stretches of the globe. The Western Allies had applied Francis Bacon's dictum that "he that commands the sea is at great liberty, and may take as much or as little of war as he will. Whereas those that be strongest by land are many times nevertheless in great straits."[44]

Nonetheless, this peripheral strategy carried risks. Soviet and Chinese resentment at having been left to face the German and Japa-nese armies alone would continue to cast a pall over Allied relations. Furthermore, Western leaders now confronted a potentially greater peril: the disposition of Allied armies at the end of the war would play a decisive role in shaping the postwar peace. By sparing American and British soldiers the horrors of major land campaigns in Europe and Asia, Roosevelt and Churchill would give embittered Soviet and Chinese leaders free rein to dictate the structure of power in postwar Europe and Asia. Command of the seas provided wide flexibility in times of war and paid great dividends in times of peace, but the degree to which maritime empires could shape continental politics remained uncertain. These concerns would rise to the surface as Allied leaders gathered in Cairo and Tehran to coordinate wartime strategy and begin planning the postwar world.

Chapter 13

PLANNING THE
POSTWAR WORLD

AT 9:35 A.M. ON NOVEMBER 22, 1943, A PLANE CARRYING PRESIDENT
Franklin Roosevelt touched down at Cairo West Air Base. The
president's plane had taken off in Tunis following an easterly
course across North Africa, then north along the Nile River, before
flying over the Sphinx and the Pyramids of Giza. Roosevelt stayed at a
villa in the Mena neighborhood of Cairo, spending much of his time
on the residence's rear patio overlooking a flower garden. The following afternoon, the president and Prime Minister Winston Churchill
made their way to the pyramids. After enlisting the services of a local
guide, they watched the sunset and the "afterglow" in the gathering
dusk. That evening, Chiang Kai-shek and his wife, Soong Mei-ling,
joined the president for dinner at his villa, where they stayed late into
the night.[1] The Allies stood at a pivotal point in the course of the war
and the history of the contemporary world. With the tide of the war

having turned in their favor, the leaders in London, Moscow, Chong-qing, and Washington would increasingly devote their attention to postwar considerations. Indeed, as Allied staffs began drawing up plans for the war's endgame, it became clear to all involved that the choices they would make in defeating the Axis powers would carry sweeping consequences for the fate of the postwar world.

Three interlocking issues sat at the heart of the ensuing debates. First, the Western Allies' refusal to launch a cross-channel invasion in 1943 remained a point of contention, rankling Soviet leaders, who accused London and Washington of shirking their responsibilities to open a second front against the Third Reich. A second, related point emerged regarding the question of postwar Europe. If the Red Army managed to defeat the Wehrmacht before an Anglo-American land-ing in France, how much influence would the Western Allies have in shaping the future balance of power on the continent? Would post-war occupations be run jointly by the Allies, or would they be used to create spheres of influence at the discretion of occupying armies? Finally, at the end of the war, would the victorious Allies extend self-determination to all the world's nations, or would they fall back into prewar patterns of imperialism and colonialism? These issues had been tabled during the crises of earlier years, but they were becom-ing increasingly urgent as Allied armies took the offensive and their leaders met at the Allied conferences in Cairo and Tehran.

THE MONTHS FOLLOWING THE JANUARY 1943 CASABLANCA CONFER-ence witnessed a sea change in American attitudes toward Moscow as a growing chorus of voices expressed concern about Soviet power in the postwar world. Officially, the Roosevelt administration remained hopeful about the prospect of postwar cooperation with the Soviet Union. The president intended to use Lend-Lease aid as a carrot to entice Moscow toward friendly relations with Washington, and many military planners continued to view Germany and Japan as the powers most likely to threaten US interests in the future. Broadly speaking, Washington placed emphasis on defeating the Axis powers rather than on planning for a coming conflict with Moscow. But this was about to change. As a key member of the War Plans Division, Brigadier General Albert Wedemeyer, later wrote, "We failed to realize that unconditional surrender and the annihilation of German power would result in a tremendous vacuum in Central Europe into which the Communist power and ideas would flow."[2]

Through early 1943, concerns about Soviet intentions had begun rising to the fore. The Soviet victory at Stalingrad convinced Western leaders that the Red Army had seized the strategic initiative in the East. Increasingly, it appeared that Stalin's regime not only would survive but would emerge in a dominant position in Europe at the end of the war. Meanwhile, Allied victories in North Africa bolstered Western confidence in their own ability to defeat German armies on the battlefield, which translated to greater American and British confidence in their dealings with Moscow. At the same time, the Casablanca Conference directed Western attention to planning for the endgame in Europe while also driving home the reality that a cross-channel invasion would not take place until 1944. The combination of these factors directed American and British deliberations away from surviving the Axis assault and toward the challenge of securing victory both on the battlefield and at the peace table. But for the time being, the Kremlin was a black box. Power in Moscow was concentrated in the hands of Stalin, and the dictator's intentions remained a mystery. "Russia was a complete sphinx to all the other nations of the world," explained Secretary of State Cordell Hull.[3] Indeed, even in the twenty-first century, the complete record of high-level Soviet decision-making remains locked away in closed Russian archives.

The enigmatic nature of Stalin's regime fueled speculation regarding one of the most vexing diplomatic questions of the war: whether the Soviets might seek a separate peace with Germany. The prospect of a rapprochement between Hitler and Stalin had haunted American and British officials since the summer of 1941. In this regard, Russia's early exit from the First World War with the 1918 Treaty of

Brest-Litovsk provided one point of reference, as did Stalin's willingness to sign onto the 1939 Molotov-Ribbentrop Pact. If Moscow chose to forge an armistice with Berlin, the Western Allies would face an exponentially tougher fight against the Wehrmacht. Following the Soviet victory at Stalingrad, the prospect of just such a deal came into view. The Wehrmacht no longer seemed invincible, the Red Army was growing in strength, and the Western Allies appeared to be dragging their feet on opening a second front. Moreover, Japanese and Italian officials had offered to serve as mediators in negotiations between Berlin and Moscow. Given the circumstances, it seemed that Stalin might well decide to halt his forces at the 1941 borders and leave the rest of the fighting to Washington and London. Reports of diplomatic feelers between Berlin and Moscow stoked Western fears through the summer of 1943.[4]

The prospect of a crushing Soviet offensive that might force the rapid collapse of Hitler's regime presented the opposite dilemma. By focusing on peripheral operations in the Mediterranean, the Western Allies had left the bulk of the land war to the Red Army—an approach that limited American and British casualties but risked leaving Stalin in control of vast stretches of the continent. If Germany collapsed before Western forces arrived in France, there would be nothing to stop the Red Army from occupying the whole of Europe. To guard against this contingency, US military leaders stressed the need to move substantial land forces onto the continent as soon as possible. As General Thomas Handy, chief of the US War Department's Operations Division, explained in early 1943, "Victory in the war will be meaningless unless we also win the peace. We must be strong enough at the peace table to cause our demands to also be respected."[5] For no small number of Western officials, the prospect of a total Soviet victory was as frightening as that of an early Soviet exit from the war.

One of the loudest voices warning of Soviet imperialism was William Bullitt, former US ambassador to Moscow and Paris. In late January 1943, Bullitt sent a lengthy memorandum to Roosevelt calling for a more focused strategy in the war and identifying Stalin as the greatest obstacle to Washington's postwar goals. While Bullitt admitted that the Soviets were vital allies who had struggled valiantly against the Nazis, he argued that Stalin remained a cunning tyrant committed to "aggressive imperialism." "No race on earth," he wrote, "not even the German, has shown such burgeoning energy as the Russian during the past hundred years. They have conquered one sixth of the earth's surface. They are still bursting with expansive energy." At a minimum, the Soviets would take over large stretches of Eastern Europe. If possible, Stalin would push Soviet influence into Germany, France, Iran, and Turkey. The Soviets would take as much territory as they were allowed, but Moscow would not risk a full-scale war with the Western powers. Nevertheless, Stalin's great opportunity would come after the Third Reich's collapse. Washington and London would be preoccupied fighting Tokyo, leaving Europe open to Soviet machinations. The Red Army would be able to "sweep through Europe from east to west" along with mobs of supporters to be greeted by "Soviet 5th columns already organized in every European country." To prevent the creation of a Soviet-dominated Europe, Bullitt argued, the United States and Britain must erect bulwarks against Soviet expansion into Western Europe. To this end, Bullitt advocated an invasion of Central Europe by way of the Balkans, which would place Western armies in the path of the Soviet juggernaut. Moreover, he argued that rather than seeking the postwar disarmament of Europe, America's goal should be to "lay the ground work for a combination of democratic governments in Europe strong enough to preserve democracy in Europe and keep the Bolsheviks from replacing the Nazis as masters of Europe." The clock was ticking, Bullitt warned. Once Germany surrendered, Washington would lose any remaining leverage over Moscow.[6]

In February 1943, the army attaché in Moscow, Brigadier General Joseph Michela, echoed this sentiment. The Soviets "intend to push their claims in Europe even to the extent of resorting to armed force, the day the war with Germany ends." The following month, Roosevelt asked Anthony Eden if he believed Bullitt's concerns about Soviet plans to dominate postwar Europe were justified. Eden remained skeptical but admitted that "Russia was our most difficult problem." The Soviet Union "had two different plans up her sleeve—one based on British-American cooperation with Russia and the other on the assumption that the U.S. would withdraw from all interest in European affairs after the war." Eden thought Stalin preferred the former, but he believed that, at the very least, Moscow would demand control over the Baltic states. While London and Washington would object to this annexation, the Red Army would be occupying the Baltic states, "and none of us can force them to get out."[7]

Two days later, on March 17, 1943, Roosevelt, his special assistant Harry Hopkins, and Secretary of State Cordell Hull met to discuss the fate of postwar Germany. Hopkins worried that without a formal agreement between the Allies regarding zones of occupation, a defeated Germany was likely to fall to communist influence or outright anarchy. Roosevelt agreed that the Allies should work out a plan for the postwar occupation. "It will, obviously, be a much simpler matter if the British and American armies are heavily in France or Germany at the time of the collapse but we should work out a plan in case Germany collapses before we get to France." At the end of the month, General Marshall warned Roosevelt that the United States must have a significant number of troops in Britain ready to enter Germany in the event of a sudden collapse. He also expressed his concerns about a potential for armed clashes at the end of the war as both Western and Soviet military forces entered Germany. On April 9, General Hap Arnold warned that, at the current rate, the Western Allies would still be planning a cross-channel invasion while the Soviets marched through the streets of Berlin.[8]

Prominent voices outside the US government had also offered their opinions on the fate of postwar Europe. In April 1943, Walter Lippmann, America's most influential columnist, published his bestselling book U.S. Foreign Policy: Shield of the Republic. Condensed for popular magazines and cartoons and sent to US troops in a paperback edition, the book outlined the emerging consensus that saw US national security interests as global in scope. Eurasia contained the bulk of the world's population and most of its industrial centers. "Our primary interest in Europe, as shown during the Napoleonic and the two German Wars," Lippmann wrote, "is that no European power should emerge which is capable of aggression outside of the European continent." Going forward, he argued, US policy must endeavor to prevent any foreign power from dominating Eurasia and thereby threatening the New World. The Allies would defeat Germany and Japan, but the shape of the postwar order depended on the actions of the victors. Peace in Europe would depend on whether Moscow intended to expand to the west. Peace in the Pacific, Lippmann continued, depended on whether Moscow and Washington could avoid conflict in Asia. Ultimately, "the crucial question of the epoch that we are now entering is the relationship between Russia and that Atlantic Community in which Britain and the United States are the leading powers." That summer, Admiral Ernest King sent Lippmann a note expressing his wish that every American read the book.[9]

In the July issue of *Foreign Affairs*, the dean of British geopolitics, Sir Halford Mackinder, also weighed in on the question of a postwar order. Moscow had emerged as the rising power that would command the pivot of history in the Eurasian landmass. Following Germany's defeat, Moscow would rank as the world's greatest land power. Soviet forces would occupy sprawling territories stretching from Central Europe to the Pacific, comprising a virtually unassailable strategic position. "The Heartland is the greatest natural fortress on the earth," Mackinder warned. "For the first time in history it is manned by a garrison sufficient both in number and quality."[10]

Diplomats with experience working with the Soviets offered even more sobering assessments. The US naval attaché in Istanbul warned Roosevelt that the "most difficult problem you will have to face in post war Europe will be Russia." More colorfully, Bullitt told Roosevelt that Stalin was nothing more than "a Caucasian bandit whose only thought when he got something for nothing was that the other fellow was an ass." In August, Bullitt again stressed that the United States must not win the war only to open the door to Soviet domination of Europe. London and Washington had already deemed Hitler's control of Europe intolerable, he explained. But Europe dominated by Stalin would represent just as great a threat. Although the Allies still needed Soviet participation to win the war against Germany, Western leaders should harbor no illusions about the Kremlin. Any thought of coming to terms with Moscow was naive, he wrote. "We can no longer reasonably hope to come to an agreed and honorable solution with the Soviet Union."[11]

As US and British leaders reconvened for the August 1943 Quadrant Conference in Quebec, questions about a second front and Soviet plans for Europe loomed large. In the run-up to the meeting, Army Air Force Intelligence had noted that a German collapse would leave the Soviet Union as the only major power on the continent. As such, Moscow would "be in a position to dictate future political arrangements and territorial assignments on the 'future' of world peace." To forestall such a scenario, US forces had to make preparations to launch a rapid invasion of the continent or "it will be too late. . . . We will merely sit on the sidelines while Russia decides the European politics." With this in mind, Army Chief of Staff George Marshall wondered whether Nazi forces might actually be willing to facilitate the entry of Western forces into Germany if it appeared that the Red Army was set to overrun the country.[12]

Perhaps the most explosive analysis of mounting US-Soviet tensions in Europe came from the Office of Strategic Services (OSS) on August 20. A paper written by OSS Soviet expert and Columbia professor Geroid Robinson argued that Europe's political future would be determined by the disposition of Allied military forces on the ground. The Soviet alliance with the Western powers would likely degenerate into a strategic rivalry within six to eight months, Robinson warned. In a broad sense, he argued, the fundamental aims of US policy must be "(1) to destroy the German domination of Europe, and (2) to prevent the domination of Europe in the future by any single power (such as the Soviet Union), or by any group of powers in which we do not have a strong influence. If we do not achieve <u>both</u> these aims, we may consider that we have lost the war." But this would be no easy task. The Soviets were certain to possess a far larger military force in Europe at the end of the war. Among several alternatives to meet the Soviet challenge, Robinson considered the possibility of attempting "to turn against Russia the full power of an undefeated Germany, still ruled by the Nazis or the generals." Such a strategy might succeed in defeating Moscow's bid for supremacy, but it would leave a largely hostile Germany in a dominant position over Europe. However, should the Western powers fail to establish a strong and lasting military presence on the continent, Soviet domination of postwar Europe would be guaranteed. Thus, Washington's best option lay in deploying Western ground forces to the continent in order to secure Western interests and block any Soviet bid for hegemony.[13]

As August drew to a close, the realization that Germany's downfall would leave Stalin in control of most of Europe east of the Rhine swept through the ranks of Allied leadership. Under the present circumstances, the Red Army was poised to become the single most powerful military force in the region—a prospect that surely sent chills down the spines of many American leaders. But this situation posed a conundrum for London and Washington. Continued Soviet participation in the war was critical for the defeat of the Third Reich, and American and British forces could not hope to stage an invasion of Europe without the Red Army tying down the bulk of German forces. As a high-level US strategic estimate explained, American and British forces in Sicily faced two German divisions. In contrast, approximately two hundred German divisions were engaged on the eastern front against the Red Army. "Whenever the Allies open a second front on the Continent, it will be decidedly a *secondary* front to that of Russia; theirs will continue to be the main effort. Without Russia in the war, the Axis cannot be defeated in Europe, and the position of the United Nations becomes precarious.

Similarly, Russia's post-war position in Europe will be a dominant one. With Germany crushed, there is no power in Europe to oppose her tremendous military forces." The prospect of a Soviet-controlled Europe presented a nightmare for US military planners. As one army general staff officer warned, on August 27, 1943: "Russia is concerned solely with Russia. . . . Any agreement or treaty will endure only so long as it is expedient for Russia. . . . The real objective of Russia is the Sovietization not only of Europe but of the world. . . . In the final analysis the only language understood by Russia is force. . . . In the course of history practically every plan has been tried to hold down powerful nations and preserve peace. The only (repeat only) effective method has been genuine 'Balance of Power.'" If the Western Allies hoped to save Europe from Soviet domination, the officer argued, they must "pour in the power and forces to the Nth degree in western Europe. . . . Get to Berlin FIRST" and then use the "threat" of an alliance with Germany "to give pause to Russia."[14]

Ongoing disagreements between London and Washington further complicated matters. British leaders remained preoccupied with defending their empire while husbanding their nation's dwindling manpower. Churchill found himself in the fraught position of leading the smallest and in many respects the weakest of the major Allied powers. London had to defeat the Axis without suffering such massive losses as to render Britain a second-class power after the war. In particular, the prime minister remained committed to defending the empire, the loss of which would reduce Britain to little more than a wealthy set of islands off the French coast. As he told a London audience in November 1942, "I have not become the King's First Minister in order to preside over the liquidation of the British Empire." But restoration of colonial rule would require manpower and wealth, both of which would be depleted by the massive bloodletting sure to result from massive land operations in Europe. In practical terms, this meant that Churchill would continue to push a peripheral strategy while working to delay a cross-channel invasion until German power had been broken on the eastern front.[15]

Hence, despite formal commitments to launch Overlord in May 1944, British officials continued to advocate for expanded operations in the Mediterranean. Churchill insisted that an Allied invasion of the Balkans coupled with Turkey's entry into the war would not only press the offensive against Germany but also give the Western Allies a foothold in southeast Europe—from there, London and Washington might counter Soviet influence after the end of the war. Such a view squared with the long-standing British approach to counterbalancing potential rivals in continental Europe. It would do no good for the British Empire to defeat the Axis merely to open the door to Soviet domination of Europe.[16]

Likewise, although Churchill had joined Roosevelt in proclaiming the Atlantic Charter in 1941, he remained committed to holding the colonies. Indeed, the prime minister did not consider the charter's calls for self-determination to be applicable to the British Empire. His personal physician, Lord Moran, observed that, while Roosevelt thought of China as a nation of four hundred million people who would play a significant role in shaping the postwar world, Churchill thought "only of the color of skin; it is when he talks of India and China that you remember he is a Victorian." Years later, Moran added that Churchill had "scarcely moved an inch from his attitude toward China since the day of the Boxer Rebellion."[17]

London's hedging on its commitment to a cross-channel operation exasperated leaders in Washington. As one Joint Chiefs of Staff paper from the autumn of 1943 complained, British officials appeared to have lost interest in a cross-channel invasion, now code-named Overlord. Instead, London was pushing for continued operations in the Mediterranean while waiting for Germany to collapse from within. "The conclusion that the forces being built up in the United Kingdom will never be used for a military offensive against western Europe, but are intended as a gigantic deception plan and an occupying force, is inescapable."[18]

Similarly, the Operations Division of the US War Department delivered an August memorandum arguing that operations in the

Mediterranean had divided Allied forces and wasted massive quantities of matériel. The report insisted that plans for further Mediterranean operations were based on the hope that German and Soviet
forces would grind each other down while the Western Allies worked
to undermine the Third Reich through raids, peripheral operations,
and strategic bombing. The continuation of this approach would
prolong the war and risk creating a stalemate in Europe. Two days
later, Secretary of War Henry Stimson warned Roosevelt that London continued to favor operations in the Mediterranean while
looking to the Soviets to shoulder the brunt of the fighting against
Germany. "To me, in light of the post-war problems which we shall
face," he told the president, "that attitude toward Russia seems terri-
bly dangerous. . . . None of these methods of pinprick warfare can be
counted on by us to fool Stalin into the belief that we have kept [the
pledge to open a second front against Germany]."[19]

And of course, London and Washington were not the only Allies
with ideas about how the war should be conducted and visions for
the future. More than any of the other Allies, Stalin sought the most
expeditious destruction of the Third Reich. Barbarossa had killed
millions of Soviet citizens, and German forces still occupied large
stretches of Soviet territory. While London and Washington could
afford to vacillate on the question of large land operations, Moscow
enjoyed no such luxury. Even so, Stalin's plans called for more than
just the defeat of the Wehrmacht. Although the full story of Stalin's
vision for the postwar world remains hidden in Russian archives, the
Soviet dictator seemed focused on four principal goals. First and foremost, Stalin pushed Churchill and Roosevelt to open a second front in
France at the earliest possible date. A cross-channel invasion would
do more than anything else to help the Soviets in their war against
the Third Reich. Second, Stalin pushed for the dismemberment of
Germany in order to prevent Berlin from launching a third invasion
of Russia. Broken up into smaller states and deprived of a first-class
military force, the Germans must never again be allowed to mount a
bid for hegemony in Europe. Third, Stalin argued for the restoration

of the 1941 borders, which would give the Soviet Union control of the Baltic republics and a substantial portion of eastern Poland. Having vanquished the Third Reich, Stalin intended to reconstitute the western borders of his empire and exercise a commanding role in Europe. Fourth, the dictator seems to have hoped for good relations with the United States and the United Kingdom. London could focus its energies on its overseas colonies while Washington maintained hegemony over the Western Hemisphere, leaving Moscow as the supreme power on the continent. Together, the victorious Allies could divide and dominate the postwar world.[20]

On their own, most of Stalin's aspirations could be reconciled with British and American priorities, but their combined implications remained problematic. If realized, Stalin's vision would make the Soviet Union the dominant military power in Eurasia. More broadly, Stalin—like Roosevelt and Churchill—recognized that the Second World War would serve as an inflection point in the arc of world history. And in this regard, the Soviet leader had every reason to believe that postwar Europe would continue on a path toward Marxist revolution. The war had devastated European economies, brought the old empires to their knees, transformed the Soviet Union into a superpower, and mobilized left-wing resistance forces across the continent. To the Kremlin leadership, the future appeared ripe for revolution. In light of the fact that the Soviet people had carried the heaviest burden in the war against Germany, Stalin believed his nation had earned the right to play a central role in shaping postwar Europe.[21]

MEANWHILE, A FOURTH ALLIED VISION FOR THE POSTWAR WORLD had appeared in Chongqing. Like Stalin, Chiang Kai-shek faced the immediate challenge of driving Axis armies out of his nation. Japanese troops had been occupying parts of his nation since 1931. The liberation of China would require close cooperation with the Allies and massive infusions of Lend-Lease aid, which was still only trickling into Chongqing. After the war ended, however, Chiang sought nothing less than the transformation of the regional order in Asia. Centuries of Western and Japanese imperialism in China and neighboring parts of Asia such as Korea and Indochina must come to an end, and China, liberated from the yoke of Japanese control, must claim its place alongside the other Allied victors as a major world power. These priorities reflected calls for change resonating across the colonial world. The old imperial order based on Western domination and white supremacy was coming to an end.

Much like Stalin, Chiang remained convinced that, having paid the wartime price in blood, his nation deserved a central role in shaping the postwar world that would follow, particularly in Asia. However, Chiang's goals clashed with British, French, and Soviet visions. While Churchill—and Free French leader Charles de Gaulle—hoped to reclaim their lost colonies after defeating Japan, Stalin sought to expand Soviet influence across his eastern frontiers. Churchill, Stalin, and de Gaulle were fighting a war to destroy Axis imperialism, but they fully intended to continue behaving as empires themselves. Meanwhile, the precise nature of Washington's vision for postwar Asia was uncertain. Whether American leaders would make good on the promises of self-determination articulated in the Atlantic Charter or continue their long-standing practice of informal imperialism remained an open question.[22]

These competing Allied visions for the postwar world collided at the conferences in Cairo and Tehran in November 1943. The first meeting took place at the luxurious Mena House Hotel overlooking the Pyramids of Giza outside of Cairo. Stalin declined an audience with Chiang: Moscow and Tokyo were still technically not at war with one another, and the Soviet leader preferred not to antagonize Tokyo. Instead, Chiang met with Churchill and Roosevelt in Egypt before the two Western leaders flew on to Tehran to meet with Stalin. Chiang recognized Cairo as a singular opportunity to assert China's role as one of the four main powers in the Grand Alliance and to argue his case for greater assistance in the war against Japan. Although overshadowed by the Tehran meeting, Cairo represented a historic milestone as the first time in contemporary history in which Western leaders met Chinese leaders as equals—a signal moment for observers around the colonial world, the significance of which was not lost on Chiang. "I don't want to bring any great shame upon myself," he wrote in his diary.[23]

With observers around the colonial world watching, Chiang faced a daunting challenge. He remained steadfast in his desire to see the end of Western imperialism in Asia but had little trust in Churchill to surrender European colonial claims. As a result, Chiang's most candid conversations took place with Roosevelt. President Roosevelt confessed that Churchill was his "biggest headache" and explained that Britain "simply does not want to see China become a power." Indeed, as recently as September, Churchill had spoken of his hope to maintain "Anglo-Saxon superiority." But there was still a war to be won—Chongqing, London, and Washington must cooperate in order to drive the Japanese out of China before the matter of Western colonialism could be resolved. To do this, Allied leaders discussed several large operations: Tarzan aimed at the invasion of Burma, Culverin called for landings on Sumatra, and Buccaneer envisioned the seizure of the Andaman Islands, which would cut Japan's communications with Southeast Asia. Each of these operations called for a new Allied commitment to reinforcing China and shifting resources away from other theaters such as the Mediterranean and the Central Pacific. In the end, however, the Allies failed to reach a firm agreement. London and Washington remained preoccupied with the war in Europe and refused to offer more than vague commitments to their Chinese allies.[24]

Chiang's private discussions with Roosevelt on Allied plans for postwar order proved more heartening. China would secure the return of Manchuria, Taiwan, and the Penghu Islands, and the nation would be recognized as a great power in Asia. Korea and Vietnam would become independent states, and the United States would join China in resisting the resurgent power of Japan, British imperialism, and creeping Soviet and communist influence throughout the region.

Despite the encouraging nature of these discussions, Chiang's hopes would fall in the coming weeks. On December 5, following a meeting with Churchill and Stalin, Roosevelt canceled Operation Buccaneer. Deprived of greater Allied support, Chiang now grew concerned about launching another disastrous operation in Burma. Meanwhile, Western observers in China warned that Chiang's regime was in trouble. US ambassador Clarence Gauss wrote that the "Chinese cannot solve their desperate economic problems." The regime had shifted to a passive strategy of defense in the war against Japan, the Chinese army was undersupplied and riddled with corruption, and the regime had adopted "fascist-like" policies to maintain its precarious position in power. For his part, Chiang worried about wasting his already-battered armies in poorly supplied campaigns across Southeast Asia. Chinese troops had been fighting mostly alone for the past six years, and Chiang had every reason to be wary of risking his troops in a theater that his allies considered to be of only secondary importance. Moreover, Chiang recognized that another, potentially deadlier conflict with Mao Zedong's communist revolutionaries lay ahead.[25]

WHILE CHIANG RETURNED TO CHONGQING, CHURCHILL AND ROOSE-velt departed to meet with Stalin in Tehran, an ancient walled city set against a backdrop of distant mountains. Their meetings were held in the heavily guarded Soviet embassy. Soviet officials warned that the US legation was a potential security risk and persuaded Roosevelt to stay inside the Soviet compound. The three leaders recognized that the meeting represented a historic moment. "We are sitting around this table for the first time as a family with the one object of winning the war," Roosevelt announced. Churchill responded that the individuals seated around the table wielded the "greatest concentration of power that the world had ever seen. In our hands; here is the possible certainty of shortening the war, the much greater certainty of victories, but also the absolute certainty that we held the happy future of mankind." After greeting the American and British representatives, Stalin called for the attendees to get to work. The dictator's primary concern remained a second front in Europe. As he had told a US diplomat in June, Stalin suspected that Churchill planned to delay a cross-channel attack—Operation Overlord—while pursuing "the classic British foreign policy of walling Russia in, closing the Dardanelles, and building a countervailing balance of power against Russia." Now, at Tehran, Stalin insisted that Overlord be the primary US and British campaign in the coming year. Any other operations, he argued, were diversionary and risked scattering Allied forces. Roosevelt hesitated, possibly for show, but then sided with the dictator. With Roosevelt and Stalin now pushing for Overlord, Churchill's hopes for continued Mediterranean operations collapsed.[26]

Having secured a commitment for Overlord to commence in the spring of 1944, Stalin promised to join the war against Japan following Germany's defeat. But sticking points remained. Stalin, wary of Germany's resurgence and eager to punish the architects of Barbarossa, hoped to impose a harsh peace on the Third Reich. Over dinner, the dictator joked that some fifty thousand German officers should be executed at the end of the war. Roosevelt, responding in jest, suggested that forty-nine thousand might suffice. In contrast, Churchill—who recognized postwar Germany's role as a counterweight to Soviet influence in Europe and was well aware that Soviet officers had murdered some twenty thousand Polish soldiers at Katyn—struggled to see the humor in the exchange. Poland's future also remained a point of contention. Stalin remained tight-lipped regarding Soviet plans to expand into Eastern Europe. "There is no need to speak at the present time about any Soviet desires," he told Churchill, "but when the time comes, we will speak." The leaders also discussed the future of colonialism, China's place in the world order, and Roosevelt's proposal for a world police force to ensure international security. While the Tehran meeting saw significant Allied progress toward winning the war, it left most of the key questions of securing the peace unanswered.[27]

Despite continuing differences between the Allies, Roosevelt struck an optimistic tone in reporting the conference's outcome to the American public. "I got along fine with Marshal Stalin," he explained. "I believe he is truly representative of the heart and soul of Russia; and I believe that we are going to get along very well with him and the Russian people." The president's words were crafted to reassure voters that America's participation in the war would indeed contribute toward postwar peace and a more just world. However, in private Roosevelt recognized that the Soviets would be difficult to work with, and he harbored doubts about Stalin's commitment to join the war against Japan, which he confided to Churchill. The prime minister expressed deep pessimism about Moscow's intentions. "There might be a more bloody war," he told his advisers. "I shall not be there. I shall be asleep. I want to sleep for billions of years."[28]

Although they lacked much of the drama and controversy associated with later conferences such as Yalta, the meetings at Cairo and Tehran proved crucial in setting the course for the rest of the war. The conferences confirmed the Anglo-American preference for peripheral operations and made it clear to both Chiang and Stalin that the Western Allies had no intention of mounting significant land campaigns in continental Asia and Europe before 1944—a postponement that effectively guaranteed that Western armies would not be in control of mainland Asia and Central Europe when the Axis empires collapsed. Instead, the huge stretches of both continents would fall under Soviet occupation or face an uncertain and possibly contested interregnum. The question of imperialism in the postwar world also remained unresolved, with Churchill refusing to disavow British colonialism and Stalin declining to renounce Soviet designs for expansion in Eastern Europe. Meanwhile, Roosevelt offered toothless reassurances about Washington's commitment to promoting self-determination.

WHILE THE ALLIED LEADERS CONVENED IN CAIRO AND TEHRAN, British and American forces engaged in a bitter struggle for Italy.

The decision to stage an invasion of the mainland following the conquest of Sicily had been made amid the turmoil of Italy's pending surrender, British pressure, and American reluctance. Eisenhower, preoccupied with negotiating Rome's surrender, had allowed his field commanders to devise a series of amphibious operations that divided Allied forces and left rival generals competing for the glory of leading the campaign. While British forces under the command of General Montgomery would land at Messina and Taranto, the US Fifth Army under the command of General Mark Clark would attack the beaches at Salerno. Clark's assault would constitute the main thrust of the Allied attack and take place at the northern edge of Allied air cover. Salerno's even tides and curving, sandy beaches would allow Allied landing craft to deliver infantry to the shore, but the mountains beyond could prove to be a problem. If German troops chose to defend this high ground, they would wreak havoc on the landing forces. Still, the Americans were confident. Sicily's liberation and Rome's surrender suggested that the rest of the campaign might be a walkover. Clark chose to forgo the customary naval bombardment of the shore in favor of a fast landing that he hoped would achieve a tactical surprise.[29]

Unfortunately for the Allies, Clark's attack played directly into the hands of the defenders. German commanders recognized Salerno as an obvious target. The beaches sat as far north as the Americans could land and still receive air support. Hence, while German commanders had pulled back from Messina and Taranto, they stationed a full-strength panzer division under the command of General Rudolf Sieckenius at Salerno. Although they would not be strong enough to stop the landing, the defenders could delay the Allied advance to allow time for reinforcements to arrive. Allied forces began landing on the beaches in the early morning hours of September 9, 1943. They met withering German gunfire but managed to push their way inland, securing a beachhead. Sieckenius's forces took heavy casualties—the division had only thirty-five operational tanks by the end of the first day of fighting—but their stubborn resistance slowed the Allied advance, buying time for German commanders to bring up more divisions. For the next three days, the Allies fought elements of six different German divisions in brutal combat. One National Guardsman from Texas remembered German tanks deliberately running over the bodies of killed Americans to demoralize the attackers: "Every time they'd go by they'd mash them," he recalled. By the evening of September 13, German forces had pushed the Allies back to a narrow beachhead a mere one and a half miles deep at some points. However, the following day, Allied commanders brought in reinforcements and deployed naval gunfire to send a hail of heavy shells down on the German counterattacks. Meanwhile, hundreds of Allied bombers pounded German positions around Salerno. This combined storm of fire finally forced German commanders to break off their counterattacks, but the Allies had paid a heavy price. One US combat engineer recalled watching the dead being brought back to the beach. "I seen about six truckloads of dead GIs and that really did open my eyes," he remembered. "Those boys . . . they got cut all to pieces there."[30]

Salerno constituted a bitter victory for the Allies. They had suffered heavy casualties and had prevailed only with the help of overwhelming naval and air support. Making matters worse, the debacle exposed divisions between the American and British generals. Many Americans suspected that Montgomery—resentful at having been given the lesser task of invading Calabria—had deliberately slowed his advance toward Salerno, which might have relieved American forces dying on the beaches. Meanwhile, Marshall rebuked Eisenhower for shoddy planning and Clark received harsh criticism for his decisions and leadership. It now seemed clear to all observers that the liberation of Italy would be far costlier than first hoped. For their part, Nazi leaders concluded that Field Marshal Albert Kesselring's plan to stage a punishing defense of the peninsula held considerable merit. More immediately, the German stand at Salerno had bought time for the Wehrmacht to prepare a series of defensive lines south of Rome. If they hoped to take the capital, the Allies would first have to fight their way through sixty thousand German soldiers dug into well-prepared positions. The battlefield was crisscrossed by flooded rivers, deep ravines, and steep mountains. Europe's soft underbelly was proving tougher than expected.[31]

Kesselring intended to use Italy's mountainous terrain to his advantage, constructing defensive echelons across the narrow peninsula. The most formidable, the Gustav Line, ran some eighty miles from coast to coast, blocking the main approaches to Rome. Lines of barbed wire snaked across steep, craggy slopes leading up to German positions blasted into the rock. Thousands of German soldiers from the Tenth Army manned machine guns and artillery trained on the narrow Allied lines of approach. At the center of the line, guarding the most direct road to the capital, sat the medieval abbey at Monte Cassino. The massive stone structure gave German observers a commanding view of the surrounding countryside. Construction of the abbey had begun in 529 CE. It had been sacked by the Lombards in the sixth century, by the Saracens in the ninth century, and again by French soldiers in 1799. It would soon be the Allies' turn. Allied forces embarked upon a grinding slog north toward Rome, fighting yard by yard against Kesselring's carefully prepared defenses. Making matters worse, preparations for the coming cross-channel invasion of France were draining resources from the Italian theater, the failure to take Rome threatened to cast the entire campaign as a failure, and each step forward called for frontal assaults into the teeth of German positions. In November, frustrated Allied commanders concluded that the only way to break the stalemate was to stage an amphibious invasion at Anzio that would outflank German positions along the Gustav Line.[32]

On the morning of January 22, 1944, some four hundred ships carrying forty-seven thousand men glided through the waters off Anzio. A seaside resort approximately forty miles south of Rome, Anzio boasted an ancient harbor and bustling waterfront. The birthplace of Nero and Caligula, the town was about to become one of the key battlefields of the Italian campaign. As the Allied armada approached, the water was calm, a light haze hung in the air, and temperatures hovered around 55 degrees Fahrenheit. On board the landing boats, nervous soldiers braced for what they feared would be a bloody fight to take the beaches. Indeed, a number of Allied commanders had warned of a catastrophe. "You need more men," General Troy Middleton argued after seeing the plans. "You can get ashore, but you can't get off the beachhead." General Lucian Truscott was even more blunt: "You are going to destroy the best damned division in the United States Army." But to the army's surprise, the initial landings went smoothly. By midnight, thirty-six thousand soldiers and three thousand vehicles had landed and established a narrow beachhead fifteen miles wide and between two and four miles deep. "[General Harold] Alexander's brave troops are pushing towards Rome," the BBC announced, "and should reach it within forty-eight hours."[33]

But the Germans had other plans. News of the landings reached Kesselring at 5:00 a.m. The field marshal immediately ordered the redeployment of artillery along the routes to Rome to block any Allied attempt to reach the capital. He then began gathering reinforcements from armies throughout Italy, southern France, the Balkans, and Germany to mount a counterattack against the landings. The Allied decision to spend the next three days consolidating the beachhead gave the Germans ample time to move their forces into place. By January 26, Kesselring's troops occupied most of the high ground overlooking the landing site. German artillery concealed in the hills unleashed a vicious rain of fire on Allied positions, forcing the invaders to spend most of the daylight hours huddling in trenches or scurrying between bunkers. The Allies' amphibious flanking move had become yet another stalemate. "Anzio was a fishbowl," remembered one American. "We were the fish."[34]

With his landing forces bottled up at Anzio, Clark turned back to the Gustav Line. On February 1, the American Thirty-Fourth Infantry Division launched a renewed offensive across the Rapido River toward Monte Cassino. This time, the Allied advance made significant progress, taking both Montes Majola and Castellone overlooking the monastery and sparking a panic among German commanders. However, a fearsome counterattack pushed Clark's forces back. Hard fighting across the rocky mountains left both sides depleted. In three weeks of fighting, the Thirty-Fourth Division suffered some 2,200 casualties. On February 15, convinced that the Germans were using the abbey as a strongpoint, British commanders authorized bombing raids and artillery strikes against the monastery. "We couldn't even see the monastery for about fifteen, twenty minutes for all the smoke and stuff coming up," remembered one American soldier. "And when they were done and left, the only thing left standing was half a wall of the monastery. And every one of those poor citizens that were underneath were all killed there, all men, women and children." The destruction of the ancient abbey and the civilians sheltering inside accomplished nothing aside from creating a set of heavy ruins ideal for the German gun positions.[35]

The forces defending the Gustav Line would hold out until late May, when a massive Allied attack—Operation Diadem—finally broke the impasse. Planned in conjunction with the upcoming cross-channel attack, Diadem was designed to breach German defenses and draw forces away from France. While British, Canadian, Polish, and Free French forces attacked the Gustav Line, American troops drove west along the coast before wheeling north to cut off retreating German units. At the same time, the forces at Anzio staged a breakout to close the trap and clear the approaches to Rome. Diadem was a larger and better-planned operation than earlier Allied attempts, and it targeted German forces that had been depleted by long months of fighting. Even so, the attacking troops faced a daunting task. The Polish units charged with taking Cassino suffered heavy casualties before finally seizing the monastery on May 18. With British and Canadian troops moving up the Liri Valley and French troops driving up from the south, Kesselring's soldiers were forced to retreat to avoid encirclement. As German lines crumbled, the American troops drove forward to take Cisterna di Latina, and the forces at Anzio finally broke out from their bridgehead.[36]

With the Germans in retreat, Clark made the controversial decision to divert his forces from their assigned role of blocking the German withdrawal and trapping Kesselring's Tenth Army and instead
directed his troops to seize Rome. Clark had abandoned the British
plan in favor of a brazen bid to seize the glory for himself and the
Americans. "Not only did we intend to become the first army in fifteen centuries to seize Rome from the south," he later wrote, "but we
intended to see that the people back home knew that it was the Fifth
Army that did the job and knew the price that had been paid for it."
With American troops closing in on the eternal city, Hitler called for
a retreat. The destruction of the great city would serve only to fuel the
Allied propaganda machine. Early on the morning of June 4, the first
American patrols entered Rome only to be thrown back by heavy fire
from the remaining German defenders. Rearguard actions and sporadic sniper fire continued throughout the day, but toward evening,
crowds of joyful citizens poured into the streets. The next morning,
Clark entered the ancient imperial capital. His motorcade soon lost
its way in the twisting streets and was forced to seek directions from
a boy on a bicycle. Finally, the general arrived at the Piazza del Cam-
pidoglio, site of Rome's city hall. As American, British, and Italian
flags fluttered in the breeze, a crowd of reporters gathered to watch
Clark declare victory. "This is a great day for the Fifth Army and for
the French, British and American troops of the Fifth that have made
this victory possible," he proclaimed. The following morning, June 6,
Clark was awakened by one of his staff with the news that the Allied
landings in Normandy had begun. "They didn't even let us have the
newspaper headlines for the fall of Rome for one day," he fumed.[37]

THE BATTLE FOR ITALY WOULD CONTINUE UNTIL THE FINAL DAYS OF
the war in Europe as German forces staged a tenacious defense in
the north, but the Italian theater had become a strategic backwater.
None now doubted that the outcome of the war would be decided

elsewhere. Nevertheless, Rome stood as the first Axis capital to be liberated by Allied forces. Beyond eliminating one of the three principal Axis powers, the Italian campaign established a precedent that would prove critical in the politics of the postwar world. American and British forces had taken Rome, but they fought as part of a larger alliance with the Soviet Union. This raised the question of how the postwar occupations would be conducted. Were each of the big three Allied powers entitled to a role in shaping the liberated Axis territories, or would that power be reserved for whoever's army occupied a given territory?

Churchill insisted that the Soviets should not be given a significant role in the occupation: "We cannot be put in a position where our two armies are doing all the fighting but the Russians have a veto and must be consulted on any minor violation of the armistice terms." But the Western powers had reason to be wary. The Red Army seemed likely to overrun large sections of Eastern Europe before the war was over. As Roosevelt warned Churchill, Allied actions in Italy would "set the precedent for all such future activities in the war." The US ambassador to London, John Winant, offered a similar assessment. "When the tide turns and the Russian armies are able to advance," he wrote, "we might well want to influence their turns of capitulation and occupancy in Allied and enemy territory."[38]

After careful consideration, US and British leaders grudgingly agreed to the creation of an Allied commission to oversee the occupation of Italy. However, the commission would operate under Western military authorities and exercise little actual power. The message to the Kremlin was clear: to the victor go the spoils. Soviet officials chafed at this blatant marginalization, but they accepted it with an understanding that the Western Allies were establishing a precedent for future liberated territories. And London and Washington would not have long to wait for Moscow to respond in kind. In March 1944, Soviet forces entered Romania, one of many Eastern European countries that would fall under the occupation of the Red Army. "The present Rumanian situation is analogous to the Italian situation at the time of her surrender to the British and ourselves," wrote the Joint Chiefs.[39]

In Italy, then, the Western Allies consciously adopted an approach to military occupation that would lead to the creation of spheres of influence in Europe. By denying Moscow a meaningful role in the occupation of Italy, Churchill and Roosevelt granted Stalin the pretext to do as he wished in territories liberated by the Red Army. In the coming months and years, Allied occupations would lay the groundwork for a slew of new governments across Europe and Asia, most of which would be modeled on the political systems of their occupying powers and integrated into the geopolitical networks that those powers controlled. Western occupations tended to create pro-Western liberal-capitalist regimes; Soviet occupations tended to produce pro-Soviet socialist governments. By conducting the occupations in this manner, the victorious Allies would embed the tensions roiling the Grand Alliance within the political infrastructure of postwar Eurasia and draw the frontiers of the approaching Cold War. Although it seems likely that Soviet leaders would have insisted on creating such a sphere in Eastern Europe regardless of Allied actions in Italy, the Anglo-American decision to sideline the Soviets in Italy effectively guaranteed that Moscow would follow the same course of action in territories conquered by the Red Army.[40]

THE MEDITERRANEAN WAS FAST BECOMING A MICROCOSM OF THE imperial transformations and geopolitical rivalries sweeping through the broader international system. As brutal land wars raged across continental Asia and the eastern front, the Western Allies pursued a strategy of naval imperialism aimed at reasserting hegemony over the inland sea and its environs. Prodded along by their British counterparts, US officials initiated a decades-long military presence in the region that would forever tie the United States to the British Empire and its legacies in the Middle East and North Africa. By the summer of 1944, Western forces had staged multiple amphibious invasions around the Mediterranean and driven the Axis fleets from its waters. US and British warships patrolled the sea while Western soldiers gawked at the ruins of ancient imperial capitals from Carthage to Alexandria to Rome.

Despite US leaders' reluctance to enter the Mediterranean, once there, Washington emerged as the dominant outside power, supplanting London and taking the first steps to banish Moscow's influence from the area. By sidelining the Soviets in the occupation of Italy, the Western Allies signaled their intention to create a de facto sphere of influence in the Mediterranean—a move that carried long-lasting implications for the postwar world. Less than three years after Clark's forces marched into Rome, President Harry Truman issued his historic call to support the governments of Greece and Turkey in their struggles against communist influence, taking over British security commitments to the eastern Mediterranean. This new policy—the Truman Doctrine—would form the basis of America's Cold War strategy aimed at containing Soviet influence around the world.[41] In this way, the Mediterranean became a launchpad for America's coming global hegemony.

By late 1943, it had become clear that the challenge of defeating the Axis armies was turning the United States and the Soviet Union into superpowers, marking a geopolitical transformation of world-historical importance. However, Washington's and Moscow's ascension triggered mutual suspicion as both governments were thrust into a position to create rival orders in the territories they conquered. As the Americans and their British partners established maritime supremacy, Soviet leaders moved toward the creation of an imperial glacis across Eastern Europe. Meanwhile China, the oft-forgotten ally, was left twisting in the wind.

Chapter 14

CRACKING THE
CO-PROSPERITY SPHERE

TARAWA ATOLL RISES A MERE TEN FEET ABOVE THE SURFACE OF THE
Pacific some 2,100 miles southwest of Hawaii. Two miles long and
less than eight hundred yards wide, the atoll's largest island, Betio,
is a speck in the vastness of the surrounding blue water. Shaded by
palm trees and swept by year-round ocean breezes, the atoll boasted,
in the words of one nineteenth-century traveler, "a superb ocean
climate, days of blinding sun and bracing wind, nights of heavenly
brightness." On the morning of November 20, 1943, Kiyoshi Ota,
warrant officer with the Japanese Special Naval Landing Forces, had
little time to enjoy this natural beauty. Ota and his men cowered in
their bunkers in the wake of a heavy preliminary bombardment from
a massive American invasion fleet. Many of Ota's marines had been
killed in the bombardment, but most had survived, along with the
bulk of their weapons. "Our men could not speak," he later wrote.

"Their faces were pale. We were surrounded by an overwhelming force of the enemy, with no hope for outside support or assistance. It was like the lonely song of an insect. We knew that we would die, one after another, as cherry blossoms fall or autumn leaves are scattered." Now he stood on the beach, "sweating in the tropical heat," and watched as the American fleet prepared to attack. The massive warships looked "like floating castles." The American landing craft rushed forward "like dozens of spiders scattering over the surface of the water," he wrote. "One of my men exclaimed, 'Heavens! The God of Death has come!'"[1]

Ota gazed out on what was at the time the largest American invasion fleet ever assembled, comprising twelve battleships, fourteen cruisers, six fleet carriers, five light carriers, eight escort carriers, fifty-eight destroyers, ten submarines, three minesweepers, dozens of landing craft, more than eleven hundred aircraft, and over thirty-five thousand troops. During the first two years of the war, US forces had fought with a shoestring battle fleet against steep odds. But by late 1943, the deployment of the new Essex-class carriers alongside state-of-the-art aircraft such as the F6F Hellcat and advanced technologies such as radar gave the US Navy the ability to mount a series of crushing offensives across the globe. Now it was Tokyo's turn to focus on conserving its dwindling personnel and resources in the face of a seemingly unstoppable enemy. The invasion of Tarawa and the operations that followed would showcase the coming American hegemony over the Pacific. "I think that for anyone that participated in the war, there were actually two wars," remembered one officer from the USS *Saratoga*. "If you went out to the Pacific after, let's say, January of 1944, you had a completely different experience and a viewpoint than those before, because it really was two different operations."[2]

The United States had become the greatest sea power the world had ever seen. In the two years since Pearl Harbor, the nation had accomplished a stunning mobilization of its engineering, financial, industrial, manufacturing, military, and political resources to amass the most powerful fleet in world history. With the strategic application of naval air power, the United States had solved a problem that had bedeviled sea powers since the Peloponnesian War: how to project power from the sea deep into the land. US aircraft carriers operating in strike groups supported by battleships, cruisers, and destroyers had gained the capacity to attack targets across the world littoral. These fast carrier task forces were supported by a network of bases that circled the globe, anchoring an unrivaled logistical chain that allowed Washington to operate as history's first planetary power—a role it would occupy well into the next century. The first major test of these new forces would come in November 1943 as American commanders orchestrated two major naval campaigns across the Central and South Pacific.

VICTORY ON GUADALCANAL GAVE US FORCES THE INITIATIVE IN THE Pacific War. In the next phase, American commanders would follow two lines of attack across the Central and South Pacific, each aimed at securing positions within striking distance of the Japanese home islands. Although the Pacific remained a secondary theater behind Europe, the US war machine had become so productive that the Americans could mount not one but two campaigns against Japan. As Admiral Nimitz prepared to launch a drive across the Central Pacific, General MacArthur fought to ensure that his operations in the South Pacific remained a coequal priority. MacArthur envisioned a massive assault northwest through the Solomon Islands that would culminate in the capture of the Japanese base at Rabaul. The campaign called for a heavy commitment of ships, troops, and aircraft precisely at the time when US military planners were working to expand their operations in Europe. The Army Air Forces remained focused on waging a strategic bombing campaign against the Third Reich, and the navy refused to place an armada under MacArthur's command. Instead, MacArthur and Admiral William Halsey would launch a scaled-down assault along the coast of New Guinea and up the Solomon Island chain. Code-named Cartwheel, the campaign called for attacks on thirteen targets, securing islands, ports, and airfields as US forces advanced toward Rabaul.[3]

Leaders in Tokyo recognized that the defeat on Guadalcanal represented a significant setback, but their larger plan for the war remained largely intact. Japanese forces must brace for the coming US attacks along the defensive periphery of the empire while the fleet searched for the long-anticipated decisive naval battle with US ships in the Central Pacific. In the meantime, Tokyo would bolster its garrisons in New Guinea and the Solomons. In September 1943, the Imperial General Headquarters ordered its forces to "hold the important southeastern area extending eastward from the eastern part of New Guinea to the Solomon Islands." Japanese troops must prepare for a "protracted defense of important positions in the Bismarck Archipelago and Bougainville areas" as well as New Guinea in order to protect the central base at Rabaul. With the euphoria of their initial victories having disappeared, Japanese leaders now spoke of a new "Hundred Years' War." But time was not on Tokyo's side. US industrial production and technological innovations had neutralized Japan's advantages from earlier in the war. Even worse, the heavy attrition of skilled aviators in the battles of the Coral Sea, Midway, and Guadalcanal meant that most Japanese aircraft were flown by raw, unseasoned pilots. Always slim, Japan's prospects for victory were narrowing.[4]

Even so, Tokyo had to reinforce its positions in the South Pacific if it had any hope of surviving the American counterattacks. In late February 1943, Admiral Yamamoto sent a convoy carrying six thousand soldiers to the base at Lae, New Guinea. US code breakers in Hawaii learned of the convoy and alerted the American air base at Milne Bay, setting the stage for the Battle of the Bismarck Sea. On March 2, US aircraft located the convoy and managed to sink one transport carrying 1,200 soldiers. Destroyer escorts rescued 875 survivors, but the convoy was in trouble. The next day, approximately one hundred aircraft attacked the Japanese ships as they approached the coast of New Guinea. American bombers employed the new technique of approaching at perilously low altitudes and then skipping their bombs across the water and into the hulls of enemy ships. The Japanese lost all seven of their remaining transports, along with four destroyers. "Hands were blown off, stomachs were blown open," remembered one survivor from the destroyer *Arishio*. Burst steam pipes turned the ship boiling hot as hundreds leaped into the sea. American pilots then turned back to strafe lifeboats and helpless men floating in the sea. US commanders justified this brutality by citing Japanese attacks on American survivors as well as the fear that the lifeboats might reach the shore of New Guinea. "I wanted . . . to kill every Japanese son of a bitch I could find," one pilot explained. "The Jap asks no quarter and expects none," MacArthur's air force commander insisted. In all, some three thousand Japanese soldiers and sailors were killed for the loss of thirteen American lives.[5]

The Battle of the Bismarck Sea constituted a resounding victory for US forces and yet another lesson of airpower's ability to threaten ships at sea. Yamamoto hoped to turn this tactic against the Americans with Operation I-Go the following month. Japanese aircraft unleashed a string of heavy attacks against Allied ships and air bases throughout the region. Although Japanese pilots returned with wildly inflated claims of the destruction they had wrought, actual damage was moderate. At the end of the operation, Yamamoto scheduled a visit to bases in New Guinea and the Solomons. After cryptographers at Pearl Harbor deciphered a message announcing Yamamoto's tour, they rushed to inform Nimitz of this rare opportunity to attack the architect of the Pearl Harbor attack. US officials deliberated on the ethics and wisdom of killing the admiral. Assassination of enemy leaders remained a taboo, and some officials wondered if Yamamoto might be replaced by a more competent commander. Ultimately, however, Nimitz chose to act. At 9:43 on the morning of April 18, a force of eighteen American P-38 fighters intercepted Yamamoto's aircraft over Bougainville. The Americans overwhelmed the admiral's escort and sent his plane screaming down into the jungle, trailing "black smoke and flames." Yamamoto was dead.[6]

Two months later, Halsey and MacArthur launched their two-pronged assault along the island approaches to Rabaul. Advance parties arriving in the dead of night found the white sand beaches of Woodlark and Kiriwina Islands deserted aside from an Australian coastwatcher and a handful of Indigenous fighters. MacArthur's forces then turned their attention to Lae and Salamaua on New Guinea's Huon Peninsula, taking both in mid-September. Lae gave the Allies an airfield as well as a good harbor. Meanwhile, Halsey's forces pushed up the eastern flank of the Solomons and staged an attack on Munda Airfield on New Georgia. American commanders opted to land on undefended beaches and then fight their way through the jungle to the airfield. Inexperienced National Guardsmen faced a grueling trek through difficult terrain, harassed by Japanese snipers who taunted them through the night. One Ohio National Guardsman recalled the Japanese "habit of jumping into [our] foxholes," which led the Americans to begin firing on one another. "We would lose four or five men every day," he remembered. Japanese soldiers staged a fierce, often suicidal resistance, but they were gradually pushed back. On August 5, the airfield finally fell to the Allies. The unexpectedly heavy resistance on New Georgia boded ill for the next target on Halsey's list, Kolombangara, on which Japanese commanders had concentrated some twelve thousand troops. Halsey was "wary of another slugging match, but . . . didn't know how to avoid it," he explained. "It was here that my staff first suggested the by-pass policy—jump over the enemy's strong points, blockade them, and leave them to starve." US forces would use their mounting control of the seas in an island-hopping campaign to isolate and starve enemy garrisons as the navy pushed ever closer to Japan.[7]

On August 15, Halsey's troops staged a surprise landing on Vella Lavella, bypassing the garrison on Kolombangara. Although the island had only a small number of Japanese troops, they put up a heavy fight. "And all at once, they cut loose and just mortared the beach," remembered a US soldier. "Just knocked the devil out of us. I went back down there and see my buddies with their legs off and everything." Despite taking casualties, Allied forces used their numerical advantage and greater firepower to make steady progress. By late September, Naval Construction Battalions had finished an airstrip that would grow into a key base in the Allied campaign against Rabaul. Vella Lavella demonstrated just how effective the strategy of leapfrogging over Japanese strongpoints could be. "The central Solomons campaign was finished," Halsey remembered. "Vella had cost us fewer than 150 dead and had abundantly justified our strategy of by-passing. The next campaign, the northern Solomons, would see this strategy win us the war in the South Pacific."[8]

There now remained only one last Japanese bastion on the path to Rabaul: Bougainville. The largest of the Solomons, Bougainville stretched some 150 miles along an axis pointing northwest. The Japanese had transformed the island into a fortress crowded with five airfields and occupied by some thirty-five thousand troops, including the division that had terrorized Nanjing in 1937. In the face of this opposition, Halsey and his staff scrapped the original plan for a frontal assault on the Japanese bases along the southern coast in favor of yet another leapfrogging campaign. This time, Allied forces would stage a surprise landing on the western coast of the island at Torokina, separated from the main body of the Japanese defenders by mountainous terrain and blanketed by tropical rainforests. If successful, Allied forces could land and "carve out [their] own airfield" before Japanese commanders had a chance to bring up reinforcements. From there, US aircraft could launch strikes against the Japanese bases on Bougainville and begin the bombing of Rabaul.[9]

AS THE SUN ROSE ON NOVEMBER 1, 1943, THE MARINES ABOARD THE US ships approaching Bougainville gazed out on a daunting sight. Beyond its narrow beaches, the island was choked by dense green jungle rising toward the forbidding highlands. In the distance, smoke curled from the top of Mount Bagana, an 8,650-foot-tall volcano. The tropical rainforest hid fifty thousand Japanese troops intent on driving the invaders from the island. But a mere 270 defenders waited at the marines' landing site at Cape Torokina. Over seven thousand troops landed in the first wave. The marines were met by Japanese gunfire and air strikes from Rabaul, but they quickly established a beachhead and began clearing the surrounding area. As the Americans settled in for a restless first night, a Japanese force of two heavy cruisers, two light cruisers, and six destroyers closed in on the US ships waiting offshore. The Japanese commander, Vice Admiral Sentaro Omori, hoped to repeat the success of the Battle of Savo Island, where Japanese ships had dealt a heavy blow to the landing force at Guadalcanal. Japanese scout planes sighted the US ships at 1:40 a.m. on November 2. American radar had already detected Omori's ships and were moving to attack. Ten minutes later, the American cruisers opened fire. "I never saw so much firing in all my life," remembered one American sailor. "This was at night. We were firing strictly by radar. We sunk the lead heavy cruiser which vanished from the screen; you could tell when one sunk on radar because the blip would vanish." The fighting continued until 2:29 a.m., when Omori retreated. The Japanese had lost one light cruiser, one destroyer, and hundreds of sailors and suffered significant damage to most of the rest of their ships for the cost of nineteen Americans lives. The American radar had neutralized Omori's superior night-fighting capabilities.[10]

Undeterred by the defeat at Empress Augusta Bay, Yamamoto's replacement, Admiral Mineichi Koga, sent a force of seven heavy cruisers to Rabaul in preparation for a second raid on the Allied beachhead. "This was the most desperate emergency that confronted me in my entire term as [Commander of the South Pacific theater]," Halsey later wrote. Rather than wait for another attack, Halsey sent the heavy carrier *Saratoga* accompanied by the light carrier *Princeton* to stage a high-risk raid on the harbor at Rabaul on November 5. "I sincerely expected both air groups to be cut to pieces and both carriers to be stricken, if not lost," he explained, "but we could not let the men at Torokina be wiped out while we stood by and wrung our hands." The fact that the admiral's son was serving on the *Saratoga* made the decision all the more agonizing. But Halsey's gamble paid off. For twenty-four minutes, beneath clear skies, American torpedo planes and dive-bombers bombarded the Japanese ships, scoring hits on four cruisers and downing dozens of Japanese aircraft. Six days later, the Americans struck again with planes from the carriers *Bunker Hill*, *Essex*, and *Independence*. Japanese forces at Rabaul staged a far more effective defense and launched a counterstrike against Halsey's carriers. Over one hundred Japanese planes attacked the American task force, but the defenders managed to fight them off, downing over a third of the Japanese planes along with twenty more shot down over Rabaul. Allied material and technological superiority had begun to overwhelm Japan's empire.[11]

The victories at Bougainville and Lae brought Rabaul within range of land-based American bombers. On October 12, 1943, Allied commanders mounted a 349-plane raid on Rabaul. Over the following weeks, Allied aircraft staged a relentless bombing campaign against the Japanese stronghold that reduced most of its buildings to rubble. In response, Rabaul's commanders mobilized their massive workforce to construct an extensive network of underground hangars, barracks, and storehouses. Meanwhile, the defenders amassed a huge stockpile of supplies to hold out against a potential siege. But Japanese preparations meant little in the face of Allied military superiority. Air raids through December and into 1944 caused a steady attrition of Japanese aircraft, pilots, and ships. Tokyo's decision in January to send carrier pilots to aid in the defense of the base proved futile. Rabaul had been reduced to a strategic liability. In February 1944, Japanese leaders decided to cut their losses. "All our fighter planes left for Truk this morning," Rabaul's commander wrote on February 20. Henceforth, Allied pilots would refer to their raids on the base as "milk runs" since they could expect little resistance from the Japanese defenders on the ground. The nearly one hundred thousand Japanese troops stranded at Rabaul now had little to do but sit in their shelters, waiting for an Allied invasion that would never come. "The Japanese Army preferred direct assault, after the German fashion," one Japanese officer later complained, "but the Americans flowed into our weaker points and submerged us, just as water seeks the weakest entry to sink a ship." Tokyo's great southern fortress had been neutralized.[12]

MEANWHILE, ANOTHER DEMONSTRATION OF ALLIED SUPERIORITY was on display 1,500 miles to the east. While MacArthur and Halsey advanced toward Rabaul, Admiral Chester Nimitz amassed an armada of ships to begin a campaign across the vast blue waters of the Central Pacific. His targets were the Gilbert and Marshall Islands. A collection of coral atolls strewn across the ocean, the tropical islands rose no more than twenty-one feet above the water. They were isolated and sparsely populated, but many were large enough to accommodate airstrips. Therefore, they gained a strategic importance as stepping stones across the vast ocean. Tokyo's engineers had transformed the atolls into bastions guarding the eastern approaches to Japan. The first step in Nimitz's campaign was the Tarawa Atoll, the largest of the Gilberts. Tarawa's main island, Betio, bristled with Japanese defenses. The shallow reef around the island formed the first, natural line of defense. Boat obstacles, barbed wire, and log barricades ringed the beaches. Behind those sat machine gun nests and pillboxes connected by a network of trenches. Japanese commanders had installed British coastal defense guns captured at Singapore and reinforced the entire system with hardened shelters. Over 4,700 defenders waited for the Americans, their guns capable of covering every inch of Betio.[13]

To lead the thrust across the Pacific, Nimitz selected Vice Admiral Raymond Spruance, commander of the American fleet at the Battle of Midway. Spruance commanded a massive fleet of twelve battleships, twenty aircraft carriers, twelve cruisers, and thirty-seven transports and landing ships. "It was the largest combat fleet the United States had ever assembled," wrote naval historian Craig Symonds, "and in terms of naval airpower the greatest armada in history." The marines tasked with landing on Tarawa fell under the command of General

Holland "Howling Mad" Smith, who faced the challenge of moving his infantry over the shallow reef surrounding Betio. Irregular tides and incomplete intelligence meant that Smith and his men would not know whether their Higgins boat landing craft could clear the reef until they actually attempted it. The marines had a number of amphibious tractors—amphtracs—capable of driving over the reefs, but they were too few to support the entire landing force. If the tides were too shallow, the marines would be forced to fight through the surf, weighed down by their gear and under heavy fire from Japanese gunners. Those who did not drown or get hit in the water would then face a brutal battle to take the beach.[14]

Early on the morning of November 20, 1943, journalist Robert Sherrod heard "a great thud in the southwest" as American ships opened fire on Betio. From the deck of a transport ship, Sherrod watched as flashes lit the predawn sky. This barrage was followed by air strikes from American carrier planes. As the island began to glow from fires and explosions, Sherrod assumed that the Japanese defenders must be all but wiped out. "Surely, we all thought, no mortal men could live through such destroying power." The bombardment stopped as the landing craft began their approach.[15]

The first wave of marines immediately ran into trouble. The tide was too shallow for the Higgins boats, which ran aground and sat exposed to withering fire from the Japanese guns. Many of the craft became death traps for passengers who would never reach the shore. The men who could leaped over the sides of the craft, plunging into the water to face a deadly fight through the waves. George Charland, with the Second Marine Division, jumped out of his landing craft only to find that the weight of his gear dragged him straight to the bottom of the water. After struggling to reach shallow water, he hid among dead bodies floating in the tide. Sheltering behind a pier, Charland realized that his leg had been shot and the bone was broken. He spent the next two days lying behind a coconut log, providing covering fire for fellow marines fighting to clear the beach. Lee Weber was fortunate enough to reach the beach, but his unit was quickly pinned down behind the seawall. Beneath the deafening roar of gunfire and explosions, Weber's unit fought back by lobbing grenades into Japanese trenches fifteen feet away. By evening, five thousand marines had landed, but they were confined to a stretch of beach of less than three hundred yards at its deepest and had suffered 1,500 casualties. "We walked into a hornet's nest on Tarawa," remembered Olian Perry.[16]

The second day of fighting opened with renewed landings that came under heavy fire from the Japanese defenders, who had moved more machine guns into position over the night. The Japanese gunners raked the Higgins boats as they approached, cutting down marines as soon as they hit the water. "Men screamed and moaned," wrote Sherrod. "Of twenty-four in one boat only three reached the shore." As Charles Pace's platoon approached Betio on the second day of the battle, their boat pushed through hundreds of dead marines floating in the warm tropical water. "We couldn't even begin to count them," he remembered. Ira Schilling remembered the bloodstained water and scores of corpses floating in the tide. "When I got on the beach," he said, "one of the first things I saw was a marine body without a head, his whole head was gone. And I just couldn't understand it." But the Americans had brought overwhelming force to Tarawa. The battle soon turned, and it was only a matter of time before the marines wore down the Japanese defenders. Most of the fighting now devolved to dealing with snipers and clearing Japanese bunkers with grenades and flamethrowers. By the third day, the marines had crushed most of the Japanese organized resistance. The remaining defenders fought from inside hardened bunkers, awaiting certain death. After the Americans torched one blockhouse using gasoline and grenades, they discovered the charred remains of three hundred Japanese fighters. Before dawn on November 23, most of the remaining defenders emerged from their bunkers on the eastern end of Betio to mount one final charge on the Americans. The marines cut them down before clearing the rest of the island.[17]

Though he was spared the worst of the combat, Charles Pace was among those who received the grisly task of burying the dead.

"On that island of about three hundred acres, or thereabouts, there were some six thousand dead bodies," he recalled. "Roughly twenty dead corpses per acre on that little island that had been laying out in the sun for upwards of a week. . . . If we found a leg, we tried to see whether it was an American leg or a Japanese leg. If it was an American leg, well, we put it on one pile; if it was a Japanese leg, we threw it in a trench and let [the bulldozers] cover it up. For a seventeen-year-old, it was a very rude awakening as to what war was really like." In just three days, the Americans had suffered one thousand killed and two thousand wounded. Nearly all of the 4,700 defenders had been killed—only 17 Japanese prisoners were taken, along with 129 Korean laborers. The American public was appalled by the images of destruction on Tarawa, but most military leaders argued that the battle had been necessary—the island was a critical stepping stone on the path across the ocean. "The lessons learned from our battle on Betio Island will be of greatest value to our future operations," insisted General Robert Richardson, commander of the US Army in the Pacific. But not all leaders agreed. "Tarawa was a mistake," General Holland Smith wrote five years after the battle. "The futile sacrifice of marines on that strategically useless coral strand makes me as sad today as it did then." Mistake or not, the next time the marines attempted an amphibious assault on a heavily defended beach, they would be better prepared.[18]

Two weeks after the Battle of Tarawa, Nimitz conferred with Spruance, Smith, and Rear Admiral Richmond Kelly Turner to plan the campaign's next move. Over the objections of the other commanders, Nimitz insisted on leapfrogging multiple Japanese positions and seizing the Kwajalein Atoll in the Marshall Islands. The admiral was confident that superior Allied forces could neutralize the bypassed bases with air strikes and establish a dominant position in the heart of the islands. "The Japanese aren't expecting us there," he explained. That Nimitz could even consider such a risky attack demonstrated just how drastically the balance of power in the Pacific had shifted.[19]

In December, Allied planes flying out of airstrips on Tarawa and Makin began battering Japanese bases across the Marshalls. The steady degradation of Japanese airpower in the area had prepared the way for the arrival of Task Force 58, under the command of Vice Admiral Marc Mitscher. In late January, twelve US carriers bearing 650 planes alongside eight battleships and a fleet of destroyers and cruisers approached Kwajalein. Tarawa had convinced the Americans of the need to throw everything they had at Japanese-held islands. Accordingly, Mitscher unleashed a torrent of fire upon the Marshalls that destroyed nearly all the remaining Japanese aircraft in the islands. Henceforth, the Americans would enjoy nearly complete aerial supremacy. Even so, Japanese commanders had prepared extensive fortifications on the principal American objectives: Kwajalein and neighboring islands of Roi and Namur. With memories of Tarawa still fresh, US commanders concluded that a far heavier bombardment was necessary to clear the islands. The admirals moved their battleships to point-blank range in a bid to blast the Japanese fortifications to rubble. Thousands of marines, supported by tanks, then stormed the beaches with overwhelming force. On one of the smaller islands, James Norwood, an American marine, found that the defenders had all died by suicide to avoid capture. "One of them killed all seven of the others and then killed himself," Norwood remembered. Though hardly bloodless, the seizure of Kwajalein demonstrated that US amphibious operations had come a long way in the months since Tarawa.[20]

Indeed, the operation had been so successful that US commanders now chose to push for a follow-up operation against Enewetak Atoll. US forces had taken Kwajalein without the assistance of their reserve forces, which could now be used in the next operation. A quick strike would carry the added benefit of occurring before Japanese forces had the opportunity to reinforce their garrison. "It would result in the savings of lives, equipment, money and effort," wrote General Smith's staff. But one key problem remained: the Japanese stronghold at Truk Lagoon, dubbed the Gibraltar of the Pacific, lay 670 miles away, well within striking distance of Enewetak. The base presented a vexing problem for the Americans. A collection of forested mountains rising from the sea and ringed by a shallow coral reef, Truk boasted a deep harbor and remained nearly impervious to naval bombardment. The atoll bristled with antiaircraft guns and shore batteries and housed 350 planes flying out of three airstrips defended by thousands of troops. Any further Allied operations in the Central Pacific would first have to deal with Truk. The Joint Chiefs faced a choice: to invade and seize the lagoon or to neutralize it as an offensive threat.[21]

Before dawn on February 17, 1944, three groups of American Hellcat fighters took off from the *Enterprise, Yorktown, Essex,* and *Bunker Hill* carriers as part of Operation Hailstone—the attack on Truk. As the attackers approached the lagoon, scores of Japanese fighters rose to intercept them. The Americans downed thirty Japanese planes in the initial dogfight and then circled back to destroy another forty aircraft on the ground. This initial wave mauled Truk's air defenses and opened a clear path for follow-up strikes from American torpedo planes and dive-bombers. While the bombers pummeled Truk's ground facilities and ships anchored in the lagoon, Admiral Spruance led a group of US battleships and destroyers on a circular sweep around the atoll to attack Japanese ships attempting to escape. Although a night attack from Japanese aircraft severely damaged the carrier *Intrepid,* the American assault resumed the following day. Having destroyed most of the ships in the anchorage, the attackers turned their attention to Truk's airstrips, storage depots, and oil tanks. Although the Americans failed to catch the Japanese Combined Fleet—which Admiral Mineichi Koga had wisely moved out of harm's way—the attacks devastated the Japanese base. In all, the Americans destroyed ten warships and thirty-one transports, 270 aircraft, 90 percent of Truk's petroleum storage, and two thousand tons of supplies. The attacks killed six hundred personnel on the atoll and an even greater number of Japanese sailors who were attempting to escape. Operation Hailstone demonstrated the crushing power of the American carrier fleet when employed against Japanese island bases.

Truk, Japan's seemingly impregnable fortress in the Central Pacific, had ceased to be a factor in the war.[22]

The neutralization of Truk and Rabaul breached Japan's outer defensive perimeter and moved Allied forces into a position to begin planning their next moves against the Marianas Islands. "The Marshalls [campaign] really cracked the Japanese shell," remembered Admiral Richard Conolly. "It broke the crust of their defenses on a scale that could be exploited at once."[23] Going forward, Allied offensives would target vital Japanese possessions and begin threatening communications with the home islands.

AS THE AMERICANS ADVANCED ACROSS THE PACIFIC TOWARD JAPAN, the brutal and largely unheralded struggle for control of Burma continued. Japanese troops had dealt a humiliating blow to British colonial forces in 1942, driving Western forces out of Malaya and across the border into India. Since then, Allied leaders had struggled to coordinate effective operations to challenge the Japanese position in Southeast Asia. Control of Burma had given Tokyo the ability to threaten the critical Allied supply route to Chiang's regime in Chongqing and left Japanese forces in a position to threaten British India. As the Japanese navy suffered a string of setbacks in the Pacific, leaders in Tokyo looked to their forces in Burma to reverse their misfortunes. In early January 1944, Imperial Army Headquarters ordered General Renya Mutaguchi, commander of the Japanese Fifteenth Army, to invade India and seize the strategic zone around Imphal. "I started off the Marco Polo Incident which broadened out into the China Incident and then expanded until it turned into the great East Asian War," wrote Mutaguchi. "If I push into India now, by my own efforts and can exercise a decisive influence on the Great East Asian War, I, who was the remote cause of the outbreak of this great war will have justified myself in the eyes of our nation." Though his forces were too small to conquer India by themselves, Mutaguchi hoped to incite a full-scale rebellion in India against British rule.

Japanese soldiers would charge across the border alongside Subhas Chandra Bose's anticolonial Indian National Army. If Bose's soldiers could march back to their homeland and liberate the subcontinent from the clutches of the British Empire, it would strike a thunderous blow for the Co-Prosperity Sphere. Tokyo hoped that a victory in India, along with the destruction of Chiang's regime in China, might finally convince the Allies to accept Japan's new role as the dominant power in Asia.[24]

On March 8, 1944, three Japanese divisions and one division of the Indian National Army crossed the Chindwin River into British-controlled India. The Indian soldiers cheered as they returned to their native soil. Their initial target was the town of Kohima, which controlled the northern approaches to Imphal, an important depot along the key roads leading deeper into India. The commander of British and Allied forces, Lieutenant General William Slim, paled upon hearing news of the attack. If Axis forces succeeded in seizing the town, the entire garrison at Imphal could be cut off. While Slim rushed in reinforcements, the troops at Kohima would need to hold out against the superior attacking force. Fortunately for the British, Allied airlift capacity was sufficient to keep the garrison at Kohima supplied even though land communications had been cut off. In contrast, Japanese forces had packed in what provisions they could carry in their packs and been told that they must feed themselves off captured Allied supplies. The attackers would either capture Kohima or starve.[25]

The siege of Kohima, which began on April 6, 1944, was among the most savage battles of the war. Japanese troops pushed the defenders back to positions along the tennis court atop Garrison Hill, where they held out through five days of ferocious fighting. "We had experienced fighting the Japs . . . bayoneting the wounded and prisoners," recalled Major John Winstanley. "They had renounced any right to be regarded as human, and we thought of them as vermin to be exterminated. Our backs were to the wall and we were going to sell our lives as expensively as we could." With the help of airlifted supplies, Allied forces continued fighting despite being sur-rounded. "Their attacks went on night after night, all night," remem-bered Major Harry Smith. "The outer part of the defences became piled with Japanese corpses." The defenders fought on, with both sides taking heavy casualties. "The smell of death increased as the days passed and bodies decomposed," Smith said. One veteran offi-cer described the fighting at Garrison Hill as being worse than the Somme. Nevertheless, the garrison held long enough for Slim to move in reinforcements and halt the Japanese advance.[26]

Meanwhile, three Japanese infantry divisions with supporting forces had launched an assault toward Imphal from the south. Slim had decided to pull his forces back to more defensible positions closer to the city, which would simultaneously shorten his supply lines and lengthen the already-strained Japanese lines. The Allied defenders met the Japanese on the Imphal Plain in a series of clashes from late March until the middle of June. Louis Mountbatten, supreme Allied com-mander in Southeast Asia, remembered the battle as a bitter struggle raging "across great stretches of wild country; one day its focal point was a hill named on no map, the next a miserable, unpronounceable village a hundred miles away. Columns, brigades, divisions marched and counter-marched, met in bloody clashes, and reeled apart, weav-ing a confused pattern hard to unravel." Though pressed, the Allied defenders held against the Japanese onslaught, turning the cam-paign into a punishing battle of attrition. Here, the Allied advantages in supply lines, motorized support, and command of the air began to take their toll on the Japanese. The arrival of the monsoon rains washed out trails and turned roads into muddy quagmires. Argu-ments between Bose and Mutaguchi compounded the Japanese pre-dicament. In June, British forces regained control of Kohima, and in July, Mutaguchi began to withdraw. Thousands of defeated Japanese soldiers, exhausted, malnourished, suffering from disease, and har-ried by Allied counterattacks, now stumbled back toward Burma. Wounds became infested with maggots, and corpses lined the trails. Men who fell sometimes sank into the mud while their fellow soldiers stripped them of their shoes. "The bodies of our comrades who had struggled along the track before us, lay all around, rain-sodden and giving off the stench of decomposition," remembered one soldier. Some men drowned in the rivers; others killed themselves with grenades. Altogether, between sixty-five thousand and eighty thousand Japanese perished in what was at the time the greatest defeat in the history of the Japanese army.[27]

While Japanese forces limped back to Burma, an even larger campaign was underway to the northeast in China. The Ichigo Offensive began in response to Japanese setbacks in the Pacific. In early 1943, Colonel Joichiro Sanada, head of the Japanese army's Operations Section, began drawing up a new long-range strategic plan. The loss of Guadalcanal and the turning tides in the Pacific War threatened Japan's maritime supply lines and increased the importance of land routes between northern China and Southeast Asia. If Tokyo hoped to wage a protracted defensive war against the Allies, it would need to secure its control of strategic rail lines across China. Moreover, the capture of this territory would put Japanese forces within striking distance of Allied air bases in China. The Ichigo Offensive, then, was designed to eliminate the threat of Allied air attacks and give Japan a continental base from which to contest the Allied advance across the Pacific. The operation was the largest in Japanese history, consisting of five hundred thousand men, one hundred thousand horses, and fifteen thousand vehicles. In all, Japanese commanders would commit 80 percent of their troops in China to the offensive.[28]

On February 25, 1944, Chiang's minister of military operations, Xu Yongchang, received reports that Japanese engineers had begun repairs on the Yellow River Bridge—a clear sign that Tokyo intended to reopen the Beijing-Wuhan railroad. Xu's intelligence apparatus was spotty and the reports he received were not always reliable. Xu assumed that Japanese forces were planning a limited operation and suspected that their moves might in fact be a feint. It was not until May that Chinese commanders realized the full scope of the Japanese offensive. By then, the Ichigo campaign was well underway.[29]

In late April, Japanese forces entered Henan Province, which had suffered years of depredation at the hands of corrupt nationalist commanders, troops who stole food from the local people, widespread famine, and the long-term effects of Chiang's 1938 decision to flood the Yellow River. As one Chinese general wrote, "People in the hills of west Henan attacked our units, taking our guns and ammo, and even mortars and telephone poles. They surrounded and killed our troops." Chiang's divisions, demoralized and understrength, collapsed before the Japanese onslaught. On May 23, Japanese troops captured the city of Luoyang after a nine-day siege. Farther south, Japanese forces were preparing for an attack on the city of Changsha. A concerted defense had beaten back three previous attempts to take Changsha, but this time two Japanese divisions managed to take the city after three days of fighting. One hundred twenty miles to the south, Chinese troops fighting from well-prepared fortifications at Hengyang held out for forty-seven days, from late June to August. Meanwhile, the offensive had touched off an exodus of hundreds of thousands of refugees moving south along the railway from Hunan to Guangxi. Chinese officials, who were already burdened by famine and crop failures and were now struggling to slow the Japanese assault, could do little to help the displaced population. Chiang's new chief of staff, US general Albert Wedemeyer, feared that the Japanese were not only poised to seize the north-south corridor but might then turn west to threaten Chongqing itself. Chiang's regime faced economic and even political collapse.[30]

Meanwhile, commander of American forces in the China-India-Burma theater, General Joseph Stilwell, treated Ichigo as yet another opportunity to excoriate Chiang's leadership. "CKS will squeeze out of us everything he can get to make us pay for the privilege of getting at Japan through China," he told George Marshall. "He will do nothing to help unless forced into it." Washington must either get tough with Chiang and insist that Chinese forces adopt a more aggressive stance against the Japanese or concentrate its efforts to maintain air bases on the mainland. "I contend that ultimately the Jap army must be fought on the mainland of Asia," he wrote. Marshall's reply made it clear that the leadership in Washington saw things differently. "Japan should be defeated without undertaking a major campaign against her on the mainland," Marshall wrote. "Subsequent operations against the Japanese ground army in Asia should then be in the nature of a mopping-up operation." Nimitz and MacArthur's success in the Pacific combined with Chiang's ongoing struggles had convinced Allied leaders to officially downgrade China—the world's most populous nation—to a backwater in the larger war effort. While Japanese soldiers rampaged through China and Chiang struggled to hold his fragile regime together, Western forces would be used elsewhere.[31]

The Ichigo Offensive devastated nationalist China. An estimated 750,000 soldiers died fighting the Japanese in what ultimately proved to be a futile defense. Chiang's financial troubles deepened, and his hold over large sections of the country deteriorated. Nevertheless, Ichigo constituted a pyrrhic victory for Tokyo. In December 1944, Japanese leaders opened their overland corridor but found that Allied bombing had severely damaged existing rail lines. Furthermore, Allied victories in the Pacific would give American long-range bombers island bases from which to attack Japan, thereby negating the value of eliminating Allied airfields in China. As a result, the strategic impact of the campaign was negligible. The real winners of the Ichigo Offensive would be Mao Zedong and the Chinese Communist Party. With Chiang's forces weakened and dispersed and Japanese troops committed to the campaign in the south, communist cadres were able to bolster their positions in the northeast. As the war entered its final year, Mao's revolutionaries laid plans for a renewed civil war against Chiang's government.[32]

FOR THE ALLIES, THE CAMPAIGNS OF 1943–1944 TOLD A TALE OF TWO wars. In the waters of the Pacific Ocean, US forces continued winning battles as Nimitz and MacArthur neutralized the twin strongholds of Rabaul and Truk, pushing ever closer toward Japan's home islands. And in the highlands around Imphal and Kohima, British and Indian troops fought off the Japanese invasion of India and prepared to launch a counteroffensive into Burma. Meanwhile, inside China, the Ichigo Offensive eviscerated the beleaguered nationalist forces and undercut Chiang's control over the country. Short on aid and relegated to a second-class position among the Allies, Chongqing teetered on the brink of collapse. As the war entered its final year, Allied leaders shifted resources away from China in order to press the offensive elsewhere. Much as in their approach in the European theater, London and Washington chose to fight a war along the continental periphery, employing advanced weaponry, amphibious operations, and air strikes to chip away at Axis positions while their allies on land suffered horrendous casualties. Certainly, this strategy maximized Anglo-American advantages, minimized their losses, and placed the Allies on a path to achieve victory. But this offshore approach kept Western armies out of most of the Eurasian landmass, effectively ceding continental Asia to Chinese and Soviet forces at war's end—a dynamic that would carry long-lasting geopolitical repercussions.[33]

Chapter 15

OVERLORD AND THE FATE OF THE WEST

O N THE MORNING OF JUNE 6, 1944, SERGEANT CARL PROFFITT OF Charlottesville, Virginia, found himself crammed alongside thirty of his men aboard a steel-plated Higgins boat in the English Channel. Fog and rain had swept through the channel the previous day, and the shallow-draft boat pitched in the choppy seas as it approached Omaha Beach, Normandy. The roar of exploding shells and aircraft streaking overhead drowned out the shouts of the men in the boat. "I didn't realize that it was actually the real thing until bullets started whizzing down, hitting in the water and hitting the side of your craft and boats being blown up out there in the water and guys going off in water over their head," he remembered. Proffitt stepped out into ankle-deep water to gaze across three hundred yards of beach strewn with barbed wire and tank obstacles. Less-fortunate soldiers jumped into deeper water only to be pulled down beneath the waves by the weight of their eighty-pound packs. He watched as gunfire from the bluffs overlooking the water raked across the beach, cutting down his fellow soldiers, their bodies "mangled all to the smithereens" while the percussion of explosions, the crackle of machine gunfire, and the screams of the wounded filled the air. The Anglo-American assault on Fortress Europe had begun.[1]

Proffitt and his fellow soldiers had stepped onto the beaches of Normandy and into the pivotal battle for hegemony in Europe. The successful defense of Normandy represented Germany's last realistic hope of splitting the Allied coalition and achieving some sort of negotiated settlement to the war short of unconditional surrender. If Hitler's troops succeeded in hurling the Allied landings back into the English Channel, Stalin might choose to cut his losses, consolidate a Soviet empire in Eastern Europe, and allow his hapless Western allies to deal with the Axis powers on their own—a grim prospect for leaders in London and Washington, who would have just suffered a crushing defeat on the beaches of Normandy. Alternatively, Soviet forces might continue their drive across Europe, absorbing enormous casualties as they blasted their way across Poland and through Germany before liberating France beneath the banners of the Red Army. The Soviet occupation of Amsterdam, Berlin, Brussels, Frankfurt, and Paris would fundamentally transform the politics of postwar Europe and the wider world. Conversely, an Anglo-American victory in the Battle of Normandy would be the first step in the liberation of Western Europe, guaranteeing a heavy British and American military presence on continental Europe, rendering Germany's unconditional surrender all but inevitable, and blocking a feared Soviet conquest of the West.

OVERLORD WAS AN OPERATION YEARS IN THE MAKING. FROM EARLY conversations between the Allies about the need to open a second front in Europe, the invasion had grown into the focus of Anglo-American planning for 1944. British and American commanders faced a dizzying array of challenges. First and foremost was Washington's desire to end the war as quickly as possible. As British leaders had pursued peripheral operations in theaters such as the Mediterranean, George Marshall and the American brass had pushed for a direct approach as the best way to win the war. Nearly as important was the desire to satisfy Soviet demands for the creation of another front in the war against the Third Reich. If the Anglo-American failure to invade Western Europe in 1943 had angered Stalin, a postponement until 1945 threatened to tear the Grand Alliance apart.

Concerns about the fate of postwar Europe also occupied a central place in Washington's calculations. Since the spring of 1943, US leaders had been considering the possibility that the Soviet onslaught might force the collapse of the Third Reich before the Anglo-Americans landed in France. Should this happen, the Red Army would be in a position to drive west across the whole of Germany and into France before American or British armies arrived. In light of these concerns, Roosevelt ordered that preparations be made for an "emergency entrance of the continent and indicated that he desired United Nations troops to be ready to get to Berlin *as soon as did the Russians*" (emphasis added). Planning for such an operation had already begun. The rapid occupation of Western Europe, code-named Rankin, envisioned several contingencies brought about by the weakening of German power. German leaders might abandon occupied countries such as France, Norway, or the Netherlands in order to consolidate their defenses; they might suddenly surrender; or they might redeploy "all available forces against the Russian menace [in order to] postpone the hour of final defeat and insure the ultimate occupation of Germany by Anglo-American rather than by Russian forces." In each scenario, US and British troops must be prepared to seize key strategic positions as quickly as possible.[2]

In a meeting with the Joint Chiefs aboard the battleship USS *Iowa* on November 19, 1943, Roosevelt noted that Soviet forces were now camped a mere sixty miles from the Polish border while Western armies were still months away from setting foot on French soil.

Nevertheless, the president insisted that the "United States should have Berlin." Once American and British forces landed on the continent, he argued, "there would definitely be a race for the capital. We may have to put the United States divisions into Berlin as soon as possible." Harry Hopkins agreed—the US military should "be ready to put an airborne division into Berlin two hours after the collapse of Germany."[3]

Allied leaders understood that the defeat of Germany was no longer their sole concern—the deployment of British, Soviet, and US armies on the continent would likely be critical to the shaping of postwar power in Europe. As Stalin himself explained, "This war is not as in the past; whoever occupies a territory also imposes on it his own social system. Everyone imposes his own system as far as his army can reach. It cannot be otherwise." No doubt with this in mind, Churchill argued that British and American troops should forgo a proposed invasion of southern France and instead land near Trieste before driving northeast through the Ljubljana Gap in a bid to capture Vienna before the Red Army. The prime minister's scheme gained few supporters—Allied armies fighting in Italy had discovered how tough Europe's "soft underbelly" could be, and most commanders feared an offensive through the Ljubljana Gap would be quickly bottled up by German defenders. Marshall and Roosevelt remained adamant: the main Anglo-American attack on Germany must come in the form of a cross-channel invasion in the spring of 1944.[4]

But landing an army capable of driving the Wehrmacht from France would be no small feat. Hitler's coastal defense network, the Atlantic Wall, snaked along the northern shore of Europe from the French border with Spain, across Belgium, the Netherlands, and Denmark, and north along the coast of Norway. Heavy concrete bunkers, pillboxes, and gun emplacements looked out over heavily mined beaches covered with antitank obstacles. Pas-de-Calais was the obvious Allied target. From there on a clear day, an observer could gaze across twenty-one miles of water at the white cliffs of Dover along the southeast coast of England. However, this same proximity had convinced German commanders to concentrate their defenses at Calais. Any attempted Allied landing would crash directly into the teeth of the Wehrmacht. The second option, an assault on the beaches of Normandy, traded a longer crossing for weaker German defenses. Normandy lay well within range of Allied aircraft, and its miles of coastline provided a wide beachhead for the American, British, and Canadian armies. If landing the Allied armies posed a challenge, supplying them presented an even greater problem. The 1943 Dieppe Raid had revealed the difficulty of seizing a German-held port, and Allied planners knew that the defenders would destroy or sabotage any shipping facilities that fell into enemy hands. Until they could move inland to seize and rebuild French harbors, the Allies would need to haul massive stores of provisions, equipment, weapons, and ammunition over the beaches quickly enough to allow their forces to withstand German counterattacks. One temporary solution to this supply problem would come in the form of Mulberry harbors: two artificial harbors made up of massive concrete caissons and obsolete ships floated across the channel and submerged to the seafloor to form a breakwater around floating piers leading to Omaha Beach and Gold Beach. Together, the two harbors weighed a staggering 1.5 million tons.[5]

Alongside these logistical plans, Allied commanders orchestrated one of the largest deception operations of the war with the creation of the First United States Army Group—a nonexistent decoy force charged with the task of staging the cross-channel attacks on Calais. Double agents in Britain fed false information about the operations to German intelligence, which remained convinced that Calais would be the target of the invasion and that General George Patton, revered in Germany as the most effective Allied commander, would be the one to lead it. In fact, Patton had been placed in command of the Third Army, which would be used in follow-up operations after the initial landings. To seal the deal, production teams from the Shepperton film studios were brought in to create a mock army composed of empty barracks, fake ammunition dumps, wooden and rubber tank

SCORCHED EARTH

models, and dummy artillery pieces in southeastern England to give the appearance of advanced preparations for an attack.[6]

The plan for Overlord also revealed the Western Allies' increasingly sophisticated amphibious war-fighting capabilities. The night before the landings, airborne divisions would stage an assault in hopes of securing the landings' flanks. Sunrise would find American and British warships sweeping the channel of seaborne threats to prepare the way for an armada of landing boats that would deliver infantry and armor onto four separate beaches. In the skies above, thousands of Allied warplanes would swarm across Normandy, pummeling any enemy target they could find in an effort to blunt a German counterattack. Soon after, Allied engineers would assemble the prefabricated Mulberry harbors. Topping it all off, the Allies planned to stage a second amphibious invasion one month later in southern France—Operation Dragoon. No power in history had attempted a landing of such size and complexity.

As night fell over southern England on June 5, 1944, three airborne divisions prepared to board a fleet of C-47 transport planes and single-use gliders. The soldiers labored under heavy packs and frazzled nerves—Eisenhower had pushed their mission back twenty-four hours due to heavy rain. But tonight they would jump. "It was cloudy, still raining, windy," remembered Sergeant George Gibbons. "The clouds got so thick we couldn't see the ground." The only light came from antiaircraft fire. "The German tracers were every fourth bullet and it looked like a steady stream of fire coming at you." At 2:15 a.m., Gibbons and his platoon leaped into the darkness over the town of Sainte-Mère-Église and soon splashed down in a field that had been flooded by the German defenders. Listening for the click of the dime-store cricket toys that had been issued to all the paratroopers, he began gathering his comrades. His lieutenant had been killed by ground fire during the descent, and his unit was scattered across two miles of sodden woodland. Their task was to set up a defensive

406

perimeter to block any German attempts to send reinforcements to the Normandy beaches. Airborne forces destroyed bridges, attacked shore batteries, and set up ambushes. The paratroopers' most important task was to stop German panzers from reaching the beaches, where they would wreak havoc upon the vulnerable landing force.[7]

While Gibbons and his fellow paratroopers dodged German patrols, the Allied fleet approached the Normandy coast. Aboard the *Empire Anvil* sat seventeen-year-old Joseph Argenzio, the youngest American soldier to participate in the Normandy landing. After eating his last meal before combat, Argenzio made his way up to the deck, where he was hustled onto a cargo net draped over the ship's side. He prayed as the landing boat tossed in the waves before a sergeant hoisted him into the wrong boat. "Who the hell are you?" the sergeant asked. As the boat began its approach, Allied warships shelled the German positions and B-17s swooped overhead. "This is going to be a piece of cake," Argenzio thought. Instead, "the Air Force dropped their bombs inland and they killed a bunch of French civilians and cows." After hitting a German obstacle, Argenzio's boat dropped its ramp. "The guys in front got killed right away," he remembered. The surviving soldiers leaped over the side into deep water. Tearing off his gear, the seventeen-year-old swam toward the beach. He survived the hail of German gunfire by sheltering behind the bodies of two dead soldiers as he hobbled toward shore. Once on land, he bolted, zigzagging, slipping, and falling toward the only cover, a seawall defiladed from enemy fire. Choking from the smell of cordite, Argenzio scrambled to pull bodies, both living and dead, into cover amid the screams of the wounded. The teenager then joined another group of soldiers, who scaled the bluffs overlooking Omaha Beach to destroy a German machine gun nest. The following morning, Argenzio's uniform had turned purple, stained with the blood of his comrades.[8]

The Americans on Omaha had started to gain the upper hand by midday. Six hours after the first landings, nearly nineteen thousand men had made it onto the beach. While infantry swept the remaining German positions on the bluffs, engineers worked to clear land mines and obstacles. The shoreline was now strewn with burning vehicles, piles of equipment, and hundreds of bodies. Smoke from burning grass in the surrounding hills drifted through the air along with the smell of burned flesh. While the Americans fought on Omaha and Utah, British and Canadian forces landed on three more beaches to the east. The troops at Gold and Juno met determined resistance but managed to establish beachheads and link up. Likewise, British forces staged an effective assault on Sword Beach, but their follow-up sputtered. Observers later reported witnessing soldiers stopping to smoke cigarettes and even brew tea after reaching the shore. Montgomery seemed to share this lack of urgency. His delay would prove costly.[9]

In all, over four thousand Allied soldiers died on June 6, 1944. The Omaha landing was the day's bloodiest, with some two thousand killed. British forces suffered about two thousand casualties in the battles for Sword and Gold Beaches, 340 Canadian soldiers were killed on Juno, and about two hundred Americans died on Utah. Another six thousand Allied troops were wounded during the landings. Out of some 150,000 troops landed at Normandy on D-Day, approximately 6.7 percent were killed or wounded. These were horrific figures—especially for the first wave to land on Omaha—but they were far from the bloodbath that some had feared. Surveying the results of the day's fighting, Eisenhower could breathe a sigh of relief. Although the Allies had done everything in their power to ensure success, the general knew the dangers of such an audacious operation. With these risks in mind, Eisenhower had scribbled a short note—sixty-five words long—announcing the failure of the operation. "If any blame or fault attaches to the attempt," he wrote, "it is mine alone." But the landings had not failed. Eisenhower would not need his note.[10]

On paper, the Third Reich's position appeared formidable. The Wehrmacht had torn through the Western armies in 1940 and now, four years later, it remained a lethal fighting force. Moreover, German commanders had had four years to prepare for an Allied invasion. However, the reality on the ground told a different story.

Germany's conquests had given the Wehrmacht a massive coastline to defend, stretching from the Spanish border to the Arctic coast of Norway. There simply were not enough Germans to garrison such a vast perimeter. While France remained relatively quiet, Hitler's legions had spent most of the last four years in a brutal struggle with the Red Army that the Reich was now losing. With the battle raging in the east, German commanders had used the west as a vast rear area—a place to rest wounded soldiers and rebuild mauled divisions for the titanic struggle against the Soviet Union. This practice drained the Reich's western reaches of manpower and resources and stymied efforts to forge a cohesive set of plans for France's defense. Adding to the disarray, Hitler had sent Field Marshal Erwin Rommel to France to command Army Group B, splitting command with Field Marshal Gerd von Rundstedt, in command of Army Group D. Not surprisingly, the redundant field marshals disagreed over battle plans. While Rommel favored keeping German panzers near the coast in hopes of stopping the expected Allied invasion on the beaches, Rundstedt insisted that German armor be kept in reserve farther inland, safe from naval bombardment and ready to launch a flexible counterattack. Hitler responded to his feuding commanders with a compromise: Rommel and Rundstedt would each receive three divisions while four would be held back under the ultimate control of Hitler himself.[11]

But none of these measures solved Germany's greatest weakness: its lack of aircraft. In January 1944, US commanders had launched Operation Argument, an extended battle of attrition against the Luftwaffe. American bombers staged attacks on vital German targets in a move designed to force the Luftwaffe into a defensive position. US fighter escorts then closed in to intercept the defenders, destroying enemy warplanes and thinning the ranks of experienced German pilots. Over the same period, British bombers concentrated attacks on key targets such as airfields, ammunition dumps, bridges, and railroads. Together, these campaigns depleted the Luftwaffe and crippled the Wehrmacht's ability to move ground forces quickly in response to Overlord. German commanders launched a paltry one hundred sorties against the Allies on D-Day. "Where is the Luftwaffe?" Axis soldiers cried as they watched enemy soldiers streaming across the channel beaches. In the following days, British and US warplanes swarmed over Normandy, devastating German ground forces and foiling attempts to mount successful counterattacks.[12]

But Allied bombs proved to be as deadly for Normandy's civilians as they were for German soldiers. While the landing forces waited in the English Channel through the waning hours of June 5, British planes swept over the countryside, dropping some five thousand tons of bombs on suspected German positions. Hours later, as the sun crept above the eastern horizon, waves of American bombers roared over Omaha Beach. But heavy clouds led most of the Americans to drop their bombs not on the beaches but on the village of Port-en-Bessin-Huppain. That afternoon and in the early hours of June 7, American and British bombers attacked the city of Caen. Allied bombs tore through buildings and left the streets strewn with the corpses of French civilians. While Allied leaders celebrated the landings, the residents of Caen battled raging fires and searched for bodies in the rubble. "The population was literally crazed, seized by panic, and trying to flee the city into the countryside," the deputy mayor of Caen remembered. "People were running about in nightshirts, bare-foot, without having had the time to put on the least clothing. The city was enveloped in a yellowish smoke and dust from all the shattered buildings." Something on the order of three thousand French civilians were killed on June 6, mostly by Allied bombs, rendering D-Day as deadly for French civilians as it was for American soldiers.[13]

The return of major operations to France also proved lethal for civilians far from the battlefields of Normandy. As German commanders gathered their troops to mount a counterattack against the Allies, the Second SS Panzer Division Das Reich launched reprisals against noncombatants suspected of aiding resistance operations. On June 9, following the deaths of several SS officers near Tulle, German troops rounded up a group of ninety-nine men and hanged them from lampposts and balconies throughout the town. The next day, SS troopers from the division arrived in the town of Oradour-sur-Glane and ordered local officials to assemble the local population. The Nazi troops led the men to a barn, where they were shot with machine guns and set on fire. Meanwhile, the women and children were forced into a church, which was then torched. The soldiers then shot any survivors who tried to flee. In all, Nazi troops butchered more than 640 civilians in the town.[14]

ALTHOUGH ALLIES HAD TAKEN THE BEACHES, THE STRUGGLE FOR Europe was only just beginning. In front of the invaders lay Normandy's verdant countryside, lined by a massive grid of impenetrable hedgerows and dozens of towns and cities infested with Nazi defenders. The Americans faced the task of linking their beachheads at Omaha and Utah and then turning west to drive up the Cotentin Peninsula and capture the vital port of Cherbourg. Although they were not fighting elite Wehrmacht forces, US troops confronted stubborn resistance aided by imposing terrain. Centuries-old hedgerows—the bocage—crept across the peninsula forming dense, leafy barricades around every field and pasture in the Americans' path. Rising several meters above the ground, the gnarled hedges proved too thick for the American tanks to break through. Advancing infantry soon discovered that their enemies had positioned their machine guns to fire on the openings and mow down any troops that tried to move through. "Lanes of fire for the guns had been prepared with great care, the grass and hedges having been cut for good fields of fire," one American sergeant reported. "The enemy held fire until we reached the open field and the [company] was a good target." Years later, army medic Raymond VanDuzer explained that his unit "learned a lot about hedgerows, the worst way." But the most lethal fire came from German 88mm flak cannons. VanDuzer remembered his futile attempts to save one crewman who had been caught inside a burning tank. "It was just like reaching down and the skin would come off, just like a chicken's skin would come off. It was just that gruesome."[15]

After nearly two weeks of heavy fighting, US forces closed in around Cherbourg. The final drive to take the city was set to begin at 3:00 a.m. on June 19. As the hour approached, the anxious men of the US Fourth Infantry Division checked their watches. Under cover of darkness, US troops crept through hedgerows, fields, and ditches to the hills above Cherbourg. The advancing troops met light resistance but made steady progress. Dawn found the Americans camped on the high ground overlooking the city. The Germans had bolstered the older fortifications with bunkers, pillboxes, and reinforced gun emplacements. The heaviest defenses had been designed to repel an attack from the sea. Now, cut off from any hope of reinforcements, the defenders pulled back into their concrete-and-brick warrens, bracing for the American onslaught. A heavy bombing raid opened the attack on June 22, followed by a slow infantry advance through the houses of Cherbourg. US soldiers cleared bunkers with grenades and bazooka fire while naval artillery offshore pounded Wehrmacht positions. By June 26, the remaining defenders had retreated into the dank tunnels beneath the town's fortress. Aware that their situation was hopeless, the commander of the German garrison, General Karl-Wilhelm von Schlieben, surrendered. Isolated resistance continued into the following day, but the Americans' greatest frustration came upon surveying the wreckage of the port, which one colonel lamented as "beyond a doubt the most complete, intensive, and best-planned demolition in history." So thorough was the destruction of the port facilities that the Allied shipping would not make full use of Cherbourg until September.[16]

To the east, British and Canadian forces were also struggling to push inland. Montgomery's plan to seize Caen on the first day of the campaign sputtered as the exhausted landing forces paused to regroup. A Canadian attack on Caen the following day slammed into the Twelfth SS Panzer Division Hitlerjugend. Fanatical SS resistance halted the Allied advance but left heavy casualties on both sides. Montgomery's slow progress allowed German reinforcements to move into position outside of Caen despite concerted attacks from Allied aircraft. As three panzer divisions filled the gap, it became clear that the Allies would face a difficult fight. On June 13, British tanks and infantry swung south toward the town of Villers-Bocage to flank the main contingent of German forces blocking the approach to Caen. As British tanker John Cloudsley-Thompson approached a bend in the road, he saw the lead tank in his column burst into flames. The advance had run into a German ambush. As he tried to turn around, Cloudsley-Thompson saw a second tank explode under enemy fire. Moments later, a massive Tiger tank broke the smoke only fifteen meters away. Covered in heavy armor and carrying an 88mm main gun, the Tiger outclassed any tank in the Allied arsenal. As Cloudsley-Thompson sped backward, one of the Tiger's shells passed within inches of his head. A second shell slammed into his tank's engine, forcing the crew to bail out and seek shelter in a nearby cellar. Only eight seconds had elapsed from the Tiger's sighting to the destruction of Cloudsley-Thompson's tank. Fighting continued through the following day, but the attackers were unable to break through. As the British pulled back, hundreds of Allied bombers converged on the town. One artillery officer remembered watching "the whole place just disappear. They were droning overhead, the bombers seemed to go on forever. . . . The place was absolutely flattened. It was what came to be known that how we liberated a village was to completely destroy it."[17]

The Battle of Villers-Bocage put an end to British hopes for the quick seizure of Caen. Instead, Montgomery would conduct a slow, grinding advance toward the city using overwhelming firepower to pummel German opposition. With the offensive stalled, Allied urgency to push forward increased. On the morning of June 13, Nazi engineers in western France launched ten V-1 rockets at London. The rockets appeared over England twenty minutes later flying at half the speed of sound. Hundreds of rockets would follow in the coming days. Terrified Londoners learned to scramble for shelter at the roar of an approaching V-1, workers removed the windowpanes from city buses, and thousands of buildings were damaged or destroyed. A furious Churchill thundered that the Allies should retaliate with poison gas attacks on Berlin. Cooler heads insisted that the only solution was to use Allied ground forces to drive the Germans from northern France.[18] Compounding Allied woes, another storm blew through the English Channel on June 19, destroying the Mulberry harbor at Omaha Beach and damaging the Mulberry at Gold Beach. Although British engineers were able to make repairs at Gold Beach, the destruction exacerbated Allied logistical problems. As challenges mounted, Allied leaders faced ever-greater urgency to expand the Normandy beachhead.

Although the German defenders continued to thwart the British and Canadian offensives, their strategic outlook remained bleak. Fierce resistance had slowed the Allied advance at the cost of heavy German losses in men and equipment that could not be replaced. Meanwhile, the Allies were able to make good their losses, sometimes in a matter of hours. "I am being bled and getting nowhere," SS commander Sepp Dietrich fumed. The tragedy of the German position in Normandy, Rommel lamented on June 13, was that "we are obliged to fight on to the very end, but all the time we're convinced that it's far more vital to stop the Russians than the Anglo-Americans from breaking into Germany." That same day, he wrote to his wife, "There's simply no answer to it. . . . It's time for politics to come into play. It will all be over with very quickly." But Hitler remained adamant: German forces must continue their hopeless fight to hold Normandy.[19]

None of which is to say that the coming weeks would be easy for the Allies. On June 26, Montgomery launched Operation Epsom. For five days, three British divisions attacked German forces west of Caen. The attackers met determined resistance across difficult terrain, taking significant losses without achieving a decisive breakthrough. On June 30, having suffered over four thousand casualties, Montgomery called off the offensive. One week later, the RAF staged a massive raid on Caen. Hundreds of aircraft pummeled the city with over two thousand tons of bombs. While Allied infantry cheered, the French residents of the city saw their city reduced to smoldering rubble. Thousands of citizens had already fled to the medieval quarries outside Caen to take shelter in dank, lice-ridden caves. There, they lived in darkness and filth, deprived of electricity, running water, and modern latrines. Montgomery's offensives continued with Operations Charnwood and Goodwood. On July 18, Allied forces finally managed to drive the Wehrmacht out of the ruined city, but fighting continued for control of the Bourguébus Ridge to the southeast.[20]

While the British and Canadians converged on Caen, US forces remained mired in the bocage. General Omar Bradley, commander of the US First Army, was intent on breaking out into open tank country. As long as the Wehrmacht kept the Allies bottled up fighting hedgerow to hedgerow, the Americans would be unable to make full use of their mechanized forces. On July 13, US forces began a punishing assault on the town of Saint-Lô despite taking eleven thousand casualties. Following delays due to bad weather, the Americans launched Operation Cobra on July 25. The offensive opened with a heavy bombing raid by hundreds of B-17 Flying Fortresses that rained bombs down on German positions. "By midday the entire area resembled a moon landscape, with the bomb craters touching rim to rim," wrote one German general. "Simultaneously with the storm from the air, innumerable guns of the American artillery poured drumfire into our field positions." Following the bombardment, US armor and infantry rushed into the freshly bombed ground. The attackers found the fighting difficult through the first day, but that was about to change. Through weeks of heavy fighting in Normandy, the Americans had continued to build up their forces while the German defenders grew weaker. Bradley now fielded fifteen divisions against nine depleted German counterparts. As Rommel had recently warned Hitler, "The moment is fast approaching when our hard pressed defences will crack." The Wehrmacht had reached its breaking point. As the assault continued into a second day, the defenders began to collapse.

With most of their reserves committed, German commanders were unable to repel the Allied onslaught. By July 28, Bradley's forces were on the verge of breaking out.[21]

With the Americans driving west out of the bocage and the British and Canadians pushing south from Caen, German forces in Normandy faced the growing threat of encirclement. The newly activated US Third Army, under the command of General George Patton, tore south through Brittany and encountered weak enemy resistance before wheeling around the southern flank of the German armies. In a last bid to stop the Americans, German commanders mounted a counterattack near Mortain. But rather than threatening the offensive, the Mortain attack drew German forces in the Allies' path. Allied intelligence had intercepted and decoded the German plans and allowed the American commanders to prepare. "This is an opportunity that comes to a commander not more than once in a century," Bradley wrote. "We are about to destroy an entire German army." Outside Caen, Montgomery's forces had begun a push to close off the Wehrmacht's escape routes to the east. Together, these three Allied prongs formed a shrinking pocket around the town of Falaise that threatened to trap all of the remaining German forces in Normandy. By August 17, the envelopment was nearly complete. Only a 4.5-mile-wide gap separated Canadian and Polish troops from Patton's forces.[22]

In a move that sparked lasting controversy, Montgomery's forces failed to close this last escape route to retreating Wehrmacht forces. Between twenty thousand and fifty thousand Germans, including a significant number of officers, escaped. Montgomery's critics later accused the general of excessive caution followed by a failure to call on American forces to move forward and fill the gap. At the very least, the British commander blundered by sending comparatively weaker Canadian and Polish units to complete the encirclement. Nevertheless, the Allies managed to trap some sixty thousand German troops. Now the Allied aircraft and artillery unleashed an apocalyptic bombardment on the remnants of the German armies.[23]

The carnage inside the pocket reached biblical proportions. West of Falaise, Canadian officer Peter Simonds gaped at the "spectacle of slaughter and destruction." German dead, blackened in the sun, lay piled by the hundreds along the sunken roads alongside dead horses and burned-out vehicles. Inside one wrecked truck, Simonds found a pair of legs "still resting over the clutch and brake pedals, but the rest of the driver was caught up in a tree ten feet above ground." Throngs of civilians scoured through the wreckage, picking the boots off corpses and stripping the tires off vehicles. As the August heat blasted the killing field, the stench of decomposing bodies spread for miles. Pilots claimed that they could smell the dead in their cockpits eight hundred feet up. Some local farmers began burning the dead in order to keep the rats away. Eisenhower visited Falaise two days after the end of the battle. There he witnessed "scenes that could be described only by Dante. It was literally possible to walk for hundreds of yards at a time, stepping on nothing but dead and decaying flesh."[24]

The Allied campaign in Normandy had obliterated the German position in France and thrown the surviving Wehrmacht forces into retreat. Despite hard fighting in the bocage and around Caen, the Normandy campaign had wrapped up ten days ahead of schedule. Meanwhile, the Americans had staged a second successful amphibious landing along the Mediterranean coast with Operation Dragoon, opening Marseille to Allied shipping and clearing German forces from the South of France. Overlord and Dragoon offered a terrifying display of US and British amphibious operations combined with overwhelming airpower, mechanized infantry, and armored operations. The arrival of the Anglo-American armies on the continent thrust Western Europe back into the maelstrom, spreading the war's devastation across gaping sections of France as brutal fighting drove German forces back toward the heart of the Reich. Meanwhile, Overlord's success also raised a host of new issues for the Allies that would carry sweeping implications for the postwar world.

On August 31, as his battered legions retreated from France, the Führer assured two of his generals that he had no intention of surrendering. "The time is not yet ripe for a political decision," he explained. "The time will come when the tension between the Allies becomes so strong that, in spite of everything, the rupture occurs. History teaches us that all coalitions break up, but you must await the moment however difficult the waiting may be. . . . Whatever happens we shall carry on this struggle until, as Frederick the Great said, 'one of our damned enemies gives up in despair!'" The Allied coalition, the Führer insisted, remained an unwieldy monstrosity composed of "the greatest extremes imaginable in this world: ultra-capitalist states on one side and ultra-Marxist states on the other." Sooner or later, he argued, the Grand Alliance would tear itself apart.[25]

The Führer's assessment of inter-Allied tensions was not far off the mark. With the opening of the second front, Western leaders' thoughts had turned toward the challenges of great power relations in the postwar world. "Winston never talks of Hitler these days," Churchill's personal doctor, Lord Moran, wrote in his diary on August 21. "He is always harping on the dangers of Communism. He dreams of the Red Army spreading like a cancer from one country to another. It has become an obsession, and he seems to think of little else."[26]

The prime minister was not alone. In late May 1944, the British representative to de Gaulle's Free France, Duff Cooper, offered his thoughts on the future of British foreign policy. British leaders had long sought to prevent any single state from dominating Europe. However, Cooper warned, Germany's imminent defeat would overturn the regional balance of power, leaving Moscow as the commanding power on the continent. The Soviet Union contained a fiercely patriotic population twice that of Germany, as well as bountiful agricultural and natural resources. Stalin's regime had staged rapid industrial development, created a ruthlessly efficient state security apparatus, and maintained a powerful ideology that resonated with millions of people both inside Russia and abroad. "It would be difficult to over-estimate the potential menace which all these advantages create," Cooper wrote. Although Soviet leaders would likely be pre-occupied with the enormous task of reconstruction after the war, long-term dangers remained. "There exist, therefore, good grounds for hope that fears of Russia may prove illusory," he argued. "But hope does not provide a satisfactory basis for policy, and preparations should always envisage the worst rather than the best eventualities."[27]

Lord Alan Brooke, chief of the British Imperial General Staff, was also devoting more attention to the question of Soviet power in post-war Europe. "Should Germany be dismembered or gradually be con-verted to an ally to meet [the] Russian threat of 20 years hence?" he wrote in his diary in late July. "I suggested the latter and feel certain that we must from now onwards regard Germany in a very different light. Germany is no longer the dominating power of Europe, Rus-sia is. Unfortunately Russia is not entirely European. She has however vast resources and cannot fail to become the main threat in 15 years from now."[28]

American officials voiced similar concerns. Like Alan Brooke, Roosevelt's Treasury secretary, Henry Morgenthau, proposed the demilitarization and dismemberment of Germany along with the dismantling of its industrial capacity. But neutering Germany would remove a crucial counterweight to Soviet power in Europe.[29]

Accordingly, in May 1944, the Joint Chiefs of Staff offered an appraisal recognizing the Red Army's military preponderance in continental Europe. The defeat of the Axis would leave the world with only three great powers, the chiefs explained: the United States, Great Britain, and the Soviet Union. Since a clash between Washing-ton and London seemed virtually inconceivable, the likeliest source of a future world war would be an armed conflict between London and Moscow. In the event of such a conflict, Britain would stand no chance of mounting "effective military opposition to Russia on the continent." Nor would the United States be in a position to challenge Soviet power in Europe: "We might be able to successfully defend Britain, but we could not, under existing conditions, defeat Russia. In other words, we would find ourselves engaged in a war which we could not win even though the United States would be in no danger of defeat and occupation."[30]

In early August, George Marshall, the US Army chief of staff, sent a memorandum to Secretary of State Cordell Hull outlining postwar concerns. The end of the war would witness a revolutionary transformation in the world balance of power, he wrote. "This is a fact of fundamental importance in its bearing upon future international political settlements and all discussions leading thereto." Germany's defeat "will leave Russia in a position of assured military dominance in eastern Europe and the Middle East." Overlord's success ensured that American and British forces would "occupy and control western Europe," but their military presence would decline as the two powers turned to the war against Japan and postwar demobilization. Furthermore, Marshall wrote, the fall of Japan would "leave Russia in a dominant position on continental Northeast Asia." Washington and Moscow would emerge from the war as the world's two dominant military powers, with the British Empire a distant third. Although the United States would maintain the capacity to project military power around the globe, neither Moscow nor Washington would be strong enough to defeat the other in a future war.[31]

The following month, as US and British leaders prepared to meet for the Second Quebec Conference, a State Department briefing paper warned that London might eventually draw Washington into a clash with Moscow. The war had transformed the Soviet Union into the dominant power in Europe, the paper explained, and British leaders might seek to draw the United States into European affairs as a counterweight to Moscow's influence. Rather than assuming the role of intermediary in a postwar Anglo-Soviet conflict, the paper argued, the United States should work to "prevent the development in Europe or elsewhere of British and Soviet spheres of influence" and instead seek to secure full Soviet participation in the postwar international security organization that would become the new United Nations.[32]

Writing from the embassy in Moscow, American diplomat George Kennan offered a gloomier assessment. The experiences of the war had kindled deep-seated Soviet paranoia and insecurity, he wrote. The resurgence of German military power during the 1930s had convinced Soviet leaders to launch their own program of territorial expansion along with a bid to create a sphere of influence, both of which drew from older traditions of czarist imperialism. The Kremlin had sought to restore influence over Finland and the Baltic states and establish control over much of Poland. Soviet leaders attempted to impose "dominant Russian influence over all the Slavs of central Europe and the Balkans" and to gain control over the Dardanelles. Ultimately, Moscow had hoped to "prevent the formation in central and eastern Europe of any power or coalition of powers capable of challenging Russian security." The German attack of 1941 had scuttled these plans, but now the Kremlin saw its chance. "This time there would be no powerful Germany to be reckoned with. An exhausted and war-torn eastern Europe would provide a plastic and yielding mass from which the objectives of Russian statesmanship could easily be moulded." The successful cross-channel invasion coupled with the Red Army's victories in the East had assured the Third Reich's eventual defeat. With German power destroyed and Soviet armies occupying vast swaths of the continent, the Kremlin would be in a position to secure its long-held goal of "becoming the dominant power of eastern and central Europe," Kennan warned. "No one can stop Russia from doing the taking, if she is determined to go through with it."[33]

By late August 1944, leaders in Berlin, London, Moscow, and Washington recognized that the Allied victory in the battle for France had fundamentally transformed the war in Europe. Germany now faced a two-front war against forces that enjoyed overwhelming numerical and material superiority. Most serious observers understood that it was only a matter of time before the Allied armies marched into Berlin. Ultimately, the successful invasion of Normandy ensured that the American and British armies would be among those forces that occupied a defeated Germany. With German defeat all but guaranteed, American, British, and Soviet leaders increasingly turned to focus on the coming struggle for influence in the postwar world. While the Western armies drove the last remnants of the Wehrmacht from France, Soviet forces were well on their way to consolidating control over a future sphere of influence in Eastern Europe.[34]

Chapter 16

BAGRATION AND
THE FATE OF THE EAST

VAN YAKUSHIN, A JUNIOR LIEUTENANT WITH THE SOVIET FIFTH
Guards Cavalry Division, first heard the news that he was headed
to the front from the landlady in charge of the house where he was
staying. "How on earth did those women always know top secret
information before we did?" he wondered. Two days later, his column
was loaded onto a train and taken to an open field. There, they disem-
barked and were marched to the edge of an old forest. "The trees in
that forest were mighty and old," he remembered. "It was like being
in the great hall of some fairy-tale castle!" There, hidden in the dark
shadows of the forest canopy, the soldiers waited.[1] Yakushin and his
comrades were small players in what would be the massive offensive
Operation Bagration. Comprising nearly 2.5 million personnel, the
operation would carry the Red Army over four hundred miles in
ten weeks, from the banks of the Dnieper River to the outskirts of

Warsaw. In the process, the Soviet juggernaut would finally crush Army Group Center and move within striking distance of Germany itself. By timing the offensive to coincide with the Allied invasion of France, Stalin ensured that Hitler's forces would feel the full force of the two-front war they had long feared. As British, Canadian, and US forces gained a foothold in Normandy, the Red Army unleashed a devastating offensive along the eastern marches of the Third Reich.

The leviathan of American sea power and the Red Army behemoth were now converging on the heart of continental Europe, leaving a trail of destruction in their wakes. The fighting further underscored the vast disparity in land power between the Western Allies and the Soviet Union. As Western troops fought to enlarge their foothold in Normandy, the Red Army's crushing advance rolled across Eastern Europe, devastating German forces and placing vast stretches of territory under Moscow's control. As they drove west through the forests of Belorussia and into Poland, Soviet forces came face-to-face with the horrors of Hitler's empire. Burned villages, ruined cities, and the ghastly remains of Nazi death camps—a vast machinery of genocide providing incontrovertible evidence of the true scope of the Führer's vision for Europe. Here, among fields strewn with ashes and bones, sat the apotheosis of Western racial ideology, civilizational hierarchy, and violent colonialism. In time, revelations of the Holocaust would give new meaning to the battle against Nazism, help to discredit notions of scientific racism, and spawn new conceptions of human rights. In the moment, however, the titanic struggle between the Red Army and the Wehrmacht took center stage as Bagration, the largest Allied offensive of the war, roared to life.

SINCE THE OPENING OF OPERATION BARBAROSSA IN THE SUMMER OF 1941, German Army Group Center had stood as the Red Army's nemesis. While Soviet forces fought through Ukraine in the south and drove the Wehrmacht from the gates of Leningrad in the north, a seemingly endless series of battles raged along the approaches to

Moscow in the center. From January 1942 until March 1943, millions of German and Soviet soldiers fought for control of the area around Rzhev, some 140 miles west of the capital. Dubbed the Rzhev Meat Grinder, this largely forgotten fourteen-month struggle generated over a million casualties. As a result, the center of the eastern front remained locked in a bloody stalemate. That was about to change.

The summer of 1944 presented Soviet leaders with a range of opportunities. The Americans and British had notified Moscow of their intention to launch in the spring a cross-channel invasion that promised, for the first time, to present a genuine second front. Significant improvements in the Red Army's fighting abilities combined with fresh troops, Lend-Lease shipments, and the erosion of German strength to dramatically enhance the Red Army's operational capacity. Along the eastern front, Soviet forces had made progress in Ukraine following their earlier victories at Stalingrad and Kursk. Moscow could choose to continue this southern thrust with a renewed offensive in 1944, focus its energy in the center toward Belorussia, or strike in the north in a bid to defeat Finland and force the Germans away from Leningrad and the Baltic republics. Soviet leaders would opt to pursue all three approaches by launching five consecutive operations, starting with the Karelian Isthmus in Finland and moving south through Belorussia and northern Ukraine, into Poland, and against southern Ukraine and Moldova. The campaign against Army Group Center would form the linchpin of the Red Army's summer offensive. With this in mind, the Stavka—the Soviet high command— assembled 178 divisions comprising nearly 1.3 million soldiers, four thousand pieces of armor, and over five thousand aircraft, giving the Soviets a nearly four-to-one advantage over the opposing German forces. Soviet commanders conducted extensive deception operations designed to convince their German counterparts that the Stavka intended to launch major offensives in the north and south that would leave Belorussia fairly quiet. The German high command took the bait and redeployed Fifty-Sixth Panzer Corps to Ukraine, giving the Soviets an even greater advantage in armor along the central front.[2]

German leaders had little inkling of the titanic forces preparing to descend on their position in Belorussia. The catastrophic defeats at Stalingrad and Kursk combined with the grinding attrition in places such as Rzhev to force the Wehrmacht into a static war of defense. Hitler's chief propagandist, Joseph Goebbels, tried to rally popular support by proclaiming that the Third Reich was defending European civilization from Eastern barbarians—an explicit invocation of the racial arguments that Europeans had used for centuries in defense of imperialism. In Goebbels's fevered rhetoric, the barbarians were at the gates and the Wehrmacht was all that stood in the path of the Jewish-Bolshevik hordes set on pillaging the West. The Nazi war for empire had been transformed into a desperate defense of the Reich. Meanwhile, the impending Allied landings in France raised the prospect of a two-front war.[3]

To counter these threats, Hitler ordered a risky new strategy. German dreams of a quick victory in the East had perished outside Moscow in the winter of 1941. Now, with American and British forces threatening the West, Germany's best hope lay in crushing the Allied landing in France. A devastating defeat along the channel coast might knock London and Washington out of the war and convince Moscow to come to terms. Meanwhile, the German troops in the East must hold the line against the Red Army through the use of fortress cities. "The 'fortified places,'" Hitler announced, "will fulfill the function of fortresses in former historical times. They will ensure that the enemy does not occupy these areas of decisive operational importance. They will allow themselves to be surrounded, thereby holding down the largest possible number of enemy forces." Although many German commanders opposed this strategy, arguing that this defensive posture would paralyze German units and do little to slow advancing Soviet forces, the Führer remained adamant. If all went according to plan, Hitler's fortresses would stop the Red Army and then function as bridgeheads for future offensives, thereby preserving the Führer's delusion of conquering a vast Eastern empire.[4]

Making matters worse, German commanders predicted that the coming Soviet offensive would seek to follow up on the previous year's successes by targeting Ukraine. Many dismissed the possibility of attack on the central sector of Belorussia because the region was choked by dense forests and the soggy Pripet Marshes, which might bog down a major offensive. Adamant that the Red Army would strike in the south, Field Marshal Walter Model convinced Hitler to move the Fifty-Sixth Panzer Corps from Army Group Center to Army Group North Ukraine, stripping the central sector of 88 percent of its tanks. As the offensive approached, then, some 336,000 German soldiers stood in the way of a force of 1.25 million Red Army troops along with thousands of partisans working behind German lines. The Wehrmacht fielded 118 tanks against 2,700 Soviet counterparts and a mere 600 aircraft would contend with 4,000 Soviet planes. In other words, the Soviets held a nearly four-to-one advantage in infantry, a nearly seven-to-one advantage in aircraft, and an over twenty-to-one advantage in tanks.[5]

OVER THE NIGHT OF JUNE 19–20, THE AREAS BEHIND ARMY GROUP Center's lines swarmed with activity as some 143,000 Soviet partisans crept through the darkness, launching a series of attacks on railways, communications, roads, and bridges. The Belorussian countryside, blanketed by forests and marshes, proved perfectly suited for guerrilla operations. In all, German command reported 9,600 explosions that set repair teams scrambling across the area and immobilized larger units. Frontline soldiers who suspected that something big was in the offing received confirmation the next day as the skies filled with thousands of Soviet aircraft flying sorties against German positions. On June 22, Soviet artillery pummeled German lines with heavy barrages. Soviet infantry followed in a massive assault that marshaled a ten-to-one advantage against the German defenders.[6]

At 6:40 a.m. on June 23, Boris Gorbachevsky, a junior officer with the Third Belorussian Front, watched as salvoes of Katyusha rockets streaked through the sky before smashing into enemy lines in front of Dubrovno. "Just try, German, to hold out!" cheered soldiers on the front line. Gorbachevsky and his comrades met "heavy walls of fire" as they charged forward. German radio broadcasts taunted the attackers as the assault ground forward. Early in the morning of the twenty-sixth, Gorbachevsky's unit finally took the town. Gorbachevsky narrowly escaped grave injury as a bullet "neatly clipped the watch off [his] left wrist and blew it to pieces."[7]

Against this onslaught, outnumbered German units staged a hopeless defense. Hitler's order to hold on to the fortified cities along the eastern front tied down thousands of German troops in the path of the Red Army. The Third Panzer Army in Vitebsk was quickly surrounded as Soviet forces enveloped the city. In a heated exchange, German chief of staff General Kurt Zeitzler begged Hitler to authorize a retreat, to no avail. Only after the Red Army had seized the last road leading out of the city did the Führer order a retreat. At 5:00 a.m. on June 26, remnants of the German garrison staged a desperate breakout. Thousands were cut down by Soviet fire as they fled across the fields outside the city. The Red Army captured ten thousand survivors. The German Fourth Army suffered a similar fate. Stationed along the eastern edge of the Belorussian salient, the army found itself facing encirclement in the early days of Bagration, but the German high command refused to authorize a retreat. Instead, Hitler demanded that his forces hold the fortress cities of Mogilev and Orsha—forcing survivors to stage another desperate retreat under heavy Soviet fire. By July 8, the Fourth Army had been destroyed aside from a few bands of soldiers who managed to find their way back to German lines weeks later. In the south, around Bobruisk, the Ninth Army was also engulfed. As the Red Army prepared to encircle the city on the morning of June 27, the defenders at Bobruisk received an order to withdraw. Fifteen minutes later, the order was rescinded, sparking panic and chaos through the German ranks. A new order to break out arrived that afternoon, but again, it came too late. Just before midnight, groups of German soldiers attempted to escape from the burning city. But dawn brought waves of Soviet warplanes that slaughtered the fleeing defenders. Soviet reports listed seventy-three thousand Germans killed, wounded, or captured at Bobruisk.[8]

While scattered bands of German soldiers fled toward Army Group Center's headquarters in Minsk, they faced a race with Soviet forces speeding toward the city. As Lieutenant Ivan Yakushin's cavalry unit rode west, he heard harrowing tales from civilians about the Nazi occupation. "In Volozhin, a small village near Molodechno, the Germans murdered the entire Jewish population," Yakushin later wrote. "They put them in barns and burned them alive." As Soviet forces pushed toward the border, they continued to face sporadic German resistance. Yakushin's unit ran across one group of defenders west of Lida. "The night was warm and quiet," he remembered. "There was no moon. Sitting in the saddle was like lying in a cradle." Suddenly, gunfire broke the silence. "The only thing we could see were the tracer bullets whizzing along the highway." The Soviet soldiers returned fire and eventually captured the German position before pressing forward. Three Soviet armies were now driving forward at a rate of nearly fifteen miles per day. On July 3, the Red Army surrounded Minsk. Soviet forces began pushing through the suburbs, past destroyed factories and into the ruined city. Over one hundred thousand German troops were now trapped. In twelve days, the Germans had lost over three hundred thousand troops.[9]

Riding in American-made Studebaker trucks and horse-drawn carts, Boris Gorbachevsky's division entered the burning city of Minsk. "After three years of German occupation," he wrote, "it represented a terrible spectacle with its emptiness, lifelessness, and destitute streets." Corpses littered the streets beneath clouds of smoke and plumes of dust drifting through the air. The crackle of gunfire and roar of explosions echoed through the ruins. Terrified citizens emerged from cellars and ditches to stare in horror at the devastation. Some residents rushed to the Soviet soldiers, offering kisses and bracing shots of homemade vodka. By evening, improvised red flags flapped from many of the buildings that still stood.[10]

The stunning success of Operation Bagration brought the Red Army to the 1941 border of the Soviet Union. As Gorbachevsky's division pushed west, it marched to the banks of the Neman River. He watched as twilight crept over the fast-moving water. "A strong, cold wind was sweeping down from the hills flanking the river," he wrote, "flinging spray from the water surface and sometimes covering me with a chilling mist." His division had passed the ruins of bread ovens dating back to the days when Napoleon's Grand Army had staged its disastrous invasion of Russia. "But Napoleon was gone," Gorbachevsky wrote, "just as Hitler himself would disappear one day." After a tense firefight with German rearguard forces, Gorbachevsky's unit continued marching westward. The following evening, the division drew within sight of the national border. Tearful soldiers embraced, cheered, and fired their guns into the air. A few men pulled out accordions and guitars and broke into song. "It seemed to all of us that the end of the war was just a stone's throw away," he wrote.[11]

From here on, the Red Army would be fighting not to drive the Nazis from Soviet territory but to liberate Eastern Europe. Stalin's vision for postwar Europe would play a seminal role in determining the shape of that liberation. From the early stages of Barbarossa, the dictator had made it clear that he intended to fight not only to reclaim Soviet territory but to "help all the peoples of Europe who were suffering under the yoke of German fascism." As his troops prepared to launch Bagration, Stalin declared, "Our tasks cannot be limited to expulsion of enemy forces from the borders of our Motherland." But the Kremlin sought more than just the downfall of the Third Reich—Soviet officials insisted that their security demanded westward expansion. As diplomat Ivan Maisky wrote in January 1944, "It is necessary to secure for the USSR peace in Europe and Asia for a period of 30–50 years. . . . With this in view, the USSR must come out of the present war with advantageous strategic borders, which must be based on the borders of 1941."[12]

Like the Western Allies, Moscow was fighting not just to defeat the Axis but to forge a new international order over which it would exercise preponderant power. Vyacheslav Molotov later echoed Maisky's thoughts: "My task as minister of foreign affairs was to expand the borders of our fatherland." And expanded borders were only the beginning. Soviet leaders would also demand friendly regimes in neighboring states.[13]

Indeed, far from simply recovering Soviet territory, Stalin intended to remake Europe. The Soviet dictator believed that the Red Army's victories would compel the Western powers to recognize a de facto Soviet sphere of influence over Eastern Europe. Meanwhile, Western Europe would remain weak, divided, and open to political competition between the great powers. Although this would not necessarily result in the communization of the continent, the Kremlin intended to emerge from the war as the preeminent power in the region. With Germany destroyed and France reduced to a third-rate power, Stalin assumed that Moscow would act as the "arbiter" of postwar European affairs.[14]

The Red Army soldiers marching into Poland would soon get their chance to put Stalin's vision of a Soviet-dominated Eastern Europe into practice. In mid-July, Soviet commanders launched the next in their series of summer operations with the Lvov-Sandomierz Offensive against Army Group North Ukraine. Soviet forces, led by General Ivan Konev, delivered a succession of devastating blows against German forces around Lvov. Making use of their overwhelming numbers, Red Army units blasted their way through enemy lines. After two weeks of heavy fighting, with Soviet troops preparing to encircle Lvov, the German defenders abandoned the city and attempted a breakout. Only five thousand Germans escaped. While Konev advanced through Ukraine, General Konstantin Rokossovsky's First Belorussian Front opened the Lublin-Brest Offensive to the north. By late July, the attackers had reached the Vistula River. Soviet commanders now wheeled north toward Warsaw.[15]

As Red Army soldiers marched deeper into Nazi-occupied territory, they heard horrific stories of starvation, forced deportation, atrocities, and mass graves. At the edge of one village, Lieutenant Yakushin saw the bodies of an entire family—parents, grandparents, and four children—who had been executed by the Germans. "Why did they kill this family?" he wondered. "And who bothered to line them up so neatly in front of that house?" Worse was yet to come.[16]

On July 22, soldiers from the Soviet Eighth Guard Army entered the partially dismantled ruins of an industrial complex on the outskirts of Lublin. They discovered about a thousand half-starved prisoners inside the vast facility that the locals called Majdanek. As the soldiers marched into the camp, they traversed a maze of barbed wire, mountains of discarded clothing, gas chambers, crematoriums, and piles of ash. Among the first to report on the camp was Soviet correspondent Konstantin Simonov. "This was a veritable slaughter house," he wrote. He saw ovens filled "with smoldering vertebrae and ashes" and walked across fields strewn with human remains. "They poured corpses like potatoes out of the trucks into the ditch. They fertilized fields with human ashes, walking like ploughmen and sowing ashes out of bags. This fertilizer stunk and contained small bits of human bones." The citizens of Lublin had learned to shut their windows when the wind blew from the southeast. "The wind brought the stench of corpses," remembered a Ukrainian writer. "It was impossible to breathe. It was impossible to eat. It was impossible to live. Majdanek's winds brought horror." British journalist Alexander Werth visited a warehouse filled with thousands of shoes and suitcases. "Then there was a long corridor with thousands of women's dresses, and another with thousands of overcoats." Outside, Werth passed mounds of cremated human remains and trenches filled with dead bodies. "The stench was still pursuing me; it now seemed to permeate everything—the dusty grass beside the barbed wire fence, and the red poppies that were naively growing in the midst of all this."[17]

Several days later, Soviet forces discovered the ruins of another camp outside of the village of Treblinka, some sixty kilometers east of Warsaw. The complex stood forlorn, surrounded by swamps, sandy soil, and thick pine forests. "These places are gloomy and deserted," wrote Jewish Ukrainian journalist Vasily Grossman. "This miserable wilderness was the place chosen by some official . . . for the construction of a vast executioner's block—an executioner's block such as the human race has never seen." Thousands of victims had arrived daily by train. Many had died en route. One survivor recalled his terrifying arrival at the camp: "Hundreds of bodies lying all around. Piles of bundles, clothes, valises, everything mixed together. SS soldiers, Germans, and Ukrainians were standing on the roofs of barracks and firing indiscriminately into the crowd. Men, women, and children fell bleeding. The air was filled with screaming and weeping." Most of those who survived the journey were stripped of their clothing and belongings before being herded into the "tube" leading to the gas chambers. Afterward, inmates forced into labor removed the bodies of those killed and carted them off to gaping ditches filled with the dead. Later, the camp's administrators ordered the corpses cremated in massive burn pits in an effort to conceal the scale of the slaughter. An estimated 925,000 Jews, along with countless Poles, Roma, and Soviet POWs, were murdered at the site.[18]

The evacuation of the camps was but one of many signs that the Third Reich had begun to crumble. As Germany's fortunes had turned over the course of 1942 and 1943, a growing number high-ranking Wehrmacht officers had come to view Hitler as a liability. The Nazi leadership had unleashed a reign of terror at home and led Germany into a disastrous war that it was now losing. Previous assassination attempts had failed. But in the summer of 1944, these disgruntled officers received another chance with the appointment of Colonel Claus von Stauffenberg to a staff position that would bring him into contact with the Führer. Stauffenberg hailed from an aristocratic Prussian family and had served in Tunisia, where he had been severely wounded, losing an arm, an eye, and several fingers. Together with a group of coconspirators, Stauffenberg hatched a plan to assassinate Hitler and stage a takeover of the German state. On July 20, 1944, Stauffenberg entered a meeting of top Nazi officials at Hitler's Wolf's

Lair headquarters outside Rastenburg in East Prussia. Stauffenberg placed a briefcase containing a bomb beneath the oak conference table near the Führer and then left the room. Some minutes later, as Stauffenberg fled the scene, the bomb exploded, killing four officers and injuring several others, including Hitler. An enraged Führer and his staff quickly rounded up Stauffenberg and his accomplices and had them executed.[19]

Stauffenberg's plot was just one of the revolts underway. As the Red Army entered Poland, the resistance fighters of the Polish Home Army prepared to rise up and liberate Warsaw. Polish leaders recognized the precarious nature of their position. Although they despised the German occupation, few Poles had reason to see advancing Soviet forces as liberators. Moscow had joined Berlin in dismembering Poland in 1939, and the Soviet NKVD had slaughtered thousands of Polish officers and intellectuals in the Katyn Forest massacre. The Home Army's commanders calculated that their best hope lay in staging uprisings timed to take advantage of the chaos of the German retreat. Polish commanders hoped that these uprisings would establish the Home Army as a credible force and bolster its claims to power in postwar Poland. The odds of success were slim, but to do otherwise would have allowed Moscow to argue that the Poles had done nothing while Soviet soldiers drove the Nazis from Poland. As July came to a close, it appeared that the time had come. Soviet tanks had been sighted in Warsaw's eastern suburbs, Hitler had narrowly survived an assassination plot, and Moscow had established a puppet government of pro-Soviet Poles in Lublin. It was now or never.[20]

At 5:00 p.m. on August 1, thousands of Polish fighters wearing red-and-white armbands poured into the streets of Warsaw to launch a series of attacks against German positions. Their objective was to hold out for two to six days, until the Red Army arrived. Fierce clashes raged across the city as German security forces—alerted earlier to the possibility of a revolt—struggled to fend off the attacks. The resistance managed to gain control of the tallest skyscraper in the city, the Prudential building, along with the main post office, rail station, and power plant. But these victories came at a heavy cost. Some two thousand partisans were killed in this initial round of fighting. The next day, resistance fighters marched through the streets as throngs of citizens cheered. One partisan remembered that "thousands of people lined the streets, throwing flowers and crying. It was a very moving scene." The revolt continued through the next day, and the next. The Home Army held out in the face of German counterattacks, but the Soviets were not yet in the city. On August 5, the German governor-general Hans Frank notified Berlin that Warsaw was in flames. "Burning down the houses is the most reliable means of liquidating the insurgent's hideouts." The toll on the population was horrendous, he explained. "Warsaw will be punished with complete destruction after the suppression or collapse of the rising."[21]

The partisans had made a fatal miscalculation. While the Home Army died on the streets of Warsaw, the Soviet advance toward the capital stalled. German forces under Field Marshal Model's command faced a potential catastrophe—Warsaw remained a vital logistical hub, and its loss would threaten the entire German position along the eastern front and leave the Soviets with an open path to the coast of the Baltic Sea. On August 1, in a desperate bid to stop the Red Army's advance, Model sent four armored divisions to attack the Soviet tanks threatening Warsaw. The attack caught Soviet forces by surprise. The Red Army was already operating at the outer limits of its supply line, and its forces were mostly spent. Model's assault tore through the Soviet vanguard, knocked out 547 tanks, and halted six weeks of Wehrmacht defeats. With their troops stalled in secure positions along the eastern banks of the Vistula River, Soviet commanders turned their attention north to the Baltic states and south to the Balkans. Moscow had no intention of overhauling its strategic plans in order to aid a group of anti-Soviet insurgents fighting through the sewers and streets of Warsaw.[22]

All of this spelled catastrophe for the Home Army and the citizens of Warsaw. After halting Soviet forces, German troops turned their wrath on the capital. One German conscript remembered seeing piles of the dead outside an Orthodox church. "Men, women, children, and old people—obviously innocent refugees who had been rounded up and shot, every last one of them. Flies swarmed round the corpses and the pools of blood. Other bodies were piled up on barrows." When the soldier complained that Azerbaijani auxiliaries were behind some of the killing, an SS officer told him that "it was very good for the Poles to see what would have happened had we not saved them from the Asiatics." As the insurgency raged on, Himmler issued an order to massacre the population, insurgent and civilian alike. Over the course of August 5 and 6, the SS troops spearheaded the brutal massacre of perhaps forty thousand civilians in the Wola neighborhood. German forces cleared barricades by using women and children as human shields and torching buildings as they pushed through the city. One pregnant woman who survived the massacre remembered seeing a "heap of bodies a meter high." A nurse working with the insurgents watched in horror as Germans and Ukrainians stormed into her hospital and "dashed the heads of those lying on the ground with their boots, screaming horribly as they did it. Blood and brains were spattered in all directions." Another eyewitness wrote that the "dead [were] buried in backyards and squares." Citizens scoured the ruins in search of food and drew water from a handful of wells around the city. "All quarters of the town are under shell fire and there are many fires."[23]

As Axis forces razed Warsaw, the Red Army lingered on the city's outskirts. Prime Minister Churchill, who had watched his nation go to war over the German invasion of Poland, was apoplectic. "Good God," he told his personal doctor, Lord Moran, in early August, "can't you see that the Russians are spreading across Europe like a tide; they have invaded Poland and there is nothing to prevent them marching into Turkey and Greece!" In a cable to Stalin, Churchill warned that the situation in Warsaw had become desperate. "Our people cannot

BAGRATION AND THE FATE OF THE EAST

understand why no material help has been sent from outside to the Poles in Warsaw," he wrote. Moscow's failure to aid the partisans, combined with its refusal to allow Allied aircraft to drop supplies to the partisans, had raised alarm in London. "Your Government's action in preventing this help being sent seems to us at variance with the spirit of the Allied cooperation to which you and we attach so much importance both for the present and the future." The US ambassador to Moscow, W. Averell Harriman, struck a similar tone in warning Soviet officials that the decision to block aid to the partisans constituted "a grave mistake and that it would have serious repercussions in Washington and London." Harriman followed up in a cable to President Roosevelt expressing his concern that Moscow's "refusal is based not on operational difficulties or denial that the resistance exists but on ruthless political considerations."[24]

Stalin scoffed at US and British appeals, insisting that the Home Army was merely a "group of criminals, who have embarked on the Warsaw adventure in order to seize power." The partisans had drawn the citizens of Warsaw into a hopeless fight, he wrote, "throwing many almost unarmed people against German guns, tanks and aircraft." Meanwhile, representatives of the Polish government in exile reported that Soviet officials had begun rounding up civil administration and Home Army troops and interning them at the Majdanek concentration camp. "In this way after 5 years of unrelenting resistance against the Germans, for which we pay with our blood, the Polish nation is coming under the no less cruel slavery of one of the Allies," the Polish chargé d'affaires wrote. "We are fighting on the ruins of Warsaw ablaze, that we shall go on fighting for independence and that we shall continue to defend the latter against any kind of imperialism."[25]

As the crisis dragged on, a dour mood fell over the US embassy in Moscow. Ambassador Harriman's personal assistant denounced Stalin's refusal to aid the insurgents as "a case of cold-blooded murder" but admitted, "There is nothing we can do about it. When the full story of this incident comes out it will certainly go down in history as one of the most infamous deeds of war. Beneath all their veneer of civilisation, the ruling elements here are nothing but a highly intelligent and ruthless gang of thugs and murderers." The chargé d'affaires, George Kennan, wrote that the massacre in Warsaw, "more than anything that had occurred to that point, brought the Western governments face to face with what they were up against in Stalin's Polish policy." The Soviet refusal to facilitate US and British supply drops to the Poles was "a gauntlet thrown down, in a spirit of malicious glee, before the Western powers." Western leaders now understood that Stalin had no intention of allowing Washington and London any say in the future of political power in Poland.[26]

Soviet leaders bristled at claims that the pause outside Warsaw was part of a plan to eliminate the Home Army. The Soviet Union had made enormous sacrifices in the fight against the Third Reich, and hundreds of thousands more soldiers would die as the Red Army drove the Wehrmacht from Poland. Soviet troops continued fighting to cross the Vistula, but they now faced fierce German opposition. The commander of Soviet forces outside Warsaw, Marshal Konstantin Rokossovsky, ridiculed the suggestion that the Red Army had halted its offensive so as to avoid having to fight the insurgents: "Do you think that we would not have taken Warsaw if we had been able to do it? The whole idea that we are in any sense afraid of the [Home Army] is too idiotically absurd." Stalin insisted that the current debacle was the result of reckless decisions by the partisans and suggested that the entire tragedy could have been avoided if Polish leaders had simply chosen to coordinate the uprising with Red Army commanders. Soviet forces would begin their own supply drops to the insurgents later in September, but they would come too late to save the partisans. By the time the Red Army finally took Warsaw, thousands of citizens had been killed, the city lay in ruins, and most of the insurgents were either dead or captured.[27]

THE WARSAW UPRISING CAST A PALL OVER THE GRAND ALLIANCE, confirming widespread suspicions that Stalin intended to establish a brutal imperial system across the lands he conquered. For the time being, however, the Red Army remained the single most powerful force contesting the Third Reich. Unless Washington and London were willing to accept far greater casualties among their own armies while risking a war with the Soviet Union, there was little Western leaders could do. Moreover, Poland was not the only nation in the Red Army's path. While the battle raged in Warsaw, Soviet troops were preparing to overrun the Balkans, the Baltic states, Czechoslovakia, Hungary, and Romania. The rapidly expanding area under Soviet control occupied the minds of Western leaders through much of 1944. In late May, the British ambassador to the United States, Lord Halifax, had approached Secretary of State Cordell Hull with a proposal to grant Moscow a controlling influence in Romania in return for recognition of a British sphere of influence in Greece. Churchill followed up with a telegram to Roosevelt urging the president to endorse the proposal. The Americans balked. "In our opinion," Roosevelt responded, "this would certainly result in the persistence of differences between you and the Soviets and in the division of the Balkan region into spheres of influence."[28]

While US officials rejected the idea of dividing Europe—at least officially—leaders in London and Moscow took a more cynical approach to planning for the postwar world. In early October, Churchill returned to the Kremlin to discuss the topic with Stalin. Late in the evening of October 9, 1944, the prime minister sat down with the Soviet dictator. "Let us settle our affairs in the Balkans," he suggested before scrawling his proposal on a sheet of paper. The Soviets would acquire 90 percent influence in Romania, and the British would receive 90 percent influence in Greece. Moscow and London would share fifty-fifty influence in Yugoslavia and Hungary, and the Soviets would receive a 75 percent influence in Bulgaria. Stalin studied the proposal for a moment before writing a large blue check on the paper. Churchill then suggested that the paper be destroyed. "Might it not be thought rather cynical if it seemed we had disposed of these issues, so fateful to millions of people, in such an offhand manner? Let us burn the paper." But Stalin demurred. "No, you keep it," the dictator replied. Churchill would later dismiss this "naughty document" as simply an attempt to gauge Stalin's position on the future status of Eastern Europe. In reality, however, the percentages agreement revealed a deeper conviction: both London and Moscow anticipated a return to the prewar imperial politics in the postwar world. Moreover, the Kremlin could justifiably argue that the Americans had already established a precedent for splitting Europe into separate spheres with their decision to lock the Soviets out of postwar Italy.[29] In addition, Washington's long embrace of the Monroe Doctrine—which effectively claimed the entire Western Hemisphere as a US sphere of influence—led many leaders in both London and Moscow to view American pearl-clutching over such matters with skepticism.

The United States maintained a deeply ambiguous relationship with imperialism and great power politics. Although the nation had been created by the imperial conquest of North America, many Americans remained ambivalent if not hostile to the concept of formal imperialism. Nevertheless, Washington controlled overseas colonies in the Caribbean and the Pacific and acted as a quasi-imperial police power in Latin America. Moreover, a growing number of American officials had begun to develop plans to exercise hegemony in the postwar order. However, in contrast to its allies, the Roosevelt administration placed its hopes for postwar peace not in a return to Machiavellian great power politics but rather in the creation of an international organization charged with overseeing world peace. Although it grew out of earlier conceptions of liberal internationalism, this new organization would avoid the pitfalls that had doomed the League of Nations. Beyond the stated role of securing world peace, the White House saw this new international organization as key to ensuring long-term American participation in the defense of the international order. Roosevelt had long understood that the nation had little appetite for traditional imperial politics. Drawing from a long history of "splendid isolation" from European affairs, American voters would turn against any elected leader who asked them to fight a war in order to restore the pre-1939 spheres of influence. Support for a world peace organization, however, promised to banish the specter of isolationism once and for all.[30]

Leadership in what would become the United Nations Organization would also give the United States a central role in shaping the postwar international order. If successful, the future United Nations would serve as the arbiter of international law, differentiating legitimate from illegitimate warfare and sanctioning the use of international violence. While the American people might recoil at the use of US military power in a straightforward colonial intervention, a military operation sanctioned by the United Nations would receive widespread public support. This same dynamic might also serve to legitimize American military power in the eyes of foreign peoples. As historian Stephen Wertheim argues, US policymakers consciously "fashioned the United Nations as an instrument to implement power politics by the United States." In this way, the future United Nations would form a cornerstone of a postwar liberal international order framed and led by the United States.[31]

In Roosevelt's vision, the victorious Allies—Britain, China, the Soviet Union, and the United States—would work in concert as four regional "policemen," ensuring collective security and facilitating economic cooperation. The result would be a new world cleansed of the treacherous diplomacy that had helped generate the last two world wars. As Secretary of State Hull told Congress in November 1943, "There will no longer be need for spheres of influence, for balance of power, or any other of the special arrangements through which, in the unhappy past, the nations strove to safeguard their security or to promote their interests." American economic dominance would provide the economic foundations for this new world order. By the end of the war, the United States would produce half of the world's manufactured goods and boast a gross national product triple that of the Soviet Union and nearly five times larger than Britain's.[32]

The July 1944 United Nations Monetary and Financial Conference, held in Bretton Woods, New Hampshire, brought together delegates from forty-four nations to deliberate on the terms of this new international economic system. Building on ideas articulated in the Atlantic Charter, the conference established the International Monetary Fund and the World Bank, which would provide the institutional infrastructure for cooperation between states in this new liberal order. The foundation of this entire system would be the US dollar—tied to gold at thirty-five dollars per ounce—which would serve as the global reserve currency used to establish the value of all currencies. This distinction would give Washington unprecedented financial influence in the postwar world, adding to the nation's overwhelming industrial might, which accounted for 60 percent of the world's combined manufacturing. The United States would thus emerge in a commanding position over the global economic order at the end of the war. In this way, Wall Street would supplant London as the world's leading financial center, completing a decades-long changing of the guard. Put together, one scholar argues, these efforts constituted "the most far-reaching international order building ever attempted."[33]

Although Roosevelt's critics castigated this internationalist approach as naive, the president's actions hinted at a sort of higher realism—an understanding that the United States could best exercise influence over a postwar order built on free-trade principles and structured by institutions such as the United Nations rather than through colonialism and brute force.[34] If successful, this postwar liberal order would render spheres of influence and formal imperialism obsolete, replacing them with a rules-based, institutional framework for collective security, free trade, and economic cooperation—all of which would be underwritten by American economic might and defended by Allied military power. The United States would exercise unprecedented global influence not through military force or economic coercion but through the creation of a worldwide institutional framework modeled on the American system. But the ultimate viability of this new order would hinge on the active support of the great powers after the end of the war. Measures such as Churchill's percentages agreement, Soviet attempts to eliminate the Polish resistance, and British and French efforts to restore their imperial privileges all threatened US plans to create a postwar collective security organization.

As August 1944 came to an end, the war's carnage enveloped an ever-growing section of continental Europe. From the ruined villages of Normandy and the heavily bombed cities of Germany to the blood-soaked ruins of Warsaw and the haunting wreckage of Poland's death camps, Europe was being transformed into a vast cemetery. Despite the destruction, Allied leaders had much to celebrate. Operation Bagration constituted one of the greatest defeats in German military history. Between that and Overlord's success, the Nazi empire had suffered two staggering blows. The Allied armies were closing in from both east and west. Having won these victories, however, the Allies faced the problem of what to do with them. Looking to the future, Germany's defeat would leave a geopolitical vacuum in Europe, raising the possibility of a new round of great power competition on the continent. Indeed, London and Washington had made it clear that they had no intention of giving Moscow a hand in occupying Italy. Now, the Kremlin's refusal to give assistance to Polish fighters in Warsaw sent an ominous signal of Soviet plans for Eastern Europe and seemed to validate the grim predictions offered by Moscow's staunchest critics in the West: Hitler's empire would fall only to be replaced by Stalin's.

Faced with this prospect, Churchill and Stalin reverted to back-room deals aimed at dividing Europe into spheres of influence. Although this approach smacked of the sort of old-fashioned imperial politics that had helped plunge Europe into two world wars, it was an attempt to arrive at a mutual understanding between the great powers. In contrast, the Roosevelt administration redoubled its efforts to use the war's massive dislocations to overhaul the entire international order, replacing it with a new American-led system guided by the ideals of free trade and collective security. The coming months would determine which of these visions would triumph.

Chapter 17

WE CAN LAND
ANYWHERE

MERICAN WAR CORRESPONDENT ROBERT SHERROD CAUGHT HIS
first sight of Saipan from the deck of the transport *Bolivar* on
the morning of June 15, 1944. To Sherrod, the island looked like
"a low-lying prehistoric monster whose high, rising spine was Mt.
Tapotchau [*sic*]." Both Tokyo and Washington recognized Saipan as
a launchpad for attacks against Japan itself. As such, Japanese commanders could be expected to mount an all-out defense. "If we can
land on Saipan," Sherrod wrote, "we can land anywhere there are Japanese." To seize the island, the Americans arrived with an armada
of 535 ships and nearly 130,000 troops. Sherrod watched as the fleet
began shelling the beaches, transforming Saipan into "a furnace seen
through a haze." As his landing craft neared shore, Sherrod caught
the bitter stink of gunpowder drifting across the water. Twenty minutes after the first marines hit the beaches, the Americans had landed

some eight thousand troops on Saipan. To a Japanese observer watching the landings, the oncoming marines looked "like a swarm of
grasshoppers." Sherrod finally made it to shore at 2:30 p.m. and threw
himself behind shelter inside a tank trap as mortar shells rained down
around him. The barrage continued through the night and into the
next morning. "Saipan was going to be a long job," Sherrod wrote,
"much longer than we had anticipated."[1]

Together with Overlord and Bagration, the invasion of Saipan
marked the third great Allied offensive of June 1944. The invasion
also promised to be a turning point in the Pacific War. The clashes
at Midway and Guadalcanal had seen a rough parity between
US and Japanese forces; the Battles of Tarawa, Rabaul, and Truk
had cracked Tokyo's outer defenses. At Saipan, US forces poured
through the breach and gained a foothold within striking distance
of the Japanese home islands. Saipan's defenders waged a suicidal
defense of the island, but they were overwhelmed by the weight of
the American assault. Few observers now doubted that this was the
beginning of the end. While American armies stormed the beaches
of Normandy and continued their slog through the mountains of
Italy halfway around the world, US leaders were able to sustain two
full-blown ocean-spanning campaigns in the Pacific. The United
States had become the first power in world history to develop planetary force-projection capabilities.

THROUGHOUT 1943, US STRATEGY IN THE PACIFIC HAD BEEN TORN BY
a heated strategic debate. As Nimitz's lethal fast carrier groups knifed
across the ocean, General Douglas MacArthur had grown increasingly concerned that his own campaign in the south was falling to
second place. The general insisted that the navy's carriers should
be used to support his drive toward the Philippines. Nimitz, fresh on
the heels of his victories in the Gilberts and Marshalls, argued that the
most direct route to Tokyo lay across the Central Pacific. Nimitz's carrier task forces constituted the most awesome constellation of naval

power ever assembled—"To confine them to narrow seas commanded by enemy land-based aircraft," wrote historian Samuel Eliot Morison, "would be idiotic." The top planners in Washington were inclined to agree. While MacArthur's forces faced a brutal slog through the jungles of the Philippines, Nimitz's carriers were poised to begin seizing island bases within striking distance of Tokyo. "The Marianas are the key of the situation," Admiral Ernest King had explained at the Casablanca Conference in January 1943, "because of their location on the Japanese line of communications." The capture of the islands would breach Japan's inner defenses and provide US forces with fleet and air bases to stage long-range air strikes against the home islands and enforce a punishing blockade against Japanese shipping. On March 12, 1944, the Joint Chiefs issued a directive outlining these priorities.[2]

That American leaders enjoyed the luxury of choosing between multiple Pacific offensives while also fighting a massive land war in Europe was testament to the United States' astonishing industrial and engineering prowess. American supply lines stretched across 7,000 miles of ocean from San Francisco to Brisbane and another 1,500 miles from Brisbane to Guadalcanal. After making this journey, supplies arrived on remote Pacific islands with no modern ports, no warehouses, and no rail networks. Ultimately, it would fall to American naval engineers to maintain these ever-lengthening lines of communication. While construction teams scrambled to build and maintain airfields and port facilities in the south, mobile supply bases composed of fuel tankers, service ships, and supply vessels ferried provisions to the American battle fleet in the Central Pacific. "The war in the Pacific," wrote historian Ronald Spector, "was an engineer's war as well as a naval, air, and amphibious war."[3]

By June 1944, the focus of these efforts had fallen on the Marianas, a chain of fifteen rocky islands, four of which were suitable for military bases. Of these, Saipan sat the closest to Japan, some 1,250 miles southeast of Tokyo. Comprising an area of some seventy square miles, Saipan was dominated by Mount Tapochau rising some 1,500 feet above the surrounding coastal plains and sugar plantations. Hills in the north met the sea along a series of dramatic cliffs while southern flatlands proved suitable for an airstrip some 3,600 feet long. Ferdinand Magellan, the first Westerner to visit the islands, arrived in 1521. Saipan remained part of Spain's empire until 1899, when it was sold to Germany. Japan established a mandate after Germany's defeat in the First World War and began working to develop the island. By the 1930s, Japanese leaders had begun making plans for naval and air bases on Saipan, and Japanese colonists outnumbered the native Chamorros. With the onset of the war, the island became an important supply depot for the empire's communications with the wider Pacific.[4]

To the west, the great blue expanse of Philippine Sea stretched some 1,500 miles to Luzon. A generation of American and Japanese planners had looked to these waters as the most likely site for a decisive battle between their two fleets. Drawing on Alfred Thayer Mahan's theories, both Washington and Tokyo believed that a climactic fleet battle would ultimately determine the outcome of the war. For Tokyo, the Marianas held an added significance as the inner ring of islands guarding the approaches to Japan itself. If Japanese defenses failed here, there would be nothing left to stop the American advance. Clouds of enemy planes would swarm over the home islands while a fleet of hostile ships plied the waters of the Japanese archipelago. The Marianas must hold if Japan had any hope left of winning the war. With this in mind, the commander of the Japanese Combined Fleet, Admiral Mineichi Koga, determined to steam forward and meet the American fleet as it approached the islands. Koga would get his decisive battle, but he would not live to see it. At the end of March 1944, the admiral's plane disappeared in a storm off the coast of the Philippines. However, his successor, Admiral Soemu Toyoda, hewed to Koga's overall plan. "We must achieve our objectives by crushing with one stroke the nucleus of the great enemy concentration of forces . . . in one decisive battle."[5]

On the morning of June 13, sailors aboard seven American battleships gazed across the water at Saipan as their heavy guns began a preparatory bombardment of the beaches. The following day, two teams of frogmen mapped the reefs and cleared the approaches for the landing ships. At 8:13 on the morning of June 15, the assault began. Eight hundred landing craft ferried eight thousand marines to shore in the first twenty minutes. Japanese defenders unleashed a hail of machine gun, mortar, and artillery fire, but the Americans managed to take all of the planned beachheads along a four-mile front. By the end of the day, twenty thousand marines had landed and advanced 1,500 yards from the shore. However, Japanese defenses were far heavier than expected.[6]

American marine Frank Borta and his unit were caught in no-man's-land between US and Japanese lines and forced to wait through the night as tracer rounds from both sides flashed just over their heads. Just before dawn, Borta's sergeant ordered the men to fix bayonets in anticipation of a Japanese counterattack that never came. After crawling back to American lines, Borta encountered a gruesome scene: "We saw bodies, Marine bodies, arms, legs, heads, from artillery." One of his close friends had had his head "blown off" and another member of his platoon had been cut in two. Dozens of dead and wounded littered the beach. The survivors now faced a savage fight against Japanese forces dug into multiple defensive echelons throughout Saipan's interior. Borta's unit pressed forward into flooded rice paddies as snipers took potshots at the Americans and artillery shells arced overhead. Borta later remembered the following days as a blur of bitter fighting, "just the process of continually fighting on ridges and hills, and casualties." Sharp coral wore holes in boots and ripped trousers to shreds. The nights were lit by the sick yellow light of flares fired up over the battlefield. Japanese infiltrators crept into American foxholes or attacked patrols bringing up supplies to the front lines. The battle became "a continued meat grinder," Borta explained. "A good day we'd lose ten percent; a bad day, anywhere from fifteen to twenty percent casualties."[7]

OUT AT SEA, SPRUANCE'S FLEET FACED A DIFFERENT THREAT. ON JUNE 13, elements of the Japanese Combined Fleet under the command of Admiral Jisaburo Ozawa steamed out of the harbor at Tawi Tawi. An American submarine lurking in the waters nearby reported the fleet's movements to American commanders. Two days later, a second American submarine sighted a second force of enemy ships heading toward Saipan. Spruance determined that the landing forces must be protected at all costs and ordered that the fleet adopt a defensive posture rather than sailing out to engage the approaching Japanese warships. Admiral Marc Mitscher, commander of the American carriers, disagreed. A former naval aviator, Mitscher was convinced that aircraft carriers were best employed as offensive weapons and was eager to unleash the US Navy's most formidable weapons against the enemy fleet. But Spruance's caution prevailed, and the American carriers moved to cover Saipan. At 7:30 a.m. on June 19, Japanese scout planes sighted Mitscher's task force and reported its position to the Japanese fleet 380 miles to the west. From this position, Ozawa could strike the US fleet while remaining out of range of a possible counterattack. At 10:00 a.m., the first group of sixty-nine Japanese aircraft appeared on American radar. Mitscher scrambled 140 planes to intercept.[8]

Although they were unable to attack Ozawa's carriers, the Americans enjoyed several distinct advantages. The fleet's radar systems gave US commanders ample warning of the Japanese attack. US fighter planes—particularly the F6F Hellcat—outclassed and outnumbered their Japanese counterparts. And perhaps most importantly, American pilots had received at least two years of training and over three hundred hours of flight time; in contrast, Japanese pilots had received no more than six months' training, and many had received as little as two. Nearly all of Japan's veteran pilots who had led the attack on Pearl Harbor had been lost in the years of fighting over Midway, Guadalcanal, Rabaul, and Truk. The American advantages would now make themselves apparent. At the controls of one F6F, Lieutenant Alex Vraciu gazed out into the clear blue sky at a group of at least fifty enemy planes. "This could develop into a once-in-a-lifetime fighter pilot's dream," he thought. Over the next eight minutes, Vraciu downed six Japanese planes. Vraciu's fellow pilots had similar luck, destroying 358 Japanese aircraft over the course of the day to a loss of only 33 American planes. "Glancing backwards to where we had begun," Vraciu remembered, "in a pattern thirty-five miles long, there were flaming oil slicks in the water and smoke still hanging in the air." The battle had been so one-sided that one pilot compared it to a turkey shoot.[9]

While American pilots tore through Ozawa's aircraft, US submarines stalked the Japanese carriers to the west. Just before 9:10 a.m., the USS *Albacore* launched six torpedoes at Ozawa's flagship, the new carrier *Taiho*. Twenty-seven seconds later, the crew heard the sound of an explosion. One torpedo had struck the carrier's starboard side, jamming its forward plane elevator and sending torrents of gasoline into its pit. The *Taiho*'s damage control teams scrambled to make repairs, but Ozawa remained confident. Three hours later, a second submarine, the USS *Cavalla*, sighted Ozawa's ships. The *Cavalla* fired a quick spread of six torpedoes at the *Shokaku*, three of which found the Japanese carrier. Gasoline fires erupted through the carrier as the submarine dodged over a hundred depth charges. At 3:00 p.m., the crew of the *Cavalla* heard a series of explosions that ripped apart the *Shokaku*, sending the carrier and 1,200 of its crew to their doom. Thirty-two minutes later, gasoline fumes aboard the *Taiho* ignited, tearing into the flight deck and destroying the engine room. Ozawa's staff abandoned ship and watched as the pride of the Japanese fleet sank below the waves along with some 1,600 sailors. By the end of June 19, Ozawa had lost two carriers and nearly four hundred aircraft.[10]

The following morning, Spruance authorized Mitscher to pursue Ozawa's fleet. The full magnitude of Japanese losses was not yet clear to either side. Ozawa believed that most of his missing pilots had landed on Guam after dealing grievous blows to the US carriers; Spruance knew that the US submarines had damaged—but not necessarily sunk—at least one Japanese carrier. American planes scoured the seas through January 20 until 3:42 p.m., when a TBF Avenger spotted Ozawa's ships 270 miles to the northwest. At that distance, American planes would be operating at the limits of their range and would be forced to perform treacherous night landings upon their return. Determined to attack the enemy fleet, Mitscher ordered 216 planes into the air. An updated report that Ozawa's ships were sixty miles farther west likewise failed to change Mitscher's mind. At 6:25 p.m., Mitscher's planes appeared over the Japanese fleet. American Helldivers sent bombs into the carrier *Zuikaku* while Avenger torpedo planes hit the carrier *Hiyo*. Japanese sailors managed to save the badly damaged *Zuikaku*, but the *Hiyo* sank that night. With darkness looming, American pilots, low on fuel, faced an arduous journey back to their carriers. Many chose to ditch in groups, hoping that by staying together, they would increase their chances of rescue. Those pilots lucky enough to make it back to the carriers were greeted with the dazzling spectacle of Mitscher's fleet illuminated by dozens of floodlights. Searchlights pointing into the night sky served as beacons to the returning planes. A crew member aboard the *Belleau Wood* compared it to "a big city at night," while a pilot likened it to "Coney Island on the Fourth of July." Eighty of the 216 American planes ditched in the sea or crashed while landing and another twenty planes went missing. US ships recovered 160 of the 209 lost aviators, bringing the total US losses in the operation to 49.[11]

As the remnants of Ozawa's fleet limped away, the lopsided nature of the Battle of the Philippine Sea came into focus. The long-awaited decisive fleet battle with the United States had resulted in the loss of three carriers and 476 planes, along with most of their pilots. Many American leaders—and Mitscher in particular—seethed over Spruance's decision to take a defensive posture. Such prudence, they insisted, had squandered an opportunity to destroy the Japanese Combined Fleet once and for all. Rarely have the victors in such a decisive battle expressed such recriminations. Although the Americans had not annihilated Ozawa's carrier force, they had delivered a mauling from which Japan's naval aviators would never recover.

Stripped of their trained pilots, Japan's six remaining carriers were of little use.[12]

DESPITE OZAWA'S CRUSHING DEFEAT, THE JAPANESE SOLDIERS ON Saipan fought on in what was now a hopeless defense engineered to extract the greatest possible price in blood from the Americans. US forces had pushed past the beaches to move east and north into the island. On the western flank, the Second Marine Division faced rough terrain crisscrossed by rocky hills and plunging ravines and choked by dense thickets of trees and vines. Japanese defenders waited for the advancing marines in machine gun nests and hidden caves, making any advance slow and treacherous. The marines took the summit of Mount Tapochau on June 25, but fierce fighting lay ahead. Meanwhile, the Fourth Marine Division worked its way up the eastern side of Saipan across more level terrain. Even so, Japanese soldiers dug into the hills used reverse-slope tactics to exact a heavy price on the American advance. This left the army's Twenty-Seventh Division with the job of pushing north up the center of the island. The Twenty-Seventh National Guard Division, which had seen its best officers reassigned to plug holes in other units and its ranks filled with draftees, faced the daunting task of moving through the valley east of Mount Tapochau beneath the watchful gaze of Japanese machine guns and artillery hidden in the surrounding heights. While the marines pushed up the flanks, the army's advance slowed to a crawl. Faced with repeated delays, the marine commander Holland Smith finally chose to sack the army's commander, General Ralph Smith, igniting a firestorm of controversy that would rage for generations. Nevertheless, the army's grinding advance continued until July 4, when the division reached Saipan's northwestern coast.[13]

On the morning of July 6, the commander of Japanese forces on Saipan, General Yoshitsugo Saito, issued an order to his remaining soldiers to launch a final suicide attack on US forces. "Whether we attack or whether we stay where we are," he wrote, "there is only death. However, in death there is life. We must utilize this opportunity to exalt true Japanese manhood. I will advance with those who remain to deliver still another blow to the American Devils and leave my bones on Saipan as a bulwark of the Pacific." That evening, thousands of Japanese soldiers began gathering at rendezvous points in order to answer Saito's call. They carried whatever weapons they still possessed—guns, knives, bamboo poles, bayonets. American forces, listening in the darkness, fired 2,666 artillery shells into the gathering ranks, disrupting the attack and pushing it back several hours. At 4:45 the next morning, the charge began. "As it was getting light all hell broke out," remembered one soldier. "We could see from our view point waves of the enemy storming south, hundreds of them, extending from the water's edge east to the hill where we were and as far north as we could see." Masses of Japanese troops swarmed over American positions, overwhelming the defenders with their sheer numbers. "There were so many of them you could just shut your eyes and pull the trigger on your rifle and you'd be bound to hit three or four with the one shot," remembered one sergeant. Fighting continued through the morning and into the afternoon as the attackers overran American positions only to be cut down as they pushed forward. By the time the fighting stopped, some four hundred Americans lay dead alongside four thousand Japanese. American commanders brought in bulldozers to clear the piles of Japanese dead, burying them in long trenches. Bodies, crawling with maggots, became swollen in the intense heat. One sergeant remembered that "you couldn't take a step without stepping on bodies or body parts."[14]

However, for many troops of Saipan, the most disturbing scenes still lay ahead. Saipan had been home to thousands of Japanese civilians who had been bombarded with tales of American brutality. Fearing rape, torture, and dishonor, throngs of civilians died by suicide, throwing themselves from cliffs into the sea or gathering around exploding grenades. Others who attempted to surrender were killed by Japanese soldiers. US interpreters and captured Japanese pleaded with the survivors to surrender, promising food, water, and medical care, but hundreds chose to take their own lives. Even battle-hardened marines were traumatized by the sight of parents throwing their children off cliffs to their deaths. Both American and Japanese propaganda would make use of the images—the former as evidence of Japanese brutality, the latter as an example of making the ultimate sacrifice for the emperor.[15]

With the impending capture of Saipan, the seizure of the other main islands in the Marianas, Tinian and Guam, were foregone conclusions. Leaders in Tokyo recognized the fall of the Marianas as irrefutable evidence that the empire was losing the war. "We can no longer direct the war with any hope of success," the War Journal of Imperial Headquarters argued in July. "The only course left is for Japan's one hundred million people to sacrifice their lives by charging the enemy to make them lose the will to fight." The Combined Fleet had lost three large carriers and most of its air wing to enemy forces, and American troops were on the verge of gaining a foothold within striking distance of Japan's major cities. "If we ever lose Saipan, repeated air attacks on Tokyo will follow," Emperor Hirohito had warned. "No matter what it takes, we have to hold there." The fleet's strategists scrambled to throw together a plan to reinforce the beleaguered troops on Saipan, but Ozawa's losses in the Battle of the Philippine Sea rendered any sustained defense of the island fantastical. On June 24, the emperor's advisers admitted that the situation was hopeless. Prime Minister Hideki Tojo's resignation followed some three weeks later. The Allied advances in the Marianas had created "an unprecedented great national crisis," he warned the nation. He then slipped back into the realm of fantasy: "The situation now approaches when opportunity will occur to crack the enemy and to win victory."[16]

For more realistic observers, the conquest of Saipan provided a vivid demonstration of the Americans' ability to project overwhelming power across the world's largest ocean and secure uncontested control over the land, air, and sea. The Americans had staged a successful amphibious assault across one thousand miles of open ocean and, in the process, all but wiped out Japan's carrier wing. The Marianas constituted a vital bastion in Japan's inner defensive ring, and the empire's failure to hold them eliminated all reasonable doubts regarding the war's ultimate outcome. "Now, as never before, the United States was truly at the Empire's threshold," the official marine history explained. "A strong, hard fist was hammering on Japan's front door." In short, the victory on Saipan represented "the beginning of the end."[17]

THE CONQUEST OF THE MARIANAS PRESENTED AMERICAN LEADERS with a new set of questions. The Joint Chiefs' plan for the defeat of Japan from 1943 had envisioned an effort to seize Formosa, Luzon, and the South China coast in order to build airfields in China that would, in turn, bring Allied forces one step closer to Japan. On paper, this plan helped justify the double-pronged offensive under MacArthur's army forces in the southwest Pacific and Nimitz's naval forces in the Central Pacific. However, the crushing success of the navy's Central Pacific campaign raised the prospect of dropping the Philippines from the list of US targets. If US carriers and marine assault troops could repeat the success of Saipan on islands such as Formosa and Okinawa—rendering them staging grounds for a possible invasion of Japan—why not bypass the more distant Philippines entirely?

Political considerations formed one rationale for keeping the campaign on the table. MacArthur insisted that he be allowed to "liberate" Manila, thereby fulfilling his promise to return to the islands. MacArthur remained a celebrity with the American public, and his potential to threaten Roosevelt's 1944 bid for a fourth presidential term should not be dismissed. However, the Philippines also served as a powerful symbol of American prestige. Occupied by US forces in the wake of the 1898 Spanish-American War, the islands remained the largest US colony through the first four decades of the twentieth century. For American leaders, the Philippines constituted a cornerstone of US power in Asia. Moreover, with the US Congress's 1934 promise to grant independence to the Philippines, the islands became a testament to Washington's commitment to supporting the global process of decolonization. Japan's 1941 invasion of the archipelago threw all of this into question. MacArthur and other proponents of the campaign to retake the Philippines now pressed the case that abandonment of the colony—as well as the American POWs on it—would leave a stain on Washington's reputation in the postwar world.[18]

However, strategic concerns also came into play. Recent intelligence reports—later found to be erroneous—suggested that the Philippines were only lightly defended, whereas Japanese forces had heavily garrisoned Formosa. As a result, MacArthur proposed an invasion of Luzon in December, well before any Formosa operation would be possible. Meanwhile, the success of Japan's Ichigo Offensive in the spring and summer of 1944 had deprived the Allies of air bases in southern China and bolstered the growing convictions that the Marianas would host the fleets of American bombers that would soon begin bombing the Japanese home islands. On the other hand, Japanese control of air bases along coastal China and the Philippines would give Tokyo well-defended lines of communication through the South China Sea to the vital oil fields of Southeast Asia.[19]

By early October 1944, support had swung decisively in favor of MacArthur's proposed invasion of the Philippines. The invasion would begin on October 20 with landings on the island of Leyte. But first, Nimitz had insisted on the seizure of Peleliu, which he hoped to use to screen the landings operations at Leyte. Intelligence on the island was all but nonexistent. Nimitz had reports of over six thousand Japanese troops on Peleliu, but little was known about its geography. Aerial photography and rudimentary maps provided little information about the island's terrain. Beneath Peleliu's dense jungle lay a craggy surface six miles long and two miles wide made up of coral and limestone and pockmarked with hundreds of caves. Sharp ridges and gulches cut through a rugged landscape strewn with rubble. Japanese troops had transformed the limestone caves into a maze of fortified tunnels, stuffed with supplies and guarded by steel doors. Camouflaged pillboxes bristled with machine guns placed to rain fire onto attacking marines. The most optimistic commanders predicted that Peleliu could be taken in four days. In reality, the battle would last over two months.[20]

Among the marines charged with seizing Peleliu was twenty-one-year-old Eugene Sledge. It was the Alabama native's first battle. Sledge and his fellow marines faced a grueling ordeal. At Peleliu, Japanese commanders abandoned their previous strategy of suicide charges and instead focused on fighting from their deep network of fortifications. From entrenched positions, the defenders fought to extract the maximum possible price for every yard of territory seized by the marines. In temperatures that sometimes reached 115 degrees Fahrenheit, opposing troops fought a grinding battle of attrition that some marine commanders considered the war's toughest. As Sledge later wrote, "To those who entered the meat grinder itself, the war was a netherworld of horror from which escape seemed less and less likely as casualties mounted and the fighting dragged on and on. Time had no meaning; life had no meaning." The rocky ground made it impossible to bury the dead. "Japanese corpses lay where they fell among the rocks and on the slopes," he wrote. "It is difficult to convey to anyone who has not experienced it the ghastly horror of having your sense of smell saturated constantly with the putrid odor of rotting human flesh day after day, night after night." The hard surface also prevented the digging of even rudimentary latrines, which added the "repulsive odor of human excrement" to the stench of the dead. Swarms of flies, bloated from their feast of both excrement and the dead, served as a constant source of harassment for the living. Nearly two thousand American troops died on Peleliu; of the fourteen thousand Japanese defenders, only four hundred survived. In retrospect, many scholars have argued that the invasion of Peleliu played no meaningful role in the larger battle for the Philippines and was ultimately unnecessary.[21]

WE CAN LAND ANYWHERE

ON THE MORNING OF OCTOBER 20, WITH THE BATTLE FOR PELELIU still raging, the invasion of the Philippines commenced. The Americans arrived with an armada of 738 ships stretching as far as the eye could see and carrying 160,000 troops. Among the vessels were eight fast carriers, nine light carriers, eighteen escort carriers, twelve battleships, twenty-four cruisers, and 116 destroyers. At 6:30 a.m., flashes lit the southwestern horizon as the American gunships began the pre-landing bombardment. Two and a half hours later, four army divisions began landing on Leyte's beaches. The moderate Japanese opposition did little to threaten the expanding beachheads. At 1:30 p.m., MacArthur splashed ashore to announce his return to America's largest colony.[22]

While a self-satisfied MacArthur preened for the cameras, the Japanese navy prepared to launch a desperate attack on the American fleet. Japanese leaders understood that the loss of the Philippines would cut off access to the vital oil fields of Southeast Asia. But the empire was running out of weapons. Without aircraft pilots, Japan's once-formidable carriers were little more than floating targets. Tokyo's best remaining hope lay in luring the American fleet into a close-quarters fight with Japan's still-intact battleship force. Accordingly, Japanese leaders devised a complex plan. Admiral Ozawa's carriers would sail forward to launch a diversionary attack on the American fleet before turning north to draw Admiral William Halsey's carriers away from the landing forces. Meanwhile, Admiral Takeo Kurita would divide his battleships into three groups, A, B, and C. While Group C approached Leyte Gulf from the south through the Surigao Strait, Groups A and B would slip through the San Bernardino Strait to the north, trapping the mostly defenseless American landing forces in the middle.[23]

As the sun rose above Brunei on October 22, Kurita's fleet set sail for the Philippines. In his path sat two American submarines, *Darter* and *Dace*, whose radar detected the Japanese ships in the early hours of October 23. The submarines reported the location of Kurita's fleet before submerging to pursue the enemy ships. At 5:30, with the dawn casting its first light over the water, *Darter* launched six torpedoes at Kurita's flagship, the cruiser *Atago*. Five explosions rocked the *Atago*, engulfing the cruiser in a mass of flames and smoke and forcing Kurita to abandon ship. *Darter* fired four more torpedoes into the cruiser *Takeo*, which was forced to turn back toward Brunei. The *Dace* then sent four of its torpedoes into the *Maya*, detonating the ship's magazine and sinking the cruiser in the space of four minutes. Kurita's attack was not off to a promising start. Still, his force steamed forward. At 8:00 a.m., American scout planes sighted the Japanese ships and relayed their position to Halsey's carrier force. Two and a half hours later, US warplanes swarmed over Kurita's force, concentrating their attacks on his largest battleships, the *Musashi* and *Yamato*. A reported seventeen bombs and twenty torpedoes slammed into the *Musashi*, mortally wounding the giant battleship. As the attacks continued, Kurita chose to withdraw out of range of the enemy aircraft to regroup. In the interim, a single Japanese dive-bomber had penetrated the screen of antiaircraft fire around the American carriers east of Leyte and scored a direct hit on the light carrier *Princeton*. Crews from the *Princeton* and the cruiser *Birmingham* scrambled to put out the resulting fires, but a devastating explosion from the carrier's magazine doomed their efforts, causing high casualties on both ships.[24]

As the crews prepared to scuttle the *Princeton*, American search planes located Ozawa's carrier force 190 miles north of Luzon. Halsey, not wanting to repeat Spruance's supposed failure at the Battle of the Philippine Sea, swallowed the bait. Eager to annihilate Ozawa's carriers, Halsey led his entire force of capital ships—battleships and fast carriers—in pursuit. After issuing his orders, the exhausted admiral retreated to his cabin. Meanwhile, indications that Kurita's force had regrouped and was now headed for the San Bernardino Strait gave some American officers cause for concern. "I thought that Admiral Halsey was making one hell of a mistake," remembered Rear Admiral Gerald Bogan. But Halsey's orders had been sent and the capital ships steamed away, leaving the San Bernardino Strait unguarded.[25]

As Kurita's flotilla approached in the center, a third group of Japanese warships commanded by Admiral Shoji Nishimura moved in from the south through the Surigao Strait. Apprised of Nishimura's progress and confident that Halsey had left a flotilla of ships to defend the northern approaches, Admiral Thomas Kinkaid prepared a devastating reception for the enemy ships. Thirty-nine PT boats waited in the dark waters off Panaon Island. At 11:30 p.m., the small American boats sighted Nishimura's battleships and launched a series of harassing attacks. The boats failed to inflict serious damage, but their reports allowed a second line of American destroyers to maneuver into positions farther north. As American destroyers fired torpedoes at Nishimura's ships—damaging the battleships *Fuso* and *Yamashiro* and sinking two enemy destroyers—battleships at the northern end of the strait opened up on the Japanese fleet. In less than fifteen minutes, six of Nishimura's seven ships were destroyed, annihilating the Japanese southern pincer.[26]

However, the greatest threat lay in the center as Kurita's group crept through the undefended San Bernardino Strait. In the early hours of October 25, Kurita, surprised at his good fortune, emerged into the empty waters off Samar and began searching for the American fleet. As dawn approached, Kurita's force sighted enemy aircraft carriers on the eastern horizon. Kurita had found Taffy 3—a task force of six small escort carriers commanded by Rear Admiral Clifton Sprague and used primarily for antisubmarine patrols in support of the invasion force at Leyte. Sprague's lookouts spotted Kurita's force at approximately the same time and reacted quickly. Turning into the wind, the Americans began frantically launching aircraft and laid a smoke screen in hopes of obscuring their force. Sprague's slow ships had no chance of escaping the attacking Japanese, but they might buy time for supporting forces to intervene. Sprague's heavily outgunned destroyers staged suicidal attacks against Kurita's ships with torpedoes. Making matters worse, MacArthur had mandated that all communications be routed through his headquarters. As a result, Sprague's calls for assistance were needlessly delayed. Kurita, apparently convinced that he faced a force of fleet carriers and heavy cruisers, launched a haphazard attack that nevertheless managed to sink the American carrier *Gambier Bay*, the destroyers *Hoel* and *Johnston*, and the destroyer escort *Samuel B. Roberts*.[27]

While Kurita's fleet battered Taffy 3, Halsey and the US capital ships were in the process of attacking Ozawa's carriers in the north. At 8:22 a.m., Halsey received Kinkaid's call for help. Still fixated on the Japanese carriers in his grasp, he chose not to divert his battleships back to engage and likely destroy Kurita's force. "It was not my job to protect the Seventh Fleet," he later insisted. As Sprague's situation grew more dire, Admiral Nimitz intervened, sending an urgent message to Halsey. "Where is Task Force 34?" he demanded. The encrypted naval communication included "padding" at both the beginning and end of messages, designed to confuse enemy surveillance. This padding was typically removed by communications officers. The full transmission of Nimitz's message read: "TURKEY TROTS TO WATER GG FROM CINCPAC ACTION COM THIRD FLEET INFO COMINCH CTF SEVENTY-SEVEN X WHERE IS REPT WHERE IS TASK FORCE THIRTY FOUR RR THE WORLD WONDERS." In this case, however, "THE WORLD WONDERS" was not removed. When Halsey read Nimitz's message, he flew into a rage. "What right does Chester have to send me a God-damned message like that?" he fumed before stomping off to his quarters, where he remained for the next hour as the fleet moved farther from Leyte. Finally, at 11:15, Halsey returned and ordered his battleships to turn back to assist Sprague. By then, it was too late for the big ships to play a role in the battle.[28]

Incredibly, just when victory appeared to be in his grasp, Kurita opted to call off his attack. A litany of factors seem to have led to this decision. The admiral was almost certainly exhausted, having slept little in the last forty-eight hours, his flagship had been sunk, and he had been forced to leap into the sea. Further, Kurita's ships had been unable to overtake the American carriers, and his fleet was running short on fuel. Finally, reports of incoming air attacks promised even greater destruction. The admiral faced the choice of launching a suicidal bid to destroy some of the American landing craft or with-drawing. The Battle of Leyte Gulf was the largest naval battle in world history. Nearly three hundred ships and two hundred thousand men— "enough to populate a mid sized city," wrote historian Ian Toll—had participated in the battle. The Americans lost six ships and suffered some three thousand killed. Japanese losses were catastrophic. The Combined Fleet lost a staggering twenty-eight ships, including four carriers, three battleships, and ten cruisers. Over twelve thousand Japanese personnel were killed. Moreover, the American seizure of the Philippines severed Tokyo's supply routes to the oil fields of Southeast Asia, depriving Japan's surviving ships of fuel necessary to conduct major operations.[29]

Fittingly, Japanese commanders chose the battle that witnessed the destruction of their fleet to unleash a deadly new weapon. At 7:40 a.m., while Kinkaid's ships were fleeing from Kurita thirty miles to the north, a single Japanese A6M Zeke fighter slammed into the escort carrier *Santee*, killing sixteen sailors and starting a raging fire. Three hours later, a Japanese Zero crashed into the escort carrier *St. Lo*, triggering a chain of explosions that quickly sank the ship. The two planes were part of a new Special Attack Unit dubbed Shinpu, "divine wind," after the storm that thwarted the Mongol invasion of Japan in 1274—better known in the West as "kamikazes." These attacks would occur with increasing frequency in the months to come. Although the suicide attacks followed a clear tactical logic— they were the most effective use of Japan's dwindling numbers of air-craft and poorly trained pilots—they came to stand as an allegory for Tokyo's continued resistance. In the face of certain defeat, Japanese forces chose self-immolation over surrender.[30]

THE BATTLES OF THE PHILIPPINE SEA AND LEYTE GULF DEVASTATED the Japanese fleet, serving as the long-anticipated decisive clash between the Japanese and American navies. "The naval battle for the Philippines represented as comprehensive and total a victory as any that had been won at sea over the previous 373 years," wrote historian H. P. Willmott. In the wake of the American victory, "the Japanese warships that escaped destruction were no more than fugitives on the run." To win this victory, the United States had assembled the largest and most powerful fleet in world history. Whereas previous generations of the Americans had entered the Pacific as one imperial power among many, by late 1944, the US Navy had established effective hegemony over the world's largest body of water, making up 30 percent of the earth's surface. Moreover, the creation of carrier-based naval aviation had allowed for the projection of sea power far inland, bringing huge sections of the world littoral within striking distance of American military power. To some of those serving in the navy, it seemed that the United States deployed two fleets during the war. The first, built before 1941 in accordance with the interwar naval treaties, managed to halt the Japanese advance south and east across the Pacific. The second, deployed after the Pearl Harbor attacks, managed to all but annihilate Tokyo's battle fleet, overwhelm Japan's defensive perimeter, and secure unchallenged supremacy in the Pacific. Meanwhile, with the capture of the Marianas, US forces had cracked the last line of defense protecting Japan from direct attacks. With the completion of airfields on Saipan and Tinian, American commanders would be able to launch a vicious bombing campaign against the home islands. The stage was now set for an unprecedented aerial offensive against Japan's population centers.[31]

Chapter 18

INTO THE REICH

A S THE LATE-SUMMER EVENING FELL OVER THE STREETS OF OCCU-
pied Paris on August 24, 1944, three Sherman tanks and sixteen half-tracks clattered up the avenue d'Italie. Elated Parisians
shouted that the Americans had arrived only to discover, to their
delight, that the detachment was in fact manned by a force of Free
French under the command of General Philippe Leclerc. Word of
the Allies' arrival raced through the city as joyous citizens filled the
streets. At 12:30 the following afternoon, the blue, white, and red
national flag was hoisted above the Eiffel Tower. While the citizens
rejoiced, sporadic skirmishes broke out across the city. "Germany's
lost the war," a German commander told his garrison, "and we have
lost it with her." On the streets, joyous celebrations mixed with vicious
retaliations against collaborators. Women believed to have taken up
with German soldiers were stripped, their heads shorn, and swasti-
kas painted on their chests. One French historian later claimed that
as many as forty thousand suspected collaborators were summarily
executed following France's liberation.[1]

As the citizens of Paris celebrated, thousands of German corpses around Falaise blackened in the summer heat. France had been liberated, but hard fighting lay ahead. Germany's borders were guarded by deep rivers, thick forests, and the daunting fortifications of the Siegfried Line. The Allied drive in the West had only been possible as the result of a remarkable American logistical feat that had linked troops fighting deep inside Europe to supply lines running hundreds of miles across the continent before traversing the Atlantic Ocean. No power in history had sustained a campaign of this size so far from its borders. While Allied forces pushed into Germany, they left a trail of destruction in their wake, transforming the heart of Western Europe into a theater of the war's brutality. As battles raged along the front lines, American commanders emerged as the driving force behind the campaign, reaffirming the eclipse of British power and signaling the emergence of American hegemony over Western Europe. Nevertheless, few doubted that the soldiers of the Wehrmacht would stage a ferocious resistance as Allied armies entered their ancestral territory. The battle of France had been won, but the battle for Germany was only just beginning.

WITH THE REMNANTS OF THE WEHRMACHT RETREATING ACROSS the Seine, Eisenhower prepared to assume the role of supreme Allied commander—a transfer agreed to prior to the Normandy landings. Not everyone was happy with this arrangement. General Montgomery now pushed for a revision to these plans that would allow him to maintain overall command of ground operations. But the prospect of a British general commanding the American armies in Europe remained politically unacceptable to Washington. Montgomery's lackluster performance in Normandy combined with his obstinate behavior toward his fellow Allied commanders only served to reinforce this decision.

Tangled up with this question of command was a debate over strategy. Eisenhower's plan for the next phase of the war envisioned an Allied advance against the Third Reich along a broad front: while British and Canadian forces under Montgomery advanced toward the Ruhr Valley in the north, Omar Bradley's First Army would attack through the Ardennes in the center and George Patton's Third Army would continue its southern drive toward the Saar. It was a conservative plan aimed at maintaining pressure all along the Reich's shrinking frontier and preventing the Wehrmacht from concentrating its defenses against any one sector of the Allied lines. However, Montgomery and Patton each called for a single, concentrated thrust into Germany. Patton, whose Third Army was now the closest to the German border, argued that he should lead this assault into the Reich, insisting that his troops would run through German defenses like "shit through a goose." But the Third Army lay far from Allied ports and faced the longest journey to the critical German industrial centers of the Ruhr Valley and Hitler's capital, Berlin. Meanwhile, Montgomery proposed a riskier single thrust into the Ruhr that would require all available resources, halting Patton's drive in the south. Montgomery insisted that such an attack could breach the defenses along the Rhine River and force a German surrender, ending the war in 1944. No one was surprised when Montgomery proposed that he be the one to lead this offensive.[2]

Eisenhower had reason to be skeptical. He insisted that Wehrmacht reserves would have little trouble outflanking and defeating a single "pencillike thrust" into Germany, and he dismissed the idea that such an attack would force the Third Reich's collapse as "completely fantastic." Years later, Montgomery's own chief of staff wrote that it "took a Russian offensive using about 160 divisions, massive offensives on our part, as well as eight months of devastating air attack, to force the Germans to capitulate. And even then Hitler and his gang never gave up." Eisenhower's chief of staff was more direct: Montgomery's scheme was "the most fantastic bit of balderdash ever proposed by a competent general." The supreme commander also worried about Montgomery's ability to lead such a risky operation—especially after the latter's delayed seizure of Caen and failure to close the Falaise Gap. Montgomery was an able commander, Eisenhower wrote, "but very conceited. . . . He is so proud of his successes to date that he will never willingly make a single move until he is absolutely certain of success—in other words, until he has concentrated rough resources as that anybody could practically guarantee the outcome." Bradley also harbored doubts about Montgomery. "I was always suspicious of Monty's plans because they were so often tied in with what will this do for Monty." Likewise, George Marshall believed that Montgomery's actual complaint concerned leadership of the Allied armies rather than genuine difference over strategy: "It was quite evident that what was wanted was complete command."[3]

Although Montgomery's notorious vanity played a role in this squabble, the controversy reflected deeper geopolitical transformations underway as the United States overtook the British Empire as a major world power. British leaders understood that their empire had entered its twilight. Five grueling years of war had depleted London's manpower and drained its treasury. Although the threat of defeat was fast receding, leaders such as Churchill and Montgomery found themselves swamped by American personnel, weapons, and money. Britain had become the junior partner in the Grand Alliance. The 1.4 million US troops on the continent outnumbered the 771,000 British soldiers nearly two to one. America's GDP was more than quadruple that of the United Kingdom; the United States was producing six times as many rifles, more than five times as many tanks, and more than triple the number of military aircraft. These dynamics would surely accelerate in the years ahead. With this in mind, Montgomery understood that his role was not only to deliver the British Empire victory in the largest war in history but also to bolster London's waning influence in the postwar world. British leaders must play a prominent role in defeating Germany, but they must do so without bleeding the empire dry. London's preferred solution was for Montgomery to command the American armies that toppled the Third Reich—reinforcing the notion of British leaders exerting moral and political leadership over the rising American empire.[4] However, US commanders scoffed at the prospect of British commanders claiming credit for a victory won by a force of primarily American soldiers. No amount of grousing from Montgomery could change these underlying dynamics.

Quarrels over national prestige aside, Eisenhower now faced the massive logistical challenge of supplying over two million troops driving into Germany. Allied armies depended on a supply chain that originated in America's heartland and traversed 3,500 miles of ocean before arriving in Europe. Victory in the Battle of the Atlantic had given US and British forces virtual control of the ocean, an asser-tion of naval hegemony as impressive as that achieved in the Pacific. Indeed, the United States had managed to deploy a commanding level of military force across the world's two largest bodies of water—covering over half the earth's surface—using the most formidable assemblage of naval power ever created. But this was just the beginning. After reaching one of the few Allied-controlled ports such as Cherbourg or Marseilles, supplies had to be hauled across a precari-ous network of damaged roads and rail links to one of the three major army groups at the front, all of which had to work together on the strategic level as constituent parts of the larger Allied war machine. Moreover, all of this needed to happen while sustaining the twin campaigns underway in the Pacific and maintaining the flows of Lend-Lease aid to the Soviet Union and China.

The rapid Allied advance through France compounded these logistical challenges. US and British planners had anticipated a ninety-day campaign to drive the Wehrmacht back to the River Seine followed by a pause to regroup. During this time, elements in the rear would construct a logistical network for the advancing armies. Instead, Allied forces had smashed Axis resistance in the West before sprinting forward to reach the German border in early September—230 days ahead of schedule. With the Germans seem-ingly in full retreat, Allied armies found themselves in danger of outracing their strained supply lines. To fill the gap, the US Army enlisted a primarily African American force of GIs as a motor pool dubbed the Red Ball Express. Fifteen hundred trucks a day hauling five-ton loads made the seventy-one-hour round trip to the front at no more than twenty-five miles per hour on the crowded roads. "We had to drive slowly at night because we had to use 'cat eyes,' and you could hardly see," remembered James Rookard. "If you turned on your headlights, the Germans could bomb the whole convoy." In less than three months, the drivers delivered over 412,193 tons of supplies.[5] Even so, the Red Ball Express was only a stopgap measure in addressing the Allied supply crisis.

The real solution to the Allies' problems lay in Antwerp, which boasted one of the largest ports in the world and was capable of off-loading massive quantities of Allied supplies and delivering them rapidly to the front lines. On September 4, tanks from the British Eleventh Armored Division rolled into the port. The startled German defenders were quickly overwhelmed before they had a chance to destroy the facilities. As they surveyed the largely intact docks, Allied officers marveled at their good fortune. But Antwerp was useless as long as German forces controlled the sixty miles of the Scheldt estuary leading to the sea. Although they could have continued across the Albert Canal and blocked German access to the Scheldt—an advance of perhaps fifteen miles—Allied forces halted. Seizing this opportunity, Wehrmacht commanders scrambled to reinforce their positions and close off the Scheldt, and the Allies' best chance to solve their supply problems slipped away. On the day the port fell, Eisenhower had ordered Allied commanders to "secure Antwerp" but had made no special mention of the Scheldt. That same day, however, the Allied naval commander, Admiral Bertram Ramsay, had warned Eisenhower that the "enemy must be prevented from . . . mining and blocking the Scheldt." As he wrote in his diary the following day, "Antwerp is useless unless the Scheldt estuary is cleared of the enemy." But other Allied leaders lacked Ramsay's sense of urgency. It was over a week before Eisenhower sent another message explaining that the "early winning of deep water ports and improved maintenance facilities in our rear are prerequisites to a final all-out assault on Germany proper." On September 20, the supreme commander sent another message explaining that "early capture of the approaches to Antwerp" was a "prerequisite" for any further advance into Germany.[6] But Eisenhower's commands fell on deaf ears. Montgomery's attention had shifted elsewhere.

HAVING FAILED TO CONVINCE EISENHOWER TO BACK HIS NARROW-thrust concept, Montgomery proposed an airborne assault aimed at seizing a series of Dutch bridges leading up to the town of Arnhem on the Rhine. Most of his staff were deeply skeptical. If successful, the Arnhem operation would give the Allies a bridgehead across the Rhine, deploy underutilized airborne forces, threaten German V-2 rocket launch sites in the Netherlands, and force Eisenhower to give priority to the British drive into Germany. Montgomery presented the plan—code-named Market Garden—during a contentious meeting aboard Eisenhower's airplane on September 10. Though he again rejected Montgomery's narrow-thrust proposal, Eisenhower endorsed the Arnhem operation as the best opportunity to cross the Rhine before the end of the year.[7]

Cobbled together with only a week's notice, the plan for Market Garden called for the paratroopers of US 82nd and 101st Airborne Divisions to capture bridges at Eindhoven, Nijmegen, and Grave, while the British 1st Airborne Division and Polish 1st Independent Parachute Brigade seized the bridge over the Rhine at Arnhem. Meanwhile, the British XXX Corps would drive forward along the narrow sixty-five-mile highway to Arnhem, reinforcing the paratroopers and opening the way across the Rhine. The parachute drops would take place during daylight hours owing to the dark moon during the short window of time. The operation's commanders, Lieutenant Generals F. A. M. Browning and Lewis Brereton were eager to demonstrate the operational potential of airborne forces—so eager, in fact, that they brushed off the advice of their more experienced subordinates and ignored reports that two SS Panzer Divisions had been sighted near Arnhem. They were not alone. Montgomery, still hoping to salvage his narrow-thrust gambit, brushed off warnings that the lightly armed paratroopers would be wiped out by German tank forces at Arnhem. Browning likewise dismissed warnings that the British drop zone was too far away from the bridges and that the plan to lift the troops over a three-day period might doom the operation. Perhaps the greatest problem of all concerned the question of success: even if the Allies managed to gain a bridgehead at Arnhem, how would they hold it against the Wehrmacht's counterattacks, especially with the vital port of Arnhem still closed?[8]

On the morning of September 17, 1944, clouds of fighter planes, bombers, transports, and gliders roared across the skies above England heading east toward the Netherlands. On board, thousands of soldiers waited, checking their gear, puffing on cigarettes, and gazing out windows. Concerns about German flak cannons led planners to select drop zones miles away from the bridges at Arnhem and Nijmegen—squandering the element of surprise and forcing the paratroopers to fight their way to the crossings. The 101st succeeded in seizing bridges near Eindhoven, but the 82nd met fierce German resistance at the road bridge over the River Waal near Nijmegen. Perhaps even more worrisome was the slow progress of the XXX Corps, which ran into heavy German fire a mere seven miles from its starting point. Rather than a costly headlong advance into enemy fire, British forces opted for a cautious approach, burning precious hours while the paratroopers fought to take the bridges ahead. Compounding these delays, the corps commander, Lieutenant General Brian Horrocks, insisted on halting at night rather than risking a treacherous advance through the darkness.[9]

To the north at Arnhem, British forces faced a tough fight against German units defending the approaches to the bridge over the Rhine. Making matters worse, malfunctioning radio sets prevented coordination between units in and around Arnhem and blocked communications with XXX Corps. To the south, the battle for Nijmegen raged as German soldiers denied the 82nd control of the Waal bridge. Finally, on the afternoon of September 20, US troops staged a perilous crossing of the river to outflank the Germans defenders and seize the bridge. Heavy machine gun fire from the Germans spattering around the boats looked to one private like "a school of mackerel on the feed." The exhausted Americans then watched in amazement as the forward elements of XXX Corps rolled to a stop across the north end of the bridge in order to avoid driving into the gathering darkness. Arnhem lay just eleven miles ahead. While the tank crews brewed tea in Nijmegen, the paratroopers in Arnhem were being cut to pieces. It was eighteen hours before Horrocks's forces resumed their drive, by which time the paratroopers fighting in Arnhem had lost their hold on the north end of the bridge over the Rhine and the Tenth SS Panzer Division had taken position to block Horrocks's armored column. British and Polish paratroopers fought on for another four days, but the battle was lost.[10]

In the decades since, American and British historians have argued over who ought to bear the blame for Market Garden's failure. With the benefit of hindsight, it seems likely that the operation was fatally flawed from its inception. At its heart, Market Garden aimed at positioning Allied forces to deliver a finishing blow to the collapsing Wehrmacht; unfortunately for the Allies, the Wehrmacht was not collapsing. Even if British troops had succeeded in capturing and holding the bridge at Arnhem, Allied forces would have encountered the daunting task of defending a narrow, sixty-mile-long corridor without adequate supply lines. Meanwhile, the Wehrmacht, operating along interior lines, would have staged concerted counterattacks and pushed Allies back toward Antwerp. Montgomery's failure to clear the Scheldt had doomed Market Garden long before any paratroopers landed in the Netherlands. All of which served to confirm the grim necessity of Eisenhower's broad front strategy.[11]

The Dutch people paid for the Allies' mistakes. In an attempt to aid the Allies, the Dutch government-in-exile had called for a nationwide railway strike to coincide with Market Garden. After Market Garden's failure, German occupation authorities retaliated by leveling a punishing embargo against the Dutch people. With food supplies already short, the nation faced the threat of widespread starvation. On September 28, the Dutch prime minister, Pieter Gerbrandy, warned Churchill of the impending disaster. "Many railway strikers and members of the resistance movement have been and are being executed, and the strongest reprisals are being taken against members of their families. Starvation in the big cities . . . is imminent." British leaders recognized the emergency, but they worried that any relief operations would likely amount to delivering food into the hands of the German occupation forces. Barring this, even a successful Allied relief effort promised to pull resources away from the war against Germany. An operation by the Swedish Red Cross began food deliveries in April, but it was too late to save some sixteen thousand Dutch citizens who had died from starvation and related diseases, casualties of a man-made famine.[12]

FOLLOWING THE FAILURE OF MARKET GARDEN, THE ALLIES TURNED back to the matter of clearing the approaches to Antwerp—a task far more difficult in early October than it would have been had Montgomery given it priority in early September. Even so, the British commander displayed a startling lack of urgency. Eisenhower continued prodding Montgomery to focus his efforts on clearing the Scheldt. "I consider Antwerp of first importance," he wrote. Some British leaders took an even stronger position. At an October 5 meeting in Versailles, Admiral Bertram Ramsay blasted Montgomery for his continuing failure to clear the Scheldt. "Monty made the startling announcement that we could take the Ruhr without Antwerp," he wrote in his diary. "I let fly with all my guns at the faulty strategy we had allowed." Field Marshal Alan Brooke agreed: "I feel that Monty's strategy for once is at fault, instead of carrying out the advance on Arnhem he ought to have made certain of Antwerp in the first place."[13]

Despite this pressure, Montgomery delegated the arduous task of clearing the Scheldt to the Canadian army. In order to force German troops out of their positions, the RAF bombed the Westkapelle dike, flooding large sections of Walcheren Island and killing 125 Dutch civilians. But it was up to Canadian forces to trudge across the sodden ground, caked in mud and soaked to the skin, while engaging in deadly firefights with German defenders. By the time the last enemy forces surrendered on November 8, Allied units had taken some eighteen thousand casualties. The Royal Navy would spend the next twenty days clearing 267 mines from the estuary, finally opening Antwerp to Allied shipping on November 28.[14]

To the south, US forces fought a series of murderous battles in their own bid to penetrate the Third Reich. To do so, the American armies would have to breach Hitler's vaunted Siegfried Line— a sprawling network of pillboxes and concrete "dragon's teeth" tank obstacles tucked into natural obstacles such as rivers, forests, and lakes. By mid-September, the US First Army had reached the approaches to Aachen. For the Germans, the city held dual significance as both the first major German city in the Allies' path and the birthplace of Charlemagne. Hitler had no intention of letting a city of such historic importance fall without a fight. While US forces paused to resupply, German commanders rushed defenders to Aachen with orders to hold the city to the last man. On October 11, American warplanes tore through the skies, dropping 62 tons of bombs while artillery pummeled the city with another 169 tons of munitions. The barrage continued through the following day in preparation for the infantry assault on October 13. US forces entered a "maze of rubble and damaged buildings" infested with German soldiers. In house-to-house fighting, American soldiers pushed their way through Aachen, blocking manhole covers to prevent sneak attacks from the sewers and using artillery to level hundreds of buildings. Machine gunners sprayed the streets while soldiers cleared buildings with flamethrowers and grenades. By October 21, the last pockets of resistance had been cleared. "The city is as dead as a Roman ruin," wrote one witness, "but unlike a ruin it has none of the grace of gradual decay. . . . Burst sewers, broken gas mains and dead animals have raised an almost overpowering smell in many parts of the city. The streets are paved with shattered glass; telephone, electric light and trolley cables are dangling and netted together everywhere, and in many places wrecked cars, trucks, armored vehicles and guns litter the streets."[15]

One hundred miles south, Patton's Third Army had reached the fortress city of Metz along the Moselle River in the province of Lorraine. The city was guarded by centuries-old fortifications with modern additions—rings of moats, walls, machine gun nests, and barbed wire—and shrouded beneath dreary clouds of falling rain. For weeks, Patton's forces blasted away at the city, taking heavy casualties and making little progress. "For God's sake, lay off it," Bradley urged his colleague. "You are taking too many casualties for what you are accomplishing." Metz would not surrender until November 22, but the last defenders held out until December 13. "I hope that in the final settlement of the war," a frustrated Patton told Secretary of War Henry Stimson, "you insist that the Germans retain Lorraine because I can imagine no greater burden than to be the owner of this nasty country where it rains every day and where the whole wealth of the people consists in assorted manure piles."[16]

American soldiers fighting in Hürtgen Forest faced an even grimmer ordeal. The commander of the US First Army, Lieutenant General Courtney Hodges, had decided to send his troops into the heavily wooded area south of Aachen in order to prevent German forces from using it as a base to threaten his flanks as he pushed east toward the Rhine. Fifty square miles of densely forested ridges and ravines neutralized American armor advantages and made air strikes difficult. Instead, infantry were forced to comb through the dark woods, often stooping beneath thick branches, in search of German positions. Heavy rains and snow left soldiers soaked and shivering in frigid waterlogged foxholes through the cold nights. Hundred-foot-tall pine trees blocked all light from hitting the forest floor and visibility was often restricted to a matter of yards. Patrols frequently lost their bearings amid the nearly impenetrable pine thickets. German soldiers littered roads and paths with land mines while snipers took positions in the trees. The greatest danger came from enemy artillery that launched bursts into the treetops, sending thousands of lethal splinters and pieces of shrapnel down on any troops below. "The forest up there was a helluva eerie place to fight," remembered army technician George Morgan. "You can't get all the dead because you can't find them, and they stay there to remind the guys advancing as to what might hit them. You can't get protection. You can't see. You can't get fields of fire. The trees are slashed like a scythe by the artillery. Everything is tangled. You can scarcely walk. Everybody is cold and wet, and the mixture of cold rain and sleet keeps falling." US forces suffered thirty-three thousand casualties in the battle, many due to trench foot, frostbite, and exhaustion. In return, six German divisions had been mauled in the bitter fighting. In a contest of attrition, the Americans held the upper hand, but few would argue that the terrible struggle for Hürtgen Forest represented a wise use of Allied resources.[17] Although the Allies did not yet know it, the fighting in Hürtgen Forest was merely a prelude to an even larger struggle in the woods between Belgium, Luxembourg, and Germany.

On September 16, as Allied forces prepared to launch the ill-fated Market Garden operation, Adolf Hitler proposed his own plan to change the tide of the war in Europe. The Führer and his generals were keenly aware that the Allied armies were closing in from both east and west. With Eisenhower's forces regrouping across the Siegfried Line and Stalin's armies massing along the Vistula, the Third Reich had one last chance to mount a counterattack. Hitler had concluded that the Red Army was too strong to fall prey to a decisive blow, but the Americans might be vulnerable. If the Wehrmacht could mount a powerful counteroffensive, smash through the American lines, and drive north to seize Antwerp, the Germans might force a second Dunkirk. If successful, the operation would encircle hundreds of thousands of Allied soldiers and rob the Western armies of the vital Belgian port. At best, Hitler hoped, the attack would be so demoralizing as to tear apart the Grand Alliance, allowing Germany to unleash the full force of its legions against the Red Army. Code-named Wacht am Rhein, the operation was the Third Reich's last desperate bid to snatch victory from the jaws of defeat.

Field Marshals Gerd von Rundstedt and Walter Model both voiced skepticism. Would it not make more sense, they asked, to attack the American units massing along the Rhine or to launch an encirclement of Allied armies near Aachen? Hitler rejected their suggestions, neither of which would be enough to change the course of the war. If the Reich was to make one last gamble, it must be one capable of delivering victory. The Führer, General Alfred Jodl explained, wanted to "stake everything on one card." Much would depend on the weather. Clear skies would allow the Allies to use their air superiority to tear through any German advance. Cloud cover, however, would conceal the German columns from Allied aircraft and negate this aerial advantage. The offensive would employ three armies across an over-one-hundred-mile front between Monschau and Echternach. The first wave of two hundred thousand soldiers would blast through the American lines while panzers made a dash to cross the Meuse and drive toward Antwerp. The operation's only hope of success lay in keeping to a tight timetable. If the German tanks got bogged down, Allied reinforcements would stop the German advance.[18]

As part of the offensive, Hitler enlisted Otto Skorzeny and a special group of English-speaking German commandos to create chaos behind Allied lines. Skorzeny, a hulking die-hard Nazi with dueling scars carved into his left cheek, had gained fame by breaking Mussolini out of prison in the Apennine Mountains. Skorzeny's men donned American uniforms taken from POWs, carried Allied weapons, rations, and identification, and even managed to scrounge fifty-seven jeeps. While the unit trained at their secret *Amerikanischschule* camps in Bavaria, rumors spread of a special mission to France to assassinate Eisenhower. Although Skorzeny's commandos would have negligible impact on the battlefield, their presence spread panic through the Allied ranks.[19]

Meanwhile, Allied commanders remained largely oblivious to the hostile armies massing in the forest to the east. German radio traffic—upon which Allied Ultra operations relied—had slackened as the Wehrmacht withdrew into the Reich, where it could rely on telephone and telegraph lines. Cloud cover and camouflage also hid German troop movements from aerial reconnaissance. The biggest blind spot, however, came from Allied convictions that the Wehrmacht, mauled by months of hard fighting on two fronts, was incapable of launching a major offensive. In early December, Eisenhower's intelligence officer, Major General Kenneth Strong, warned that the Germans might be planning an attack in the Ardennes, but Bradley paid little attention. Soon after, Colonel Benjamin Dickson of the US First Army warned of German tank concentrations in the Eifel mountain range and rumors of an attack on Aachen, but his superiors dismissed his concerns and suggested that Dickson take a leave in Paris.[20]

Just before 5:30 on the cold morning of December 16, an American sentry perched atop a concrete water tower in the Belgian village of Hosingen reported a curious sight. Distant flashes of light danced across the eastern horizon. Moments later, the rumble of artillery announced the beginning of the offensive. With dawn still hours away, most soldiers were sleeping in cabins, barns, and cowsheds. The Ardennes was supposed to be a quiet sector, a place to train new replacements or to allow battle-weary veterans to recuperate over the winter. But now, the German onslaught was bearing down on the stunned American defenders. Elements of the green 106th Infantry Division and the lightly armed 14th Cavalry Group could do little to stop the German armor streaming through the Losheim Gap. To the north at Büllingen, the 99th Infantry Division learned of the attack when a crewman in a passing armored car yelled a warning: "The whole damned German army is just down the road!" Soon after, the town was overrun by German tanks. American troops with the 395th Regiment to the west at Höfen had more success, pouring small-arms fire into advancing German forces at point-blank range. Even more effective was the American artillery at Elsenborn Ridge, which employed brand-new proximity fuses timed to detonate twenty feet above their targets, raining lethal airbursts over German troops. The arrival of the veteran 2nd Infantry Division bolstered the defenses at Elsenborn, presenting a firm northern shoulder against the German assault.[21]

Through the first day of the attack, Allied headquarters remained calm. Bradley, whose forces stood in the direct path of the German assault, had made the trip to Versailles to celebrate Eisenhower's promotion to the rank of general of the army. The two men had attended a wedding ceremony for one of Eisenhower's aides as intelligence reports from the front streamed in. Bradley was nonchalant—the Germans had simply launched a localized attack in the Ardennes. Eisenhower disagreed. "That's no spoiling attack," he insisted, and he resolved to take the immediate actions of placing the 82nd and 101st Airborne Divisions on alert and transferring units from Patton's army in the south to the Ardennes. The two men then spent a restless night drinking champagne and Scotch and waiting for more news from the front. The following day, Eisenhower and his staff drew up plans for the Allied response. The 101st would be rushed to Bastogne—a vital hub in the region's sparse road network—to reinforce the 10th Armored Division and an effort would be made to hold the crossroads at St. Vith. At a meeting in Verdun on the nineteenth, Eisenhower and his generals drew a line along the Meuse River as the bulwark of their defense. Allied forces must stop the offensive at the Meuse and then launch their own counterattack against the German salient. Patton, fully in his element, insisted that he needed only forty-eight hours to mount a counterattack. "The Kraut's stuck his head in a meatgrinder," he said, waving his cigar, "[and] this time I've got hold of the handle."[22]

In the interim, beleaguered American forces at the front fought a series of desperate clashes to slow the German onslaught. Spearheading one prong of the German armored advance was twenty-nine-year-old SS-Obersturmbannführer Joachim Peiper. An ardent Nazi who had acquired a vicious reputation for slaughtering noncombatants and burning villages on the eastern front, Peiper had been tasked with driving his tanks hard through Allied lines to secure a crossing over the Meuse River. Once in Belgium, however, the tank commander found his panzers bogged down by poor roads and difficult terrain. On December 17, the second day of the offensive, Peiper's troops captured 130 American soldiers from the 285th Field Artillery Observation Battalion southeast of Malmédy. After stripping their captives of valuables, the SS troops opened fire on the defenseless Americans, killing eighty-four and leaving their bodies in the snow. News of the massacre soon spread to US commanders, who publicized the incident to rally their troops, who would soon have the opportunity to take revenge on the Germans. Peiper's forces drove on, guzzling fuel, but struggling to make a breakthrough. Late the next morning, as Peiper's tanks wheeled north toward Spa, soldiers from the 51st Engineer Battalion detonated charges on the bridges spanning the Amblève and Salm Rivers at Trois-Ponts, blocking the German advance.[23]

In the center of the growing bulge, remnants of the 106th Division joined with units from the 7th Armored, 9th Armored, and 28th Infantry Divisions to fight a bitter holding action at St. Vith that delayed an entire German corps until December 21. By denying the vital crossroads to the attacking forces, the defense of St. Vith choked the German advance and ruined the operation's tight timetable. Having failed to break through American defenses at Elsenborn and St. Vith, the German advance was now funneled into a narrow corridor aimed directly at the town of Bastogne. If the Allies could hold there, the German offensive would almost certainly fail.[24]

As the cold winter night crept over the Ardennes on the evening of December 18, the first truckload of paratroopers from the 101st Airborne arrived in the town of Bastogne. By noon the next day, the rest of the division had crowded into the town, along with units from the 10th Armored Division. A total of eighteen thousand Americans would face three German panzer divisions numbering some forty-five thousand men. Bastogne was now the linchpin of the German offensive. US soldiers harassed enemy columns along the approaches to the town, but by Thursday, December 21, the defenders found themselves surrounded. The next morning, German envoys approached the American lines. The Germans presented a note beseeching the defenders to surrender, sparing themselves and the civilians of Bastogne inevitable destruction at the hands of the Wehrmacht. The commander of the 101st, Brigadier General Anthony McAuliffe, responded with a single word: "Nuts!" German commanders launched a series of probing attacks through the following days. The American defenders, camouflaged in white capes fashioned from bedsheets and fighting with rationed ammunition, held against the Germans and the swirling snow. On December 23, the combatants awoke to a blast of frigid temperatures that swept away the clouds and gave way to bright-blue skies.[25]

American soldiers watched from foxholes as squadrons of Allied bombers and fighters roared through the skies overhead. No longer grounded by the weather, the Ninth Air Force would fly nearly 1,300 sorties. C-47 transport planes dropped 144 tons of supplies to the garrison at Bastogne. Meanwhile, snow-covered fields silhouetted German units for attacking bombers, which blasted the frozen landscape with burning walls of napalm. By the end of the day, Bastogne was ringed with fire. But the fighting was not yet over. At 8:30 p.m. on Christmas Eve, Dr. John Prior was sharing a bottle of champagne with his staff when a magnesium flare flashed through the darkness, filling the sky with a searing white light. The next instant, the concussion of a German bomb shook the building. German bombers would dump two tons of ordnance on Bastogne. Bombs ripped through the American aid station, killing twenty wounded along with a volunteer Belgian nurse, Renée Lemaire, and ignited fires through the town. Prior found the three-story building that served as his hospital reduced to a pile of rubble six feet high. Among the survivors was a half-Congolese nurse named Augusta Chiwy. She remembered the bitter cold and heavy blanket of fog that lay over the town. But the siege was nearly at an end. Patton's counterattack had gotten off to an impressive start, but, like the Germans', his tanks had soon gotten bogged down as a result of poor weather, icy roads, and determined resistance. By December 26, however, the American Fourth Armored Division had reached the approaches to the Bastogne. At 2:00 p.m., the commander of III Corps asked to mount a direct lunge through the village of Assenois that would break through German lines and reach the garrison. Patton agreed. While aircraft and artillery attacked the village, a group of American tanks led by Lieutenant Colonel Creighton Abrams fought their way north through German defenders. At 4:45 p.m., the first American tank reached the outer defenses of Bastogne. Within hours, Patton's forces had opened a corridor to the town.[26]

Although fierce fighting still lay ahead, the twin stands at Bastogne and Elsenborn dashed the Wehrmacht's hopes of sustaining the offensive. Even if German panzers reached the Meuse, their supply lines would be so strained by the bottleneck created by American defenses that they stood little chance of moving farther. Moreover, with Patton's army driving north, the German salient risked encirclement. But in late December, Eisenhower directed Montgomery to mount a counteroffensive on the north beginning no later than January 3. Instead of launching the assault, the British field marshal seized the opportunity to once again pester Eisenhower about giving him total command of a larger counteroffensive. Valiant efforts by British staff talked the supreme commander down from calling for Montgomery's dismissal. Montgomery then rewarded Eisenhower's clemency with what may have been his most obnoxious action of the war, erroneously suggesting during a January 7 press conference that it was his marginally engaged British forces who had turned the tide of the battle rather than the Americans.[27]

Montgomery's relationship with US commanders would never recover. Years later, Eisenhower would tell journalist Cornelius Ryan that Montgomery was a "psychopath. . . . He is such an egocentric. . . . He has never made a mistake in his life." The British commander's goal, Eisenhower insisted, was "to make sure that the Americans, and me in particular, had no credit, had nothing to do with this war. I just stopped communicating with him." Meanwhile, in keeping with the signature caution he had exercised at Caen, Falaise, and Antwerp, Montgomery conducted a plodding counterattack that squandered any chance of cutting off the German armies in the Ardennes. Shortly after reaching Bastogne, a frustrated Patton wrote that if only Eisenhower would put Bradley in charge—rather than Montgomery—the Allies could "bag the whole German army. . . . Monty is a tired little fart. War requires the taking of risks and he won't take them." As a result, thousands of German troops escaped, regrouped, and continued their fight against Allied forces advancing on the Siegfried Line. Altogether, the Americans suffered 76,980 casualties. German casualty estimates range from sixty-seven thousand to eighty-four thousand. Tank losses stood at 733 for the Allies and 600 for the Germans. Although the casualties were numerically similar, their impacts could hardly have been more disparate. While the Allies brought up reinforcements and new vehicles, German losses were irreplaceable.[28]

THE THIRD REICH HAD MOUNTED ITS LAST STRATEGIC OFFENSIVE OF the war and failed. Meanwhile, Germany's redeployment of forces to the west depleted its defenses to the east on the eve of the Red Army's winter offensive. Although they had suffered nothing as intense as the fighting on the eastern front, American and British forces had taken Germany's best shot, survived, and were now pushing deeper into the Reich. In doing so, Western commanders had accomplished a master stroke of coordination. Three major army groups sustained by a transatlantic supply chain were conducting a multipronged offensive along a broad front deep inside continental Europe. Western armies relied on sophisticated machinery, massed artillery, and combined arms operations that drew on infantry, armor, and airpower. Even German officers credited the proficiency of their opponents. The Americans exploited their advantages in equipment, unleashing rolling artillery barrages, deploying multiple smoke screens, and orchestrating coordinated, systematic attacks that minimized casualties and kept pressure on German lines.[29] Employing these methods, Western armies had moved from the English Channel across France and the

Low Countries to breach the borders of Germany itself, placing the Allies in a position to achieve near-certain victory. The Third Reich now found itself caught in an ever-tightening vise between the Red Army and the Western powers. As Allied leaders entered the final months of the war against Germany, their focus turned primarily to the matter of destroying the German leadership and maneuvering for power in postwar Europe.

Chapter 19

THE RACE TO BERLIN

T 5:00 A.M. ON JANUARY 12, 1945, THE FIRST UKRAINIAN FRONT, commanded by General Ivan Konev, opened a renewed offensive from the Sandomierz bridgehead along the Vistula River. Falling snow shrouded prisoner battalions marching forward to clear minefields as thousands of Soviet guns fired on German positions. The Red Army fielded one piece of artillery for every four meters along the front. One German officer likened the bombardment to "the heavens falling down on earth." Rifle battalions and tanks covered with graffiti such as "Forward into the fascist lair!" surged forward. The next day, General Ivan Chernyakhovsky's Third Belorussian Front launched its assault against East Prussia, followed by attacks on January 14 from Zhukov's First Belorussian Front and Konstantin Rokossovsky's Second Belorussian Front. Soviet tanks splashed into the freezing waters of the Pilica River in a deep thrust through enemy lines. The cascading offensives threw the German defenses into disarray as the Red Army charged forward. Stalin would later claim that he had launched the operation early to remove pressure on his Western Allies. In truth, the Ardennes Offensive in the West had stripped key units from the eastern front and left the Wehrmacht even more vulnerable to the Soviet assault.[1]

The Red Army tore through German positions at a blistering pace. Zhukov's forces advanced nearly eight miles on the first day of their attack and were racing toward the Oder River by the end of January 18. Konev's front advanced twelve miles on the first day of fighting and seized Krakow on January 19. That same day, General Vasily Chuikov's Eighth Guards Army took the city of Lodz. By the end of the month, Soviet troops had advanced some 250 miles to the banks of the Oder River.[2]

As Soviet troops advanced through Poland, they stumbled on further evidence of the Third Reich's horrors. On January 27, elements of the 322nd Rifle Division rode into the sprawling camp complex at Auschwitz. Instead of Nazi defenders, they met groups of emaciated prisoners staring at them from behind barbed wire. Guards had evacuated most of the inmates, leaving only the weakest behind—some seven thousand in all. Six hundred corpses lay on the grounds along with 370,000 men's suits, 837,000 women's outfits, and 7.7 tons of human hair. The Nazis had murdered over a million people here in the Reich's largest death camp. While Jews made up the overwhelming majority of the victims, tens of thousands of Poles, Roma, and Soviet POWs had also been killed. Yulia Pozdnyakova, a signaler with the Red Army, remembered the piles of children's shoes and the stench of death that hung in the air throughout the camps. "The ghosts of the dead were all around us," she recalled. "It was very hard to sleep at night. For weeks afterwards, I could not stand the smell of fried meat."[3]

With Allied armies closing in from both east and west, the horrifying reality of the Nazi empire came into focus. Hitler's regime had achieved the apotheosis of racial imperialism: a brutal empire forged by war, sustained by slave labor, and committed to the systematic extermination of entire peoples. And now, even as Germany's last hope of staving off a catastrophic defeat winked out, Nazi leaders committed to fighting to the bitter end. From his subterranean bunker deep beneath the streets of Berlin, the Führer ordered national suicide rather than surrender. But in these closing months of the war, as the Third Reich entered its death throes, the Allies crossed into open competition both on the ground and at the summit table. While American, British, and Soviet commanders vied to be the first to enter Berlin, teams of scientists raced to plunder the spoils of Nazi weapons technology, diplomats turned away from amity and toward suspicion, and strategists began drawing up plans for World War III. Amid the blackened ruins of Berlin, a new imperial struggle was born.

WHILE THE RED ARMY PICKED THROUGH THE GHASTLY REMAINS OF Auschwitz, the leaders of Great Britain, the Soviet Union, and the United States converged on the resort town of Yalta in the Crimean Peninsula. Roosevelt, in the advanced stages of congestive heart failure, made the five-thousand-mile journey across the Atlantic, stopping at Malta before boarding a plane to Crimea and driving the final eighty miles to Yalta by car. Along the way, the Americans gaped at the devastation around them. "The rolling countryside was littered with burned-out tanks, gutted buildings, and destroyed German freight trains that had been abandoned and burned by the Nazis in their retreat from the Crimea," wrote one bodyguard. The Americans stayed in Livadia Palace, a prerevolutionary estate perched 150 feet above the sea that had once been a favorite summer destination of Czar Nicholas II. The retreating Nazis had ransacked the palace in the spring of 1944, and Soviet workers had scrambled to make repairs and find furniture in the weeks leading up to the conference. Even so, the accommodations remained sparse. "If we had spent ten years in our research we could not have found a worse place in the world than Yalta," grumbled Churchill. "It is good for typhus and deadly on lice which thrive in those parts."[4]

Roosevelt arrived in Yalta with high hopes for building an amicable relationship with Stalin, speaking confidently of his plans to charm the Soviet leader and affirming the need for good relations between Washington and Moscow in the postwar world. But not all Americans shared the president's optimism. A series of foreign service officers stationed in Moscow had embarked on their assignments eager to build better relations with the Soviets only to grow disillusioned in the face of the Kremlin's duplicity, obstinance, and suspicion. Certainly an atmosphere of suspicion pervaded Soviet preparations for the conference. Stalin's intelligence had bugged Livadia Palace as well as the British delegation's rooms at Vorontsov Palace. Moreover, Soviet spies had penetrated US and British security, giving Stalin access to the Allied negotiating strategies.[5]

In the weeks before the conference, a growing list of American diplomats had voiced concerns about Moscow's behavior. In early December 1944, the head of the US military mission to Moscow, General John Deane, warned that relations between the two allies had begun to sour. "We never make a request or proposal to the Soviets that is not viewed with suspicion," he wrote. "They simply cannot understand giving without taking, and as a result even our giving is viewed with suspicion. Gratitude cannot be banked in the Soviet Union. Each transaction is complete in itself without regard to past favors. The party of the second part is either a shrewd trader to be admired or a sucker to be despised." US officials, Deane explained, had secured only trifling concessions from Moscow while doing everything in their power to grant the Soviets any and all requests. Relations between the Americans and the Soviets were almost entirely one-sided. "Our files are bulging with letters to the Soviets and devoid of letters from them. . . . In short, we are in the position of being at the same time the givers and the supplicants. This is neither dignified nor healthy for U.S. prestige." Going forward, Deane argued, Washington must insist on a quid pro quo in its dealings with Stalin's regime.[6]

Five weeks later, US ambassador to Moscow Averell Harriman warned that Soviet officials had begun installing puppet regimes throughout the liberated territories of Eastern Europe. Rather than pursuing formal incorporation into the Soviet Union, Stalin's forces were working to establish "regimes which, while maintaining an outward appearance of independence and of broad popular support, actually depend for their existence on groups responsive to all suggestions emanating from the Kremlin." Worse still, Soviet officials seemed to be making no distinction "between members of the United Nations whose territory is liberated by Soviet troops and ex-enemy countries which have been occupied."[7]

Harriman's reservations had been mounting over the preceding months. He had warned in September 1944 that the Soviets had "misinterpreted our generous attitude toward them as a sign of weakness, and acceptance of their policies." Going forward, Washington "must make clear what we expect of them as the price of our good will. Unless we take issue with the present policy there is every indication the Soviet Union will become a world bully wherever their interests are involved." Harriman's chargé d'affaires, George Kennan, took the more fatalistic view that US-Soviet relations would be marked by deep tensions if not outright hostility. "Why should we not make a decent and definite compromise with [Moscow]—divide Europe frankly into spheres of influence—keep ourselves out of the Russian sphere and keep the Russians out of ours?" he asked.[8]

Stalin also had his doubts about the long-term prospects of good relations with the Western powers. Although he hoped for a period of peace following the war, he believed future tensions with the capitalist world were inevitable. In a meeting with Yugoslav and Bulgarian communist leaders on January 28, 1944, Stalin explained that the "capitalist world is divided into two hostile blocs—democratic and fascist." Moscow was currently aligned with the democratic bloc against the fascists, "but in the future we will be allied against the first faction of capitalists too." In the long run, the "crisis of capitalism" would create conditions "favourable for the victory of socialism in Europe."[9]

This logic took concrete form at Yalta. Through eight days of meetings, the Allies wrangled over key issues such as the fate of Poland, the partition of Germany, Axis reparations, France's status at the end of the war, the United Nations Organization, and Soviet entry into war against Japan. Yalta, as a wartime conference, was not a meeting of equals. The Red Army had shouldered the heaviest burden in the war against Germany and even now was marching west toward Berlin. Soviet forces occupied a large chunk of Eastern Europe and were set to overrun much of the rest of the region. As British secretary of state for foreign affairs Anthony Eden later explained, "We had not very much to offer them, but . . . we required a great deal from them." Similarly, British diplomat Alexander Cadogan "feared Stalin would say: we've done our bit, we can't do much more," leaving the Western Allies to finish off the Wehrmacht without the support of the Red Army. Instead, Stalin committed to finishing the war and joining the battle against Japan after Berlin's defeat. Moscow also agreed to join the United Nations Organization and to allow the restoration of France's status as a major power in Europe.[10]

But Stalin also made his own demands. The Western Allies must recognize Moscow as a great power in world affairs and accept a Soviet sphere of influence over much of Eastern Europe, and Germany must pay heavy reparations to the Soviet Union. Nevertheless, the question of German partition was still very much open. US officials had initially supported proposals to dismember Germany, the most prominent of which, the Morgenthau Plan, called for Germany to be divided, stripped of its industry, and reduced to a pastoral existence. However, such punitive schemes had fallen out of favor by the end of 1944. Calls for a harsh settlement would bolster German resistance, create an unstable balance of power in Europe, and sow seeds of resentment among the German people. Instead, Allied leaders agreed to create temporary occupation zones. In the long term, the Allies hoped, the spirit of cooperation would prevail following victory, leading to a joint postwar administration in Germany. In the coming months, however, disputes over Poland, Stalin's demands for harsh reparations from Germany, and Moscow's efforts to extend control over the Turkish Straits would cause inter-Allied relations to sour. As the spirit of cooperation faded, the temporary occupation zones would harden, eventually solidifying in the form of a divided postwar Germany.[11]

Correspondingly, Poland's status remained a key point of contention. British leaders remained committed to the creation of a free and independent Poland after the war, and the US delegation understood that the defense of the Atlantic Charter principles extended to self-determination for the Poles. However, Stalin insisted that postwar Soviet security required that a "friendly" regime be in place in Warsaw. While the precise language concerning Poland's status remained ambiguous, more cynical Western leaders suspected that such a regime was likely to be nothing more than a Kremlin puppet. Nevertheless, London and Washington possessed little leverage. While American and British armies sat camped along the western reaches of Germany, the Red Army had taken Warsaw and was crossing the Oder River. In retrospect, it is difficult to imagine any possible chain of events that would have allowed Churchill and Roosevelt to change Stalin's stance on Poland. Churchill and Roosevelt could not gain through negotiation what the Red Army had purchased in blood.

Nevertheless, Western spirits ran high in the immediate wake of the conference. "The Conference in the Crimea was a turning point," Roosevelt told Congress. "We shall have to take the responsibility for world collaboration, or we shall have to bear the responsibility for another world conflict." Allied leaders at Yalta had found a "common ground for peace. It ought to spell the end of the system of unilateral action, the exclusive alliances, the spheres of influence, the balances of power, and all the other expedients that have been tried for centuries—and have always failed." The president's key adviser Harry Hopkins was even more enthusiastic: "We were absolutely certain that we had won the first great victory of the peace—and by 'we,' I mean all of us, the whole civilized human race." Kennan, however, remained characteristically gloomy. Yalta's plan for Germany was nothing more than a "meaningless platitude," he lamented. "Since we ourselves have no constructive ideas for the future of Germany, our influence can only be negative. And without our support the British can do nothing. The result is that the Russians will do as they please, first within their own zone and then, in increasing measure, in ours." The result would be economic collapse, a decline in living standards, and general upheaval leading to a "gulf of human despair, which will cover the heart of Central Europe."[12]

In truth, the Yalta Conference was neither a great success nor a dismal failure. The Western powers achieved as much as they could have at the conference; the Allied war effort was too heavily dependent on the Red Army to demand more. Nothing Roosevelt or Churchill could have done would have changed the reality that the Red Army occupied Poland, and Stalin would never allow an anti-Soviet government to take power in Warsaw. Ultimately, each of the three Allies attained their primary goals at Yalta. Weeks later, as the post-conference enthusiasm waned and the grim fate of Soviet-controlled Poland came into better focus, Roosevelt offered a more muted appraisal. "I didn't say the result was good," he noted. "I said it was the best I could do."[13]

AFTER YALTA, STALIN TURNED TO THE TASK OF CONSOLIDATING CONtrol over Eastern Europe. On February 10, the second-to-last day of the conference, Zhukov had informed Stalin that he intended to attack German forces before they could regroup and that he would then continue toward Berlin. Three days later, Zhukov ordered his commanders to prepare for this offensive, aiming at taking the capital by the end of February. Soon thereafter, however, Stalin ordered Zhukov to halt the attack and instead focus on Pomerania and Silesia. On February 17, the Soviet high command issued orders to the Second and Third Ukrainian Fronts to move on Vienna and eastern Austria. The Kremlin explained this change of plans as an effort to clear the Red Army's flanks and begin the buildup for the final assault on Berlin. Years later, however, Marshal Vasily Chuikov argued that this halt had been unnecessary. "Berlin could have been taken in February," he wrote. "And that, of course, would have hastened the end of the war." A chorus of voices—including Zhukov's—rushed to refute Chuikov, and Soviet censors excised the argument from subsequent editions of the marshal's memoirs.[14]

Historians David Glantz and Jonathan House argue that Stalin's real motivation for halting the Red Army's advance on Berlin lay in postwar political calculations. While the newly inked Yalta agreements had demarcated occupation zones for Germany, they had made no such provisions for Austria. If the Red Army had taken Berlin in February, it would have been capturing territory that had been designated for Soviet occupation. By capturing Vienna, however, Stalin's forces guaranteed a sizable zone of Soviet occupation in eastern Austria. "It seems clear," Glantz and House write, "that as the Red Army conducted its final campaign in eastern and central Europe to defeat Germany, Stalin manipulated his military strategy not only to capture Berlin but also to secure Vienna and the Danube basin." The Vistula-Oder Offensive had ripped through Poland, shredded two German army groups, and brought the Red Army to within forty miles of Berlin. Now, as Stalin's forces swept west, they left in their wake "the nuclei of governments that would ensure Soviet political dominance over central and eastern Europe for decades to come."[15]

The creation of pro-Soviet states across Eastern Europe sat at the core of Stalin's plans. Through early 1944, Soviet leaders anticipated a postwar Europe divided into British- and Soviet-controlled spheres of influence. Roosevelt had conveyed his intention to withdraw American forces from the continent after the end of the war, which would divide Europe between Britain, a sea power, and the Soviet Union, Europe's great land power. Although he hoped for good relations in the initial postwar period, Stalin remained pessimistic about long-term harmony with the capitalist world. The dictator believed that bourgeois capitalists were untrustworthy and history had revealed a long pattern of manipulation at the hands of the Western powers. As Stalin told Foreign Minister Vyacheslav Molotov, in the past, Russia had been able "to win wars but was unable to enjoy the fruits of its victories. . . . Russians are remarkable warriors, but they do not know how to make peace: they are deceived, underpaid." As historian Vladimir Pechatnov writes, the Soviet leader had no intention of allowing his Western allies to use Soviet soldiers as "cannon fodder, lure them with promises of major strategic gains, and then leave them empty-handed in the end." To guard against such a betrayal and against another catastrophic invasion from the west, the Kremlin intended to build a "glacis of 'friendly states'" across Eastern Europe.[16]

The precise details of Stalin's plans for this Eastern European glacis remain the subject of some debate. Although some Western observers warned that Stalin was instituting a forced Sovietization in capitals under the Red Army's control, recent scholars have argued that regimes across Eastern Europe in fact chose to adopt Soviet models of their own accord. Officially, Moscow pushed a "popular front" strategy that allowed for a variety of communist and noncommunist parties to vie for political power within liberated states. Only over time and in response to perceived provocations from the West did Moscow's grip tighten over Eastern Europe. On the other hand, the Soviet dictator outlined some of his thinking with fellow communist leaders. "This war is not as in the past," he told Yugoslav communist Milovan Djilas in April. "Whoever occupies a territory also imposes on it his own social system. Everyone imposes his own system as far as his army has power to do so. It cannot be otherwise."[17]

For their part, American and British leaders saw the Polish case as the clearest indication of Soviet plans for Eastern Europe. The Yalta agreements had been ambiguous regarding the postwar government of Poland, stipulating merely that the "Provisional Government which is now functioning in Poland should . . . be reorganized on a broader democratic basis with the inclusion of democratic leaders from Poland itself and from Poles abroad." The exact makeup of the government would be determined by negotiations between American, British, and Soviet officials. Accordingly, Ambassador

Harriman soon found himself in bare-knuckled negotiations with Foreign Minister Molotov. While Harriman pushed for representation for pro-Western Polish exiles in London, Molotov insisted that the pro-Soviet Lublin Poles dominate the postwar government in Warsaw. Churchill warned that "every day the Lublin Government is becoming more and more the Warsaw Government and the Rulers of Poland." As the negotiations dragged on, Moscow closed off Western access to Poland. "An impenetrable veil has been drawn across the scene," Churchill wrote. Harriman, too, was growing increasingly frustrated. On March 21, he wrote in dire tones that the Soviets were "attempting to wear us down step by step." In response, the United States must "reorient our whole attitude and our methods of dealing with the Soviet Government . . . unless we wish to accept the 20th century Barbarian invasion of Europe." The only course of action going forward was for Washington to adopt "a forceful policy of supporting those people that have the same general outlook . . . and concept of life that we do."[18]

Regardless of these top-level Allied discussions, the Wehrmacht fought on. Although the Americans had beaten back the German assault in the Ardennes, the shock of the offensive triggered a new round of controversy. British commanders leaped at the chance to once again castigate Eisenhower's broad front strategy and lobby for a single thrust against Berlin, to be led by Montgomery. Even Marshall now wondered if the burden of the campaign had overwhelmed his commander. However, after weeks of maneuvering and a contentious meeting in Malta, Eisenhower emerged still in command. It now seemed clear that the Wehrmacht would fight a hopeless battle to exact the highest possible price in blood from the Allied armies driving into the Reich. Eisenhower intended to launch a multipronged assault across the Rhine, with Montgomery's troops massing for a northern attack from the Netherlands, Lieutenant General Courtney Hodges and Brigadier General William Simpson attacking the Ruhr in the center, and Patton's and General Jacob Dever's armies moving in from the south toward Czechoslovakia, Austria, and the Elbe.[19]

In the Allies' path sat two massive dams along the Roer River. The previous October, a German prisoner of war had warned of plans to blow up the dams in the event of an Allied advance through the Roer Valley, unleashing a deluge of one hundred million metric tons of water that would drown any offensive. In early February, American forces captured the first of the dams with little resistance before pushing forward to take the battered towns of Kommerscheidt and Schmidt. After sunset on February 8, advance units from the Seventy-Eighth Division caught sight of the Schwammenauel Dam. German artillery fell as the advancing forces made their way toward the massive structure—1,200 feet across, 1,000 feet thick, and 170 feet high. Just before daybreak, American engineers slid down the spillway to access the dam's interior while others moved toward the control room. A half-dozen German defenders surrendered immediately. Though the dam remained intact, the retreating forces had destroyed the sluice gates and discharge valves, unleashing a torrent of water fifteen feet in diameter into the valley below. Fifteen American divisions were now forced to wait two weeks for the floodwaters to recede before continuing their advance.[20]

As Allied forces prepared to resume their ground campaign, American and British bombers pummeled German cities from the air. At 10:15 on the evening of February 13, British Pathfinder aircraft began dropping marker flares over Dresden, using the city's football stadium as the central target. Germany's seventh-largest city, Dresden was now filled with one hundred thousand refugees who had fled the advancing Red Army from the east, filling hospitals, schools, and public buildings as local officials scrambled to find space. Allied flares left a burning red "bull's-eye" for the following wave of Mosquito bombers dropping incendiaries. A second wave of five hundred bombers arrived just past 1:30 a.m. to a burning city lighting up the night sky. As the last bombers disappeared into the night, the inferno cast a glow visible from up to one hundred miles away. Morning brought another wave of 311 American B-17s, which dropped 771 tons of bombs on the city. The next day, a fourth wave of American bombers hit Dresden with 461 tons of bombs. The uncharacteristic accuracy of the attacks combined with steady westerly winds to whip the fires into a conflagration. As the inferno grew, it sucked in surrounding air, creating a vortex that built into a firestorm. Inside the conflagration, fiery winds ripped buildings apart, tore trees out of the ground, and melted asphalt. Many of those lucky enough to find shelter from the flames were suffocated by poisonous clouds of carbon monoxide. Between twenty-five thousand and thirty-five thousand people died in Dresden, most of them civilians.[21]

Allied leaders still held out hope that massive terror bombing might finally succeed in breaking German morale and bringing about a final surrender. In addition, Allied intelligence had identified Dresden as an important communications hub. Although the Americans had begun the war hoping to restrict strategic bombing to specific industrial targets, bad weather, German air defenses, and imprecise technology had led planners to incorporate attacks on cities as a necessary evil. Nevertheless, some officers complained that such operations amounted to little more than "baby killing schemes." One American general warned that such attacks would "absolutely convince the Germans that we are the barbarians they say we are, for it would be perfectly obvious to them that this is primarily a large-scale attack on civilians. . . . Of all the people killed in this attack over 95% of them can be expected to be civilians." British officers—for whom the Blitz was still a recent memory—seemed to harbor fewer reservations about destroying German cities, although Churchill later expressed concerns about the attacks.[22]

Beyond their questionable strategic value, large-scale bombing raids on German cities served a political purpose. The war in Europe had entered its final months, and American and British leaders were at pains to demonstrate their contributions to defeating the Third Reich. While the Red Army was tearing across Poland and into East Prussia, Eisenhower's forces remained stalled west of the Rhine. Strategic bombing appeared to some Allied leaders to be the clearest means of demonstrating their nations' contributions to the war. However, as General Henry "Hap" Arnold had lamented in the run-up to the Yalta Conference, the Soviets had yet to witness the ferocious power of the Allied bombing campaigns. "Stalin hasn't the faintest conception of the damage done to Germany and Japan by strategic bombing," he wrote in January 1945. In this spirit, American officials had carried photographs of bombed German cities to Yalta in hopes of impressing Stalin. But these images could not capture the full scale of the destruction. Dresden's immolation, only days after Yalta's end, provided further evidence of the fearsome power of Allied bombing. When the Red Army marched into the blackened ruins of Dresden, they found a city reduced to ashes—a vivid demonstration and a potential warning to any Soviet leaders who thought of turning their armies against the Western powers after Hitler's defeat.[23]

By the beginning of March, Allied armies were preparing to resume their assault against the last major geographic barrier in their path. The Rhine River cut a wide, deep channel as it flowed north through Germany from Swiss glaciers to empty in the North Sea. Any attempt to cross the river, Allied planners warned, would be comparable to "a short sea voyage." Engineers from the US Ninth Army considered the operation "their most important and carefully-planned since 'D' day." In preparation for the crossing, Allied commanders amassed over one thousand assault boats, six thousand bridge floats, fifty-four thousand tons of steel beams, and five million feet of lumber. While Allied forces finished off the remnants of the Wehrmacht west of the river, German engineers scrambled to set charges on the handful of bridges still standing. Explosives sent the Hohenzollern Bridge at Cologne into the waters of the Rhine on March 6, one day before General Courtney Hodges's First Army took the medieval city. Farther south, at the town of Remagen, however, the Ludendorff Bridge remained standing. Wehrmacht forces had set sixty charges across the bridge's thousand-foot span and received orders to wait until Allied forces approached before blowing the crossing. Just before 1:00 p.m., lead elements of the First Army sighted the still-intact outline of the bridge at Remagen. Two black stone towers guarded the entrances to the span on either bank. "Jesus, look at that," one sergeant gasped. "Do you know what the hell river that is?"[24]

American troops under the command of Lieutenant Karl Timmermann now raced through Remagen toward the bridge, fighting off a handful of stubborn defenders. At 4:00 p.m., Timmermann's company reached the western end of the bridge as enemy forces blew a crater in the road. The Americans responded by firing white-hot phosphorous shells to create a smoke screen. On the eastern bank, panicked civilians cowered in a railroad tunnel bored into the bluff overlooking the river as German engineers finished their preparations to blow the bridge. The lead engineer threw the switch to ignite the charges, but there was no detonation. Concluding that the circuit was broken, German volunteers ran out to light the fuse manually. Moments later, the combatants watched as an explosion shook the span, releasing billows of dust and black smoke. But the bridge stood. Timmermann's soldiers rushed forward to secure the crossing, cutting wires to the demolition boxes as they went. "Hot damn!" one sergeant exclaimed after relaying the news to headquarters. "We got a bridge over the Rhine and we're crossing over!" Bradley expressed a similar reaction. "This will bust him wide open. . . . Shove everything you can across it." The reaction at Allied headquarters was more muted as some planners warned that the crossing at Remagen led to nowhere, diverting forces away from Eisenhower's objectives farther north. Nevertheless, an intact bridge over the Rhine seemed too good to pass up. Eisenhower authorized five divisions to cross the river to establish a bridgehead on the eastern bank.[25]

News of the defeat at Remagen sent shock waves through the German leadership. Hitler ordered the arrest of four German officers to be held responsible for the debacle. Field Marshal Walter Model personally tried the accused on March 13–14 and ordered their immediate execution. Meanwhile, Wehrmacht commanders launched a series of furious counterattacks against the American bridgehead as well as the bridge itself. An attack by frogmen failed, as did the Luftwaffe's attempt to bomb the bridge. But on March 17—ten days after falling into American hands—the bridge finally collapsed. By then, however, the Allies had secured their bridgehead on the eastern bank and erected two pontoon bridges across the river.[26]

While the coup at Remagen seized headlines, Allied armies all along the front lines prepared to cross the Rhine. In the south, Patton's forces were once again on the move, charging through the Palatinate and pushing their lead elements across the Rhine at Nierstein on the night of March 22. "I peed in the Rhine today," Patton scribbled at the bottom of his official report. The following night, Montgomery's forces launched their own crossing near Wesel. Months in preparation, Montgomery's ponderous operation was the largest since D-Day. Two thousand guns, a fleet of RAF bombers, two airborne divisions, and almost one million troops stormed across the river to assault the depleted German defenses. Three days later, as Allied forces blasted their way forward, a British intelligence officer offered his assessment: "This is the collapse. The German line is broken. They no longer have a coherent system of defence between the Rhine and the Elbe. It is difficult to see what there is to stop us now."[27]

WHILE HIS ALLIES TORE THROUGH GERMAN DEFENSES AND DROVE into the heart of the Reich, Stalin was growing increasingly suspicious. The Red Army had made little progress in the weeks since Yalta, and the drive on Vienna had stalled. On March 25, Churchill himself surveyed the banks of the Rhine River. Two days later, Reuters reported that the Americans and British were no longer encountering resistance as they pushed toward Berlin. On the western front, Allied forces were killing sixty Germans a day while the Red Army was killing eight hundred. Meanwhile, the number of German soldiers reported as "missing" in the West outnumbered those on the eastern front by a factor of ten. To many in the Kremlin, it appeared as if the Wehrmacht was effectively standing down in the West while throwing its last reserves against the Red Army. The ever-paranoid Stalin now worried that the Americans and British might strike a deal with Hitler's commanders to surrender Germany to the Western powers in order to stave off the horrors of a vengeful Soviet occupation. And it was not too far-fetched to imagine a scenario in which the Western Allies chose to unleash surrendered German troops against the Red Army in a campaign to liberate Eastern Europe. On this point, Stalin's paranoia was justified: Western officials had been considering just such a possibility since August 1943. Thus, reports of rapid American and British progress in the West were met with "extreme reserve" in Moscow, Ambassador Harriman explained in early April. "The Russians evidently conclude . . . that the Germans are putting up only token resistance to our advance, and suspect that they may be acting this way either in pursuance to some tacit understanding with our military authorities or in the hope of obtaining some sort of assurance of mild treatment from our side."[28]

Stalin's suspicions had been further inflamed by the news that German forces in Italy commanded by Field Marshal Albert Kesselring had arranged a meeting with American intelligence officer Allen Dulles to negotiate a surrender. Led by Waffen-SS general Karl Wolff, the German efforts were aimed at ending increasingly hopeless resistance in Italy and securing a pardon for Wolff himself. The American refusal to allow Soviet representation at the meeting seems to have convinced Stalin that his allies might be plotting against him. In response, the irate dictator sent a series of angry telegrams to Roosevelt accusing the Western Allies of striking a separate deal with the Wehrmacht: "As a result of this at the present moment the Germans on the Western front in fact have ceased the war against England and the United States. At the same time the Germans continue the war with Russia, the Ally of England and the United States. It is understandable that such a situation can in no way serve the cause of preservation of the strengthening of trust between our countries." Roosevelt vehemently denied Stalin's accusations, insisting that the negotiations concerned purely military conditions and carried no wider political implications. Churchill suggested that Soviet leaders were dismayed by the rapid advance of the American and British armies and that Stalin's messages were an attempt to bully the Anglophone powers. Churchill also warned that the Kremlin had not yet agreed to occupation zones in Austria despite the fact that the Red Army was close to taking Vienna. "All this makes it the more important that we should join hands with the Russian armies as far to the east as possible and if circumstances allow, enter Berlin."[29]

Stalin's outburst took place amid an even more momentous set of events at Eisenhower's headquarters. In late March, Eisenhower had decided to halt the Western drive toward Berlin and instead focus on the Hamburg-Kiel area in the north, the Leipzig area in the center, and the Nurnberg-Regensburg-Munich area in the south. "Berlin as a strategic area is discounted as it is now largely destroyed," he wrote, "and we have information that the Ministries are moving to the Erfurt-Leipzig region. Moreover, it is so near to the Russian front that once they start moving again they will reach it in a matter of days."[30]

Churchill and the British chiefs insisted that Hitler's capital must not be left to the Red Army. "I say quite frankly that Berlin remains of high strategic importance," wrote Churchill. "Nothing will exert a psychological effect of despair upon all German forces of resistance equal to that of the fall of Berlin. It will be the supreme signal of defeat to the German people." Moreover, the Soviets were on the brink of overrunning Austria and capturing Vienna. "If they also take Berlin," he wrote, "will not their impression that they have been the overwhelming contributor to our common victory be unduly imprinted in their minds, and may this not lead them into a mood which will raise grave and formidable difficulties in the future? I therefore consider that from a political standpoint we should march as far east into Germany as possible and that should Berlin be in our grasp we should certainly take it."[31]

But Eisenhower remained steadfast in his decision. "I am the first to admit that a war is waged in pursuance of political aims," he wrote. If the capital could be seized "at little cost we should, of course, do so. But I regard it as militarily unsound at this stage of the proceedings to make Berlin a major objective, particularly in view of the fact that it is only 35 miles from the Russian lines."[32]

Stalin, for his part, seemed pleased by Eisenhower's decision. "Berlin has lost its former strategic importance," the dictator wrote in an April 1 message to Eisenhower. "The Soviet High Command therefore plans to allot secondary forces in the direction of Berlin." That same day, Stalin summoned his top generals, Zhukov and Konev, to his wood-paneled Kremlin study lined with portraits of great Russian generals of past centuries. The Americans and British were preparing to take Berlin, he explained. "Well, who is going to take Berlin, we or the Allies?" he asked. Konev insisted that Soviet forces would take the city before the Allies. "So that's what you're like," Stalin responded, grinning. The dictator then proceeded to trace out positions on the map between Konev's and Zhukov's armies leading toward the capital, goading his generals into a two-way race to take Berlin. The glory would go to the first Soviet commander to take the city.[33]

WHILE SOVIET COMMANDERS PREPARED TO SEIZE BERLIN, AMERIcan officials mounted a campaign to alert Roosevelt to the rising Soviet threat. Harriman was among the most vocal. "The Soviet Government views all matters from the standpoint of their own selfish interests," he wrote in early April. Communist forces were exploiting Europe's economic difficulties to promote Moscow's influence at the expense of the Western powers. "We must clearly recognize that the Soviet program is the establishment of totalitarianism, ending personal liberty and democracy as we know and respect it," he wrote. "Unless we are ready to live in a world dominated largely by Soviet influence, we must use our economic power to assist those countries that are naturally friendly to our concepts in so far as we can possibly do so." Two days later, Harriman sent another telegram stressing the need to reevaluate Washington's relationship with Moscow. Soviet leaders, he said, were building "a unilateral security ring through the domination of their border states" while simultaneously working to undermine democracy and Western influence in other countries. The Roosevelt administration had expressed reservations about Kremlin policies but had not been firm enough. Lend-Lease shipments continued despite Stalin's actions, and Roosevelt had refrained from challenging the dictator in the hopes of maintaining good relations with Moscow. This approach had backfired, Harriman insisted. The Kremlin interpreted Washington's generosity "as a sign of weakness," he wrote. "They do not understand that their present actions seriously jeopardize the attainment of satisfactory relations with us and unless they are made to understand this now, they will become increasingly difficult to deal with."[34]

But Harriman's efforts to redirect the administration's approach to Moscow were derailed by Roosevelt's sudden death. The president had been diagnosed with high blood pressure and congestive heart failure in March 1944 but had hidden his condition from the public. Roosevelt's aides had tried to keep him to a reduced schedule, but the president had been clearly exhausted. In late March, Roosevelt's cardiologist noted his poor appearance: "Color is poor (grey). Very tired." At the end of the month, the president departed to his personal retreat in Warm Springs, Georgia. There, his health seemed to improve, but on April 12, while working his way through a batch of papers, he looked up with a pained expression. "I have a terrific pain in the back of my head," he said, and then he collapsed. At 3:30 p.m., the president was declared dead, the result of a stroke.[35]

Roosevelt's death sent shock waves through Moscow. Molotov, the Soviet foreign minister, rushed to the US embassy at 3:00 a.m. to pay his condolences. "He seemed deeply moved and disturbed," reported Harriman. Hours later, Harriman paid a visit to Stalin. "He greeted me in silence and stood holding my hand for about 30 seconds before asking me to sit down," he wrote. The Soviet leader asked about the details of Roosevelt's death before the conversation turned toward his successor. Harriman assured Stalin that Truman would carry on the late president's plans. However, the exact nature of those plans remained subject to interpretation—and the ambassador intended to shape that interpretation.[36]

Following his meeting with Molotov, Harriman received permission to return to the United States to brief Truman on the state of US-Soviet relations. While Roosevelt had conducted relations with Stalin according to his own designs, the change in power presented an opportunity to change course. The ambassador rushed back to Washington via Italy and North Africa in a record-setting forty-nine hours, arriving just before midnight on April 18. At noon on April 20, President Harry Truman received Harriman in the Oval Office. The ambassador was blunt, warning Truman that the United States was faced with a "barbarian invasion of Europe." The Kremlin was pursuing two lines of policy: the first sought cooperation with Washington and London; the second pursued unilateral control over Eastern Europe. Moscow had interpreted Washington's "generosity and desire to cooperate" as an "indication that the Soviet Government could do anything that it wished without having trouble with the United States." While it would be possible to establish a working relationship with the Kremlin, Harriman explained, it would require the "abandonment of the illusion that for the immediate future the Soviet Government was going to act in accordance with the principles which the rest of the world held to in international affairs." Washington must take a tougher line in future negotiations with Moscow. Truman appeared to take the ambassador's warnings to heart and expressed his intention to be firm in his dealings with the Soviets.[37]

Harriman made the same case to leaders in the State Department during his visit to Washington. "The basic and irreconcilable difference of objective between the Soviet Union and the United States," he argued, "was its urge for its own security to see Soviet concepts extend to as large an area of the world as possible." As the Kremlin expanded its influence along its frontiers, he warned, it "would attempt to penetrate the next adjacent countries." The United States should not overestimate Moscow's strength. The Red Army was powerful but disorganized; the nation as a whole remained poor and "fantastically backward"; its road and rail networks were underdeveloped; and most Muscovites lived in "slum"-like conditions. As a result, the Kremlin would not provoke a direct conflict with the West. "But they will take control of everything they can by bluffing." Looking forward, the ambassador offered a stark assessment: "Russian plans for establishing satellite states are a threat to the world and to us. The excuse offered that they must guard against a future German menace is only a cover for other plans. . . . The extent to which the Soviet [*sic*] will go in all directions will depend on the extent of our pressure." The ambassador had proposed an early version of what was to become the Cold War policy of containment.[38]

This debate came to a head two days later, on April 23. In preparation for a meeting with Molotov, Truman called together his top foreign policy advisers. The Soviets were working to install a puppet government in Poland, Secretary of War Stimson told the group. Truman explained that to date, Washington's agreements with Moscow "had been a one way street and that could not continue; it was now or never." The president then asked his advisers' opinions on the matter. Stimson urged caution. The Soviets "had kept their word" on military matters, and cooperation in the war remained of paramount importance. He then added that "25 years ago virtually all of Poland had been Russian." Ultimately, he believed that the "Russians perhaps were being more realistic than we were in regard to their own security." Secretary of the Navy James Forrestal worried that the Kremlin seemed to believe that the Western Allies had given it a free hand in Eastern Europe. This had to change: "If the Russians were to be rigid in their attitude we had better have a show down with them now [rather] than later." Harriman warned that a confrontation risked a "real break" with Moscow, but if "properly handled it might be avoided." Army Chief of Staff Marshall also urged caution: "The possibility of a break with Russia was very serious." General Deane responded that, based on his experiences in Moscow, "if we were afraid of the Russians we would get nowhere. . . . We should be firm when we were right." Truman thanked his advisers and announced his determination to press Molotov on the issue of Poland: "There was no reason why we should fail to stand up to our understanding of the Crimean agreements."[39]

Several hours later, the president welcomed Molotov to what was to be a fateful meeting. Truman was "sorry to learn that no progress had been made towards a solution of the Polish question." Moscow seemed to be pushing a set of Polish officials who were not "representative of all Polish democratic elements," at the expense of other elements of Polish society. When Molotov protested, Truman responded that "all [he was] asking was that the Soviet Government carry out the Crimean decision on Poland. . . . An agreement had been reached on Poland. . . . It only remained for Marshal Stalin to carry it out in accordance with his word." Truman then handed Molotov a press release to be shared with Stalin warning that "the failure to go forward at this time with the implementation of the Crimean decision on Poland would seriously shake confidence in the unity of the three [Allied] Governments and their determination to continue the collaboration in the future as they have in the past."[40]

One observer who watched Molotov leave the meeting noted that he had "never seen a man come out more ashen in my life." Truman seemed pleased. "I gave it to him straight," he boasted. "I let him have it. It was straight one-two to the jaw." Reflecting on the meeting, the new president asked one adviser, "Did I do it right?" Harriman worried that Truman had come on too strong. "I think it was a mistake," he explained later. "His behavior gave Molotov an excuse to tell Stalin that the Roosevelt policy was being abandoned." Assistant Secretary of State Charles Bohlen remembered the meeting as "probably the first sharp words uttered during the war by an American President to a high Soviet official."[41]

WHILE LEADERS IN WASHINGTON REASSESSED THEIR RELATIONSHIP with Moscow, frontline forces in Europe were already preparing for a future confrontation with the Red Army. As Allied troops drove deeper into the Third Reich, special teams of British and US soldiers scoured the German countryside in search of the Nazis' military, scientific, and engineering secrets. Hitler's scientists had made great strides in the areas of rocket engineering, jet propulsion, and chemical and biological weapons. These were the Führer's "wonder weapons" that promised to save his crumbling empire. While V-2 rocket attacks terrorized London and Antwerp—one killed 567 people in Antwerp's Cinema Rex—they did nothing to slow the Allied armies crashing across the Reich's borders. Even so, the minds and the engineering behind the weapons represented prizes of the first order for the Allied militaries quick enough to claim them. Whoever could seize and repurpose these Nazi weapon technologies would gain a marked advantage in any future war.

In late March, British teams hunting German scientists caught a break. While Allied forces poured into Bonn, German scientists at the local university scrambled to destroy documents, burning large caches and flushing others down toilets. A Polish lab technician had retrieved a batch of documents that had proved too large for the toilet and handed the papers to a British soldier. Upon closer inspection, the documents contained a list of German scientists compiled by Werner Osenberg, a mechanical engineer and SS officer who had been charged with rounding up leading German scientists and engineers to run Hitler's weapons programs. The list together with files from Osenberg's office provided the names of thousands of scientists and engineers, many of whom now became prime targets for Allied forces.[42]

Among the greatest prizes was the Mittelwerk V-2 weapons factory outside of Nordhausen. In an effort to elude Allied aerial attacks, Nazi officials had hidden the factory in an old gypsum mine bored into the Harz Mountains. Thousands of slave laborers from a nearby concentration camp worked twelve-hour shifts to expand the tunnels to accommodate V-2 production. The tunnels themselves were unventilated and had no running water or sanitation. For half those sent to Mittelwerk, the assignment amounted to a death sentence. Prisoners died from starvation, disease, and savage beatings. American troops with the 104th Infantry Division captured the facilities on the morning of April 11. "The camp was literally a charnel house, with the distinction that a small proportion of the bodies therein were not quite dead," explained one colonel. The living lay "intermingled indiscriminately" with the dead. Medical personnel had to scrutinize the victims to "ascertain whether they contained life. Those that were living were in such advanced stages of starvation, and frequently tuberculosis, that there was little hope for them."[43]

But to the Allied teams hunting Hitler's wonder weapons, Nordhausen constituted a gold mine. In all, the Americans recovered enough parts to assemble one hundred V-2 rockets. However, the components themselves were of limited use without Germany's rocket scientists. Making matters worse, Mittelwerk lay deep inside the Soviet zone of occupation. Soviet forces were set to take control of Nordhausen in the coming weeks. The Americans now raced to salvage as much material and information as possible to be packed and shipped back to the United States before the Red Army's arrival. Meanwhile, the lead scientist behind the Nazi rocket program, Wernher von Braun, had fled south to the Bavarian Alps along with hundreds of his colleagues to await the Allies' arrival. Well aware of his value on the international market, von Braun had spent the closing days of the war sunbathing in an Alpine ski resort, gazing at the surrounding peaks and enjoying a well-stocked larder courtesy of Hitler's SS. As an added insurance policy, he and his associates had stashed fourteen tons of the most important engineering documents in an abandoned mine outside of Dörnten.[44]

On May 2, von Braun sent his brother, Magnus, down the mountain by bicycle to contact the American forces below. Fearing a trap, US intelligence ordered Magnus to return to his brother and bring the scientists down for a formal surrender. When von Braun and his colleagues arrived that evening, they were treated to a meal of eggs and coffee, given clean beds, and gathered for celebratory photographs with American soldiers the next morning. The Americans had Hitler's top rocket scientists in their grasp, but they would need to act quickly if they hoped to harness their knowledge. In late May, Major Robert Staver, head of the army's special V-2 mission, sent an urgent telegram to his superiors: "Have in custody over 400 top research development personnel. . . . Developed V-2. . . . The thinking of the scientific directors of this group is 25 years ahead of U.S. . . . Later version of this rocket should permit launching from Europe to U.S. . . . Immediate action recommended to prevent loss of whole or part of this group to other interested parties. Urgently request reply as early as possible." Staver's telegram helped convince American leaders that the Nazi scientists must be recruited to serve the United States. In the coming months, von Braun, along with much of his team, V-2 rocket parts, and fourteen tons of documents, would depart for the United States.[45] In addition to von Braun's research materials, Allied forces recovered jet-powered Messerschmitt 262 aircraft, Henschel Hs 293 glide bombs, and key components of Germany's chemical and biological weapons programs.

Soviet officers on the eastern front were just as eager to salvage what they could of the Third Reich's armaments for the anticipated postwar contest with the United States. The Soviet Military Administration in Karlshorst coordinated these efforts, which aligned with broader initiatives to dismantle Germany's industrial base and send it to the Soviet Union as partial reparations for the destruction wrought by the Wehrmacht. Unfortunately for Moscow, many of the Third Reich's most important scientists had either been stationed in areas slated to fall under Western occupation or had fled west before the Red Army's advance. Among the most important were Werner Heisenberg and Otto Hahn, who had been working with the Kaiser Wilhelm Institute for Physics, which had been moved to the outskirts of the Black Forest. Even so, significant numbers of scientists and engineers remained in territories that had fallen under Red

Army control. So, too, did many laboratories that contained valuable research and equipment that the Kremlin was more than happy to seize. Entire facilities were broken down, crated up, and shipped to the Soviet Union. In some cases, even water faucets and doorknobs were removed and sent east.[46]

As the Red Army advanced, teams of Soviet scientists and military officials appeared at key installations bearing vodka and lard in an attempt to win over German technical experts. While they failed to capture the most coveted individuals, such as von Braun and Heisenberg, leading scientists such as Peter Adolf Thiessen, Ludwig Bewilogua, and Max Steenbeck fell into Soviet hands, along with the Kaiser Wilhelm Institutes for Biology, Biochemistry, Chemistry, and Silicate Research. In short order, German laboratories, machinery, and scientists and their families were packed up and sent to the communist empire. Soviet officials also came into possession of substantial stockpiles of V-2 rocket technology from the Mittlewerk factory at Nordhausen, as well as 60 percent of Germany's aeronautical industry.[47]

Once integrated into each nation's military-industrial complex, Nazi military technology would form critical components of what would become Moscow and Washington's Cold War arsenals. Post-1945 missile technology, biological and chemical weapons, jet propulsion, and even the space race all trace components of their lineage back to Nazi engineering. Although the Third Reich perished, its weapons systems and the men who built them lived on as foundational elements of the Cold War.

WHILE THE ALLIES SWEPT UP THE THIRD REICH'S LEADING SCIENtific minds, the stage was set for the final climactic battle for Berlin. For twelve years, Berlin had stood as the capital of Hitler's empire. From his seat at the Reich Chancellery, the Führer had directed the conquest of Europe, his armies tearing through Poland and France and into the heart of the Soviet Union. Now, in the spring of

1945, the tattered remnants of the Wehrmacht braced to defend Hitler's capital from the Soviet host massing at its gates. Since February, Soviet forces had camped along the banks of the Oder River, clearing their northern flanks and preparing for the final assault against Berlin. Across the river, the floodplain presented a maze of marshes, streams, and ditches that would slow any advancing force. Farther west, a line of bluffs crowned by the Seelow Heights rose above the floodplain, forming a natural bastion for the defenders. German commanders had used the pause to prepare an intricate network of trenches, bunkers, antitank traps, and gun positions along the main approaches to the capital.[48]

Alarmed by the swift American and British advances across the Rhine and worried that Eisenhower might try to seize Berlin before the Red Army, Soviet leaders had accelerated their timetable, leaving their commanders with a mere two weeks to complete their preparations. The Soviet plan called for a full-scale assault on Berlin by three separate fronts. Rokossovsky's Second Belorussian Front would attack from the north, Konev's First Ukrainian Front would push up from the south, and Zhukov's First Belorussian Front would strike west in the center. Soviet troops were to crush the German defenders in their path, take Berlin, and link up with the Western Allies on the banks of the Elbe River. Altogether, Soviet forces consisted of seventeen combined-arms armies, four air armies, four tank armies, and thirteen mobile corps comprising 2.5 million troops, over 6,000 tanks, 41,600 guns, and 7,500 aircraft. Against this massive force, German commanders had assembled some eight hundred thousand troops, no small number of whom were second-rate Volkssturm battalions composed of poorly trained youths or men too old for regular military service. The Luftwaffe still numbered 1,600 aircraft, but severe fuel shortages grounded most of them. Soviet tank forces likewise vastly outnumbered German panzers.[49]

German officials had paid little attention to the plan for defense of Berlin. Hitler had declared the capital to be a fortress in February but refused to assign troops to its defenses. The Nazi leadership, sinking into ever-deeper levels of delusion, seemed to believe that the Wehrmacht could stop the Red Army along the banks of the Oder. No detailed plans were in place to feed the city's 3.5 million residents in the event of a siege. When asked how he intended to nourish the 120,000 infants still inside the city, Hitler insisted that all young children had already left. Goebbels proposed bringing in cows to provide milk but declined to explain how said cattle would be fed. There also was no adequate plan for evacuation of Berlin's civilian population. Rather, Hitler looked to a different approach. On March 19, the Führer issued his infamous Nero Decree. As they withdrew, German forces were to destroy everything that might be of use to the Red Army. But this scorched-earth policy would leave nothing for the civilian population after the end of the war. "If the war is lost," Hitler explained, "the people will also be lost [and] it is not necessary to worry about their needs for elemental survival. On the contrary, it is best for us to destroy even these things. For the nation has proved to be weak, and the future belongs entirely to the strong people of the East. Whatever remains after this battle is in any case only the inadequates because the good ones will be dead." Although Albert Speer ultimately blocked the most severe elements of the Nero Decree, it had become clear that the Führer intended to drag the entire nation with him into the abyss.[50]

A COLD, QUIET DARKNESS HUNG OVER THE ODER FLOODPLAIN IN THE early hours of April 16. The predawn gloom hid thousands of troops preparing to launch one of the largest offensives of the war. A Soviet captain gazing across the assembled ranks watched "swarms of assault troops, lines of tanks, platoons of engineers with sections of pontoon bridges and rubber boats. Everywhere the bank of the river was jammed with men and equipment and yet there was complete silence." Soviet tanks festooned with graffiti reading "From Moscow to Berlin" and "50 kilometers to the lair of the Fascist Beast" waited alongside rifle regiments for the order to attack. An artillery chief warned his crew to yell once the barrage began to equalize the air pressure in order to avoid bursting their eardrums. In his command bunker overlooking the bridgehead, Zhukov checked his watch before peering through his field glasses at his forces. "Now, comrades. Now," he ordered. Moments later, 140 searchlights snapped on, blasting German positions with blinding light as thousands of Soviet guns roared in the darkness. It was 4:00 a.m. Thirty-five miles to the west, on the outskirts of Berlin, residents living amid the bombed-out ruins heard what sounded like distant thunder across the horizon as the city's dogs began howling in the night.[51]

Despite its initial fury, the Soviet onslaught soon slowed. "What the hell do you mean—your troops are pinned down?" Zhukov roared upon hearing the news. Soviet tanks had become bogged down on the marshy floodplain, making them easy targets for German artillery atop the Seelow Heights. German commanders had withdrawn their frontline troops in anticipation of the Red Army's opening bombardment, leaving their defenses largely intact. Making matters worse, Zhukov's searchlights had blinded his own forces and done little to confuse the enemy. Now, burning wrecks and Soviet corpses littered the approaches to the heights. To the south, Konev's armies were making better progress, having secured 133 of their 150 planned Neisse River crossings. While Zhukov's troops battered away at the hardened defenses along the Seelow Heights, Konev eyed the prospect of being the first to reach Berlin. Meanwhile, inside the city, Hitler warned that the enemy's final assault had begun. "This time the Bolshevist will experience the old fate of Asia: he must and shall fall before the capital city of the German Reich," he told his commanders. "If every soldier at the Eastern Front does his duty in the coming days and weeks, the last onrush of Asia will be broken. . . . Berlin will remain German, Vienna will be German once more and Europe will never be Russian."[52]

The clashes outside the city told a different story. Zhukov's troops had slogged through three days of heavy fighting for the Seelow Heights as German commanders fed their reserves into the battle. Soviet soldiers dashed from one shell crater to another as a steady drizzle soaked both the living and the dead. "Everywhere lay smashed German guns, vehicles, burning tanks and many corpses," wrote one officer. The rain had cleared by April 17, giving way to columns of smoke drifting across the battlefield. Soviet artillery began shelling every building in sight, igniting countless fires that sent the stench of burning flesh—human and beast—across the countryside. The Red Army had suffered some thirty thousand casualties, but Zhukov continued grinding forward. Soviet superiority in aircraft, armor, artillery, and infantry were wearing the German defenses down. On April 20, Zhukov's forces achieved breakthroughs in the north and south, pushing toward Bernau and Diedersdorf and moving into position to begin shelling Berlin. Konev's armies were also driving up from the south and took the German general staff headquarters on April 21. The converging Soviet fronts enveloped the German Ninth Army in the forest outside of Halbe, trapping many of the last Wehrmacht forces that might have been used to fight inside Berlin itself. Two days later, Konev's and Zhukov's armies met near Potsdam, completing their encirclement of the capital.[53]

Inside the Führerbunker, the Nazi regime's last holdouts were participating in a macabre drama. Hitler, his face worn and haggard, broke down on the afternoon of April 22, howling that he had been betrayed. The war was lost. All that was left was to watch as his thousand-year Reich went up in flames. But he would not flee like some bandit to his Alpine fortress in Berchtesgaden, as his aides suggested. Instead, he would choose suicide. Joining him, he determined, would be his closest supporters, his longtime girlfriend—and soon-to-be wife—Eva Braun, and his German shepherd, Blondi. Most disturbing, Joseph Goebbels and his wife, Magda, brought their six children to the bunker to join Hitler in death. "If all goes well," Goebbels insisted, "then it's in any case good. If things don't go well and the Führer finds in Berlin an honourable death and Europe were to become bolshevized, then in five years at the latest the Führer would become a legendary personality and National Socialism would have attained mythical status."[54]

On the surface above, Zhukov unleashed General Chuikov's Eighth Guards Army, experienced urban fighters who had honed their tactics in the ruins of Stalingrad. The most stalwart German defenders took positions in basements and cellars to attack advancing Soviet tanks at short range with lethal Panzerfausts while riflemen fired from upper floors. Soviet forces resorted to blasting every window with submachine gun fire or leveling whole buildings with artillery and tank rounds. Infantry advanced by using smoke screens, firing at any movement, and lobbing grenades into cellars and clearing suspected enemy positions with flamethrowers. Red Army troops used captured Panzerfausts to blast gaping holes in the walls of tightly packed structures, advancing from building to building as they fought their way deeper into Berlin. The carnage took a terrible toll on civilians trapped in the city. "We didn't have time to distinguish who was who," one Red Army officer explained. "Sometimes we just threw grenades into the cellars and passed on." German women standing in queues for food or water braved shellfire and air strikes. Survivors scrounged for food before rushing back to dark, filthy cellars.[55]

Women faced the additional danger of sexual assault. As Soviet forces approached the borders of Germany, propagandists had ramped up their calls for vengeance. "Woe to the land of the murderers," read Zhukov's orders to his armies in January. "We will get our terrible revenge for everything." Another message from the Red Army announced that "on German soil there is only one master—the Soviet soldier, that he is both the judge and the punisher for the torments of his fathers and mothers, for the destroyed cities and villages." Reports from some villages in East Prussia told of burning houses, looted food and alcohol, and the mass rape of every female over the age of thirteen. The violence appeared to reach a crescendo as the Red Army fought its way into Berlin. American diplomat Robert Murphy reported that credible sources claimed that "the majority of the eligible female population" of Berlin were raped. While Murphy's account was probably exaggerated, credible accounts suggest hundreds of thousands and possibly millions of assaults. As the Red Army advanced and rumors of widespread sexual violence at the hands of Soviet soldiers raced through the country, women learned to hide through the night and emerge only in the morning, when drunken soldiers were likely to be asleep. Horror stories of gang rapes, repeated assaults, rampant venereal disease, and victims dying by suicide would cast a shadow over the opening weeks and months of the Soviet occupation.[56]

Berlin now descended into a maelstrom. From his vantage point atop the Zoo flak tower, one German colonel gazed at a "panoramic view of the burning, smouldering and smoking great city, a scene which again and again shook one to the core." As the battle for the capital entered its final stages, Soviet commanders focused on the last great symbol of Nazi power: the Reichstag. The massive gray building had housed the German parliament until 1933, when an arsonist had set the structure on fire. It nevertheless had retained its iconic status. As the first rays of light fell on the burning city on April 30, Soviet troops peered across the ruined Königsplatz at the building, some four hundred meters away. "If there had been no fighting," wrote one Soviet journalist, "this distance could be crossed in a few minutes, but now it seemed impassable, covered with shell holes, railway sleepers, pieces of wire and trenches." A collapsed tunnel had flooded to form a moat in the attackers' path. Soviet troops began their assault at 6:00 a.m. but quickly found themselves pinned down by fire from the surrounding buildings. They pushed forward with the help of artillery support and Katyusha rocket launchers, but progress remained slow. As night fell, the attackers finally burst into the building. As combat raged inside the main hall, blood spattered across the surrounding columns and grenades ignited fires throughout the corridors. Soviet soldiers fought their way up to the second floor, taking heavy casualties. Shortly before 11:00 p.m., Red Army commanders claimed victory, but fighting continued into the next day.[57]

As the battle for the Reichstag raged, another drama was unfolding some five hundred meters to the south beneath the Reich

Chancellery. Just before 3:00 a.m. on April 30, Hitler received word from Field Marshal Wilhelm Keitel that the Ninth Army was surrounded and unable to break through to rescue Berlin. Having lost his last hope, the Führer began saying his goodbyes. Dawn brought the thunder of Soviet artillery reverberating from the surface down through the bunker. Hitler ordered that his body be cremated. Several minutes before 3:30 p.m., Hitler and Eva Braun retired to his study and shut the door. The pair were found ten minutes later, slumped over on a sofa. Braun had swallowed poison. Hitler had shot himself in the temple. Their bodies were wrapped in blankets, taken up to the garden above the bunker, doused with gasoline, and set ablaze.[58]

WHILE ZHUKOV'S TROOPS FOUGHT THEIR WAY INTO BERLIN, EISEN-hower's armies kept watch along the banks of the Elbe. On the morning of April 24, Lieutenant Albert Kotzebue led a patrol out of the town of Trebsen. His orders were to drive east toward the Elbe in search of Red Army units rumored to be in the area. Kotzebue's patrol ran across assorted groups of Germans, most of whom were eager to surrender to the Americans and fearful of being turned over to the Russians. The patrol spent the night in a farm compound in the town of Kühren while German stragglers continued drifting in to offer their surrender. Kotzebue's force set out again the next morning after a breakfast of eggs and bacon. At 11:30 a.m., the patrol sighted a lone horseman several hundred yards away in the village of Leckwitz. The rider disappeared into a courtyard as the Americans approached. Kotzebue's men soon located the man in the middle of a crowd of refugees and confirmed their suspicions: he was a Soviet cavalryman. Kotzebue's patrol had made the first Western contact with the Red Army. The Russian soldier seemed withdrawn and suspicious and directed the Americans to a Polish partisan who was eager to lead them to the Soviet command post. Thirty minutes later, the patrol found a group of brown-shirted soldiers milling around a column of wrecked vehicles on the other side of the Elbe. Kotzebue's men fired two green

flares—the agreed signal between the two armies. Their Polish companion hollered "Amerikanski" to the Russians on the opposite bank
as both groups now rushed toward the river. After securing a boat,
the Americans paddled across. The two sides exchanged salutes and
shook hands while photographers scrambled to take pictures.[59]

This was the first of many meetings as word of the linkup circulated. A US soldier and Soviet soldier met several hours later on
a ruined bridge spanning the Elbe at Torgau. Not knowing what to
say, the American "just grinned and reached out to pound the Russian on the knees." After crawling across the eastern bank, soldiers
from the two forces united in celebration. "Both sides pumped arms
and slapped each other on the back, grinned and exchanged greet-
ings," the after-action report said.[60] Soon after, commanders from the
two armies met up to drink toasts to Roosevelt, Truman, Stalin, and
Churchill.

The official German surrender took place at Eisenhower's headquarters in Reims at 2:41 a.m. on May 7. Bursts from reporters' flash-
bulbs lit the room as General Alfred Jodl and Admiral Hans-Georg
von Friedeburg signed the 234-word document. Eisenhower waited
down the hall, puffing on a cigarette. "The German people and the
German armed forces are, for better or worse, delivered into the victors' hands," Jodl declared. "In this hour I can only express the hope
that the victor will treat them with generosity." The general was then
marched into Eisenhower's office. The supreme commander warned
Jodl that he would be held personally responsible for any breach of
the surrender's terms. Then he said, "I suppose this calls for a bottle
of champagne."[61] As news of Germany's surrender spread, throngs of
joyous citizens flooded the streets of cities and towns across the world.
But even as millions celebrated in London, Moscow, Paris, and Washington, Allied leaders in both the East and West sensed the darker
implications of their victory: while the struggle for Europe had ended,
the struggle for the postwar world was only just beginning.

On May 22, 1945, British planners delivered Churchill their
top secret assessment of a potential war against the Soviet Union,

code-named Operation Unthinkable, with the goal of imposing "upon Russia the will of the United States and the British empire." While initial success in a surprise attack might convince Moscow to pull out of Eastern Europe, in the absence of a quick, decisive victory, Soviet forces would be able to wage total war against the Western powers. "There is virtually no limit to the distance it would be necessary for the Allies to penetrate in order to render further resistance impossible," the report warned, and the risk of repeating Germany's mistakes with Barbarossa appeared high. The British chiefs of staff estimated that the Red Army outnumbered US and British forces by a factor of two to one. Allied forces could likely be supplemented with ten intact German divisions, which could be expected to resume their fight against the Red Army. While Western forces would enjoy distinct advantages in the air and sea, these would by no means negate Soviet superiority on land. The result, the report concluded, was likely to be a long, drawn-out war—in short, a bloodbath. After reviewing the chiefs' analysis, Churchill stressed that Unthinkable remained "a precautionary study of what, I hope, is still a highly improbable event."[62]

In all likelihood, Soviet spies in the United Kingdom alerted Stalin to the existence of Operation Unthinkable in the following weeks—a revelation that would have confirmed the dictator's abiding distrust of his Western allies and reinforced his determination to consolidate his hold over Eastern Europe in anticipation of a future war against the capitalist states.[63]

American officials would also soon shift their attention from fighting the Axis powers to confronting the Red Army. In October 1945, US military intelligence submitted a comprehensive assessment of Moscow's military capabilities and strategic ambitions that would form the basis of future war plans against the Soviet Union. The authors warned that the Kremlin was pursuing a foreign policy that was "expansion, nationalistic and imperialist in character." Moreover, the Red Army remained "capable of overrunning all of Europe now or by 1 January 1948" and seizing Turkey and Iran at any point in the near future. In addition, Soviet scientists were likely to develop an atomic bomb in the next five to ten years, if not sooner. However, American analysts concluded that the war against Germany had exhausted the Soviet economy, and US intelligence predicted that the Kremlin would be incapable of sustaining a major war in the next five years. Nevertheless, in the interim, Soviet leaders could be expected to continue to pursue their ambitions by all means short of open war.[64]

WITH THE DEFEAT OF GERMANY, THE GRAND ALLIANCE HAD secured victory in Europe. But the Allied triumph also heralded the dawn of a fractious new era in which the United States and Soviet Union—transformed by the war into massive military powers—would jockey for domination of the international order. The euphoria of victory was already giving way to an atmosphere of deep suspicion that would endure into the next century. Germany's destruction as a continental power removed the primary bulwark against Soviet influence in Europe. Although few observers questioned the necessity of ending the Nazi reign of terror, many Western officials soon concluded that they had traded one threat for another. In the coming years, the early proposals put forward by the Office of Strategic Services and the British chiefs to rearm German military forces to stand against the Red Army would be realized. But first, the war against Japan was racing toward its deadly finish.

Chapter 20

STARING INTO THE
MOUTH OF HELL

I
N THE FIRST HALF OF AUGUST 1945, THE MOST FEARSOME CONCEN-
tration of military power in world history converged on the Japanese
Empire. At 8:16 a.m. on August 6, a searing flash of light appeared
above Japan's seventh-largest city, Hiroshima, followed by a deafening
roar. Moments later, the skies darkened beneath a mushroom cloud
rising sixty thousand feet into the air. On the ground, shock waves
ripped across the city, destroying everything within a two-kilometer
radius of ground zero and blasting lethal shards of glass and building materials across the decimated landscape. The US Strategic Bomb
Survey reported that steel girders "twisted like jelly" and reinforced
concrete "crumbled and collapsed." Heat from the explosion sent fire
winds howling across the irradiated fields of rubble, soon escalating
into a firestorm. Approximately sixty-five hours later and 1,300 miles
to the northwest, the Red Army unleashed a massive offensive against

the Imperial Japanese Army in Manchuria. Nearly 1.7 million troops supported by thousands of tanks and heavy artillery poured across the frontier, crushing Japanese resistance and driving deep into the heart of the empire's most important colony. Meanwhile, in the waters of the vast Pacific Ocean, the United States prepared to gather the largest fleet the world had ever seen to launch an invasion of the home islands and American commanders drew plans to storm beaches turned to glass by atomic bomb strikes.[1]

The end of the Pacific War played out like the opening chapter of the apocalypse. The eight years since the 1937 Marco Polo Bridge incident had witnessed a sweeping transformation of weapons technologies and military power. Allied forces had established a network of bases across the world's largest ocean capable of sustaining multiple campaigns. The US Navy now exercised mastery over the sea, mounting amphibious assaults against heavily defended coastlines and staging punishing air strikes hundreds of miles inland. Beneath the waters, US submarines conducted a devastating campaign against Japanese shipping that helped to cripple Tokyo's maritime empire. In the skies above, American forces orchestrated a bombing campaign of unprecedented ferocity against Japanese cities. Back in the United States, American scientists had completed work on an unimaginably powerful new weapon that promised to transform warfare itself. And in the closing weeks of the war, the Kremlin prepared to unleash the colossal forces of the Red Army on Japan's continental empire. Japan thus found itself at the receiving end of imperial power on a scale unprecedented in human history, heralding the dawn of a new geopolitical age in Asia and beyond.

BEFORE OPENING THE FINAL ATTACK ON JAPAN, THE AMERICANS sought to retake their lost colony in the Philippines. Having devastated the Japanese fleet in the waters off Leyte, US forces turned to the island itself as the launchpad for clearing the larger archipelago. Control of the airfields on Leyte would give the Americans the air

superiority necessary for clearing the rest of the archipelago. MacArthur's troops hit Leyte's beaches on October 20, 1944, as Japanese commanders rushed reinforcements to the island. The Americans seized
their key target of Tacloban Airfield on the first day of operations and
continued into Leyte's interior. The attackers trudged through a wet,
swampy landscape of rice paddies crisscrossed by streams fed by torrential rain. Thirty-five inches of rain would fall on Leyte over the
coming two months. Forced to march and fight in sodden boots, soldiers soon began suffering from "bad feet"—shriveled skin became
infected and in some cases tore off. Fever and dysentery took a similar toll on the combatants. The swampy terrain also complicated US
efforts to build airstrips on the island. Meanwhile, American infantry
pushed up into the highlands to drive Japanese defenders from their
positions. The attackers faced heavy resistance along a line of hills
that they dubbed Breakneck Ridge, where Japanese forces had prepared a network of trenches and spider holes. Fighting raged through
November and much of December as US troops slowly cleared Leyte.[2]

The fierce battle for Leyte combined with the slow progress of
airstrip construction to force Halsey's fleet to remain off the coast in
order to provide air support. The American ships now became targets
for Tokyo's lethal new weapon, the mass suicide attack. Beginning
in late October and intensifying through November and December,
Japanese commanders launched over four hundred kamikaze attacks
against US ships off the Philippines. The attacks sank sixteen ships,
including two escort carriers, and damaged another eighty-seven. By
the end of the war, kamikaze attacks had killed thousands of American sailors. A successful attack left fires raging across a ship's deck
and often set off secondary explosions by igniting fuel and ammunition. Those sailors fortunate enough to survive an attack faced the
grim task of clearing the burned wreckage of machines and mangled bodies. Naval aviator Paul Ignatius remembered cleaning up the
remains of one kamikaze attack on the escort carrier *Manilla Bay* and
finding the attacker's wallet. Inside was the photograph of the young
pilot and his two parents. The steady string of attacks mauled the US

fleet and forced American commanders to send scores of ships back for repairs.[3]

For all their ferocity, kamikaze attacks could do nothing to alter the strategic realities of the Pacific War. After securing control of Leyte, MacArthur turned to the main island of Luzon. As the first rays of light fell across the waters of Lingayen Gulf on January 9, 1945, they revealed an armada of over eight hundred ships. "On the dark purple water, as far as the eye could carry," wrote one reporter, "hundreds of ships of every type completely surrounded us—transports and cruisers, cargo vessels and battleships, landing craft and destroyers." The calm waters of the gulf rolled onto some twenty miles of beaches, beyond which lay 110 miles of highway leading to the capital, Manila. The Americans landed four divisions on the first day of operations. Troops from the Sixth Army drove south to capture the constellation of airstrips at Clark Field while elements of the Eighth Army, which had landed fifty miles southwest of Manila, advanced north toward the city. The landings met little opposition aside from kamikaze attacks against the fleet, and MacArthur's troops were soon pushing south toward Manila. With US forces advancing, the Japanese commander, General Tomoyuki Yamashita issued orders to withdraw in order to wage a defense of the three strongholds in the mountains east of the capital, Corregidor, and the northern highlands near Baguio.[4]

However, Rear Admiral Sanji Iwabuchi, commander of a contingent of some 12,500 sailors and 4,500 soldiers, was determined to fight the Americans inside Manila. Iwabuchi anchored his defenses around the Intramuros, a sixteenth-century Spanish citadel in the heart of Old Manila. Japanese defenders transformed the castle and the heavy concrete buildings of the city into a ring of fortresses bristling with barbed wire, pillboxes, sandbags, machine guns, and antitank weapons. Resigned to their own deaths in the battle for Manila, Japanese troops unleashed their fury on the Filipino civilians. Reports of systematic rape, pillaging, and massacres spread through the city as American troops reached its outskirts. On

February 6, MacArthur announced the fall of the city. President Roosevelt congratulated the general on "an historic moment in the reestablishment of freedom and decency in the Far East." But weeks of heavy fighting lay ahead. "The view of Manila last night was a terrible thing as the whole part of one side of the city seemed to be on fire," wrote General Robert Eichelberger that same day. "Great sheets of flame swept across the roof-tops, sometimes spanning several city blocks in their consuming flight," wrote another officer. "We saw the awful pyrotechnics of destruction, spreading ever faster to encompass and destroy the most beautiful city in the Far East." The view on the ground was worse. At the Dy Pac Lumberyard, American soldiers found the corpses of scores of men, women, and children. The victims' hands had been tied and their bodies cut to pieces and left to rot in the tropical heat.[5]

US forces faced increasingly determined Japanese defenders as they fought their way deeper into the burning city. As one infantry report stated, "From now on until the final day of the battle for Manila we were to encounter an unbroken succession of heavily fortified buildings, mutually supporting pillboxes at all street intersections, thickly sown mine fields, mined buildings, an abundance of all types of weapons, innumerable snipers, and an enemy who elected death over surrender." Soldiers fought building by building, clearing one structure before blasting a hole into the neighboring one. "Japs organize each big reinforced concrete building into a fortress," complained one American commander, "and fight to the death in the basement, on each floor, and even to the roof." As they pushed forward, American troops found hundreds of bodies of massacred civilians. Women, children, and whole families had been butchered with swords and bayonets, their mangled bodies thrown into the rubble. By February 23, MacArthur's troops were prepared to storm the Intramuros. Two thousand Japanese defenders waited inside, manning a network of machine guns, booby traps, and elaborate tunnels bored into the citadel. At 7:30 a.m., American artillery began a heavy bombardment. "Forty feet thick at the bottom and 20 feet at the top, this century-old wall dissolved in great geysers of black smoke, showering rubble and shrapnel," wrote one reporter. American soldiers wielding flame-throwers, bazookas, and grenades poured into the breach to assault pillboxes and drive the defenders back. Bitter firefights raged through the old streets as US troops pushed forward, discovering grisly piles of massacred bodies as they went. "When the Japanese realized that Manila was lost," a report explained, "they engaged in a final orgy of mass murder by shooting, bayonetting and burning alive all prisoners remaining inside the fort." Fighting continued until March 3, when US forces eliminated the last organized Japanese resistance—one month after MacArthur's premature declaration of victory. Over one thousand Americans had died in the battle, along with 16,665 Japanese troops—and an estimated one hundred thousand Filipino civilians had been killed. "In the night," wrote American internee Natalie Crouter, "when the wind is from a certain direction over the Walled City, the air is laden with the smell of charred wood, wet cement, gun powder, pungent chemicals, and over all that the sickish sweetish odor which is rotting flesh and blood. Once in the nostrils, it is never forgotten."[6]

With Manila in their grasp, the Americans turned to the rest of the Philippines. Most of the islands held little strategic value, but MacArthur insisted on launching a series of landings throughout the archipelago. US forces carried out thirty-eight landings over the next forty-four days, but these operations came at a cost. With large contingents of their forces fighting in the south, US troops faced a prolonged struggle against Yamashita's remaining troops on Luzon, which would continue until the end of the war.[7]

WHILE MACARTHUR'S FORCES FOUGHT THEIR WAY THROUGH THE ruins of Manila, US Marines prepared to storm Iwo Jima. The island's strategic significance stemmed from its location astride the most direct bombing routes between Japan and the massive B-29 air base on Tinian. The B-29 was one of the greatest technological achievements of the war. First conceived in the 1930s as a long-range, high-altitude heavy bomber, the aircraft was designed to defend the Western Hemisphere against foreign powers. Heavy bombers cruising at thirty thousand feet could defend shipping lanes against foreign navies and conduct air strikes against any enemy forces that landed in North or South America. The outbreak of the war in Europe had added a new urgency to the efforts of engineers at Boeing who were drafting plans for the aircraft. In May 1941, the Army Air Force ordered 250 of the planned aircraft; within a year the order had grown to 1,644. With a wingspan of 140 feet and a takeoff weight of seventy tons, the B-29 was at the time the largest aircraft ever produced in mass quantities. A marvel of engineering, the four-engine plane could carry a crew of eleven inside a heated, pressurized cabin to a height of thirty thousand feet and fly a distance of some five thousand miles. The bomber's development carried a heavy price tag, with a development cost of $3 billion—greater than the atomic bomb's cost of $1.9 billion. The first squadrons of B-29s began operating out of China in June 1944, but the logistical difficulties of sending fuel, personnel, munitions, and supplies over the Himalayas convinced American commanders to seek alternative bases. The capture of Tinian in the summer of 1944 provided an ideal launchpad for the long-range bombing campaign against Japanese cities. By the end of 1944, US commanders were pulling the B-29 groups out of China and India to focus on attacks from the Marianas.[8]

Nevertheless, Japanese control of Iwo Jima remained a thorn in the side of B-29 aircrews. The island's radar could detect incoming bombers and provide Japanese air defenses with an early warning of American attacks. Moreover, the threat from Japanese fighter aircraft based on Iwo Jima forced B-29s to chart longer flight paths to avoid the island. These longer flights required more fuel, which meant reducing the number of bombs in order to stay under weight. In October 1944, Nimitz was ordered to capture the island—a move designed to eliminate the Japanese threat, establish a base for American fighter escorts to support the bombing campaign, and provide an emergency landing site for damaged B-29s returning from bomb runs over Japan.[9]

But seizing Iwo Jima would be no simple task. Rising from the sea 670 miles south of Tokyo, the barren volcanic island comprised a mere eight square miles. Known for its large sulfur deposits that polluted the air with the stench of rotten eggs, the rocky island depended on rainfall collected and stored in cisterns for most of its fresh water. The 550-foot-tall volcano Mount Suribachi dominated the southern tip of Iwo Jima. A plateau with some arable land rose at the northern end. In the middle lay a plain covered in a deep layer of soft ash that made walking difficult and wheeled traffic all but impossible. Japan had claimed Iwo Jima in the 1860s, but by 1943, only 1,100 colonists lived on the island. Most of the population worked at the sugar mill or in the sulfur mines.

In early 1944, Japanese leaders began building up Iwo Jima's defenses in anticipation of an Allied assault. In May, Tokyo sent General Tadamichi Kuribayashi to Iwo Jima with orders to defend the island to the death in hopes of buying time to prepare the defenses of Japan itself. Kuribayashi transformed the island into a fortress. In Iwo Jima's volcanic soil Japanese forces dug a sprawling network of tunnels, bunkers, and caves designed to withstand bombardment from Allied ships and aircraft. The ash that covered much of the island provided ample material for the construction of concrete pillboxes, blockhouses, and bunkers, which further hardened Kuribayashi's defenses. The work proved grueling as geothermal vents heated many of the tunnels to a stifling 120 degrees Fahrenheit and filled the stagnant air with toxic sulfur fumes. By February, however, Kuribayashi commanded a force of some twenty-one thousand men garrisoning perhaps the most heavily fortified patch of land on the planet. Kuribayashi's troops received orders to defend the island to the last man. "Each man will make it his duty to kill ten of the enemy before dying. Until we are destroyed to the last man, we shall harass the enemy by guerrilla tactics."[10]

On the morning of February 19, 1945, a fleet of 450 American ships arrived off Iwo Jima. Clear skies and gentle surf greeted the Americans. The air temperature stood at 68 degrees Fahrenheit. On board the transports, fifty thousand marines wolfed down a hot breakfast of steak and eggs. Among them was George Raffield, a machine gunner with the Fifth Marine Division. After finishing his meal, he returned to his compartment, grabbed two extra bandoliers of ammunition and extra grenades, and rechecked his pack. As dawn arrived, he headed above deck for his first look at Iwo Jima, now under heavy bombardment by the American gunships. "It looked [like] a pork chop in a skillet, a red hot skillet that was on fire," he remembered. "It was smoking and burning." The first assault wave headed toward the beaches at 8:30 a.m. The island's terrain proved more problematic than the sporadic Japanese fire that met the attackers. Heavily armed marines slogged through the loose volcanic ash that covered the beaches; a fifteen-foot-tall terrace blocked fields of fire. However, as the marines pushed inland, they began encountering stiffer enemy resistance. Japanese defenders firing from pillboxes, blockhouses, and caves swept the advancing American troops with machine gun fire while mortars and artillery targeted landing vessels.[11]

Undaunted, the Americans landed some thirty thousand troops before dusk. The marines were crowded into a narrow beachhead 4,400 yards wide and 1,100 yards deep. Through the night, Japanese mortars and rockets rained down on the beaches, leaving a mess of torn bodies and wounded marines across the sand. "The first night on Iwo Jima can only be described as a nightmare in hell," wrote correspondent Robert Sherrod. At 8:30 the next morning, the Americans renewed their attack beneath a cold drizzle falling from the sky. The marines pushed forward to reach the base of Mount Suribachi on the afternoon of February 21. Two days later, US troops had fought their way up the slopes to reach Suribachi's summit. There, a group of marines raised a makeshift flagpole, prompting a chorus of cheers and the sounding of ships' horns from the sea. The raising of a second, larger flag was immortalized by the photographer Joe Rosenthal in what became the Pacific War's most iconic photograph. Secretary of the Navy James Forrestal, who witnessed the scene, recognized the gravity of the moment: "The raising of that flag on Suribachi means a Marine Corps for the next five hundred years." But the battle for Iwo Jima had only just begun.[12]

Having taken Suribachi, American forces prepared to clear the rest of Iwo Jima. The marines formed a line across the island running east to west, from which they would force their way north. Their initial objective of Airfield No. 1 sat on a relatively flat patch of ground containing little besides runways and sand dunes. Airfield No. 2 lay a mile beyond, in front a fifty-foot ridge guarding the more heavily fortified northern end of Iwo Jima. The marines had reached Airfield No. 2 by the fifth day of the battle and pushed through the first line of Japanese defenses. As the battle continued, advancing US troops blasted their way forward against enemy forces entrenched within the craggy landscape of rocks and rubble. "This was a broad, deep belt of fortifications running from coast to coast, a mass of mutually supporting pillboxes and concrete bunkers, many of them almost buried underground," wrote General Holland Smith.

> Behind were thousands of caves and subterranean positions, in the rocky fastness of the north. This was the "masterpiece of impregnability" produced by the specialists from Japan, who utilized natural caves and dug hundreds more, all interconnected with tunnels, and linked them to underground fortresses 30 to 40 feet below ground, hiding guns and mortars. Beyond the first line of pillboxes, protected by mine fields and accurately placed overlapping fire from hidden guns, the island was a huge warren of holes, caves and passages in rocky ridges and cliff faces. Every day of our advance on Iwo Jima showed us another marvel of defensive construction.

The fighting grew bloodier as the marines drove deeper into Kuribayashi's network of fortifications. Japanese troops hiding in caves,
tunnels, and spider holes mounted a vicious defense against advancing US forces. By March 9, the marines had reached the northern coast
of Iwo Jima, but the fighting continued as the Americans struggled to
clear Japanese fortifications.[13]

Iwo Jima's forbidding landscape exacerbated the misery on both
sides. The island's lack of water left soldiers parched and forced the
military to cart in drinking water in old gasoline cans—not all of
which had been thoroughly cleaned. The ground itself was often
hot to the touch. Some men took to heating their rations in shallow
holes dug in the ash. The stench of sulfur mixed with smoke, cordite, and rotting flesh. "It was almost like a piece of the moon that had
dropped down to the earth," one marine said. Iwo Jima was so small
and Japanese fortifications so extensive that the entire island was a
battlefield. No area was safe from possible attack or artillery fire. The
ordeal remained significantly worse for Kuribayashi's forces. As the
battle raged on, Japanese stores of water and food began to run short.
Crowded into dark subterranean bunkers and choking on hot sulfu-
ric fumes, Kuribayashi's men slept and ate beside the decomposing
corpses of their comrades. The living could look forward only to the
near-certain prospect of death. The Americans were "making a desert
out of everything before them," one Japanese commander explained.
"They fight with the mentality as though exterminating insects."
On the morning of March 26, the last organized force of Japanese
defenders emerged from their caves for a final charge against the
Americans—300 Japanese troops launched a suicidal attack, killing
170 American personnel. Kuribayashi's body was never identified.[14]

The Americans had suffered 24,053 casualties in the struggle to
seize the island. Of these, 6,140 were killed, making Iwo Jima the cost-
liest battle in the history of the US Marine Corps. The entire Japanese
garrison of twenty-two thousand was killed or captured. Iwo Jima
earned the distinction of being the only major battle of the Pacific War

in which American casualties outnumbered Japanese. The bloodbath unleashed a public outcry and led some later scholars to question the necessity of taking the island. Certainly, Iwo Jima saved the lives of a significant number of American aviators—some twenty thousand aircrew members landed on the island in the remaining months of the war. But the use of Iwo Jima as a base for American fighter aircraft did not, ultimately, prove pivotal to the war. Nor was the island required to provide support for the planned invasion of Kyushu, the southernmost of Japan's home islands. However, US planners could not have known that such an invasion would prove unnecessary.[15]

WHILE FIGHTING RAGED ON LUZON AND IWO JIMA, A FIRESTORM WAS bearing down on Japan. As early as the 1920s, proponents of airpower had identified Japanese cities as prime targets for aerial bombing campaigns. America's foremost prophet of air war, army general William Mitchell, famously argued that Japan's cities, constructed from "paper and wood," stood as "the greatest aerial targets the world has ever seen." Japan's six largest cities were home to the majority of the empire's war production and one-fifth of the country's population. As the Pacific War ground on with ever-greater casualties, American leaders turned to strategic bombing as a means of forcing Tokyo into submission. But the challenge of inflicting catastrophic damage on Japan's war production remained maddeningly difficult.[16]

Through a series of large-scale raids beginning in November 1944, American B-29s had failed to destroy their targets while suffering significant losses. The aircrews' task was complicated by frequent cloud cover and the presence of the jet stream—a current of 130-mile-per-hour winds some thirty thousand feet aboveground—which rendered precision bombing nearly impossible. On January 23, 1945, seventy-three B-29s attacked the aircraft engine plant in Nagoya. Only twenty-three managed to drop bombs near their primary target, and of these, only four bombs hit the plant, none of which caused serious damage. Two B-29s were lost during the raid. Three weeks later, 118 bombers attacked the engine plant at Ota. The B-29s scored ninety-seven hits—half of which were duds—but suffered a loss of twelve planes. Through seven weeks of bombing in early 1945, B-29s conducted a total of 1,065 sorties against Japan, but only 386 managed to hit their targets—thirty-six planes were lost along with a total of 324 aviators killed, missing, or wounded. The commander of the army's bombing forces operating out of the Marianas, General Curtis LeMay, offered a blunt assessment: "My general comment on the bombing is that it was poor."[17]

The dismal results of these high-altitude daytime bombing raids led LeMay and his fellow commanders to consider another option: night attacks against urban targets using incendiary bombs. Fire-bombing had yielded mixed results in European cities built of brick, concrete, and steel. But Japan's cities, composed of tightly packed wooden structures, were virtual tinderboxes. To test their theories, Army Air Forces engineers built four experimental ranges—dubbed "Little Tokyos"—in Florida. The tests revealed the devastating impact of incendiary attacks. While conventional explosives destroyed structures in their immediate blast radius, well-placed incendiaries ignited whole neighborhoods. The most potent weapons used a substance called napalm. Developed in 1943 by a team of researchers at Harvard, napalm consisted of gasoline thickened with aluminum salts to give the substance the consistency of applesauce. The jellied fuel stuck to anything it touched and burned at a temperature of 1,800 degrees Fahrenheit. Packed into six-pound steel pipes and dropped in clusters of thirty-eight, the incendiaries sprayed burning napalm across vast areas. B-29s had conducted small firebombing raids against Nagoya and Kobe in January and February to encouraging results, but a large-scale raid had not yet been attempted. On February 25, LeMay sent 202 bombers loaded with 454 tons of incendiaries to attack Tokyo. Although snow limited the damage, the attacks burned twenty-eight thousand buildings and left thirty-five thousand people homeless. Judged a success by American commanders, the raid revealed just a glimpse of the coming devastation.[18]

At 5:36 on the evening of March 9, 1945, the first of 325 bombers took off from airstrips on Saipan en route to Tokyo. For this massive raid, LeMay had abandoned previous doctrine. The B-29s would fly at low altitude to increase the precision of their attacks, and the aircraft had been stripped of their defensive machine guns in order to carry a greater weight in bombs. LeMay was convinced that Japanese air defenses would be unable to inflict serious damage on his bombers. Still, he was taking a risk. "For almost a week," remembered one officer, "most of us wondered if we were planning the greatest disaster in aviation history." Seven and a half hours later, as searchlights flashed across the skies and the drone of heavy engines echoed through the darkness, the first American planes appeared over Tokyo. In seconds, burning napalm rained down from above, igniting countless fires across the capital. Air-raid sirens wailed in the night as terrified citizens burst into the streets. "In every direction I looked," remembered one Japanese boy, "it was a sea of flaming red fire." In the skies above, approaching American pilots could see the glow of the burning city from two hundred miles away. "As far as the eye could see, to the east and the north, there was a sea of flame, a mass of roaring fire that seemed to cover the city like a boiling cauldron," one radar operator wrote. "It felt like you were staring into the mouth of hell," said another officer. "You cannot imagine a fire that big." The inferno illuminated the B-29s' cabins and filled the air with the stench of the flaming city. "You could smell the flesh burning," remembered one flight engineer.[19]

As the conflagration grew, it sucked in the surrounding air, creating a raging firestorm. Gale-force winds blasted embers through the air, igniting new fires as the blaze spread. Superheated air caused hair and clothing to burst into flames as throngs of panicked residents fled in search of safety. Thousands perished. "In the black Sumida River," wrote one witness, "countless bodies were floating, clothed bodies and naked bodies, all as black as charcoal." Dawn cast a cold light over the ruined city. The largest fires had burned themselves out, leaving dazed survivors to pick their way through the devastation.

LeMay's B-29s had dumped 1,665 tons of napalm on Tokyo, devastating nearly sixteen square miles and destroying a quarter of the city's buildings. The raid killed more than one hundred thousand men, women, and children. The Americans lost fourteen B-29s—4.3 percent of the attacking force. "It was a hell of a good mission," reported the raid's commanding officer, General Thomas Power. "If the Japs persist," LeMay announced on an army radio show, "I now promise that they have nothing more to look forward to than the complete destruction of their cities." He was as good as his word. On March 11, nearly three hundred B-29s firebombed Nagoya. Two days later, 274 bombers attacked Osaka, killing nearly four thousand of the city's residents. LeMay's B-29s attacked Kobe on March 16, killing 2,500 people, and returned to Nagoya two days later, on March 18. Over the course of ten days, American B-29s had incinerated thirty-two square miles of Japan's largest cities. "We ran out of bombs," LeMay explained. "Literally."[20]

WHILE LeMAY'S B-29S PUMMELED JAPAN FROM THE AIR, AMERICAN commanders prepared to continue their drive toward Kyushu. MacArthur's progress in the Philippines and the decision to table the Formosa invasion left Okinawa as the next step in the march toward Japan. The island would provide airfields for an estimated 780 medium-range bombers to strike Japan and serve as a staging area for the invasion of Kyushu. The largest island in the Ryukyu chain, Okinawa ran sixty miles from north to south and was eighteen miles across at its widest point, comprising an area of 485 square miles. Rugged hills and plunging ravines cut across the terrain, and pine forests covered large swaths of the island. Terraced fields and rice paddies lay scattered across the lowlands and near the coasts beyond Okinawa's coral sand beaches. Most of the prewar population of 435,000 lived in the southern end of the island, with 65,000 residents in Okinawa's largest city, Naha. Control of the Ryukyus was critical to the defense of the Japanese home islands. Okinawa was the last line of defense before an invasion of Japan itself. Following the fall of Saipan, Japanese commanders had built up the island's garrison to a force of approximately seventy-seven thousand men under the command of General Mitsuru Ushijima. Rather than defending the beaches, Japanese forces would adopt a defensive strategy using prepared fortifications concentrated along the Shuri Line to tie down enemy ground forces while kamikaze attacks eroded American fleet strength in the surrounding waters. Once these air and sea attacks severed American lines of communication, Japanese troops would counterattack, wiping out enemy infantry on the island. However, Ushijima offered a less sanguine assessment. The best the Japanese defenders could hope for, he felt, was a long, punishing battle of attrition to buy time and kill as many Americans as possible before the garrison's inevitable defeat.[21]

Thirty minutes before dawn on April 1, 1945, the US fleet unleashed a massive bombardment of the beaches at Hagushi, Okinawa. Over the next three hours, American gunships fired 44,825 shells and 33,000 rockets. That the Americans could mount such an operation at all stood as a testament to the American ability to project force around the world. Hundreds of Allied ships had carried 183,000 assault troops and 747,000 tons of cargo from eleven ports across the Pacific Ocean. The core supply line from the West Coast traversed 6,250 miles of open water. This globe-spanning network of troops and weapons converged on Okinawa at precisely 8:20 a.m. as the first wave of landing boats set off for the beaches. The first American forces to set foot on Okinawa were surprised to find almost no resistance. "It is a walk-on," wrote one marine. "How great." By nightfall, the Americans had landed nearly sixty thousand troops on the island to little opposition. Twelve miles south of the beaches, Ushijima stood atop Shuri Castle, watching the landings through a pair of binoculars. "It is as if the sea itself were advancing with a great roar," wrote one Japanese officer observing the landings. "They must be thinking gleefully that they have passed through a breach in the Japanese defenses. They will be wrong."[22]

Ushijima's soldiers had been hard at work constructing an elaborate network of fortifications running from coast to coast across the approaches to Naha. Rings of tunnels, strongpoints, and trenches had been burrowed into a landscape of rocky cliffs and precipitous ravines. The defenders had expanded natural caves into fortified bunkers complete with cisterns, storerooms, and ammunition dumps, linked by tunnels cut through rock and earth. Japanese leaders called on the civilian population—composed of many Okinawans with uncertain allegiance to Tokyo's ambitions—to kill ten enemy soldiers each before dying for the empire. While Ushijima's soldiers prepared to defend their subterranean fortress, Japanese commanders in Kyushu gathered their dwindling supply of aircraft to launch the most concentrated kamikaze campaign of the war against the US fleet in the waters around Okinawa. On the morning of April 6, American radar picked up a large number of Japanese planes heading toward the fleet off Okinawa. Combat air patrol moved to intercept as nearby carriers scrambled additional fighters. American patrols shot down sixty Japanese planes, but the sheer number of attackers—some seven hundred aircraft, half of which were kamikazes—meant that about two hundred breached the defenses. Waves of kamikazes now screamed down on the Americans. Antiaircraft guns swept the skies with flak, but dozens of aircraft slammed into the fleet. By dusk, twenty ships had been damaged and six sunk.[23]

While swarms of kamikazes rained down upon the US invasion fleet, the battleship *Yamato* and nine escorts set a course for Okinawa. The *Yamato* and its sister ship *Musashi*—the largest battleship ever built—had spent most of the war idle as carrier battles rendered the old gunships obsolete. With its defenses collapsing, its navy all but destroyed, and its fuel supplies draining away, Japanese commanders now ordered the *Yamato* into one last attack. The battleship would charge toward Okinawa, pulling fighters and ships away from the American carriers to provide an opening for further kamikaze strikes. After expending its ammunition, the *Yamato* would beach itself on the island and its crew of 3,500 would join Ushijima's garrison. The ship's officers realized that they had been ordered on a suicide mission meant to redeem the honor of the Imperial Navy, but they had no other choice. On the evening of April 6, American submarines reported the hulking battleship and its escorts were steaming out of Japan's Inland Sea toward Okinawa. The next morning, long-range US search planes sighted the *Yamato*. US carriers sent 280 aircraft to attack the Japanese force. At noon, clouds of American bombers and torpedo planes descended on the *Yamato* and its escorts. One Japanese officer remembered "silvery streaks of torpedoes . . . silently converging on us from all directions." Without a fighter escort, the battleship was all but defenseless. Explosions shook the massive ship as compartments below deck began flooding. The battleship's crew was ordered above deck as the ship began to list. At 2:30 p.m., a massive explosion ripped the *Yamato* apart. Observers one hundred miles away on Kyushu saw the tower of smoke rising above the sinking ship. Around three thousand of the *Yamato*'s crew were lost at the cost of ten American planes.[24]

While fighting raged in the surrounding waters, US troops on Okinawa approached the first echelon of Ushijima's defenses. Here, Japanese forces had dug into the island itself, transforming each successive hill and ridgeline into a heavily armed fortress. US troops pushed forward with the help of overwhelming firepower, suffering heavy casualties with every new clash. Torrential rains exacerbated the misery on both sides. "The whole area was pocked with shell craters and churned up by explosions," wrote one marine. "Every crater was half full of water and many of them held a Marine corpse. The bodies lay pathetically just as they had been killed, half submerged in muck and water, rusting weapons still in hand. Swarms of big flies hovered around them." The grinding battle carried on through April and into May as soldiers and marines seized Kakazu Ridge, the Pinnacle, and Sugar Loaf Hill. On May 11, US forces launched their final assault, into the ruins of Shuri Castle. At each line, Japanese forces put up a ferocious defense before withdrawing to their next position to continue the battle. By mid-June, the defenders' supplies and ammunition had started to run short. Fierce fighting continued, however, as American forces rooted out the last isolated pockets of resistance. On June 18, Japanese artillery killed the commander of US forces on Okinawa, General Simon Bolivar Buckner Jr., as he was surveying the fighting. He was the highest-ranking US officer killed in battle during the war. Four days later, General Ushijima killed himself. The struggle for Okinawa had been enormously costly for both sides. The Americans suffered 12,520 killed and another 36,631 wounded; Japanese losses stood at 110,000 killed and 3,700 captured.[25]

Tragically, tens of thousands of Okinawan civilians were also killed in the carnage. Many had been forcibly conscripted by Japanese commanders and used as cannon fodder in the defense against the Americans. Others had been slaughtered by Japanese forces in order to clear areas for battlefield operations or murdered in the closing stages of the battle. Even more had been caught in the cross fire as the Americans used their heavy guns to blast their way across the island. Most harrowing of all were the suicides that were spurred on by Tokyo's propaganda. Although definitive numbers will never be known, some estimates place civilian deaths at nearly one hundred thousand.[26]

THE STRUGGLE FOR OKINAWA PROVED TO BE THE AMERICANS' bloodiest battle of the Pacific War, and it provided a harsh warning to leaders in Washington contemplating an invasion of the Japanese home islands. With Germany defeated and Japan in retreat, American leaders faced mounting pressure to finish the war quickly and with minimum further loss of life. In early July, Secretary of Defense Henry Stimson told President Truman that an invasion of Kyushu would be a bloodbath. Japanese forces, Stimson warned, would mount "a last ditch defense such as has been made on Iwo Jima and Okinawa." In order to prevent such a devastating battle, he encouraged the president to make one last push to reason with Tokyo. Japan found itself stripped of its allies and facing the combined power of the United States, Great Britain, China, and soon, the Soviet Union. The Japanese population was suffering through a massive strategic bombing campaign from the air and a tightening blockade of the seas. Given the hopelessness of their cause, Japanese leaders might be induced to surrender. "On the other hand," Stimson wrote, "I think that the attempt to exterminate her armies and her population by gunfire or other means will tend to produce a fusion of race solidity and antipathy which had no analogy in the case of Germany."[27]

On June 18, Truman called a meeting of his top advisers to assess plans for the defeat of Japan. General Marshall identified November 1 as the target date for an invasion of Kyushu, which would put the Allies in position to stage an attack on the Kanto Plain. He expressed his hope that the landing, combined with the ongoing bombing campaign, the navy's blockade, and Soviet entry into the war, might be sufficient to force Tokyo's surrender. Marshall suggested that "the impact of Russian entry on the already hopeless Japanese may well be the decisive action levering them into capitulation at that time or shortly thereafter if we land in Japan." An invasion would be costly but necessary: "Air power alone was not sufficient to put the Japanese out of the war. It was unable alone to put the Germans out."[28]

Just how bloody such an invasion might be remained a matter of debate. Conservative estimates offered by Marshall projected thirty-one thousand casualties in the first month of an invasion. The highest estimates ran all the way up to four million casualties—including eight hundred thousand killed. Truman likely never saw these higher estimates, and historians have questioned their accuracy. Nevertheless, the president and his advisers were by no means eager to send tens of thousands of American soldiers to their deaths in the final push to end the war.[29]

While Truman and his advisers hashed out their plans, leaders in Tokyo prepared to mount a suicidal defense. Having correctly identified the beaches of southern Kyushu as the most likely point of attack, Japanese commanders launched a massive troop buildup over the summer of 1945. American intelligence initially estimated that there was an enemy force of between six and ten divisions constituting 280,000 troops on Kyushu. By late July, however, intercepted Japanese communications had identified thirteen divisions totaling 560,000 men, nearly all of whom could be expected to fight to the death in defense of the homeland. Japanese engineers were hard at work building a complex network of fortifications that included underground aircraft hangars, airstrips, minefields, trenches, and pillboxes. Japanese commanders assembled an estimated 5,400 kamikaze aircraft to meet the invasion forces with the slow-moving troop transports, which were identified as prime targets. As Japanese troop totals climbed, Marshall inquired about the possibility of using atomic weapons to clear Kyushu's beaches. Official estimates predicted that an atomic bomb would immediately kill all forces within one thousand feet of ground zero, incapacitate troops within a mile, and slow all forces within five miles. US commanders expected to have eleven or twelve bombs available for the invasion. Had it come to pass, this scenario would have witnessed the spectacle of American troops storming the irradiated, blackened beaches of Kyushu to face the dazed survivors of a dozen atomic bombs—and this would have been merely a prelude to the march on Tokyo.[30]

As American forces drew ever closer to the home islands, Japanese leaders recognized that the war was lost. But they were not yet ready to accept US demands for unconditional surrender. Although some officials in Tokyo were now working to push the government toward peace, key factions in the government—the Imperial Army in particular—remained committed to continuing the war. If Japanese soldiers managed to kill enough Americans on Kyushu's beaches, the pro-war faction in Tokyo hoped, the bloodshed might convince the Americans to offer better terms, such as allowing Japan to keep control of its colonies in Korea and Manchuria, permitting the nation to maintain its military forces, and, most importantly, preserving the institution of the emperor. The wild card in these calculations remained the Soviet Union. If Moscow remained neutral, Soviet diplomats might serve as mediators in a negotiated settlement with the other Allied powers. However, if Moscow joined the war, the combined might of the US and Soviet militaries would crush Japan. As the top leaders in Tokyo explained in May, "Soviet entry into the war will deal a death blow to the empire."[31]

Unbeknownst to Tokyo, leaders in the Kremlin had already made their decision. In December 1941, with the battle for Moscow still raging, Soviet leaders had resolved to enter the war against Japan following Germany's defeat. In a memorandum to Stalin and Molotov, Deputy Foreign Commissar Solomon Lozovsky looked to the future. The postwar world, he predicted, would be characterized by a clash between the Soviet Union and the capitalist world. Therefore, Moscow must work to ensure its own security. In the coming war against Japan, Soviet forces should seize the Soya Strait, the Kuril Islands, and the Tsugaru Strait in order to guarantee unfettered access to the Pacific Ocean. The Allies learned of Stalin's intentions two years later at the November 1943 Tehran Conference, where the dictator achieved the diplomatic coup of framing Soviet strategic designs in the Far East as a concession to his Anglo-American allies. A long-term strategic analysis written in early 1944 by diplomat Ivan Maisky, argued that Moscow must seek to create postwar peace and security in both Europe and Asia. To this end, Soviet leaders should endeavor to gain control over southern Sakhalin and the Kuril Islands. But Maisky insisted that Moscow must not rush to join the war against Japan. Rather, Soviet leaders should wait for American and British forces to wear down Japanese resistance and enter the conflict only once Tokyo neared defeat—a sort of mirror image of the war in Europe. In this way, Moscow could gain these territories "without firing a shot in the Far East." Following Germany's defeat, Moscow began massing its forces in the East. By May 1945, Soviet commanders had gathered the equivalent of fifty-nine divisions totaling 1,185,000 troops along the Manchurian frontier.[32]

By the spring and summer of 1945, US attitudes regarding Soviet participation in the war against Japan had begun to change. The string of hard-won victories in the Pacific coupled with dramatic progress on building the atomic bomb had convinced many that Soviet forces were no longer necessary to defeat Japan. Moreover, Moscow's brutal record in Eastern Europe in the previous months had led many US officials to conclude that Soviet involvement in the Far East constituted a long-term threat to Washington's interests in Asia. "Unless we kid ourselves we know damn well the only Asiatic enemy we are guarding against is Russia," army planner Colonel Charles Bonesteel argued in May. Secretary of War Henry Stimson voiced a similar concern in August: "It was of great importance to get the [Japanese] homeland into our hands before the Russians could put in any substantial claim to occupy and help rule it." Truman expressed comparable sentiments: "It was to our interest that the Russians not push too far into Manchuria." More broadly, the president remained deeply suspicious of Soviet aims in the Far East. "I was not willing to let Russia reap the fruits of a long and bitter and gallant effort in which she had had no part," he later wrote. Thus, as the Pacific War entered its endgame, Moscow and Washington found themselves in what historian Tsuyoshi Hasegawa has called a "race" to establish their positions in Asia. Soviet leaders hoped to conquer as much territory as possible in order to establish themselves as central players in the Far East, and American leaders hoped to knock Tokyo out of the war before the Red Army overran large stretches of Japan's fallen empire. With Soviet troops massing on the Manchurian border and the Allied leaders en route to their final wartime conference at Potsdam, the Americans prepared to play what they hoped would be their trump card.[33]

AT 5:30 ON THE MORNING OF JULY 16, A PIERCING WHITE LIGHT TORE through the darkness in the desert outside Alamogordo, New Mexico. The flash was immediately followed by a massive fireball that rose ten thousand feet into the sky before dissolving into an even larger mushroom cloud reaching into the stratosphere. Observers one hundred miles away in El Paso and two hundred miles away in Albuquerque and Santa Fe saw the light from the explosion and heard the distant boom. Nothing remained at the site of the explosion but a gaping crater lined with pulverized soil. The hundred-foot steel tower holding the world's first atomic bomb had simply evaporated. Scientists detected radioactive material from the blast as far away as 120 miles from the test site. The first test of a nuclear weapon "was successful beyond the most optimistic expectations," wrote the Manhattan Project's director, General Leslie Groves.[34]

Word of the successful test reached Truman that evening in Potsdam, where he was meeting with Churchill and Stalin to discuss the fate of Germany and provisions for the postwar international order. Groves's full report—which arrived on July 21—had a noticeable effect on Truman. "The President was tremendously pepped up by it," wrote Stimson in his diary, "and spoke to me of it again and again when I saw him. He said it gave him an entirely new feeling of confidence." Churchill made a similar observation: "Truman was evidently much fortified by something that had happened and that he stood up to the Russians in a most emphatic and decisive manner, telling them as to certain demands that they absolutely could not have and that the United States was entirely against them. . . . When he got to the meeting after having read this report he was a changed man. He told the Russians just where they got on and off and generally bossed the whole meeting." Alan Brooke, chief of the British general staff, wrote that Churchill seemed "completely carried away" upon learning of the bomb and spoke as if "it was now no longer necessary for the Russians to come into the Japanese war; the new explosive alone was sufficient to settle the matter. Furthermore, we now had something in our hands which would redress the balance with the Russians. The secret of this explosive and the power to use it would completely alter the diplomatic equilibrium which was adrift since the defeat of Germany." Stimson had expressed similar thoughts on the shifting balance of power between the Allies in May:

My own opinion was that the time now and the method now to deal with Russia was to keep our mouths shut and let our actions

548

speak for words. The Russians will understand them better than anything else. It is a case where we have got to regain the lead and perhaps do it in a pretty rough and realistic way. They have rather taken it away from us because we have talked too much and have been too lavish with our beneficences to them. I told him this was a place where we really held all the cards. I called it a royal straight flush and we mustn't be a fool about the way we play it.

Such statements leave little doubt that leaders in both Washington and London hoped that the bomb would provide the leverage necessary to force Moscow into a more compliant relationship with the Western Allies.[35]

Nevertheless, some in Washington warned that the Soviets—still technically wartime allies—must be informed of the bomb's existence before its first use in combat. Following the plenary session at Potsdam on July 24, Truman pulled Stalin aside to reveal his trump card. The Americans had just successfully tested "a new weapon of unusual destructive force." Stalin seemed surprisingly nonchalant. His spies had already informed him of the Manhattan Project. Truman remembered his reply: "He was glad to hear it and hoped we would make 'good use of it against the Japanese.'" Behind closed doors, Stalin struck a different tone. "They simply want to raise the price," he told Zhukov and Molotov. "We've got to work on Kurchatov [director of Soviet atomic energy research] and hurry things up."[36]

Potsdam was also the site from which Truman issued one final warning before launching an atomic strike on Japan. Since June 18, American leaders had been working on a statement designed to be one last bid to convince Japanese leaders to surrender. The key issue for American leaders concerned the status of the emperor. Ambassador Joseph Grew and others had argued that Truman should amend US calls for unconditional surrender so as to provide for the survival of Japan's imperial house. Uncertainty about the emperor's fate remained a major obstacle to surrender, and US military leaders had already suggested that the emperor's position ought to be maintained as a means of facilitating the surrender of Japanese forces and preserving some modicum of order in occupied Japan. Despite Grew's efforts to insert such a clause into Truman's statement, Secretary of State James Byrnes removed any explicit reference to preserving the emperor's position—likely because of worries about a potential domestic political backlash. "We will issue a warning statement asking the Japs to surrender and save lives," wrote Truman. "I'm sure they will not do that, but we will have given them the chance."[37]

On July 26, the United States, Great Britain, and China jointly issued the Potsdam Declaration. "The time has come for Japan to decide whether she will continue to be controlled by those self-willing militaristic advisers whose unintelligent calculations have brought the Empire of Japan to the threshold of annihilation or whether she will follow the path of reason," the statement read. Moscow was notably absent from the list of signatories. US leaders, fearing that the Soviets would use the opportunity to demand further territorial concessions, had chosen not to allow Stalin the option to sign the declaration. Beyond snubbing Soviet leaders at the conference they were in the process of hosting, this exclusion appeared to send a signal to Tokyo that Moscow might still be in a position to serve as a mediator between Japan and the United States. Japanese leaders responded by stating that they would ignore the Potsdam Declaration. The way was now clear for the United States to launch the world's first nuclear assault.[38]

HIROSHIMA BUSTLED WITH LIFE ON THE MORNING OF MONDAY, August 6, 1945. Workers pedaled their bicycles through the streets, dodging pedestrians, while streetcars clattered along their tracks and schoolchildren prepared to start their day. Though it was still early, the morning air was already warm and humid. "Shimmering leaves, reflecting from a cloudless sky, made a pleasant contrast with shadows in my garden," remembered one physician. As the city hummed, some residents cast their eyes up into the bright-blue morning sky and watched as three silver shapes drifted high above. In an instant, a blinding flash of light appeared 1,900 feet above. The flash was immediately followed by a blast of intense heat that incinerated exposed flammable material within a half mile of ground zero. Birds flying through the air burst into flames and people walking in the streets simply vaporized. The bomb's shock wave tore through the city at two miles per second, shattering houses and driving a supersonic cloud of dust and debris outward in all directions. Witnesses outside the city remembered watching the sky turn golden yellow as a deafening roar shook the city. The blast ignited thousands of fires as stupefied survivors struggled to make sense of the instantaneous devastation. "I just could not understand why our surroundings had changed so greatly in one instant," recalled one writer. "I thought it might have been something which had nothing to do with the war, the collapse of the earth which it was said would take place at the end of the world." Towers of black smoke soon darkened the sky while raging fires threw an orange glow across the landscape. Throngs of survivors wandered through the ruins, their skin burned, blackened, and hanging from their limbs like rags. One witness remembered watching a burning horse standing in the devastation. The smell of fire, ash, and burning flesh hung in the air as residents searched for their families. Soon a black rain began to fall. Rivers and cisterns became clogged with the swollen, charred corpses of victims who had spent their last bit of strength searching for a drink of water. "Nothing remained except a few buildings of reinforced concrete," recalled one witness. "For acres and acres the city was like a desert except for scattered piles of brick and roof tile."[39]

As news of the apocalypse above Hiroshima filtered out to the world, leaders in Tokyo, Moscow, and Washington scrambled to make sense of this new atomic age. Because the bomb had destroyed all communications in and out of Hiroshima, details of the attack did not reach the Japanese cabinet until the evening of August 6. Although they were shaken by reports of the bomb's devastation, Japanese officials did not appear convinced of the need to accept unconditional surrender. Rather, the bombing simply increased the urgency to seek a negotiated settlement through Soviet channels. "Now that such a new weapon has appeared," Emperor Hirohito said on August 8, "it has become less and less possible to continue the war. We must not miss a chance to terminate the war by bargaining for more favorable conditions now."

Soviet leaders took a very different lesson from the bombing. Stalin seems to have interpreted the Hiroshima attack as an act of hostility aimed at blocking Moscow from seizing the spoils of the war in the Far East. As British correspondent Alexander Worth wrote, "It was clearly realized that this was a New Fact in the world's power politics, that the bomb constituted a threat to Russia, and some Russian pessimists I talked to that day dismally remarked that Russia's desperately hard victory over Germany was now 'as good as wasted.'" On August 7, with fires in Hiroshima still burning, the Soviet dictator ordered his commanders to accelerate the planned invasion of Manchuria to commence at midnight on August 9, two days ahead of schedule. The Red Army would not sit on the sidelines as its Allies claimed victory in the war against Japan.[40]

At the appointed hour, Soviet reconnaissance troops stole across the darkened frontier into Japanese-occupied Mongolia and Manchuria. Hoping to maintain the element of surprise, Red Army commanders had dispensed with their customary artillery bombardments. Advance troops encountered little opposition as they pushed forward. Four hours later, the main Red Army contingent launched its assault, charging thirty-four miles into the Mongolian desert on the first day of the offensive. To the north, Soviet soldiers driving into Manchuria had larger problems with the weather than with Japanese defenders. "It was the worst thunderstorm I've ever seen," one soldier remembered. "The lightning caused us to lose our night vision, our sense of direction—and lit us up for the enemy on Camel Hill." In the largest operation of the war in Asia, Stalin unleashed a force of 1.5 million troops on Manchuria. Soviet troops were to slash through

Japanese positions in Manchuria before moving forward to seize Sakhalin and the Kuril Islands. If the situation permitted, Red Army commanders would then stage an amphibious invasion of Hokkaido. Outnumbered two to one, the Japanese defenders waited in fortified zones, stretched thin across a sprawling territory roughly the size of Western Europe.[41]

Soviet troops attacking across the Ussuri River found themselves mired in deep marshes strewn with barbed wire. Forests along the border presented different obstacles. "Between the trees thick undergrowth created a carpet of thorns, each as long as a man's finger and sharp as a sewing needle," wrote one Soviet officer. "Streams and creeks were so swampy that even tanks as powerful and manoeuvrable as T-34s became bogged." Troops fighting with the Transbaikal Front faced relentless sun and daytime temperatures of 95 degrees Fahrenheit as they trudged across the dry Mongolian landscape. Poorly equipped and realizing that the end of the war was approaching, many Japanese soldiers showed little desire to fight. Others strapped on explosive charges and hurled themselves in suicide attacks against enemy tanks. Undeterred, Soviet spearheads simply bypassed stronger Japanese positions, leaving defenders to wait out the final days of the war in their besieged fortresses.[42]

Reports of the Soviet invasion struck a leadership in Tokyo still reeling from the atomic bombing of Hiroshima. Early on August 9, top leaders in the Foreign Ministry concluded that Japan must now accept the terms of the Potsdam Declaration along with a unilateral insistence that such an acceptance "shall not have any influence on the position of the imperial house." Emperor Hirohito also seems to have recognized that the Soviet entry represented the end. "The Soviet Union declared war against us, and entered into a state of war as of today," he told his most trusted adviser. "Because of this it is necessary to study and decide on the termination of the war." Former prime minister Fumimaro Konoe, who had been advocating a negotiated peace with the Allies, believed that the Soviet attack might be enough to persuade the military leadership to accept surrender. "This might be God's gift to control the army," he observed. Reports of the Soviet offensive received a frosty reception in Washington. Shortly after hearing the news, Truman delivered the shortest press conference in White House history. "Russia has declared war on Japan," he told reporters. "That's all." While the president addressed reporters in Washington, a B-29 named *Bock's Car* flying out of the air base on Tinian made its way north toward Japan. On board was a second atomic bomb. At 11:02 a.m., Japan time, a terrible, blinding flash lit the skies above Nagasaki.[43]

The end of the war was fast approaching. While the Red Army charged forward to seize as much territory as possible, leaders in Tokyo debated their next moves. At 11:30 that evening, the Japanese Supreme War Council convened a meeting in the air-raid shelter beneath the Imperial Palace. Foreign Minister Shigenori Togo opened with a proposal to accept a modified version of the Potsdam Declaration. "The military situation is now more favorable to the United States and Britain given the current state of the enemy forces and because of Soviet participation in the war, so it is difficult for us to demand that they change the terms of the ultimatum any further," he explained. While the imperial house must be preserved, he argued, no further conditions were necessary. The minister of the army, Kore-chika Anami, disagreed. "We should live up to our cause even if our hundred million people have to die side by side in battle," he insisted. "We have no choice other than to continue the war by all means." Pushed on the question of further atomic bombings, Chief of the Army General Staff Yoshijiro Umezu admitted, "Though we haven't made sufficient progress so far in dealing with air raids, we should expect better results soon since we have revised our tactics. But there is *no reason we should surrender to our enemies as a result of air raids*" (emphasis added). The army's dismissal of the atomic bombings as air raids was indicative of both the callousness with which the military viewed civilian casualties and the willingness of Japanese leaders to fight on in the face of further nuclear attacks.[44]

HAVING FAILED TO REACH A CONSENSUS AFTER THREE HOURS OF deliberation, the council presented the matter to the emperor himself. Although Hirohito still hoped to maintain the imperial institution in Japan, he had determined that the war must end. "We will risk losing everything if we continue a hopeless war. I have no expectation for victory after considering our material power compared to [the enemy's] and various situations in and out of the country." With tears in his eyes, Hirohito concluded that the military's confidence in victory was not supported by the available evidence. "In this situation, there is no prospect of victory over the American and British forces with such technological power. It is very unbearable for me to take away arms from my loyal military men and to hand them over to the Allied Forces as war criminals. But I should bear the unbearable from a broader perspective . . . so I decide this way in order to save the people from disaster and bring about happiness to mankind around the world." The assembled ministers "burst into wails" and resolved to accept the terms of the Potsdam Declaration with the single condition that their acceptance did "not comprise any demand which prejudice[d] the prerogatives of His Majesty as a sovereign ruler." A telegram outlining the decision was sent to Switzerland and Sweden at 7:00 a.m. on August 10.[45]

That same afternoon in Washington, Truman and his cabinet gathered to consider the Japanese message. The Americans would accept the surrender, although Secretary of State James Byrnes insisted that the "top dog over Hirohito be an American." The British had signaled their agreement, but the Soviets had not yet replied. Truman doubted that Moscow would respond but decided that he "would go ahead without them anyway." Secretary Stimson suggested that the Soviets were playing for time in order to seize as much of Manchuria as possible. Truman then told the cabinet that he had ordered a halt to further atomic strikes. "He said the thought of wiping out another 100,000 people was too horrible," wrote Secretary of Commerce Henry Wallace in his diary. "He didn't like the idea of killing, as he said, 'all those kids.'" Wallace then went on to record his own thoughts on the growing tensions between Washington and Moscow: "It is obvious to me that the cornerstone of the peace of the future consists in strengthening our ties of friendship with Russia. It is also obvious that the attitude of Truman, Byrnes and both the War and Navy Department is not moving in this direction. Their attitude will make for war eventually."[46]

While Wallace worried about a future war, not everyone was prepared to stop fighting the current one. Many figures in the Imperial Japanese Army still hoped to continue the struggle against the Allies, but Emperor Hirohito pushed back. "The military situation has changed suddenly," he told senior officers on the morning of August 14. "The Soviet Union entered the war against us. Suicide attacks can't compete with the power of science. Therefore, there is no alternative but to accept the Potsdam terms." Prime Minister Suzuki Kantaro had made an even more pointed argument the previous day. "If we don't act now," he said, "the Russians will penetrate not only Manchuria and Korea but northern Japan as well. . . . We must act now while our chief adversary is still only the United States." Astute observers in Tokyo must have understood that the dangers of a potentially permanent Soviet occupation outweighed the risk of surrender to the Americans.[47]

Nevertheless, a hardened cadre of junior officers in Tokyo remained determined to block the government's surrender. Late that evening, the insurrectionists staged a coup against the Japanese government. Although the insurgents managed to seize control of the Imperial Palace through the early morning hours of August 15, their attempt failed when Japan's senior military leadership refused to support the uprising. At 7:21 that same morning, Japanese radio called on the entire nation and its forces abroad to tune in for a special announcement from the emperor to be read at noon. As millions of Japanese gathered around radio sets, a recording of Hirohito announced the government's decision to surrender. Japan was losing the war, he explained. "Moreover, the enemy has begun to employ a new and most cruel bomb, the power of which to do damage is indeed incalculable, taking the toll of many innocent lives. Should we continue to fight, it would result not only in an ultimate collapse and obliteration of the Japanese nation, but also in the total extinction of human civilization." Two days later, Hirohito offered a second rescript to the armed forces: "Now that the Soviet Union entered the war, to continue under the present conditions at home and abroad would only result in further useless damage and eventually endanger the very foundation of the empire's existence. Therefore, although the fighting spirit of the Imperial Navy and Army is still vigorous, I am going to make peace with the United States, Britain, the Soviet Union, and Chungking, in order to preserve our glorious *kokutai* [national polity]."[48] In his message to the Japanese people, Hirohito had cited the bomb as the factor driving his decision to surrender, but in his message to the military, he had pointed to the Soviet invasion.

Although Tokyo had resolved to surrender, Moscow remained determined to press forward in a blatant attempt to seize more territory. As Red Army soldiers continued their drive through Manchuria, Soviet naval forces prepared to stage an attack across five hundred miles of the Sea of Okhotsk on the Kuril Islands. On August 18, three days after Hirohito's radio address accepting the Potsdam Declaration, Soviet troops landed on the northernmost of the Kurils. Some eight thousand Japanese soldiers mounted a determined defense, but they were forced to retreat after three days of combat. Meanwhile, fighting raged on Sakhalin Island off the coast of Siberia. Again, Japanese forces staged a fierce but hopeless resistance before the island fell to Soviet control on August 26. In the case of the Kurils and Sakhalin, Soviet officials could reasonably claim that they were occupying the territories that they had been promised under the terms of the Yalta agreements. However, Stalin's bid for seizing Hokkaido in an operation set to begin at midnight on August 23 was an even bolder attempt to gain territory in the closing days of the war. So, too, were American considerations of landing in the Kurils to occupy the port of Dalian.

In both cases, leaders in Moscow and Washington backpedaled, forestalling what might have been a clash between their forces in the Far East.[49]

The race to the finish in the Pacific War presented a mirror image of the Allied race to Berlin. Where the Western Allies had delayed the Normandy invasion until the Wehrmacht was on its heels, the Red Army entered the war against Japan when Tokyo teetered on the brink of defeat. Both Washington and Moscow had waited until the final stages of the war to rush in and claim spheres of influence in Western Europe and the Far East, respectively. In conducting the postwar occupations that followed, both superpowers would reconfirm Stalin's assertion that "whoever occupies a territory also imposes his own social system."

JAPANESE LEADERS HAD SIGNED THE OFFICIAL INSTRUMENT OF SUR-render on the USS *Missouri* on September 2, 1945. "It is my earnest hope," General MacArthur told the assembled leaders, "and indeed the hope of all mankind, that from this solemn occasion a better world shall emerge out of the blood and carnage of the past—a world dedicated to the dignity of man and the fulfillment of his most cherished wish for freedom, tolerance and justice." Not everyone was so optimistic. Watching the closing stages of the most destructive war in human history, Joseph Stalin voiced his concerns about the geopolitical fallout from America's new monopoly on atomic weapons. Washington had emerged as the first power in world history with the ability to annihilate any population center on the globe in a matter of hours. "Hiroshima has shaken the whole world," he told two leaders of the Soviet atomic program. Any semblance of strategic parity between Moscow and Washington was now gone: "The balance has been destroyed."[50]

Several weeks later, US Foreign Service officer John Emmerson arrived in Tokyo, where he would serve as aide to General MacArthur in the postwar occupation. Much of the city still lay in scorched, blackened ruins as the result of the March firebombing raids. The Japanese nation was just beginning the long, painful process of reconstruction. Inside his new office, Emmerson encountered a junior Mitsui executive cleaning out the last odds and ends from his desk. On his way out the door, the executive gestured to a wall map of the Greater East Asia Co-Prosperity Sphere. "There it is," he told Emmerson with a grin. "We tried. See what you can do with it!"[51]

Conclusion

FOREVER WAR

I N July 1945, US ambassador to the Soviet Union Averell
Harriman greeted Joseph Stalin in the devastated city of Berlin.
Harriman remarked that the Soviet leader must be pleased to finally
enter the capital after four years of brutal warfare. Stalin paused. "Czar
Alexander got to Paris," he grumbled. The triumphant dictator's chilling response fed Harriman's deep suspicions. Vast stretches of Europe
had been reduced to smoking piles of rubble. Countless bodies lay
buried in the ruins while the Allies met in Potsdam to determine the
shape of the postwar world. For Harriman, the stakes could not have
been greater. Moscow had unleashed a "twentieth-century barbarian
invasion of Europe," he had written months earlier. Unless American leaders could meet the Soviet threat, "history [would] record the
period of the next generation as the Soviet Age." Now, gazing across
the smoldering ruins of the Third Reich, his mood turned back toward
the apocalyptic. "The greatest crime of Hitler was that his actions
had resulted in opening the gates of Eastern Europe to Asia," he
lamented.[1]

Barbarians at the gates, threats from the East—Harriman's dark visions portrayed a struggle for the very fabric of civilization. His language evoked a sense of racial anxiety, imperial collapse, and world historical upheaval that would have resonated with an observer witnessing the fall of Rome. And the ambassador was not the only American thinking of falling empires. Months earlier, the Joint Chiefs of Staff had warned that the global transformations unleashed by the war would be "more comparable indeed with that occasioned by the fall of Rome than with any other change occurring during the succeeding fifteen hundred years."[2]

Like many, these men seemed to sense that the Second World War marked the end of an old era and the dawn of a new one. Some sixty million people had been killed. If all of the dead were laid out in a straight line, head to toe, they would circle the earth twice. Two out of every three were civilians. Savage fighting had ripped through societies across Europe and Asia, reducing whole cities to rubble. In the countryside, farms lay in ruin, herds of livestock had been wiped out, and prewar rail and shipping networks had been devastated. Emaciated prisoners languished and died in concentration camps. Millions more faced the threat of famine as throngs of refugees roamed in search of shelter and sustenance. The war had devastated every major industrial economy in the world except that of the United States. Seventy-five percent of Berlin's buildings lay in ruins; twenty million Germans had lost their homes. Half a million French homes had been leveled. But the destruction in the West was dwarfed by the devastation in the East. One in five Poles had been killed. Seventy thousand Soviet villages had been destroyed along with 1,700 towns, leaving twenty-five million homeless.[3]

The war in Asia had killed nearly twenty-four million people, and another eighty-five million had been wounded, raped, enslaved, or made homeless. Hospitals, irrigation systems, railways, and power plants lay in ruins. Fifty percent of Shanghai's industry lay in ruins; 60 percent of Wuhan's industry had been destroyed; 96 percent of nationalist-controlled China's rail network had been wrecked.

Catastrophic famines killed as many as two million in French Indochina and another two million in British India. Meanwhile, Allied bombing had obliterated an estimated 40 percent of Japan's total urban area across sixty-six cities, leaving almost one in three Japanese citizens homeless. And the irradiated ruins of Hiroshima and Nagasaki now stood as grim testaments to the terrifying power of nuclear weapons.[4]

Beyond this staggering physical destruction, the war had dealt a lethal blow to a centuries-old international order. The Axis bid for world power—a brutally violent effort to consolidate Africa, Eurasia, and Oceania under the direct control of imperial sovereigns in Berlin, Rome, and Tokyo—marked the climax of five hundred years of colonial expansion. As the age of formal colonialism entered its twilight, many in the Western world noted what they saw as the decline of white supremacy. As the novelist Pearl Buck had warned Franklin Roosevelt in late 1941, "More basic than Chinese antagonism to Japan was [the] colored races' antagonism to white." This sentiment was echoed by Malayan independence fighter Mustapha Hussain: "When the British returned to rule Malaya in 1945, they no longer faced Malays of the pre war mould. They were confronted instead by a Malay community whose souls and spirits were no longer static and no longer accepting." Surveying the aftermath of the war in Asia, American reporter Robert Trumbull offered a similar take: "Respect for the white man's attainments remains, but in the eyes of the Asiatic he is no longer a master who is invincible." The West, he explained, had "lost face" in Asia. Across the entire region, "the power and prestige of the white man have waned."[5]

To many, the global edifice of colonialism and white supremacy appeared to be disintegrating. Nazi and Japanese racial policies had weakened the intellectual foundations of eugenics and scientific racism that had been so prevalent before the war. Overtly racist language began to lose favor in mainstream political, intellectual, and business circles. Similarly, the war's brutalities helped to establish a growing human rights consciousness that was codified in documents such as the United Nations' 1948 Universal Declaration of Human Rights and in the efforts of Raphael Lemkin, a Jewish Polish lawyer, to recognize genocide under postwar international law.[6] The war had also weakened the old colonial empires and empowered anticolonial forces across the globe. Although British, French, and Dutch leaders would wage a series of struggles to reclaim their lost empires, the old colonial powers were fighting a losing battle. The tide of history had turned and the worldwide decolonization movement would not be denied. Within a generation, nearly all of Europe's former colonies had achieved independence and self-determination.

But appearances were deceiving. Even as overt expressions of white supremacy diminished, veiled manifestations of racism proliferated. Official racism survived in forms such as the American Jim Crow system of segregation, white-minority regimes in Rhodesia and South Africa, and a host of other institutions. Informal racism remained even more widespread in everyday expressions of discrimination, prejudice, and little-recognized structures of systemic racism. The resurgence of far-right nationalist groups and ethnic violence in the twenty-first century serves as a reminder that strong currents of ethnocentrism remain across much of the world. Likewise, despite international efforts to eradicate the scourge of genocide, ethnic violence surged across large parts of the world through the twentieth and twenty-first centuries.[7]

The demise of colonialism followed a similar trajectory. For all the Atlantic Charter's lofty rhetoric about self-determination, the United States had already emerged as a grudging defender of the dying colonial order. The Office of Strategic Services had explained this shift in April 1945. The United States "should realize . . . its interest in the maintenance of the British, French and Dutch colonial empires. We should encourage the liberalization of the colonial regimes in order to better maintain them and to check Soviet influence in the stimulation of colonial revolt." A State Department officer at the San Francisco conference of May 1945 that established the United Nations offered a similar assessment: "When perhaps the inevitable struggle comes between Russia and ourselves . . . would we have the support of Great Britain if we had undermined her [imperial] position [in the Far East]?" The United States should be careful "not to undermine the influence of the West," especially in light of the fact that "Soviet ideology will be a rising force throughout the Far East." Rather than dismantling colonialism, then, Washington would seek to facilitate the gradual transition to a more subtle mode of imperial influence, governed by the American dollar, defended by US naval, atomic, and air power, and justified by the threat of the Soviet Union.[8]

INDEED, LEADERS IN BOTH WASHINGTON AND MOSCOW RECOGNIZED that the Second World War had set off a revolution in the geopolitical order, fatally undermining the old colonial system and propelling the twin American and Soviet juggernauts into positions to dominate the post-1945 era. The new superpowers' wartime experiences could hardly have been more different. Stalin colluded with Hitler to dismember Poland before suffering a surprise attack in June 1941; Roosevelt nudged the United States toward war over a period of eighteen months until the Pearl Harbor attacks pushed the nation over the edge. The Soviet Union sustained the heaviest casualties of any nation in the war; the Americans were blessed to emerge with some of the lightest losses of any of the war's principal belligerents. The USSR suffered the near annihilation of its industrial base; the US gross national product increased by over 50 percent. Seven hundred thousand square miles of Soviet territory came under German occupation; not one inch of the continental United States fell under enemy control.

The superpowers also prosecuted the war in dramatically different ways. The United States fought in close cooperation with the British Empire, relying on London's colonial outposts and imperial supply lines. The Soviet Union conducted its campaigns largely alone, with the supplemental infusion of Lend-Lease aid from the West. Washington fought as a maritime power, building a worldwide network of bases from which it launched primarily offensive operations at places and times of its own choosing. Moscow fought as a continental empire, relying on its massive armies to absorb devastating casualties before staging equally punishing counterattacks and spending much of the war in strategic defensive operations. Western forces relied heavily on naval and aerial actions, sinking ships and burning cities across the globe. Soviet forces relied on colossal land campaigns that crushed the German and Japanese armies through sheer weight of numbers. By war's end the United States had built the infrastructure to support a worldwide naval empire that could command the Atlantic and Pacific Oceans and threaten the skies above nearly all the world's major cities. In contrast, the colossal Red Army dominated most of Eurasia, from Manchuria in the east to the Inner German border in the west.

In the process, the war fundamentally transformed the architecture of global power. Never before had a single conflict wrought such profound change at a planetary level. The superpowers' ascendency had rendered traditional colonialism obsolete, but the legacy of imperialism survived. The Second World War had served as a laboratory for the articulation of new forms of imperial and neo-imperial power that came to life in the Cold War. American leaders oversaw an empire of capital built on the foundations of Lend-Lease and structured by financial mechanisms outlined at the 1944 Bretton Woods Conference—all while presiding over a domestic political system still mired in the racism of Jim Crow. On the other side of the Iron Curtain, Soviet leaders established a system of vassal states in Eastern Europe led by client regimes that the Red Army had installed at the end of the war. Soviet leaders disguised imperial ambitions dating back to the czarist era beneath the rhetoric of Marxist-Leninism and proletarian revolution. The combined effect of these transformations amounted to a sweeping reconfiguration of imperial power in the postwar world.

The genius of the new American empire was its ability to dispense with formal colonies in favor of extraterritorial hegemony— offshore military, political, and financial machinery designed to direct American power and influence deep into continental interiors without exposing large numbers of US citizens to the perils of colonial warfare. The Second World War had taught leaders in Washington that they could exercise power from far beyond the horizon, whether through an armada of fleet carriers floating hundreds of miles off the coast, through long-distance bombers operating from distant airstrips on coral atolls, or through the virtue of its massive wealth. Forged in wartime, this global infrastructure of imperial control gave Washington the capacity to project military force across the oceans with unprecedented speed and flexibility. Ringed by an expanding archipelago of forward bases from Greenland to Germany, through Turkey and the Philippines to South Korea and Japan, the continental United States remained effectively invulnerable to all conventional attacks from a potential adversary. But the offshore nature of American power left Washington with little influence over armed struggles far inland during the war and after.

The Soviet empire, for its part, emerged from the war in command of the largest land army in human history. From the citadel of Moscow deep in the heart of the Eurasian landmass, Soviet leaders wielded a brutally efficient state security apparatus and cultivated a worldwide network of foreign agents. The Red Army had played the starring role in vanquishing the Nazi beast, delivering Europe from the clutches of Hitler and his genocidal vision. Moreover, the Soviets achieved overwhelming victory while laying claim to the legacy of the most sweeping political revolution since 1789. Untainted by close association with Europe's old colonial powers, Soviet leaders presented themselves as champions of revolutionary forces across the globe engaged in liberation struggles against Western colonialism. And although the Soviet Union remained vulnerable to attack along its western and southern borders, Moscow's crushing victory over the Wehrmacht combined with a vast continental rear area to render any potential invasion of the Soviet empire virtually unthinkable. Nevertheless, as a land power, Moscow struggled to acquire the capacity to project dominating force far from its own borders.

Surrounded by rampant destruction, confronted with the horrors of the Holocaust, and preparing for the terror of atomic war, the triumphant Allies' fears turned to one another. Indeed, as the new superpowers claimed their spots atop the geopolitical hierarchy, the last vestiges of wartime cooperation dissolved. To be sure, Moscow and Washington had been unlikely allies, forced together by their shared Axis enemies. But the war's unprecedented violence had induced both nations to reimagine their national security in global terms. The war had removed Britain and France as arbiters of the international order, creating a power vacuum into which the new superpowers were now drawn. At the same time, Germany's and Japan's surprise attacks had revealed new strategic vulnerabilities for both superpowers. The development of arsenals designed to defeat the Axis exacerbated the sense of insecurity in both Moscow and Washington. In addition, the fact that the two superpowers had incurred vastly disproportionate costs in fighting the war sowed lasting resentments. So, too, did opposing visions of postwar order that took shape in the military occupations of Germany, Japan, Italy, Poland, Manchuria, and a host of other nations after 1945. Going forward, Washington would work to construct a postwar liberal-capitalist world order while Moscow sought to forge a new international system rooted in the tenets of Marxism-Leninism.

These contending visions of world order set the geostrategic agenda for the next eighty years of great power struggle. While America and its allies patrolled the Mediterranean, the Middle East, and Western Europe, the Soviet Union garrisoned the Eurasian heartland. As this new imperial rivalry took hold, Washington and Moscow embraced many of the Axis powers' key goals. Both superpowers recruited Nazi scientists to build their new Cold War arsenals and conscripted former Wehrmacht officers to impart their experience in waging military campaigns against US and Soviet armies. Where

Berlin, Rome, and Tokyo had formed the Anti-Comintern Pact as an alliance against Moscow, Washington worked to build a collective security system composed of anticommunist states focused on containing Soviet influence. On the other side of the Iron Curtain, Stalin forged the Soviet-dominated Eastern Bloc on the same territory where Hitler had tried to build the Third Reich's lebensraum. Likewise, after 1945, Moscow would take up Germany's and Japan's quests to derail America's rising economic hegemony. And in one of the war's greatest ironies, Washington rebuilt West Germany and Japan as the dominant economic powers in Europe and East Asia.

Collectively, these developments challenge orthodox interpretations of the Second World War. If the war was a struggle against fascism, why were the superpowers so eager to enlist former Nazis into their Cold War national security states? If the war was an effort to restrain Germany and Japan, why did Washington devote so many resources to rebuilding them as economic powers? Although both Moscow and Washington entered the conflict in response to Axis surprise attacks, the nascent superpowers quickly determined that true victory would entail establishing control over the postwar international order. Viewed broadly, World War II was a pivotal moment in global history: an imperial succession whereby the United States replaced Britain's waning hegemony and prepared to fend off challenges from the Soviet Union. The Cold War materialized as a new imperial struggle between the war's principal victors for supremacy in the post-1945 global order.

Although the United States maintained its prewar sphere of influence over Latin America and the Soviet Union functioned as an imperial suzerain in Eastern Europe, the Cold War was no simple redux of colonial empire. The failures of Britain, France, Germany, and Japan had demonstrated that outright colonialism was no longer a viable mechanism for exercising hegemony. Instead, the superpowers would wield power through more subtle means such as economic controls, ideology, foreign aid, and arms sales. When these measures failed, Washington and Moscow staged covert operations and military interventions to police their respective spheres of influence and defend their standing in the wider world. Although this arrangement delivered a measure of peace to Europe, it fostered military conflict across the postcolonial world, where dozens of newly sovereign states were coming to grips with the challenges of independence.

None of these postcolonial states had a greater impact on world affairs than China—World War II's forgotten ally.[9] The destruction of Japan's empire ended China's "century of humiliation," but it set the stage for the resumption of the decades-long civil war between Chiang Kai-shek's regime and Mao Zedong's Communist Party. Chiang's catastrophic losses in the war with Japan combined with the absence of large numbers of American ground forces on the mainland and the presence of the Red Army in Manchuria to boost communist fortunes. Mao's victory in 1949 reverberated across the postcolonial world, inspiring millions of revolutionary fighters around the globe. Within a generation, Beijing emerged as a third great power, serving as the pivot in a triangular competition between Beijing, Moscow, and Washington. Propelled by its meteoric economic rise, China moved to the center of world politics in the twenty-first century.

The decades after World War II also witnessed a long chain of conflicts across Asia, Africa, and the Middle East as rival factions fought for control of postcolonial governments, worked to consolidate control over political territory, and struggled to assert regional influence. These rivalries presented a multitude of openings for the superpowers to recruit clients around the world to serve as willing agents of US and Soviet imperial influence, all under the overarching framework of formal state sovereignty. The blueprint for these postcolonial wars was drawn from the World War II campaigns of the eastern front and the Second Sino-Japanese War. Rather than traditional armies squaring off on defined battlefields, these Cold War–era conflicts were characterized by genocidal violence and systematic civilian atrocities—hallmarks of pre-1945 colonial warfare.

Meanwhile, Moscow and Washington maintained their respective spheres of influence and engaged in a massive arms race in both conventional and nuclear weaponry.

Viewed from the perspective of the twenty-first century, the end result of the Second World War was to create a new global order maintained in a state of perpetual nuclear terror, riven by permanent colonial warfare, and justified by the logic of the Cold War.

This is not the narrative that appears in textbooks, popular histories, novels, and films. Instead, standard accounts of the Second World War have been hijacked by nationalist mythology. Russian schoolchildren learn of the "great patriotic war" in which the peoples of the Soviet Union fought as one to repel the Nazi invasion and liberate Europe—a narrative that erases widespread resistance to Moscow's rule. This framing also serves to justify the creation of a Russian-controlled sphere of influence in Eastern Europe and brands international objections to this policy as efforts by the perfidious Western powers to weaken Moscow. Similarly, collective memory of the war in Britain commemorates an "England alone" version of the conflict that celebrates the British Empire and portrays Dunkirk, the Blitz, and El Alamein as the critical turning points of the war. In these accounts, the British Empire emerges as the savior of Western civilization: a role to which it had laid claim in the Napoleonic Wars and when it defeated the Spanish Armada, and which it would reprise during the 1956 Suez Crisis and the Falklands War.[10]

In China, the war's history was frequently invoked to support a narrative of national unity that celebrated Mao's communist guerrillas while downplaying the central contributions of Chiang and the Guomindang. At the same time, the war served as a warning against foreign efforts to intervene in Chinese affairs and as justification for Beijing's efforts to assert its influence more widely across East Asia. More recently, "good war" narratives about China's role in defeating fascism have been mobilized to provide a moral basis for Beijing's bid for global hegemony.[11]

Perhaps no memorialization has had a more far-reaching impact than that of the United States. Americans have embraced a narrative of the "good war" fought by the "greatest generation." This account portrays the United States as an unwitting victim of Axis aggression that launched a heroic, selfless crusade to save the world from fascism and totalitarianism.

In this telling, Soviet and Chinese contributions are downplayed and the United States emerges as the central player in winning the war—a characterization that both justifies America's postwar hegemony and nourishes the delusion that victory in major wars can be purchased at a comparatively low price in blood. American leaders are portrayed as unfailingly honest, while their Soviet counterparts are portrayed as congenitally deceitful. The lessons of Munich and Pearl Harbor demand constant military vigilance and muscular responses to foreign aggression—providing a convenient template for framing later clashes with the likes of Joseph Stalin, Fidel Castro, Ho Chi Minh, and Saddam Hussein. American claims to absolute moral superiority have also been used to whitewash Washington's long record of indiscriminate bombing campaigns against civilian populations. Above all, this version of the war has served to rationalize Washington's pursuit of Pax Americana, recasting America's global empire as vital for the defense of global democracy and civilization itself.

Collectively, then, the victorious Allies chose to narrate the history of the war as a series of patriotic fairy tales designed to justify postwar national ambitions. The tragic result is that a conflict born of unbridled colonial ambition was used to legitimize Cold War imperialism; a conflict shaped by virulent racism was used to fan the flames of postwar nationalism; a war marked by unrestrained militarism and civilian atrocities was used to rationalize a suicidal nuclear arms race and brutal Third World interventions; a war that was won through sustained cooperation between the great powers was used to promote bitter postwar rivalries between those same powers.

THIS BOOK HAS LAID OUT AN ALTERNATE APPROACH TO UNDER-
standing the war. Viewed in the long historical perspective, the Second World War remains central to understanding the contours of
our twenty-first-century world. The war served as the catalyst for the
transformation of the international order, tearing down the crumbling facade of formal colonialism and refashioning the United States
and Soviet Union as global empires vying for hegemony over the postwar world. For the next forty-five years, Moscow would stand as the
dominant land power in Europe; US maritime supremacy survived
into the next century. The Axis conquests of Eastern Europe and East
Asia transplanted tactics of indiscriminate violence from the colonial periphery to metropolitan centers of Europe and the Far East,
assembling a repertoire of civilian atrocities from which the Allies
and later generations of Cold Warriors would draw. Within this larger
structure, the war's principal victors pursued objectives that would
have been all too familiar to the architects of the Second World War:
the domination of Europe—or the prevention thereof; the pursuit
of supremacy in the Far East; shepherding China's reemergence as a
world power; and intervening in the political, economic, and military
affairs in Asia, Africa, and the Middle East.

These dynamics would live into the twenty-first century, with
Moscow waging a long campaign to reconstitute the old Russian
Empire in Eastern Europe, Washington struggling to defend an
embattled Pax Americana, and Beijing asserting its growing great
power influence in Asia and beyond. On this point, aspiring strategists would be wise to remember that the last time a world leader
launched a war to dominate Eastern Europe and a rising Asian power
sought to challenge American power in the Pacific, it led to the bloodiest war in human history.

IN THE END, IT IS THIS CONTINUED SALIENCE OF THE WAR THAT
makes grappling with the darker dimensions of its history so critical.

For billions of people around the world, the Second World War represents the origin story for understanding contemporary world affairs—the central point of reference for making sense of diplomacy, war, genocide, and the very structure of international power. By ignoring the imperial dimensions of the war and the global order it created, we conceal the enduring legacies of violence and colonialism that formed the foundations of our contemporary world. Ultimately, if we hope to understand world affairs in the twenty-first century, we must come to terms with a basic, underlying truth: the war did not end imperialism; imperialism ended the war.

ACKNOWLEDGMENTS

In the early morning hours of November 13, 1942, my great-uncle, Paul Grey Wisenberger, was killed serving aboard the USS *San Francisco* during the Naval Battle of Guadalcanal. Thirty-seven years later, my parents gave me his name. Millions of people around the world have similar stories about the Second World War. Perhaps no event in contemporary history touched so many lives—surely none destroyed so many. The moral weight of this reality and the tragedy that the war brought to so many people around the world should not be lost on anyone studying the topic. It certainly was not lost on me.

I incurred many debts in the course of writing this book. The History Department and the Weatherhead East Asian Institute at Columbia University provided generous financial support. Katherine Owens served as my research assistant, helping me to track down a number of the oral histories that appear in the book. Thomas Zeiler read the entire manuscript and provided thoughtful suggestions. I benefited from conversations with Frank Costigliola, Daniel Immerwahr, Ryan Irwin, Rashid Khalidi, Dirk Moses, Andrew Preston, Mark Stoler, and Adam Tooze. My thanks also go to Jeremy Collins and the staff at the National WWII Museum in New Orleans and to Larry Berman, John Burns, and Rudy Shapee at the USS *Midway* Museum in San Diego. For the last eight years, I have been blessed to be a member of the History Department at Columbia University, where I have the privilege to work with an outstanding group of colleagues. A special thanks also goes out to my brilliant students, particularly those who participated in my 3011 seminar over the last several years.

I was fortunate to work with a phenomenal editor at Basic Books, Brian Distelberg, whose sage advice was instrumental throughout the writing of this book. His assistant, Alex Cullina, helped to keep me on task through the closing stages of the process. Erin Granville copyedited the entire manuscript and saved me from numerous typographical errors. My thanks also go to Kate Blackmer, who created the maps, and to Tony Bui, who took my author photo. Two of my mentors passed away while writing this book. My literary agent, John Wright, was one of my strongest advocates and one of my most incisive critics. My writing and my work as a scholar have greatly benefited from having known him. The late George Herring was a role model in so many ways—as a scholar, teacher, senior colleague, and friend.

As always, I owe a special debt to my family: my parents, Tom and Connie; my brother Dan and sister-in-law Rachel. But no one deserves more gratitude than my amazing wife and my incredible daughters. Mia never hesitated to let me know when it was time to stop typing and do something more worthwhile, like kick a soccer ball around Riverside Park. Leila served as one of my earliest readers even though she still can't fathom why anyone would choose to write history books instead of fantasy novels. And for the last sixteen years, Hang Nguyen has been my partner and best friend, putting up with me and the ever-growing pile of books that has taken over our dining room table.

Paul Thomas Chamberlin
Morningside Heights, New York
September 2024

NOTES

INTRODUCTION: UNTHINKABLE

1. Churchill's original draft reads "highly improbable event." These words are crossed out in red and replaced with the handwritten "purely hypothetical contingency." Joint Planning Staff, "Operation 'Unthinkable,'" 22 May 1945, CAB 120/691, Russian Threat to Western Civilisation; Ismay to Churchill, 8 Jun. 1945, CAB 120/691; Churchill to Ismay, 10 Jun. 1945, CAB 120/691. All in the National Archives, Kew, Richmond, England (hereinafter UKNA).

2. Joint Chiefs of Staff (JCS), Memorandum for Information No. 121, "Strategy and Policy: Can America and Russia Cooperate?," 20 Aug. 1943, World War II: U.S. Documents on Planning, Operations, Intelligence, Axis War Crimes, and Refugees, ProQuest History Vault.

3. Although a comprehensive list would be too long for this book, the most influential traditional accounts include the following: Peter Calvocoressi and Guy Wint, *Total War* (New York: Pantheon, 1972), one of the first attempts at a deep, comprehensive account of the global war; Gerhard Weinberg, *A World at Arms* (New York: Cambridge University Press, 1995), the most authoritative and detailed international history; Williamson Murray and Allan Millett, *A War to Be Won* (Cambridge, MA: Belknap Press of Harvard University Press, 2000), the most comprehensive and trenchant account of the American war effort; Andrew Roberts, *The Storm of War* (London: Allen Lane, 2009), which provides an updated strategic analysis focusing on Hitler's mistakes; and Max Hastings, *Inferno* (New York: Alfred Knopf, 2011), which offers a wealth of firsthand accounts from everyday participants. Although each is an impressive work of scholarship with valuable insights, together they do little to challenge the underlying tenets of the established orthodox interpretation.

4. While revisionism remains rare in broad global histories, pioneering interpretations abound at the local and regional levels. A short list includes A. J. P. Taylor, *The Origins of the Second World War* (New York: Atheneum, 1983); Gabriel Kolko, *The Politics of War* (New York: Random House, 1968); Ernest Mandel, *The Meaning of the Second World War* (London: Verso, 1986); Mark A. Stoler, *Allies and Adversaries* (Chapel Hill: University of North Carolina Press, 2000); Tsuyoshi Hasegawa, *Racing the Enemy* (Cambridge, MA: Belknap Press of Harvard University Press, 2005); Timothy Snyder, *Bloodlands* (New York: Basic, 2010); and Stephen Wertheim, *Tomorrow the World* (Cambridge, MA: Belknap Press of Harvard University Press, 2020).

5. Some of the more provocative recent surveys of the war that offer compelling new interpretations include Evan Mawdsley, *World War II*, 2nd ed. (Cambridge, UK: Cambridge University Press, 2020); Thomas Zeiler, *Annihilation* (New York: Oxford University Press, 2011); Antony Beevor, *The Second World War* (New York: Little, Brown, 2012); the three-volume *Cambridge History of the Second World War* (Cambridge, UK: Cambridge University Press, 2015); and Victor Davis Hanson, *The Second World War* (New York: Basic, 2017). Thomas Zeiler and Daniel M. DuBois, eds., *A Companion to World War II* (Hoboken, NJ: Wiley-Blackwell, 2013), provides an indispensable guide

to recent literature on the war. Richard Overy, *Blood and Ruins* (New York: Viking, 2022), deserves special mention. Overy's masterful account articulates an emerging line of argument—echoed in this book as well as in a number of specialized monographs—that approaches World War II as a clash of imperial powers. In contrast to Overy, this book argues that imperialism survived the war and played a foundational role in shaping the Cold War imperial confrontation that followed.

6. I use Jane Burbank and Frederick Cooper's definition of empires as "large political units, expansionist or with a memory of power extended over space, polities that maintain distinction and hierarchy as they incorporate new people. The national-state, in contrast, is based on the idea of a single people in a single territory constituting itself as a unique political community." *Empires in World History* (Princeton, NJ: Princeton University Press, 2010), 8. Colonialism represents the formal application of imperialism on subject populations, whereas imperialism often operates through informal mechanisms such as economic, political, and cultural influence. For a recent discussion of the "imperial turn" in US foreign relations history, see the articles in Into the Stacks in *Modern American History* 7, no. 1 (March 2024).

7. On Cold War violence, see Paul Thomas Chamberlin, *The Cold War's Killing Fields* (New York: Harper, 2018).

8. For the *longue durée* story of great power competition, see Paul Kennedy, *The Rise and Fall of the Great Powers* (New York: Vintage, 1989).

9. Hannah Arendt, *The Origins of Totalitarianism* (New York: Harcourt, Brace, 1951); Aimé Césaire, *Discourse on Colonialism*, trans. by Joan Pinkham (New York: Monthly Review Press, 2000).

10. On this dynamic, see Andrew Buchanan, *From War to Postwar* (London: Bloomsbury, 2023), 3, 6.

CHAPTER 1: A WORLD OF EMPIRES

1. Walter Duranty, "Signing Provides Brilliant Pageant," *New York Times* (hereinafter *NYT*), 29 Jun. 1919; "Enemy Envoys in Truculent Spirit," *NYT*, 29 Jun. 1919.

2. "Terrible Atrocities by Turks," *Scotsman*, 30 Jul. 1919; "Aidin a Vast Sepulchre," *NYT*, 29 Aug. 1921; Vasileios Th. Meichanetsidis, "The Genocide of the Greeks of the Ottoman Empire, 1913–1923," *Genocide Studies International* 9, no. 1 (Spring 2015): 104–173.

3. Jeffrey Veidlinger, *In the Midst of Civilized Europe* (New York: Metropolitan, 2021), 2–5.

4. Zara Steiner, *The Lights That Failed* (New York: Oxford University Press, 2005), 6; Robert Gerwarth, "The Continuum of Violence," in *The Cambridge History of the First World War*, vol. 2, *The State*, ed. Jay Winter (Cambridge, UK: Cambridge University Press, 2016), 640; Robert Gerwarth, "The Sky Beyond Versailles," *Journal of Modern History* 93, no. 4 (Dec. 2021).

5. "Peace with Germany," *Times* (London), 30 Jun. 1919.

6. Quoted in Margaret MacMillan, *Paris 1919* (New York: Random House, 2002), 86.

7. Numbers come from Evan Mawdsley, *World War II* (Cambridge, UK: Cambridge University Press, 2009), 14. On America's empire in the interwar years, see Daniel Immerwahr, *How to Hide an Empire* (New York: Farrar, Straus and Giroux, 2019).

8. Alfred Thayer Mahan, *The Influence of Sea Power upon History* (Boston: Little, Brown, 1890), 28, 83.

9. Halford Mackinder, *Democratic Ideals and Reality* (New York: H. Holt and Company, 1919), 186.

10. For more on colonialism, see Frederick Cooper and Ann Stoler, eds., *Tensions of Empire* (Berkeley: University of California Press, 1997).

11. On the concept of civilization, see Bruce Mazlish, *Civilization and Its Contents* (Stanford, CA: Stanford University Press, 2004); on the civilizing mission, see Alice Conklin, *A Mission to Civilize* (Stanford, CA: Stanford University Press, 1997).

12. Quoted in Merz Tate, "The War Aims of World War I and World War II and Their Relation to the Darker Peoples of the World," *Journal of Negro Education* 12, no. 3 (Summer 1943).

13. On the mandate system, see Susan Pedersen, *The Guardians* (New York: Oxford University Press, 2015).

14. On the centrality of racial thought to international relations scholarship, see John Hobson, *The Eurocentric Conception of World Politics* (New York: Cambridge University Press, 2012); Erroll Henderson, "Hidden in Plain Sight," *Cambridge Review of International Affairs* 26, no. 1 (2013); and Robert Vitalis, *White World Order, Black Power Politics* (Ithaca, NY: Cornell University Press, 2015).

15. See Vitalis, *White World Order*; and Raymond Leslie Buell, *International Relations* (New York: H. Holt, 1929), 56–57, 73–76.

16. Madison Grant, *The Passing of the Great Race* (New York: Charles Scribner's Sons, 1918), xv, 139, 193; Frederick Adams Woods, review of *The Passing of the Great Race*, by Madison Grant, *Science*, 25 Oct. 1918; Review, *Annals of the American Academy of Political and Social Science*, 1 Mar. 1917; Book Review, *Journal of Race Development*, 1 Apr. 1918.

17. Vitalis, *White World Order*, 62; "A New Basis for History," *NYT*, 11 Jul. 1920; "White Supremacy Challenged," *New York Tribune*, 2 May 1920; Stoddard quoted in Vitalis, *White World Order*, 63.

18. "Nordic Race Supremacy," *Chicago Defender*, 5 May 1923; "Mrs. F. D. Roosevelt Hostess at Concert," *NYT*, 31 Jan. 1939; Hope Ridings Miller, "Informality Rules Meem and Stoddard Parties," *Washington Post*, 9 May 1940.

19. Charles Tripp, *A History of Iraq*, 2nd ed. (Cambridge, UK: Cambridge University Press, 2002), 40–44.

20. Michael Provence, "French Mandate Counterinsurgency and the Repression of the Great Syrian Revolt," in *The Routledge Handbook of the History of the Middle East Mandates*, ed. Cyrus Schayegh and Andrew Arsan (New York: Routledge, 2015), 137–138, 140, 147. For more on the persistence of empire after 1919, see Jane Burbank and Frederick Cooper, "Empires After 1919," *International Affairs* 95, no. 1 (2019): 81–100.

21. Robert Gerwarth, *The Vanquished* (New York: Farrar, Straus and Giroux, 2016), 7, 71–73, 98–99, 139.

22. Gerwarth, *Vanquished*, 34–35, 78–82, 92–93.

23. Jonathan Haslam, *Spectre of War* (Princeton, NJ: Princeton University Press, 2021), 2, 5, 24.

24. Mawdsley, *World War II*, 14, 20–21. The classic work on the Open Door thesis is William Appleman Williams, *The Tragedy of American Diplomacy*, rev. ed. (New York: Dell, 1962).

25. Adam Tooze, *The Deluge* (New York: Viking, 2014), 3–6. See also Melvyn Leffler, *The Elusive Quest* (Chapel Hill: University of North Carolina Press, 1979); and Michael J. Hogan, *Informal Entente* (Columbia: University of Missouri Press, 1977).

26. Erez Manela and Robert Gerwarth, introduction to *Empires at War*, ed. Erez Manela and Robert Gerwarth (New York: Oxford University Press, 2014), 1; Robert Mallett, *Mussolini in Ethiopia, 1919-1935* (New York: Cambridge University Press, 2015), 7–8.

27. G. Bruce Strang, "Places in the African Sun," in *Collision of Empires*, ed. G. Bruce Strang (New York: Routledge, 2013), 14, 16–17.

28. Shelley Baranowski, *Nazi Empire* (Cambridge, UK: Cambridge University Press, 2011), 110, 112, 147–152.

29. Baranowski, *Nazi Empire*, 113–114, 123, 145. Ludendorff is quoted in A. Dirk Moses, "Colonialism," in *The Oxford Handbook to Holocaust Studies*, ed. Peter Hayes and John K. Roth, 68–80 (New York: Oxford University Press, 2010).

30. Ian Kershaw, *Hitler, 1889-1936* (New York: W. W. Norton, 1998), 240, 243, 249.

31. Good starting points for some of these ideas include Louise Young, *Japan's Total Empire* (Berkeley: University of California Press, 1998); Louise Young, "When Fascism Met Empire in Japanese-Occupied Manchuria," *Journal of Global History* 12, no. 2 (2017): 274–296; and S. C. M. Paine, *The Japanese Empire* (New York: Cambridge University Press, 2017).

32. Paine, *Japanese Empire*, 6–8.

33. For more on America's Pacific territories, see Immerwahr, *How to Hide an Empire*.

34. Young, *Japan's Total Empire*, 23.

35. See Walter LaFeber, *The Clash* (New York: W. W. Norton, 1997).

36. Naoko Shimazu, *Japan, Race, and Equality* (New York: Routledge, 2003), 20.

37. Quoted in Iris Chang, *The Rape of Nanking* (New York: Basic, 1997), 27.

38. William Keylor, *The Twentieth-Century World and Beyond*, 6th ed. (New York: Oxford University Press, 2011), 100–101.

39. Stephen Kotkin, *Stalin* (New York: Penguin, 2017), xiii.

40. See Haslam, *Spectre of War*.

41. See, for instance, Mark Mazower, *Hitler's Empire* (New York: Penguin, 2008), 43.

42. Ian Kershaw, *To Hell and Back* (New York: Viking, 2015), 93.

CHAPTER 2: DESTROYING THE VERSAILLES ORDER

1. Rodney Gilbert, "Mukden: Its Modes and Modernity," 22 Dec. 1928, *North China Herald*.

2. Seki Hiroharu, "Manchurian Incident," in *Japan Erupts*, ed. James William Morley (New York: Columbia University Press, 1984), 228.

3. Michael A. Barnhart, *Japan Prepares for Total War* (Ithaca, NY: Cornell University Press, 1987), 27–31.

4. Jay Taylor, *The Generalissimo* (Cambridge, MA: Belknap Press of Harvard University Press, 2009), 11, 20.

5. See Rana Mitter, *Forgotten Ally* (Boston: Houghton Mifflin, 2013), 40–47.

6. Mitter, *Forgotten Ally*, 48–50.

7. Barnhart, *Japan Prepares*, 27–32; Military History Section, Army Forces Far East, *Political Strategy Prior to the Outbreak of War, Part I*, Japanese Monograph 144 (Washington, DC: Office of the Chief of Military History, Department of the Army, 1952), 1.

8. Akira Iriye, *The Origins of the Second World War in Asia and the Pacific* (London: Longman, 1987), 5–7.

9. Louise Young, *Japan's Total Empire* (Berkeley: University of California Press, 1998), 28–31, 38. For the official Japanese history of the Kwantung Army's buildup, see Military History Section, Army Forces Far East, *Japanese Preparations for Operations in Manchuria Prior to 1943*, Japanese Monograph 77 (Washington, DC: Office of the Chief of Military History, Department of the Army, 1954).

10. Stephen S. Large, *Emperor Hirohito and Showa Japan* (London: Routledge, 1992), 40.

11. Seki, "Manchurian Incident," 148–149, 170.

12. Seki, 171, 212–213.

13. Peck to Johnson, Chinese Ministry of Foreign Affairs, aide-mémoire, 10 Sep. 1931, in *Foreign Relations of the United States* (hereinafter *FRUS*), 1931, vol. 3, *The Far East*, ed. Joseph V. Fuller (Washington, DC: Government Printing Office, 1946), document 4.

14. Johnson to Secretary of State, 19 Sep. 1931, in *FRUS*, 1931–1941, vol. 1, *Japan*, ed. Joseph V. Fuller (Washington, DC: Government Printing Office, 1943), document 1; "Japanese Occupy Manchuria," *North China Herald*, 22 Sep. 1931.

15. Lynch to Johnson, 20 Sep. 1931, in *FRUS*, 1931, vol. 3, document 21.

16. Japanese embassy to the US Department of State, undated (9 Oct. 1931), in *FRUS*, 1931–1941, vol. 1, document 14; Military History Section, Army Forces Far East, *Japanese Preparations*, 7; Military History Section, Army Forces Far East, *Political Strategy*, 3–4.

17. Neville to Secretary of State, 22 Sep. 1931, in *FRUS*, 1931–1941, vol. 1, document 4; Chinese Ministry of Foreign Affairs at Nanking to the Foreign Legation, 9 Oct. 1931, in *FRUS*, 1931, vol. 3, document 155; Secretary of State to the Chargé d'Affaires in Japan, 11 Oct. 1931, in *FRUS*, 1931–1941, vol. 1, document 20.

18. Statement by the Japanese government, 27 Dec. 1931, in *FRUS*, 1931–1941, vol. 1, document 55.

19. John Murnane, "Japan's Monroe Doctrine?," *History Teacher* 40, no. 4 (Aug. 2007): 508, 510–511.

20. "Japanese Set Chapei Afire," *NYT*, 29 Jan. 1932; "Memorandum by the Secretary of State of a Conversation with the British Ambassador at Woodley at 2:15 pm," 25 Jan. 1932, in *FRUS*, 1932, vol. 3, *The Far East*, ed. Gustave A. Nuermberger, Victor J. Farrar, John G. Reid, and William R. Willoughby (Washington, DC: Government Printing Office, 1948), document 71; Stimson's diary quoted in Walter LaFeber, *The Clash* (New York: W. W. Norton, 1997), 168.

21. Chinese Ministry of Foreign Affairs, "Statement of the Chinese Government Concerning the So-Called Independence Movement in Manchuria," 23 Feb. 1932, document 457; Forbes to Secretary of State, February 23, 1932, document 454; Atherton to Secretary of State, 19 Feb. 1932, document 410. All in *FRUS*, 1932, vol. 3.

22. Young, *Japan's Total Empire*, 87–88; Ian Nish, *Japanese Foreign Policy, 1869–1942* (New York: Routledge, 1977), 182–183.

23. Christopher Thorne, *The Issue of War* (New York: Oxford University Press, 1985), 27.

24. G. Bruce Strang, ed., *Collision of Empires* (New York: Routledge, 2017), 19, 22, 26.

25. Ian Campbell, *The Addis Ababa Massacre* (New York: Oxford University Press, 2017), 19, 21.

26. Georgio Rochat, "The Italian Air Force in the Ethiopian War (1935–1936)," in *Italian Colonialism*, ed. Ruth Ben-Ghiat and Mia Fuller (New York: Palgrave McMillan, 2005), 38, 40.

27. Alberto Sbacchi, "Poison Gas and Atrocities in the Italo-Ethiopian War (1935–1936)," in Ben-Ghiat and Fuller, *Italian Colonialism*, 50.

28. Haile Selassie, speech to the League of Nations, Geneva, Switzerland, 30 Jun. 1936; Alden Whitman, "Haile Selassie of Ethiopia Dies at 83," *NYT*, 28 Aug. 1975.

29. Campbell, *Addis Ababa Massacre*, 55, 115, 118–131, 328.

30. Rashid Khalidi, *The Iron Cage* (Boston: Beacon, 2006), 107–108.

31. For a more complete discussion of the rise of the Third Reich, see Richard Evans, *The Coming of the Third Reich* (London: Allen Lane, 2003).

32. Shelley Baranowski, *Nazi Empire* (Cambridge, UK: Cambridge University Press, 2010), 193; Adam Tooze, *The Wages of Destruction* (New York: Penguin, 2006), 56; Associated Press, "Hitler to Increase Army to 480,000," *Baltimore Sun*, 17 Mar. 1933.

33. Secretary of State to Straus, 18 Mar. 1935, in *FRUS*, 1935, vol. 2, *The British Commonwealth, Europe*, ed. Rogers P. Churchill and N. O. Sappington (Washington, DC: Government Printing Office, 1952), document 236.

CHAPTER 3: A NEW ORDER IN EAST ASIA

1. F. Tillman Durdin, "Japanese Atrocities Marked Fall of Nanking After Chinese Command Fled," *NYT*, 9 Jan. 1938.

2. "IMTFE Judgment (English Translation): Chapter VIII," p. 1008 (publisher not identified, 1948) (hereinafter IMTFE); Louise Young, *Japan's Total Empire* (Berkeley: University of California Press, 1998). On Japan's decision to fashion itself as a continental power, see S. C. M. Paine, *The Japanese Empire* (New York: Cambridge University Press, 2017), chapter 2.

3. Akira Iriye, *The Origins of the Second World War in Asia and the Pacific* (London: Longman, 1987), 32–33.

4. Iriye, 22, 34–35.

5. Navy Headquarters (Tokyo), "General Principles of National Policy," Apr. 1936, reprinted in *Japan's Greater East Asia Co-Prosperity Sphere*, ed. Joyce Lebra (London: Oxford University Press, 1975), 58–60.

6. Army General Staff Headquarters (Tokyo), "General Principles of National Defence Policy," 30 Jun. 1936, reprinted in Lebra, *Japan's Greater East Asia Co-Prosperity Sphere*, 61–62.

7. Five Ministers' Conference (Tokyo), *Fundamentals of National Policy*, 7 Aug. 1936, reprinted in Lebra, *Japan's Greater East Asia Co-Prosperity Sphere*, 62–64.

8. Ministry of Health and Welfare, Research Bureau, *An Investigation of Global Policy with the Yamato Race as Nucleus*, 1 Jul. 1943, quoted in John Dower, *War Without Mercy* (New York: Pantheon, 1986), 262–266, 277.

9. Hata Ikuhiko, "The Marco Polo Bridge Incident," in *The China Quagmire*, ed. James William Morley (New York: Columbia University Press, 1983), 245–248.

10. Jay Taylor, *The Generalissimo* (Cambridge, MA: Belknap Press of Harvard University Press, 2009), 125–127.

11. Iriye, *Origins*, 42–43. On the importance of Beijing, see Rana Mitter, *Forgotten Ally* (Boston: Houghton Mifflin, 2013), 81.

12. Ian Nish, *Japanese Foreign Policy in the Interwar Period* (Westport, CT: Praeger, 2002), 218–220; Walter LaFeber, *The Clash* (New York: W. W. Norton, 1997), 182–183; Jeremy Yellen, *The Greater East Asia Co-Prosperity Sphere* (Ithaca, NY: Cornell University Press, 2019), 14; quotation from Konoe's 1933 essay appears in Herbert Bix, *Hirohito and the Making of Modern Japan* (New York: HarperCollins, 2000), 267.

13. Iriye, *Origins*, 45.

14. "Peiping Buzzes as Army Withdraws," *North China Herald*, Jul. 1937 (published 4 Aug.); "The Massacre at Tungchow," *North China Herald*, 31 Jul. 1937 (published 4 Aug.).

15. Taylor, *Generalissimo*, 147.

16. "Three Killed in Affray Near Aerodrome," *North China Herald*, 10 Aug. 1937 (published 11 Aug.); Gauss to Secretary of State, 12 Aug. 1937, in *FRUS*, 1937, vol. 3, *The Far East*, ed. Matilda F. Axton et al. (Washington, DC: Government Printing Office, 1954), document 415.

17. Hattori Satoshi with Edward Drea, "Japanese Operations from July to December 1937," in *The Battle for China*, ed. Mark Peattie, Edward Drea, and Hans van de Ven (Stanford, CA: Stanford University Press, 2011), 168–175.

18. "Settlement Bombed," *North China Herald*, 18 Aug. 1937; "170 Dead in Nanking Road Explosion," *North China Herald*, 25 Aug. 1937; F. Tillman Durdin, "All Captives Slain," *NYT*, 18 Dec. 1937. The figure of three hundred thousand comes from Peter Harmsen in Michael Peck, "Shanghai 1937," *The Buzz* (blog), *National Interest*, 30 May 2016, https://nationalinterest.org/blog/the-buzz/shanghai-1937-chinas-forgotten -stalingrad-16396.

19. Mitter, *Forgotten Ally*, 102–103; figures from Satoshi and Drea, "Japanese Operations," 174.

20. Taylor, *Generalissimo*, 150–151; "How Lieutenants Mukai and Nota Exceeded Murder Quotas," *China Weekly Review*, 1 Jan. 1938; F. Tillman Durdin, "Japanese Atrocities Marked Fall of Nanking After Chinese Command Fled," *NYT*, 9 Jan. 1938.

21. Fujiwara Akira, "The Nanking Atrocity: An Interpretive Overview," in *The Nanking Atrocity, 1937–38*, ed. Bob Tadashi Wakabayashi (New York: Berghan, 2007), 34, 36; Durdin, "Japanese Atrocities"; Durdin, "All Captives Slain."

22. Akira, "Nanking Atrocity," 38, 42.

23. Akira, 49; IMTFE, pp. 1011, 1002. The death toll figures are disputed. Iris Chang claims the figure of three hundred thousand, though the IMTFE placed figures at two hundred thousand. Some Japanese scholars argue that the atrocity was largely a fabrication of Chinese propaganda, though these claims are dismissed by most scholars. See Iris Chang, *The Rape of Nanking* (New York: Basic, 1997). On the scholarly debates, see Wakabayashi, *Nanking Atrocity*.

24. Taylor, *Generalissimo*, 152.

25. Jay Taylor, "China's Long War with Japan," in *The Cambridge History of the Second World War*, vol. 1, *Fighting the War*, ed. John Ferris and Evan Mawdsley (Cambridge, UK: Cambridge University Press, 2015), 51, 57.

26. Paine, *Japanese Empire*, 130–132.

27. Mitter, *Forgotten Ally*, 145–147, 151–154; Johnson to Secretary of State, 19 Apr. 1938, in *FRUS*, 1938, vol. 3, *The Far East*, ed. Matilda F. Axton et al. (Washington, DC: Government Printing Office), document 149; Peter South, "Nanking and Taierchwang: Where Japan Lost the War," *China Weekly Review*, 11 Jun. 1938.

28. Mitter, *Forgotten Ally*, 155–156; Reuters, "Hsuchow a Mass of Flames," *North China Herald*, 1 Jun. 1938.

29. Diana Lary, *The Chinese People at War* (New York: Cambridge University Press, 2010), 60–62.

30. Edward J. Drea and Hans van de Ven, "An Overview of Major Military Campaigns During the Sino-Japanese War, 1937–1945," in Peattie, Drea, and van de Ven, *Battle for China*, 34–35; "Japanese Bombard Last Strongholds on Way to Hankow," *NYT*, 25 Oct. 1938.

31. Lary, *Chinese People at War*, 62–64.

32. Bix, *Hirohito*, 359–361; Mitter, *Forgotten Ally*, 2–3.

33. Bix, *Hirohito*, 365; "Statement by the Japanese Prime Minister," 22 Dec. 1938, in *FRUS*, 1931–1941, vol. 1, *Japan*, ed. Joseph V. Fuller (Washington, DC: Government Printing Office, 1943), document 332.

34. Edward Drea, *Nomonhan*, Leavenworth Papers 2 (Fort Leavenworth, KS: Combat Studies Institute, US Army Command and General Staff College, 1981), ix, 1, 9–11; "Japanese Form 'Suicide Corps' in Mongol Fight," *New York Tribune/Herald Tribune*, 10 Jul. 1939; Drea and van de Ven, "Overview," 36.

35. Bix, *Hirohito*, 352–353; Grew to Secretary of State, 18 May 1939, in *FRUS*, 1931–1941, vol. 2, *Japan*, ed. Joseph V. Fuller (Washington, DC: Government Printing Office, 1943), document 2; Hull to Horinouchi (Japanese ambassador), 26 Jul. 1939, in *FRUS*, 1931–1941, vol. 2, document 115.

36. Navy National Policy Research Committee, "Summary Draft of a Policy for the South," April 1939, in Lebra, *Co-Prosperity Sphere*, 64–67.

37. Kamikawa Hikomatsu, "The American and Japanese Monroe Doctrines," in Lebra, *Co-Prosperity Sphere*, 25–30.

38. Ronald Spector, "The Sino-Japanese War in the Context of World History," in Peattie, Drea, and van de Ven, *Battle for China*, 467–468.

CHAPTER 4: BLOOD, SOIL, AND EMPIRE

1. Roger Moorhouse, *Poland 1939* (New York: Basic, 2020), chap. 1, Kindle.

2. Adolf Hitler, *Mein Kampf* (Boston: Houghton Mifflin, 1943), 290, 289, 296, 305.

3. Hitler, 642–643, 649. Although scholars have long debated the question of just how central Hitler was to determining the Third Reich's fate, prevailing interpretations lean toward the view that he was indeed the pivotal figure in this story. On these debates and on Hitler's view of race and living space, see Gerhard Weinberg, *Hitler's Foreign Policy* (New York: Enigma, 2005). On the broader world history of these ideas, see Ben Kiernan, *Blood and Soil* (New Haven, CT: Yale University Press, 2009).

4. Cabinet memorandum, "Notes on Anglo-German Conversations, Held at the Chancellor's Palace, Berlin, on March 25 and 26, 1935," UKNA, http://filestore.nationalarchives.gov.uk/pdfs/small/cab-24-254-CP-69-1.pdf. See also Jonathan Haslam, *Spectre of War* (Princeton, NJ: Princeton University Press, 2021).

5. Timothy Snyder, *Bloodlands* (New York: Basic, 2010), 61; Hitler, *Mein Kampf*, 660–661.

6. Hitler, *Mein Kampf*, 139, 90, 289, 439–440; Hans Weigert, "Haushofer and the Pacific," *Foreign Affairs*, July 1942.

7. Duncan Bell, *Reordering the World* (Princeton, NJ: Princeton University Press, 2016), 89, 197–198; Charles Mills, "Race and Global Justice," in *Empire, Race and Global Justice*, ed. Duncan Bell (New York: Cambridge University Press, 2019); Stephen Wertheim, *Tomorrow the World* (Cambridge, MA: Belknap Press of Harvard University Press, 2020).

8. Peter Uwe Hohendahl, *Perilous Futures* (Ithaca, NY: Cornell University Press, 2018), 63, 68–69.

9. Adolf Hitler, *Hitler's Second Book*, trans. Krista Smith (New York: Enigma, 2003), 107, 113, 116; Adam Tooze, *The Wages of Destruction* (New York: Penguin, 2006); Adam Tooze, *The Deluge* (New York: Viking, 2014).

10. Hitler, *Second Book*, 167.

11. Hitler, *Mein Kampf*, 624–625, 658, 666.

12. Richard J. Evans, *The Third Reich in Power* (New York: Penguin, 2005), 543–555. See also Shelley Baranowski, *Nazi Empire* (Cambridge, UK: Cambridge University Press, 2011), 187–190.

13. Stanley G. Payne, *The Spanish Civil War* (New York: Cambridge University Press, 2012), 132–135, 140, 143.

14. Payne, *Spanish Civil War*, 208–210; Canon Alberto Onaindia, "Priest Who Saw Plane Attack Tells of Guernica 'Massacre,'" *Washington Post*, 30 Apr. 1937; "Guernica," *Manchester Guardian*, 30 Jul. 1937.

15. "Hossbach Memorandum," 10 Nov. 1937, Avalon Project (website), Lillian Goldman Law Library, Yale Law School, accessed 20 Jul. 2024, https://avalon.law.yale .edu/imt/hossbach.asp.

16. Evans, *Third Reich in Power*, 621–622, 648–653; "Nazi Crowds Rout Enemies in Vienna," *NYT*, 12 Mar. 1938.

17. Mark Mazower, *Hitler's Empire* (New York: Penguin, 2008), 55; Ian Kershaw, *Hitler, 1936–1945: Nemesis* (New York: W. W. Norton, 2000), 95–98. Hitler's assessment of British military readiness comes from a note handed to Mussolini by Prince Philipp of Hesse, who was "used as a special envoy between Hitler and Mussolini. The document presumably represents a statement of the Führer's policy intended for Mussolini personally." "Memorandum Transmitted by Prince Philip [*sic*] of Hesse to the Duce," Sep. 1938, in *Documents on German Foreign Policy, 1918–1945*, series D, vol. 2, *Germany and Czechoslovakia, 1937–1938* (Washington, DC: US Government Printing Office, 1949), document 415.

18. Carr to Secretary of State, 29 Dec. 1938, in *FRUS*, 1938, vol. 1, *General*, ed. Matilda F. Axton et al. (Washington, DC: Government Printing Office, 1955), document 712; "Conclusions of a Meeting of the Cabinet held at 10, Downing Street, S.W.1.," 14 Sep. 1938, 11:00 a.m., CAB 23/95, UKNA.

19. "The Premier's Broadcast," *Manchester Guardian*, 28 Sep. 1938; "The German Ambassador in the United States to the German Foreign Ministry," 27 Sep. 1938, in *Documents on German Foreign Policy*, series D, vol. 2, document 651.

20. G. S. Messersmith, "Memorandum by the Secretary of State to President Roosevelt," in *FRUS*, 1938, vol. 1, document 685. See also Gerhard Weinberg, *Visions of Victory* (New York: Cambridge University Press, 2005), 37; and Weinberg, *Hitler's Foreign Policy*, 932, 951–952.

21. Max Hastings, *Inferno* (New York: Knopf, 2011), 6; Gerhard Weinberg, *A World at Arms*, 2nd ed. (New York: Cambridge University Press, 2005), 49–51.

22. International Military Tribunal, *Trial of the Major War Criminals Before the International Military Tribunal* (hereinafter *TMWC*), "Blue Series" (Nuremberg, Germany: n.p., 1947–1949), 2:279–280; *TMWC*, "Red Series" (Washington, DC: Government Printing Office, 1947), 1:699, 3:585–593.

23. Edward Beattie, *Freely to Pass* (New York: Thomas Y. Crowell, 1942), 135–136; Richard Hargreaves, *Blitzkrieg Unleashed* (Barnsley, England: Pen and Sword, 2008), chapter 4; Marian Chodacki, "Nazi-Made Horror in Danzig," *Los Angeles Times*, 30 Sep. 1939.

24. Geoffrey Roberts, *Stalin's Wars* (New Haven, CT: Yale University Press, 2006), 31–32. On the deeper history of German-Soviet cooperation through the interwar period, see Ian Ona Johnson, *Faustian Bargain* (New York: Oxford University Press, 2021).

25. Roberts, *Stalin's Wars*, 32–36.

26. Snyder, *Bloodlands*, 128–130, 135–137, 140.

27. Roberts, *Stalin's Wars*, 43–44, 47.

28. Weinberg, *World at Arms*, 64–66.

29. Hitler quoted in Richard J. Evans, *The Third Reich at War* (New York: Penguin, 2010), 11; Christopher Browning and Jürgen Matthäus, *The Origins of the Final Solution* (Lincoln: University of Nebraska Press, 2004), 14.

30. Alexander Rossino, *Hitler Strikes Poland* (Lawrence: University Press of Kansas, 2003), xiv, 62, 71–72, 125.

31. Rossino, 14; Snyder, *Bloodlands*, 126–127; Browning and Matthäus, *Origins of the Final Solution*, 17–18.

32. Mazower, *Hitler's Empire*, 71–74.

33. Richard Hargreaves, *Blitzkrieg Unleashed* (Mechanicsburg, PA: Stackpole, 2010), chapter 10, ebook.

34. *TMWC*, "Red Series," 3:472–474.

CHAPTER 5: EMPIRE BESIEGED

1. Julian Jackson, *The Fall of France* (New York: Oxford University Press, 2003), 11–13, 37; Adam Tooze, *The Wages of Destruction* (New York: Penguin, 2006), 371.

2. David Reynolds, "1940: Fulcrum of the Twentieth Century?," *International Affairs* 66, no. 2 (Apr. 1990): 325–350.

3. "The Fateful Hour," *NYT*, 11 May 1940; Dorothy Thompson, "The Problem Child of Europe," *Foreign Affairs*, Apr. 1940.

4. André Siegfried, "War for Our World," *Foreign Affairs*, Apr. 1940.

5. Chief of Imperial Staff, "British Strategy in the War," 7 Sep. 1939, WO 193/147, UKNA; War Cabinet, "Review of the Strategical Situation on the Assumption That Germany Has Decided to Seek a Decision in 1940," 4 May 1940, WO 193/132, UKNA.

6. G. H. Archambault, "15,000 Tanks Battle for Hours; Enemy Beaten," *NYT*, 13 May 1940.

7. Jackson, *Fall of France*, 30–31, 39; Tooze, *Wages of Destruction*, 376–377.

8. Basil Henry Liddell Hart, *The Other Side of the Hill*, 2nd rev. ed. (London: Cassell, 1973), 169–183.

9. Lynn Heinzerling, "Rotterdam Left in Ruins by Lighting Air Attack," *NYT*, 23 May 1940.

10. "Text of Lord Lothian's Address Here," *NYT*, 15 May 1940.

11. Duncan Bell, *Reordering the World* (Princeton, NJ: Princeton University Press, 2016), 89, 189, 196–197; George Blakeslee, "Introduction," *Journal of Race Development* 1, no. 1 (Jul. 1910): 1–4. For a longer discussion, see Robert Vitalis, *White World Order, Black Power Politics* (Ithaca, NY: Cornell University Press, 2015).

12. Bullitt to Secretary of State, 15 May 1940, in *FRUS*, 1940, vol. 1, *General*, ed. Matilda F. Axton and Shirley L. Phillips (Washington, DC: Government Printing Office, 1959), document 180; Kennedy to Secretary of State, 16 May 1940, in *FRUS*, 1940, vol. 1, document 184.

13. Bullitt to Secretary of State, 18 May 1940, in *FRUS*, 1940, vol. 1, document 189.

14. Antony Beevor, *The Second World War* (New York: Little, Brown, 2012), 102–103. On the question of the German pause, see Gerhard Weinberg, *A World at Arms*, 2nd ed. (New York: Cambridge University Press, 2005), 130–131; and Hart, *Other Side of the Hill*, 186–193.

15. War Cabinet Minutes (40) 139th Conclusions, Minute 1, 26 May 1940, CAB 65/13, UKNA.

16. "Future Policy," 28 May 1940, WO 193/132, UKNA.

17. The unsigned memo was probably written by the secretary of the general staff. Mark Skinner Watson, *Chief of Staff* (Washington, DC: Historical Division, Dept. of the Army, 1950), 104–107.

18. Basil Bartlett, *My First War* (New York: Macmillan, 1941), 110, 116–119.

19. Ralph Barnes, "Reporter Views Decisive Fight for Dunkerque," *New York Herald Tribune*, 5 Jun. 1940.

20. Bartlett, *My First War*, 123, 129.

21. Winston Churchill, "Future Military Policy," 2 Jun. 1940, WO 193/132, UKNA.

22. War Cabinet, "Western Front—British Military Policy: Report by the Chiefs of Staff Committee," 3 Jun. 1940, CAB 66/8, document 94, UKNA; Max Hastings, *Winston's War* (New York: Knopf, 2010), 49.

23. "Conclusions of a Meeting of the War Cabinet Held at 10 Downing Street," 15 Jun. 1940, CAB 65/7, p. 467, UKNA; Kennedy to Secretary of State, 12 Jun. 1940, in *FRUS*, 1940, vol. 1, document 209.

24. E. R. Noderer, "Finds Dunkirk Is a Pile of Shell Wrecked Ruins," *Chicago Tribune*, 6 Jun. 1940; Ralph Barnes, "Nazis Looking to Invade UK," *New York Herald Tribune*, 8 Jun. 1940.

25. "Eiffel Tower Visible to Nazis Troops Ringed About Paris," *Daily Boston Globe*, 13 Jun. 1940; Demaree Bess is quoted in *The Voice of War*, ed. James Owen and Guy Walters (London: Viking, 2004), 53–54; Louis Lochner, "Paris Called Ghost City as Nazis Take over Control," *Los Angeles Times*, 16 Jun. 1940.

26. Richard Leighton and Robert Coakley, *Global Logistics and Strategy: 1940–1943* (Washington, DC: Center of Military History, 1995), 28. A summary of Strong's memo appears in the official army history: Watson, *Chief of Staff*, 109–110. For more on the impact of France's fall on US policymakers, see Stephen Wertheim, *Tomorrow the World* (Cambridge, MA: Belknap Press of Harvard University Press, 2020).

27. Quoted in Nicholas Murray Butler, "A Bell Is Ringing," *Washington Post*, 9 Jun. 1940.

28. Barnet Nover, "Pall of Darkness," *Washington Post*, 19 Jun. 1940.

29. Walter Lippmann, "The American Destiny," *Life*, 5 Jun. 1939, 73; Nicholas Wapshott, *The Sphinx* (New York: W. W. Norton, 2015), 114–115. My thinking on this transition owes much to Stephen Wertheim's excellent dissertation, "Tomorrow, the World" (PhD diss., Columbia University, 2015), 63–65.

30. Walter Lippmann, "The Economic Consequences of German Victory," *Life*, July 1940; Mark A. Stoler, *Allies and Adversaries* (Chapel Hill: University of North Carolina Press, 2000), 32.

31. Christopher O'Sullivan, *Sumner Welles, Postwar Planning, and the Quest for a New World Order* (New York: Columbia University Press, 2003), 33–35; Seventy-Seventh US Congress, Committee on Foreign Relations, *To Promote the Defense of the United States* (Washington, DC: Government Printing Office, 1941), 157–160; Henry Stimson and McGeorge Bundy, *On Active Service in War and Peace* (New York: Harper and Brothers, 1948), 320.

32. Leon Trotsky, "Manifesto of the Fourth International on Imperialist War and the Proletarian World Revolution," 19–26 May 1940, marxists.org.

33. Chiefs of Staff, "Urgent Measures to Meet Attack," 19 Jun. 1940, CAB 66/8, WP (40) 213, UKNA.

34. Bullitt to Secretary of State, 28 May 1940, in *FRUS*, 1940, vol. 2, *General and Europe*, ed. Matilda F. Axton and Shirley L. Phillips (Washington, DC: Government

Printing Office, 1957), document 524; Biddle to Secretary of State, 18 Jun. 1940, in *FRUS*, 1940, vol. 2, document 530; Kennedy to Secretary of State, 22 Jun. 1940, in *FRUS*, 1940, vol. 2, document 532.

35. Sumner Welles, "Memorandum of Conversation," 24 Jun. 1940, in *FRUS*, 1940, vol. 2, document 533; Cordell Hull, "Memorandum of Conversation," 27 Jun. 1940, in *FRUS*, 1940, vol. 2, document 535.

36. Quotations are Bullitt's descriptions of his conversations. Bullitt to Secretary of State, 1 Jul. 1940, in *FRUS*, 1940, vol. 2, document 536.

37. Bullitt to Secretary of State, 1 Jul. 1940.

38. Heath to Secretary of State, 2 Jul. 1940, in *FRUS*, 1940, vol. 2, document 569.

39. War Cabinet, "Weekly Resume, No. 44," 5 Jul. 1940, WP (4) 250, CAB 66/9, UKNA, http://filestore.nationalarchives.gov.uk/pdfs/large/cab-66-9.pdf; Admiralty to F. O. Force H, 2 Jul. 1940, CAB 65/8, pp. 36–37, UKNA, http://filestore.nationalarchives.gov.uk/pdfs/large/cab-65-8.pdf.

40. Craig Symonds, *World War II at Sea* (New York: Oxford University Press, 2018), 75–76.

41. Barnet Nover, "The Battle of Oran," *Washington Post*, 5 Jul. 1940; Leighton and Coakley, *Global Logistics*, 30.

42. Geoffrey Roberts, *Stalin's Wars* (New Haven, CT: Yale University Press, 2006), 56–57.

43. Hans Umbreit, "Plans for Landing in England," in *Germany and the Second World War* (hereinafter *GSWW*), vol. 2, *Germany's Initial Conquests in Europe*, ed. Klaus A. Maier, Horst Rohde, Bernd Stegemann, and Hans Umbriet (New York: Oxford University Press, 1991), 366–369.

44. Ibid.

45. Klaus Maier, "The Battle of Britain," in *GSWW*, 2:379–380; W. F. Leysmith, "Factories Target: British Industrial Areas, Airfields and Ports Are Heavily Pounded," *NYT*, 16 Aug. 1940.

46. Drew Middleton, "Eyewitness Account: Fiery Glow Turns London into Fantastic Dreamworld," *NYT*, 8 Sep. 1940. See also Richard Overy, *The Battle of Britain* (New York: W. W. Norton, 2001), 85–91.

47. "British Bomb Reichstag Building in Berlin, Nazis Blast London with Increasing Force," *Hartford (CT) Courant*, 11 Sep. 1940; figure from Andrew Roberts, *The Storm of War* (London: Allen Lane, 2009), 108.

48. These numbers are from Overy, *Battle of Britain*, 162.

49. Ralph Ingersoll, *Report on England, November 1940* (New York: Simon and Schuster, 1940), 5.

CHAPTER 6: COLONIAL RAMPARTS

1. Harold Stark, "Memorandum for the Secretary" ("Plan Dog"), 12 Nov. 1940, Navy Department, box 4, Safe File, Franklin D. Roosevelt, Papers as President: The President's Secretary's File (PSF), 1933–1945, Franklin D. Roosevelt Presidential Library and Museum, Hyde Park, NY, http://www.fdrlibrary.marist.edu/_resources/images/psf/psfa0048.pdf; Maurice Matloff and Edwin Snell, *Strategic Planning for Coalition Warfare, 1941–1942* (Washington: Center of Military History, 1999); Stephen Wertheim, *Tomorrow the World* (Cambridge, MA: Belknap Press of Harvard University Press, 2020); James Lacey, "Toward a Strategy," in *The Shaping of Grand Strategy*, ed. Williamson Murray, Richard Hart Sinnreich, and James Lacey (New York: Cambridge University Press, 2011), 186.

2. Hornbeck to Secretary of State, 24 May 1940, document 375; Hull to Grew, 30 May 1940, document 376; Grew to Secretary of State, 3 Jun. 1940, document 377. All in *FRUS*, 1940, vol. 4, *The Far East*, ed. John G. Reid, Ralph R. Goodwin, and Louis E. Gates (Washington, DC: Government Printing Office, 1955).

3. Robert Cressman, *The Official Chronology of the U.S. Navy in World War II* (Annapolis, MD: Naval Institute Press, 1999).

4. Grew to Secretary of State, 26 Jun. 1940, in *FRUS*, 1940, vol. 4, document 398; "Regulations Governing the Exportation of Articles and Materials Designated in the President's Proclamation," 2 Jul. 1940, in *FRUS*, 1931–1941, vol. 2, *Japan*, ed. Joseph V. Fuller (Washington, DC: Government Printing Office, 1943), document 134; Military History Section, Army Forces Far East, *Political Strategy Prior to Outbreak of War, Part II*, Japanese Monograph 146 (Washington, DC: Office of the Chief of Military History, Department of the Army, 1953), 13–15. The Japanese Monograph series is a unique source in that it was prepared by former Japanese military officers working under the direction of the US government following the end of the war. For more information, see http://ibiblio.org/pha/monos/.

5. Jeremy Yellen, *The Greater East Asia Co-Prosperity Sphere* (Ithaca, NY: Cornell University Press, 2019), 3, 29–30, 33–35.

6. Military History Section, Army Forces Far East, *Political Strategy [. . .], Part II*, 18–20.

7. Yosuke Matsuoka, "Proclamation of the Greater East Asia Co-Prosperity Sphere," reprinted in *Japan's Greater East Asia Co-Prosperity Sphere*, ed. Joyce Lebra (London: Oxford University Press, 1975), 71–72; Yellen, *Co-Prosperity Sphere*, 4, 37.

8. "Japanese Continue Indo-China Attack," *NYT*, 24 Sep. 1940; "Japanese Resisted," *NYT*, 25 Sep. 1940; "Indo-China Allows Japanese to Enter," *NYT*, 27 Sep. 1940.

9. Steinhardt to Secretary of State, 23 Sep. 1940, in *FRUS*, 1940, vol. 1, *General*, ed. Matilda F. Axton and Shirley L. Phillips (Washington, DC: Government Printing Office, 1959), document 692; "Summary of the Three-Power Pact Between Japan, German, and Italy, Signed at Berlin," 27 Sep. 1940, in *FRUS*, 1931–1941, vol. 2, document 100.

10. War Cabinet, "Future Strategy," Aug. 1940, WO 193/148, UKNA.

11. Chief of the Imperial General Staff, "The General Strategical Situation: Outline of the Position and British Policy," 15 Oct. 1940, WO 193/132, UKNA; War Cabinet, "Future Strategy," Aug. 1940, WO 193/148, UKNA.

12. David Reynolds, *From Munich to Pearl Harbor* (Chicago: Ivan R. Dee, 2001), 83–87; Lothian to Roosevelt, 5 Aug. 1940, in *FRUS*, 1940, vol. 3, *The British Commonwealth, the Soviet Union, the Near East, and Africa*, ed. Roger P. Churchill et al. (Washington, DC: Government Printing Office), document 54; Kennedy to Secretary of State, 15 Aug. 1940, in *FRUS*, 1940, vol. 3, document 59.

13. Warren Kimball, *Forged in War* (New York: W. Morrow, 1997), 58.

14. Lothian to Roosevelt, aide-mémoire, 8 Jul. 1940, in *FRUS*, 1940, vol. 3, document 69; Paul Kennedy, *Engineers of Victory* (New York: Random House, 2013), 60; David Zimmerman, *Top Secret Exchange* (Stroud, England: Alan Sutton, 1996).

15. Churchill to Roosevelt, 27 Oct. 1940, in *FRUS*, 1940, vol. 3, document 18.

16. Lacey, "Toward a Strategy," 186.

17. William Franklin, *Western Hemisphere Security*, Studies of American Interests in the War and in the Peace, W-60-A-B7, Council on Foreign Relations, 25 Nov. 1940.

18. Churchill to Roosevelt, 7 Dec. 1940, in *FRUS*, 1940, vol. 3, document 20.

19. Quotes from an unofficial summary of Roosevelt's comments to reporters. Hull to Johnson, 20 Dec. 1940, in *FRUS*, 1940, vol. 3, document 22; "Radio Address by

President Roosevelt," 29 Dec. 1940, in *FRUS*, 1931–1941, vol. 2, document 109.

20. Reynolds, *From Munich to Pearl Harbor*, 108–110.

21. Acheson, memorandum of conversation, 28 Jul. 1941, in *FRUS*, 1941, vol. 3, *The British Commonwealth; The Near East and Africa*, ed. N. O. Sappington, Francis C. Prescott, and Kieran J. Carroll (Washington, DC: Government Printing Office, 1959), 9. Historian Warren Kimball writes that Lend-Lease became a "lever to force Britain to eliminate the imperial preference system and extend the Open Door to America." Warren Kimball, *The Juggler* (Princeton, NJ: Princeton University Press, 1991), 49.

22. Military History Section, Army Forces Far East, *Political Strategy Prior to the Outbreak of War, Part III*, Japanese Monograph 147 (Washington, DC: Office of the Chief of Military History, Department of the Army, 1953), 24.

23. FDR to Ambassador Joseph Grew, 21 Jan. 1941, in *FRUS*, 1941, vol. 4, *The Far East*, ed. John G. Reid, Louis E. Gates, and Ralph R. Goodwin (Washington, DC: Government Printing Office, 1956), document 5; Richard Frank, *Tower of Skulls* (New York: W. W. Norton, 2020), 175.

24. Henry R. Luce, "The American Century," *Life*, 17 Feb. 1941.

25. Louis Morton, "Germany First," in *Command Decisions*, ed. Kent Roberts Greenfield (Washington, DC: Center of Military History, 2000), 20.

26. Alan Moorehead, *The March to Tunis* (New York: Harper and Row, 1967), 175; Ashley Jackson, *The British Empire and the Second World War* (London: Bloomsbury, 2006). Key works on the historical controversies surrounding the Mediterranean strategy include Chester Wilmot, *The Struggle for Europe* (New York: Harper, 1952); Michael Howard, *The Mediterranean Strategy in the Second World War* (London: Weidenfeld and Nicolson, 1968); John Ellis, *Brute Force* (New York: Viking, 1990); Douglas Porch, *The Path to Victory* (New York: Farrar, Straus and Giroux, 2004); and Simon Ball, *The Bitter Sea* (London: HarperPress, 2009).

27. War Cabinet, Chiefs of Staff Committee, "Future Strategy," August 1940, WO 193/148, UKNA.

28. Quoted in Andrew Stewart, *The First Victory* (New Haven, CT: Yale University Press, 2016), 72–73, 87–88.

29. War Cabinet, "General Directive for Commander-in-Chief, Middle East," 23 Aug. 1940, in *Principal War Telegrams and Memoranda, 1940–1943*, Great Britain Cabinet Office, vol. 1, *Middle East* (Nendeln, Liechtenstein: KTO Press, 1976) (hereinafter *PWTM*).

30. Porch, *Path to Victory*, 100–101.

31. I. S. O. Playfair, *The Mediterranean and the Middle East*, vol. 1, *The Early Successes Against Italy (to May 1941)* (London: Her Majesty's Stationery Office, 1954), 266–272; Moorehead, *March to Tunis*, 67–68, 70, 73–74.

32. Churchill to Wavell, 13 Dec. 1940, in *PWTM*; Archibald Wavell, "Operations in the Western Desert from December 7, 1940 to February 7, 1941," *London Gazette*, 25 Jun. 1946.

33. Wavell, "Operations in the Western Desert"; Moorehead, *March to Tunis*, 90–91.

34. Wavell to War Office, 3 Feb. 1941; Heywood to Wavell and Dill, 4 Feb. 1941; Wavell to War Office, 12 Feb. 1941. All in *PWTM*.

35. Robin Higham, *Diary of a Disaster* (Lexington: University Press of Kentucky, 1986), 113, 167; Antony Beevor, *The Second World War* (New York: Little Brown, 2012), 156, 160. Robin Higham calls Wavell's change of heart one of the great "puzzles" of the Greek campaign.

Notes to Chapter 7

36. Higham, *Diary of a Disaster*, 89; Bernd Stegemann, "The Italo-German Conduct of the War in the Mediterranean and North Africa," in *GSWW*, vol. 3, *The Mediterranean, South-East Europe, and North Africa, 1939–1941*, ed. Gerhard Schrieber, Bernd Stegemann, and Detlef Vogel (New York: Oxford University Press, 1995), 654–655, 657; Erwin Rommel, *The Rommel Papers*, ed. B. H. Liddell Hart (New York: Harcourt, Brace, 1953), 514–515.

37. Rommel, *Rommel Papers*, 95, 106, 109, 118.

38. Walid Hamdi, *Rashid Ali al-Gailani and the Nationalist Movement in Iraq, 1939–1941* (London: Darf, 1987), 84, 186–187.

39. Winston Churchill, *The Grand Alliance* (New York: Houghton Mifflin, 1950), 254–261; I. S. O. Playfair, *The Mediterranean and the Middle East*, vol. 2, *The Germans Come to the Help of Their Ally (1941)* (London: Her Majesty's Stationery Office, 1954–1988), 183; War Office to Wavell, 2 May 1941, in *PWTM*.

40. Churchill, *Grand Alliance*, 263–266.

41. Churchill, 323–324, 326–327; Moorehead, *March to Tunis*, 152.

42. Playfair, *Mediterranean and the Middle East*, 2:207, 210, 213, 220–221; Moorehead, *March to Tunis*, 168, 170.

43. Winston Churchill, *The Second World War*, vol. 3, *The Grand Alliance* (Boston: Houghton Mifflin, 1950), 339, 344.

44. "Log of the President's Cruise on Board the USS *Potomac* and USS *Augusta*," Atlantic Charter (1), box 1, Safe File, Franklin D. Roosevelt, Papers as President: The President's Secretary's File (PSF), 1933–1945, Franklin D. Roosevelt Presidential Library and Museum, Hyde Park, NY, http://www.fdrlibrary.marist.edu/_resources/images/psf/psfa0007.pdf.

45. Joint statement by Roosevelt and Churchill, 14 Aug. 1941, in *FRUS*, 1941, vol. 1, *General, the Soviet Union*, ed. Matilda F. Axton et al. (Washington, DC: Government Printing Office, 1959), document 372.

46. Nigel Ashton, "Harold Macmillan and the 'Golden Days' of Anglo-American Relations Revisited, 1957–63," *Diplomatic History* 29, no. 4 (2005): 691–723.

CHAPTER 7: A WAR OF ANNIHILATION

1. David Stahel, *Operation Barbarossa and Germany's Defeat in the East* (Cambridge, UK: Cambridge University Press, 2009), 2.

2. For more on Hitler's intentions, see Stephen Fritz, *Ostkrieg* (Lexington: University Press of Kentucky, 2011), xxi–xxii; and Geoffrey Megargee, *War of Annihilation* (Lanham, MD: Rowman and Littlefield, 2006).

3. Adolf Hitler, *Hitler's Table Talk, 1941–1944*, ed. H. R. Trevor-Roper (New York: Enigma, 2008), 14–15, 21; Mark Mazower, *Hitler's Empire* (New York: Penguin, 2008), xxxix, 2. For examples, see Carroll Kakel III, *The American West and the Nazi East* (New York: Palgrave Macmillan, 2014), 1; Fritz, *Ostkrieg*, 18, 93; Timothy Snyder, *Black Earth* (New York: Tim Duggan Books, 2015), 19–21; and Adam Tooze, *The Wages of Destruction* (New York: Penguin, 2006), 469–470.

4. Fritz, *Ostkrieg*, 43, 51; Hitler, *Hitler's Table Talk*, 27–28, 73; Evan Mawdsley, *Thunder in the East* (New York: Oxford University Press, 2005), 6–7.

5. Hitler, *Hitler's Table Talk*, 54–55.

6. Hitler, 31, 33.

7. Peter Longerich, *Holocaust* (New York: Oxford University Press, 2010), 182–186.

8. Fritz, *Ostkrieg*, 66, 69–70.

9. Oberkommando der Wehrmacht, "Directives for the Treatment of Political

591

Commissars ('Commissar Order')," 6 Jun. 1941, German History in Documents and Images, German Historical Institute, https://ghdi.ghi-dc.org/pdf/eng/English58.pdf.

10. Walter von Reichenau, "Conduct of Troops in Eastern Territories," 10 Oct. 1941, pp. 585–587; Walter von Reichenau, "Protection of Troops Against Partisans and Sabotage," 26 Nov. 1941, translation of document UK-81, pp. 583–584. Both in *Nazi Conspiracy and Aggression*, vol. 8, Office of the United States Chief of Counsel for Prosecution of Axis Criminality (Washington, DC: Government Printing Office, 1946), https://phdn.org/archives/www.ess.uwe.ac.uk/genocide/USSR2.htm.

11. *TMWC*, 1:798, 810–811.

12. Mawdsley, *Thunder in the East*, 18, 41, 45–46; Fritz, *Ostkrieg*, 73.

13. Tooze, *Wages*, 472–485, 538–549; *TMWC*, 5:378; *TMWC*, 1:832, 814–815.

14. Timothy Snyder, *Bloodlands* (New York: Basic, 2010), 51, 53.

15. David Glantz and Jonathan House, *When Titans Clashed*, rev. ed. (Lawrence: University Press of Kansas, 2015), 39, 48–49.

16. Mawdsley, *Thunder in the East*, 13–15.

17. *TMWC*, 1:796–797, 803.

18. I. V. Tiulenev, "At Moscow District Headquarters," in *Stalin and His Generals*, ed. Seweryn Bialer (New York: Pegasus, 1969), 200–203.

19. Hans Schäufler, "From the Bug to the Dnjepr," in *Knight's Cross Panzers*, ed. Hans Schäufler (Mechanicsburg, PA: Stackpole, 2010), 72; Glantz and House, *When Titans Clashed*, 34; Fritz, *Ostkrieg*, 77–78.

20. Alexander Hill, *The Red Army and the Second World War* (New York: Cambridge University Press, 2017), 203, 207–209.

21. "Text of Reichsfuehrer Hitler's Proclamation That Revealed Germany's War Against Soviet Union," *NYT*, 23 Jun. 1941; "Moscow Predicts Crushing of Nazis," *NYT*, 23 Jun. 1941.

22. Quotations in Jonathan Haslam, *Russia's Cold War* (New Haven, CT: Yale University Press, 2022), 10–11.

23. Turner Catledge, "Our Policy Stated," *NYT*, 24 Jun. 1941.

24. Waldo Heinrichs, *Threshold of War* (New York: Oxford University Press, 1989), 102, 139–140; George Kennan, *Memoirs*, vol. 1, *1925-1950* (Boston: Little, Brown, 1967–1972), 146.

25. Quoted in Turner Catledge, "Our Policy Stated," *NYT*, 24 Jun. 1941.

26. Steinhardt to Secretary of State, 29 Jun. 1941, in *FRUS*, 1941, vol. 1 *General, the Soviet Union*, ed. Matilda F. Axton et al. (Washington, DC: Government Printing Office, 1959), document 731.

27. Georgy Zhukov, *The Memoirs of Marshal Zhukov* (New York: Delacorte, 1971), 255–256; Mawdsley, *Thunder in the East*, 58–61.

28. Franz Halder, *The Halder Diaries* (Boulder, CO: Westview, 1976), 2:1000; Zhukov, *Memoirs*, 262, 268–269.

29. Snyder, *Bloodlands*, 188–189, 192, 198, 202.

30. Geoffrey P. Megargee, ed., *The United States Holocaust Memorial Museum Encyclopedia of Camps and Ghettos, 1933-1945* (Bloomington: Indiana University Press, 2009) (hereinafter *USHMM*), 1:1233–1236.

31. *TMWC*, 2:267–268.

32. *TMWC*, 2:266.

33. Omer Bartov, *Germany's War and the Holocaust* (Ithaca, NY: Cornell University Press, 2003), 8; Omer Bartov *Hitler's Army* (New York: Oxford University Press, 1991), 95; Megargee, *War of Annihilation*, 59–60; Glantz and House, *When Titans Clashed*,

67–68; G. H. Bidermann, *In Deadly Combat* (Lawrence: University Press of Kansas, 2000), 13.

34. "Text of Stalin Broadcast," *NYT*, 3 Jul. 1941.

35. Stahel, *Operation Barbarossa*, 232–233; Bidermann, *In Deadly Combat*, 16.

36. Zhukov, *Memoirs*, 266–267; Fritz, *Ostkrieg*, 115–116. On the partisans, see Kenneth Slepyan, *Stalin's Guerrillas* (Lawrence: University Press of Kansas, 2006).

37. Stahel, *Operation Barbarossa*, 259.

38. Heinz Guderian, *Panzer Leader* (New York: Ballantine, 1965), 140–142, 144, 148, 151–152; Halder, *Halder Diaries*, 2:1071.

39. David M. Glantz, *Barbarossa Derailed* (Solihull, England: Helion, 2020), 1:45; S. M. Shtemenko, *The Soviet General Staff at War, 1941–1945* (Moscow: Progress Publishers, 1970), 43; Zhukov, *Memoirs*, 273, 275.

40. Bidermann, *In Deadly Combat*, 25; quotations in Stahel, *Operation Barbarossa*, 288–290.

41. Stahel, *Operation Barbarossa*, 266; Glantz and House, *When Titans Clashed*, 73.

42. Timoshenko quoted in Stahel, *Operation Barbarossa*, 347; Zhukov, *Memoirs*, 286.

43. Glantz and House, *When Titans Clashed*, 81; Hill, *Red Army*, 232.

44. *USHMM*, 2:1821–1823.

45. David Stahel, *Kiev 1941* (New York: Cambridge University Press, 2011), 9–10; Mawdsley, *Thunder in the East*, 69, 71.

46. Zhukov, *Memoirs*, 288, 294.

47. Geoffrey Roberts, *Stalin's Wars* (New Haven, CT: Yale University Press, 2006), 101–102.

48. Stahel, *Kiev 1941*, 255–258.

49. Karel Berkhoff, "The Corpses in the Ravine Were Women, Men, and Children," *Holocaust and Genocide Studies* 29, no. 2 (Fall 2015): 251, 260, 263, 265.

50. *USHMM*, 2:1066–1067.

51. *USHMM*, 2:1148–1150.

52. Harrison Salisbury, *The 900 Days* (New York: Harper and Row, 1969), 204–207, 209.

53. Richard Bidlack, *The Leningrad Blockade, 1941–1944* (New Haven, CT: Yale University Press, 2012), 34–36.

54. Elena Kochina, *Blockade Diary*, trans. Samuel C. Ramer (Ann Arbor, MI: Ardis, 1990), 42, 44, 52, 64.

55. Georgy Zhukov, *Marshal Zhukov's Greatest Battles* (New York: Harper and Row, 1969), 31–33.

56. Mawdsley, *Thunder in the East*, 88–91; David Stahel, *Operation Typhoon* (Cambridge, UK: Cambridge University Press, 2015), 64.

57. Stahel, *Operation Typhoon*, 55, 66, 77, 80–81.

58. Guderian, *Panzer Leader*, 176, 181–183, 194.

59. Rodric Braithwaite, *Moscow 1941* (New York: Knopf, 2006), 213–214, 250–251.

60. Zhukov, *Memoirs*, 328–331, 334.

61. Heinrich Haape, *Moscow Tram Stop* (Guilford, CT: Stackpole, 2020), 103–106.

62. Peter Bamm quoted in *The Voice of War*, ed. James Owen and Guy Walters (London: Viking, 2004), 156; Hans von Luck, *Panzer Commander* (New York: Praeger, 1989).

63. David Stahel, *The Battle for Moscow* (Cambridge, UK: Cambridge University Press, 2015), 246, 250–251.

64. Ian Kershaw, *Hitler, 1936–45* (London: Penguin, 2001), 441; Guderian, *Panzer Leader*, 199.

65. Zhukov, *Memoirs*, 343, 344–346, 348.

66. Glantz and House, *When Titans Clashed*, 108–110; Guderian, *Panzer Leader*, 200.

67. Mawdsley, *Thunder in the East*, 116.

CHAPTER 8: JAPAN'S GRAND OFFENSIVE

1. Mitsuo Fuchida, "The Air Attack on Pearl Harbor," in *The Japanese Navy in World War II*, 2nd ed., ed. David Evans (Annapolis, MD: Naval Institute Press, 2017), 51, 53–55; Ada Margaret Olsen interview by Chris Conybeare, 4 Dec. 1986, Oral History Interviews, Pearl Harbor National Memorial Oral History Project, National Park Service, accessed May 2020, https://www.nps.gov/valr/learn/historyculture /oral-history-interviews.htm.

2. Oscar Villadolid, *Surviving World War II* (Passig City, Philippines: Colet-Villadolid, 2005), 3–5.

3. Yeoh Siang Aun, "8 Dec 1941: The Battle Begins," in *A Battle to Be Remembered* (Singapore: Oral History Dept., 1988), 8.

4. "Outline Narrative of Hong Kong Campaign," WO 106/5359, UKNA.

5. I borrow "Japan's grand offensive" from James MacGregor Burns, *Roosevelt* (New York: Harcourt Brace Jovanovich, 1970), 201.

6. Grew to Roosevelt, 14 Dec. 1940, in *FRUS*, 1940, vol. 4, *The Far East*, ed. John G. Reid, Ralph R. Goodwin, and Louis E. Gates (Washington, DC: Government Printing Office, 1955), 493.

7. Roosevelt to Grew, 21 Jan. 1941, in *FRUS*, 1941, vol. 4, *The Far East*, ed. John G. Reid, Louis E. Gates, and Ralph R. Goodwin (Washington, DC: Government Printing Office, 1956), 5.

8. For more, see H. P. Willmott, *Empires in the Balance* (Annapolis, MD: Naval Institute Press, 2008), 108.

9. William Michael Morgan, *Pacific Gibraltar* (Annapolis, MD: Naval Institute Press, 2011); Jon Thares Davidann, introduction to *Hawai'i at the Crossroads of the U.S. and Japan Before the Pacific War*, ed. John Thares Davidann (Honolulu: University of Hawai'i Press, 2008), 1–8.

10. Charles Groves, "Pacific N.E. 'Colony' Future Hangs on Report to Congress," *Daily Boston Globe*, 19 Dec. 1937; American Civil Liberties Union, *Civil Liberties in American Colonies* (New York: ACLU, 1939); Daniel Immerwahr, *How to Hide an Empire* (New York: Farrar, Straus and Giroux, 2019), 7, 12.

11. Clark Reynolds, *Admiral John H. Towers* (Annapolis, MD: Naval Institute Press, 1991), 237–238.

12. US Congress, Senate, *Investigation of the Pearl Harbor Attack: Report of the Joint Committee on the Investigation of the Pearl Harbor Attack*, July 20 (Legislative Day July 5), 1946, 79th Cong., 2d sess., 1946, S. Doc. 244, 263–266.

13. US Congress, Senate, *Investigation of the Pearl Harbor Attack*, 27; Grew to Secretary of State, telegram, 27 Jan. 1941, exhibit 15 in *Pearl Harbor Attack: Hearings Before the Joint Committee on the Investigation of the Pearl Harbor Attack*, part 14, 79th Cong. (1946), 1042.

14. Ronald Spector, *Eagle Against the Sun* (New York: Vintage, 1985), 2; Gordon Prange, *At Dawn We Slept* (New York: McGraw-Hill, 1981), 122; US Congress, Senate, *Investigation of the Pearl Harbor Attack*, 167, http://www.ibiblio.org/pha/pha/congress

Notes to Chapter 8

/part_4.html; Waldo Heinrichs, *Threshold of War* (New York: Oxford University Press, 1989), 37–38.

15. Mark Skinner Watson, *Chief of Staff* (Washington, DC: Center of Military History, 1991), 374–376; "United States—British Staff Conversations: Report," 27 Mar. 1941, exhibit 49 in *Pearl Harbor Attack: Hearings*, part 15, 79th Cong. (1946), 1485–1550; *Pearl Harbor Attack: Hearings*, part 3, 79th Cong. 1226 (1946) (testimony of General George C. Marshall).

16. Brian Farrell, *The Defence and Fall of Singapore* (Singapore: Monsoon, 2015), 16, 48; "Notes on Situation," 27 Apr. 1941, WO 143/146, UKNA; Chiefs of Staff Committee, "Immediate Measures Required in the Far East," CAB 66/9/2, UKNA; War Office, telegram, 16 Aug. 1941, WO 143/146, UKNA.

17. Military History Section, Army Forces Far East, *Political Strategy Prior to the Outbreak of War, Part III*, Japanese Monograph 147 (Washington, DC: Office of the Chief of Military History, Department of the Army, 1953), 13–14.

18. Military History Section, Army Forces Far East, *Political Strategy [. . .], Part III*, 27–29, 32.

19. "Japanese Landing in Indo-China," *North China Herald*, 30 Jul. 1941; "Press Release Issued by the Department of State," 24 Jul. 1941, in *FRUS, 1931–1941*, vol. 2, *Japan*, ed. Joseph V. Fuller (Washington, DC: Government Printing Office, 1943), document 230; Louis Morton, *Strategy and Command* (Washington, DC: Center of Military History, 2000), 125. Stark recounted his conversation with the Japanese ambassador years later. There is no date for when it supposedly took place, although Stark's memo to Roosevelt from 21 Jul. 1941 mentions the following exchange: "I have also told Nomura that were our two nations to clash there could be only one ending, because, regardless of how long it took, once we had started it, the United States would finish it in its own way, etc., etc." See Stark to Secretary of State, 22 Jul. 1941, in *FRUS, 1941*, vol. 4, document 661.

20. Welles to Grew, 1 Aug. 1941, in *FRUS, 1941*, vol. 4, document 673; Heinrichs, *Threshold of War*, 180–182; Sadao Asada, *From Mahan to Pearl Harbor* (Annapolis, MD: Naval Institute Press, 2013), 252.

21. Asada, *From Mahan to Pearl Harbor*, 243–244, 250.

22. Military History Section, Army Forces Far East, *Political Strategy [. . .], Part III*, 36; Military History Section, Army Forces Far East, *Political Strategy Prior to the Outbreak of War, Part IV*, Japanese Monograph 150 (Washington, DC: Office of the Chief of Military History, Department of the Army, 1952), 21.

23. Willmott, *Empires in the Balance*, 72, 74–75.

24. Spector, *Eagle Against the Sun*, 44–45, 48–49.

25. Asada, *From Mahan to Pearl Harbor*, 270–272.

26. Asada, 276.

27. Quoted in Prange, *At Dawn We Slept*, 16.

28. S. C. M. Paine, *The Japanese Empire* (New York: Cambridge University Press, 2017), 154–155.

29. Browne to Secretary of State, 29 Oct. 1941, in *FRUS, 1941*, vol. 5, *The Far East*, ed. G. Bernard Noble, E. R. Perkins, and Gustave A. Nuermberger (Washington, DC: Government Printing Office, 1956), document 349; Heinrichs, *Threshold of War*, 202–204.

30. "Report by the Commercial Attaché in Japan," 10 Nov. 1941, enclosure in Grew to Secretary of State, 13 Nov. 1941, in *FRUS, 1941*, vol. 4, document 437; Netherlands Legation to Dept. of State, 21 Nov. 1941, in *FRUS, 1941*, vol. 5, document 367;

"Memorandum of Conversation, by the Assistant Chief of the Division of Far Eastern Affairs," 22 Nov. 1941, in *FRUS*, 1941, vol. 5, document 372; Reed to Secretary of State, 25 Nov. 1941, in *FRUS*, 1941, vol. 5, document 376; Browne to Secretary of State, 26 Nov. 1941, in *FRUS*, 1941, vol. 5, document 379; *Pearl Harbor Attack: Hearings*, part 11, 79th Cong. 5187–5188 (1946) (testimony of General George C. Marshall).

31. Robert Dallek, *Franklin D. Roosevelt and American Foreign Policy* (New York: Viking, 2017), 308; "Document Handed by the Secretary of State to the Japanese Ambassador," 26 Nov. 1941, in *FRUS*, 1931–1941, vol. 2, document 409; Military History Section, Army Forces Far East, *Political Strategy [. . .], Part IV*, 63–64.

32. Otto Tolischus, *Tokyo Record* (New York: Reynal and Hitchcock, 1943), 321–322.

33. G. Hermon Gill, *Royal Australian Navy, 1939–1942*, Australia in the War of 1939–1945, Series 2—Navy (Canberra: Australian War Memorial, 1957), 485; Peck to Secretary of State, 7 Dec. 1941, in *FRUS*, 1941, vol. 5, document 406; Farrell, *Defence and Fall*, 140–143; Patton to Secretary of State, 8 Dec. 1941, in *FRUS*, 1941, vol. 5, document 405; Edwin Maurice Glover, *In 70 Days* (London: F. Muller, 1946), 75.

34. *Japanese Navy in World War II*, 57, 59–60; George Phraner quoted in *The Voice of War*, ed. James Owen and Guy Walters (London: Viking, 2004), 174; George Charland, interview, 7 Dec. 1998, World War II Veterans Oral History Collection, National Museum of the Pacific War, digitalarchive.pacificwarmuseum.org.

35. Morton, *Strategy and Command*, 133–134.

36. John Correll, "Disaster in the Philippines," *Air Force Magazine*, 1 Nov. 2019.

37. Koichi Shimada, "The Opening Air Offensive Against the Philippines," in Evans, *Japanese Navy in World War II*, 72, 92–93; Louis Morton, *The Fall of the Philippines* (Washington, DC: Center of Military History, 1993), 88.

38. Dallek, *Franklin D. Roosevelt*, 311–312.

39. For more on this reframing, see Immerwahr, *How to Hide an Empire*, 3–6.

40. S. Woodburn Kirby, *The War Against Japan* (London: Her Majesty's Stationery Office, 1957–1969), 194–199; Frank, *Tower of Skulls*, 354.

41. Churchill to Eden, telegram, 12 Dec. 1941, CHAR 20/46/88-89, UKNA; Churchill to Curtin, telegram, 12 Dec. 1941, CHAR 20/46/91, UKNA.

42. Churchill to Auchinleck, 12 Dec. 1941, WO 193/135, UKNA.

43. "Extracts from Summary of Information Compiled at G.H.Q. India," undated, "Atrocities Committed by the Japanese in Hong Kong," WO 141/101; "Extract from Second List of Japanese Atrocities Compiled at G.H.Q. India," undated, "Atrocities Committed by the Japanese in Hong Kong," WO 141/101; "Extract from Paper on Japanese Atrocities Compiled at G.H.Q. India," undated, "Japanese Atrocities," WO 141/101. All in UKNA.

44. Anthony Eden, "Treatment of Prisoners at Hong Kong: Memorandum by the Secretary of State for Foreign Affairs," 5 Mar. 1942, "Japanese Atrocities," WO 141/101, UKNA.

45. Gerald Horne, *Race War!* (New York: New York University Press, 2004), 77–79.

46. Bruce Gamble, *Fortress Rabaul* (Minneapolis: Zenith, 2010), 47–50.

47. King to FDR, "Memorandum for the President," 5 Mar. 1942, folder King, Ernest J., box 3, Safe File, Franklin D. Roosevelt, Papers as President: The President's Secretary's File (PSF), 1933–1945, Franklin D. Roosevelt Presidential Library and Museum, Hyde Park, NY, http://www.fdrlibrary.marist.edu/_resources/images/psf /psfa0039.pdf.

48. "Minutes of War Council Meeting," 17 Dec. 1941, WO 106/2568, UKNA;

"Minutes of War Council Meeting," 19 Dec. 1941, WO 106/2568, UKNA.

49. George Seabridge, "Notes Found in Baggage of Mr. Seabridge," 28 Feb. 1942, WO 106/2550A, UKNA.

50. John Bull, "Massacre by Japanese Troops in Alexandria Military Hospital, Singapore," box 87/50/1, Private Papers of Major JWD Bull CBE MD FRCP, Imperial War Museum, London.

51. "Some Notes and Personal Observations on the Malayan Campaign," 29 Sep. 1942, WO 106/2550B, UKNA; Lance-Bombardier S. Lord, WO 106/2550A, UKNA.

52. Fred Glueckstein, "Churchill and the Fall of Singapore," *Finest Hour* 169, Summer 2015, 32; Akira Iriye, *Power and Culture* (Cambridge, MA: Harvard University Press, 1981), 50.

53. Christopher Thorne, *The Issue of War* (New York: Oxford University Press, 1985), 145, 155.

54. War Cabinet, "Far East Appreciation," 21 Feb. 1942, CAB 66/22/24, UKNA; Frank, *Tower of Skulls*, 462–464. Some accounts report the destruction of the bridge on February 22, but the majority cite February 23. I follow the Imperial War Museum's designation of February 23.

55. Christopher Bayly and Tim Harper, *Forgotten Armies* (Cambridge, MA: Belknap Press of Harvard University Press, 2004), 159–162, 164.

56. Geoffrey Tyson, *Forgotten Frontier* (Calcutta: W. H. Targett, 1945), 19; Philip Woods, *Reporting the Retreat* (Oxford, UK: Oxford University Press, 2016), 113–116; Bayly and Harper, *Forgotten Armies*, 182–183.

57. Frank, *Tower of Skulls*, 386, 389, 391–395.

58. Spector, *Eagle Against the Sun*, 110, 113–114; Quezon to FDR, message, 8 Feb. 1942, folder Philippines, box 5, http://www.fdrlibrary.marist.edu/_resources/images /psf/psfa0059.pdf; FDR to Quezon, message, 9 Feb. 1942, folder Philippines, box 46. Both in Safe File, Franklin D. Roosevelt, Papers as President: The President's Secretary's File (PSF), 1933–1945, Franklin D. Roosevelt Presidential Library and Museum, Hyde Park, NY.

59. MacArthur to Marshall, 4 Feb. 1942; "Message from General Marshall to General MacArthur," 8 Feb. 1942. Both in folder Philippines, box 5, Safe File, Franklin D. Roosevelt, Papers as President: The President's Secretary's File (PSF), 1933–1945, Franklin D. Roosevelt Presidential Library and Museum, Hyde Park, NY.

60. Spector, *Eagle Against the Sun*, 115–119.

61. Spector, 119; John Dower, *War Without Mercy* (New York: Pantheon, 1986), 51–52, 328; Donald Knox, *Death March* (New York: Harcourt Brace, 1981), 118, 121.

62. Tim Harper, "A Long View on the Great Asian War," in *Legacies of World War II in South and East Asia*, ed. David Koh Wee Hock (Singapore: Institute of Southeast Asian Studies, 2007), 11; Morrison quoted in Horne, *Race War!*, 2.

CHAPTER 9: THE BATTLE FOR THE PERIPHERY

1. Clive Moore, *Tulagi* (Canberra: Australian National University Press, 2019) 1, 4; Office of Naval Intelligence, *The Battle of the Coral Sea*, Combat Narratives (Washington, DC: Office of Naval Intelligence, US Navy, 1943), 5.

2. H. P. Willmott, *The Barrier and the Javelin* (Annapolis, MD: Naval Institute Press, 1983), 33, 39–42.

3. Willmott, 46–52.

4. John Lundstrom, *The First South Pacific Campaign* (Annapolis, MD: Naval Institute Press, 2014), 42–45; Willmott, *Barrier and the Javelin*, 37.

5. John Wukovits, *One Square Mile of Hell* (New York: NAL Caliber, 2006), 21.

6. Winston Churchill, memorandum, 16–20 Dec. 1941, in *FRUS, The Conferences at Washington, 1941–1942, and Casablanca, 1943*, ed. Fredrick Aandahl, William M. Franklin, and William Slany (Washington, DC: Government Printing Office, 1958), document 114.

7. Churchill, memorandum, 16–20 Dec. 1941.

8. Liddell Hart quoted in Alex Danchev, "Liddell Hart's Big Idea," *Review of International Studies* 25, no. 1 (Jan. 1999): 29–48.

9. "Papers by the Joint Board," 21 Dec. 1941, in *FRUS, Conferences at Washington, 1941–1942, and Casablanca, 1943*, document 34.

10. Editorial note, in *FRUS, Conferences at Washington, 1941–1942, and Casablanca, 1943*, document 44; Maurice Matloff and Edwin Snell, *Strategic Planning for Coalition Warfare, 1941–1942* (Washington, DC: Center of Military History, 1999), 104–105.

11. Memorandum by the British chiefs of staff, 24 Dec. 1941, in *FRUS, Conferences at Washington, 1941–1942, and Casablanca, 1943*, document 114.

12. Paul Dull, *A Battle History of the Imperial Japanese Navy* (Annapolis, MD: Naval Institute Press, 1978), 104, 107–111; Churchill to FDR, 7 Apr. 1942, CHAR 20/73/68, UKNA.

13. Winston Churchill, *Hinge of Fate* (Boston: Houghton Mifflin, 1950), 183; second Churchill quotation in Ashley Jackson, "Ceylon's Home Front During the Second World War," in *Home Fronts*, ed. Mark Crowley and Sandra Trudgen Dawson (Rochester, NY: Boydell, 2017).

14. Churchill to Smuts, 24 Mar. 1942, CHAR 20/72/89-91, UKNA; Churchill to Wavell, 1 May 1942, CHAR 20/74/93-94, UKNA; Martin Thomas, "Imperial Backwater or Strategic Outpost? The British Takeover of Vichy Madagascar, 1942," *Historical Journal* 39, no. 4 (1996): 1056, 1059.

15. War Cabinet, "Weekly Resume," 7 May 1942, CAB 66/24, UKNA.

16. Office of Naval Intelligence, *Early Raids in the Pacific Ocean*, Combat Narratives (Washington, DC: Office of Naval Intelligence, US Navy, 1943), https://www.history.navy.mil/.

17. This number may be exaggerated. Richard Frank, *Tower of Skulls* (New York: W. W. Norton, 2020), 511–512.

18. S. C. M. Paine, *The Wars for Asia, 1911–1949* (New York: Cambridge University Press, 2012), 192.

19. Lundstrom, *First South Pacific Campaign*, chapters 6, 8.

20. Frederick Parker, *A Priceless Advantage* (Fort George Meade, MD: National Security Agency, Center for Cryptologic History, 1993); "Estimate of the Situation," 22 Apr. 1942, in *Command Summary of Fleet Admiral Chester W. Nimitz, USN* (hereinafter *Gray Book*), vol. 1, *7 December 1941 to 31 August 1942* (Newport, RI: US Naval War College, 2013), 371–407.

21. Office of Naval Intelligence, *Battle of the Coral Sea*, 3–6, 16; Ronald Spector, *Eagle Against the Sun* (New York: Vintage, 1985), 159–160.

22. Office of Naval Intelligence, *Battle of the Coral Sea*, 22, 25–26, 30, 34–35, 40–42; *Gray Book*, 1:443.

23. US Strategic Bombing Survey, Naval Analysis Division, *The Campaigns of the Pacific War* (Washington, DC: Government Printing Office, 1946), 58.

24. Lundstrom, *First South Pacific Campaign*, chapter 13; Craig Symonds, *The Battle of Midway* (New York: Oxford University Press, 2011), 176–178.

25. Rochefort's ploy also embarrassed his superiors in Washington. According to Edwin Layton, the combat intelligence officer in Hawaii, intelligence officers in Washington who had initially dismissed Rochefort's analysis pivoted and took credit for identifying Midway as the target of Japan's attack. These same officers then smeared Rochefort and had him transferred from the Hawaii station. Parker, *Priceless Advantage*, 50–51; Edwin Layton, *"And I Was There"* (New York: W. Morrow, 1985), 420–422, 449–452.

26. 16 May 1942, *Gray Book*, 1:482; "Estimate of the Situation," 26 May 1942, *Gray Book*, 1:512, 519–520; Office of Naval Intelligence, *Battle of Midway*, Combat Narratives (Washington, DC: Office of Naval Intelligence, US Navy, 1943), 5, 7.

27. Mitsuo Fuchida and Masatake Okumiya, "The Battle of Midway," in *The Japanese Navy in World War II*, 2nd ed., ed. David Evans (Annapolis, MD: Naval Institute Press, 2017), 121–133.

28. Symonds, *Battle of Midway*, 218–221, 224, 232; Office of Naval Intelligence, *Battle of Midway*, 12, 15.

29. Spector, *Eagle Against the Sun*, 171–174.

30. Symonds, *Battle of Midway*, 301–305; Fuchida and Okumiya, "Battle of Midway," 141; Office of Naval Intelligence, *The Japanese Story of the Battle of Midway* (Washington, DC: Office of Naval Intelligence, US Navy, 1947), 10.

31. Dull, *Battle History*, 157–161.

32. Masataka Chihaya, "An Intimate Look at the Japanese Navy," in *The Pearl Harbor Papers*, ed. Donald M. Goldstein and Katherine V. Dillon (Washington, DC: Brassey's, 1993), 349.

33. US Strategic Bombing Survey, *Campaigns of the Pacific War*, 60.

34. US Strategic Bombing Survey, *Campaigns of the Pacific War*, 60. Figures are from Ernest King, *U.S. Navy at War, 1941–45* (Washington, DC: US Navy Department, 1946), 252–286. See David C. Evans and Mark R. Peatie, *Kaigun* (Annapolis, MD: Naval Institute Press, 1997), 366–367.

35. Clark Reynolds, *Fast Carriers* (Huntington, NY: R. E. Krieger, 1978), 53.

CHAPTER 10: RISE OF THE SUPERPOWERS

1. Albert Speer, *Inside the Third Reich* (New York: Macmillan, 1970), 189–190.

2. David Glantz and Jonathan House, *When Titans Clashed*, rev. ed. (Lawrence: University Press of Kansas, 2015), 151, 384.

3. Geoffrey Roberts, *Stalin's Wars* (New Haven, CT: Yale University Press, 2006), 114–115.

4. Stephen Fritz, *Ostkrieg* (Lexington: University Press of Kentucky, 2011), 235; Bernd Wegner, "The Historical Topos of the Second Campaign Against the Soviet Union," in *GSWW*, vol. 6, *The Global War*, ed. Horst Boog, Werner Rahn, Reinhard Stumf, and Bernd Wegner (New York: Oxford University Press, 2001), 1206–1208.

5. Bernd Wegner, "Hitler's 'Second Campaign': Military Concept and Strategic Foundations," in *GSWW*, 6:844; Fritz, *Ostkrieg*, 169; Adam Tooze, *The Wages of Destruction* (New York: Penguin, 2006), 554.

6. Christian Gerlach, *The Extermination of the European Jews* (Cambridge, UK: Cambridge University Press, 2016), 66, 80; Christian Gerlach, "The Wannsee Conference, the Fate of the German Jews, and Hitler's Decision in Principle to Exterminate All the European Jews," *Journal of Modern History* 70, no. 4 (Dec. 1998): 786; Ian Kershaw, *Hitler, 1936–45* (London: Penguin, 2001), 477, 491, 493.

7. Robert Citino, *Death of the Wehrmacht* (Lawrence: University Press of Kansas,

2007), 52; Wegner, "Hitler's 'Second Campaign,'" 844; Adolf Hitler, "Fuhrer Directive No. 41," 5 Apr. 1942.

8. Bernd Wegner, "The Spring Battles of 1942," in *GSWW*, 6:929–930; Evan Mawdsley, *Thunder in the East* (London: Bloomsbury, 2005), 135–136.

9. For a vivid description of the clash at Kharkov, see Citino, *Death of the Wehrmacht*, 1–2, 94, 99, 102–103, 110; and Earl Ziemke, *Moscow to Stalingrad* (Washington, DC: Center of Military History, 1987), 282.

10. Hitler, "Directive No. 45"; Mawdsley, *Thunder in the East*, 160.

11. Fritz, *Ostkrieg*, 266–267, 276–277.

12. Citino, *Death of the Wehrmacht*, 180–181, 233–234, 240, 243.

13. Bernd Wegner, "Stalingrad," in *GSWW*, 6:1060–1061, 1064–1066; Hans Wijers, *Eastern Front Combat* (Mechanicsburg, PA: Stackpole, 2008), 54–55, 61.

14. S. M. Shtemenko, *The Soviet General Staff at War, 1941–1945* (Moscow: Progress Publishers, 1970), 94–93, 103.

15. Jochen Hellbeck, *Stalingrad* (New York: PublicAffairs, 2015), 104–108; Glantz and House, *When Titans Clashed*, 147.

16. Wijers, *Eastern Front Combat*, 60, 76; Fritz, *Ostkrieg*, 298–299.

17. Chris Bellamy, *Absolute War* (New York: Knopf, 2007), 523–524.

18. Glantz and House, *When Titans Clashed*, 148.

19. Wijers, *Eastern Front Combat*, 72–73.

20. General Georgy Zhukov claims credit for Uranus in his *Reminiscences and Reflections* (Moscow: Progress, 1985), 93–95, but Geoffrey Roberts disputes these claims in *Stalin's Wars* (New Haven, CT: Yale University Press, 2006), 149, and Glantz and House dismiss them completely, identifying General Andrey Yeremenko as Uranus's architect in *When Titans Clashed*, 172.

21. Bellamy, *Absolute War*, 531–535.

22. Citino, *Death of the Wehrmacht*, 299–300; Mawdsley, *Thunder in the East*, 162.

23. Jonathan Bastable, *Voices from Stalingrad* (Barnsley, England: Pen and Sword, 2019), 187, 227; Panse quoted in Wijers, *Eastern Front Combat*, 1.

24. Bastable, *Voices from Stalingrad*, 262, 264–265.

25. Wegner, "Historical Topos," 1214–1215.

26. Mawdsley, *Thunder in the East*, 181.

27. Abbas Amanat, *Iran* (New Haven, CT: Yale University Press, 2017), 495–498.

28. P. J. Vatikiotis, *The History of Modern Egypt*, 4th ed. (Baltimore, MD: Johns Hopkins University Press, 1991), 348–351.

29. Citino, *Death of the Wehrmacht*, 123, 127–128, 133; CINC Middle East to War Office, 27 May 1942, *Principal Telegrams Relating to Operations in the Middle East*, 27 May–21 June 1942 (Nendeln: KTO Press, 1976).

30. Weekly Résumé of the Naval Military and Air Situation, 4 Jun. 1942, CAB 66/25, UKNA, 4–5; Weekly Résumé of the Naval Military and Air Situation, 11 Jun. 1942, CAB 66/25, UKNA, 5; Weekly Résumé of the Naval Military and Air Situation, 18 Jun. 1942, CAB 66/25, UKNA, 4; Mideast to Air Ministry, 21 Jun. 1942, *Principal Telegrams Relating to Operations in the Middle East*, 27 May–21 June 1942.

31. Martin Kitchen, *Rommel's Desert War* (New York: Cambridge University Press, 2009), 244, 246–249, 252–254.

32. Alan Moorehead, *The March to Tunis* (New York: Harper and Row, 1967), 362; Douglas Porch, *The Path to Victory* (New York: Farrar, Straus and Giroux, 2004), 273, 280.

33. Reinhard Stumpf, "The Advance to El Alamein (Operation Theseus)," in

GSWW, 6:715; Reinhard Stumpf, "El Alamein," in *GSWW*, 6:722.

34. Citino, *Death of the Wehrmacht*, 206–210, 213.

35. Winston Churchill, *Hinge of Fate* (Boston: Houghton Mifflin, 1950), 457.

36. Erwin Rommel, *The Rommel Papers*, ed. Basil Henry Liddell Hart (New York: Harcourt, Brace, 1953), 264, 276–281, 283.

37. Richard Hammond, *Strangling the Axis* (New York: Cambridge University Press, 2020), 20–23; Simon Ball, *The Bitter Sea* (London: HarperPress, 2009).

38. Bernard Montgomery, *The Memoirs of Field-Marshal the Viscount Montgomery* (New York: New American Library, 1959), 107–111.

39. Bernard Montgomery, *El Alamein to the River Sangro* (London: Hutchinson, 1948), 16–17, 22–23; Rommel, *Rommel Papers*, 303–309, 320.

40. Rommel, *Rommel Papers*, 321, 327.

41. Winston Churchill, *Hinge of Fate* (Boston: Houghton Mifflin, 1950), 603. Casualty estimates include Italian forces and are imprecise due in no small part to the haphazard Axis retreat across North Africa.

CHAPTER 11: THE PATH TO GLOBAL HEGEMONY

1. John Toland, *Rising Sun* (New York: Random House, 1970), 351–356.

2. Winston Churchill, *Hinge of Fate* (Boston: Houghton Mifflin, 1950), 376–377, 380–382.

3. For one of the best discussions of these debates, see Mark A. Stoler, *Allies and Adversaries* (Chapel Hill: University of North Carolina Press, 2000).

4. Stoler, *Allies and Adversaries*, 53, 55, 289n43.

5. Raymond E. Lee, "Possibility of a Negotiated Russo-German Settlement," 12 Feb. 1942, G-2 Military Attaché Reports on Petroleum, Petroleum Refineries, and USSR Armed Services, 1 Feb. 1942–28 Feb. 1943, World War II: U.S. Documents on Planning, Operations, Intelligence, Axis War Crimes, and Refugees, ProQuest History Vault; Mark Stoler, "The 'Second Front' and American Fear of Soviet Expansion, 1941–1943," *Military Affairs* 39, no. 3 (Oct. 1975): 136–141.

6. Stoler, *Allies and Adversaries*, 79–84, 88.

7. Churchill, *Hinge of Fate*, 382–383; Robert Lester, ed., *Papers of George Marshall* (Bethesda, MD: University Publications of America, 1992), 3:245–246, 248–249. For Roosevelt's views on the Middle East, oil, and Suez, see Robert Dallek, *Franklin D. Roosevelt and American Foreign Policy* (New York: Viking, 2017), 348.

8. Churchill, *Hinge of Fate*, 438.

9. For more, see Stephen Kotkin, *Stalin* (New York: Penguin, 2017), 2:777, 780, 818.

10. Jonathan Haslam, *Russia's Cold War* (New Haven, CT: Yale University Press, 2022), 11; I. M. Maiski to Stalin, 7 Aug. 1942, in "New Documents about Winston Churchill from Russian Archives," *International Affairs* 47, no. 5 (2001): 133; Geoffrey Roberts, *Stalin's Wars* (New Haven, CT: Yale University Press, 2006). See also Standley to Secretary of State, 14 May 1942, in *FRUS*, 1942, vol. 3, *Europe*, ed. G. Bernard Noble and E. R. Perkins (Washington, DC: Government Printing Office, 1961), document 376.

11. Churchill, *Hinge of Fate*, 474–475, 478–480.

12. Churchill, 481–482.

13. John Campbell, *Dieppe Revisited* (London: F. Cass, 1993), 1; Churchill, *Hinge of Fate*, 509–511.

14. Standley to Secretary of State, 25 Aug. 1942, in *FRUS*, 1942, vol. 3, document 530; Winant to Secretary of State, 5 Oct. 1942, in *FRUS*, 1942, vol. 3, document 393.

15. Roberts, *Stalin's Wars*, 141–142.

16. Walter Lord, *Lonely Vigil* (New York: Open Road, 2021), 2–5.

17. Louis Morton, *Strategy and Command* (Washington, DC: Office of the Chief of Military History, 2000), 89–90.

18. Richard Frank, *Guadalcanal* (New York: Random House, 1990), 21–22, 31, 35–36; James Boston, interview, 13 Sep. 2005, World War II Veterans Oral History Collection, National Museum of the Pacific War, digitalarchive.pacificwarmuseum.org.

19. Toland, *Rising Sun*, 351–356.

20. Craig Symonds, *World War II at Sea* (New York: Oxford University Press, 2018), 302–303, 306–309.

21. Ronald Spector, *Eagle Against the Sun* (New York: Vintage, 1985), 195–196; Robert Leckie, *Strong Men Armed* (New York: Random House, 1962), 35, 45–47; Ian Toll, *Conquering Tide* (New York: W. W. Norton, 2015), 74.

22. Samuel Eliot Morison, *The Struggle for Guadalcanal* (London: Oxford University Press, 1948–1962), 82–84, 88–90, 94, 97, 107.

23. Sid Phillips, "Sid Phillips Oral History: Life on Guadalcanal," YouTube video, 4:31, posted by the National WWII Museum on 29 Sep. 2017, https://www.youtube.com/watch?v=q0LokYgWQN4; Seth Paridon, "Life on Guadalcanal," 2 Oct. 2017, National WWII Museum, https://www.nationalww2museum.org/war/articles/life-guadalcanal.

24. Frank, *Guadalcanal*, 194, 199.

25. Leckie, *Strong Men Armed*, 56–62.

26. Morison, *Struggle for Guadalcanal*, 131–135.

27. Paul Dull, *A Battle History of the Imperial Japanese Navy* (Annapolis, MD: Naval Institute Press, 1978), 215–220, 238.

28. Spector, *Eagle Against the Sun*, 209–211.

29. James Hornfischer, *Neptune's Inferno* (New York: Bantam, 2011), 235.

30. Symonds, *World War II at Sea*, 364–369.

31. Symonds, 369–371.

32. "As a rule of thumb," historian John Prados writes, "the Imperial Navy needed to eliminate three or four warships for each one it lost." John Prados, *Islands of Destiny* (New York: New American Library, 2012), 351–352. Casualty figures are from Frank, *Guadalcanal*, 614.

33. George Howe, *Northwest Africa* (Washington, DC: Office of the Chief of Military History, Department of the Army, 1957), 89–90; Hollis Stabler, *No One Ever Asked Me* (Lincoln: University of Nebraska Press, 2005), 40; Harold Boyle, "Greatest Amphibious Action Described," *Christian Science Monitor*, 16 Nov. 1942.

34. Douglas Porch, *The Path to Victory* (New York: Farrar, Straus and Giroux, 2004), 350–352.

35. Dwight Eisenhower, *Crusade in Europe* (Garden City, NY: Doubleday, 1948), 107.

36. Howe, *Northwest Africa*, 277, 280–282.

37. Reinhard Stumpf, "The Allied Landing in North-west Africa and the German-Italian Panzerarmee's Retreat to Tunisia," in *GSWW*, 6:802–806.

38. Rick Atkinson, *An Army at Dawn* (New York: Henry Holt, 2002), 339–342; Porch, *Path to Victory*, 383–389.

39. Simon Ball, *The Bitter Sea* (London: HarperPress, 2009), 203–205; Atkinson, *Army at Dawn*, 420, 424–428.

40. Williamson Murray and Alan Millett, *A War to Be Won* (Cambridge, MA: Belknap Press of Harvard University Press, 2000), 299–301.

41. Maurice Matloff and Edwin Snell, *Strategic Planning for Coalition Warfare, 1941–1942* (Washington, DC: Center of Military History, 1999), 2:18–25; Stoler, *Allies and Adversaries*, 103.

42. "C.C.S. 55th Meeting," 14 Jan. 1943, 10:30 a.m., 1:172; and JCS Meeting with the President, 16 Jan. 1943, 1700 hours, 1:390, both in *Casablanca Conference* (Washington, DC: Office of the Combined Chiefs of Staff, 1943), https://www.jcs.mil/About/Joint-Staff-History/.

43. Stoler, *Allies and Adversaries*, 109–110.

44. Stoler, *Allies and Adversaries*, 49–50, 124, 133, 141; Lloyd Gardner, *Spheres of Influence* (Chicago: I. R. Dee, 1993), 148–149, 153.

45. Stoler, "'Second Front,'" 136–141.

46. Stoler, *Allies and Adversaries*, 133.

47. Combined Chiefs of Staff minutes, 16 Jan. 1943, 10:30 a.m., in *FRUS*, 1943, *The Conferences at Cairo and Tehran*, ed. William M. Franklin and William Gerber (Washington, DC: Government Printing Office, 1961), document 346.

48. Combined Chiefs of Staff minutes, 18 Jan. 1943, 5:00 p.m., in *FRUS*, 1943, *Conferences at Cairo and Tehran*, document 355.

49. Marc Gallicchio, *Unconditional* (New York: Oxford University Press, 2020), 8–10.

CHAPTER 12: COLONIAL INTERVENTIONS AND CONTINENTAL SLAUGHTERHOUSES

1. Nicholas Spykman, *The Geography of the Peace* (New York: Harcourt, Brace, 1944), 44; Paul Chamberlin, *The Cold War's Killing Fields* (New York: Harper, 2018).

2. Mark A. Stoler, *Allies and Adversaries* (Chapel Hill: University of North Carolina Press, 2000), 144–145. For the concept of an empire of bases, see Chalmers Johnson, "Empire of Bases," *NYT*, 13 Jul. 2009.

3. Jonathan Dimbleby, *The Battle of the Atlantic* (New York: Oxford University Press, 2016), 105, 123.

4. The figure of six hundred thousand tons appears to be losses from all shipping, not just losses due to U-boat attacks. Craig Symonds, *World War II at Sea* (New York: Oxford University Press, 2018), 104, 185, 187–188.

5. See John Ferris, "Intelligence," in *The Cambridge History of the Second World War*, vol. 1, *Fighting the War*, ed. John Ferris and Evan Mawdsley (Cambridge, UK: Cambridge University Press, 2015), 637–663.

6. Paul Kennedy, *Engineers of Victory* (New York: Random House, 2013), 51–56, 61.

7. Evan Mawdsley, *War for the Seas* (New Haven, CT: Yale University Press, 2019), 315–316.

8. Duncan Redford, "The March 1943 Crisis in the Battle of the Atlantic," *History* 92, no. 1 (Jan. 2007): 70. Over thirty thousand members of the British Merchant Navy died. Terry Hughes and John Costello, *The Battle of the Atlantic* (New York: Dial, 1977), 303.

9. "Newport News Launches Big Carrier," *Austin (TX) Statesman*, 31 Jul. 1942.

10. Owen Gault, "Evolution of the Essex-Class Carriers," *Sea Classics*, Dec. 2007.

11. Kennedy, *Engineers of Victory*, 320–321.

12. Clark Reynolds, *Fast Carriers* (Huntington, NY: R. E. Krieger, 1978), 22, 51–52, 75–76, 80, 167.

13. Stoler, *Allies and Adversaries*, 139–140, 143–144.

14. Daniel Yergin, *Shattered Peace* (Boston: Houghton Mifflin, 1977), 202–203.

15. Stoler, *Allies and Adversaries*, 128.

16. Memorandum by the Combined Chiefs of Staff, 21 Jan. 1943, in *FRUS, The Conferences at Washington, 1941-1942, and Casablanca, 1943*, ed. Fredrick Aandahl, William M. Franklin, and William Slany (Washington, DC: Government Printing Office, 1958), document 412.

17. Michael Sherry, *The Rise of American Air Power* (New Haven, CT: Yale University Press, 1987), 24, 27, 30; House of Commons, *Times* (London), 11 Nov. 1932, 7; Richard Overy, *The Bombing War* (London: Allen Lane, 2013), 48, 52.

18. "The Whirlwind of 'Bomber' Harris," *Air Force Magazine*, 1 Sep. 2011.

19. Overy, *Bombing War*, 325, 342, 346.

20. RAF Bomber Command, "Campaign Diary, July 1943," archived webpage, archived 6 Jul. 2007, UKNA, https://webarchive.nationalarchives.gov.uk/200707060 55428/http://www.raf.mod.uk/bombercommand/jul43.html; Richard Overy, "Allied Bombing and the Destruction of German Cities," in *A World at Total War*, ed. Roger Chickering, Stig Förster, and Bernd Greiner (Cambridge, UK: Cambridge University Press, 2005), 290.

21. Overy, *Bombing War*, 356–357, 619; US Strategic Bombing Survey, *Summary Report (European War)*, 30 Sep. 1945 (Maxwell Air Force Base, AL: Air University Press, 1987), https://www.airuniversity.af.edu/Portals/10/AUPress/Books/B_0020_SPANGRUD _STRATEGIC_BOMBING_SURVEYS.pdf. Phillips Payson O'Brien offers a spirited defense of strategic bombing in *How the War Was Won* (Cambridge, UK: Cambridge University Press, 2015). The most focused critique of airpower as a means of winning wars comes from Robert Pape, *Bombing to Win* (Ithaca, NY: Cornell University Press, 1996).

22. Adam Tooze, *The Wages of Destruction* (New York: Penguin, 2006), 597–598.

23. Carlo D'Este, *Bitter Victory* (London: Collins, 1988), 49–50.

24. Combined Chiefs of Staff minutes, 12 May 1943, in *FRUS, 1943, Conferences at Washington and Quebec*, ed. William Slany and Richardson Dougall (Washington, DC: Government Printing Office, 1970), document 29.

25. Combined Chiefs of Staff minutes, 13 May 1943, in *FRUS, 1943, Conferences at Washington and Quebec*, document 31; Henry Stimson and McGeorge Bundy, *On Active Service in Peace and War* (New York: Octagon, 1971), 527.

26. Combined Chiefs of Staff minutes, 14 May 1943, document 35; Combined Chiefs of Staff minutes, 18 May 1943, document 41; Combined Chiefs of Staff minutes, 19 May 1943, document 46; "Memorandum by the Combined Staff Planners," 25 May 1943, document 99. All in *FRUS, 1943, Conferences at Washington and Quebec*.

27. Harry L. Hopkins, memorandum, 17 Mar. 1943, in *FRUS, 1943*, vol. 3, *The British Commonwealth, Eastern Europe, the Far East*, ed. William M. Franklin and E. R. Perkins (Washington, DC: Government Printing Office, 1963), document 17; George Marshall, memorandum for General Handy, 30 Mar. 1943, in *The Papers of George Catlett Marshall*, vol. 3, *The Right Man for the Job*, ed. Larry Bland and Sharon Ritenour Stevens (Baltimore: Johns Hopkins University Press, 1991), 620–621. See also Gabriel Kolko, *The Politics of War* (New York: Random House, 1968), 28–29.

28. Denis Smyth, *Deathly Deception* (Oxford, UK: Oxford University Press, 2010), 1–4.

29. Douglas Porch, *The Path to Victory* (New York: Farrar, Straus and Giroux, 2004), 425–427, 432–433, 444.

30. D'Este, *Bitter Victory*, 430–431.

31. Porch, *Path to Victory*, 464–470.

32. Robert Citino, *The Wehrmacht Retreats* (Lawrence: University Press of Kansas, 2012), 119, 122, 124.

33. Georgy Zhukov, *The Memoirs of Marshal Zhukov* (New York: Delacorte, 1971), 2:151–152; David Glantz and Jonathan House, *When Titans Clashed*, rev. ed. (Lawrence: University Press of Kansas, 2015), 210–211, 214–217.

34. Many scholars now claim that Soviet commanders exaggerated German casualties in order to justify their own massive losses. If true, this challenges the notion that Kursk was a climactic tank battle. Stephen Fritz, *Ostkrieg* (Lexington: University Press of Kentucky, 2011), 344–350; *T-34 in Action*, ed. Artem Drabkin and Oleg Sheremet (Barnsley, England: Pen and Sword, 2006), 130–131.

35. Karl-Heinz Frieser, "The Battle of the Kursk Salient," in *GSWW*, vol. 8, *The Eastern Front, 1943–1944*, ed. Karl-Heinz Frieser (New York: Oxford University Press, 1990), 139–140, 145–146; David Glantz, *The Battle of Kursk* (Lawrence: University Press of Kansas, 1999), 217.

36. Evan Mawdsley, *Thunder in the East* (London: Bloomsbury, 2005), 267; Frieser, "Battle of the Kursk Salient," 170; Erich von Manstein, *Lost Victories* (Chicago: H. Regnery, 1958), 449–450.

37. Memorandum by the United States chiefs of staff, undated, document 85; Combined Chiefs of Staff minutes, 20 May 1943, document 52, both in *FRUS, 1943, Conferences at Washington and Quebec*.

38. Jan Karski, review of *A Most Unsordid Act*, by Warren Kimbal, *Annals of the American Academy of Political and Social Science* 388, no. 1 (Mar. 1970); Hsi-sheng Ch'i, "The Military Dimension, 1942–1945," in *China's Bitter Victory*, ed. James Hsiung and Steven Levine (Armonk, NY: M. E. Sharpe, 1992), 157, 159–160.

39. Hans van de Ven, *China at War* (Cambridge, MA: Harvard University Press, 2018), 165–166.

40. James Scott, *Target Tokyo* (New York: W. W. Norton, 2015), 375, 381–384.

41. Scott, 385–390.

42. Edward J. Drea and Hans van de Ven, "An Overview of Major Military Campaigns During the Sino-Japanese War, 1937–1945," in *The Battle for China*, ed. Mark Peattie, Edward Drea, and Hans van de Ven (Stanford, CA: Stanford University Press, 2011), 43–44.

43. Atcheson to Secretary of State, 28 May 1943, document 46; and Chiang Kai-shek to Roosevelt, 9 Dec. 1943, document 142, both in *FRUS, 1943, China*, ed. G. Bernard Noble and E. R. Perkins (Washington, DC: Government Printing Office, 1957).

44. Quoted in Alex Danchev, "Liddell Hart's Big Idea," *Review of International Studies* 25, no. 1 (Jan. 1999): 29–48.

CHAPTER 13: PLANNING THE POSTWAR WORLD

1. "Log of the Trip," in *FRUS, 1943, The Conferences at Cairo and Tehran*, ed. William M. Franklin and William Gerber (Washington, DC: Government Printing Office, 1961), document 246.

2. Warren Kimball, *Churchill and Roosevelt*, vol. 1, *Alliance Emerging October 1933–November 1942* (Princeton, NJ: Princeton University Press, 1984), 421; Michael Sherry, *Preparing for the Next War* (New Haven, CT: Yale University Press, 1977), 159–160; Albert Wedemeyer, *Wedemeyer Reports!* (New York: Holt, 1958), 94–95.

3. Lloyd Gardner, *Spheres of Influence* (Chicago: I. R. Dee, 1993), 148–149, 153.

4. See Vojtech Mastny, "Stalin and the Prospects of a Separate Peace in World War II," *American Historical Review* 77, no. 5 (Dec. 1972): 1365–1388.

5. Mark A. Stoler, *Allies and Adversaries* (Chapel Hill: University of North Carolina Press, 2000), 133.

6. William Bullitt to Roosevelt, 29 Jan. 1943, in *For the President, Personal and Secret*, ed. Orville H. Bullitt (Boston: Houghton Mifflin, 1972), 576–590.

7. Thomas Boghardt, *Covert Legions* (Washington, DC: Center of Military History, 2022), 9; Edward Moore Bennett, *Franklin D. Roosevelt and the Search for Security* (Wilmington, DE: Scholarly Resources, 1985), 71; Eden's comments as recorded by Harry Hopkins, in Robert Sherwood, *Roosevelt and Hopkins*, rev. ed. (New York: Harper, 1950), 708–709; Eden and Welles, memorandum of conversation, 16 Mar. 1943, in *FRUS*, 1943, vol. 3, *The British Commonwealth, Eastern Europe, the Far East*, ed. William M. Franklin and E. R. Perkins (Washington, DC: Government Printing Office, 1963), document 15.

8. Hopkins, memorandum, 17 Mar. 1943, in *FRUS* 1943, vol. 3, document 17; Mark Stoler, "The 'Second Front' and American Fear of Soviet Expansion, 1941–1943," *Military Affairs* 39, no. 3 (Oct. 1975): 136–141.

9. Stoler, *Allies and Adversaries*, 131–132; Walter Lippmann, *U.S. Foreign Policy* (Boston: Little, Brown, 1943), 146, 164.

10. Stoler, *Allies and Adversaries*, 129.

11. Stoler, 134; Bullitt to Roosevelt, 10 Aug. 1943, in Bullitt, *For the President*, 595–596.

12. Stoler, "'Second Front.'"

13. JCS, Memorandum for Information No. 121, "Strategy and Policy: Can America and Russia Cooperate?," 20 Aug. 1943, World War II: U.S. Documents on Planning, Operations, Intelligence, Axis War Crimes, and Refugees, ProQuest History Vault.

14. Maurice Matloff and Edwin Snell, *Strategic Planning for Coalition Warfare, 1941–1942* (Washington, DC: Center of Military History, 1999), 292–293; Burns to Hopkins, 10 Aug. 1943, in *FRUS*, 1943, *Conferences at Washington and Quebec*, ed. William Slany and Richardson Dougall (Washington, DC: Government Printing Office, 1970), document 317. This document is possibly the same as the one mentioned in the previous note from Matloff and is partially reproduced in Sherwood, *Roosevelt and Hopkins*, 748–749. Matloff notes that the original has not been found in Pentagon records: Matloff and Snell, *Strategic Planning for Coalition Warfare*, 293n45; Colonel Ordway, memo, 27 Aug. 1943, quoted in Matloff and Snell, *Strategic Planning for Coalition Warfare*, 287–288.

15. Richard Toye, *Churchill's Empire* (New York: Cambridge University Press, 2023), 230.

16. Jeremy Black, "Churchill as Strategist in the Second World War," in *Winston Churchill: Politics, Strategy, and Statecraft*, ed. Richard Toye (London: Bloomsbury Academic, 2017), 145–146.

17. Gerhard Weinberg, *Visions of Victory* (New York: Cambridge University Press, 2005), 144–145.

18. Max Hastings, *Overlord* (New York: Simon and Schuster, 1985), 22.

19. "Memorandum Prepared in the Operations Division of the War Department General Staff," 8 Aug. 1943, in *FRUS*, 1943, *Conferences at Washington and Quebec*, document 223; Henry Stimson and McGeorge Bundy, *On Active Service in War and Peace* (New York: Octagon, 1971), 437.

20. On Stalin's thinking, see Geoffrey Roberts, *Stalin's Wars* (New Haven, CT: Yale University Press, 2006), 188–191.

21. Roberts.

22. Rana Mitter, *Forgotten Ally* (Boston: Houghton Mifflin, 2013), 308–309.

23. Mitter, 307.

24. Jay Taylor, *The Generalissimo* (Cambridge, MA: Belknap Press of Harvard University Press, 2009), 245–253; Mitter, *Forgotten Ally*, 308, 310–313. On the choice between Mediterranean and Southeast Asian operations, see Combined Chiefs of Staff minutes, 24 Nov. 1943, in *FRUS*, 1943, *Conferences at Cairo and Tehran*, document 263.

25. Mitter, *Forgotten Ally*, 308–313.

26. Matloff and Snell, *Strategic Planning for Coalition Warfare*, 356, 360; Bohlen, minutes of the first plenary meeting, 28 Nov. 1943, in *FRUS*, 1943, *Conferences at Cairo and Tehran*, 360; Frank Costigliola, *Roosevelt's Lost Alliances* (Princeton, NJ: Princeton University Press, 2012), 192.

27. Costigliola, *Roosevelt's Lost Alliances*, 199–202; Bohlen, minutes, 29 Nov. 1943, in *FRUS*, 1943, *Conferences at Cairo and Tehran*, document 368.

28. Robert Dallek, *Franklin D. Roosevelt and American Foreign Policy* (New York: Viking, 2017), 439–441.

29. Douglas Porch, *The Path to Victory* (New York: Farrar, Straus and Giroux, 2004), 485–488, 493–494.

30. Robert Citino, *The Wehrmacht Retreats* (Lawrence: University Press of Kansas, 2012), 255–257, 260–261, 263–264; Orby Ledbetter, interview, 15 May 2001, World War II Veterans Oral History Collection, National Museum of the Pacific War, digitalarchive.pacificwarmuseum.org/; Lowell Hughes, interview, National WWII Museum, accessed July 26, 2024, https://www.ww2online.org.

31. Porch, *Path to Victory*, 504–507, 509–511.

32. The Gustav Line connected to a series of other positions, but for the sake of simplicity I refer to them collectively. Robert Citino, *Wehrmacht's Last Stand* (Lawrence: University Press of Kansas, 2017), 64–66; Martin Blumenson, *The Mediterranean Theater of Operations: Salerno to Cassino* (Washington, DC: Office of the Chief of Military History, US Army, 1969), 401; Carlo D'Este, *Eisenhower* (New York: Henry Holt, 2002), 459.

33. Rick Atkinson, *The Day of Battle* (New York: Henry Holt, 2007), 323, 327, 351, 360–363.

34. Citino, *Wehrmacht's Last Stand*, 79–84.

35. Porch, *Path to Victory*, 539–543; Richard J. Andrew, interview, 3 Aug. 2018, World War II Veterans Oral History Collection, National Museum of the Pacific War, digitalarchive.pacificwarmuseum.org.

36. Porch, *Path to Victory*, 547–560.

37. Atkinson, *Day of Battle*, 549, 568–575; "Gen. Clark Sees 2 Armies Beaten," *NYT*, 6 Jun. 1944.

38. John Lewis Gaddis, *The United States and the Origins of the Cold War* (New York: Columbia University Press, 1972), 89–90.

39. Gaddis argues in his footnotes that Stalin would have created a sphere of Soviet influence in Eastern Europe regardless of Allied actions in Italy. Gaddis, *Origins of the Cold War*, 90–91; Gabriel Kolko, *The Politics of War* (New York: Random House, 1968), 50–51.

40. Gaddis, *Origins of the Cold War*, 90–91.

41. For more on the importance of the Mediterranean for postwar American hegemony, see Andrew Buchanan, *American Grand Strategy in the Mediterranean During World War II* (Cambridge, UK: Cambridge University Press, 2014).

CHAPTER 14: CRACKING THE CO-PROSPERITY SPHERE

1. John Wukovits, *One Square Mile of Hell* (New York: NAL Caliber, 2006), 90, 101, 104, 112; Ian Toll, *The Conquering Tide* (New York: W. W. Norton, 2015), 319.

2. S. Matthew Cheser and Nicholas Roland, *Galvanic* (Annapolis, MD: Naval Institute Press, 2020), 29–30; Toll, *Conquering Tide*, 384–385.

3. Ronald Spector, *Eagle Against the Sun* (New York: Vintage, 1985), 224–226.

4. Paul Dull, *A Battle History of the Imperial Japanese Navy* (Annapolis, MD: Naval Institute Press, 1978), 267–268; John Rentz, *Bougainville and the Northern Solomons* (Washington, DC: Historical Section, Division of Public Information, US Marine Corps, 1948), 6.

5. Craig Symonds, *World War II at Sea* (New York: Oxford University Press, 2018), 402–407; Masuda Reiji, "Transport War," in *Japan at War*, ed. Haruko Taya Cook and Theodore F. Cook (New York: New Press, 1992), 300–302.

6. Toll, *Conquering Tide*, 203–206.

7. John Miller, *Cartwheel* (Washington, DC: Office of the Chief of Military History, 1959), 55; Spector, *Eagle Against the Sun*, 232–239; James E. T. Hopkins, interview, 20 Sep. 2003, World War II Veterans Oral History Collection, National Museum of the Pacific War, digitalarchive.pacificwarmuseum.org; William F. Halsey and J. Bryan, *Admiral Halsey's Story* (New York: Whittlesey House, 1947), 170–171.

8. Ernest Latta, interview, 23 Jul. 2004, World War II Veterans Oral History Collection, National Museum of the Pacific War, digitalarchive.pacificwarmuseum.org; Halsey and Bryan, *Admiral Halsey's Story*, 172.

9. Halsey and Bryan, *Admiral Halsey's Story*, 173–174.

10. Samuel Eliot Morison, *Breaking the Bismarcks Barrier* (London: Oxford University Press, 1948–1962), 299–304; Dull, *Imperial Japanese Navy*, 288–289; Robert Tippen, interview, 7 Dec. 2003, World War II Veterans Oral History Collection, National Museum of the Pacific War, digitalarchive.pacificwarmuseum.org.

11. Dull, *Imperial Japanese Navy*, 290–294; Halsey and Bryan, *Admiral Halsey's Story*, 180–181.

12. Morison, *Breaking the Bismarcks Barrier*, 286–287, 393–394, 400–402, 405; Toll, *Conquering Tide*, 240.

13. Samuel Eliot Morison, *Aleutians, Gilberts and Marshalls* (London: Oxford University Press, 1952), 70–75, 146–148; James Stockman, *The Battle for Tarawa* (Washington, DC: Historical Section, Division of Public Information, US Marine Corps, 1947).

14. Symonds, *World War II at Sea*, 490–493.

15. Robert Sherrod, *Tarawa* (New York: Skyhorse, 2013), 60–62.

16. Spector, *Eagle Against the Sun*, 259–265; George Charland, interview, 7 Dec. 1998; Lee Weber, interview, 23 Sep. 1999; and Olian Perry, interview, 22 Dec. 2008, all in World War II Veterans Oral History Collection, National Museum of the Pacific War, digitalarchive.pacificwarmuseum.org.

17. Toll, *Conquering Tide*, 354–355, 358–360; Charles Pace, interview, 12 Apr. 2001, World War II Veterans Oral History Collection, National Museum of the Pacific War, digitalarchive.pacificwarmuseum.org; Ira Schilling, interview, 2015, National WWII Museum, accessed 27 Jul. 2024, ww2online.org.

18. Charles Pace, interview; Morison, *Aleutians, Gilberts and Marshalls*, 183–184; Holland Smith, "Tarawa Was a Mistake," *Saturday Evening Post*, 6 Nov. 1948.

19. Toll, *Conquering Tide*, 384–385.

20. Spector, *Eagle Against the Sun*, 268–271; James Norwood, interview, 14 Nov. 2008, World War II Veterans Oral History Collection, National Museum of the Pacific War, digitalarchive.pacificwarmuseum.org.

21. Lieutenant Colonel Robert D. Heinl Jr. and Lieutenant Colonel John A. Crown, *The Marshalls* (Washington, DC: Historical Section, Division of Public Information, US Marine Corps, 1954); Morison, *Aleutians, Gilberts and Marshalls*, 317–319.

22. Marc Bernstein, "Hail Storm at Truk," *Naval History*, February 1994.

23. Morison, *Aleutians, Gilberts and Marshalls*, 332.

24. Louis Allen, *Burma* (London: Phoenix Giant, 1998), 166–167; Christopher Bayly and Tim Harper, *Forgotten Armies* (Cambridge, MA: Belknap Press of Harvard University Press, 2004), 361.

25. John Toland, *Rising Sun* (New York: Random House, 1970), 612–613.

26. Julian Thompson, *Forgotten Voices of Burma* (London: Ebury, 2010), 215–217, 227.

27. Thompson, *Forgotten Voices of Burma*, 252; Jon Latimer, *Burma* (London: John Murray, 2004), 272; Bayly and Harper, *Forgotten Armies*, 381–382, 388–390; Toland, *Rising Sun*, 613–615.

28. Hara Takeshi, "The Ichigo Offensive," in *The Battle for China*, ed. Mark Peattie, Edward Drea, and Hans van de Ven (Stanford, CA: Stanford University Press, 2011), 392, 395.

29. Wang Qisheng, "The Battle of Hunan and the Chinese Military's Response to Operation Ichigo," in Peattie, Drea, and van de Ven, *Battle for China*, 404–407.

30. Hans van de Ven, *China at War* (Cambridge, MA: Harvard University Press, 2018), 182–190.

31. Toland, *Rising Sun*, 619–620.

32. Takeshi, "Ichigo Offensive," 402.

33. See Andrew Buchanan, *From War to Postwar* (London: Bloomsbury, 2023), 3, 6.

CHAPTER 15: OVERLORD AND THE FATE OF THE WEST

1. Carl D. Proffitt, interview, 17 Feb. 2005, Military Oral History Collection, John A. Adams '71 Center for Military History and Strategic Analysis, VMI Archives, Virginia Military Institute, https://vmi.contentdm.oclc.org/digital/collection/p15821 coll13/id/434/.

2. Combined Chiefs of Staff minutes, 23 Aug. 1943, in *FRUS, 1943, Conferences at Washington and Quebec*, ed. William Slany and Richardson Dougall (Washington, DC: Government Printing Office, 1970), document 415; Maurice Matloff and Edwin Snell, *Strategic Planning for Coalition Warfare, 1941–1942* (Washington, DC: Center of Military History, 1999), 226; "Memorandum by the Chief of Staff to the Supreme Allied Commander Designate," 14 Aug. 1943, in *FRUS, 1943, Conferences at Washington and Quebec*, document 448.

3. "Minutes of the President's Meeting with the Joint Chiefs of Staff," 19 Nov. 1943, in *FRUS, 1943, The Conferences at Cairo and Tehran*, ed. William M. Franklin and William Gerber (Washington, DC: Government Printing Office, 1961), document 238; Mark A. Stoler, *Allies and Adversaries* (Chapel Hill: University of North Carolina Press, 2000), 164; Cornelius Ryan, *The Last Battle* (New York: Simon and Schuster, 1966), 148.

4. Daniel Harrington, "As Far as His Army Can Reach," *Diplomacy and Statecraft* 20, no. 4 (2009): 580–594. For an assessment of Churchill's proposal, see Thomas Barker, "The Ljubljana Gap Strategy," *Journal of Military History* 56, no. 1 (Jan. 1992): 57–86.

5. Paul Kennedy, *Engineers of Victory* (New York: Random House, 2013), 276.

6. Carlo D'Este, *Eisenhower* (New York: Henry Holt, 2002), 505.

7. George Gibbons, interview, 26 Aug. 2004, World War II Veterans Oral History Collection, National Museum of the Pacific War, digitalarchive.pacificwarmuseum.org.

8. Joseph L. Argenzio, interview, 30 Oct. 2006, Military Oral History Collection, John A. Adams '71 Center for Military History and Strategic Analysis, VMI Archives, Virginia Military Institute, https://digitalcollections.vmi.edu/digital/collection/p15821 coll13/id/22/rec/1.

9. Antony Beevor, *D-Day* (New York: Viking, 2009), 109–110, 142–145.

10. Dwight D. Eisenhower, "In Case of Failure Message," 5 Jun. 1944, Butcher Diary, 28 Jun.–14 Jul. 1944 (2), box 168, Principal File, "Papers, Pre-Presidential, 1916–52," Dwight D. Eisenhower Presidential Library, Museum, and Boyhood Home, Abilene, KS, https://www.eisenhowerlibrary.gov/sites/default/files/research/online-docu ments/d-day/in-case-of-failure-message.pdf. Precise casualty figures remain elusive because most units did not track them for the landings alone—rather, they calculated figures for the larger operation, including fighting after 6 Jun. 1944. The British losses seem to be the least defined. For estimates from the National D-Day Memorial Foundation, see Dave Roos, "How Many Were Killed on D-Day?," 3 Jun. 2019, https:// www.history.com/news/d-day-casualties-deaths-allies.

11. Robert Citino, *The Wehrmacht's Last Stand* (Lawrence: University Press of Kansas, 2017), 113, 117–120, 125–126.

12. Tami Davis Biddle, "Anglo-American Strategic Bombing," in *The Cambridge History of the Second World War*, vol. 1, *Fighting the War*, ed. John Ferris and Evan Mawdsley (Cambridge, UK: Cambridge University Press, 2015), 508–513; Beevor, *D-Day*, 153.

13. William Hitchcock, *The Bitter Road to Freedom* (New York: Free Press, 2008), 3, 28–31.

14. Rick Atkinson, *The Guns at Last Light* (New York: Henry Holt, 2013), 94.

15. Samuel D. Morris, interview, 22 Jun. 1944, "4th Infantry Division Action in Normandy, June 1944," p. 42, World War II: U.S. Documents on Planning, Operations, Intelligence, Axis War Crimes, and Refugees, ProQuest History Vault; Raymond VanDuzer, interview, 1 Jul. 2014, National WWII Museum, https://www.ww2online .org/view/raymond-vanduzer.

16. [Combat report of 12th Infantry Regiment, title illegible], "4th Infantry Division Action in Normandy, June 1944," p. 102, World War II: U.S. Documents on Planning, Operations, Intelligence, Axis War Crimes, and Refugees, ProQuest History Vault; Max Hastings, *Overlord* (New York: Simon and Schuster, 1985), 163–166; Atkinson, *Guns at Last Light*, 120.

17. Hastings, *Overlord*, 124, 127; John Cloudsley-Thompson, interview, 1 Aug. 2008, sound recording, reel 7, object 31558, Imperial War Museums, https://www.iwm .org.uk/collections/item/object/80031261; Edward Ronald Douglas Palmer, interview, 29 Nov. 1994, sound recording, reel 3, object 14800, Imperial War Museums, https: //www.iwm.org.uk/collections/item/object/80014400.

18. Atkinson, *Guns at Last Light*, 107–110. On Churchill's call to use poison gas, see Gerhard Weinberg, *A World at Arms*, 2nd ed. (New York: Cambridge University Press, 2005), 691.

19. Hastings, *Overlord*, 174–176.

20. Hitchcock, *Bitter Road to Freedom*, 32–35.

21. John Keegan, *Six Armies in Normandy* (New York: Penguin, 1994), 231–232.

22. Hastings, *Overlord*, 283.

23. Carlo D'Este, *Decision in Normandy* (New York: HarperPerennial, 1991), 428, 430–432.

24. Peter Simonds, *Maple Leaf Up, Maple Leaf Down* (New York: Island, 1946), 253–255; D'Este, *Decision in Normandy*, 431–432.

25. Chester Wilmot, *The Struggle for Europe* (New York: Harper, 1952), 444–446; Karl-Heinz Frieser, Part V, in *GSWW*, vol. 8, *The Eastern Front, 1943–1944*, ed. Karl-Heinz Frieser (New York: Oxford University Press, 1990), 491–492.

26. Frank Costigliola, *Roosevelt's Lost Alliances* (Princeton, NJ: Princeton University Press, 2012), 219.

27. Duff Cooper to Anthony Eden, 30 May 1944, Post-War General Policy, Part 3, WO 193/262, UKNA.

28. Lord Alan Brooke, entry of 27 Jul. 1944, in *War Diaries, 1939–1945*, ed. Alex Danchev and Daniel Todman (London: Weidenfeld and Nicolson, 2001), 575.

29. Henry Morgenthau, "Suggested Post-Surrender Program for Germany," 1944, folder Germany, 1944–1945, box 31, Safe File, Franklin D. Roosevelt, Papers as President: The President's Secretary's File (PSF), 1933–1945, Franklin D. Roosevelt Presidential Library and Museum, Hyde Park, NY, http://docs.fdrlibrary.marist.edu /PSF/BOX31/a297a01.html.

30. The letter, signed by Admiral William Leahy and dated 16 May 1944, is attached to "Briefing Book Paper," *FRUS*, 1945, *The Conferences at Malta and Yalta*, ed. Bryton Barron (Washington, DC: Government Printing Office, 1955), document 104.

31. This document includes JCS 973, "Fundamental Military Factors in Relation to Discussions Concerning Territorial Trusteeships and Settlements," drafted on 28 Jul. 1944; Marshall to Secretary of State, 3 Aug. 1944, in *FRUS*, 1944, vol. 1, *General*, ed. E. Ralph Perkins and S. Everett Gleason (Washington, DC: Government Printing Office, 1966), document 410.

32. Department of State briefing paper, undated [early September], in *FRUS*, 1944, *The Quebec Conference*, ed. Richardson Dougall, Arthur G. Kogan, Richard S. Patterson, and Irving L. Thomson (Washington, DC: Government Printing Office, 1972), document 122.

33. Memorandum by the counselor of embassy in the Soviet Union (Kennan), in *FRUS*, 1944, vol. 4, *Europe*, ed. E. Ralph Perkins et al. (Washington, DC: Government Printing Office, 1966), document 826.

34. As David Reynolds writes, "By the time Anglo American armies finally landed in Normandy, Germany had lost the war in Europe. What remained to be decided were the scale or its defeat and the division of the spoils." Reynolds, "World War II and Modern Meanings," *Diplomatic History* 25, no. 3 (Summer 2001): 464. Stephen Ambrose expressed a similar view, arguing that D-Day determined who would "rule in this world in the second half of the twentieth century," Nazism, communism, or the democracies. Stephen Ambrose, "D-Day: June 6, 1944," interview by Brian Lamb, *Booknotes*, C-SPAN, 25 May 1994, https://www.c-span.org/video/?57267-1/historian -stephen-ambrose-discusses-d-day-june-6-1944.

CHAPTER 16: BAGRATION AND THE FATE OF THE EAST

1. Ivan Yakushin, *On the Roads of War* (Barnsley, England: Pen and Sword, 2005), 96.

2. David Glantz and Jonathan House, *When Titans Clashed*, rev. ed. (Lawrence: University Press of Kansas, 2015), 256–257, 264–266.

3. Stephen Fritz, *Ostkrieg* (Lexington: University Press of Kentucky, 2011), 376–377.

4. Karl-Heinz Frieser, Part V, in *GSWW*, vol. 8, *The Eastern Front, 1943–1944*, ed. Karl-Heinz Frieser (New York: Oxford University Press, 1990), 515, 521.

5. On Soviet partisans, see Kenneth Slepyan, *Stalin's Guerrillas* (Lawrence: University Press of Kansas, 2006). Fritz, *Ostkrieg*, 406–410.

6. Karl-Heinz Frieser, Part V, in *GSWW*, 8:534–535.

7. Boris Gorbachevsky, *Through the Maelstrom* (Lawrence: University Press of Kansas, 2008), 313–314.

8. Robert Citino, *The Wehrmacht's Last Stand* (Lawrence: University Press of Kansas, 2017), 177–181, 189–190, 195–197.

9. Yakushin, *Roads of War*, 117, 120–121; David M. Glantz and Harold S. Orenstein, trans. and eds., *Belorussia 1944: The Soviet General Staff Study* (London: Frank Cass, 2001), 91; John Erickson, *The Road to Berlin* (Boulder: Westview, 1983), 227; Glantz and House, *When Titans Clashed*, 272.

10. Gorbachevsky, *Through the Maelstrom*, 314.

11. Gorbachevsky, 325, 327–329.

12. Evan Mawdsley, *Thunder in the East* (London: Bloomsbury, 2005), 307, 309–311.

13. Mawdsley, 307, 309–311.

14. Vojtech Mastny, *The Cold War and Soviet Insecurity* (New York: Oxford University Press, 1996), 20.

15. Glantz and House, *When Titans Clashed*, 272–277.

16. Yakushin, *Roads of War*, 140.

17. Quoted in Dan Stone, *The Liberation of the Camps* (New Haven, CT: Yale University Press, 2015), 36–38; and Anita Kondoy Anidi, "The Liberating Experience," *Russian Review* 69, no. 3 (Jul. 2010): 444, 446–447.

18. Vasily Grossman, "The Hell of Treblinka," in *The Road*, ed. Robert Chandler (New York: New York Review Books, 2010); Yitzhak Arad, *The Operation Reinhard Death Camps* (Bloomington: Indiana University Press, 2018), 121–123. The estimate of the number killed at Treblinka is from "Treblinka," Holocaust Encyclopedia (website), United States Holocaust Memorial Museum, 3 Mar. 2021, https://encyclopedia.ushmm .org/content/en/article/treblinka.

19. Thomas Childers, *The Third Reich* (New York: Simon and Schuster, 2017), 536–539.

20. Timothy Snyder, *Bloodlands* (New York: Basic, 2010), 298–299.

21. Norman Davies, *Rising '44* (London: Macmillan, 2003), 245–246, 251–252.

22. Karl-Heinz Frieser, Part V, in *GSWW*, 8:569, 580–583; Richard Overy, *Blood and Ruins* (New York: Viking, 2022), 700–701.

23. Davies, *Rising '44*, 266–267, 299; Snyder, *Bloodlands*, 304–305; Churchill to Roosevelt, eyewitness account of the Warsaw rising, 24 Aug. 1944, CAB 120/852, UKNA.

24. Bruce Kuniholm, *The Origins of the Cold War in the Near East* (Princeton, NJ: Princeton University Press, 1980), 104; Churchill to Roosevelt, text of telegram to Stalin, 4 Sep. 1944, CAB 120/852, UKNA; Harriman to Secretary of State, 15 Aug. 1944, document 1260, and Harriman to Secretary of State, 15 Aug. 1944, document 1261, both in *FRUS*, 1944, vol. 3, *The British Commonwealth and Europe*, ed. E. Ralph Perkins et al. (Washington, DC: Government Printing Office, 1965).

25. Stalin to Churchill and Roosevelt, 22 Aug. 1944, document 1271; Schoenfeld to Secretary of State, 24 Aug. 1944, document 1274. Both in *FRUS*, 1944, vol. 3.

26. R. P. Meiklejohn, quoted in Geoffrey Roberts, *Stalin's Wars* (New Haven, CT:

Yale University Press, 2006), 215; George Kennan, *Memoirs*, vol. 1, *1925–1950* (Boston: Little, Brown, 1967–1972), 221.

27. Roberts, *Stalin's Wars*, 206–207, 214–215.

28. Cordell Hull, *Memoirs* (New York: Macmillan, 1948), 1:1451–1453; Roosevelt to Churchill, 11 Jun. 1944, in *FRUS*, 1944, vol. 5, *The Near East, South Asia, and Africa, the Far East*, ed. E. Ralph Perkins et al. (Washington, DC: Government Printing Office, 1965), document 120.

29. This somewhat-embellished account is from Churchill's memoirs, as related in Lloyd Gardner, *Spheres of Influence* (Chicago: I. R. Dee, 1993), 198, 203.

30. See Robert Dallek, *Franklin D. Roosevelt and American Foreign Policy* (New York: Viking, 2017), 482–483.

31. Stephen Wertheim, *Tomorrow the World* (Cambridge, MA: Belknap Press of Harvard University Press, 2020), 12.

32. John Thompson, *A Sense of Power* (Ithaca, NY: Cornell University Press, 2015), 223, 230.

33. G. John Ikenberry, *A World Safe for Democracy* (New Haven, CT: Yale University Press, 2020), 178, 181; Adam Tooze and Jamie Martin, "The Economics of the War with Nazi Germany," in *The Cambridge History of the Second World War*, vol. 3, *Total War*, ed. Michael Geyer and Adam Tooze (Cambridge, UK: Cambridge University Press, 2015), 52–53; Randall Woods, *A Changing of the Guard* (Chapel Hill: University of North Carolina Press, 1990).

34. For more on Roosevelt's higher realism, see Warren Kimball, *The Juggler* (Princeton, NJ: Princeton University Press, 1991).

CHAPTER 17: WE CAN LAND ANYWHERE

1. Quoted in Ray Boomhower, *Dispatches from the Pacific* (Bloomington: Indiana University Press, 2017), 148–152.

2. Samuel Eliot Morison, *New Guinea and the Marianas* (London: Oxford University Press, 1953), 4–9.

3. Ronald Spector, *Eagle Against the Sun* (New York: Vintage, 1985), 299–300.

4. Carl Hoffman, *Saipan* (Washington, DC: Historical Division, US Marine Corps, 1950), 2–4.

5. Craig Symonds, *World War II at Sea* (New York: Oxford University Press, 2018), 539–540.

6. Ian Toll, *The Conquering Tide* (New York: W. W. Norton, 2015), 464–466.

7. Frank Borta, interview, undated, World War II Veterans Oral History Collection, National Museum of the Pacific War, digitalarchive.pacificwarmuseum.org.

8. Symonds, *World War II at Sea*, 543–546.

9. Spector, *Eagle Against the Sun*, 306; Alex Vraciu, interview, 9 Oct. 1994, World War II Veterans Oral History Collection, National Museum of the Pacific War, digitalarchive.pacificwarmuseum.org.

10. Morison, *New Guinea and the Marianas*, 279–282.

11. Toll, *Conquering Tide*, 488–497.

12. William Y'Blood, *Red Sun Setting* (Annapolis, MD: Naval Institute Press, 1981), 213.

13. Waldo Heinrichs and Marc Gallicchio, *Implacable Foes* (New York: Oxford University Press, 2017), 111–122.

14. Harold Goldberg, *D-Day in the Pacific* (Bloomington: Indiana University Press, 2007), 172–174, 180, 188–191.

15. John Dower, *War Without Mercy* (New York: Pantheon, 1986), 45; Haruko Taya Cook, "The Myth of the Saipan Suicides," *MHQ*, Spring 1995.

16. Richard Frank, *Downfall* (New York: Random House, 1999), 89; Toll, *Conquering Tide*, 530–534.

17. Hoffman, *Saipan*, 261–262.

18. Ian Toll, *Twilight of the Gods* (New York: W. W. Norton, 2020), 76.

19. Spector, *Eagle Against the Sun*, 418–419; Heinrichs and Gallicchio, *Implacable Foes*, 152–153.

20. Heinrichs and Gallicchio, *Implacable Foes*, 160, 162.

21. E. B. Sledge, *With the Old Breed* (New York: Presidio, 2007), 55–56, 120, 140–142.

22. Spector, *Eagle Against the Sun*, 426.

23. Paul Dull, *A Battle History of the Imperial Japanese Navy* (Annapolis, MD: Naval Institute Press, 1978), 315.

24. Symonds, *World War II at Sea*, 566–572.

25. Toll, *Twilight of the Gods*, 237–240.

26. Spector, *Eagle Against the Sun*, 434–435.

27. Heinrichs and Gallicchio, *Implacable Foes*, 183–186.

28. Symonds, *World War II at Sea*, 582.

29. Toll, *Twilight of the Gods*, 291–292, 295–297.

30. Evan Mawdsley, *War for the Seas* (New Haven, CT: Yale University Press, 2019), 457–459.

31. H. P. Willmott, *The Battle of Leyte Gulf* (Bloomington: Indiana University Press, 2005), 3, 240–241.

CHAPTER 18: INTO THE REICH

1. Rick Atkinson, *The Guns at Last Light* (New York: Henry Holt, 2013), 173–178.

2. Cornelius Ryan, *A Bridge Too Far* (New York: Simon and Schuster, 1974).

3. Carlo D'Este, *Eisenhower* (New York: Henry Holt, 2002), 606. The most thorough analysis of the debate can be found in G. E. Patrick Murray, *Eisenhower Versus Montgomery* (Westport, CT: Praeger, 1996), 56–61, 72, 81–84, 175.

4. John Buckley, *Monty's Men* (New Haven, CT: Yale University Press, 2013), 16–17. For troop figures, see Forrest Pogue, *The Supreme Command* (Washington, DC: Center of Military History, 2017), 542–543. For GDP and war production figures, see Mark Harrison, *The Economics of World War II* (New York: Cambridge University Press, 1998), 10, 15.

5. Roland Ruppenthal, *Logistical Support of the Armies* (Washington, DC: Office of the Chief of Military History, Department of the Army, 1958), 5–7, 134–137; Rookard quoted in Rudi Williams, "African Americans Gain Fame as World War II Red Ball Express Drivers," American Forces Press Service, 15 Feb. 2002, reproduced in George Johnson, *Profiles in Hue* (Xlibris, 2011), 178–180.

6. Alistair Horne, "Antwerp," *MHQ*, Summer 2004, 36–47.

7. Buckley, *Monty's Men*, 212–213.

8. D'Este, *Eisenhower*, 612–615.

9. Max Hastings, *Armageddon* (London: Macmillan, 2004), 48–49, 55–56.

10. Hastings, *Armageddon*, 61–63; Combat Interviews, 82nd Airborne Division, Holland, 17–26 Sep. 1944, ProQuest History Vault, 213.

11. Cornelius Ryan's *A Bridge Too Far* is the classic account of Market Garden. For a more recent study, see Antony Beevor, *The Battle of Arnhem* (New York: Viking, 2018).

12. William Hitchcock, *The Bitter Road to Freedom* (New York: Free Press, 2008), 101–122.

13. Horne, "Antwerp."

14. Hastings, *Armageddon*, 154–158.

15. Charles MacDonald, *The Siegfried Line Campaign* (Washington, DC: Center of Military History, 1993), 29, 34, 309–311, 320.

16. Atkinson, *Guns at Last Light*, 343, 348–349; Hastings, *Armageddon*, 79.

17. Antony Beevor, *Ardennes 1944* (London: Viking, 2015), 57, 61–63; MacDonald, *Siegfried Line Campaign*, 493; David Roderick, interview, 2 Jun. 2008, National WWII Museum, https://www.ww2online.org/view/david-roderick; 4th Infantry Division in the Battle of Hürtgen Forest, 7 Nov.–11 Dec. 1944, p. 297, World War II Combat Interviews: Armed Forces Oral History, ProQuest History Vault.

18. Detlef Vogel, "The Battles on the Western Front from September 1944 to January 1945," in *GSWW*, vol. 7, *The Strategic Air War in Europe and the War in the West and East Asia, 1943-1944/5*, ed. Horst Boog, Gerhard Krebs, and Detlef Vogel (New York: Oxford University Press, 2006), 679–681.

19. Peter Caddick-Adams, *Snow and Steel* (New York: Oxford University Press, 2015), 99–101.

20. Beevor, *Ardennes 1944*, 104.

21. Charles MacDonald, *A Time for Trumpets* (New York: W. Morrow, 1984), 102; Caddick-Adams, *Snow and Steel*, 374–376.

22. D'Este, *Eisenhower*, 639–646.

23. Beevor, *Ardennes 1944*, 96–97, 145–147, 164.

24. Hugh Cole, *The Ardennes* (Washington, DC: Center of Military History, 1993), 422; Atkinson, *Guns at Last Light*, 428.

25. Atkinson, *Guns at Last Light*, 451–456, 462–467.

26. MacDonald, *Time for Trumpets*, 521–523, 526–527, 532; Beevor, *Ardennes 1944*, 290, 292; Michael Collins and Martin King, *Voices of the Bulge* (Minneapolis: Zenith, 2011), 212–215.

27. D'Este, *Eisenhower*, 655–658.

28. Beevor, *Ardennes 1944*, 367; Patton, diary entry, 27 Dec. 1944, in Martin Blumenson, ed., *The Patton Papers*, vol. 2, *1940 to 1945* (Boston: Houghton Mifflin, 1974), 608; Caddick-Adams, *Snow and Steel*, 635.

29. See Peter Mansoor, *The G.I. Offensive in Europe* (Lawrence: University Press of Kansas, 1999), 184–185.

CHAPTER 19: THE RACE TO BERLIN

1. Antony Beevor, *The Fall of Berlin, 1945* (London: Viking, 2002), 16–18.

2. David Glantz and Jonathan House, *When Titans Clashed*, rev. ed. (Lawrence: University Press of Kansas, 2015), 307–308, 310–312.

3. Ishaan Tharoor, "What a Soviet Soldier Saw When His Unit Liberated Auschwitz 70 Years Ago," *Washington Post*, 27 Jan. 2015; Max Hastings, *Armageddon* (London: Macmillan, 2004), 285–286.

4. S. M. Plokhy, *Yalta* (New York: Viking, 2010), 37–39, 43–44.

5. Plokhy, 17, 78–79.

6. Deane to Marshall, 2 Dec. 1944, in *FRUS*, 1945, *The Conferences at Malta and Yalta*, ed. Bryton Barron (Washington, DC: Government Printing Office, 1955), document 287.

7. Harriman to Secretary of State, 10 Jan. 1945, in *FRUS*, 1945, *Conferences at Malta and Yalta*, document 288.

8. Harriman to Hopkins, 10 Sep. 1944, in *FRUS*, 1944, vol. 4, *Europe*, ed. E. Ralph Perkins et al. (Washington, DC: Government Printing Office, 1966), document 901; Michael Dobbs, *Six Months in 1945* (New York: Knopf, 2012), 7.

9. Geoffrey Roberts, *Stalin's Wars* (New Haven, CT: Yale University Press, 2006), 236.

10. Plokhy, *Yalta*, 91, 393.

11. See Marc Trachtenberg, *A Constructed Peace* (Princeton, NJ: Princeton University Press, 1999), 17–23; and Michael Neiberg, *Potsdam* (New York: Basic, 2015), 176–183.

12. Roosevelt, address to Congress, 1 Mar. 1945, transcript from the American Presidency Project, University of California, Santa Barbara, https://www.presidency.ucsb.edu/documents/address-congress-the-yalta-conference; Hopkins quoted in Dobbs, *Six Months*, 95–96.

13. Plokhy, *Yalta*, 392–395; Dobbs, *Six Months*, 108.

14. Glantz and House, *When Titans Clashed*, 315–318, 324.

15. Glantz and House, 318.

16. Vladimir Pechatnov, "The Soviet Union and the World, 1944–1953," in *The Cambridge History of the Cold War*, vol. 1, *Origins*, ed. Melvyn P. Leffler and Odd Arne Westad (Cambridge, UK: Cambridge University Press, 2010), 92–95.

17. Norman Naimark, "The Sovietization of Eastern Europe," in Leffler and Westad, *Cambridge History of the Cold War*, 1:195–197; Evan Mawdsley, *Thunder in the East* (London: Bloomsbury, 2005), 311.

18. Dobbs, *Six Months*, 133–134.

19. See Carlo D'Este, *Eisenhower* (New York: Henry Holt, 2002), 672–678.

20. "78th Infantry Division's Capture of the Roer Dams," 30 Jan.–10 Feb. 1945, World War II Combat Interviews, ProQuest History Vault; Rick Atkinson, *The Guns at Last Light* (New York: Henry Holt, 2013), 315, 536–538.

21. Tami Davis Biddle, "Dresden 1945," *Journal of Military History* 72, no. 2 (Apr. 2008).

22. Michael Sherry, *The Rise of American Air Power* (New Haven, CT: Yale University Press, 1987), 260; Biddle, "Dresden 1945."

23. Sherry, *Rise of American Air Power*, 260–261.

24. Atkinson, *Guns at Last Light*, 546–550; "9th Army Engineering Problems and Operations in Crossing of the Rhine River," 24 Mar.–1 May 1945, World War II Combat Interviews: Armed Forces Oral Histories, ProQuest History Vault.

25. Charles MacDonald, *The Last Offensive* (New York: Barnes and Noble, 1995), 215–219.

26. Robert Citino, *The Wehrmacht's Last Stand* (Lawrence: University Press of Kansas, 2017), 439–440.

27. D'Este, *Eisenhower*, 683; Peter Caddick-Adams, *Fire and Steel* (New York: Oxford University Press, 2022), 233.

28. JCS, Memorandum for Information No. 121, "Strategy and Policy: Can America and Russia Cooperate?," 20 Aug. 1943, World War II: U.S. Documents on Planning, Operations, Intelligence, Axis War Crimes, and Refugees, ProQuest History Vault; Dobbs, *Six Months*, 145–146; Harriman to Secretary of State, 2 Apr. 1945, in *FRUS*, 1945, vol. 5, *Europe*, ed. Rogers P. Churchill et al. (Washington, DC: Government Printing Office, 1969), document 621.

29. Averell Harriman to Secretary of State, 12 Mar. 1945, document 516; Bohlen to Secretary of State, 13 Mar. 1945, document 518; Stalin to Roosevelt, 3 Apr. 1943,

document 532; Churchill to Roosevelt, 5 Apr. 1945, document 535, all in *FRUS*, 1945, vol. 3, *European Advisory Commission, Austria*, ed. William Slany et al. (Washington, DC: Government Printing Office); Gerhard Weinberg, *A World at Arms*, 2nd ed. (New York: Cambridge University Press, 2005), 818–819.

30. Supreme Headquarters Allied Expeditionary Force (SHAEF) to War Department, 31 Mar. 1945, folder: Allied Western Front Offensive and Invasion of Germany, 1 Mar.–30 Apr. 1945, Map Room Files, FDRL, ProQuest History Vault.

31. Churchill to Roosevelt, 1 Apr. 1945, folder: Allied Western Front Offensive and Invasion of Germany, 1 Mar.–30 Apr. 1945, Map Room Files, FDRL, ProQuest History Vault.

32. SHAEF to War Department, 7 Apr. 1945, folder: Allied Western Front Offensive and Invasion of Germany, 1 Mar.–30 Apr. 1945, Map Room Files, FDRL, ProQuest History Vault.

33. I. S. Konev, "Strike from the South," in *Stalin and His Generals*, ed. Seweryn Bialer (New York: Pegasus, 1969), 516–517; Dobbs, *Six Months*, 150–151.

34. Harriman to Secretary of State, 4 Apr. 1945, document 622; and Harriman to Secretary of State, 6 Apr. 1945, document 624, both in *FRUS*, 1945, vol. 5.

35. Frank Costigliola, *Roosevelt's Lost Alliances* (Princeton, NJ: Princeton University Press, 2012), 256.

36. Harriman to Secretary of State, 13 Apr. 1945, document 627; and Harriman to Secretary of State, 13 Apr. 1945, document 628, both in *FRUS*, 1945, vol. 5.

37. Dobbs, *Six Months*, 163–164; Bohlen, memorandum of conversation, 20 Apr. 1945, in *FRUS*, 1945, vol. 5, document 190.

38. "Minutes of the Secretary of State's Staff Committee," 20 Apr. 1945, document 632; "Minutes of the Secretary of State's Staff Committee," 21 Apr. 1945, document 633, both in *FRUS*, 1945, vol. 5.

39. Bohlen, memorandum of a meeting at the White House, 23 Apr. 1945, in *FRUS*, 1945, vol. 5, document 195.

40. Bohlen, memorandum of conversation, 23 Apr. 1945, in *FRUS*, 1945, vol. 5, document 196; Diane Clemens, "Averell Harriman, John Deane, the Joint Chiefs of Staff, and the 'Reversal of Co-operation' with the Soviet Union in April 1945," *International History Review* 14, no. 2 (May 1992): 277–306.

41. Costigliola, *Roosevelt's Lost Alliances*, 326.

42. Annie Jacobsen, *Operation Paperclip* (New York: Little, Brown, 2014), 41–42.

43. Jacobsen, *Operation Paperclip*, 12–14; "VII Corps Discovery and Cleaning Out of Concentration Camp at Nordhausen, Germany," 14 Apr. 1945, World War II Combat Interviews: Armed Forces Oral Histories, ProQuest History Vault.

44. Jacobsen, *Operation Paperclip*, 33–34, 66–69, 98–100.

45. Ibid.

46. Norman Naimark, *The Russians in Germany* (Cambridge, MA: Belknap Press of Harvard University Press, 1995), 206–212.

47. Naimark, 206–212; Paul Maddrell, *Spying on Science* (New York: Oxford University Press, 2006), 25–26.

48. Stephen Fritz, *Ostkrieg* (Lexington: University Press of Kentucky, 2011), 459–460.

49. Glantz and House, *When Titans Clashed*, 327–332; Fritz, *Ostkrieg*, 461.

50. Beevor, *Fall of Berlin*, 155–156, 177–178.

51. Cornelius Ryan, *The Last Battle* (New York: Simon and Schuster, 1966), 331–334, 343.

52. Ryan, 342, 345, 347.

53. Citino, *Wehrmacht's Last Stand*, 458–459; Beevor, *Fall of Berlin*, 226, 234.

54. Ian Kershaw, *Hitler, 1936–1945* (London: Penguin, 2001), 803–804, 811.

55. Beevor, *Fall of Berlin*, 310–311, 316–318.

56. Naimark, *Russians in Germany*, 72, 80, 133.

57. Beevor, *Fall of Berlin*, 340, 354–356, 365–366, 372.

58. Kershaw, *Hitler*, 826–828.

59. "The Russian-American Linkup, 25 April 1945," 69th Infantry Division Contacts with Russian Forces on the Banks of the Elbe River, 25–26 Apr. 1945, World War II Combat Interviews: Armed Forces Oral Histories, ProQuest History Vault.

60. Ibid.

61. Atkinson, *Guns at Last Light*, 625–626.

62. Joint Planning Staff, "Operation 'Unthinkable,'" 22 May 1945, CAB 120/691, "Russian Threat to Western Civilisation," UKNA; Ismay to Churchill, 8 Jun. 1945, CAB 120/691; Churchill to Ismay, 10 Jun. 1945, CAB 120/691; all in UKNA.

63. Max Hastings, *Winston's War* (New York: Knopf, 2010), 6; Andrew Lownie, *Stalin's Englishman* (London: Hodder and Stoughton, 2015), 148.

64. Joint Intelligence Staff, "Russian Capabilities," 23 Oct. 1945, JIC 250/3/M, World War II: U.S. Documents on Planning, Operations, Intelligence, Axis War Crimes, and Refugees, ProQuest History Vault.

CHAPTER 20: STARING INTO THE MOUTH OF HELL

1. US Strategic Bombing Survey, *The Effects of the Atomic Bombs on Hiroshima and Nagasaki* (Washington, DC: Government Printing Office, 1946), 3; David Glantz and Jonathan House, *When Titans Clashed*, rev. ed. (Lawrence: University Press of Kansas, 2015), 378.

2. Waldo Heinrichs and Marc Gallicchio, *Implacable Foes* (New York: Oxford University Press, 2017), 194–204.

3. Ian Toll, *Twilight of the Gods* (New York: W. W. Norton, 2020), 370–374, 378; Rikihei Inoguchi, *The Divine Wind* (Annapolis, MD: US Naval Institute Press, 1958), appendix A; Paul Ignatius, interview, 8 Sep. 2022, National WWII Museum, https://www.ww2online.org/view/paul-ignatius.

4. James Scott, *Rampage* (New York: W. W. Norton, 2018), 52, 76–77, 88, 97.

5. Scott, 92–97, 203–205, 222–223.

6. Scott, 277–278, 351–353, 393–398, 403, 422–424.

7. Ronald Spector, *Eagle Against the Sun* (New York: Vintage, 1985), 526–527.

8. Toll, *Twilight of the Gods*, 336–339.

9. Joseph Alexander, *Storm Landings* (Annapolis, MD: Naval Institute Press, 2012), 127.

10. George Garand and Truman Strobridge, *History of U.S. Marine Corps Operations in World War II*, vol. 4, *Western Pacific Operations* (Washington, DC: Historical Division, US Marine Corps, 1971), 444–447, 449–450, 453, 455, 458.

11. Garand and Strobridge, 502, 505–506, 508; George B. Raffield, interview, undated, World War II Veterans Oral History Collection, National Museum of the Pacific War.

12. John Toland, *Rising Sun* (New York: Random House, 1970), 653–657.

13. Heinrichs and Gallicchio, *Implacable Foes*, 276–278; Holland Smith and Percy Finch, *Coral and Brass* (New York: Charles Scribner's Sons, 1949), 265.

14. Toll, *Twilight of the Gods*, 499, 509, 513–515.

15. Toll, 515–516. For a debate on the need to take Iwo Jima, see Robert Burrell, *The Ghosts of Iwo Jima* (College Station: Texas A&M University Press, 2006), and a response from Brian Hanley, "The Myth of Iwo Jima: A Rebuttal," *Journal of Military History* 69, no. 3 (July 2005): 801–808.

16. Richard Frank, *Downfall* (New York: Random House, 1999), 48, 53, 58–59, 62.

17. Ibid.

18. Barrett Tillman, *Whirlwind* (New York: Simon and Schuster, 2010), 102, 137–139.

19. James Scott, *Black Snow* (New York: W. W. Norton, 2022), 192–193, 209–210, 220–223.

20. Scott, 225–226, 238–240, 248–250, 253–257.

21. Roy Appleman et al., *Okinawa* (Washington, DC: Center of Military History, 1993), 3, 6–10, 84, 92–93, 485.

22. Saul David, *Crucible of Hell* (New York: Hachette, 2020), 2–11.

23. Toll, *Twilight of the Gods*, 575–581.

24. Craig Symonds, *World War II at Sea* (New York: Oxford University Press, 2018), 626–629.

25. Heinrichs and Gallicchio, *Implacable Foes*, 384–388, 395, 406–407, 411–412.

26. See Toll, *Twilight of the Gods*, 640.

27. Stimson to Truman, 2 Jul. 1945, in *FRUS*, 1945, vol. 1, *The Conference of Berlin (The Potsdam Conference)*, ed. Richardson Dougall et al. (Washington, DC: Government Printing Office, 1960), document 592.

28. "Memorandum by the Secretary of the Joint Chiefs of Staff," 18 Jun. 1945, in *FRUS*, vol. 1, document 592.

29. For discussions of the casualty estimates and the enduring scholarly debates surrounding them, see Frank, *Downfall*, 339–343; and J. Samuel Walker, *Prompt and Utter Destruction*, rev. ed. (Chapel Hill: University of North Carolina Press, 2004), 116–119.

30. Edward Drea, "Previews of Hell," *American Intelligence Journal* 16, no. 1 (Spring/Summer 1995): 51–57.

31. Tsuyoshi Hasegawa, *Racing the Enemy* (Cambridge, MA: Belknap Press of Harvard University Press, 2005), 72–73.

32. Hasegawa, *Racing the Enemy*, 19, 25; David Glantz, *August Storm: The Soviet 1945 Strategic Offensive in Manchuria* (Washington, DC: Government Printing Office, 1984), 6–7.

33. Hasegawa, *Racing the Enemy*, 220–221, 265.

34. Groves to Stimson, "The Test," 18 Jul. 1945, RG 77, MED Records, Top Secret Documents, File no. 4, National Security Archive, George Washington University, Washington, DC, https://nsarchive.gwu.edu/document/28465-document-46-memo randum-general-l-r-groves-secretary-war-test-july-18-1945-top-secret.

35. Both quotes are observations from the Stimson diary entries for 16–25 Jul., Sterling Library, Yale University, copy available on the National Security Archive website, https://nsarchive.gwu.edu/document/28467-document-48-stimson-diary-entries -july-16-through-25-1945; Gar Alperovitz, *The Decision to Use the Bomb* (New York: Knopf, 1995), 143–144, 260–261.

36. Martin Sherwin, *A World Destroyed*, 3rd ed. (Stanford, CA: Stanford University Press, 2003), 227.

37. Walker, *Prompt and Utter Destruction*, 69–72.

38. Ibid.

39. Richard Rhodes, *The Making of the Atomic Bomb* (New York: Simon and Schuster, 1986), 806–824.

40. Hasegawa, *Racing the Enemy*, 185–186; David Holloway, *Stalin and the Bomb* (New Haven, CT: Yale University Press, 1996), 127.

41. David Glantz, *The Soviet Strategic Offensive in Manchuria, 1945* (London: Frank Cass, 2003), 48, 180–181; Max Hastings, *Retribution* (New York: Knopf, 2008), 482, 487.

42. Hastings, *Retribution*, 492–496.

43. Hasegawa, *Racing the Enemy*, 193–194, 197–198.

44. Zenshiro Hoshina, *Daitoa Senso Hishi* (Tokyo: Hara-Shobo, 1975), 139–149, unpublished translation by Hikaru Tajima, National Security Archive, George Washington University, Washington, DC, https://nsarchive.gwu.edu/briefing-book/nuclear-vault/2020-08-04/atomic-bomb-end-world-war-ii.

45. Hoshina, *Daitoa Senso Hishi*, 139–149.

46. Henry Wallace, diary entry, 10 Aug. 1945, Papers of Henry A. Wallace, Special Collections Department, University of Iowa Libraries, Iowa City, IA, available through National Security Archive, George Washington University, Washington, DC, https://nsarchive.gwu.edu/briefing-book/nuclear-vault/2020-08-04/atomic-bomb-end-world-war-ii.

47. Hasegawa, *Racing the Enemy*, 241–242; Yukiko Koshiro, *Imperial Eclipse* (Ithaca, NY: Cornell University Press, 2013), 243; S. C. M. Paine, *The Japanese Empire* (New York: Cambridge University Press, 2017), 170.

48. Hasegawa, *Racing the Enemy*, 242–250.

49. Hastings, *Retribution*, 526–528.

50. Douglas MacArthur, *Reports of General MacArthur*, vol. 1, *The Campaigns of MacArthur in the Pacific* (Washington, DC: Government Printing Office, 1966), 455; David Holloway, *Stalin and the Bomb* (New Haven, CT: Yale University Press, 1996), 132.

51. Michael Schaller, "Securing the Great Crescent," *Journal of American History* 69, no. 2 (Sep. 1982): 392.

CONCLUSION: FOREVER WAR

1. Walter Isaacson and Evan Thomas, *The Wise Men* (New York: Simon and Schuster, 1988), 303–304; Walter Millis, ed., *The Forrestal Diaries* (New York: Viking, 1951), 79.

2. George Marshall to Secretary of State, 3 Aug. 1944, in *FRUS*, 1944, vol. 1, *General*, ed. E. Ralph Perkins and S. Everett Gleason (Washington, DC: Government Printing Office, 1966), document 410.

3. Tony Judt, *Postwar* (New York: Penguin, 2005), 13–17.

4. Werner Gruhl, *Imperial Japan's World War Two* (New Brunswick, NJ: Transaction, 2007), 20, 149–153.

5. Frank Costigliola, *Roosevelt's Lost Alliances* (Princeton, NJ: Princeton University Press, 2012), 158; Tim Harper, "A Long View on the Great Asian War," in *Legacies of World War II in South and East Asia*, ed. David Koh Wee Hock (Singapore: Institute of Southeast Asian Studies, 2007), 12–13; Robert Trumbull, "The West Loses 'Face' in the East," *NYT*, 1 Dec. 1946; Yukiko Koshiro, *Trans-Pacific Racisms and the U.S. Occupation of Japan* (New York: Columbia University Press, 1999), 18.

6. The direct connection between Holocaust consciousness and the human rights movement remains controversial. See G. Daniel Cohen, "The Holocaust and the

'Human Rights Revolution,'" in *The Human Rights Revolution*, ed. Akira Iriye, Petra Goedde, and William Hitchcock (New York: Oxford University Press, 2012).

7. See Paul Thomas Chamberlin, *The Cold War's Killing Fields* (New York: Harper, 2018).

8. Christopher Thorne, *The Issue of War* (New York: Oxford University Press, 1985), 196.

9. I borrow the term from Rana Mitter's *Forgotten Ally* (Boston: Houghton Mifflin, 2013).

10. See Marc Gallicchio, "World War II in Historical Memory," in *A Companion to World War II*, ed. Thomas Zeiler and Daniel M. DuBois (Hoboken, NJ: Wiley-Blackwell, 2013), 978–988.

11. Rana Mitter, *China's Good War* (Cambridge, MA: Belknap Press of Harvard University Press, 2020).

INDEX

INDEX

INDEX

INDEX

trans-Pacific offensive of, 239
US code-breaking of, 217, 250
US intelligence on, 216–217
imperialism. *See also* colonial warfare;
colonialism; Germany; Great Britain;
Italy; Japan; United States
as international order after World War
I, 14–15
League of Nation mandates as, 12,
19–20
in Mediterranean theater, 376–377
US relationship with, 440
Inahara, Katsuji, 51
India, 230, 238, 246, 395, 400
Indian Ocean, British forces in, 248
Indochina, Japanese occupation of,
211–212
Indonesia, 232
The Influence of Sea Power upon History
(Mahan), 15
Ingersoll, Ralph, 136
International Military Tribunal for the
Far East, 77–78
International Monetary Fund, 442
international relations, 16–17, 19
International Relations (Buell), 17
Ioffe, Ezri, 271
Iowa, USS, 403–404
Iraq, 162
Allied troops in, 159
British troops in, 157–158
establishment as League of Nation
mandate, 12, 19–20
rebellion against imperialism in, 20
Iraqi Revolt, 276
Ishikawa, Shingo, 213
Ishiwara, Kanji, 46–47
Ismay, Hastings, 159
Itagaki, Seishiro, 47
Italy. *See also* Mussolini, Benito
Allied forces struggle over, 368–376
Anti-Comintern Pact and, 66, 142
Battle of Anzio, 371–374
establishment as imperial power, 35,
54–58

Grand Council of Fascism in, 339
invasion of Sicily, 337–340
in Mediterranean theater, 245
National Fascist Party in, 25–26
occupation of Ethiopia, 54–58
Operation Diadem, 373–374
Operation Mincemeat, 338
territorial gains after World War I, 25
in Tripartite Pact, 142
Iwabuchi, Sanji, 528

Japan. *See also* Greater Asia
Co-Prosperity Sphere; *special topics*
anticolonialism in, 142
Anti-Comintern Pact and, 66, 142
assassination of civilian leaders
in, 53
atomic bomb attacks in, 9, 525
attack on Shanghai, China, 51–52
attempted invasion of India, 400
Battle of Iwo Jima, 530–536
Battle of Okinawa, 539–543
biological weapons used by, 346
bombing campaigns against, 536–543
in Burma, 394–399
Cherry Blossom Society in, 45
Chinese conflict with, 31
colonial warfare and, 7
colonialist expansion by, 30–35, 72
establishment as imperial power, 35
expansion into Russia, 84–85
expansion into Southeast Asia, 218
First Sino-Japanese War, 33
Fundamentals of National Policy, 68
*General Principles of National Defence
Policy*, 67
Great Depression in, 45
Hiroshima, 9, 525, 550–552
home islands, 34, 543–545
Ichigo Offensive, 397, 399, 457
imperial expansion of, 66–69
Imperial Navy, 239, 252–260
Kwantung Army in, 45–48
Manchukuo as puppet state of, 64–65
military strength of, 32–33

INDEX

Credit: Tony Bui

Paul Thomas Chamberlin is an associate professor of history at Columbia University. The author of *The Cold War's Killing Fields* and *The Global Offensive*, his writing has appeared in the *New York Times*, *Washington Post*, and *Christian Science Monitor*. He lives in New York.